WORLD
PREHISTORY
AND
ARCHAEOLOGY
PATHWAYS THROUGH TIME

WORLD
PREHISTORY
AND
ARCHAEOLOGY

PATHWAYS THROUGH TIME

SECOND CANADIAN EDITION

MICHAEL CHAZAN

UNIVERSITY OF TORONTO

Pearson Canada
Toronto

Library and Archives Canada Cataloguing in Publication

Chazan, Michael
World prehistory and archaeology : pathways through time / Michael Chazan. — 2nd Canadian ed.
ISBN 978-0-205-71954-9

1. Prehistoric peoples—Textbooks. 2. Anthropology, Prehistoric—Textbooks.
3. Archaeology—Textbooks. I. Title.

GN740.C43 2011   930.1   C2010-906193-4

ISBN 978-0-205-71954-9

Vice-President, Editorial Director: Gary Bennett
Editor-in-Chief: Ky Pruesse
Senior Acquisitions Editor: Lisa Rahn
Sponsoring Editor: Carolin Sweig
Marketing Manager: Lisa Gillis
Senior Developmental Editor: Paul Donnelly
Project Manager: Sarah Lukaweski
Production Editors: Rohini Herbert, Lila Campbell
Copy Editor: Nancy Mucklow
Proofreader: Kelly Coleman
Compositor: Glyph International
Permissions and Photo Researcher: Julie Pratt
Art Director: Julia Hall
Cover and Interior Designer: Miriam Blier
Cover Image: With permission of the Royal Ontario Museum © ROM
Photo Credit: Brian Boyle

2 3 4 5   15 14 13 12

Printed and bound in Canada.

FOR **MICHELLE**

BRIEF CONTENTS

CONTENTS

PART TWO

HUMAN EVOLUTION 54

Introduction: Our Place in Nature 55

6
THE PEOPLING OF AUSTRALIA AND THE NEW WORLD 151

PART FOUR

THE DEVELOPMENT OF SOCIAL COMPLEXITY 264

Introduction: Defining Social Complexity 265

LIST OF BOXED FEATURES

TOOLBOX

FROM THE field

ARCHAEOLOGY in the world

CANADIAN research

PREFACE

Archaeology is the study of how humans have created the world we live in—a voyage of exploration into the human past. The goal of this voyage is to gain new perspectives and insights into who we are and how our world came into being. As is true of all sciences, archaeology is not a search for absolute and final answers. Archaeologists develop knowledge of the past that can be continuously questioned and improved. The goal of this book is to involve students in the current state of archaeological research—to reveal how archaeologists work and what they know. The fascination of archaeology is found in the continual process of human self-discovery. This book will help connect students to that process and show them not only the discoveries that have been made but also the challenges that remain. In archaeology, it is not enough to raise questions; one must also think of methods for providing the answers. People often think of archaeology as a random accumulation of artifacts or a series of chance discoveries. In practice, archaeology is a far more active and creative undertaking. Certainly, the excitement of discovery plays an essential role. Even in the most carefully planned project, the possibility always exists that the next shovel of soil will lead to an unexpected revelation.

In this second Canadian edition, you will read about a range of new discoveries, including an early human ancestor recovered in Ethiopia, ancient art and musical instruments excavated in a cave site in Germany, and the spectacular burial remains found in the Moon Pyramid at Teotihuacán, Mexico. Much of the excitement of archaeology comes from asking questions and finding answers. In this edition, you will also read about the application of new perspectives and methods such as the use of surveying to understand the development of social complexity in China and the role metallurgical analyses play in elucidating the ancient technologies of the Andes.

In preparing this edition, I have been struck by three characteristics of archaeology today. The first is that archaeology is a truly global discipline. One can no longer remain up to date simply by relying on the information emerging from a small number of centres of research. The challenge today is to keep abreast of a torrent of information coming from archaeologists all over the world. Thus, even while writing this book, I was painfully aware that I might have missed some of the information and failed to incorporate vital insights. However, thanks to a wealth of resources available through university library websites, research that in the past would have taken weeks to conduct can now be completed in minutes with a few mouse clicks.

The second characteristic of archaeology today is that it often involves deploying methods from the study of natural sciences. In many cases, research requires collaboration between natural scientists and archaeologists. One of the most important skills for a present-day archaeologist is to be able to collaborate with specialists in other fields. Collaboration is a tricky business that requires trusting our partners and stretching our perspectives, but the result is a significant increase in scientific capacity.

The third characteristic of archaeology is that, paradoxically, while archaeology is becoming more entwined with the natural sciences, there is an enhanced sense that the field is engaging with the contemporary world. Archaeologists around the globe find themselves enmeshed in complex issues ranging from community identity to the tourist industry. The recognition of the fragility and importance of the archaeological record is central to contemporary archaeology.

Preparing the second Canadian edition has involved some reorganization and expansion of coverage. However, the main outcome of the revision is a book with a stronger conceptual core: Archaeology is presented as a dynamic, scientifically rigorous, and socially engaged inquiry into the remains of the human past that survive in the world today.

New to This Edition

The second Canadian edition includes a new chapter (Chapter 4, From *Homo erectus* to Neanderthals), expansions of existing chapters, and updated information throughout. Recent discoveries are examined, including the discovery of a complete skeleton of *Ardipithecus ramidus*, early evidence for exploitation of marine resources on sites in South Africa and Gibraltar, and early art and flutes at the early Upper Paleolithic site of Hohle Fels, Germany.

- The chapter on the initial occupation of Australia and the Americas (Chapter 6) now includes coverage of the spread of human populations across the islands of Micronesia, as well as material on the Archaic Period in North America.

- Part Four has been reorganized and expanded to four chapters, including new data on Minoan and Mycenaean societies and enhanced coverage of early states in China, Mesoamerica, and the Andes.

- New *Toolboxes* deal with the topics of "Archaeoacoustics" (Chapter 2), "Faunal Analysis and Taphonomy" (Chapter 2), "*Chaîne Opératoire* and the Levallois Method" (Chapter 4), "Experimental Archaeology" (Chapter 6), "Archaeology and Genetics" (Chapter 11), "Underwater Archaeology" (Chapter 12), "Space Syntax" (Chapter 12), and "Human Osteoarchaeology" (Chapter 13).

- The new *Archaeology in the World* boxes feature the topics of "Community Archaeology" (Chapter 1), "Political Borders and Archaeology" (Chapter 7), "Who Owns the Past?" (Chapter 8), "Archaeology and the Environment" (Chapter 9), "Archaeology and Development" (Chapter 12), "Archaeology and Tourism" (Chapter 13), and "Ancient Agriculture and Modern Development" (Chapter 14).

- New *Canadian Research* boxes include "The Gender of Tomb 7 at Monte Albán" (Chapter 13), and "Excavating in the Peruvian Desert" (Chapter 14).

- New *From the Field* boxes include the essays "The Archaeological Consultant" by Carla Parslow (Chapter 2); "Doing Regional Archaeological Settlement Patterns Survey in Northeast China" by Christian Peterson (Chapter 12); and "Discovering a Ceremonial Site of the Ancient Moche People" by Katrina Joosten (Chapter 14). I have also contributed new essays on my own field work in South Africa (Chapter 1), Jordan (Chapter 7), and Egypt (Chapter 11).

- New *MyAnthroKit* at **www.myanthrokit.com** includes a wealth of resources to help you succeed. Online resources are as diverse as ethnographies and include case studies, practice quizzes, research assignments, and online academic reference sources.

Organization

The first section of this book, Part One, "The Past Is a Foreign Country: Getting From Here to There," presents an introduction to archaeological method and theory. The first chapter, "Getting Started in Archaeology," begins in the field and discusses how archaeologists locate and excavate sites. From the field, we move into the laboratory to look at how the remains recovered in an excavation are analyzed. Archaeology involves not only field and laboratory work but also developing a framework for thinking about the past. In Chapter 2, "Putting the Picture Together," we consider how well we know the past and how much we can learn about it. This chapter presents a brief history of the ways archaeologists have thought about the past.

From here, we turn to what we currently know about prehistory. The next three sections of the text examine prehistory in three parts: human evolution, agricultural beginnings, and the development of political complexity. Part Two, "Human Evolution," covers the periods from the first evidence of tool manufacture to the spread of modern humans (*Homo sapiens*) throughout the globe. Human evolution involves the interaction between changes in human anatomy and changes in the way humans lived and in the tools they used. The four chapters in this section follow the process of biological evolution while tracking the geographic spread of human populations and developments in the way they lived.

Part Three, "Perspectives on Agriculture," examines the shift to an agricultural way of life. The development of agricultural societies demanded a profound reorientation of the way humans related to plants and animals, along with equally significant changes in society and technology. Because the transition to agriculture took place independently in several distinct regions, it is possible to take a comparative approach to the origins of this new way of life to gain a broad understanding of the process. Chapter 7, "Towers, Villages, and Longhouses," presents the archaeological record pointing to the beginnings of agriculture in the Middle East and the spread of agriculture into Europe. Chapter 8, "Mounds and Maize," focuses on the origin of maize (corn) agriculture in Mesoamerica and its spread into North America. The adoption of maize agriculture in eastern North America is particularly interesting and complex, as maize was integrated into an existing indigenous agricultural system. Chapter 9, "A Feast of Diversity," broadens the comparative perspective by briefly considering a number of other civilizations in Africa, China, New Guinea, and Peru. It becomes clear that the development of agriculture often spanned a period of several thousands of years and that the process differed significantly among regions.

Following the adoption of agriculture, societies in many parts of the world expanded in scale and increased in population, which, in turn, led to increased social inequality. Power and access to resources came to be controlled by a smaller segment of people, resulting in the emergence of state societies. Part Four examines "The Development of Social Complexity." This final section covers many of the world's most spectacular and enigmatic archaeological sites, including Stonehenge, the pyramids at Giza, and the cities of the Maya. As with agriculture, social complexity developed independently in a number of regions. Thus, it is again possible to use a comparative approach to gain a broad understanding of this process.

The first chapter of Part Four, Chapter 10, "Complexity Without the State," considers four monumental sites—Stonehenge, Pueblo Bonito, Cahokia, and Great Zimbabwe—constructed by societies that were characterized by emerging social inequality. The remaining chapters have been revised so that case studies of early states and empires are organized geographically. Coverage has been expanded to include the Minoan and the Mycenaean societies of the Aegean. Coverage of early states in China, Mesoamerica, and the Andes has also been expanded. The text concludes with an Epilogue entitled "Bringing It Back Home," in which we look at the traces of the past in our familiar world.

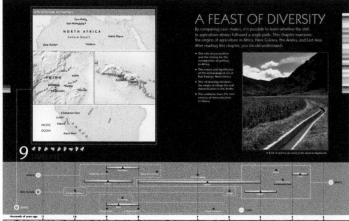

A FEAST OF DIVERSITY

By comparing case studies, it is possible to learn whether the shift to agriculture always followed a single path. This chapter examines the origins of agriculture in Africa, New Guinea, the Andes, and East Asia. After reading this chapter, you should understand:

- The role of pastoralism and the timing for the introduction of pottery in Africa.
- The culture and significance of the archaeological site at Kuk Swamp, New Guinea.
- The relationship between the origins of village life and domestication in the Andes.
- The evidence from the two centres of domestication in China.

TIMELINE

Pedagogy

Every chapter contains a number of pedagogical elements to guide students through. Each chapter opener includes satellite location maps and timelines to orient students in time and place to the sites discussed. Learning objectives help students focus on their reading of each chapter. Within the text, key terms, concepts, and place names are defined or described when they first appear; they are also defined in the margin of the page. Subsequently, they are all listed together in a section at the end of each chapter called *Key Terms*, along with a chapter *Summary* and a list of *Review Questions*. Each chapter contains dozens of stunning illustrations and photographs to engage students in the subject matter, demonstrate key concepts, and visually convey the spectacular nature of our stops along the pathways through time.

Distinctive Features

The main purpose of this book is to present an integrated picture of prehistory as an active process of discovery. From this perspective, we cannot relegate methodological issues to the opening chapters alone. After the student is introduced to archaeological method in the first two chapters, the question of *how* we know the past comes up on numerous occasions throughout the remaining text. A number of features have been developed to draw together an integrated presentation of prehistory.

■ Toolbox Sections

Toolboxes introduce aspects of archaeological methods that are particularly relevant to the material covered. There are two toolboxes in each chapter. Toolboxes are critical for achieving the aim of this book: to integrate prehistory with an introduction to archaeological methods. New toolboxes in this second Canadian edition include "Archaeoacoustics" (Chapter 2), "Faunal Analysis and Taphonomy" (Chapter 2), "*Chaîne Opératoire* and the Levallois Method" (Chapter 4), "Experimental Archaeology" (Chapter 6), "Archaeology and Genetics" (Chapter 11), "Underwater Archaeology" (Chapter 12), "Space Syntax" (Chapter 12), and "Human Osteoarchaeology" (Chapter 13).

■ Archaeology in the World

Despite the stereotype of the archaeologist as a cloistered academic, archaeology is very much a discipline that takes place in the real world. Issues such as control over human burial remains, the antiquities trade, and the preservation of threatened cultural resources are every bit as important to the field as trowels and levels. Archaeology is not only the study of what happened in the past, but also the examination of the role of the past in today's world.

To emphasize the significance of the role of the past in the present, every chapter includes a boxed feature called *Archaeology in the World*. These boxes pinpoint ethical issues

TOOLBOX

Experimental Archaeology

Voyaging across the sea figures prominently in Polynesian oral history; however many anthropologists have viewed these voyages as myths rather than stories based on actual experience. There is good reason for skepticism. Hawaiian oral history speaks of repeated trips between Hawaii and an ancestral land that appears to be Tahiti. Is such a voyage conceivable in a canoe without a compass? The trip from Hawaii to Tahiti covers over 3,620 kilometres of open sea, but the actual distance is quite a bit farther, since it is necessary to curve eastward against the trade winds and currents that flow across the course. Archaeologists came to view the ancient Polynesians as hapless sailors blown off course until they reached fortuitous landfall.

A set of experiments has led to a reversal of opinion about the voyaging of ancient Polynesians and the veracity of Polynesian oral history. The first experiment was a computer simulation. In 1973, Michael Levison and colleagues used a computer model of Pacific Ocean currents and wind speeds to run over 100,000 simulations of what would happen to a vessel drifting away from various Polynesian islands. They found that while hitting an island by drifting from east to west was possible, drifting from west to east and hitting an island was virtually impossible. These results cast doubt on the claim made by Thor Heyerdahl, based on his voyages on the raft Kon-Tiki, that Polynesia was settled by drifting sailors from South America. Perhaps most significantly, the computer simulation showed that out of 16,000 trials from various Polynesian islands, none reached Hawaii. The implication is that Hawaii was reached by sailors who set their course intentionally.

In 1976, to push the experiment a step farther, Bill Finney and colleagues

formed the Polynesian Voyaging Society and built a double-hull canoe. The goal was to sail from Hawaii to Tahiti using only traditional methods of navigation. Mau Pialiug, a master navigator from Satawal Atoll in the Caroline Islands, guided the canoe, christened the *Hokulé'a*, to a successful landfall in Tahiti. Since that time, the *Hokulé'a* has continued to voyage across the Pacific. The experiment successfully showed that controlled voyaging across Polynesia using traditional methods was possible, and has sparked a rebirth of pride and interest among Polynesian and Hawaiian communities in their legacy of sea voyaging. The project has also led to a complex "dialogue developing between indigenous peoples in search of their own past and anthropologists seeking to reconstruct ancient practices" (Finney 1991, 398).

Finney's research is an example of an application of experimental archaeol-

ogy, which allows archaeologists to test ideas about the past in a controlled setting. The range and scope of experimental archaeology is vast. At Butser Farm in England, researchers have recreated a working Bronze Age farm. In a very different setting, archaeologists working in engineering laboratories have tested the fracture mechanics that underlie stone tool manufacture. At the root of all these activities is the spirit of the inquiry, an effort to explore the dynamics of the past by carrying out experiments in the present. Experimental archaeology is closely associated with ethnoarchaeology, taphonomic analysis, and other aspects of archaeological methodology that use studies set in the present as a source of insight into the dynamics that formed the archaeological record. ⊕

For more information on the Polynesian Voyaging Society see http://pvs.kcc.hawaii.edu/index.html.

FIGURE 6.9 The canoes of the Polynesian Voyaging Society have provided insight into the archaeology of the Pacific Islands. These vessels have also served as a powerful means for local people to explore their history and identity.

relevant to the archaeology of the periods discussed in the chapter. Through reading these features, students will see that archaeology plays a role in the present. *Archaeology in the World* topics include "A History of Canadian Archaeology" (Chapter 2), "Religion and Evolution" (Chapter 4), "Repatriation of Indigenous Burial Remains" (Chapter 6), "The Fate of Iraq's Antiquities" (Chapter 11), and "The Trade in African Antiquities" (Chapter 10). This second Canadian edition includes new features on "Community Archaeology" (Chapter 1), "Political Borders and Archaeology" (Chapter 7), "Who Owns the Past" (Chapter 8), "Archaeology and the Environment" (Chapter 9), "Archaeology and Development" (Chapter 12), "Archaeology and Tourism" (Chapter 13), and "Ancient Agriculture and Modern Development" (Chapter 14).

From the Field

A primary goal of this text is to draw students into the process of archaeological research. Rather than sitting on the sidelines observing the game, students should be on the playing field. This does not mean that this book is suitable only for future archaeologists; rather, it is meant to provide the tools to give any student a lifelong engagement with archaeology, whether through travelling, visiting museums, reading, or joining in a research project. Toward that end, we have also included in each chapter a feature called *From the Field*, in which people—including students—who are actively involved in archaeological research write an informal report about a project relevant to the chapter subject. *From the Field* segments include "The Archaeological Consultant" by Carla Parslow (Chapter 2); "Following the Footsteps of Our Ancestors," by Andrew Du, a student at Rutgers University, (Chapter 3); "A Paleoepiphany," by Dr. Lynne A. Schepartz (Chapter 4); "Towns They Have None": In Search of New England's Mobile Farmers," by Dr. Elizabeth S. Chilton (Chapter 8); "Doing Regional Archaeological Settlement Patterns Survey in Northeast China" by Christian Peterson (Chapter 12); "The Socialization of Ancient Maya Children," by Rissa M. Trachman (Chapter 13); and "Discovering a Ceremonial Site of the Ancient Moche People" by Katrina Joosten (Chapter 14). I have also contributed features on my own fieldwork experiences in South Africa, Jordan, and Egypt. I hope that these sections will inspire some readers to consider volunteering on an excavation or enrolling in a field school. No words can replace the experience of uncovering the buried remains of the human past.

Canadian Research and Canadian Archaeologists

Canadian content is integrated throughout the book. In some cases, particularly the coverage of the Arctic in Chapter 6 and the Northwest Coast in Chapter 10, sections not found in the U.S. edition cover aspects of the archaeology of Canada. The research of Canadian researchers working around the world is also included in every chapter, augmented by a brief history of Canadian archaeology in Chapter 2. Furthermore, two special features are dedicated to the unique contributions of Canadian archaeology: "Canadian Research," which is a brief essay that covers a

ARCHAEOLOGY in the world

Who Owns the Past?

Who owns the past? This is a rather vague question, but for archaeologists it takes on a very concrete meaning. For example, the Metropolitan Museum recently returned the Euphronios vase, a 2,500 year old Greek vessel with exquisite paintings of mythological scenes, to Italy because it was resolved that the vase had been illegally acquired. In this case, the Metropolitan Museum's claim of property rights to an artifact was found to be legally faulty; therefore the object was returned to the Italian government, whose claims to property rights are supported by international law.

But should laws of property rights always determine who owns archaeological artifacts or sites? What happens when property rights clash with other claims to ownership and access? This question is particularly pertinent in North America,

where property rights are highly prized. The Newark Earthworks provide an illustration of this problem. Squier and Davis documented the Newark Earthworks in 1848 in their study of Ohio Valley mounds. In 1853, the local agricultural society purchased the northwestern part of the earthworks, and in 1891 the land was sold to the City of Newark for State Encampment Grounds. The state militia used the Encampment Grounds for a number of years before the land was leased to its current tenants, the Moundbuilders Country Club. In 1933 the deed to the property was transferred to the Ohio Historical Society.

It is quite incredible that one of the most impressive monuments in the Americas is today a golf course. Two events have brought renewed attention to the earthworks. The first was an unsuccessful attempt by the country

club to build a new clubhouse that would have damaged the mounds. The second was the identification of a lunar orientation for the octagon-shaped enclosure. The archaeologist Chris Scarre has included the Newark Enclosures among his seventy wonders of the ancient world (Scarre 1999). But for the club manager, it is the right of the club to limit access to this site because the club holds the lease (Maag 2005).

As with many significant archaeological sites, the planning for the long-term conservation of the Newark Earthworks is an extremely delicate undertaking. The Ohio Historical Society has set out a management plan for the site that does include removing the golf course. In the meantime, procedures have been put in place to provide at least limited access to visitors wishing to experience this spectacular site. ◉

FIGURE 8.14 The return of the Euphronios vase to Italy.   **FIGURE 8.15** The golf course on the Newark Earthworks.

source of data for reconstructing diet. However, identifying diets using bone chemistry is successful only if the consumers ate foods that had a particular chemical signature. One type of chemical signature is the relative frequency of two isotopes of the same element. Fortunately for the study of maize agriculture, the ratio of carbon-13 (^{13}C) to carbon-12 (^{12}C) varies in plants with different photosynthetic pathways. The ratio of carbon-13 to carbon-12 is expressed as the value $\delta^{13}C$, which is the deviation from an international standard. Trees, bushes, and

MOUNDS AND MAIZE   CHAPTER 8   **233**

FROM THE field

The Author on His Fieldwork at Wonderwerk Cave, South Africa

Wonderwerk Cave is a spectacular site located in the Northern Cape Province of South Africa, on the edge of the Kalahari. Although this is a remote area, our living conditions are quite good. We stay in small brick chalets built near the site and most of the roads are tarred. The view from the cave is of an immense open space, a flat grassland that reaches to the horizon. A nice part of working at the site is that not only do we lack Internet access, but we have to walk out to the main road to even get cell phone reception—a welcome break from my heavily connected life in Canada. However, this remote place is also the nexus of an international research team as well as a diverse range of community interests. My role at Wonderwerk makes me think that of a ringmaster in a circus than that of an archaeologist.

It might be best to begin by explaining how I ended up working at this site. In the late 1990s I was completing a project in Israel with my colleagues Liora Horwitz and Naomi Porat. Liora is a faunal analyst, Naomi is a geologist, and I am an archaeologist who specializes in stone tools, so we make a good team. We began looking for a new project that would allow us to continue to study the shift from the Lower Paleolithic to the Middle Paleolithic, or as they are known in Africa, the Earlier to the Middle Stone Age. By chance Liora was off to South Africa to visit family, which included a visit to her uncle's farm in the Free State. En route she stopped off in Kimberley, a diamond mining city that is home to Peter Beaumont. Peter is famous for excavating sites at the time range we were interested in, and before I knew it I was off to South Africa for an unforgettable tour with Peter. The wealth of sites he showed us and the extent of the excavations he had carried

out was simply staggering. We resolved to develop a project to analyze the collections from Peter's excavations at Wonderwerk Cave housed at the McGregor Museum, carry out small-scale field projects to document the stratigraphy on the site, and collect samples for geological and botanical analysis.

Seven years later we are still hard at work. Our research team has swelled to over fifteen members from South Africa, England, Israel, Canada, and the United States. Our most exciting result is the dating of the base of the deposit at Wonderwerk to 2 million years ago. The stone tools from this stratum provide the earliest evidence for hominin cave occupation in the world. My job as the codirector of this project is not simply to analyze stone tools but to coordinate the activities of all the scientists working at the site. This is a fascinating undertaking, since each member of the team

comes to the project with his/her own perspective, and meshing these perspectives is a tremendous challenge. We have also found ourselves involved in ongoing discussions with the local community. Wonderwerk Cave is a candidate for a World Heritage status and a critical element of the tourism development in this area. Wonderwerk is also integrated into local school curriculum, and all children from the area schools visit the site during their primary years. Combining the educational, tourism, and scientific potential of this site is every bit as complex as the analysis of Earlier Stone Age stone tools. Days at Wonderwerk tend to be a bit unpredictable and are almost always interesting. A day that begins with conversations with local Tswana chiefs might also involve careful excavation and complex discussions of stratigraphy and geophysics. One couldn't ask for much more. ▲

FIGURE 1.12 Taking samples for paleomagnetic dating of the early hominin occupation at Wonderwerk Cave, South Africa.

18   PART ONE   THE PAST IS A FOREIGN COUNTRY: GETTING FROM HERE TO THERE

research project by a Canadian archaeologist found in each chapter; "Canadian Archaeologists," which includes a listing of some Canadian archaeologists and a link to their website. I hasten to add that this is not a comprehensive listing of Canadian archaeologists. My focus has been on providing information about Canadian archaeologists whose research is particularly relevant to the chapter.

A Final Note

Australian aboriginal societies speak of the *dreamtime* as the time when their ancestors walked the land. The actions of ancestors are inscribed in the land and experienced in the landscape. Archaeology explores the "scientific dreamtime"—the time of our ancestors that we discover through archaeological research. This book is an introduction to the current state of archaeology. It is not a simple catalogue of finds but rather an attempt to give coherence to the vast expanses of human experience studied by archaeologists. Our hope is that readers will keep in mind the uncertainty that characterizes the study of prehistory. What is meant by "uncertainty"? Archaeology is a constant process of questioning and improving our understanding of the past. As in any science, all claims can and should be questioned. Archaeology is a report on the current state of the human endeavour to understand our own past. We invite you to join this endeavour, in which we reveal the present state of archaeological knowledge and introduce you to the methods used to gain that knowledge. We hope that these tools will enable you to actively engage in thinking about humanity from the perspective of archaeology, to think about processes that stretch over millennia and are global in scale, and to walk the pathways of our own "scientific dreamtime."

Support for Instructors and Students

This book is accompanied by an extensive learning package designed to enhance the experience of both instructors and students.

PEARSON myanthrokit™ is an online resource that offers a wealth of tools to help student learning and comprehension, including practice quizzes, flashcards for studying images and terms, timelines, and more. MyAnthroKit also includes a rich array of interactive tools enhanced with audio and video to engage students in learning. Visit **www.myanthrokit.com.**

INSTRUCTOR'S RESOURCE CD-ROM (ISBN 0-205-02466-1). This resource CD includes the following instructor supplements:

INSTRUCTOR'S MANUAL. This manual includes chapter outlines, learning objectives, key terms and concepts, classroom activities and student projects, suggested videos and readings, and internet links.

TEST ITEM FILE. The test bank includes between 75 and 100 questions per chapter in four formats: multiple choice, true/false, fill-in-the-blank, and essay questions. The Test Item File is also available online through Pearson Canada's MyTest platform.

MYTEST. This is an online tool that allows instructors to create their own personalized exams, edit any or all of the existing test questions, and add new ones. Other special features of this program include random generation of test questions, creation of alternate versions of the same test, scrambling question sequences, and test previews before printing.

POWERPOINT™ PRESENTATIONS. These PowerPoint™ slides combine text and graphics for each chapter to help instructors convey archaeological principles in a clear and engaging way.

Most of these instructor supplements are also available for download from a password-protected section of Pearson Canada's online catalogue (vig.pearsoned.ca). Navigate to your book's catalogue page to view a list of supplements that are available. See your local sales representative for details and access.

TECHNOLOGY SPECIALISTS. Pearson's Technology Specialists work with faculty and campus course designers to ensure that Pearson technology products, assessment tools, and online course materials are tailored to meet your specific needs. This highly qualified team is dedicated to helping schools take full advantage of a wide range of educational resources, by assisting in the integration of a variety of instructional materials and media formats. Your local Pearson Canada sales representative can provide you with more details on this service program.

COURSESMART. CourseSmart goes beyond traditional expectations—providing instant, online access to the textbooks and course materials you need at an average savings of 60%. With instant access from any computer and the ability to search your text, you'll find the content you need quickly, no matter where you are. And with online tools like highlighting and note-taking, you can save time and study efficiently. See all the benefits at **www.coursesmart.com**.

Acknowledgments

In writing this book, I have drawn on practically every experience I have had as an archaeologist. First, I would like to thank some of my teachers. The late James Sauer taught me much of what I know about pottery and showed me that archaeology has the potential to build bridges across the chasms created by conflict. Andrew Moore and Frank Hole supported me as I stepped out of the classroom and into research and provided me with the freedom that I now try to give my own students. Learning to be an archaeologist takes place in the field as much as in the classroom. I have had the opportunity to work with project directors who somehow had the patience to put up with a novice. I am very grateful to Avi Gopher, Nigel Goring-Morris, and François Valla for teaching me how to excavate a Neolithic site; to Ofer Bar-Yosef, Liliane Meignen, and Bernard Vandermeersch for showing me why the Paleolithic is fascinating; and to Mark Lehner for the incredible experience of working at the Giza pyramids. I would also like to thank my friend Zahi Hawass for making it possible for me work in Egypt.

My views of archaeology have been greatly enriched by my association with research groups in France and Israel. Catherine Pèrles warmly welcomed me into the Prehistory and Technology Research Group of the Centre Nationale de la Recherche Scientifique in Meudon, outside of Paris. During my year at Meudon, I learned from researchers Eric Boëda, Anne Delagnes, Jacques Pelegrin, and Valentine Roux, among others, how to look at technology as an aspect of human behaviour. In Jerusalem, I have long enjoyed a connection with faculty at the Hebrew University, where I have been welcomed by Na'ama Goren-Inbar, Anna Belfer-Cohen,

Erella Hovers, and Nigel Goring-Morris. Most recently, I have developed a number of collaborative projects with colleagues, including Joel Janetski, Liora Kolska-Horwitz, Naomi Porat, Hagai Ron, Peter Beaumont, and David Morris. I thank them for their patience, as I sometimes have had to balance my responsibilities to these projects with the excitement of writing this book.

I have been lucky to find an ideal home in the city of Toronto and wonderful colleagues and students at the University of Toronto. Much of this book stems from the courses that I teach at the university as well as from courses I taught at Tufts and Brandeis before coming to this city. The dynamism of the University of Toronto is built on an appreciation of diversity that I hope is reflected in the book.

The actual process of developing the first U.S. edition was facilitated by the people at Allyn & Bacon, who believed that we could pull off the project. I never imagined the amount of effort that goes into such a book. I want to thank Jennifer Jacobson, who shepherded me through that first edition with a skill that combined patience and enthusiasm.

I would like to thank the team at Pearson Canada for making the second Canadian edition of this book happen: Lisa Rahn, Senior Acquisitions Editor; Carolin Sweig, Sponsoring Editor; Paul Donnelly, Senior Developmental Editor; Sarah Lukaweski, Project Manager; Rohini Herbert and Lila Campbell, Production Editors; Nancy Mucklow, Copy Editor; Kelly Coleman, Proofreader; and Miriam Blier, Designer.

I would also like to thank the Canadian reviewers who provided excellent overall input as well as specific insight on portions of the text during development. This edition and future editions of this text are improved by your feedback.

Michael S. Bisson, McGill University

Diana E. French, UBC Okanagan

Sheila Greaves, Athabasca University

Ross Jamieson, Simon Fraser University

Peter Johansen, University of British Columbia

Hugh McKenzie, Grant MacEwan University

Laurie Milne, Medicine Hat College

Peter Timmins, University of Western Ontario

Since *World Prehistory and Archaeology: Pathways through Time* is used as a course text, I hope that instructors and students may wish to contact me. I would appreciate receiving questions, comments, and criticisms at mchazan@chass.utoronto.ca.

I would like to take the opportunity to thank my parents, who have been a constant source of inspiration and support. I am delighted to have shared this project with my wife Michelle Fost and our children Gabriel and Nathan. This has been, in every sense, a team effort.

Michael Chazan, mchazan@chass.utoronto.ca

ABOUT THE AUTHOR

Michael Chazan is an Associate Professor in the Department of Anthropology and the Director of the Archaeology Centre at the University of Toronto. He earned his Ph.D. in anthropology at Yale University. Before coming to Toronto, Dr. Chazan was a postdoctoral fellow with the *Centre National de la Recherche Scientifique* in Paris and at the Hebrew University in Jerusalem. Among his field experience are excavations in New Jersey, France, Israel, Jordan, Egypt, and South Africa. Dr. Chazan's publications include a monograph on the Lower Paleolithic site of Holon, Israel, co-authored with Liora Kolska-Horwitz. Dr. Chazan is currently engaged in a project on the Earlier Stone Age of South Africa. The project pulls together an international team of researchers to study a series of spectacular sites located in the Northern Cape Province.

PART ONE

THE PAST IS A FOREIGN COUNTRY: GETTING FROM HERE TO THERE

Archaeology is the study of the human past through the traces of the past that exist in the present. After reading this introduction, you should understand:

- The structure of the discipline of archaeology.

- The fundamental elements of archaeological ethics.

Introduction: Questions of Time and Ethics

The thing the Time Traveller held in his hand was a glittering metallic framework, scarcely larger than a small clock, and very delicately made. There was ivory in it, and some transparent crystalline substance. "This little affair," said the Time Traveller, resting his elbows on the table and pressing his hands together above the apparatus, "is only a model. It is my plan for a machine to travel through time." (Wells 1895, 39)

Time travel, as imagined by H. G. Wells in his visionary novel, *The Time Machine*, and in countless subsequent films and books, remains a tantalizing impossibility. We cannot mount the saddle of an apparatus, or for that matter the seat of a DeLorean, that will whisk us back in time. We are rooted firmly in the present.

Archaeologists have developed a solution to the problem of time travel that is every bit as intricate as the mechanism built by Wells's hero. Archaeological excavation and analysis is a highly developed scientific discipline that allows us a means of access to the human past. Archaeology does not take us into the past, but enables us to read the traces of the past that exist with us in the present.

A simple "thought experiment" can give a sense of how archaeology works. Imagine a building that you are familiar with, perhaps your family home or a school you have attended. Picture how this structure looks today, and then attempt to remove any elements that were added in the past twenty years. If the building is old, try pushing back forty, sixty, or even a hundred years. Now extend your view to encompass a larger landscape, perhaps a neighbourhood or a town. Although we cannot re-enter the past, we are surrounded by its material traces. Uncovering and understanding these traces is the archaeologist's task (Figure I.1).

Because archaeological remains can take many forms—objects made or modified by people, organic material, or geological features—the discipline of archaeology is diverse. As a result, archaeology is often found spread across academic disciplines. In Canada, archaeology is considered a subfield of anthropology, and departments of archaeology are rare. The University of Calgary, Memorial University, and Simon Fraser University are universities with departments of archaeology. Anthropologists study the diversity of human experience, and archaeology provides an important bridge between biological anthropologists and anthropologists studying modern society and culture. Archaeology also provides time depth and gives a clear material focus to anthropology. Archaeologists working on the ancient civilizations of Mesopotamia, Egypt, and the biblical world are often found in departments of Near or Middle Eastern civilizations, while archaeologists of classical Greece and Rome are usually in departments of classics or art history. Archaeologists are also employed as curators in museums.

Archaeologists today tend to work outside of the university or museum setting. In Canada, most professional archaeologists are employed by private companies, dedicated to excavating and surveying areas in advance of impending construction. This type of archaeology, usually referred to as cultural resource management, or CRM, is critical to preserving our heritage in the face of development. CRM is increasingly a global enterprise and includes firms that operate internationally. Other archaeologists work in various branches of the government. Archaeologists working in the public sector play a critical role in both the preservation and the presentation of cultural heritage (Figure I.2). Archaeologists have also begun to find employment in law

Figure I.1 In Montreal, Christ Church Cathedral, built in 1859, stands in stark contrast to the surrounding modern city.

FIGURE I.2 Archaeologists excavating in the backyard of Robert Service's cabin in the Dawson National Historic Site in the Yukon.

enforcement, prohibiting illegally traded artifacts and halting illegal excavation. Finally, archaeologists contribute to the development of methods of forensic science and remain active in projects documenting crime scenes, both locally and internationally, in conjunction with investigations of war crimes.

Training in archaeology is based on a combination of university course work and practical experience. Most professional archaeologists have advanced training, at least at the master's level. Archaeological research is expensive, supporting both the process of excavation and scientific analysis of the recovered materials. For CRM firms, the costs of excavation are paid by the landowner, as required by law. In most cases, the firm has to bid for a contract, the terms of which bind and limit the firm. Academic and museum-based archaeologists have the luxury of pursuing projects that develop from a program of research rather than from the imperatives of development. However, to pursue research, it is necessary to raise funds from government and private agencies. In Canada, the Social Sciences and Humanities Research Council provides significant funding for archaeological research.

Archaeology is a varied field of study, and archaeologists follow a range of career paths. However, the discipline is bound both by shared methods and interests and by a shared ethic. Archaeologists have recently begun to recognize the importance of exploring and codifying archaeological ethics (Figure I.3). The Register of Professional Archaeologists (RPA) was founded in 1998 as a listing of archaeologists with both graduate training and practical experience who agree to abide by an explicit code of conduct and standards of research performance (http://www.rpanet.org/). The Society for American Archaeology has set out the following eight principles of archaeological ethics (http://www.saa.org/public/resources/ethics.html):

- Stewardship. The archaeological record is irreplaceable, and archaeologists are responsible for acting as stewards, working for long-term conservation and protection of the archaeological record. Stewards are caretakers and advocates who work for the benefit of all people. The archaeological record includes archaeological materials, sites, collections, records, and reports.

- Accountability. Archaeologists are accountable to the public and must make an effort to consult actively with all groups affected by their research.

- Commercialization. Archaeologists should discourage and avoid the enhancement of the commercial value of archaeological objects, particularly those not curated in public institutions or those inaccessible to the public.

- Public Education and Outreach. Archaeologists should reach out to and cooperate with interested members of the public.

- Intellectual Property. Original materials and documents from archaeological research should not be treated as personal possessions. After a limited and reasonable time, these materials should be made available to others.

- Public Reporting and Publication. Knowledge gained from archaeological research should be published within a reasonable length of time to a wide range of interested publics. If necessary for the preservation of a site, its location and nature may be obscured in publications.

- Records and Preservation. Archaeologists should actively work for the preservation of archaeological records and reports.
- Training and Resources. Archaeologists must have adequate training, facilities, and support before carrying out research.

The Canadian Archaeological Association has developed a detailed framework for ethical conduct pertaining to aboriginal peoples (http://www.canadianarchaeology.com/ethical.lasso). Three principles are laid out regarding the excavation of sacred sites:

FIGURE I.3 In Jerusalem, the close juxtaposition of the sacred remains of the past and the modern city creates a landscape fraught with tension, highlighting the ethical dimension of archaeology.

1. To recognize and respect the spiritual bond that exists between aboriginal peoples and special places and features in the landscape.
2. To acknowledge the cultural significance of human remains and associated objects to aboriginal peoples.
3. To respect protocols governing the investigation, removal, curation, and reburial of human remains and associated objects.

Archaeologists study the past, but they work for the present and the future. Although we are motivated by the excitement of discovery, we are also compelled by the importance of conservation. The practical decision of how much of a site to excavate offers an example of maintaining a balance between exploration and conservation. While archaeologists might like to clean out every nook and cranny of a site as they search for critical pieces of data, such an approach is acceptable only in situations where the site faces imminent destruction. In all other cases, the desire to explore is tempered by the imperative of leaving material for future generations of archaeologists who may arrive with new methods capable of unlocking aspects of the archaeological record that are inaccessible today.

From Indiana Jones to Lara Croft, archaeologists have become popular movie heroes. The irony is that the reality of archaeology is much closer to moviemaking than to the exploits of a movie hero. Like making a film, archaeology involves the logistics of working with a team on location, for long hours, and with an eye toward pragmatic compromise. Like filmmakers, archaeologists do a great deal of unglamorous pre- and postproduction work. Archaeology calls less for bravery in battle than it does for the courage to take creative leaps based on intuition. The result of archaeological research is not triumphantly grasping a trophy, but rather reaching conclusions that open an entirely new vista of questions.

SUMMARY

- Because archaeological remains can take many forms, including objects made or modified by people, organic material, and even geological features, the discipline of archaeology is highly varied.
- In the Canada, the academic discipline of archaeology is usually found in departments of anthropology, as well as in departments of Near or Middle Eastern civilizations, classics, and fine arts.
- Most archaeologists today work outside of academia, in either cultural resource management firms or government agencies.
- Archaeological ethics are based on the idea that archaeologists should act as stewards of the archaeological record.

REVIEW QUESTIONS

1. Can you think of a place you are familiar with where the physical remains of the past are apparent?

2. How does stewardship of the archaeological record differ from ownership?
3. In what ways do archaeologists work for the future?

A surveyor works at the Chac restoration site in Mexico.

1

GETTING STARTED IN ARCHAEOLOGY

This chapter introduces you to how archaeologists find and excavate sites,
as well as to the basics of archaeological laboratory research.
After reading the chapter, you should understand:

- The goals of archaeological survey.
- The methods of horizontal and vertical excavation.
- The use of quantification in artifact and ecofact analysis.
- The methods used to construct an archaeological chronology.

We experience the past at almost every instant. Think of how you hear a piece of music. You do not simply hear a succession of notes as they unfold in time. Rather, your hearing of each note is shaped by your memory of the preceding notes and your anticipation of what is to come. The human present is created through a fusion of past, present, and future.

As humans, we live in a present shaped by our consciousness of the past. Our sense of the past exists in our memories—in our visual, auditory, and olfactory images and sensations. Athletes also speak of a "body memory" that allows them to carry out elaborate, fine-tuned sequences of action. But memory goes far beyond our minds and our bodies. Writing systems and, more recently, computer technologies store memory externally. Anthropologists speak of collective memories, particularly memories of traumas, such as the events of September 11, that are held by a group rather than being the property of an individual. Objects and places can also embody memory; most families have heirlooms that carry a memory and a direct connection to previous generations (Lillios 1999).

Archaeology is a science that probes the depths of the human past. But archaeology is not time travel: Archaeologists and the objects they study remain firmly anchored in the present. The essential trick of archaeology is how to use static objects that exist in the present to infer the dynamics of past societies (Binford 1983). Put more simply, the goal of archaeological method is to be able to use the objects we dig up to understand the lives of people who lived in the past.

The goal of this chapter is to introduce you to archaeological method—to show you how archaeologists look at the world. We begin with fieldwork, first the way that archaeologists locate sites and then how sites are excavated. Archaeological excavation draws heavily on tools used in geology, so we also take time to consider aspects of geological stratigraphy. We then move to the laboratory to see how the objects recovered in excavations and surveys are analyzed. We pay particular attention to the quantitative methods archaeologists use to glean information from the totality of the recovered material.

1.1 Reading the Landscape

The first challenge facing archaeologists is finding the traces of human action. The purpose of an archaeological **survey** is to map the physical remains of human activity. The scale of surveys can range from an entire region to the surface of a single site. The evidence recorded can be as fine grained as individual stone tools and potsherds, or as massive as large standing structures.

■ Survey Design

The most obvious reason for carrying out an archaeological survey is to discover sites, be they sunken ships, buried cities, or hunter–gatherer camps. But archaeologists also use surveys to understand the distribution of sites within a region, how sites are distributed across the landscape, or where different activities took place within a site. In some cases, the goal is to determine whether sites will be destroyed by construction projects. Often, there is pressure to gain as complete a picture as possible at the lowest possible cost.

Archaeological surveys must be designed with the goals of the project in mind (Banning 2002). Simply recording everything is rarely possible, or even necessary, so archaeologists usually determine a strategy to sample the survey area. Statistical sampling in archaeological survey works on the same basis as a public-opinion poll. In both cases, a carefully selected sample is used to represent a larger population. The

survey An archaeological survey maps the physical remains of human activity.

goals of survey research can range widely. In an important survey project carried out in southern Iraq, Robert McCormick Adams and his colleagues were able to trace the hierarchy of settlements surrounding the large urban centres of early Mesopotamia (Adams and Nissen 1972). Archaeologists working across the western United States have used similar survey methods to track the mobility of small-scale societies of hunter–gatherers (Kelly 1988).

in situ Archaeological material is considered to be *in situ* when it is found in the place where it was originally deposited.

■ Geological Factors

It would be naïve to expect that we can simply walk across the landscape and find traces of all past human activity. Archaeological survey must take into consideration geological factors that affect the preservation and visibility of sites. Often, sites are so deeply buried that no artifacts are visible on the surface. Early prehistoric sites in East Africa, such as Olduvai Gorge, are examples of this kind of deeply buried context. At Olduvai Gorge, sites can be discovered only where natural erosion has cut through the accumulation of sediments, exposing fossil- and artifact-bearing levels.

Although erosion is often the archaeologists' indispensable ally, erosion can also complicate the interpretation of survey results. In many cases, stream channels have cut through archaeological sites and redeposited material far downstream. Archaeologists must take care to determine whether archaeological material picked up on a survey is actually in the place where it was originally deposited or whether it has been redeposited by erosion. Archaeologists refer to material that is in the place where it was originally deposited as **in situ**. It is often possible to identify archaeological material that has been transported by water on the basis of characteristic wear patterns and the absence of very small fragments.

■ Recovery Methods and GIS

Most surveys involve little more than a team of archaeologists walking slowly, with heads bent, across the landscape. The problems faced in surface collection vary tremendously according to the context of the research. On the one hand, in locations where there is heavy brush coverage, actually seeing artifacts can be extremely challenging (see Figure 1.1). On the other hand, there are areas where one is walking on a "carpet of artifacts"—a situation that is problematic because one has to decide what to pick up and record.

In a depositional environment, where there is a constant buildup of sediments, artifacts may not always be found on the surface. In such a context, many archaeologists rely on a strategy of digging small test pits to find buried artifacts. The type of survey and the extent of available resources together determine the placement of the test pits.

FIGURE 1.1 Surveyors in Cyprus carefully work their way up a slope looking for archaeological remains. Compare this setting to that shown in Figure I.2 on page 4.

Archaeologists draw on a wide range of technologies to increase their ability to detect archaeological deposits and to collect and organize spatial information.

- Methods of remote sensing, including aerial and satellite photography, play a critical role both in discovering sites and in orienting exploration (see Toolbox in Chapter 10, p. 291).

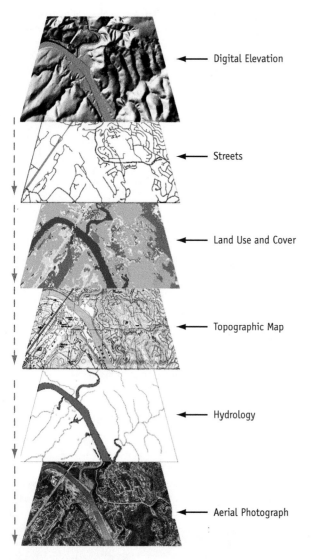

Digital Elevation

Streets

Land Use and Cover

Topographic Map

Hydrology

Aerial Photograph

FIGURE 1.2 Geographical information systems (GIS) work by creating a series of georeferenced overlays.

- Geophysical techniques are used to gain an idea of what lies below the surface of a site without having to excavate, allowing archaeologists to detect invisible features. The two main geophysical methods used in archaeological survey are magnetometry and ground-penetrating radar (see Toolbox in Chapter 13, p. 373).
- The precise location of archaeological sites can be determined with handheld Global Positioning System (GPS) receivers.

Archaeologists have access to a wide range of geographical information. Satellite images, aerial photographs, topographic maps, and the coordinates of locations of sites already found make up a rich body of data. **Geographical information systems (GIS)** are a suite of software applications that allow spatial data to be brought together and consolidated. GIS software works as a series of layers or overlays that the software sets to the same scale (see Figure 1.2). Imagine that you have a series of "documents," including an aerial photograph of a site, a topographic map of the region in which the site is located, a soil map of the same region, and, from a survey, the coordinates of archaeological finds at the site (Wheatley 2002). For any one of these documents to be used in a GIS environment, the exact longitude and latitude of two or three points in the area covered by the map must be known, allowing the document to be georeferenced. Once the image is georeferenced, it must be digitized as either a digital or a raster image. A digital image is an image all of whose points are digitized; a raster image is simply a scanned picture. Once each of the documents is digitized and georeferenced, all of them are ready to be treated as layers by a GIS program. The program will overlay the images at a uniform scale and location. One can then see how a particular site lies relative to the find spots identified in survey, the distribution of soils, the hydrology, and the topography of the area. GIS programs come with tools to both visualize and analyze these data. To help archaeologists visualize a region, topographic maps can be used to create three-dimensional models of the terrain and to statistically test the association of find spots with elevation, slope, and soils. One popular application is to analyze the "viewshed"—what would have been visible to a person from a given spot in the landscape.

When GIS systems were first introduced, they were used largely within an ecological framework, looking at relationships between site locations and the availability of natural resources. Other applications were developed to model migration routes and to predict where sites would likely be found. In recent years, a number of archaeologists have begun to use GIS as a means of exploring the way people in the past would have experienced the environment.

1.2 Excavation

The archaeological "time machine" consists of simple tools such as trowels, screens, and levels. The fundamental characteristic of archaeological excavation is the careful attention paid to recording the context in which artifacts are discovered. Intensive documentation is what distinguishes archaeological excavation from vandalism and looting.

geographical information systems (GIS) Software applications that allow spatial data to be brought together and consolidated.

Horizontal Excavation

In A.D. 79, the Roman city of Pompeii was rapidly buried by volcanic material from the eruption of Mount Vesuvius. The archaeological site at Pompeii preserves the last moments of the city in often gruesome detail (see Figure 1.3). Pompeii provides a unique snapshot of life in a Roman city at a single moment in time. The effort to reconstruct such a moment is one of the major goals of archaeological excavation. At most sites, time is not frozen quite as spectacularly as at Pompeii, and archaeologists must work with fragmentary remains that have been significantly altered by both subsequent occupants of the site and natural processes.

When archaeologists work to reconstruct a particular moment in time, it is necessary to excavate broad areas of a site. Such an approach is referred to as **horizontal excavation**. This is contrasted with **vertical excavation**, which focuses on the sequence of occupations of the site. Figures 1.4 and 1.5 show examples of horizontal and vertical excavations.

Horizontal excavations can be carried out on any type of site, from simple hunter–gatherer camps to large urban centres. The French prehistorian André Leroi-Gourhan was among the pioneers of horizontal excavation (Leroi-Gourhan 1984). At the site of Pincevent in the Paris Basin, Leroi-Gourhan excavated a prehistoric hunter–gatherer encampment from the Magadalenian period. These people left behind no traces of architecture, yet by carefully mapping every stone tool and every animal bone found on the site, Leroi-Gourhan was able to reconstruct the locations of tents and estimate the number of family groups using the site. Pincevent was a perfect site for this undertaking because it had only one major layer of occupation, which had been rapidly buried by river silts.

FIGURE 1.3 A moment frozen in time. Excavation of bodies trapped in volcanic ash at Pompeii.

horizontal excavation An excavation for which the goal is to excavate a broad area in order to expose the remains of a single point in time.

vertical excavation An excavation for which the goal is to excavate a significant depth of deposits in order to expose the record of a sequence of occupation.

FIGURE 1.4 Example of a horizontal excavation: An Iroquoian longhouse at Crawford Lake, Ontario. Remains of this structure are postholes (marked by sticks), pits, and a large sweat lodge.

FIGURE 1.5 Excavations at the Koster site in Illinois uncovered a long sequence of occupation and provide an example of a vertical excavation. The archaeologists working at the Koster site were able to chart changes in the environment and human activities over a period spanning 8,000 years.

law of superposition In any undistributed depositional sequence, each layer of sediments is younger than the layer beneath it.

strata Discrete layers in a stratigraphic sequence.

Another ideal setting for horizontal excavation, on a much grander scale, is offered by the city of Amarna in Egypt. A new capital city, Amarna was constructed by Akhenaton as part of his program of religious reformation (1350 B.C.). Following Akhenaton's death, his reforms were repudiated and his city abandoned, never to be reoccupied. Excavations at Amarna have exposed large parts of the city plan, giving us an invaluable perspective on New Kingdom Egyptian town planning (Kemp 1989).

■ Vertical Excavation

Most archaeological sites include more than a single period of occupation. Many archaeologists are drawn to sites with a lengthy history of occupation because their interest is in long-term processes of culture change. Several archaeologists have emphasized that sites such as Pincevent and Amarna are in fact quite rare and also more complex than they at first seem. Thus, for all archaeologists, an understanding of how sites develop over time is critical. Vertical excavations focus on exposing the record of a sequence of occupation. Emphasis is placed more on excavating the entire depth of deposits than on opening large horizontal areas. In vertical excavation, archaeologists analyze the sequence of deposits, or stratigraphy, of the site. The basic concepts of stratigraphy are drawn from geology; applied to archaeology, they have led to the development of methods of archaeological stratigraphy that take into account the particular characteristics of archaeological sites.

FIGURE 1.6 Roadcut in Arizona showing layers of sedimentary rocks. Note the fault line that creates a slight offset in the layers.

GEOLOGICAL STRATIGRAPHY. When sediments are deposited in an undisturbed environment, a stratigraphic sequence will develop over time. The buildup of sediments is said to be stratigraphic in that it follows the **law of superposition**, which states that, in any undisturbed depositional sequence, each layer is younger than the layer beneath it. A stratigraphic sequence can be either continuous or discontinuous. In a continuous sequence, the sediments or rocks are uniform throughout, with no clear breaks. In a discontinuous sequence, there are clear breaks in either the types of rocks or the types of sediments. In a discontinuous sequence, it is possible to identify discrete layers, or, as they are often called in archaeology and geology, strata. Geological **strata** can be characterized either by the type of rock or sediment they consist of or by the fossils they contain.

The surface of the earth is not an undisturbed depositional environment. The movements of the plates of the earth's crust cause mountain chains and rift valleys to form. Volcanic activity brings igneous rocks from the earth's mantle to the surface. Erosion by wind, water, and glaciers breaks down and transports rocks and sediments. As a result of all of this activity, the law of superposition applies only in localized contexts where deposition has taken place. The geological science of stratigraphy has as its goal the correlation of strata across wide areas.

In many cases, geologists drill deep into the earth to gather samples for stratigraphic analyses. Such exploratory work is essential in prospecting for minerals and oil. In other cases, such as road-cuts that slice through part of a hill, it is possible to see stratigraphy directly. The exposure left by a road cut, like the one shown in Figure 1.6, is called a stratigraphic *section* or *profile*. If the rocks in the profile are sedimentary rocks—rocks that have formed from sediments in a depositional environment—we can apply the law of superposition to deduce that the rocks lower down in the sequence are older than those higher up. Often in road cuts the folding of the rocks from the processes associated with mountain building is apparent, and we can follow strata along their folds. Of course, one does need to make sure that what one is looking at is actually sedimentary rock. In many cases, what one sees in a road cut consists of either metamorphic rocks, which have formed deep in the earth's crust at high temperature and pressure, only to be thrust out onto the surface as the result of uplift, or igneous rocks, which have squeezed through the crust from the earth's mantle. The law of superposition does not necessarily apply to these kinds of rocks.

HOW ARCHAEOLOGICAL SITES FORM. Most environments on the surface of the earth can be classified as either erosional or depositional—locations where sediment is being either carried away or deposited, respectively. Buried archaeological sites form in depositional environments. In some cases, artifacts are deposited on a surface and then, over time, become incorporated into the geological strata. Most early prehistoric sites were formed in this way. In discussing the stratigraphy of such sites, one is usually referring to the position of the archaeological deposits in geological strata.

On most archaeological sites, *stratigraphy* refers to the accumulation of strata that result from a combination of geological and anthropogenic deposits. **Anthropogenic deposits** are produced by human activities ranging from building fires on ephemeral hunter–gatherer campsites to erecting the palaces and fortifications of great cities. For village and city sites, it is necessary to understand the methods and materials used in their construction, and it is also important to understand how structures decay and collapse. In many areas the main construction material used until recently has been unbaked mud brick. As mud brick structures fall out of use, they are usually eroded along the base, which causes them to collapse. The resulting collapsed house forms a mound of earth that was simply levelled out before new structures were built. As layers of collapsed mud brick houses accumulate, large artificial mounds, known in the Middle East as tels, often develop. In areas where wood or stone was the main building material, such mounds will not form, because wood will decay and stones are liable to be reused.

ARCHAEOLOGICAL STRATIGRAPHY. Archaeological sites are rarely, if ever, a simple "layer cake" of strata. Archaeological layers or strata emerge only through the process of stratigraphic analysis (see Figure 1.7). The basic units of archaeological sites are **depositional units**—material that was deposited at a particular point in time. In practice, depositional units go by many names, including *locus* and *stratigraphic feature*.

Any process that has led to the accumulation of material on an archaeological site is considered to be a depositional event. Because deposition is not continuous on archaeological sites, archaeologists are able to define depositional units. What makes the concept of depositional units confusing is that they can be of many types, including walls, floors, and the infill of pits.

FIGURE 1.7 At the site of Hammath Tiberius in northern Israel, a crude stone wall and pillars cut into an earlier mosaic floor. In most archaeological contexts it is more difficult to identify construction phases.

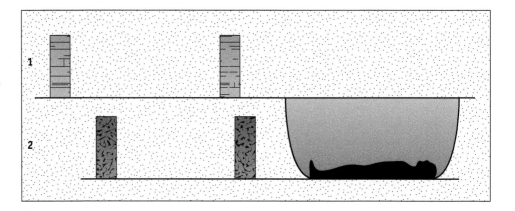

FIGURE 1.8 In this diagram of a stratigraphic profile, the surface of origin for the burial pit is in the upper level (1). Which building was contemporary with the burial?

In practice, interpreting an archaeological sequence often hinges on paying attention to the relationships among depositional units. One example of the types of problems faced in the field is determining the date of a burial pit (see Figure 1.8). The burial is not part of the depositional unit it cuts into. Rather, it is in superposition to the depositional unit, even though they are at exactly the same height. It is critical to find the surface of origin of the pit—the surface from which the pit was excavated.

Archaeologists use a range of methods to assist in a stratigraphic analysis.

- Soil micromorphology is used to characterize the accumulation of sediments at a microscopic scale (see Toolbox in Chapter 4, p. 113).
- The Harris matrix is a method for placing depositional units in stratigraphic order (see Toolbox in Chapter 7, p. 204).
- Taphonomic analysis examines the natural and cultural processes that have affected the formation of archaeological sites (see Toolbox in Chapter 2, p. 45).

■ Controlling Horizontal and Vertical Space

provenience The precise context in which an object is recovered in an excavation.

The critical task for archaeologists is to record the precise context, or **provenience**, of objects recovered during excavation. Control of horizontal and vertical space is essential to modern archaeological excavation. The first job on an archaeological site is to create a grid that covers the intended excavation area (see Figure 1.9). The size

FIGURE 1.9 A datum point provides a point of reference for measuring depth while a grid provides a means of controlling horizontal space.

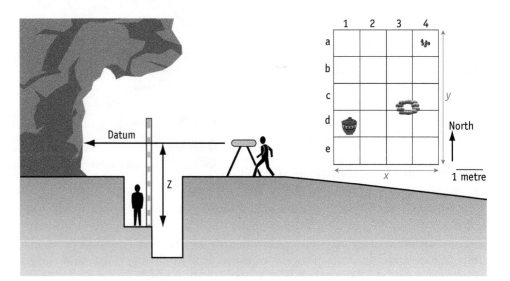

FIGURE 1.10 Excavation of Tel Knedig, Syria. The excavation consists of a series of square excavation units. Most of the baulks have been removed at this stage of excavation to provide a continuous view of the architecture.

of the squares forming the grid varies from 1 square metre on early prehistoric sites to 25 square metres (5 metres × 5 metres) on large excavations (see Figure 1.10). In some contexts, linear trenches are used rather than squares. The size of the squares and their spacing will depend on the goals of the excavation. If the goal is to get a sample representing an entire settlement, small squares might be distributed randomly across the site. If the goal is to get a broad exposure, excavation squares will cover a single continuous area. The grid is usually laid out with pegs and string. However, in cave sites, the grid can be suspended from high-tension wires anchored into the walls of the cave.

Control of vertical space requires the establishment of a fixed **datum point**, or, simply, datum, that serves as a reference for all depth measurements on the site (see Figure 1.9). Ideally, this datum is at a known elevation above or below sea level. It is essential, though not always easy, for the datum to be marked on an object or a location that will not be moved or damaged in the future. The datum point is the linchpin for the control of the excavation; loss of the datum point would make it difficult to return to the site and continue the excavation.

A wide range of tools is used for laying out grid squares and measuring depths relevant to the datum. Most excavations make use of a theodolite, which is able to measure both distance and elevation relative to a given point. Increasingly, archaeologists use digital surveying equipment during excavation, allowing for the precise recording and automatic storage of spatial data.

Excavating in square units makes it easier to draw plans of the layout of architectural remains and artifacts because one can measure the locations of objects and features with reference to the sides of the excavation square. The other advantage of excavating in square units is that the sides of the holes provide a record of the stratigraphic sequence. The sides of excavation units, known as stratigraphic profiles, show the stratigraphy of the site much in the way that a road cut gives a view of the geological stratigraphy (see Figure 1.11). Often, a one-half-metre area called a baulk is left standing around each excavation square to provide profiles. Baulks also facilitate movement around the excavation without trampling on newly exposed deposits. Drawings of the profiles left in baulks are critical records of a site's

datum point The linchpin for the control of excavation. It serves as a reference point for all depth measurements on the site.

FIGURE 1.11 Stratigraphic profile from the site of Abu Hureyra, Syria. The numbers in circles indicate discreet depositional units. These units include walls, floors, and fill. The scale on the left shows depth above mean sea level. How does this archaeological stratigraphy differ from the geological stratigraphy shown in Figure 1.6 on page 12?

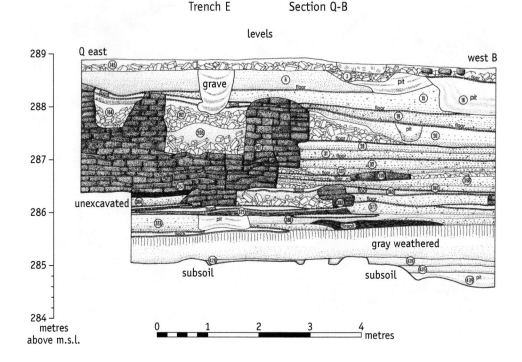

stratigraphy. Great care is taken during the excavation to ensure that these profiles are protected and that they are as straight as possible.

During excavation, it is necessary to keep moving between a horizontal and a vertical perspective. In excavating an urban site, it is critical to think in terms of the architecture being excavated. However, if, at the same time, one does not keep in mind the site's stratigraphy, there is the danger of erroneously combining walls from different phases of occupation.

■ Recovery Methods

The digging tools used in an archaeological excavation vary with the scale and goals of the project. Backhoes and bulldozers are often employed to dig exploratory trenches or to clear overlying deposits. Hand tools range from shovels and hoes to trowels and dental picks. Most excavations involve screening the excavated sediments to make sure that all artifacts are recovered. The size of the screen mesh is important in determining what sizes of objects will be recovered. If one of the goals of the excavation is the recovery of small artifacts and bones, then it is necessary to use a very fine mesh, together with water, to break up the sediments and move them through the screen. This process, called **wet screening**, is usually carried out by spraying water onto the sieve.

The recovery of botanical material (wood and seeds) requires special methods. In many locations, the most effective method is **flotation**, which involves vigorously mixing sediments in water. In the process, charred remains of seeds and wood float to the surface while the mineral sediments settle to the bottom. The charred botanical material can then be skimmed off and dried for analysis. On sites where recovering botanical material is a high priority, it is possible to set up a system that will process sediments rapidly.

At every step of recovery, whether collecting objects from excavation, from the sieve, or from flotation, it is essential that the context from which the objects were recovered be carefully tracked. Every bucket of earth that goes to the sieve must be

wet screening The process of spraying water onto a sieve to break up sediments and move them through the mesh to make sure that all artifacts are recovered during an excavation.

flotation The process used to recover botanical material (wood and seeds) which involves mixing sediments vigorously in water. In the process, charred remains of seeds and wood float to the surface while the mineral sediments settle to the bottom. The charred botanical material can then be skimmed off and dried for analysis.

clearly labelled so that its precise context is known. After the earth is sieved, the label must be transferred to the bag of recovered objects. Ultimately, each object should be labelled in ink, with the label stating the exact provenience of the find.

▪ Recording Methods

Archaeological excavation is essentially a destructive act. One cannot go back and excavate an area a second time. What is destroyed in excavation is not, one hopes, archaeological objects. Rather, it is the context within which these objects are found—the matrix of depositional units—that is destroyed. The goal of recording methods is to allow archaeologists to go back and reconstruct that context on paper after excavation. Also, it is essential that all recovered objects be linked with as precise a provenience as possible.

There are almost as many recording systems as there are archaeologists. The basic unit is usually the depositional unit, also called a locus or stratigraphic feature. Each depositional unit has its own recording sheet, which includes plan maps at various stages of excavation, stratigraphic sections showing the relation among different depositional units, and a description of the contents of the depositional unit. A careful description of soil colour and texture is often also included.

Architectural features can be treated as depositional units. In practice, many archaeologists prefer to treat walls and buildings separately from other depositional units. On excavations of urban sites, the excavation team often includes an architect whose job is to draw plans of architectural remains. Increasingly, digital media are being integrated into the process of excavation. Digital photography allows excavators to annotate photographs during the excavation and to point out significant details. Digital video allows for an ongoing recording of the excavation process.

1.3 Artifacts and Ecofacts

The objects recovered in excavations can be divided into artifacts and ecofacts. **Artifacts** are objects that show traces of human manufacture. Artifacts include tools and vessels, as well as the waste resulting from a manufacturing process. An example of a waste artifact is slag, a by-product of smelting ores. These are some of the major areas of archaeological artifact analysis:

- Lithic analysis is the study of stone tools (see Toolbox in Chapter 3, p. 73).
- Ceramic analysis is the study of pottery and other objects made of fired clay (see Toolbox in Chapter 8, pp. 226–227).
- Metallurgy is the study of metal artifacts and the by-products of smelting (see Toolbox in Chapter 14, p. 404–405).

Ecofacts are objects recovered from an archaeological context that are either the remains of biological organisms or the results of geological processes. The major areas of biological analysis include the following:

- Faunal analysis is the study of animal bones recovered on archaeological sites (see Toolbox in Chapter 2, p. 45).
- Paleoethnobotany is the study of archaeological plant remains, such as charred seeds and pollen (see Toolbox in Chapter 7, p. 208).
- Human osteoarchaeology is the study of the biological characteristics of human skeletal material recovered on archaeological excavations (see Toolbox in Chapter 13, p. 369).

artifacts Objects that show traces of human manufacture.

ecofacts Objects recovered from an archaeological context that are either the remains of biological organisms or the results of geological processes.

The Author on His Fieldwork at Wonderwerk Cave, South Africa

Wonderwerk Cave is a spectacular site located in the Northern Cape Province of South Africa, on the edge of the Kalahari. Although this is a remote area, our living conditions are quite good. We stay in small brick chalets built near the site and most of the roads are tarred. The view from the cave is of an immense open space, a flat grassland that reaches to the horizon. A nice part of working at the site is that not only do we lack Internet access, but we have to walk out to the main road to even get cell phone reception— a welcome break from my heavily connected life in Canada. However, this remote place is also the nexus of an international research team as well as a diverse range of community interests. My role at Wonderwerk seems more like that of a ringmaster in a circus than that of an archaeologist.

It might be best to begin by explaining how I ended up working at this site. In the late 1990s I was completing a project in Israel with my colleagues Liora Horwitz and Naomi Porat. Liora is a faunal analyst, Naomi is a geologist, and I am an archaeologist who specializes in stone tools, so we make a good team. We began looking for a new project that would allow us to continue to study the shift from the Lower Paleolithic to the Middle Paleolithic, or as they are known in Africa, the Earlier to the Middle Stone Age. By chance Liora was off to South Africa to visit family, which included a visit to her uncle's farm in the Free State. En route she stopped off in Kimberley, a diamond mining city that is home to Peter Beaumont. Peter is famous for excavating sites of the time range we were interested in, and before I knew it I was off to South Africa for an unforgettable tour with Peter. The wealth of sites he showed us and the extent of the excavations he had carried out was simply staggering. We resolved to develop a project to analyze the collections from Peter's excavations at Wonderwerk Cave housed at the McGregor Museum, carry out small-scale field projects to document the stratigraphy on the site, and collect samples for geological and botanical analysis (Figure 1.12).

Seven years later we are still hard at work. Our research team has swelled to over fifteen members from South Africa, England, Israel, Canada, and the United States. Our most exciting result is the dating of the base of the deposit at Wonderwerk to 2 million years ago. The stone tools from this stratum provide the earliest evidence for hominin cave occupation in the world. My job as the codirector of this project is not simply to analyze stone tools but to coordinate the activities of all the scientists working at the site. This is a fascinating undertaking, since each member of the team comes to the project with his/her own perspective, and meshing these perspectives is a tremendous challenge. We have also found ourselves involved in ongoing discussions with the local community. Wonderwerk Cave is a candidate for a World Heritage status and a critical element of the tourism development in this area. Wonderwerk is also integrated into local school curriculum, and all children from the area schools visit the site during their primary years. Combining the educational, tourism, and scientific potential of this site is every bit as complex as the analysis of Earlier Stone Age stone tools. Days at Wonderwerk tend to be a bit unpredictable and are almost always interesting. A day that begins with conversations with local Tswana chiefs might also involve careful excavation and complex discussions of stratigraphy and geophysics. One couldn't ask for much more. ▲

FIGURE 1.12 Taking samples for paleomagnetic dating of the early hominin occupation at Wonderwerk Cave, South Africa.

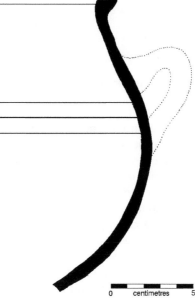

FIGURE 1.13 This archaeological illustration of a ceramic vessel shows the exterior of the vessel on the left side and a section through the vessel wall on the right.

Ecofacts are studied with an eye toward reconstructing the ecological setting of the site or looking for evidence of human activity on the site. Often, these two goals are closely linked. For example, in studying the animal bones from a hunter–gatherer site, one needs to reconstruct the ecological setting in order to understand the occupants' hunting strategies.

Archaeologists have developed conventions for representing objects in drawings. One example is the illustration of ceramic vessels, shown in Figure 1.13. The convention is to show a view of the outside of the vessel, including any surface treatment and decoration, on one side of the drawing. The other side of the drawing reveals a section through the vessel wall, which gives a sense of the thickness of the vessel and the shape of the rim and base. This convention can be used both with complete vessels and with fragments from the rim of the vessel— what archaeologists refer to as rim sherds. In drawing a rim sherd, the original diameter of the vessel is calculated on the basis of the arc of the fragment of the rim.

1.4 Biases in Preservation

Look around the room you are sitting in, and imagine what would be preserved thousands of years from now. Most organic materials, such as paper and leather, would be preserved only under remarkable conditions, such as rapid burial in an environment with no oxygen (e.g., a bog; see Figure 1.14). Valuable metals are likely to have been reused, unless they are left behind when a site is abruptly abandoned or they are placed in a ritual context such as a tomb. Differences in preservation create a bias in what is found on archaeological sites. Archaeologists must take into consideration **postdepositional processes**—those events that take place after the site was occupied.

FIGURE 1.14 The soft tissue of this one-thousand-year-old burial, known as Lindow Man, has been preserved because it was buried in a bog, resulting in a process of natural mummification.

postdepositional processes
Events that take place after a site has been occupied.

Arctic Explorers of the Nineteenth Century

The Arctic explorers of the Franklin Expedition were the astronauts of the mid-nineteenth century. Setting out in 1845, the HMS *Erebus* and HMS *Terror* ventured into a forbidding environment that Europeans thought of as the ultimate unknown. The expedition ended not in the triumphant discovery of the Northwest Passage but in tragedy, with all hands lost to an unknown fate.

In 1981, Owen Beattie of the University of Alberta began a project combining methods from archaeology and forensics to untangle the mystery of the fate of the Franklin Expedition. Beattie and his colleagues disinterred the frozen corpses of three sailors who died early in the voyage of the expedition. The analysis of these bodies, together with a collection of artifacts left behind by the expedition, cast a chilling new light on the fate of these explorers.

When he analyzed bone, tissue, and hair samples, Beattie found that they held highly elevated levels of lead; these men were suffering from lead poisoning. They probably did not die from the lead poisoning, but this affliction would have left them vulnerable to pneumonia and other diseases. The source of the lead was the seemingly innocuous lead solder that had been applied to the insides of the tin cans the expedition had used to carry its provisions. Beattie suggested that lead poisoning contributed to the weakening of the crew, ultimately leaving them unable to survive the rigours of the Arctic environment. ◆

REFERENCE: Owen Beattie and John Geiger. (1998). *Frozen in Time: The Fate of the Franklin Expedition.* Vancouver: Greystone Books.

Postdepositional processes can be caused by climate (such as frost heave) and biological agents (including termites, earthworms, and rodents), both of which can move material around the site and distort its stratigraphy. A number of archaeologists have pointed out that cultural practices, such as where garbage is disposed, will also shape the archaeological record (Schiffer 1987).

Taphonomy is the study of the processes that affect organic remains after death. An important line of evidence for all taphonomic studies is traces found on the surface of bones recovered on archaeological sites. The overall condition of the surface of the bone can indicate whether it has been transported by water or has suffered significant chemical weathering. Chewing by animals ranging from rodents to bears often leaves characteristic marks on the surface of the bone. If a bone has passed through the digestive tract of an animal such as a hyena or a dog, the surface of the bone will show characteristic etching. Human action can often be detected through the identification of cut marks left when meat was sliced off the bone or the carcass was disarticulated with a stone tool. Human action can also be detected on the basis of percussion marks left when the bone is smashed open to access marrow.

1.5 Quantification and Sampling

In early excavations, representing what had been found was a simple process. One just took all the complete vessels and tools, placed them in a row, and snapped a photograph or made a sketch of the collection. Figure 2.8 shown on page 39 provides an excellent example of this. But this approach works only so long as one recovers complete artifacts and discards everything else. Today, archaeologists recover all artifacts, including broken pieces and waste, as well as a wide range of ecofacts. Only in rare cases is it possible to present each object individually. Certainly, unique pieces and artifacts of particular historical or artistic merit receive individual attention. However, the vast bulk of the material can be represented only by quantitative methods. The methods of **quantification** used by archaeologists range from simple databases, which provide counts of various types of objects, to sophisticated statistical techniques.

taphonomy The study of the processes that affect organic remains after death.

quantification Methods used by archaeologists to represent the large quantities of material recovered in excavations and surveys.

In analyses of large bodies of data, it is often possible to use a sampling strategy such that only a portion of the material is analyzed. In studying artifacts and ecofacts, archaeologists often rely on statistical sampling strategies to allow a true representation of the site to emerge without having to measure or describe every single object recovered. On many sites, the number of artifacts and ecofacts recovered is in the hundreds of thousands, making sampling an essential tool.

Counting Bones

Using quantitative methods requires that one understand the way these methods work. Problems that at first glance seem quite simple often turn out to be far more complex. For example, counting animal bones would seem to be quite a straightforward undertaking (Davis 1987). If one is able to identify the bones by species, then one should be able to make a chart illustrating the relative frequency of bones of different animals found on the site. This method of counting is known as number of identifiable specimens (NISP). Some archaeologists have argued that NISP does not provide an accurate quantitative picture of the relative frequency of different animals that make up an assemblage. To illustrate this point, imagine a site that produced the complete skeleton of a rabbit and ten left tibia from cows. According to NISP, there would be more rabbits represented on the site than cows. But in fact, there are the remains of one rabbit and five cows. To get around this problem, some archaeologists prefer to use a method known as minimum number of individuals (MNI). According to this method, each skeletal element (i.e., left tibia or first upper premolar) is counted individually. The number of examples of a given element is then divided by the number of bones of that type that occur in an individual skeleton. For example, there are two first upper premolars in any individual skeleton, so the number of upper premolars found would be divided by 2. It is quite likely that not all skeletal elements will indicate the same number of animals, so the largest number is used to determine the MNI of animals at the site. In the case just described, the MNI for rabbits would be 1 and the MNI for cows would be 5 (see Figure 1.15). Of course, we still have the problem that the meat yield of a rabbit is quite a bit smaller than the meat yield of a cow. One way to overcome this challenge is to multiply the number of individuals by the average weight of a carcass of the species. What this example highlights is the fact that the way objects are counted will shape the picture that emerges.

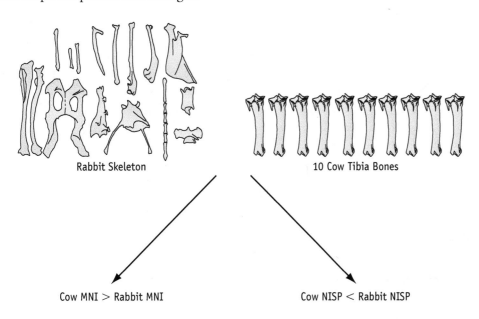

Rabbit Skeleton

10 Cow Tibia Bones

Cow MNI > Rabbit MNI

Cow NISP < Rabbit NISP

FIGURE 1.15 The method used to quantify the animal bones found on an archaeological site will have a major impact on the picture that emerges. In this case, the use of NISP or MNI leads to very different conclusions about the proportion of rabbits and cows.

■ Counting Artifacts

If you were asked to go through your kitchen and inventory its contents, you would create a list of appliances, utensils, and vessels. You would be unlikely to have much difficulty coming up with names for these various objects. Archaeologists working on colonial and historical periods in the United States have access to inventories, known as probate records, drawn up by assessors who went carefully through a person's home after their death (Orser 2004). However, archaeologists working on prehistoric sites do not have access to lists of artifacts drawn up by the people who lived there at the time. One of the first steps of artifact analysis is to create a classification of the objects.

Most artifact classifications begin by defining major categories of objects. In your kitchen, you would be likely to separate appliances from vessels and utensils. You might then define vessels as objects used to hold food and utensils as tools used to process food by hand. It would then be rather simple to divide vessels into pots, pans, plates, and bowls and to divide utensils into forks, knives, and spoons. Archaeologists follow such a process, often sorting artifacts on the basis of their material of manufacture (e.g., bone tools, stone tools, pottery, metal).

Archaeologists usually want to go beyond simply reporting how many bowls and plates were found on a site. It is often critical to describe the detailed characteristics of the artifacts. Including this type of information, even in the inventory of your own kitchen, might be challenging. How do you describe a plate, a fork, or a knife? Archaeologists often develop detailed systems of classification based on types of artifacts. A **typology** is a list of artifact types for a particular archaeological context. Archaeologists use typologies to draw up an inventory of the artifacts they have found.

A good example of a typology is the list of types of ceramic vessels used in classical Greece (see Figure 1.16). These vessel types are known by the names the ancient Greeks gave them. Most archaeological typologies, however, are far more refined than a simple description of vessel types. The purpose of detailed archaeological typologies is to register nuances of style that reflect when and where an artifact

typology A list used to draw up an inventory of types of artifacts found by archaeologists in a particular archaeological context.

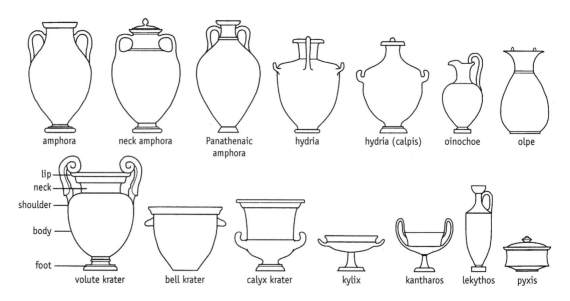

FIGURE 1.16 Greek pottery vessels with their Greek names. Do we have a similar system for the vessels we use?

TOOLBOX

Ethnoarchaeology

Ethnoarchaeology refers to research carried out by archaeologists living with and observing communities in order to make a contribution to archaeology. Archaeologists bring to the study of modern cultures an intense interest in the material aspects of human lives. Ethnoarchaeological research covers a wide range of domains, including subsistence, technology, ideology, and site formation.

Much of our understanding of stone tool manufacture comes from ethnoarchaeological studies of societies that still use stone tools or have used them recently. Among the stone tool techniques studied by ethnoarchaeologists are ground stone axe manufacture in Papua New Guinea, flint knapping in Australia, obsidian tool manufacture and use in Ethiopia, and stone bead manufacture in India. All of these studies provide an insight into the process of tool manufacture and the way tools are used. Ethnoarchaeological studies have also provided an insight into how people think about the tools they are making. For example, on the basis of ethnoarchaeological research in Australia, Brian Hayden has questioned whether people making stone tools ever think about making a specific type of tool. Interestingly, in the group Hayden worked with, the focus of attention was on the type of edge produced, and the actual form of the tool was of little importance.

Ethnoarchaeological research also can provide a reminder of the limitations of the archaeological record. In 1974 and 1975, Robert and Priscilla Janes lived for twenty-two weeks with the Slavey Dene people in the Northwest Territories (Janes 1983). The Slavey Dene spend most of the year in Fort Norman but move to seasonal camps during the late winter or early spring. The Janeses' research examined the structure of one of these camps. Their experience living with the Slavey Dene led them to recognize the "potential immensity of the gap . . . between the results of field archaeology and the richness of a living culture" (David and Kramer 2001, 288). This gap is particularly wide in the case of hunter–gatherer societies, which made most artifacts out of perishable material.

In some cases, ethnoarchaeologists do not simply make observations, but rather collaborate with members of local communities to carry out experiments. During the 1970s, Peter Schmidt and his colleagues collaborated with members of a Haya community from northeastern Tanzania to smelt iron by traditional methods (Schmidt 1997). Because the Haya had not practised traditional smelting for over fifty years, this project was guided by Haya elders who remembered participating in smelting operations as children. The resulting smelt was only partially successful, but it did provide an opportunity to carefully document the functioning of the iron furnace, as well as the processes involved in producing charcoal and in mining the clay used to build the furnace. The furnace produced in the experiment served as an important point of reference for the interpretation of archaeologically excavated furnaces.

Despite the obvious value of ethnoarchaeological research, some archaeologists have reservations about the use of ethnographic analogies in archaeology. Martin Wobst (1978) has written of the "tyranny of the ethnographic record," which leads archaeologists to assume that the cultures they are investigating were similar to ethnographically known cultures. A slavish adherence to analogy can dull our awareness of those aspects of past societies that are unique and different from characteristics of societies living in the present. The use of ethnographic analogy is also not helpful in studying long-term processes of cultural change that last hundreds, thousands, or even tens of thousands of years and that are of particular interest to archaeologists (see Figure 1.17). ●

REFERENCE: Nicholas David and Carole Kramer. (2001). *Ethnoarchaeology in Action*. Cambridge: Cambridge University Press.

FIGURE 1.17 An ethnoarchaeologist with a Hadza hunter in Tanzania, East Africa. What kind of questions might the ethnoarchaeologist be asking?

was manufactured. A modern artifact that has undergone regular changes in form is the ubiquitous Coca-Cola bottle. Ever since a standard bottle was adopted for Coca-Cola in 1916, the shape and decoration of the bottle have changed regularly. These changes can be used as chronological indicators. For example, if you find a bottle with the logo "Coca-Cola" painted on it, the bottle must date to after 1958, the date when painted bottles first appeared (Orser 2004).

Archaeological typologies are often highly detailed, with dozens of types for each category of artifact. Once a typology has been developed, the number of objects belonging to each type can be counted to create a quantitative inventory of artifacts found in a particular context. Typologies are built from combinations of artifact attributes that the archaeologist intuitively selects to define the various types. An **attribute** is a particular characteristic of an artifact. For a simple ceramic bowl, one can observe a surprising number of attributes. Some of these attributes describe the clay out of which the bowl was made and the decoration applied to the bowl. Other attributes describe the shape of the bowl, including the form of the base, the curvature of the walls, and the shape of the rim. Still other attributes measure the size of the bowl. Some archaeologists see the value of typologies as limited, arguing that types can be defined only on the basis of a statistical analysis of the attributes of all of the vessels found in a context. Other archaeologists argue that the idea of vessel types should be discarded completely in favour of the analysis of attributes. From this perspective, artifact types are an unjustified abstraction that distort our picture of the archaeological record.

1.6 Creating a Chronology

Depositional units are dated on the basis of material recovered within the unit during excavation. This is one of the reasons it is so important to know the exact provenience of every recovered object. Objects can be dated by a variety of methods. Some artifacts are of a known date of manufacture. Coins are a good example of such artifacts. Artifacts with a known date of manufacture allow archaeologists to create an **absolute chronology** stated in terms of calendar years. Other artifacts can be placed within a regional chronology on the basis of style. Often, pottery is used to date archaeological sites because of frequent, identifiable changes in the shape and decoration of vessels. Frequently, chronologies based on artifact typology are **relative chronologies** that place assemblages in a temporal sequence not directly linked to calendar dates.

In most regional chronologies, artifacts are used to correlate the stratigraphic sequence of a site with the chronological framework for a region. In the absence of artifacts with a known date of manufacture, the relative frequency of different artifacts is used to fit a particular context into a regional chronology. The method of comparing the relative frequency of artifact types between contexts is known as **seriation**. The assumption behind seriation is that the frequency of an artifact form will increase gradually over time and then decline gradually after reaching a peak.

An important illustration of the principle that the frequency of an artifact form will increase gradually over time and then decline gradually after reaching a peak is found in shifting preferences for design motifs on gravestones in Colonial America, like the one shown in Figure 1.18 (Deetz 1996). From 1720 to 1750, the main motif used on gravestones was the death's head. Between 1760 and 1780, the frequency of death's heads declined as cherub motifs increased. The number of cherub motifs reached a peak between 1780 and 1789. After 1780,

attribute A particular characteristic of an artifact.

absolute chronology A chronology stated in terms of calendar years.

relative chronology A chronology that places assemblages in a temporal sequence not directly linked to calendar dates.

seriation The method of comparing the relative frequency of artifact types between contexts.

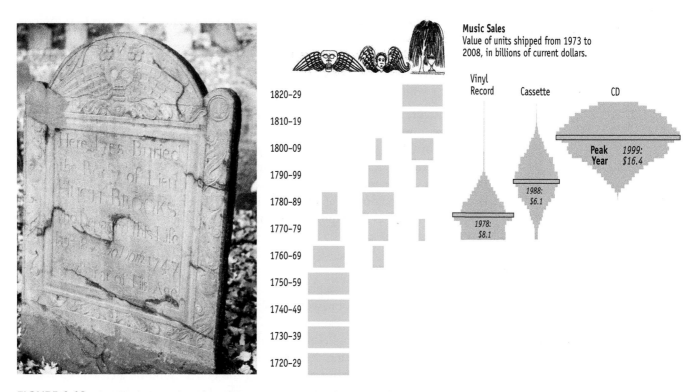

Music Sales
Value of units shipped from 1973 to 2008, in billions of current dollars.

1820–29

1810–19

1800–09

1790–99

1780–89

1770–79

1760–69

1750–59

1740–49

1730–39

1720–29

Vinyl Record — 1978: $8.1

Cassette — 1988: $6.1

CD — **Peak Year** *1999: $16.4*

FIGURE 1.18 Two illustrations of seriation. Shifts over time in the designs carved on New England headstones, such as the winged skull carved on the top of this headstone from 1747. The changing frequency of death's head, cherub, and willow and urn motifs provides an excellent illustration of the principles underlying seriation. In a more contemporary context the shifts in technologies used by the recorded music industry demonstrate the same principles.

the frequency of cherub motifs gradually declined as that of urn and willow motifs increased.

A number of scientific methods have been developed for determining absolute dates of material recovered from archaeological sites.

- Radiocarbon dating measures the decay of carbon isotopes. Charcoal, bone, and other organic material can be dated with this method. Radiocarbon dating can be used for sites younger than 40,000 years. Accelerator mass spectrometry (AMS) radiocarbon dating is an advanced method that can date extremely small samples (see Toolbox p. 27).

- Argon dating identifies the time of a volcanic eruption. Argon dating can be used on early hominin sites in contexts where there are layers of volcanic ash (see Toolbox in Chapter 3, p. 80–81).

- Paleomagnetism measures reversals in the earth's magnetic field. Paleomagnetism is most useful for dating early hominin sites (see Toolbox in Chapter 3, p. 80–81).

- Luminescence dating methods are used to measure the uptake of radioactive material. Luminescence methods can be used to date soils (optically stimulated luminescence), animal teeth (electron spin resonance), and burnt flint (thermoluminescence) from early hominin sites. Particularly useful for the period between 300,000 and 30,000 years ago, luminescence can also be used for more recent periods to learn when pottery vessels were fired (see Toolbox in Chapter 5, p. 130–131).

- Dendrochronology uses sequences of tree rings to date wood found on archaeological sites. In some areas of the world, the dendrochronological sequence has been established for a period of thousands of years (see Toolbox in Chapter 10, p. 293).

- Obsidian hydration measures the decay of the surface of obsidian artifacts. Obsidian hydration is often used on sites several thousand years old or younger.

Absolute dates can be expressed on a number of time scales. In this text, we employ a time scale that uses the birth of Christ as the point of reference. Dates after the birth of Christ can be expressed as years A.D. or years C.E. In this book, we use years A.D. Years before the birth of Christ can be expressed as years B.C. or years B.C.E. In this book, we use years B.C. When archaeologists work on early prehistoric sites, they tend to count years back from the present rather than using years B.C. In this book such dates are expressed as years before present, or years B.P.

1.7 Comparison

Much of the work that takes place in an archaeological laboratory involves comparison. A comparative collection, which serves as a point of reference, is an important tool in archaeological research. Faunal analysis laboratories usually have an extensive reference collection of modern skeletons from known species. Preparing these collections is a laborious process involving the collection and defleshing of carcasses. Faunal reference collections are essential for identifying the bones found on archaeological sites.

The spatial scale of comparisons can vary. **Intrasite** comparisons look at differences between contexts within a single site. Comparing the size and contents of different houses to try to determine the social structure of a society is an example of an intrasite analysis. **Intersite** comparisons examine differences between two or more sites. Comparing the number of houses between sites in a region is an example of intersite analysis.

The temporal scale of comparisons can also vary. **Synchronic studies** make comparisons within a single period. An example of a synchronic study is the comparison of burial practices from a single period. The goal of synchronic studies is to understand the workings of a society at a given point in time. A synchronic study of burial practices might indicate the presence of social inequality within a society. **Diachronic studies** make comparisons between different periods. An example of a diachronic study is a comparison of burial practices between periods. The goal of diachronic studies is to understand processes that change through time. A diachronic study of burial practices might provide evidence about the emergence of social inequality.

Archaeologists have often relied on analogies to descriptions of living cultures to help interpret archaeological remains. Some archaeologists practise "living archaeology," using observations made in the present to help interpret archaeological remains. Two such techniques are the following:

- Ethnoarchaeology is research carried out by archaeologists living with and observing communities in order to make a contribution to archaeology (see Toolbox p. 23).
- Experimental archaeology involves attempts to replicate archaeological features or objects (see Toolbox in Chapter 6, p. 160).

1.8 Conservation and Display

The process of excavation also includes the conservation of excavated areas and, in some cases, the consolidation of remains for display (Figure 1.21). At the most basic level, it is essential that excavated areas be filled back in after excavation, unless there

intrasite Having to do with contexts within a single site—for example, an analysis comparing the sizes and contents of different houses to try to determine the social structure of a society.

intersite Comparisons between two or more sites—for example, an analysis comparing the number of houses between sites in a region.

synchronic studies Studies that make comparisons within a single period.

diachoronic studies Studies that make comparisons between different periods and look at processes of change through time.

TOOLBOX

Radiocarbon Dating

The story of radiocarbon dating begins in the upper atmosphere, where neutrons from cosmic rays bombard atoms of nitrogen to produce carbon-14 atoms. Carbon-14 is an isotope of carbon, which means that it is chemically identical to other forms of carbon, including carbon-12 and carbon-13. However, because of its extra neutron, carbon-14 is unstable, or radioactive. The half-life of carbon-14 is 5,730 years. Thus, in a sample of carbon-14, half of the atoms will decay to a more stable carbon isotope over a period of exactly 5,730 years. In other words, 1% of the sample will decay every 83 years.

Once carbon-14 atoms form in the atmosphere, they rapidly combine with oxygen to form molecules of carbon dioxide (CO_2). These molecules then spread through the atmosphere, the oceans, and the biosphere, entering plants through photosynthesis. Remarkably, the ratio between carbon-14 and nonradioactive molecules of carbon is the same throughout the atmosphere, the oceans, and the biosphere, known collectively as the "carbon exchange reservoir." (see Figure 1.19.)

Carbon-14 decays at a constant rate and is found in the same concentration throughout the carbon exchange reservoir. How do these facts allow us to use carbon-14 to date archaeological remains? Animals, trees, and plants are all part of the carbon exchange reservoir. While they live, these organisms maintain the same concentration of carbon-14 found throughout the reservoir. This is as true for you as it is for a tree. The tree exchanges carbon through photosynthesis, and you participate in the exchange reservoir by eating plants, or animals that eat plants. However, when a plant or animal dies, it ceases to exchange carbon. From that point in time,

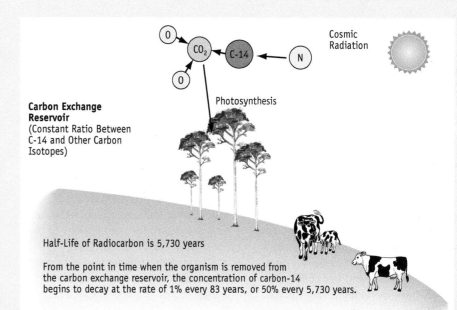

Carbon Exchange Reservoir (Constant Ratio Between C-14 and Other Carbon Isotopes)

Photosynthesis

Cosmic Radiation

Half-Life of Radiocarbon is 5,730 years

From the point in time when the organism is removed from the carbon exchange reservoir, the concentration of carbon-14 begins to decay at the rate of 1% every 83 years, or 50% every 5,730 years.

FIGURE 1.19 Radiocarbon dating is based on the participation of all living organisms in the carbon exchange reservoir.

when the organism is removed from the carbon exchange reservoir, the concentration of carbon-14 begins to decay at the rate of 1% every 83 years, or 50% every 5,730 years.

Radiocarbon dating calculates the time since an organism was removed from the carbon exchange reservoir by measuring the concentration of carbon-14 relative to stable isotopes of carbon (carbon-13 and carbon-12). By calculating the amount of carbon-14 that has decayed, it is possible to determine when the organism stopped exchanging carbon. This event usually marks the death of the organism; however, in trees it marks the end of an annual growth cycle (see Dendrochronology Toolbox in Chapter 10, p. 293).

The impact of radiocarbon dating on archaeology has been nothing short of revolutionary. Carbon-14 provided the first means of finding an absolute

age for archaeological discoveries, an achievement that earned W.F. Libby the Nobel Prize. In later chapters, we will look at two further developments of this method: calibration (see Toolbox in Chapter 6, p. 164) and accelerator mass spectroscopy (see Toolbox in Chapter 8, p. 221).

Radiocarbon dating works for samples less than 40,000 years old, although some researchers are attempting to transcend this frontier. Almost all organic materials, including bone and wood, can be dated. All radiocarbon dates are reported with an error range that reflects statistical limits of the method, as well as limits in the precision of laboratory equipment. (To simplify the presentation, the error range is not given with dates in this book.) ●

REFERENCE: R.E. Taylor and Martin Aiken. (1997). *Chronometric Dating in Archaeology*. New York: Plenum.

Community Archaeology

There is a general trend in archaeology toward including local communities in the process and the benefits of archaeological research (McGuire 2008). In recent years some archaeologists have taken this idea a step further and worked to develop a truly community-based archaeology in which the archaeologists relinquish to the local community at least partial control over their program of research (Marshall 2002). In many cases archaeologists are trying to react with sensitivity to painful histories of colonialism and disenfranchisement. In a project at the site of Quseir in Egypt, Stephanie Moser and her colleagues (2002) have developed some guidelines for the practice of Community Archaeology. They outline the following components for Community Archaeology projects:

1. Communication and collaboration
2. Employment and training
3. Public presentation
4. Interviews and oral history
5. Development of educational resources
6. Creation of a photographic and video archive
7. Community-controlled merchandising

Moser and her colleagues make it clear that not all circumstances will fit this template and that Community Archaeology must be sensitive to local conditions. However, the range of topics included gives a good sense of the complexity of adopting a community-driven approach. The project at Quseir addresses elements of economic development including employment and training as well as merchandising; aspects of local identity through the development of archives and oral history; as well as initiatives related to educa-

tion. Some archaeologists, while appreciating the importance of a community-based approach, stress the complexities involved in such an undertaking. One of the most difficult problems is the definition of the community that is at the very root of Community Archaeology (Chirikure and Pwiti 2008). In many areas of the world the definition of communities is deeply contested. However, this issue can feed into the process of Community Archaeology as archaeologists are drawn into discussions of the construction of local identities.

Community engagement is increasingly a significant component of many archaeological projects in Canada. The Tla'amin-Simon Fraser University Archaeology and Stewardship Program (http://www.sliammonfirstnation.com/archaeology/) is a fieldschool and

research project that sets out explicit goals that go well beyond the scope of traditional archaeological research:

1. Sustaining collaborations between the university and the Tla'amin First Nation
2. Identifying, documenting, and investigating heritage sites
3. Training university students and Tla'amin youth in archaeology and heritage stewardship
4. Increasing awareness and knowledge about Tla'amin history
5. Facilitiating exchanges of information and experience among Tla'amin Elders, youth, and the university
6. Advancing Tla'amin goals of self-governance, self-determination, and self-representation ●

FIGURE 1.20 Tla'amin cultural expert and project collaborator Siemthlut (Michelle Washington) and her daughter help screen for artifacts at one of the project's excavation sites. Courtesy of Georgia Combes and Dana Lepofsky.

is a clear plan for exhibition in place. When exhibition of the site is involved, the exposed remains need to be consolidated.

Recent excavations at the Neolithic site of Çatal Höyük, Turkey, directed by Ian Hodder, are unusual in that a consideration of the use of the site for exhibition is fundamental to the project as a whole (http://www.catalhoyuk.com). Çatal Höyük is well known for spectacular frescoes discovered in earlier excavations. Hodder and his team have worked to develop methods of preserving these frescoes and allowing them to be viewed by the public. They are also working to integrate the archaeological process into the exhibit. In a similar vein, excavations in historical Annapolis, Maryland, aim at providing the public the opportunity to engage in the reinterpretation of the history of that city (Leone, Potter, and Shackel 1987).

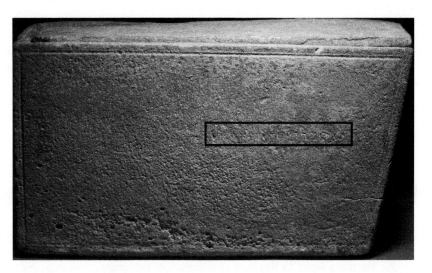

FIGURE 1.21 The James ossuary on display at the Royal Ontario Museum. Note the inscription that reads "James, brother of Jesus" (indicated by the black rectangle). This exhibit has been debated by archaeologists who are divided on the question of the authenticity of this object. How important is authenticity in shaping our experience of museum exhibits?

Courtesy of the Royal Ontario Museum © ROM.

CHAPTER SUMMARY

- Archaeological surveys involve mapping sites of the physical remains of human activity.
- Horizontal excavations have as their goal the reconstruction of a single occupation. Vertical excavations focus on exposing the record of a long sequence of occupations.
- A stratigraphic sequence develops where sediments are deposited over time. Strata can be identified when the deposition is discontinuous. The law of superposition states that, in an undisturbed depositional sequence, each layer is younger than the layer beneath it.
- Archaeological sites are made up of depositional units.
- Grids are used to control horizontal space at the site of an excavation, while measurement from a datum point is used to control the vertical dimension. Recovery methods used on excavations include sieving, wet sieving, and flotation.
- Artifacts are objects that show traces of human manufacture. Ecofacts are objects recovered from an archaeological context that are either the remains of biological organisms or the results of geological processes.

- Quantification is used to represent the large samples of artifacts and ecofacts recovered from archaeological excavations. Often, a sampling strategy is used to select a representative group of artifacts for study.
- Minimum number of individuals (MNI) and number of identifiable specimens (NISP) are two methods for quantifying animal bones.
- Quantitative studies of artifacts often rely on the use of typologies, in which the artifacts are classified according to a list of discrete types.
- In some cases, archaeologists analyze artifacts on the basis of a statistical analysis of their attributes. Attributes are particular characteristics of an artifact.
- A range of scientific methods is used to date archaeological contexts. Artifact typology and seriation can also be used to date archaeological contexts.
- Synchronic studies make comparisons within a single period, while diachronic studies make comparisons across periods. Intrasite comparisons are made within a site, while intersite comparisons are made between sites.

KEY TERMS

absolute chronology, 24
anthropogenic deposits, 13
artifacts, 17
attribute, 24
datum point, 15
depositional units, 13

diachronic studies, 26
ecofacts, 17
flotation, 16
geographical information systems (GIS), 10
horizontal excavation, 11
in situ, 9

REVIEW QUESTIONS

1. What is the difference between horizontal and vertical excavations? How would you decide which type of approach to choose in a given archaeological situation?
2. Are there limits to the kind of information archaeologists can recover?
3. Why do archaeologists use sampling?
4. Why is quantification important for archaeological analysis? What methods of quantification are used in the analysis of animal bones?
5. What is the difference between an analysis based on typology and an analysis based on attributes?

CANADIAN ARCHAEOLOGISTS

- E.B. Banning, professor in the Department of Anthropology at the University of Toronto, has carried out extensive field research on the Neolithic societies of the Near East. He has published on archaeological survey methods, including *Archaeological Survey* (2002), Academic/Plenum Publishing, New York.
  http://www.chass.utoronto.ca/~banning/

- James Conolly, professor in the Department of Anthropology at Trent University, currently directs a landscape survey of the small Aegean island of Antikythera. He has published research on the use of geographical information systems in archaeology, including *Geographical Information Systems in Archaeology* (Cambridge University Press, 2006).
  http://naxos.tuarc.trentu.ca/~jconolly/jamesconolly.html

- Nicholas David, professor in the Department of Archaeology at the University of Calgary, has directed the Mandara Archaeological Project in Cameroon, Nigeria, and Ghana since 1984. He has published extensively on ethnoarchaeology, including *Ethnoarchaeology in Action,* written with Carol Kramer (Cambridge University Press, 2001).
  http://homepages.ucalgary.ca/~ndavid/Homepage/

- Dana Lepofsky, professor in the Department of Archaeology at Simon Fraser University, carries out field research on sites in the Pacific Northwest and in Polynesia. She is currently engaged in a collaborative research project with the Tla'amin First Nation that involves a significant component of community archaeology.
  http://www.sfu.ca/archaeology/faculty/lepofsky/index.html

PEARSON
myanthrokit™

Visit **www.myanthrokit.com**, where you will find a variety of tools and resources to enhance your learning, including:
- Practise quizzes with Study Plans
- Videos
- Listening Activities
- And much more!

Unsealing the tomb of Tu

2 ''

n the mid-1700s, two philosophers of the French Enlightenment began one of the most audacious schemes in the history of publishing. Diderot and D'Alembert planned to write an encyclopedia that would collect all human knowledge into a series of massive tomes (see Figure 2.1). The resulting lavishly illustrated volumes fell far short of this goal. Today, however, the Enlightenment dream embodied in Diderot and D'Alembert's *Encyclopedia* is alive and well, particularly on the Internet, where attempts to collect massive quantities of information have reached a level unimaginable even a decade ago. Still, regardless of technological advances, the Internet is likely to fail just as the two French philosophers failed 250 years ago.

The basic flaw in Diderot and D'Alembert's plan was that they failed to realize that knowledge does not emerge from a collection of facts. If nothing else, data in the absence of ideas simply overwhelms our capacity to assimilate information; nobody could actually read the entire *Encyclopedia*. This is a critical insight for archaeologists. The archaeological record includes the totality of traces left by human activity over a period of more than 2 million years, across almost the entire surface of the globe. If archaeology were simply the collection of data, then we would be engaged in a futile task, one in which we would rapidly drown in masses of information. Methods of recovery, recording, and analysis are not enough for archaeology to function. Archaeologists cannot simply be technicians (Taylor 1948); archaeologists must also develop the ideas that guide and give meaning to their search through the human past.

The previous chapter discussed the methods archaeologists use in the field and in the laboratory. These methods are tightly linked to ways of thinking about the past and about what we can learn about it from the material remains found on archaeological sites. This chapter presents a brief history of the development of **archaeological theory** and method. Archaeological theory consists of the ideas archaeologists have developed about the past and about the ways we come to know it. We begin the chapter with an examination of the origins of archaeology and the recognition of the depth of human antiquity. We then consider the growing awareness that archaeologists must develop a body of self-reflexive theory—theory that addresses the question of how we use the archaeological record to gain access to the past. We will look at the powerful set of ideas advanced by the New Archaeologists of the 1960s and the sharp reaction to their ideas developed by the postprocessual archaeologists beginning in the 1980s. We will finish by briefly surveying some of the emerging new directions in archaeological theory.

FIGURE 2.1 A page from Diderot and D'Alambert's *Encyclopedia* showing a pottery factory. Notice that the authors try to show both the manufacturing process in the upper part of the plate and the products on the bottom.

archaeological theory Ideas that archaeologists have developed about the past and about the ways we come to know the past.

2.1 Origins of Archaeology

Relics of human activity have been present in the landscape for millions of years. However, the earliest evidence of a conscious recognition of ancient objects comes from the early state societies of Mesopotamia, Egypt, and China. For example,

FIGURE 2.2 The stela in front of the sphinx records a dream in which Thutmose IV was told to free the sphinx from the sands that buried it.

FIGURE 2.3 A fifteenth-century drawing with the oldest known representation of an archaeological excavation. The accompanying text reads "Time conquers all, it embraces all human endeavors and all human handicrafts."

Nabonidus, who ascended to the throne of Babylon in 556 B.C., wrote about the city of Ur: "At that time Egipar, the holy precinct, wherein the rites of the high priestess used to be carried out, was an abandoned place, and had become a heap of ruin.... I cut down the trees, removed the rubble of its ruins, I set eyes on the temple and its foundation terrace became visible" (Schnapp 1997, 41). In Egypt, King Thutmose IV (1412–1402 B.C.) set up a monumental inscribed stone, or stela, between the paws of the great Sphinx at Giza (see Figure 2.2). The inscription relates a dream Thutmose had as a young man in which the sun god promises him kingship in return for freeing the sphinx from the sands that bury it (Hallo and Simpson 1971, 265). When Nabonidus and Thutmose IV excavated antiquities, they both did so out of reverence. There is no evidence in either case for the use of the physical remains they found to explore the past.

The first clear evidence for the use of excavation to recover and explore the past was in Renaissance Europe. An emblem book written by Johannes Sambucus (see Figure 2.3) in 1564 provides the earliest depiction of excavation for antiquities. The interest of Renaissance antiquarians (as the early archaeologists are known) was drawn to Greek and Roman antiquities and to questions about the origins of the Celts. By the eighteenth century, there was increasing sophistication among European antiquarians in the way they drew monuments and documented and collected artifacts.

Until the nineteenth century, antiquarians struggled with a number of inter-related problems. The most striking problem was the difficulty in distinguishing objects of human manufacture from objects created by natural processes. For example, ground stone axes were believed to be "**thunderstones**"—objects that formed in spots where lightning struck the earth. Arrowheads were identified as fossilized serpent tongues.

thunderstones Objects such as ground stone axes that people in Medieval Europe believed were formed in spots where lightning struck the earth.

A Brief History of Canadian Archaeology

Archaeology developed relatively late in Canada, compared to Europe and the United States (Kelley and Williamson 1996). The first major figure in Canadian archaeology was Sir Daniel Wilson, a Scottish archaeologist who arrived in Toronto in 1853 and eventually became the first president of the University of Toronto (see Figure 2.4). Wilson did little archaeological field-work, but his book, *Prehistoric Man: Researches into the Origin of Civilization in the Old and the New World*, was "a remarkable synthesis of all that was known about the anthropology of the New World" (Trigger 1989, 120). Wilson has been credited by some with coining the term *prehistory* and is widely recognized for resisting racial explanations of human behaviour (Kehoe 1991).

The professionalization of Canadian archaeology took its first small step in 1887 with the provision of provincial funding, at the sum of $1,000 per year, for David Boyle to act as curator of the Canadian Institute in Toronto (Killian 1983). Boyle set in motion the collection and curation of archaeological artifacts from across Ontario and initiated a series of field projects. Perhaps most significantly, he began publication of an annual *Archaeological Report*. Although Boyle can be regarded as Canada's first professional archaeologist, he lacked any form of training in the discipline. Before assuming his position at the Canadian Institute, he had been a blacksmith, teacher, and bookseller.

The first anthropology department at a Canadian university was founded by Thomas McIlwraith at the University of Toronto in 1926. The appointments of Phileo Nash in 1938 and Norman

Emerson in 1946 marked the addition of archaeology to this program. In the early 1950s, there were still fewer than 10 archaeologists active in the field in Canada (Kelley and Williamson 1996, 8).

The 1950s and 1960s saw tremendous growth in Canadian universities and widespread development of archaeology as an academic discipline. New faculty were drawn largely from the United States, strengthening existing ties between Canadian and American archaeology. At the same time, provincial regulations led to the beginning of cultural resource management in Canada. Kelley and Williamson (1996) argue that because many areas of the country remained unexplored well into the 1960s, Canadian archaeologists were forced to focus on the fundamentals of

culture history. As a result, few Canadians were able to respond to the challenges laid out by Lewis Binford and the New Archaeologists (see The New Archaeology, p. 42). Kelley and Williamson stress that the "lack of commitment in Canada to the passing 'isms'" is actually an advantage as archaeology moves forward, leaving Canadian archaeologists flexible and open to new directions (Kelley and Williamson 1996, 12). ●

REFERENCES: A. Kehoe. (1991). The invention of prehistory. *Current Anthropology* 43: 467–476.

Jane H. Kelley and Ronald Williamson. (1996). The positioning of archaeology within anthropology: A Canadian historical perspective. *American Antiquity* 61(1): 5–20.

Gerald Killian. (1983). *David Boyle: From Artisan to Archaeologist*. Toronto: University of Toronto Press.

FIGURE 2.4 · Sir Daniel Wilson was the first major figure in Canadian archaeology.

Against this background of traditional beliefs, methods for recognizing objects of human manufacture emerged. Experience with societies that still used stone tools certainly had an effect on that recognition. Michele Mercati, a Vatican doctor who lived from 1541 to 1593, wrote of the thunderstones that "those who study history judge that before the use of iron they were struck from very hard flint for the folly of war" (Schnapp 1996, 347). In 1732, the French naturalist Antoine de Jussieu compared the thunderstones with stone tools from the American Islands and Canada. On the basis of this comparison, he wrote that "the savages of these countries have different ways of using nearly similar stones which they have fashioned by almost infinite care by rubbing them against other stones, lacking any tool of iron or steel" (Heizer 1962, 68).

However, there was still no method for determining the age of artifacts. In the absence of such a method, all prehistoric relics were assumed to have come from a fairly brief period of time. In 1797, John Frere reported on the discovery of elephant remains together with stone tools (what he called "weapons of war") at the site of Hoxne, England. His conclusion was that "the situation in which these weapons were found may tempt us to refer them to a very remote period indeed; even beyond that of the present world" (Heizer 1962, 71). This report was ignored for over 50 years.

2.2 The Emergence of Archaeology

The development of Darwin's theory of evolution was one of the most far-reaching achievements of nineteenth-century science. That century also saw a tremendous growth in the scope of scientific research in almost every domain. The nineteenth century was the period when archaeology emerged as a clearly defined discipline. Two of the major achievements of nineteenth-century archaeologists were the creation of the **Three-Age system** and the determination of the depth of human antiquity. It is important to realize that the growth of archaeological research was closely linked to the expansion of European empires. The archaeology of the nineteenth century often reflects the ideology and biases of European colonists.

▪ Organizing Time

Throughout the nineteenth century, prehistoric artifacts poured into museums and other collections, but nobody knew how old these objects were or how to group them. The first step toward solving this problem was the development of the Three-Age system by the Danish antiquarian Christian Jürgensen Thomsen (Trigger 1989). In 1816, Thomsen was given the job of cataloguing collections for the newly founded National Museum of Antiquity. His solution was to divide the collections into the relics of three periods—the Stone Age, the Bronze Age, and the Iron Age—based on the material of manufacture. Thomsen assumed that he had arranged these periods chronologically, with the Stone Age being the earliest and the Iron Age the latest. Thomsen also recognized that some stone and bronze artifacts continued to be manufactured in later periods. He therefore augmented his classification with attention to the designs found on the objects.

▪ The Establishment of Human Antiquity

Already in the early 1800s, scientists were beginning to talk about the evolution of life on earth and even the possibility that humanity was the product of evolution. The French zoologist Jean Baptiste Lamarck developed an evolutionary framework for the history of life on earth based on the inheritance of acquired characteristics. Lamarck was not alone. Many scientists were beginning to question a strict acceptance of the biblical chronology of life, which, according to the Bishop James

Three-Age system A system developed by Danish antiquarian Christian Jürgensen Thomsen that catalogues artifacts into relics of three periods—the Stone Age, the Bronze Age, and the Iron Age—based on the material of manufacture.

FIGURE 2.5 Artifacts excavated by Boucher de Perthes at the site of Abbeville.

Ussher, placed creation at 4004 B.C. Because the early nineteenth century was a period of political struggle between Christianity and materialism, the resistance to evolution was fierce. Theologians objected strenuously to removing divinity from creation and ridiculed the idea that "man descended from the apes."

Beginning in the late 1850s, everything began to change (Grayson 1983). Within a number of years, the evidence for the existence of human remains together with the remains of extinct animals was irrefutable. In 1857, a Neanderthal skull was discovered near Düsseldorf (Germany), providing evidence of a premodern human. In 1859, the publication of Charles Darwin's *On The Origin of Species* put the theory of evolution on new and more solid ground.

The turning point in the recognition of the depth of human antiquity came from the interaction between two very different scientists (Cohen and Hublin 1989). Jacques Boucher de Perthes was a customs officer at Abbeville in northwestern France. Far from the centres of power in Paris and London, Boucher de Perthes wrote a series of idiosyncratic books describing his discovery of tools of human manufacture together with bones of extinct mammoths and rhinoceros in the deep gravel deposits of the Somme Valley (Figure 2.5). Alone, these books had little impact.

Unlike Boucher de Perthes, Charles Lyell was a powerful scientific figure and an authority in the field of geology. In 1859, Lyell visited Boucher de Perthes in Abbeville and became convinced of the authenticity of the association between tools that were clearly produced by humans and the remains of animals that had long been extinct. On the basis of this observation, Lyell concluded that human existence dates far back in geological time. When Lyell, who had been a critic of claims about evidence of early humans, presented his findings to the Royal Academy, the recognition of the depth of human antiquity shifted from a position held by a few mavericks to the consensus of the scientific establishment.

Neolithic The period in which there are polished stone tools. Also called the New Stone Age.

Paleolithic The period in which humans lived with now-extinct animals. Also called the Old Stone Age.

The vast new expanses of time opened up by these discoveries soon led to the division of Thomsen's Stone Age into two periods. In 1865, John Lubbock defined the **Neolithic** (New Stone Age) as the period in which there are polished stone tools, and the **Paleolithic** (Old Stone Age) as the period during which humans lived with now-extinct animals. At the same time, excavations in southern France showed that Paleolithic sites included not only stone tools but also art objects (see Figure 2.6).

FIGURE 2.6 Drawing of Paleolithic incised bones from southern France published by Lartet and Christy in 1875. These are among the first art objects found on Paleolithic sites.

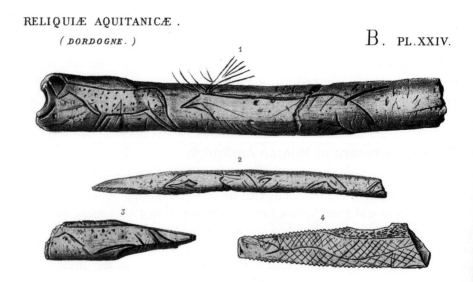

RELIQUIÆ AQUITANICÆ .

(*DORDOGNE.*)

B. PL.XXIV.

Imperial Archaeology

The nineteenth century also saw an explosion of exploration in the expanding European empires. Often, this was the work of treasure hunters with little in the way of scruples. An extreme example is Giovanni Belzoni, a circus strongman turned Egyptian explorer. Belzoni writes of moving through a passageway "choked with mummies, and I could not pass without putting my face in contact with that of some decayed Egyptian ... I could not avoid being covered with bones, legs, arms and heads rolling from above. . . . The purpose of my researches was to rob the Egyptians of their papyri" (Fagan 1996, 77–78). In other cases, such as Champollion's decipherment of Egyptian hieroglyphs in 1822, the motivations were more scholarly. The German archaeologist Heinrich Schliemann's identification of the site of Hissarlik, Turkey, with Troy of the Iliad captured the imagination of the world (see Figure 2.7). Other archaeologists began to dig at the biblical-period foundations of Jerusalem and in the ancient cities of Mesopotamia. In far-flung colonies from Africa to Tasmania, archaeologists were also at work. In many areas, archaeologists created a picture of the "unchanging savage," which supported the racist underpinnings of colonial empires (Trigger 1989).

2.3 Developing Method and Theory

The basic tools of archaeology (including stratigraphic excavation and the quantitative analysis of artifacts) began developing during the early part of the twentieth century. Archaeological theory also began to develop during this period, particularly in the writing of V. Gordon Childe.

Stratigraphic Method and Culture History

By the end of the nineteenth century, archaeology was an established and increasingly professional discipline. The professionalization of archaeology saw the emergence of modern methods of excavation and analysis. In Egypt and Palestine, Sir Flinders Petrie pioneered the methods of stratigraphic excavation and seriation (see Figure 2.8).

FIGURE 2.7 Heinrich Schliemann displayed the treasures he recovered at Troy in this striking photo of his wife. Recent scholarship has shown that Schliemann's flair for the sensational often led to misrepresentation of his findings.

FIGURE 2.8 Flinders Petrie examining pots from an excavation. Petrie was one of the first archaeologists to use stratigraphy to create a chronology.

In North America, particular attention was given to the development of culture history through the elaboration of formal schemes for the classification of archaeological sites into culture groups. The resultant methods included the Pecos Classification in the southwestern United States and the Midwestern Taxonomic method. These developments were driven in part by the increasing amount of archaeological activity. In the United States, archaeology carried out under the Depression-era public works acts was a particular stimulus.

Although the focus on defining cultures generated an enormous amount of research, it also began to generate a degree of dissatisfaction. In 1948, Walter Taylor wrote, "the archaeologist, as archaeologist, is nothing but a technician" (Taylor 1948, 43). While they were focusing on classifying artifacts, archaeologists at times ignored the societies whose remains they were excavating. In some cases, the focus on defining the extent and spread of culture took on a more insidious tone. Gustaf Kossinna used a culture history approach to reinforce German nationalism, and his work became central to the ideology of Nazi Germany (Arnold 1990).

■ V. Gordon Childe

Although his only excavation was of a small village in Orkney, V. Gordon Childe is a towering figure in the history of archaeology (Harris 1994). Childe was born in Australia in 1892, but he lived most of his life in England. His early work was firmly within a culture history framework. He was aided in this work by what is said to have been a near-photographic memory. A powerful visual memory allowed him to make comparisons and recognize patterning in the archaeological collections across Europe.

In his later work, Childe went beyond mapping cultures to asking fundamental questions about the nature of prehistory. Archaeology showed him that across the globe, societies have undergone two revolutions. The first was the Neolithic revolution, which led to the emergence of settled villages practising agriculture. The second was the urban revolution, which led to the appearance of cities and complex forms of government. We can compare Childe's ideas with Thomsen's Three-Age system discussed earlier. Thomsen focused on the classification of objects and thus created major periods—the Stone Age, Bronze Age, and Iron Age. Similarly, Lubbock split the Stone Age into the Paleolithic and Neolithic. Childe shifted the focus from artifacts to societies of people living in a network of social and economic relations. The great changes we see in the archaeological record, Childe held, are evidence of changes in society, because the material aspects of culture are intimately connected to social and economic relations. Thus, for Childe, the presence of bronze artifacts presupposes a society that was able to gain access to tin and copper and that could support specialists with the skills necessary to practise metallurgy.

Childe was a committed and politically active Marxist. In his writing, he stressed the social organization of production and revolutionary change in human societies. His ideas were influenced by his contacts with Soviet archaeologists, and also drew heavily on the U.S. ethnographer Lewis Henry Morgan.

2.4 Archaeology as Science

Childe's work is significant in that he pushed archaeology away from defining itself in terms of the recovery and classification of artifacts and toward a focus on the study of ancient societies. This is a significant shift, and it has resulted in ongoing debates about how archaeology can go beyond describing objects to explore past societies.

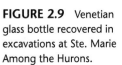

Ste. Marie Among the Hurons

Ste. Marie, a small town near Georgian Bay in Ontario, was a remote Jesuit mission station established in Huron territory in 1639. After a decade as a centre for Jesuit mission work, Ste. Marie Among the Hurons was burned and abandoned following the destruction of the Huron confederacy by Iroquois and Neutral aggression (Trigger 1985).

In 1855, Father Félix Martin, a Jesuit priest from Montreal, carried out a survey and partial excavation at the site. His report can be considered the first real archaeological excavation in Canada and is therefore worth quoting:

> "An excavation at this point [the Northwest bastion] allowed us to discover at a depth of approximately two feet the foundation and traces of a burnt plank; we also found large carpentry nails, beaver bones and a piece of copper, that might have been part of a household utensil" (translated from a passage reproduced in Kidd 1949, 169).

In 1941, new excavations were undertaken at the site by the Royal Ontario Museum (Kidd 1949). One discovery made during this excavation provides a particularly vivid picture of the lives of the early European missionaries in Huronia. The remains of a drop-shaped glass bottle were recovered embedded in the vegetable refuse of a storage pit (see Figure 2.9). Although most of the shards were very small, it was possible to piece together an almost complete bottle. This graceful and fragile vessel, its walls an average of less than 0.5 mm in thickness, was of Venetian origin. The excavator writes:

> "We may speculate on its having been given to the Jesuit Fathers as a parting gift from some noble or wealthy patron . . . and the story of its dangerous journey across the ocean, up the St. Lawrence, and Ottawa Rivers and across country by way of the Mattawa and French Rivers to its final resting place at Fort Ste. Marie, would make a saga in itself. We shall probably never know where it was shattered . . . it could have happened on the journey and not been discovered until it was unpacked, or it may have done long and honourable duty at Ste. Marie until, broken at last, it was thrown away. Restored now to something like its original condition, it stands out as one of the fine examples of early European glass in the New World, and was probably the first of all real art treasures to reach Canadian shores" (Kidd 1949, 172–173). ◆

REFERENCE: Kenneth E. Kidd. (1949). *The Excavation of Ste Marie I.* Toronto: University of Toronto Press.

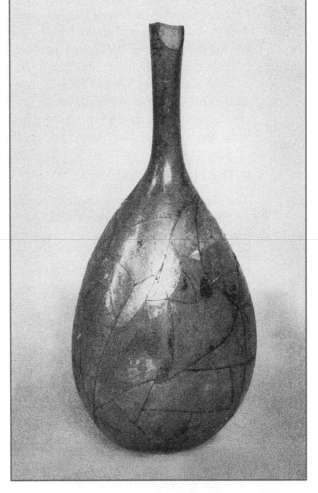

FIGURE 2.9 Venetian glass bottle recovered in excavations at Ste. Marie Among the Hurons.

Developing Scientific Methods

Beginning in 1949, the Cambridge-based archaeologist Graham Clark brought together botanists, zoologists, and archaeologists to excavate Star Carr, a prehistoric hunter–gatherer site in East Yorkshire, England. Because the site is waterlogged, many artifacts not usually found on archaeological sites, such as wood, are well preserved. Clark opened wide excavation areas at Star Carr, with the explicit goal of gaining insight into the subsistence practices of late prehistoric hunters. The term *subsistence* refers to the activities involved in procuring and processing food. Clark's student Eric Higgs extended Clark's emphasis on economy. Indeed, Higgs took the position that archaeology should concern itself only with economy. Higgs also pioneered methods for recovering botanical remains from archaeological sites.

Similar developments took place in the United States, stimulated by the work of the ecological anthropologist Julian Steward, who explored the relationship between nature and culture and developed the school of thought known as cultural ecology. In 1946, Gordon Willey carried out a pioneering survey project in the Virú Valley of Peru. The importance of this survey is that its goal was to gather evidence of settlement patterning that would provide information relevant to social organization.

Alongside the development of methodologies for the archaeology of economy and society found in the work of Clark and Willey, a number of archaeologists began to develop and stress the importance of statistical methods for archaeology. A. C. Spaulding argued, on the basis of pottery studies in the Lower Mississippi Valley and the southwestern United States, that archaeologists should not impose categories on material culture, but rather should discover clustering through statistical analysis of attributes. One of the important aspects of Spaulding's position is that he was championing a statistical method not because it was better for building chronologies—the goal of the culture history approach—but because his methods were necessary to explore how societies changed through time.

The New Archaeology

The rumblings of discontent with the culture history approach could be heard as early as 1948, with the publication of Walter Taylor's *A Study of Archaeology*. At the same time, Clark and Willey were working to develop scientific methods for the study of the economy and organization of ancient societies, and Spaulding was urging the adoption of statistical methods. One can easily imagine these trends causing a gradual eclipse of culture history by an increasing sophisticated social and economic archaeology—but that is not what happened.

Rather than a gradual transition, what took place in the 1960s was a fierce confrontation initiated by a group of young archaeologists calling their approach the **New Archaeology** or **processual archaeology**. The catalyst in this movement was Lewis Binford (see Figure 2.10). In a series of fiercely polemical articles, Binford pronounced that archaeology should be a science or it should be nothing at all. Clearly, he did not view the work of traditional archaeologists as science. Why was the debate so heated? Perhaps its tone was an extension of the

New Archaeology (or processual archaeology) An approach to archaeology based firmly on scientific method and supported by a concerted effort aimed at the development of theory.

FIGURE 2.10 Lewis Binford spearheaded the emergence of the New Archaeology in the 1960s.

excitement and vitality of campus life in 1960s America. Perhaps it was the sense that traditional archaeologists had a stranglehold on the field that could be loosened only by confrontation. It is clear that the tone of the debate reflected the fact that radically new ideas were being brought into archaeology. The New Archaeologists were the first to argue that the central problem of the field was not the need for more data or even better methods; rather, they questioned the way archaeologists could know the past. This is essentially an intellectual, or, as it has come to be known, a theoretical, problem.

Binford was an ideal ringleader for a gang of intellectual revolutionaries. A tireless master at the cut and thrust of debate (and not shy about drawing blood), he has carried out wide-ranging research from the midwestern United States to the Arctic to South Africa.

Binford set out a fundamental problem facing archaeologists. Their interest is the *dynamics* of past societies, but what they have to study are the *static* objects recovered in an excavation or a survey. Archaeologists tend to work by **induction**, drawing inferences on the basis of available data. James Deetz has described induction as "the archaeologist providing the flesh for the bare bones of his data" (quoted in Binford and Binford 1968, 17). Drawing on the work of philosopher of science Carl Hempel, Binford saw induction as dangerously naïve. For archaeology to be a science, he believed, it must work by **deduction** from general laws and models. The fundamental methodology of archaeology should be testing hypotheses. This stress on hypothesis testing, which was meant to ally archaeology with the hard sciences such as physics, created a breach between the New Archaeologists and the rest of the discipline.

The excitement of the New Archaeology flowed from the argument that archaeologists were not limited to describing the archaeological record. Theory and method have the potential to enable archaeological research to extend into all realms of past societies. Binford expressed this potential when he wrote that "facts do not speak for themselves . . . data [will] tell us nothing about cultural process or past lifeways unless we [ask] the appropriate questions" (1968, 13).

The key to the optimism of the New Archaeologists was the linkage they made between material remains and other aspects of society (Watson, Leblanc, and Redman 1984). To Binford, it was inconceivable that any cultural item functioned independently of nonmaterial aspects of society. Thus, the potential scope of archaeologists' knowledge of past societies would be almost limitless.

Paradoxically, processual archaeology often involved an extremely reductive view of culture. In Binford's (1962) famous formulation, "Culture is man's extrosomatic [i.e., external to the body] means of adapting to the environment." What is striking is that, in Binford's view, all aspects of symbolic behaviour are relegated to insignificance.

As archaeological theory matured, the insistence of the New Archaeologists on strict adherence to hypothesis testing and the rejection of induction tended to moderate. This trend was strongly influenced by the work of Alison Wylie, who showed through careful analysis that all archaeologists have to use induction at some points in their research. By 1984, Patty Jo Watson, Steven LeBlanc, and Charles Redman, important proponents of the New Archaeology, recognized that archaeological research involves a "to-and-fro" between induction and deduction (Watson, LeBlanc, and Redman 1984, 60). Quoting Kent Flannery, who states that the New Archaeologists "assume that truth is just the best current hypothesis, and that whatever they believe now will ultimately be proved wrong" (Flannery 1967, 122), Watson, LeBlanc, and Redman stressed that the New Archaeology adopted a scientific approach to truth.

Because the search for covering laws in archaeology yielded at best only modest results, Binford returned to his initial question about how we can know

induction Drawing general inferences on the basis of available empirical data.

deduction Drawing particular inferences from general laws and models.

middle-range research Research investigating processes that can be observed in the present and that can serve as a point of reference to test hypotheses about the past.

cultural resource management (CRM) Public archaeology carried out with the goal of mitigating the effects of development on archaeological resources.

systems theory An archaeological theory that views society as an interconnected network of interacting elements.

about processes that took place in the past. In the absence of covering laws, Binford emphasized the importance of **middle-range research**, which allows us to make secure statements about past dynamics on the basis of observations made on archaeological material. The key to middle-range research is to look at processes that we can observe in the present and analyze the material patterning left by those processes. We can then develop hypotheses about the past that can be tested by reference to our observations in the present. As an example, Binford carried out a project in which he fed bones to hyenas and recorded the patterns of breakage and the markings on the bones. He could then compare these patterns with those found on early human sites to test the hypothesis that these sites were produced partially by carnivore activity.

The development of the New Archaeology overlapped with changes in legislation that led to a significant increase in public archaeology. New laws resulted in a demand for archaeologists who could assess the potential damage of construction projects and, when necessary, carry out excavations to salvage endangered sites (see Figure 2.11). The field of public archaeology has come to be known as **cultural resource management**, or **CRM**. CRM archaeologists are found in the private sector, in government agencies, and in academia. The development of the methods of CRM archaeology has been strongly influenced by the scientific methods espoused by the New Archaeologists.

■ Systems Theory

One direction pursued by the New Archaeologists is the application of **systems theory** to the study of past societies. A system is an interconnected network of elements that together form a whole. A classic example of a system is the combination of a thermostat and the furnace in a house. The ambient temperature affects the thermostat, which turns the furnace on and off. The heat of the furnace raises the temperature in the house, which in turn causes the thermostat to turn off the furnace. The thermostat and furnace together control the temperature through feedback within the system. When you set the temperature in your house, this system works to produce a steady state. Archaeologists

FIGURE 2.11 A modern salvage excavation in England. Notice the combination of heavy equipment and more traditional recovery methods.

Faunal Analysis and Taphonomy

Faunal Analysts (also known as zoo-archaeologists or archaeozoologists) study animal bones found on archaeological sites. The fundamental skill needed to practise faunal analysis is the ability to recognize the species of animal from the scraps of bone that survive in the archaeological record (see Figure 2.12). Comparative collections of skeletons of modern animals are an essential tool in developing this skill and for confirming identification. But the work of the faunal analyst goes far beyond the technical demands of species recognition, or even the more complex tasks of identifying the age and sex of an individual. Faunal analysts bridge zoology and archaeology and seek to understand the interaction between humans and animals through prehistory.

Understanding the processes that have shaped the collections of bones recovered on archaeological sites is a critical first step in any faunal analysis. Taphonomy is the study of postdepositional processes that shape the archaeological assemblage. In many cases, determining whether humans were actually responsible for the accumulation of bones is a central concern, and taphonomy leads faunal analysts to a close consideration of the activities of scavengers such as hyenas. Excavating hyena dens, while an unpleasant and often smelly undertaking, can provide critical tools to evaluate faunal assemblages. Taphonomy can also contribute to understanding how carcasses were processed.

Faunal analysts have also been at the forefront of developing excavation methods that ensure complete recovery of an unbiased sample. These accomplishments are often remarkable. On some coastal sites it has been possible to track the seasonality of human occupation by analyzing the ear stones, or otoliths, of fish that are less than 1 centimetre in length. Faunal analysts combine meticulous recovery and detailed observation with a knowledge of animal biology and behaviour to provide critical insight into the archaeological record. ●

REFERENCES: Simon Davis. (1987). *The Archaeology of Animals*. New Haven: Yale University Press.

Elizabeth Reitz and Elizabeth Wing. (1999). *Zooarchaeology*. Cambridge: Cambridge University Press.

FIGURE 2.12 Cleaning the upper canine tooth of a bear, discovered at the Lower Paleolithic site of Isernia de la Pineta, Italy.

---

argued that societies can be viewed as systems that normally operate at such a steady state. David Clarke and Kent Flannery were among those who went to great lengths to try to formalize the elements of archaeological systems. One attraction of the systems approach is that it made it possible to investigate periods of rapid change in the archaeological record in terms of feedback among elements of a complex system. As a result, change could be understood as the effect of internal processes—processes that took place within society. Although today formal systems theory plays a minor role in archaeology, the recognition of the complexity of social systems and the degree to which various aspects of the archaeological record are interrelated are of critical importance. Systems theory has been particularly valuable in giving archaeologists tools to integrate evidence of ecological change into models of social change.

2.5 Alternative Perspectives

Lewis Binford proclaimed that archaeology should be a science based on deduction and hypothesis testing. The New Archaeologists worked to create the guidelines for an explicitly scientific approach to archaeology—what has come to be known as processual archaeology—an approach strongly associated with systems theory and with an emphasis on ecology. Although the emphasis on pure deduction was gradually toned down, and the search for general laws was replaced by middle-range research, the basic premises of processual archaeology remained largely unchallenged until the mid-1980s, by which time processual archaeology had become the dominant approach to archaeological theory in the United States. Indeed, processual archaeology strongly influenced the development of CRM.

■ Postprocessual Archaeology

The central argument of processual archaeology is that archaeology should be a science, a discipline that emulates the hard sciences such as physics. The only apparent alternative to processual archaeology was culture history based on naïve induction. It took over twenty years for processual archaeology to be effectively challenged. The challenge came from British archaeologists led by Ian Hodder in a movement that came to be known as **postprocessual archaeology**. Hodder's challenge to Binford went to the core of processual archaeology. Why, Hodder asked, should archaeologists not choose to emulate historians rather than physicists? Perhaps archaeology is more similar to reading a text than carrying out an experiment. After all, is a science based on predicting the outcome of experiments appropriate to the study of processes that took place in the past? How can archaeologists ever replicate their results, as is expected of a laboratory scientist?

Hodder was not arguing for naïve induction or advocating a return to culture history. To parry Binford's reliance on the philosopher of science Hempel, Hodder drew on the theoretical writing of historians such as R.G. Collingwood, who espoused the idea that it is necessary for the historian to get at the "inside" of events. The historian should try to understand the past from the perspective of the people who lived through those events.

Binford had defined culture as a means of adaptation and had argued that there is no need to understand how the people themselves viewed their own culture. Following Binford, one can adopt an external, or what anthropologists term an **etic**, approach and still get at a true understanding of the society. Hodder argued that culture must be understood as the result of the meaningful and purposeful actions of people, and that only an internal understanding of these meanings—what anthropologists call an **emic** approach—produces a real knowledge of the past.

The strength of Hodder's position is readily apparent. Clearly, we all experience the world as meaningful and would have a difficult time thinking of the way we live as our "extrasomatic means of adaptation." Should we not assume that this was the case for people who lived in the past? Some cultural anthropologists have argued persuasively for an etic approach to living societies. For example, Marvin Harris has studied the taboo on eating cattle in Hindu societies and has argued that the emic understanding of this taboo in religious terms hides the fact that the taboo actually serves an important ecological function. However, Harris is certainly in the minority among people who study living societies.

The problem faced by archaeologists who embrace Hodder's position is that archaeologists do not work with living societies. Archaeologists cannot simply ask their informants what something means. To meet this challenge, Hodder emphasized the importance of context in providing clues to understanding the meaning of artifacts. As he writes, "as soon as the context of an object is known it is no longer

postprocessual archaeology
A movement, led by British archaeologist Ian Hodder, which argues that archaeologists should emulate historians in interpreting the past.

etic An approach to archaeological or anthropological analysis that does not attempt to adopt the perspective of the members of the culture that are being studied.

emic An approach to archaeological or anthropological analysis that attempts to understand the meanings people attach to their actions and culture.

totally mute" (Hodder 1986, 4). Where objects are found and what they are found with provide the basis for making interpretations about their meaning. To use a very simple example, if a type of object is found only in a tomb setting, this fact tells us something about the object's meaning.

But even allowing for the use of context, it is hard to see how one could try to "work from the inside" and still meet the New Archaeologists' criteria for scientifically valid deductive research. Not surprisingly, Hodder dismissed the position that the deductive method is the appropriate framework for archaeological research.

The goal of postprocessual archaeology is not to test hypotheses, but rather to offer interpretations based on contextual data. Some have argued that this means that "anything goes," and that all interpretations are equally valid. Unlike processual archaeology, which ultimately holds that proper scientific procedure will lead archaeologists to the truth about the past, postprocessual archaeology argues that the process of interpretation is ongoing. This does not, however, mean that all interpretations are equally valid. For example, our legal system is based on the ability of a judge or a jury to reach a consensual interpretation of events. Clearly, we care very much that these interpretations be sound and well grounded.

The analogy to a jury trial is useful in introducing the concept of **hermeneutics**, which is critical to the way that Hodder views archaeology. When a jury renders its verdict, there is a degree of finality to the decision. However, the verdict is not necessarily the end of the interpretation of the past events examined in the trial; such interpretation can continue in the courts if new evidence is found or out of the courts in the investigations of reporters and historians. Hermeneutics is a theory of interpretation that stresses the interaction between the presuppositions we bring to a problem and the independent empirical reality of our observations and experiences. Rather than coming to an archaeological situation with a hypothesis, in following a hermeneutic approach we come with preexisting knowledge and questions. Hermeneutic interpretation is an open-ended cycle of continual inquiry. Because this process results in an understanding that is continuously enriched through a confrontation with empirical reality, it is often depicted as a spiral—a process through which we arrive at a deeper understanding of the past (see Figure 2.13).

Postprocessual archaeologists have also taken the lead in seriously considering the position of archaeology in modern society and contemporary politics (Figure 2.14). If interpretation is the continuous confrontation of presuppositions with empirical reality, then how we arrive at our presuppositions about the past becomes far more important than it would be in a processual archaeological approach. With their stress on a pure scientific method, the New Archaeologists could do little but urge their followers to do their best to separate politics from archaeology. Postprocessual archaeologists have embraced the idea that archaeology is an activity that takes place in the present and that the archaeologist is a person working in a particular historical setting. In two books published in the late 1980s, Michael Shanks and Christopher Tilley went as far as to deny that archaeologists could ever do more than simply project the present onto the past and to assert that the major role of archaeology is to legitimate the modern political order. (See, e.g., Shanks and Tilley 1987.)

hermeneutics A theory of interpretation that stresses the interaction between the presuppositions we bring to a problem and the independent empirical reality of our observations and experiences.

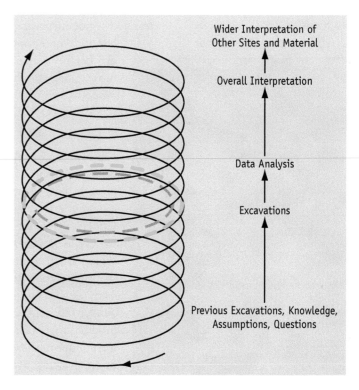

Wider Interpretation of Other Sites and Material

Overall Interpretation

Data Analysis

Excavations

Previous Excavations, Knowledge, Assumptions, Questions

FIGURE 2.13 The hermeneutic spiral represents a process of continually refining knowledge through an ongoing process of confronting pre-existing knowledge with new information.

FIGURE 2.14 An image of the archaeological site of Great Zimbabwe on a banknote from modern Zimbabwe provides an example of the use of archaeology in contemporary society. Why do you think this image was chosen for a banknote?

Although most of those in the field reject this argument, Shanks and Tilley were instrumental in spurring archaeologists to look critically at the history of the science in relation to factors such as colonialism, nationalism, and racism.

For processual archaeologists, archaeology should ideally be a unified science with agreed-upon procedures and standards. By contrast, postprocessual archaeology is far more open to a multiplicity of approaches and interpretations. Depending on what presuppositions one brings to a situation, the resulting interpretation will differ. At the same time, because postprocessual archaeology is supposed to work from the inside, it follows that a multiplicity of interpretations are expected, since they would reflect the diversity of perspectives held by people in the past. As a result, it is not surprising that postprocessual archaeologists have developed a number of different approaches to archaeology. In recent years, archaeological theory has been characterized by a wide diversity of approaches, ranging from those more closely allied to postprocessual archaeology to those allied with processual archaeology.

feminist archaeology An approach that focuses on the way archaeologists study and represent gender and brings attention to gender inequities in the practice of archaeology.

■ Gender and Agency

Feminist archaeology and agency theory are two approaches that have developed out of postprocessual archaeology. **Feminist archaeology** has brought new attention both to the way that archaeologists study and represent gender and to gender inequities in the practice of archaeology (Gero and Conkey 1991; see Figure 2.15). Archaeologists have had a tendency to treat society as homogeneous. Feminist archaeologists have drawn on studies by sociocultural anthropologists to show that the experience of individuals is shaped by their role in society. The challenge to archaeologists is how to study gender with the tools of archaeology. Studies focusing on identifying gender differences have looked at a wide range of topics, including stone tool production, textiles, and plant food processing. The difficulty is that identifying gender in these realms can be elusive. In cultures with written documents or art showing people at work, it has been possible to combine the information contained therein with archaeology to reach significant conclusions about gender in ancient societies. Studies of skeletal remains have also produced important insights into the relation between gender and other factors, such as diet, activity, and burial practices.

Feminist archaeology has also brought attention to the way that archaeologists represent gender. The invisibility of gender in archaeology has often masked a strong

FIGURE 2.15 American archaeologist Harriet Boyd Hawes, photographed on the island of Crete in 1902. The contributions of women to archaeology have often been overlooked.

TOOLBOX

Archaeoacoustics

It is hard to imagine a world without sound, but archaeologists often feel limited to the visual and tactile aspects of culture. The discovery of bone flutes from the Upper Paleolithic of Germany (see p. 141, in Chapter 5) and the Neolithic of China (see p. 256, in Chapter 9) has drawn attention to the central importance of music in human experience. However, a small group of archaeologists has cast a far wider net. Researchers in the emerging field of archaeoacoustics aim to explore the archaeological record to understand the role of sound in human behaviour (Scarre and Lawson 2006). Archaeoacoustics is one element of an "archaeology of the senses" that has developed out of postprocessual archaeology. Some of the first studies of ancient music focused on the Lurs, a wind instrument from the Scandinavian Bronze Age. Already in the 1960s John Coles (1979) was carrying out experiments to determine how this instrument would have sounded. More recent studies in archaeoacoustics include analysis of Mesoamerican hieroglyphic signs relating to sound (Houston and Taube 2000); studies of the acoustic properties of the ceremonial centre of Chavin de Huantar in Peru (Burger 1992; see

p. 396, in Chapter 14); and examination of the placement of rock art in relation to places with acoustic resonance (Waller 2006). One of the most interesting acoustic phenomena uncovered by archaeologists is the association of rock art with "rock gongs" found in both South Africa and India (see Figure 2.16). These are rocks that produce a clear tone when struck (Parkington and Morris 2008; Boivin 2004). In the case of rock gongs there is little question that people were drawn to a location for its aural qualities. One can clearly see the places

where the rocks have been struck, and when this action is repeated it produces a clear tone. In other cases the connection between the acoustics of a place and the actions of people in the past is more tenuous, and the archaeologist has to take great care in drawing inferences about how sound shaped behaviour. However, as Chris Scarre notes, "the study of archaeoacoustics has much to offer, and has scarcely begun" (Scarre 2006, 9). ●

REFERENCE: Chris Scarre and Graeme Lawson. (2006). *Archaeoacoustics*. Cambridge: Cambridge University Press (McDonald Institute Monographs).

FIGURE 2.16   Rock gong site in South Africa. The indentations on the rock are marks left when it was struck to produce a loud sound. How would the location of this site in the landscape have shaped the way this sound was experienced?

bias toward viewing men as the active and productive agents of change and women as passive "fellow travellers." One humorous example is found in the rather implausible title of one of Childe's books: *Man Makes Himself!* Feminist archaeologists have done important work identifying the pervasiveness of gender bias in archaeology and offering alternative images. In a number of intriguing studies, feminist archaeologists have used fiction as a way to bring attention to the active role of women in society (Spector 1991).

Feminist archaeologists have made an important contribution by demonstrating that societies are not uniform. Recently, archaeologists working with agency theory have taken this idea further by arguing that the basic unit of archaeology is not society, but individuals living in society (Dobres and Robb 2000). Based on the theory of practice developed by the sociologists Pierre Bourdieu and Anthony Giddens, **agency theory** emphasizes the agency of individuals—the purposeful actions of the people

agency theory A theory that emphasizes the interaction between the agency of individuals and social structure.

The Archaeological Consultant

CARLA PARSLOW

I have to admit, working in the archaeological consulting industry is not at all what I had imagined it would be. For starters, I had to learn how to juggle . . . well! Also known as multi-tasking, I was keeping track of many things at the same time. In university, I focused on my Ph.D. research, with a few projects on the side and a teaching assistant position. Today, I am managing twelve different projects that are all going on at once, at different stages of completion. In short, multi-tasking is very important in this field, and if you enjoy doing many things at the same time, you will enjoy working as an archaeological consultant.

Consulting work also focuses more on the business side of archaeology than on research. A business focus means there are schedules to maintain, budgets to stay within, and external clients to work with. I essentially become a spokesperson for archaeology when talking to prospective clients.

Any mining or construction company is a prospective client because its projects involve development or land disturbance. Land disturbance can also be equated with archaeological site disturbance, and knowingly disturbing or destroying an archaeological site in Ontario is an offence and can result in large fines, up to $50,000. To ensure that their project does not involve archaeological issues, companies call in the professionals—such as a consulting archaeologist.

The consulting archaeologist's job can be divided into two stages:

- Assessment of property: The goal is to find out if there are archaeological sites on the land. If there is a potential to find such sites, we go to the next stage.

- Property survey: We can do the property survey using either a pedestrian survey or a test pit survey.

We use a pedestrian survey on ploughed agricultural fields. We walk the field at 5 metre intervals looking for artifacts on the ground surface.

We use test pit surveys on land that cannot be ploughed. We start by digging a test pit, approximately the diameter of a shovel, down to the subsoil. We screen the dirt for artifacts. If we find a scatter of artifacts, we might recommend further testing, which would involve excavating 1 metre square units over the area of the original dig. These secondary digs help us get a better understanding of the type of site, as well as the size of the site.

Once an archaeologist is finished the survey stage, and if he/she then deems the site to have some heritage value or be of heritage interest, he/she may recommend to have the land excavated or protected. The archaeologist will have discussions with the client about the possibility of changing the scope of their development, or even moving it, to avoid any further disturbance of the site.

One factor that impacts my work (as any Canadian will know) is the weather. Dealing with weather means I have to be good at scheduling the work so that I can accomplish as much as possible between late spring and freeze-up. Once there is snow on the ground, archaeological field work stops. Agricultural fields get special consideration, since they would need to be ploughed prior to a pedestrian survey; if there is a crop growing on the field, chances are we would not be able to assess it until the late fall, after

harvesting season. Late summer and fall end up being the busiest time of the year, during which time I can be working on several sites.

The consulting archaeologist needs to find a balance between the needs of the client and those factors that are beyond his/her control. These challenges do make for an exciting career, and I am glad that I took this path. Where else could I have the experience of excavating an early Euro-Canadian homestead, a War of 1812 battleground, and an Iroquoian village, all in the same year? ▲

FIGURE 2.17 Carla Parslow screening sediments at a property survey on a golf course.

who lived in the past. Agency theory is a constant balancing act between the recognition that history consists of the choices and actions of individuals, and an awareness that the choices people make are strongly shaped by structure, the social world, and material conditions in which they live.

Archaeologists working from a foundation of agency theory have tackled a wide range of topics. One of the most interesting directions this research has taken is in reconsidering the nature of the landscape. By putting people at the centre of the landscape, agency theorists have led archaeologists to investigate how ancient monuments were experienced by the people who built them and lived with them (Thomas 1996). Adopting an agency perspective also pushes archaeologists to look for particular variations in material culture that might express the actions of the individual. For example, in a detailed study of Mimbres pottery from the American Southwest (A.D. 1000–1300), Michelle Hegmon and Stephanie Kulow (2005) view the act of painting a design as agency and the overall style of the design as a form of structure. Potters work within a style while expressing their individual agency in their painting. However, agency is not expressed only through personal style or deviation from social norms. Rosemary Joyce (2005) has pointed out that agency also involves recapitulating valued practices of the past and thus is responsible for the maintenance of tradition as well as the development of innovation.

Some archaeologists have questioned whether agency should be limited to people (Knappett 2008). Perhaps objects can also be said to have agency. Carl Knappett offers the example of a young sailor circumnavigating the globe in a hi-tech trimaran. This vessel is capable at times of virtually sailing on its own, so who exactly is circling the the world—the sailor or the ship? Knappett draws on the idea of assemblages and argues that archaeologists need to explore the networks that connect human and nonhuman collectives, such as the sailor and the boat. In a similar vein, Christopher Watts develops an approach to the analysis of Iroquois pottery in Ontario that draws on the theory of signs, or semiotics, developed by Charles Pierce (Watts 2008). Like Knappett, Watts expands the perspective beyond the actions of the potter, writing that "it is the possibilities afforded by and encapsulated within the materials themselves, along with the context of their creation and use" that led to the styles of pottery recognized by archaeologists" (Watts 2008, 201).

■ Evolutionary Archaeology

There has been a diversification of approaches aligned with both processual and postprocessual archaeology. **Evolutionary archaeology** was developed by processual archaeologists who stress the importance of evolutionary theory as a potential unifying theory. Robert Dunnell pioneered this approach in his studies of archaeological systematics. In recent years, evolutionary archaeology has come to encompass a range of approaches, from ecological studies that look at changes in culture as changes in human adaptation, to attempts to apply Darwinian theory to changes in the frequencies and types of artifacts found at a site (O'Brien and Lyman 2002).

One critical issue for evolutionary archaeologists is determining whether human cultures evolve through a splitting of cultural lineages (phylogenesis) or through a process of borrowing and blending (ethnogenesis). In an innovative analysis of the decoration woven into carpets by Turkmen tribes in Central Asia, Jamshid Tehranin and Mark Collard found little evidence for the borrowing and blending of ideas (Tehrani and Collard 2002). They found that the methods used to analyze the relationships between biological lineage applied well to the development of decorative styles in Turkmen rugs.

evolutionary archaeology
A range of approaches that stress the importance of evolutionary theory as a unifying theory for archaeology.

2.6 Archaeology at the Trowel's Edge

Along with the growth and diversification of archaeological theory has come a sense of a disconnection between the way archaeologists write about their discipline and what they actually do. Most archaeologists would argue that the labels "processualist" and "postprocessualist" obscure what they actually do. In practice, it is quite possible to borrow liberally from many theoretical perspectives. Ian Hodder has proposed that we change archaeological theory from a top-down approach to one that begins "at the edge of the trowel" (Hodder 1999, 92). Drawing on the theory of hermeneutics, Hodder argues that archaeological theory should build on what archaeologists *actually* do, rather than prescribing what they *should* do.

Archaeology has developed from the simple recognition of the extent of the human past to a discipline that involves intense debate about how we gain knowledge of the past. Archaeology today has a rich theoretical "tool kit"—a diversity of approaches that can be used to think about the past. This diversification of approaches has led to confusion, confrontation, and, at times, a degree of despair. Surely, processualists and postprocessualists cannot both be right! Or perhaps they can. Alison Wylie has given us a beautiful image comparing archaeology to sailing, wherein one tacks back and forth in the wind in order to make progress. Our subject matter is over 2 million years of human experience. Our evidence is all of the physical remains of that experience. Given the immensity of the venture, we are really in a very small boat on an enormous ocean. The ability to manoeuver between approaches may be just what is needed in such a voyage.

SUMMARY

- The earliest use of archaeology to learn about the past was in Renaissance Europe. However, until the nineteenth century, there were no methods for determining the age of prehistoric artifacts, and in many cases the human manufacture of artifacts was not recognized.
- The development of the Three-Age system of Stone, Bronze, and Iron Ages was a major accomplishment of nineteenth-century archaeologists.
- The recognition that tools of human manufacture were found in the same layers as the bones of extinct animals, together with the development of the theory of evolution, changed the scope of archaeological research.
- The professionalization of archaeology during the early part of the twentieth century led to a focus on culture history and stratigraphic method.

- V. Gordon Childe shifted the focus of archaeologists from changes in the material remains recovered on archaeological sites to what those remains told us about ancient and prehistoric societies.
- The New Archaeologists, also known as processual archaeologists, led by Lewis Binford, argue that archaeologists should follow an explicitly scientific method of testing hypotheses.
- One of the approaches widely used by the New Archaeologists is systems theory.
- The postprocessual archaeologists, led by Ian Hodder, argue that archaeology is closer to history than to the exact sciences. The postprocessualists emphasize the role of interpretation and context in archaeological research.
- Gender and agency theory are two of the approaches used by postprocessual archaeologists.

KEY TERMS

agency theory, 49
archaeological theory, 34
cultural resource management (CRM), 44
deduction, 43
emic, 46
etic, 46
evolutionary archaeology, 51
feminist archaeology, 48
hermeneutics, 47

induction, 43
middle-range research, 44
Neolithic, 38
New Archaeology/processual archaeology, 42
Paleolithic, 38
postprocessual archaeology, 46
systems theory, 44
Three-Age system, 37
thunderstones, 35

REVIEW QUESTIONS

1. What kind of impact do you think the establishment of human antiquity has had on the way we think about humanity?

2. Do you agree with the New Archaeologists' stress on the importance of scientific method in archaeology?

3. What are the critiques raised by the postprocessualists? Do you think these critiques are valid?

CANADIAN ARCHAEOLOGISTS

- Mark Collard, professor in the Department of Archaeology at Simon Fraser University, pursues research in evolutionary anthropology. His research covers a range of topics in paleoanthropology and uses methods and theory from evolutionary biology to understand patterns of material culture variation.

  http://www.sfu.ca/archaeology/faculty/collard/index.html

- Bruce Trigger (1937–2006) was a professor in the Department of Anthropology at McGill University and the leading voice in the history of archaeology. His landmark book *History of Archaeological Thought* was reprinted in a revised edition by Cambridge University Press in 2006.

  http://mqup.mcgill.ca/book.php?bookid=2033

- Christopher Watts is a postdoctoral research fellow at the Royal Ontario Museum who specializes in the archaeology of the First Peoples of Northeastern North America, particularly the Late Woodland Traditions of the lower Great Lakes region. His research explores the application of semiotics and material culture theory in archaeology.

  http://www.rom.on.ca/collections/curators/watts.php

- Alison Wylie is a professor of philosophy at the University of Washington. She has published widely on the philosophy of archaeology, research ethics, and feminist archaeology. Her volume of collected essays, *Thinking From Things: Essays in the Philosophy of Archaeology* (University of California Press, 2002) presents an overview of her work.

  http://faculty.washington.edu/aw26/

PEARSON
myanthrokit™

Visit **www.myanthrokit.com**, where you will find a variety of tools and resources to enhance your learning, including:

- Practise quizzes with Study Plans
- Videos
- Listening Activities
- And much more!

PART TWO

HUMAN EVOLUTION

The study of human evolution draws insight from a multitude of disciplines, including paleontology, genetics, the reconstruction of past climates, and archaeology. This section of the book synthesizes the current state of research in human evolution with a strong emphasis on the unique perspective provided by archaeology. Particular topics are the timing of hominin dispersals and changes in adaptation and technology. After reading this introduction, you should understand:

- The place of humans in biological classification.

- The genetic evidence for the timing of the split between the human and chimpanzee lineages.

- The fossil record of homonoid phylogeny.

Introduction: Our Place in Nature

Charles Darwin is an odd choice for a hero. Plagued by everything from boils to self-doubt, he hardly fits the picture of a revolutionary figure. However, the theory of evolution developed in Darwin's *On the Origin of Species* is among the cornerstones of modern science. Almost all of Darwin's ideas were based on what he was able to observe on his voyage around the world on the *Beagle* and on walks around his country home in England. Darwin was obsessed by the question of how one explains the incredible variation in the living world. The theory of evolution begins with the observation that there is significant variety within populations. Whether one is looking at a bed of roses, a flock of pigeons, or a room of people, such variation exists. Darwin suggested that if some variations offered advantages to survival, they might come to be prevalent. Drawing on an analogy to the way humans breed domesticated animals for certain traits, he proposed that natural selection would act on the variation within populations to favour organisms with traits that were adaptive. Over vast periods of time, natural selection in different settings would lead to the splitting of populations into distinct species. Darwin's conception of evolution derives much of its power from its simplicity. According to Darwin, all the spectacular variety of life on earth can be explained as the result of the action of selection on variation over very long periods of time. Thus, the emergence of new species need not be explained by an appeal to metaphysics, but rather could be rendered intelligible through a detailed understanding of shifts in environments and adaptation over time.

In *On the Origin of Species*, Darwin wrote little about human evolution. Only at the end of the concluding chapter did he write that, on the basis of his theory, "light will be thrown on the origin of man and his history" (Darwin 1859). The theory of evolution is not a formulation that provides ultimate answers, but rather is a doorway to an endlessly fascinating exploration of humanity and the natural world. The next four chapters examine what we have learned in the last 150 years about the evolutionary history of humans.

■ Phylogeny

Before turning to a consideration of human evolution, it is necessary to define some of the fundamental aspects of biological terminology and to situate humans within an evolutionary framework. The basic unit of biological classification is the **species**, which is defined as a group of organisms that can produce fertile offspring. A genus (plural *genera*) refers to a grouping of similar species. All living humans are members of the species *Homo sapiens*, which belongs to genus *Homo*. Similar genera are grouped into families and superfamilies, and similar families are grouped into orders. Humans, the great apes (orangutans, gorillas, and chimpanzees), and gibbons make up the biological superfamily Hominoidea, or the **hominoids**. Together with monkeys and prosimians (lemurs, lorises, tarsiers, and their relatives), the hominoids belong to the order Primates. Most primates are tree-dwelling animals. Primates rely heavily on sight in dealing with the environment and are highly social, with a tendency to live in groups.

Table II.1 gives a biological classification of humans. Biological classifications are not based only on the degree of similarity between species; rather, they are also

species A group of intimately related and physically similar organisms that can produce fertile offspring.

hominoids The biological superfamily that includes humans, great apes, and gibbons.

TABLE II.1 BIOLOGICAL CLASSIFICATION OF HUMANS

Species	Homo sapiens	All living humans
Genus (pl. *genera*)	Homo	Humans and immediate ancestors
Superfamily	Hominoidea (hominoids)	Humans, orangutans, gorillas, chimpanzees, and gibbons
Order	Primates	Hominoids, monkeys, and prosimians

Common Ancestor

FIGURE II.1 In biological classification, chimpanzees and humans are closely related, reflecting their recent branching from a common ancestor.

phylogeny The evolutionary history of a species.

ontogeny The growth and development of an individual organism.

nuclear DNA DNA located in the cell nucleus; combines from each parent.

mitochondrial DNA DNA located outside of the cell nucleus; inherited exclusively from the mother.

molecular clock Method that allows the timing of the split between lineages to be calculated on the basis of the degree of genetic similarity.

paleoanthropologists Scientists who study the evolutionary history of the hominoids.

Aegyptopithecus A fossil primate that lived 56–23 million years ago.

meant to reflect the branching pattern of evolution. Popular media often misrepresent evolution as a linear process of progress through stages (see Figure II.2). Evolution is actually a process of splitting ancestral populations into distinct lineages. A common example of the popular misconception of evolution is found in the statement, "Humans evolved from apes." The correct statement is that humans and chimpanzees share a common ancestor, as is depicted in Figure II.1.

Reconstructing evolutionary history, or **phylogeny**, is based on a combination of information from fossils and genetics. The nature of the evidence provided by each of these sources differs. Genetic evidence is derived largely from living populations of humans and animals, although in a small number of cases it is possible to recover genetic material from fossils. Genetics provides insight into the evolutionary relationship between living species and the timing of the split between the lineages leading to those species (see Figure II.3). Fossils are the physical remains of prehistoric life. It is only through fossils that we can learn about our now-extinct human ancestors.

■ Genetic Evidence

The path of our growth and development as individuals (called **ontogeny**) is the result of the interaction between genetics and the environment. A copy of the DNA molecules that encode our genetic inheritance is contained in the nucleus of every one of our body cells. This **nuclear DNA** is a combination of genes inherited from each of our parents. **Mitochondrial DNA**, which is located outside of the cell nucleus, differs from nuclear DNA in that it is inherited exclusively from the maternal lineage. The DNA of all living humans is similar, so, genetically, humans are a quite homogeneous species.

Constructing a phylogeny, or evolutionary history, of the hominoids (humans, great apes, and gibbons) on the basis of genetic evidence involves comparing the degree of genetic similarity between species. Most genetic phylogenies of the hominoids emphasize the high degree of similarity between humans and chimpanzees. Chimpanzees consist of two living species: common chimpanzees (*Pan troglodytes*) and pygmy chimpanzees (*Pan paniscus*). The degree of similarity of humans to gorillas (*Gorilla gorilla*) is only slightly lower than the similarity of humans to chimpanzees. Orangutans (*Pongo pygmeaus*) are genetically less similar to humans than either chimpanzees or gorillas, and gibbons (*Hylobates*) are even more distantly related.

The degree of genetic similarity between species can be used to infer the timing of the split between lineages. Calculating when lineages diverged on the basis of the degree of genetic similarity rests on the concept of the **molecular clock**. The assumption underlying this concept is that genetic mutations accumulate at a constant rate. One can think of the DNA in the cell nucleus as an extremely lengthy series of coded messages. A genetic mutation is a random change in some part of this message. If one knows the degree of genetic similarity between two species, one can use the molecular clock to calculate the date when their lineages diverged. In practice, the use of the molecular clock is quite complex, and the results are controversial. However, some agreement has been reached over the timing of the divergence between the lineages of humans and the great apes (see Figure II.3). The split between the chimpanzee and human lineages is now placed between 4 and 6 million years before the present. The split between the human lineage and gorillas is said to have taken place 6 to 8 million years before the present, and that between humans and orangutans is held to be 12 to 15 million years before the present.

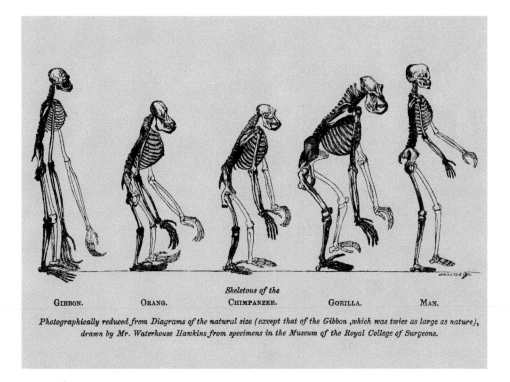

FIGURE II.2 This image from Thomas Huxley's book *Evidence as to Man's Place in Nature,* published in 1873, presents a picture of evolution as a linear directional process. This image has had a powerful influence on popular perceptions of evolution.

GIBBON. ORANG. *Skeletons of the* CHIMPANZEE. GORILLA. MAN.

Photographically reduced from Diagrams of the natural size (except that of the Gibbon ,which was twice as large as nature),
drawn by Mr. Waterhouse Hawkins from specimens in the Museum of the Royal College of Surgeons.

■ The Fossil Record

Although genetic evidence provides a framework for the timing of the split of the lineages leading to living species, it does not provide information about the extinct species that make up these lineages. **Paleoanthropologists**—scientists specializing in the study of the hominoid lineage—rely on fossils to construct the evolutionary history of humanity. As Darwin recognized in *On the Origin of Species*, the study of the fossil record is like reading a book with many pages missing. Because the preservation and discovery of fossils relies heavily on chance, there are significant gaps in the fossil record. Of course, one of the exciting elements of paleoanthropology is the role new discoveries play in developing knowledge and challenging ideas.

The earliest fossils that appear to be ancestral to the order Primates date to the Cretaceous period, 90 to 65 million years ago. A particularly important locality for the study of early primates is the Fayum Depression, south of Cairo, Egypt. The rich fossil remains recovered from the Fayum date to the Eocene and Oligocene periods (56 million to 23 million years ago). At that time, the Fayum, which is today a desert, was a marshland inhabited by a wide array of animals. Included in the Fayum assemblage are some of the earliest ancestors of monkeys. *Aegyptopithecus*, a fairly well represented species from the Fayum, might be ancestral to old world monkeys and apes.

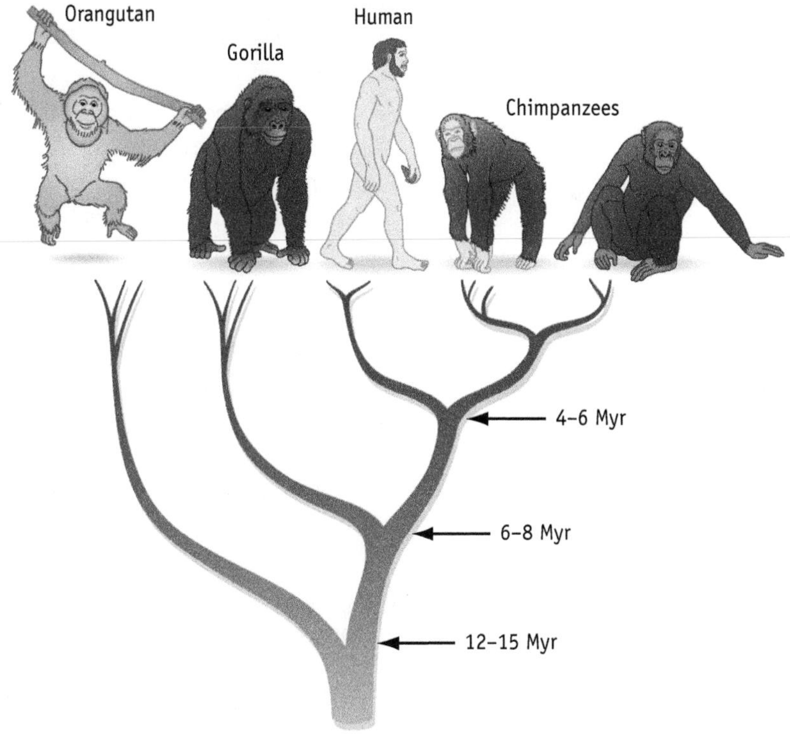

Orangutan

Gorilla

Human

Chimpanzees

4–6 Myr

6–8 Myr

12–15 Myr

FIGURE II.3 Homonoid phylogeny based on molecular data. How does this differ from Huxley's image found in Figure II.2?

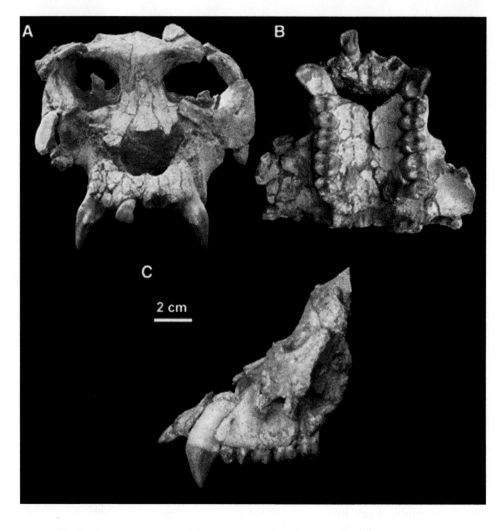

The **Miocene era** (23 million to 5 million years ago) saw an explosion in the number of hominoid species. During this period, hominoids filled many of the ecological niches now filled by monkeys. The range of Miocene hominoids is impressive. Species ranged from the size of a very small monkey to that of a gorilla (Figure II.4). One of the greatest challenges facing paleoanthropologists working with Miocene fossils is to determine where they fit on the hominoid evolutionary tree. Several Miocene species show traits that are characteristic of the orangutan, to the exclusion of the other hominoids. Thus, although it is possible to identify Miocene ancestors of modern orangutans, it is still difficult to identify a clear Miocene ancestor of the chimpanzee–human lineage. One of the major gaps in the fossil record is a representative of the common ancestor of humans and chimpanzees.

David Begun (2010) has pointed out that many Miocene homonoid fossils are found on sites in Europe. While he does not question that the last common ancestor of chimpanzees and humans lived in Africa, he stresses the possibility that Europe was the geographic context for the evolution of the earlier precursors of both the African ape and human lineages.

■ Culture and Human Evolution

One of the defining characteristics of biological evolution is that selection operates on traits that are transmitted genetically between generations. We pass on our genes, not our experiences, to our children. The early French zoologist Jean-Baptiste Lamarck famously made the argument that giraffes evolved long necks through the

Miocene era The period 23 million to 5 million years ago when there was an explosion in the number of hominoid species.

FIGURE II.5 A teacher working with eight- to nine-year-old children. How does the teacher guide the children's attention?

inheritance of acquired characteristics. This means that as giraffes stretched their necks to reach the tops of trees, their necks grew longer, and the lengthened-neck trait was then passed on to the next generation. A more contemporary example would be to argue that the children of fans of loud music are born partly deaf because their parents' hearing was damaged when the parents stood near loud speakers. We now know that Lamarck made one of the great errors in the history of science: Traits acquired during life are not transmitted genetically to the next generation.

Throughout the animal world, we often find that acquired traits are in fact transmitted. However, their transmission takes place not through genetics, but rather through learning. Learning provides a mechanism for transmitting experience from generation to generation (see Figure II.5). We frequently refer to the complex of learned behaviours found in human societies as culture. Is culture unique to humans? This is partly a matter of definition, but there is significant evidence that suggests that there is a patterning of learned behaviour between chimpanzee groups that warrants the label "culture" (Whiten et al. 1999). Regardless of how one resolves this issue, it is unquestionable that the specific nature of human culture is unique in the animal world. Change in human culture has been both rapid and cumulative. There is a clear sense that developments in human culture build on themselves, creating a kind of "ratchet" effect. When we study human evolution, we are studying not only biological evolution, but also cultural evolution. The fascination inherent in the archaeology of human origins lies in the exploration of the relationship between biological and cultural evolution. Did biological evolution drive cultural change and innovation? Or is it possible that innovations in culture led to events in biological evolution?

Underlying these questions is one of the most engaging mysteries in biological science: Why is it that human culture is of a unique nature? One intriguing answer examines the solely human capability to recognize others as "beings *like themselves* who have intentional and mental worlds like their own" (Tomasello 1999, 5). As far as we know, this capability is not found in any other animals, although chimpanzees can recognize themselves in a mirror (see Figure II.6 on page 60). Michael Tomasello (1999) argues that the capability to see another as like oneself opens the door to powerful new mechanisms of learning, in which humans learn by identifying with another rather than simply by observing.

FIGURE II.6 A chimpanzee examining itself in a mirror. Notice that the chimpanzee uses its hands to explore, guided by its reflection.

Language is also critical to human interaction and plays an essential role in the transmission of cultural knowledge between generations. The timing of the first appearance of language is a central topic in the archaeology of human origins. Unfortunately, language does not leave fossil evidence. We must infer what cultural behaviours would have required language. One intriguing idea is that the evolution of the human brain took place within the context of the evolution of language. Terrence Deacon (1997) has suggested that there was a coevolutionary relationship between language and the brain. If he is correct, the implication is that the archaeology of human origins traces the intricate give-and-take between genetic evolution and the evolution of culture. It is this interaction that makes the archaeology of human origins a unique and challenging field of study.

SUMMARY

- Reconstructing evolutionary history (phylogeny) is based on genetic and fossil evidence.
- Genetic evidence indicates a close relationship between humans and the great apes. Chimpanzees show the greatest genetic similarity to humans. On the basis of the molecular clock, the split of the human and chimpanzee lineages is placed at 4 to 6 million years ago.

- During the Miocene era 23 to 5 million years ago, there was an explosion in the diversity of homonoids.
- Learning, self-recognition, and language are critical components of human culture and the transfer of cultural knowledge between generations.

Aegyptopithecus, 56
hominoids, 55
mitochondrial DNA, 56
Miocene era, 58
molecular clock, 56

nuclear DNA, 56
ontogeny, 56
paleoanthropologists, 56
phylogeny, 56
species, 55

REVIEW QUESTIONS

1. What is the evidence for the timing of the split between the human and the chimpanzee lineages?
2. What are some characteristics of the Oligocene and Miocene homonoid fossil record?
3. What is the difference between biological evolution and cultural evolution?

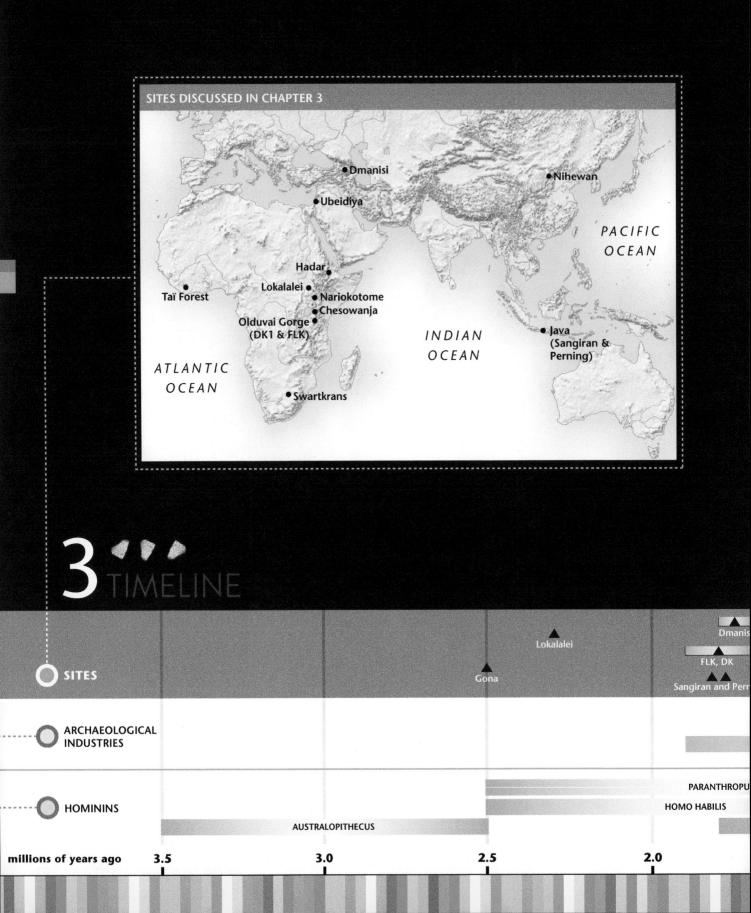

SITES DISCUSSED IN CHAPTER 3

Dmanisi

Nihewan

Ubeidiya

PACIFIC
OCEAN

Hadar

Lokalalei

Taï Forest

Nariokotome

Chesowanja

Olduvai Gorge
(DK1 & FLK)

INDIAN
OCEAN

Java
(Sangiran &
Perning)

ATLANTIC
OCEAN

Swartkrans

3 TIMELINE

					Dmanis
			Lokalalei		
SITES			Gona		FLK, DK
					Sangiran and Perr
ARCHAEOLOGICAL INDUSTRIES					
					PARANTHROPU
HOMININS					HOMO HABILIS
		AUSTRALOPITHECUS			
millions of years ago	3.5	3.0	2.5	2.0	

EARLY HOMININS

The early hominin record includes species belonging to four distinct genera. After reading this chapter, you should understand:

- The hominin radiation between 4 million and 2 million years ago.

- The major characteristics of Lower Paleolithic stone tool industries.

- The evidence for the origin of tool use.

- The debates about hunting and food sharing by early hominins.

- The evidence for the first dispersal of hominins out of Africa.

Excavating an early hominin site in East Africa.

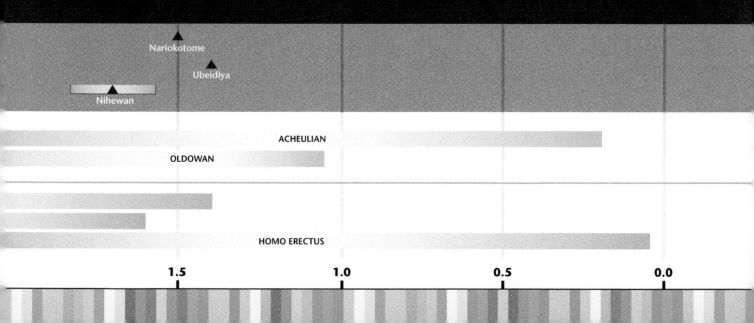

Nariokotome

Ubeidiya

Nihewan

ACHEULIAN

OLDOWAN

HOMO ERECTUS

1.5   1.0   0.5   0.0

FIGURE 3.1 The toothless *Homo erectus* from Dmanisi, Georgia.

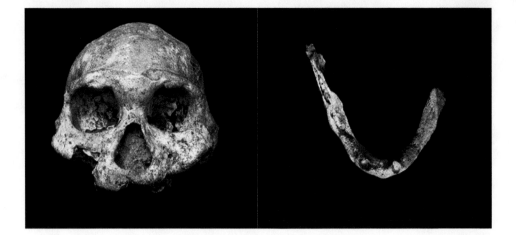

One-and-a-half million years ago, a male *Homo erectus* lived in the Caucasus Mountains, in what is today the Republic of Georgia. When archaeologists discovered his skull (see Figure 3.1) at the site of Dmanisi, they were surprised to find that he had lost all but one of his teeth, years before he died at the age of forty (Lordkipanidze et al. 2005). How did he survive without teeth? Did he rely on the compassion of members of his social group for food he could eat? The toothless man from Dmanisi raises many of the fundamental questions that occupy archaeologists studying early human ancestors. What was the nature of their society? How did they get food? How did they use tools?

In this chapter, we examine the archaeology of the early members of the hominin lineage. **Hominins** include all members of the human lineage after it split with the chimpanzee lineage. Until recently, hominins were refered to as hominids; however, the term hominin has now been adopted because it more properly fits with the rules of biological nomenclature (Wood and Richmond 2000). We begin by setting the stage for the study of early hominins by examining the fossil record, the geological context of early sites, and the definition of archaeological periods. With this background, the chapter moves on to three major themes in the archaeology of early hominins: tool use, adaptation, and social organization. Tool use is often thought to be a distinctive marker of the human lineage. We consider the evidence for tool use by animals and then move on to the timing and nature of the earliest archaeological evidence for tool manufacture. Beyond tool use, we are interested in the way that early hominins lived, including how they got their food and how their societies were organized. We focus on the evidence for hunting and food sharing by early hominins. Finally, the chapter turns to the archaeological evidence for the expansion of the hominin lineage beyond Africa and into Europe and Asia. One can imagine the toothless grin of the old man from Dmanisi as we struggle to understand the basic outlines of the lives of our early hominin ancestors.

3.1 The Fossil Record

The oldest fossils thought to belong to the hominin lineage are of ***Sahelanthropus tchadensis*** (Brunet et al. 2005; Zollikofer et al. 2005). The fossils of *Sahelanthropus* have been found in Chad in levels dating to 7 million years ago. A complete skull of *Sahelanthropus* has been discovered, but it is badly deformed, leaving room for differing interpretations of the species. Some have argued that *Sahelanthropus* is an African ape ancestor, while the discoverers of the fossil argue that it is, in fact, a hominin.

Ardipithecus ramidus is another early hominin (White et al. 1994, 1995). This species, which lived approximately 4.5 million years ago, is known from fossils discovered beginning in 1992 at the site of Aramis in Ethiopia. A picture of this early human ancestor has begun to emerge from the dramatic discovery of the fairly complete skeleton of a female *Ardipithecus* (White et al. 2009) (see Figure 3.2). This individual, nicknamed "Ardi," appears to have combined the ability to walk upright with anatomical traits, such as an opposable large toe, that would have facilitated climbing in trees. Ardi lacks anatomical features of the hands and wrists required for moving around on all four limbs using knuckle walking as is found in chimpanzees and gorillas. Ardi also differs from the great apes in that it lacks the pronounced canines found in these species. At this point many questions remain about *Ardipithecus* but the discovery of Ardi forces paleoanthropologists to reconsider the adaptations of the earliest members of the hominin lineage.

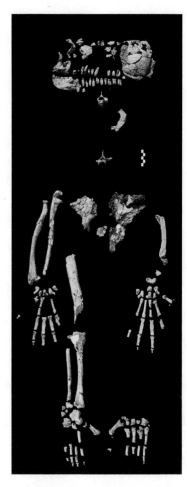

FIGURE 3.2 The partial skeleton of *Ardipithecus ramidus* discovered at Aramis, Ethiopia, provides a challenging new perspective on the early members of the hominin lineage.

■ The Early Hominin Radiation

The period between 4 million and 2 million years ago saw an explosion in the diversity of hominin species (Wood and Richmond 2000). Such an event is known in evolutionary biology as a **radiation**. The hominin radiation that took place between 4 million and 2 million years ago included three distinct genera: *Kenyanthropus*, *Australopithecus*, and *Paranthropus*.

Despite the wide variation found in these three genera, there are certain broad similarities among them. Members of the three genera appear to have been distinct from living great apes in that they were adapted to walking upright. However, it is possible that some species were also adapted to moving easily through trees by climbing. It is notable that these hominins, like *Ardipithecus,* lacked the pronounced canine teeth characteristic of living great apes. The mean brain size for members of the three genera was consistently between 450 and 475 cubic centimetres, at the high end of brain size for living apes. Thus, within the hominin lineage, bipedalism (walking upright) and the loss of large canines preceded a significant increase in brain size. Table 3.1 presents some important aspects of *Kenyanthropus*, *Australopithecus*, and *Paranthropus*, as well as of the two later species *Homo habilis* and *Homo erectus*.

TABLE 3.1

GENUS OR SPECIES	DATE	BRAIN SIZE	CHARACTERISTICS	FOUND IN
Australopithecus	4.0–2.5 million years ago	450–475 cc	Bipedal	East Africa, West Africa, and South Africa
Kenyanthropus	3.5 million years ago	450–475 cc	Similar to *Australopithecus*	East Africa
Paranthropus	2.5–1.4 million years ago	450–475 cc	Massive molars and chewing muscles	East Africa and South Africa
Homo habilis	2.5–1.6 million years ago	500–800 cc	Increased brain size	East Africa and South Africa
Homo erectus	1.9 million–45,000 (?) years ago	750–1,250 cc	Further increase in brain size, dispersal out of Africa	Africa, Asia, and Europe

FIGURE 3.3 The footsteps at Laetoli preserved in a bed of volcanic ash dated to 3.8 million years ago. Notice the hominin trackways and the tracks of other animals running off to the right.

AUSTRALOPITHECINES. The **australopithecines** are known from as many as six distinct species. Australopithecine fossils are known from sites dating between 4 million and 2.5 million years ago (Leakey et al. 1995). Most specimens come from East Africa and South Africa; however, a new species, *Australopithecus bahrelghazali*, which lived 3.5 million years ago, was discovered in 1996 in Chad in Central Africa (Brunet et al. 1995). The nearly complete skeleton of an *Australopithecus afarensis* discovered by Donald Johanson in the Hadar, Ethiopia, famously nicknamed Lucy after the Beatles song "Lucy in the Sky with Diamonds," provides the first evidence that australopithecines walked on two legs. Graphic evidence that the species walked upright is found in a trail of footprints left in volcanic ash at the site of **Laetoli** in Tanzania, shown in Figure 3.3 (Leakey and Harris 1987). A team of excavators working with Mary Leakey in 1978 discovered fossil footprints left by three individuals walking on a surface of volcanic ash. The prints at Laetoli clearly show that these three individuals were walking upright. Because the ash dates to 3.8 million years ago, the footprints were most likely produced by members of the species *Austrolopithecus afarensis.* The recent discovery of the remarkably well-preserved remains of an australopithecine child in the Dikka research area in Ethiopia sheds new light on this species (Alemseged et al. 2006). Much of the skeleton shows ape-like traits that suggest that australopithecines were adapted to climbing trees as well as to walking upright.

KENYANTHROPUS. *Kenyanthropus*, which dates to 3.5 million years ago, was first discovered in 2001 by Meave Leakey and her colleagues on the shores of Lake Turkana in northern Kenya (Leakey et al. 2001). *Kenyanthropus* is still poorly understood; however, in general terms, it seems similar to the australopithecines.

PARANTHROPUS. *Paranthropus*, also known as robust *Australopithecus*, is characterized by massive molars and muscles for chewing (Wood and Richmond 2000). Louis Leakey nicknamed the *Paranthropus boisei* skull he recovered at Olduvai Gorge in Tanzania "Nutcracker Man," and it is thought that the massive chewing mechanisms of these species is related to a diet that included seeds or fruits with a hard outer coating (Figure 3.4). The earliest known *Paranthropus* dates to 2.5 million years ago, while the most recent dates to 1.4 million years ago.

HOMO HABILIS. Contemporary with *Paranthropus* there was a very different hominin living in East Africa. This hominin lacked the heavy chewing muscles and large teeth characteristic of *Paranthropus* and had a larger brain, which had a volume of 500 to 800 cubic centimetres. This was the first primate with such a large brain and also the earliest species to be assigned to the genus *Homo*. **Homo habilis** is known from sites in East Africa dating to between 2.5 million and 1.6 million years ago, including Olduvai Gorge, Tanzania, and Koobi Fora, Kenya (Wood and Richmond 2000).

FIGURE 3.4 Louis Leakey examines the skull of a *Paranthropus* fossil. Notice how the skull is assembled from fossil fragments.

HOMO ERECTUS. The next member of genus *Homo* to appear in the fossil record is ***Homo erectus***. The oldest evidence of *Homo erectus* dates to the period between 1.9 million and 1.5 million years ago. *Homo erectus* fossils are known from East Africa and South Africa, as well as from sites in Europe and Asia. Some paleoanthropologists separate the earliest *Homo erectus* fossils from sites in Africa into a distinct species called *Homo ergaster* (Wood and Collard 1999).

The discovery of the complete skeleton of a juvenile adolescent *Homo erectus* at the site of Nariokotome, Kenya, has provided a unique picture of this hominin species (Leakey and Walker 1993). The fossil found at Nariokotome is the skeleton of a boy who was approximately 160 cm (5 ft. 3 in.) tall when he died, roughly 1.5 million years ago (see Figure 3.5). Not only was he tall, but he also was thin, with a body shape typical of tropical populations among modern humans. He lived on the rich floodplain grasslands along the banks of a channel of the Omo River, in a landscape that was mostly open grassland and swamps, with trees limited to the river's edge and high spots. It is unclear why the boy died. There is no evidence of any trauma or attack by a carnivore. The only evidence of pathology is a pocket of gum disease related to the loss of one of his milk teeth. It is possible that infection of this inflammation was the cause of death.

3.2 Setting the Scene

The lives of early hominins left behind few traces. The only remains are the stone tools and bones discarded as they moved around the landscape. The richest context for the recovery of early hominin archaeological sites is the **East African Rift Valley**. The stone tools found on early hominin sites are grouped as belonging to the Lower Paleolithic, or, as it is known in Africa, the Early Stone Age. The Oldowan and the Acheulian are the two main industries identified within the Lower Paleolithic.

■ The East African Rift Valley

The East African Rift Valley is a massive geological feature stretching from Malawi in southern Africa to Turkey and Syria in the Middle East. This formation can be thought of as an enormous trough that is in constant formation as the surface of the earth pulls apart along the rift. Three characteristics of the Rift Valley make it invaluable in the search for early hominin sites. The first is that, because it is a trough, it is filling up with sediments. It is thus a depositional environment that preserves archaeological and paleontological sites. Second, because it is tectonically active, there is a great deal of erosion. The result is the formation of badlands, landscapes in which enormous deposits of earth are cut by gullies and ravines (see Figures 3.7 and 3.8 on page 69). Third, as a sort of icing on the cake, the Rift Valley is also volcanically active, so there are levels of volcanic ash, known as tuffs, that can be dated using the argon method (see Toolbox on page 80).

OLDUVAI GORGE. Of all the gullies and ravines of the East African Rift Valley, none is more impressive or more important for the study of human evolution than **Olduvai Gorge** in Tanzania. Olduvai Gorge has come to be synonymous with the names Louis and Mary Leakey. The Leakeys' decades of research

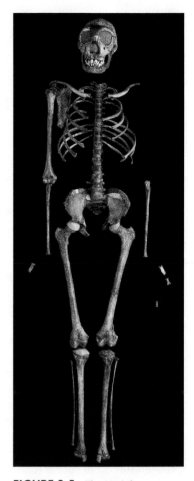

FIGURE 3.5 The Nariokotome *Homo erectus* fossil gives a very complete picture of the anatomy of this species. Notice how low the cranial vault (forehead) is compared to that of modern humans.

▲▲ **Laetoli** Location in Tanzania where tracks of australopithecine footprints were found, showing that australopithecines walked upright.

Homo habilis This hominin is the earliest species to be assigned to the genus *Homo*.

Homo erectus The first hominin found on sites outside of Africa. The earliest known *Homo erectus* fossils date to the period between 1.9 and 1.5 million years ago.

▲▲ **East African Rift Valley** A geological feature stretching from East Africa to the Middle East that is the richest context for the recovery of early hominin archaeological sites.

▲▲ **Olduvai Gorge** The most impressive and important location in the East African Rift Valley for the study of human evolution.

Fraud—Piltdown and Kama-takamori

On December 28, 1912, the *Illustrated London News* announced "a discovery of supreme importance to all who are interested in the history of the human race." The discovery, made at the site of Piltdown in East Sussex, England, included fragments of a skull and jaw that appeared to be the oldest known fossils of a human ancestor. When the skull of Piltdown man was reconstructed, a picture emerged of an individual with a large cranium similar to the skull of living humans. However, the jaw (mandible) was in many ways ape-like. The Piltdown fossils became the basis for a new genus of human ancestor: *Eoanthropus*, or "dawn man."

In 1954, 42 years after the discovery, the fossil remains from Piltdown were unmasked as an elaborate fraud. The jaw was from a modern orangutan and had been stained to appear fossilized. The teeth had been filed down to alter their shape into a slightly more human configuration and parts of the mandible had been deliberately broken off in order to make it more difficult to identify as the mandible of an ape. The skull fragments were from a modern human of recent archaeological origin. All of the bones found at Piltdown were deliberately introduced into the site.

Of course, the intriguing question is, Who concocted and carried out this scheme? The most likely suspect is Charles Dawson, the amateur scientist and solicitor who discovered the fossils. However, Dawson did not have a clear motive, and many doubt that he had the expertise to make the fakes, as well as access to paraphernalia such as an orangutan jaw. It seems likely that Dawson was himself duped or had an accomplice. Among the list of suspects were two of the most prominent scientists of the day, Arthur Smith Woodward and Arthur Keith. Both had the expertise and access to the site, but their motive is unclear. Would they risk everything and sacrifice

the most basic of scientific ethics in such an undertaking? The Catholic priest and paleontologist Teilhard de Chardin has also been implicated as a suspect, particularly given the fact that he discovered some of the Piltdown fossils himself during brief visits to the site. Even Sir Arthur Conan Doyle, the author of the Sherlock Holmes mysteries, has been suggested as a suspect. To this day, the file on the Piltdown hoax remains open.

Frauds like Piltdown are exceptionally rare in archaeology. However, a similar scandal recently rocked Japanese archaeology. In 1993, Japanese archaeologists announced the discovery of stone tools at the Kama-takamori site in a context dated to roughly 500,000 years ago. The discovery was widely reported, primarily in the Japanese popular press, as the earliest evidence of human occupation of Japan. In 1995, a pit was found with fifteen tools arranged in an oval, with two tools in the centre, one made of a particularly beautiful white rock and the other from an unusual red rock.

In 2002, the archaeological community was stunned to learn that the artifacts at the Kama-takamori site had been deliberately planted by one of the excavators. Videotapes caught the excavator in the act of digging out a pit, planting the tools, covering them up, and then carefully tamping down the earth with his boot. The events at the site have cast confusion over the early prehistory of Japan, as this same excavator was involved in many projects.

It is important to distinguish between fraud, as practised at Piltdown and Kama-takamori, and error. Fraud is inimical to scientific research, while error plays a large role in increasing our knowledge of the past. A fraud is an intentional attempt to deceive. An error is a false interpretation based on the best available evidence. Errors often form the basis for further testing and refutation of a scientific theory. ●

REFERENCE: Frank Spencer. (1990). *Piltdown: A Scientific Forgery*. Oxford, UK: Oxford University Press.

FIGURE 3.6 A painting of the examination of the Piltdown skull. The painting underscores the fact that this forgery was perpetrated on the scientific establishment of the time.

at Olduvai revolutionized ideas of prehistory and brought attention to the tremendous potential of the East African Rift Valley for the study of early hominins. Two million years ago in the area that is now Olduvai Gorge, there was a small lake surrounded by a grassland and marsh landscape within a large basin or depression. The lake was salty, but it supported a diversity of fish and reptiles, including crocodile. The surrounding grassland and swamps of the basin supported mammals such as elephants, bovids (ancestors of cows), hippos, antelope, and hominins. Over time, the basin filled with sediments carried by wind and water, until it was scarcely discernible on the landscape of the Serengeti Plain.

Two hundred thousand years ago, modern streams began to carve a canyon through the soft sediments filling the basin at Olduvai. Over time, this erosion created the spectacular landscape of Olduvai Gorge, a main gorge and side gorge that meet to form a Y shape. The erosion that created the Gorge provides a point of access to the fossils and stone tools deposited around Lake Olduvai. Without the erosion, this critical evidence would remain inaccessible, locked under tens of metres of accumulated sediments. Research at Olduvai first involves walking along the gorge, looking for places where tools or fossils are eroding out of the cliffs. As one walks up the walls of the gorge, one is walking up through geological time. In the spots where material is found eroding out of the sections, it is possible in some cases to dig into the cliff face to expose ancient living surfaces.

The sequence at Olduvai Gorge is based on geological rather than archaeological strata. Bed I is the earliest unit, Bed IV the latest, and overlying Bed IV is a unit known as the Masek Beds. Table 3.2 gives a chronology of the formation of the beds.

FIGURE 3.7 A view of the badlands landscape in the Rift Valley near Dikka, Ethiopia, where the fossil of an australopithecine child was discovered. The erosion of sediments is what allows archaeologists and paleoanthropologists to find hominin sites.

FIGURE 3.8 Searching for hominin fossils at the Dikka site, Ethiopia.

▓ Lower Paleolithic

The period during which early hominins began making stone tools is known as the **Lower Paleolithic**. In Africa, the Lower Paleolithic is often called the Early Stone Age. The Lower Paleolithic includes two major industries: the Oldowan and the Acheulian. An archaeological industry is a period characterized by a certain approach to making stone tools. Prehistorians working on very early periods tend to

TABLE 3.2

Masek Beds	0.6–0.4 million years ago
Bed IV	0.8–0.6 million years ago
Bed III	1.15–0.8 million years ago
Bed II	1.7–1.15 million years ago
Bed I	1.9–1.7 million years ago

Lower Paleolithic The period when hominins began producing stone tools.

Discovering the Past: Early Hominins in the Nihewan Basin

BY CHEN SHEN, ROYAL ONTARIO MUSEUM

When I began working in the Nihewan Basin in 1998, Professor Wei Qi from the Institute of Vertebrate Paleontology and Paleoanthropology (IVPP), Chinese Academy of Sciences, had been working in the area for 26 years, searching for fossil remains of early hominins. He told me, "Richard Leakey found his first *Homo* fossil in the Olduvai Basin after working there for 28 years; so my luck of finding them here will come pretty soon." Now, a decade later, Professor Wei Qi is still hoping to find the first Nihewan hominin fossil, but the hope is much greater than ten years ago. Today we have clear archaeological evidence to suggest that the Nihewan Basin in northern China was the site of the earliest occupations of early hominins. More than a dozen Lower Pleistocene sites dating between 1.7 and 1 million years ago have now been identified in this area.

The Nihewan Basin, about 300 km away from the Zhoukoudian *Homo erectus* site near Beijing, is regarded as the "Asian Olduvai Gorge" in Chinese Palaeolithic studies because of its similar geological formation and abundant archaeological materials from Lower Pleistocene deposits. Prior to 1990, the field investigation methods used by those eager to find the first *Homo* fossil remains caused some problems. At one of the most important sites—Xiaochangliang, the first known Lower Pleistocene site in the basin, identified in 1978—the excavations were not systematic, and no artifacts and faunal remains were recorded with precise provenances *in situ*. On a hot day in July 1998, I arrived at the site with Dr. Chen Chun.

We began to excavate at Xiaochangliang using the latest field techniques, including a digital camera, GPS device, and computer database

application for recording, none of which had ever been used previously in Nihewan archaeology. Careful excavation along with sediment analysis revealed that the site was very close to a water source—an archaic lake, which, according to geological studies, dried out around 25,000 years ago. A large number of stone tools were recovered. These were studied under a microscope for use-wear by examining microfractures, rounding, and polish caused by forces from use. The results show that Xiaochangliang hominins used unmodified flakes as expedient tools, probably for the scavenging of dead animals for food.

In 2000 and 2001, the Nihewan project, a collaborative endeavour between the Royal Ontario Museum and the IVPP, undertook two field sessions of excavation at another important site, Donggutuo, of which Wei had identified and excavated a

---

be cautious about using the term *culture* because it implies that the groups that lived during those periods resemble modern cultures in sharing a common set of beliefs and values and, in many cases, also a common language. We do not know whether that is true of the people who made Oldowan and Acheulian types of stone tools; therefore, the term *industry* is used.

THE OLDOWAN. The **Oldowan** was defined on the basis of the archaeological material from Olduvai Gorge Beds I and II dated between 1.9 million and 1.15 million years ago. The question of which hominin made the Oldowan tools is not yet resolved. *Paranthropus*, *Homo habilis*, and *Homo erectus* all lived during the time Oldowan tools were manufactured. Fossils of all these hominins are found either on or near Oldowan archaeological sites.

Oldowan tools have been described as a least-effort solution to creating sharp-edged tools (Schick and Toth 1993). The basic distinction between Oldowan tools is that they are either flakes or cores. Flakes are slivers of rock that

Oldowan Lower Paleolithic stone tool industry, dated between 1.9 and 1.15 million years ago, characterized by choppers and flakes.

limited portion in the early 1980s. It is the only known multiple-layered Lower Pleistocene site in the basin. Most artifacts were found in clusters indicative of some kind of hominin activities. Our study of cores from Donggutuo suggests that a bipolar technique—striking a core that rested on an anvil stone—was used to produce small artifacts. This is the earliest evidence in China for this type of tool manufacture.

The sites in the Nihewan Basin were dated by applying the palaeomagnetic technique. This method indicated that Donggutuo is about 1.1 million years old, while Xiaochangliang is roughly 1.36 million years old. As important as these dates are, the most exciting find in the Nihewan Basin was the Goudi site, discovered in 2001. Here we found evidence of hominin presence dating back to 1.66 million years ago; this is so far the oldest hominin occupation in East Asia with abundant cultural remains. The faunal remains discovered include birds (e.g., ostrich), rodents, carnivores, elephantids, rhinoceros, and cervids. Excavations revealed an activity area where natural rock hammerstones and other stone artifacts were densely integrated with a cluster of elephant bones. The cultural remains of hominin activities also are evident from a large number of artifacts that can be refitted together from adjacent excavation areas.

FIGURE 3.9
Excavations at the Donggutuo site in 2000.

have been struck off of a stone. Cores are the pieces from which the flakes have been struck. The characteristic tool of the Oldowan is the chopper, the tool shown being used to smash a bone in Figure 3.10 on page 72. To manufacture a chopper, one begins with a rounded stone and strikes a series of flakes off one edge. The process can be continued by flipping the stone over and striking a series of flakes along the same edge off the other side. When Mary Leakey began work at Olduvai Gorge, she identified choppers as tools and imagined them as being useful for butchering animals. However, when archaeologists began making Oldowan tools and using them to butcher carcasses, they found that choppers were not very useful for this task. These experiments demonstrated that it was the sharp-edged flakes that were most useful. As a result, it has been argued that the actual desired product was the flake and that the chopper was simply waste from manufacture. An alternative is that both flakes and choppers were used. The choppers might have been useful for working wood or breaking bones to get at marrow, while the flakes were used for butchery. Unfortunately, we have no preserved wood from Oldowan sites.

Acheulian Lower Paleolithic stone tool industry dated in Africa between 1.7 million and 200,000 years ago, characterized by bifacial tools including handaxes and cleavers.

bifaces Characteristic tools of the Acheulian. Bifaces include handaxes and cleavers.

FIGURE 3.10 An archaeologist uses a chopper to break a bone to get at the marrow inside.

THE ACHEULIAN. The earliest **Acheulian** industries in East Africa date to the period between 1.7 and 1.5 million years before the present. The date for the end of the Acheulian is currently unclear, but it is in the range of 400,000 and 200,000 years ago. Acheulian sites are found throughout Africa, including major sites in both eastern and southern Africa, as well as in Europe, the Middle East, and India. The Acheulian began at the same time as the first appearance of *Homo erectus* and the extinction of *Homo habilis*.

The characteristic tool of the Acheulian is the biface. Unlike the Oldowan flakes and cores, the Acheulian tool can hardly be described as a least-effort solution. The Acheulian **bifaces** are better described as the earliest evidence of design. Bifaces can be either handaxes, if they are pointed at the end, or cleavers, if they have a wide working end (see Figure 3.11). Bifaces were carefully and skillfully fashioned tools, not simply cores. One aspect of their design is their symmetry with reference to a central axis. The actual function of bifaces has remained an enigma. Clearly, they were highly effective tools if hominins continued to use them for over 1 million years. The handaxe is perhaps the most successful tool humans have ever invented. But what was it used for? Recently, an archaeologist studied botanical remains known as phytoliths on handaxes from the site of Peninj, Tanzania. Phytoliths are mineral elements of plant cells that survive after the rest of the plant has disintegrated. The phytoliths adhering to the handaxes from Peninj suggest that these tools were used for woodworking. There is some evidence of worked wood at the Acheulian site of Kolambo Falls, Zambia.

FIGURE 3.11 An Acheulian cleaver (left) and handaxe (right). Archaeologists stress the symmetry of many Acheulian handaxes. (Scale in centimetres.)

TOOLBOX

Stone Tools

The archaeological study of stone tools is known as lithic analysis, and the manufacture of stone tools is known as knapping. When looking at stone tools, archaeologists see not only the formal properties of the artifact (colour, shape, size, weight), but also evidence of how it was manufactured and used. To understand the process of knapping, archaeologists take great care to recover all stone artifacts, including waste products from manufacture.

Lower Paleolithic tools were made by delivering a sharp blow to a rock in order to break off a smaller piece, a technique known as percussion. The piece that is struck off is called a flake, and the piece from which the flake is struck is called the core. The goal of percussion is to produce either flake tools or core tools. In many cases, both flakes and cores were used as tools.

Flakes have several important features. The surface that is split off of the core, known as the ventral face, has a convex area called the bulb of percussion at the end where it was struck. This end is known as the proximal end of the flake. The bulb of percussion is produced when the force of the blow enters the rock. The force enters the rock as a cone, much like the cone produced when a bullet strikes glass or a stone is thrown into a body of water. The force from the blow ripples out from this initial cone, eventually splitting the flake from the core.

Percussion techniques can be classified on the basis of the way the blow is delivered. In *direct percussion*, it is delivered directly to the core. In *hard-hammer direct percussion*, a rock is used as a hammer. In *soft-hammer direct per-*

cussion, either an antler or a piece of hardwood is used. Using a soft hammer allows the knapper to produce thin flakes with a less pronounced bulb of percussion. *Indirect percussion* involves the use of an intermediary device known as a punch between the hammer and the core. The advantage of indirect percussion is that the precise placement of the blow can be controlled. Indirect percussion is often used in making long blades or shaping arrowheads.

Pressure techniques follow the same principles as percussion, except that the force is applied by pressure rather than a blow. In practice, the knapper presses the tip of an antler or, in some cases, a copper tip, against the edge of a tool to push off a flake. Pressure techniques involve the exertion of a great deal of force by the knapper, and usually the entire upper body is involved. Pressure techniques are normally used in the very fine shaping of tools. Because no blow is involved, the bulb of percussion is extremely diffuse, and very thin flakes can be removed.

In some cases, a flake would simply be used as struck. In other cases, however, a core or a flake was carefully

modified to create a desired shape or edge. The careful secondary shaping of a core or flake is known as retouch.

In Canadian archaeology, arrowheads—usually referred to as projectile points—and other carefully shaped tools, such as drills and endscrapers, are a major focus of lithic analysis (Kooyman 2000). Analyzing projectile points involves detailed measurements of shape and application of well-developed regional typologies. Lithic analysts are also able to identify preforms—pieces abandoned in the early stages of making a projectile point—as well as biface thinning flakes produced in the final stages of shaping projectile points.

It is critical that the knapper have control of the way the rock fractures. Many rocks are not suitable for these techniques, because they either fracture along cleavage planes in the rock or crumble when struck. The stones used by knappers are brittle and fine grained, and do not have internal features that determine the direction in which they break. A wide variety of rocks, including flint (also known as chert), basalt, and obsidian, fits these criteria and can be used to make stone tools. ●

Retouch

Bulb of Percussion

Core

Flake

Flake Ventral Surface

FIGURE 3.12 Cores and flakes bear traces of the manufacture process such as retouch and the bulb of percussion.

FIGURE 3.13 A New Caledonian crow grasps a hooked tool, which it uses to probe for insects.

▲▲ Taï Forest Location where chimpanzees use stone hammers and anvils to break open hard nuts. The tools are not manufactured, but, rather, are used as found.

3.3 The Origin of Tool Use

Tool use is often considered a trait that separates humans from animals, although research by ethologists—scientists who study animal behaviour—casts doubt on tool use as a uniquely human behaviour. Nonetheless, the development of stone tool technology marks an important point in human evolution. Stone tools dating to 2.4 million years ago are the earliest known archaeological artifacts. Recent research indicates that the manufacture of these early stone tools was a more complex process than previously imagined.

■ Tool Use by Animals

Most evidence for tool use and manufacture comes from studies of chimpanzees and the other great apes. However, surprising evidence for tool manufacture by birds has emerged in a study of crows on New Caledonia, a string of islands approximately 1450 kilometres northeast of Australia. While observing the behaviour of New Caledonian crows, Gavin Hunt noticed that the birds were carrying objects in their beaks and using the objects to extract insects from trees (see Figure 3.13). Closer investigation showed that the objects the crows were using were strips cut out of leaves from pandanus trees. The edges of these leaves are spiked, so when a strip is cut off of the edge of the leaf, it has a series of hooks. It is these hooks that the birds use to search out their prey. Hunt found that the birds often cut off strips of leaves and then stepped them in shape, with hooks pointed toward the narrow end.

Jane Goodall was among the first to document tool use by chimpanzees in the wild. The chimpanzee group she studied at Gombe in Tanzania used twigs, bark, or grass to fish termites and ants out of mounds. In subsequent years, tool use was discovered in a number of distinct groups of chimpanzees. Perhaps the most dramatic of these discoveries comes from the studies of the chimpanzees in the Taï Forest, Ivory Coast (Boesch and Boesch-Achermann 2000). The **Taï Forest** chimpanzees use stone hammers and anvils to break open hard nuts (see Figure 3.14). The tools are not manufactured, but, rather, are used as found. However, the use of these tools is a skilled activity that young chimpanzees acquire by observing their mothers over a period of years. The skills the young chimpanzees learn include both the selection of the right hammers and anvils and the appropriate use of force.

On their own, dipping for ants and cracking nuts seem like rather modest examples of tool use. However, an interesting pattern emerges when the distribution of chimpanzee tool use behaviours is examined across Africa (Whiten et al. 1999). The tools and the way they are used are not uniform across the continent, but rather are distinctive of particular groups. This pattern is true not only of tool use, but also of other behaviours, such as greeting and grooming. Ecological factors alone do not dictate where particular tools are used. For example, there are populations of chimpanzees living in West Africa that have access to the same nuts as those in the Taï Forest, but that do not use stone hammers to break the nuts. These groups either ignore the nuts completely or break them with their teeth, a far less efficient technique. These observations have led some ethologists to argue that chimpanzees have culture.

FIGURE 3.14 A chimpanzee in Liberia, West Africa, uses a hammerstone and an anvil to crack nuts. Notice how the intent gaze of the chimpanzee guides its actions, much like the baseball player who is urged to "keep your eye on the ball."

In 1990, a group of archaeologists and primatologists began an experiment to determine whether they could teach Kanzi, a pygmy chimpanzee born and raised at the Language Research Center at Georgia State University, to make stone tools (Toth et al. 1993; Schick et al. 1999). Kanzi was shown a box with a transparent door held closed by a piece of rope. A piece of fruit was placed inside the box, and Kanzi was shown that the rope could be cut with a stone flake struck off a rock with a hammer. The chimpanzee was then shown how to create sharp flakes by striking one piece of rock (a hammer) against another (a core). Kanzi was able to carry out this task; however, his preferred method was to smash a rock by throwing it onto the concrete floor of the laboratory. In all cases, the method of flake production was very crude. Still, Kanzi did manage to make some tools bearing a resemblance to the earliest tools produced by hominins.

Kanzi's skill at breaking rocks seems to indicate that the ability of chimpanzees to manufacture tools is at best quite limited. However, this test might actually have more to do with the qualities of the human hand than with any abstract conceptual abilities. Humans are unique in having a thumb and fingers that are able to rotate, allowing for a wide range of grips. Chimpanzee hands, like all ape hands, are largely limited to folding their fingers over objects or gripping small objects between the thumb and the index finger (Panger et al. 2002). Perhaps Kanzi's difficulties in stone tool manufacture reflect the limited range of grips he is capable of compared to those the human demonstrator is able to assume.

■ The Archaeological Evidence

The earliest occupation at Olduvai Gorge, in Bed I, dates to approximately 1.8 million years ago. On the basis of discoveries made at **Hadar**, it is now clear that the earliest stone tools are at least half a million years older. The Hadar region, located in the East African Rift Valley in Ethiopia, has produced some of the most important fossils of australopithecines, including Lucy. In the early 1990s, two teams discovered stone tools at sites in the Hadar in levels that date to approximately 2.5 million years ago.

▲▲ **Hadar** Location in the East African Rift Valley where many important fossils, including the near-complete fossil of an australopithecine, and the earliest known stone tools have been discovered.

Primate Tool Use

Anne Russon of Glendon College at York University is an ethologist who studies orangutans in the rain forest of Borneo. Orangutans in Borneo are threatened by drought, fire, logging, and poaching. A major challenge for conservationists is to reintroduce captive orangutans to free forest life. Russon has focused her research on observing how captive orangutans learn to gain access to food resources once they have been returned to the forest. Russon has been impressed by the extent to which captive orangutans rely on social learning and high-level reasoning to gain skills related to food acquisition. She suggests that her results have impli-

cations not only for our understanding of orangutan cognition, but also for how conservation programs should habituate captive orangutans to their new environment after they have been returned to the forest.

Julio Mercader, an archaeologist at the University of Calgary, has carried out excavations of sites in the Ivory Coast where chimpanzees use stone tools to crack nuts. One question that has plagued researchers of primate tool use is whether it developed based on primate observation of human tool use. In the case of chimpanzees using hammer stones, it has been argued that they might have "aped" this behaviour based

on exposure to agricultural groups pounding grains. Mercader and his colleagues were able to radiocarbon date levels with evidence of chimpanzee tool use back as far as 4,300 years ago. This places the beginning of chimpanzee tool use before the development of village farming communities in the region. ◆

REFERENCES: Anne E. Russon. (2001). Return of the Native: Cognition and site-specific expertise in orangutan rehabilitation. *International Journal of Primatology* 23(3): 461–478.

Julio Mercader, Huw Barton, Jason Gillespie, Jack Harris, Steven Kuhn, Robert Tyler, and Christophe Boesch. (2007). 4,300-year-old chimpanzee sites and the origins of percussive stone technology. *Proceedings of the American Academy of Sciences* 104(9): 3043–3048.

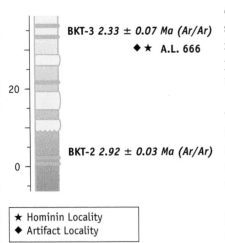

BKT-3 *2.33 ± 0.07 Ma (Ar/Ar)*

◆ ★ A.L. 666

20 —

BKT-2 *2.92 ± 0.03 Ma (Ar/Ar)*

0 —

★ Hominin Locality
◆ Artifact Locality

FIGURE 3.15 Stratigraphic context of the stone tools from the Hadar. Notice the position of the artifacts (indicated by a diamond) and the hominin fossil (known as A.L. 666 and indicated by a star). Both the tools and hominin are above BKT-2 and below BKT-3. Dates are in millions of years ago (Ma). The vertical scale on the left is in metres.

At the Gona site, close to 3,000 stone tools were found in a single layer in two excavation areas covering an area of 22 square metres (Semaw 2000). The tools were discovered in a clay soil that showed no signs of river activity. Although the tools are simple, there is no question that they were manufactured by hominins. Given what is known about the geological context, it is not possible that any geological process produced the uniform patterns of flaking found on these tools. The major types of tools found are sharp-edged flakes and cores, including choppers.

The archaeological horizon at the Gona site is sandwiched between layers of volcanic ash known as tuff (see Figure 3.15) (Semaw et al. 1997). Fortunately, these tuff layers are ideal for argon dating. The BKT-2 tuff, which underlies the site, dates to 2.9 million years ago, while the BKT-3 tuff, which overlies the site, is dated to 2.3 million years ago. Therefore, the stone tools were produced and deposited during the time interval between 2.9 million and 2.3 million years ago.

Another team of researchers working near Gona has found a smaller assemblage of tools from a similar context (Kimbel et al. 1996). Adding to the interest of this discovery is a hominin fossil found at the same level. The fossil is a well-preserved maxilla (palate) that has been identified as belonging to the genus *Homo*. Due to the fossil's fragmentary nature, it was not possible to determine what species it belongs to, but given the age of the site *Homo habilis* is the most likely candidate.

The tools from the Hadar site seem to be the simplest possible form, showing the least possible elaboration. Indeed, were it not for the geological context, one might even cast doubt on whether these tools are evidence of human manufacture.

Lokalalei, situated in the west Turkana region of northern Kenya, is yet another East African Rift Valley site to produce evidence of tool manufacture from an early date (Roche et al. 1999). Based on the argon dating method, **Lokalalei** is

FIGURE 3.16 A refit core from Lokalalei, Kenya, shows the complexity of the earliest stone tool manufacture. This refit includes a large number of flakes struck from a single core.

approximately 2.3 million years old, younger than the Hadar sites. At Lokalalei 2C, a horizontal area of 17 square metres has been excavated, and slightly over 2,000 stone flakes and cores were recovered from a single surface. A wide range of animal remains was also found, including twelve mammal species as well as reptiles and fish. There is no indication of cut marks or other signs of human activity on the animal bones.

In studying the stone tools from Lokalalei, Hélène Roche and her colleagues focused on trying to understand the process through which the tools were manufactured. By carefully fitting the flakes back onto the cores from which they were struck, the researchers showed that the simple tools at Lokalalei were produced through a fairly elaborate process (Figure 3.16). The cores included coarse-grained cobbles from which only two or three flakes had been removed, but also more fine-grained cobbles and pebbles from which up to thirty flakes had been removed. The analysis of how the flakes were removed in these lengthy sequences demonstrates that the knapping was not random and haphazard, but rather followed a clear and consistent strategy. The complexity of tool manufacture at Lokalalei demonstrates that the first stone tools were not the simplest of all possible, only a step removed from the hammers used by the chimpanzees in the Taï Forest or similar to the flakes produced by Kanzi the chimpanzee. The first tools manufactured by hominins involved a sequence of manufacture more complex than any process known from studies of animal behaviour.

3.4 Hunting and Sharing Food

Western philosophy has developed two opposing pictures of "man in a state of nature." For Thomas Hobbes, humans were essentially violent, and it was only through the development of institutions that it was possible for humanity to tame its destructive nature. Other philosophers, such as Jean Jacques Rousseau, imagined a life of leisure and peace that was disrupted only by the development of social inequality. Prehistorians have carried this debate into the study of early hominins. While some archaeologists view early hominins as killer apes, others envision societies of hunter–gatherers sharing meat and other food.

▲▲ **Lokalalei** An archaeological site in Kenya dating to 2.3 million years ago. Analysis of refit cores from the site indicates that stone tool manufacture at this early date was more complex than anticipated.

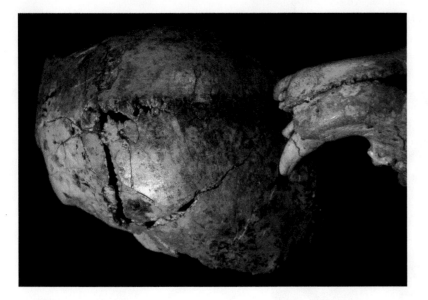

FIGURE 3.17 The hunted, not the hunter. The skull of an australopithecine from Swartkrans, South Africa, with a puncture wound that matches the spacing of the lower canines of a leopard.

■ Were They Hunters?

As a young professor of anatomy in South Africa, Raymond Dart was the first to identify the remains of an australopithecine. Dart subsequently became convinced that australopithecines used tools made of fractured pieces of bone. He labelled these tools the osteodontokeratic (bone, tooth, and horn) culture. The tools Dart identified included cutting tools, scoops, and spears. Dart developed a vision of australopithecines as brutal hunters "slaking their ravenous thirst with the hot blood of victims and greedily devouring livid writhing flesh" (Dart 1953, 209).

In the 1970s, archaeologists began to question Dart's interpretation with a series of studies into how bones are accumulated and what processes affect them after their burial. Such studies, known as taphonomic analyses, have included scrambling into hyena dens to collect bones gnawed by these carnivores. When bones from hyena dens were compared with the bones Dart had identified as tools, it became clear that the "tools" were actually produced by carnivores' gnawing. It also turns out that the hominins at these sites were not the hunters, but rather the hunted. In a particularly vivid illustration, the puncture marks on the skull of a juvenile australopithecine from the site of Swartkrans closely match the spacing of the lower canines of a leopard (see Figure 3.17).

Some archaeologists began to question whether early hominins were even capable of hunting large animals. Lewis Binford vocally advanced the idea that early hominins were scavengers, living off carcasses left behind by carnivores or fallen through natural mortality. Binford left archaeologists with a tremendous challenge. Rather than being able to assume that the bones found on archaeological sites were the traces of human hunting, they now had to prove that those bones were neither scavenged nor brought onto the site by geological processes.

Before looking at the archaeological evidence, it is worth considering whether it is even plausible to think that early hominins were hunters. Here again, information from the study of wild populations of chimpanzees is useful. There has long been a popular conception of chimpanzees as peaceful vegetarians, but we now know that this is far from the truth. Chimpanzees fight, often to the death, and hunt. The range of animals hunted by chimpanzees is quite limited, including small monkeys and very small antelope. Chimpanzees hunt without tools, but rely on cooperation to catch and kill animals. When the Taï Forest chimpanzees hunt monkeys, some members of the group chase them up a tree, while others wait quietly in a strategic spot to catch the monkeys as they run away. The monkeys are usually killed by biting and then ripped apart and eaten on the spot. The hunters are males, and the distribution of meat from the hunt seems to be an important element of how particular males gain dominance in the group.

From the way chimpanzees hunt, it is safe to assume that early hominins might have hunted small animals. It should be kept in mind, however, that early hominins would have lacked the chimpanzees' prominent canine teeth and their ability to move rapidly through trees. What is most interesting about chimpanzee hunting is that it is a group activity characterized by cooperation. It is likely that early hominins were capable of similar behaviour. The problem posed by Binford is that the animal bones found on early hominin sites are not only of small animals, but also of midsize ones such as antelope, and of very large animals, including hippopotamuses and elephants. Could early hominins armed with choppers and flakes have taken down such animals, even if they were working cooperatively?

It turns out that it is very difficult to prove archaeologically that animals were hunted rather than scavenged. Perhaps the clearest evidence would be a site with the remains of a single animal carcass and stone tools. One such site is **FLK North (FLKN)** in Olduvai Gorge, Bed I (see Figure 3.20 on page 82). FLK North is a site with six distinct occupation levels. In the lowest, the nearly complete skeleton of an extinct elephant (*Elephas recki*) was found together with a small number of choppers and flakes. At least one cut mark from a stone tool has been found on the elephant bones. Fragments of a wide range of smaller animals were also found concentrated in the area around the elephant skeleton. This is clearly a butchering site, but the Leakeys were uncertain to what degree the kill was planned. One possibility is that the elephant was "deliberately driven . . . into a swamp to be slaughtered" (Leakey 1971, 64). However, it is also possible that the hominins came upon an elephant carcass that they then scavenged for meat. Even at a site as seemingly simple as FLK North, it is not possible to determine with certainty that the hominins were actually hunting.

Although the association of stone tools with the remains of very large animals such as elephants might best be explained as the result of hominin scavenging, the same is not clearly the case for midsized to large animals. Field studies of the bones left behind after carnivores finish with a kill have raised a significant challenge to the theory that early hominins were scavengers. In general, these studies show that very little is left behind and that most of the carcass is consumed. If the early hominins were collecting the leftovers from the meals of lions and other carnivores, their yield would have been very small.

The most promising studies of how early hominins acquired meat are analyses of the surface of the animal bones found on archaeological sites. If these bones are well preserved, they bear the marks of three distinct processes: (1) gnawing by carnivores, which leaves characteristic pit marks and striations; (2) butchery with stone tools, resulting in clearly identifiable cut marks (see Figure 3.21); and (3) smashing the bones to gain access to their marrow, which produces distinctive fracture patterns known as bulbs of percussion. By studying which bones show evidence of which kind of modification, researchers can develop a picture of meat processing that provides clues whether the animals were hunted or scavenged. Studies such as these point to a complex interaction among carnivores, and early hominins.

Almost all early hominin sites with well-preserved bone surfaces produce evidence of carnivore gnawing, cut marks, and bulbs of percussion. The problem therefore is not whether both hominins and carnivores were involved in the formation of the recovered bone assemblage; rather, the difficulty lies in determining the order of events. Did carnivores kill the animals before hominins scavenged the remains, or did hominins kill animals whose remains were then scavenged by hyaenas or other carnivores? What was the role of smashing bones for marrow in this process? In the current state of research, the answer to these questions remains contentious. Some archaeologists, pointing to cut marks on the most meat-rich bones, argue that hominins had access to fresh kills. This pattern would not be expected if the hominins had access only to scraps of flesh that a carnivore had left behind. However, other scientists, emphasizing the frequency of carnivore gnaw marks on the midshaft of long bones, maintain that hominins scavenged bones mostly for marrow. Such a pattern fits with studies of bone damage found when carnivores deflesh carcasses.

▲▲ **FLK North (FLKN)** The site in Olduvai Gorge where the remains of an elephant were found together with stone tools.

Dating Early Hominin Sites

Precisely dating early hominin sites is extremely challenging. Archaeologists are often forced to rely on a combination of methods to arrive at a reliable age for a site. The main methods used to date early hominin sites are paleomagnetic dating and argon dating. Recently a new method known as Cosmogenic Burial Age dating has begun to have an impact, particularly on cave sites (Granger and Muzikar 2001).

Paleomagnetic Dating

Paleomagnetic dating is a method used to determine when sediments were deposited. The method dates the soils in which artifacts are found, rather than the artifacts themselves. To use paleomagnetism for dating artifacts or fossils, one must be confident that these objects are in the context in which they were initially deposited. If this is not the case—for example, if artifacts have been transported by water and redeposited in a new location—then the paleomagnetic date will be for the redeposition event rather than the manufacture of the artifacts.

The scientific basis for paleomagnetic dating is the observation that the earth's geomagnetic field has repeatedly switched polarity. The current state of the earth's geomagnetic field is known as normal polarity. In periods of

reversed polarity the field was switched, so a compass that points north today would have pointed south. It has been possible to build up a chronology of these switches so as to divide geological time into a sequence of epochs of normal and reversed polarity.

When particles containing iron are deposited, they orient themselves in accordance with the earth's geomagnetic

FIGURE 3.18
Eruption of ash from Mount St. Helens, Washington, in 1980. Such an eruption can blanket a wide area in a layer of ash that can be dated using the argon method.

■ Living Floors and Base Camps

When chimpanzees hunt, they consume the meat on the spot. They do share parts of the carcass, and as ethologist Craig Stanford (1999, 201) has written, "meat eating is about politics as well as nutrition." For chimpanzees, the sharing of the meat plays an important role in creating the social structure of the group. Modern human groups that subsist on hunting and gathering place a great emphasis on sharing. On the basis of research on the !Kung San hunter–gatherers of Botswana, ethnographers have found that sharing is the fundamental ethos of such societies (Lee 2003). Unlike chimpanzee sharing, which takes place at the spot where the kill was made,

field. This orientation is preserved as long as the particles are not moved. Almost all soils on earth contain iron. By studying the orientation of their iron particles, a geophysicist can determine the direction of the earth's geomagnetic field at the time the soil was deposited. Thus, on most archaeological sites it is possible to determine whether the site formed during a period of normal or reversed polarity.

In some cases, archaeologists working in recent periods have been able to use the paleomagnetic record of subtle shifts in the geomagnetic field to date artifacts or sites. The materials dated with these methods are usually hearths or pottery.

Argon Dating

Unlike paleomagnetic dating, argon dating provides a numerical age rather than assigning a deposit to an epoch or event. Argon dating works by means of an accumulation clock. The unit that is accumulating is ^{40}Ar, an isotope of the element argon. Isotopes are forms of a chemical element that have the same number of protons and electrons but vary in the number of neutrons in the nucleus. Because ^{40}K, an isotope of the element potassium, decays into ^{40}Ar at a constant rate, the rate at which ^{40}Ar accumulates is also a constant.

The trick with any accumulation clock is that it must be set to zero at the point in time of interest. Argon diffuses rapidly at high temperatures while potassium does not. This means that when a material containing argon is heated, the argon will be diffused out of the material while the potassium will remain stable. If a material containing both ^{40}Ar and ^{40}K is heated to a very high temperature, the resulting product will be a material containing ^{40}K and no ^{40}Ar. From that point on, ^{40}K will begin to decay, resulting in a steady accumulation of ^{40}Ar.

Fortunately for archaeologists, the magma that explodes out of volcanoes to form ash or lava is rich in potassium. The magma is superheated until it cools after eruption. As a result, any volcanic material can be dated by determining how much ^{40}Ar has accumulated since cooling. Time zero is the point of eruption, and the time since eruption is determined by measuring the accumulation of ^{40}Ar.

In potassium–argon dating, the measure of accumulation of ^{40}Ar is based on the ratio of ^{40}K to ^{40}Ar. The development of single-crystal argon dating has significantly improved the reliability of the argon method. With the use of lasers to vaporize the sample, it is possible to date single crystals of lava or ash by measuring the ratio of ^{39}Ar to ^{40}Ar. Argon dating has been critical to the study of human evolution, particu-larly at East African sites such as Olduvai Gorge. Unfortunately, in areas with limited volcanic activity, argon dating is not useful. ●

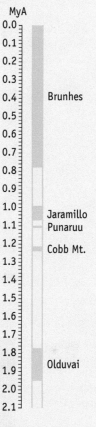

FIGURE 3.19 Paleomagnetic time scale. Time in millions of years ago. Periods of normal polarity are in dark blue; periods of reverse polarity are in light blue.

---

sharing among hunter–gatherers takes place when meat is brought back to a camp. This distinction forms the basis of the **home-base/food-sharing model** developed by Glynn Isaac. According to this model, hominins created places on the landscape to which meat was brought for sharing among members of a community. According to Isaac, it is the ability to share and cooperate, rather than the ability to kill, that is the driving force behind human evolution.

THE STONE CIRCLE AT DK. When Isaac developed his home-base/food-sharing model, he had in mind site **DK** in Bed I at Olduvai Gorge. Excavations at DK in

home-base/food-sharing model
Model developed by Glynn Isaac that sees the sharing of meat at base camps as a fundamental part of the lives of early hominins.

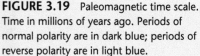 **DK** The site at Olduvai Gorge where a stone circle was found, suggesting evidence of a temporary structure built on a home-base site.

FIGURE 3.20 The plan of the excavation of the FLK North site, Olduvai Gorge, showing the association between the stone tools and the elephant bones.

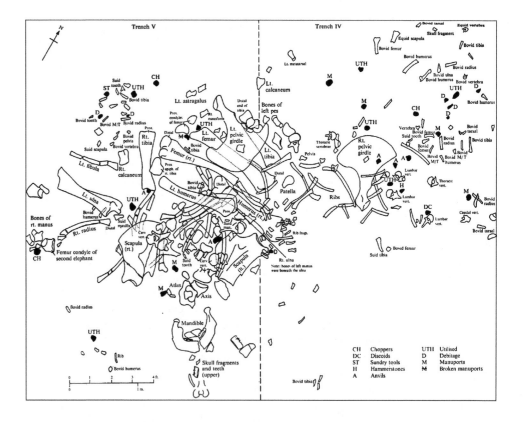

CH	Choppers	UTH	Utilised
DC	Discoids	D	Debitage
ST	Sundry tools	M	Manuports
H	Hammerstones	M̶	Broken manuports
A	Anvils		

1962 uncovered a circle of lava blocks on what the Leakeys identified as an "occupation floor" (Leakey 1971)—a clearly defined level of animal bones and stone tools (see Figures 3.22 and 3.23). The circle measures roughly 4 metres in diameter. Blocks are piled around the circumference to a maximum height of approximately 30 centimetres, and there are scattered stones on the inside. The Leakeys interpret

FIGURE 3.21 A cut mark left by a stone tool on an animal bone found on an archaeological site. This photograph was taken with a scanning electron microscope (SEM).

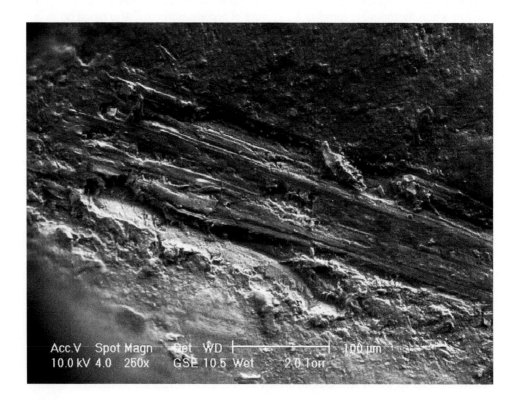

this circle as the remains of a temporary shelter or windbreak of branches, which were then covered with grass or skin. In the area in and around the structure, stone tools and animal bones were found. The density of these remains was greater outside the stone circle than inside.

DK offers a vivid picture of what an early hominin base camp would look like and suggests that these sites would have resembled the camps of modern human hunter–gatherers. However, there is some need for caution. The stone circle at DK was found in a level immediately above the volcanic bedrock—the same material out of which the circle is constructed. The Leakeys note that "the area immediately outside the circle is relatively clear of loose stones, which become more numerous again at a distance of approximately 2 feet (0.6 metres) from the outer circumference" (Leakey 1971, 24). Thus, the possibility that the stone circle is a natural feature cannot be completely ruled out. The animal bones recovered from the DK site included the bones of mid- and large-sized mammals, with crocodile and turtle bones predominating. This suggests that the stone circle was at the edge of a swamp or lagoon.

ASSESSING THE ARCHAEOLOGICAL EVIDENCE. As was the case with the distinction between hunting and scavenging, it appears that the answer to the question of which activities led to the concentrations of stone tools and animal bones found on archaeological sites is complex. In some cases, the association of stone tools and animal bones is the result of geological processes, primarily transport by rivers or streams. However, most other sites suggest an overlay of activities that took place at a single location. Such a situation is referred to as a **palimpsest**—an archaeological surface that is the result of multiple distinct occupations. A palimpsest exists on a site that was revisited on at least several occasions and is distinct from a base camp that a single group occupied continuously. From this perspective, the early hominin sites were built up over

palimpsest An archaeological site produced by a series of distinct brief occupations.

FIGURE 3.23 A shelter made by the Okombambi of Namibia that the Leakeys compared to the DK circle. Notice that flat stones are used at the base of the structure. How might such a construction result in the kind of circle found on the DK site?

time as different butchery and meat-processing events took place. For example, at FLK North, the elephant butchery was distinct from the events that led to the deposition of the fragmentary remains of other animals. It is possible that the DK site is a palimpsest site, rather than the base camp the Leakeys reconstructed. One problem with maintaining that DK is a base camp is that doubts have been raised about the evidence for the remains of a shelter at the site. Equally problematic is that the site is in close proximity to a source of fresh water. It seems unlikely that such an area, which would attract predators, would be selected as a place for sharing meat from kills.

But if these sites were not base camps, why did early hominins continuously return to the same spots on the landscape? The DK site is only one of a number of early sites with large concentrations of stone tools and animal bones. One possibility is that hominins were drawn by natural features, such as tree cover, that would have provided shelter from carnivores and scavengers. Richard Potts (1988) has suggested that stone tools might have been cached at certain locations and carcasses dragged to those locations for processing. This is certainly possible, but it does not explain every case. For example, at FLK North, only a small number of stone tools was found.

There is clear evidence that early hominins moved stone tools around the landscape, and the same appears to be true for parts of animal carcasses. However, it is still not possible to demonstrate unequivocally that the animal carcasses were coming into base camps, where the members of hominin groups shared the meat in the fashion that is so characteristic of societies of modern hunter–gatherers.

■ The Use of Fire

There is very little evidence for the controlled use of fire from Oldowan and Acheulian sites in Africa. At site FxJj 20 in the Okote member at Koobi Fora, two round features roughly 1 metre in diameter are thought to be evidence of the use of fire. The soil in these circles is reddish in colour, and the magnetic properties of the soil suggest that it was burnt. At the site of **Chesowanja**, Kenya, dated to 1.4 million years ago, lumps of burnt clay were found in the same context as stone tools and animal bones. The excavators argue that these lumps are the remains of a hearth that has become broken up and dispersed. Because the possibility that the burnt clay was the result of natural fires cannot be ruled out, the lumps of clay from Chesowanja cannot be taken as evidence that early hominins used fire.

3.5 The Expansion of the Hominin World

By 1.4 million years ago, the hominin radiation was over. Of the four genera that flourished beginning 4 million years ago, only genus *Homo* survived. Within genus *Homo*, there was at this point only a single species, *Homo erectus*. By this time a sophisticated tool technology, the Acheulian, had developed in Africa. Overlapping with the end of the hominin radiation, the hominin colonization of areas outside of Africa began. In a **dispersal** event, a single species dramatically expands its geographic range. Dispersal, which often involves a species moving into a new ecological niche, contrasts with radiation in that a single species expands both its geographical range and the range of ecological niches it inhabits. By contrast, in a radiation event, a wide diversity of new species evolves, each of which adapts to a particular ecological niche. What took place in the hominin lineage around 4 million years ago was a radiation. The first event of hominin dispersal began around 1.8 million years ago, soon after the first appearance of *Homo erectus* in Africa.

What is the significance of the spread of *Homo erectus* beyond Africa? We need to be careful to avoid seeing this process through the lens of the heroic modern image of the explorer. The dispersal of *Homo erectus* does not track the paths of individual wanderers; rather, it follows the expansion of populations into new ecological settings. What is it about *Homo erectus* that allowed this species to move into areas that earlier hominins did not occupy? Did *Homo erectus* possess some new ability that spurred its expansion? We will return to these questions at the end of the chapter, but first we must follow the archaeological evidence for the timing of the dispersal.

■ Ubeidiya and Dmanisi

The site of **Ubeidiya** is located south of the Sea of Galilee in Israel. The Sea of Galilee is part of the northern extension of the East African Rift Valley, and the setting of the site is not very different from that at Olduvai Gorge. When the site was in use, it was at the edge of a large freshwater lake in an area occupied by a wide diversity of mostly African species of animals. The stone tools from Ubeidiya also look much like the material from Olduvai. The lower part of the sequence includes tools characteristic of the Oldowan, including choppers and flake tools along with a small number of crude handaxes.

The dating of Ubeidiya is complex and draws on a number of methods. The site can be dated to the period between 1.4 million and 1.0 million years ago, with the most accurate estimate being 1.4 million years ago. Fragmentary hominin remains from the site are attributed to *Homo erectus*.

The prehistoric site of **Dmanisi**, in the Republic of Georgia, was discovered during the excavation of a medieval village (see Figure 3.24). When the excavators were clearing out the cellars that had been dug into the ground by the site's inhabitants, they found bones eroding out of the earthen walls. A paleontologist identified the bones as

Chesowanja Site located in Kenya and dated to 1.4 million years ago that has produced tentative evidence for the use of fire by early hominins.

dispersal An event where a single species dramatically expands its range.

Ubeidiya One of the earliest archaeological sites outside of Africa, located in Israel south of the Sea of Galilee and dated between 1.4 and 1.0 million years ago.

Dmanisi The oldest known archaeological site outside of Africa, located in the Republic of Georgia and dated between 1.7 and 1.8 million years ago.

FIGURE 3.24 The site of Dmanisi, Georgia, was discovered during the excavation of a medieval village. This site has produced a series of hominin fossils and the earliest evidence of hominin occupation outside of Africa.

fossils dating to around 1.8 million years ago. In 1994, a limited paleontological project began to recover more of these fossils, which, to the surprise of the excavators, included a *Homo erectus* mandible (jaw). This spectacular discovery was followed by the identification of stone tools on the site and the recovery of three fairly complete crania of *Homo erectus*.

The dating of the Dmanisi site is of critical importance to understanding the initial spread of hominins out of Africa. Although dated using the argon method to 1.8 million years ago, the lava at the site is below the level in which the hominin remains were found. Accordingly, following the law of superposition, one can only assume that the hominin occupation was later than 1.8 million years ago. Paleomagnetic dating adds some further information, restricting the hominin occupation to between 1.8 million and 1.1 million years ago. However, some animal species, including both large mammals and rodents, found with the hominin remains were either extinct or not found in the region after 1.7 million years ago. For this reason, Dmanisi is widely accepted today as the earliest evidence of human occupation outside of Africa.

The nature of the hominin activity at Dmanisi remains unclear. None of the animal bones have signs of cut marks, and it does not seem likely that the hominins had anything to do with accumulating these bones. The stone tools are found widely dispersed on the site and are not found in association with the hominin and animal fossils. The fossils and some of the tools come from irregularly shaped pits in the soil. It is possible that these pits were formed by water action that created depressions into which hominin and animal carcasses tumbled. Alternatively, the pits could have been natural features altered and used as dens by carnivores.

The stone tools found at Dmanisi are mostly simple flakes (De Lumley et al. 2005). There are none of the bifaces characteristic of the Acheulian industry. A small number of choppers have been found at the site.

■ East Asia

The discovery at Dmanisi of strong evidence for a hominin dispersal soon after the first appearance of *Homo erectus* in Africa is supported by recent research on sites in China and Indonesia. Like Dmanisi, the East Asian sites have produced no evidence of Acheulian technology. The early dates for sites in China and Indonesia are currently the subject of heated debate. However, if these early dates hold up to scrutiny, they suggest that the initial dispersal of *Homo erectus* was a remarkably rapid event.

JAVA. The first discovery of a *Homo erectus* fossil took place far from Africa, at the site of Trinil on the Indonesian island of Java. The Trinil fossil, discovered in 1892 by the Dutch paleontologist Eugene Dubois, created a sensation and much controversy. Many scientists were unwilling to accept Dubois' claim that he had found the "missing link" between apes and humans, and argued instead that the fossil was either an ape or a human. Dubois was so infuriated by the controversy that he stopped allowing researchers direct access to the fossils, keeping them locked in a safe in his office.

Today, controversy again surrounds the *Homo erectus* from Java. There is little dispute about the taxonomic status of the fossils; all appear to belong to the species *Homo erectus*. The subject of contention now is the dating of the fossils, specifically those from the sites of **Sangiran and Perning**. These fossils are found

▲▲ **Sangiran and Perning** Sites on the island of Java where fossils of *Homo erectus* dating to 1.8 million years ago were found.

in an early geological position within the Javan sequence known as the Upper Sangiran Formation. The date of this formation was long thought to be approximately 1 million years ago, on the basis of paleomagnetism and the types of animal fossils found in the formation. In 1994, argon dates were published for the Upper Sangiran Formation at Sangiran and Perning that place the fossils at 1.8 million years ago. However, a number of archaeologists have questioned whether this date is accurate.

Although Java is now an island, it was not so throughout the Pleistocene era. A land bridge, known as the Sunda shelf, connected Java to mainland southeast Asia during periods of low sea level. One oddity of the early *Homo erectus* sites on Java is that none have produced evidence of stone tools. Still, it is not yet clear whether these hominins lacked stone tools or whether they made tools that have not been identified.

NIHEWAN BASIN. The **Nihewan Basin** in the Northern China Plain near Beijing is an area rich in paleontological sites. A number of sites with stone tools have been found at Nihewan in contexts that appear to be Early Pleistocene. Four of these sites have been dated by paleomagnetism to the period around 1.6 million years ago (Zhu et al. 2004). The stone tools from the Nihewan Basin are flakes, mostly made of poor raw material.

■ Summing Up the Evidence

The evidence from Ubeidiya and Dmanisi makes it clear that the initial hominin dispersal took place soon after the first appearance of *Homo erectus* in Africa. If one accepts the early dates from Java, it would appear that the initial dispersal was a widespread event. Whether it is best to reconstruct a single migration or multiple migrations is open to question. It is quite possible that the dispersal of hominins to Java followed a southerly route across the Arabian Peninsula and around the Indian subcontinent. Such a route would have required crossing the minor body of water known as the Straits of Bab el Mandeb at the mouth of the Red Sea.

It is particularly difficult to try to tie the hominin dispersal in with a particular climatic event. In a general sense, climatic instability might have played a role in the dispersal. Another possibility is that some aspect of technology gave these hominins the ability to adapt to new environments. Clearly, this ability is not tied to any particular type of stone tool, as these elaborate tools are lacking in all of the early sites. One interesting suggestion is that it was the development of technologies of food processing, particularly the use of fire, that led to the hominin dispersal (Wrangham et al. 1999). However, to date none of the early sites outside of Africa has produced evidence for the use of fire.

Some archaeologists have suggested as an explanation of the dispersal the increased cognitive capacity of *Homo erectus*, reflected in a larger brain, which might have led to the development of new forms of social organization. Clive Gamble has argued that before *Homo erectus*, the social organization of hominins required frequent face-to-face interactions. The cognitive ability of *Homo erectus* to retain information for increased periods of time allowed for the "stretching of society in time and space," as the social group could then maintain its coherence even when individuals met infrequently (Gamble 1993, 142). As a result, *Homo erectus* social groups would be able to survive in areas where seasonal scarcity forced the group to disperse across a wide territory during parts of the year. Groups of *Homo erectus* thus were able to survive in ecological niches that could not support earlier hominin species. One can easily imagine how such wide-ranging social groups would discover new territories, perhaps as young adults explored the edges of the range of the core group, leading to its expansion into previously uninhabited areas.

▲▲ **Nihewan Basin** Location in northern China where there is solid evidence of human occupation around 1.6 million years ago.

SUMMARY

- The hominin radiation between 4 million and 2 million years ago included four distinct genera.
- The earliest evidence for walking upright is found in *Australopithecus afarensis*.
- *Homo habilis* is characterized by an increased brain size relative to that of other early hominins.
- The earliest known *Homo erectus* dates between 1.9 and 1.5 million years ago. *Homo erectus* is characterized by an increase in brain size compared with *Homo habilis*.
- Chimpanzee tool use includes fishing for termites and breaking nuts with stone hammers and anvils.
- The earliest evidence for hominin stone tool manufacture is found at the Gona site in the Hadar region of Ethiopia, dated to 2.5 million years ago.
- Analyses of stone tools from the site of Lokalalei indicate that the manufacture of the earliest stone tools was a complex process.
- There is debate over whether early hominins gained access to meat by hunting or by scavenging.
- The home-base/food-sharing model suggests that meat sharing at base camps played an important role in the lives of early hominins.
- A stone circle that might have been the base of a hut was found at the DK site, Olduvai Gorge. This type of site is predicted by the home-base/food-sharing model.
- The earliest tentative evidence for the controlled use of fire was found at Chesowanja, Kenya, a site dated to 1.4 million years ago.
- The earliest archaeological sites outside of Africa are Dmanisi, Georgia (1.8 to 1.7 million years ago), and Ubeidiya, Israel (1.4 to 1.0 million years ago).
- *Homo erectus* fossils found on the Indonesian island of Java at the sites of Sangiran and Perning have been dated to 1.8 million years ago. No other archaeological material has been found with these fossils.
- The oldest reliable evidence for human occupation of China is from the Nihewan Basin, dated to around 1.6 million years ago.

KEY TERMS

Acheulian, 72
Ardipithecus ramidus, 65
australopithecines, 66
bifaces, 72
Chesowanja, 85
dispersal, 85
DK, 81
Dmanisi, 85
East African Rift Valley, 67
FLK North, 79
Hadar, 75
home-base/food-sharing model, 81
hominins, 64
Homo erectus, 67

Homo habilis, 66
Laetoli, 66
Lokalalei, 76
Lower Paleolithic, 69
Nihewan Basin, 87
Oldowan, 70
Olduvai Gorge, 67
palimpsest, 83
radiation, 65
Sahelanthropus tchadensis, 64
Sangiran and Perning, 86
Taï Forest, 74
Ubeidiya, 85

REVIEW QUESTIONS

1. Why is the period between 4 million and 2 million years ago referred to as the hominin radiation?
2. Which hominin produced the earliest stone tools?
3. What is the significance of the discoveries made at FLK North, Olduvai Gorge?
4. What is the home-base/food-sharing model? Does the archaeological evidence support it?
5. Is the initial dispersal of *Homo erectus* best described as gradual or rapid?

- David Begun, professor in the Department of Anthropology at the University of Toronto, is a paleoanthropologist who focuses on the study of Miocene homonoids. He carries out field work at the site of Rudabánya in Hungary as well as on sites in Turkey.
  http://anthropology.utoronto.ca/Faculty/Begun/index.htm

- Brian Kooyman, professor in the Department of Anthropology at the University of Calgary, is the author of *Understanding Stone Tools and Archaeological Sites* (University of Alberta Press, 2000). Along with lithic analysis he also carries out research in faunal and botanical analysis and has worked on a range of sites in Alberta, including the Head-Smashed-In Buffalo Jump.
  http://arky.ucalgary.ca/profiles/brian-patrick-kooyman

- Yin Lam, professor in the Department of Anthropology at the University of Victoria is a specialist in faunal analysis and taphonomy. His research focuses on how biases in preservation effect the interpretation of the archaeological record of early hominin behaviour. He has extensive field experience in Africa and now works on sites in China.
  http://anthropology.uvic.ca/people/faculty/lam.php

- Julio Mercader, professor in the Department of Archaeology at the University of Calgary, is a Paleolithic archaeologist who directs a field project in Mozambique. He has also published on the archaeology of chimpanzee tool use.
  http://www.ucalgary.ca/mercader/

- Jack Rink is a professor in the School of Geography and Earth Sciences at McMaster University and an expert in the use of luminescence and electron spin resonance dating methods on early hominin sites. His projects include the dating of *Homo erectus* in Java and China.
  www.science.mcmaster.ca/geo/faculty/rink

- Anne Russon, professor in the Department of Psychology at the Glendon Campus of York University, has carried out extensive field studies of orangutan tool use in Borneo. Her publications include *The Evolution of Thought: Evolutionary Origins of Great Ape Intelligence*, a volume co-edited with David Begun (Cambridge University Press, 2004).
  www.yorku.ca/arusson/

- Chen Shen, curator at the Royal Ontario Museum, is engaged in a wide range of research projects on the early prehistory of China. He is also an expert in the analysis of use wear on stone tools and has carried out studies of stone tool function in China, Jordan, and Ontario.
  http://www.rom.on.ca/collections/curators/shen.php

PEARSON
myanthrokit™

Visit **www.myanthrokit.com**, where you will find a variety of tools and resources to enhance your learning, including:
- Practise quizzes with Study Plans
- Videos
- Listening Activities
- And much more!

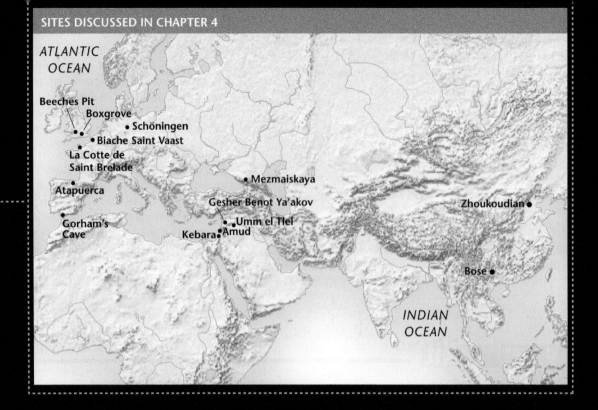

SITES DISCUSSED IN CHAPTER 4

ATLANTIC
OCEAN

Beeches Pit
Boxgrove
• Schöningen
• Biache Saint Vaast
La Cotte de
Saint Brelade
Atapuerca
Gorham's
Cave
• Mezmaiskaya
Gesher Benot Ya'akov
• Umm el Tlel
Kebara• Amud
Zhoukoudian •
Bose •
INDIAN
OCEAN

4  TIMELINE

SITES

Gran Dolina (TD-6 level),
Atapuerca

Boxgrove

Gesher Benot Ya'akov

Isernia la Pineta

Bose

Zhoukoukian

ARCHAEOLOGICAL
INDUSTRIES

HOMININS

HOMO ERECTUS

thousands of years ago · 800 · 700 · 600 · 500

FROM HOMO erectus TO NEANDERTHALS

Neanderthals occupied Europe and the Middle East between 175,000 and 30,000 years ago. After reading this chapter, you should understand:

- The *oxygen isotope* glacial sequence.
- The spread of hominins through Europe and the characteristics of the European Lower Paleolithic.
- The major anatomical features that characterize Neanderthals.
- The three major theories of the evolution of Neanderthals.
- The evidence for Neanderthal stone tool technology hunting, use of fire, burial of the dead, and artwork.

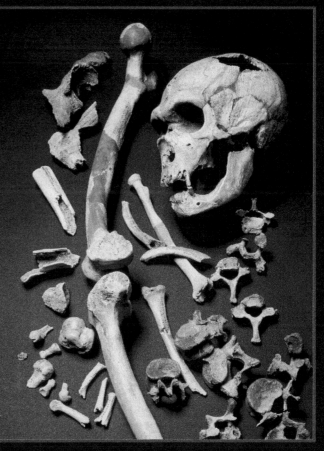

The Neanderthal fossil from La Chapelle-aux-Saints.

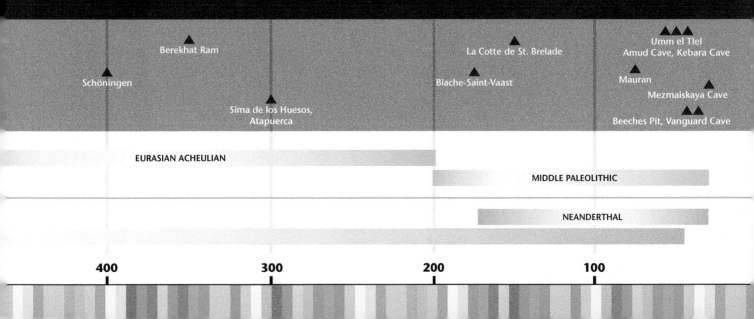

Berekhat Ram

Schöningen

Sima de los Huesos, Atapuerca

La Cotte de St. Brelade

Biache-Saint-Vaast

Umm el Tlel
Amud Cave, Kebara Cave

Mauran

Mezmaiskaya Cave

Beeches Pit, Vanguard Cave

EURASIAN ACHEULIAN

MIDDLE PALEOLITHIC

NEANDERTHAL

400   300   200   100

FIGURE 4.1 Marcelin Boule's reconstruction of a Neanderthal as a stooped, hairy brute. Notice the club grasped firmly in the Neanderthal's right hand. Why do you think this detail is included?

Pleistocene The geological era that began 1.8 million years ago, characterized by the frequent buildup and retreat of continental ice sheets.

he picture of Neanderthals as hulking ape-men dates back to 1908 and the discovery of the "Old Man of La Chapelle-aux-Saints." The La Chapelle fossil was the most complete skeleton of a Neanderthal ever recovered, and it provided a unique opportunity to understand the characteristics of this intriguing hominin. The task of analyzing the skeleton fell to Marcelin Boule, a prominent paleoanthropologist who came to the job convinced that Neanderthals were "a degenerate side branch of human evolution" (Bowler 1986, 88). Not surprisingly, the portrait that emerged from Boule's analysis was a hairy, stooped creature (see Figure 4.1). Subsequent studies show that Boule had largely ignored the effects of arthritis and other pathologies on the posture of the fossil from La Chapelle. Contemporary studies of Neanderthals paint a far more intriguing picture of a hominin that is in numerous respects similar to modern humans, but at the same time is distinctive. In many ways, the dramatic picture of Neanderthals as our apish ancestors has been replaced by the image of Neanderthals as an enigma.

In this chapter, we begin by examining the environmental record pertaining to the Pleistocene Ice Age. We then pick up where we left off in the last chapter to follow the record for the continued spread of populations of *Homo erectus* into Western Europe. We also look at aspects of the Lower Paleolithic archaeology of Europe and Asia that shed light on the behaviour and society of *Homo erectus*. We then turn to the Neanderthal fossil record and offer an extended consideration of the archaeological record of Neanderthal behaviour and society.

4.1 Defining the Ice Age

The evolution of Neanderthals took place within the context of the geological period known as the Pleistocene, or the Ice Age. The boundary between the **Pleistocene** and the preceding Pliocene era is fixed at almost precisely 1.8 million years ago, although geologists are considering moving the boundary back to 2.6 million years ago. The Pleistocene is characterized by periods with a significant buildup of ice sheets, known as glacial eras, and periods during which the ice sheet subsequently retreated, known as interglacial eras.

Geologists first developed a record of Pleistocene climate change on the basis of features of the landscape. One such feature is the terminal moraine, a characteristic raised ridge that formed at the point where the glacial ice sheet reached its maximum extent. Cape Cod in Massachusetts is a classic example of a terminal moraine. By looking at such features in both North America and Europe, geologists developed a glacial chronology for the Pleistocene involving four major cycles of advance and retreat of the ice sheets. In Europe, the four major glacial advances were named, from earliest to latest, Günz, Mindel, Riss, and Würm. In North America, the last two glacial advances are known as the Illinoian and the Wisconsin.

The bottom of the sea might seem to be an unlikely place to search for a record of the advance and retreat of ice sheets, but analyses of cores drilled from the ocean floor have revolutionized our view of Pleistocene climate change. The development of glaciers is only one element of a global process. As glaciers build up, water is locked up in ice at the expense of water otherwise held in the oceans. When glaciers advance, sea levels drop, and when glaciers retreat, sea levels go up. During some past periods of glacial advance, the global sea level was close to 140 metres below what it is today

(Rohling et al. 1998). Today's sea level reflects the fact that we are living in an interglacial period.

Analysis of cores drilled from the sea floor allows scientists to measure and date fluctuations in the amount of water in the ocean and thus develop a global "thermometer" for the Ice Age. The secret behind this thermometer is foraminifera, tiny organisms that live on the surface of the ocean. The skeletons of these organisms are made of calcium carbonate, which absorbs oxygen from sea water and drifts to the sea floor after the organisms die. Over millennia, the sea floor deposits incorporate a continuous stratigraphic sequence of foraminifera. A core drilled out of the sea floor can recover a sequence of foraminifera covering millions of years. Such sequences can be dated by the uranium series method.

Foraminifera absorb two isotopes of oxygen. ^{18}O is the heavier isotope and ^{16}O is the lighter. During periods of glacial buildup, the oceans become isotopically heavy because ^{16}O is drawn off with the moisture that builds the ice sheets. During glacial periods, the oceans have a high ratio of ^{18}O to ^{16}O. The reverse is true during interglacial periods, when sea levels rise. Measuring the ratio of ^{18}O to ^{16}O in the foraminifera collected in deep-sea cores provides a record of the advance and retreat of glaciers during the Pleistocene. The record provided by sea cores is very different from the model of four major glacial periods. The picture that emerges is of an unstable climate with many glacial and interglacial periods over the last 1.8 million years. In the last 700,000 years there have been eight full glacial–interglacial cycles (see Figure 4.2). The climate

FIGURE 4.2 The oxygen isotope curve provides a record of Pleistocene climate change by measuring shifts in the ratio of oxygen isotopes in foraminifera, microscopic organisms that live on the surface of the ocean.

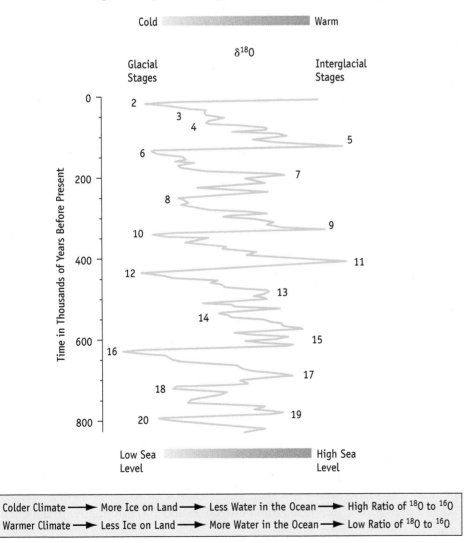

record produced by the analysis of deep-sea cores is known as the oxygen isotope curve. Glacial and interglacial events are given numbers, from the most recent (we now live in Oxygen Isotope Stage 1) to the oldest. If one looks closely at the **oxygen isotope curve**, it becomes evident that the extent of glaciation and the rapidity of climate change vary considerably. For instance, the boundaries between stages 5 and 6 and stages 9 and 10 are examples of particularly abrupt climate change.

4.2 Before the Neanderthals

In the last chapter we examined the evidence for the initial dispersal of *Homo erectus*. To understand the evolution of Neanderthals, we need to know more about what happened after this initial dispersal. We need to know when hominins first spread into Western Europe. We also need to know about the Lower Paleolithic cultures of Europe and Asia. We will focus on the challenge of interpreting the variability found in this period. Finally, we want to know about aspects of Lower Paleolithic culture beyond stone tools. Is there evidence for tools made from other materials? Is there artwork? Are there burials? And did hominins have control over the use of fire?

■ The Initial Occupation of Western Europe

Although Dmanisi, at the eastern edge of Europe, has evidence of occupation going back approximately 1.7 million years, hominin sites more than 500,000 years old in Western Europe are rare and often unconvincing. However, the 500,000-year barrier has been dramatically shattered by research at a system of caves located at **Atapuerca** in north-central Spain. The construction of a railroad through the hill at Atapuerca exposed a massive cave filled with 18 metres of deposits. Archaeologists perched on an elaborate system of scaffolding have swarmed over the Gran Dolina sequence, digging into eleven archaeological levels that have been dated by paleomagnetism and electron spin resonance. In the TD-6 level, dated to 800,000 years ago, a rich collection of stone tools and fossil bones were recovered along with thirty hominin fragments. TD-6 is the earliest securely dated archaeological level in Western Europe (Carbonell et al. 1999).

The stone tools from Gran Dolina TD-6 are flakes and cores. The hominin remains from TD-6 have been classified as a new species, *Homo antecessor*. Because most of the remains are fragmentary and the single fairly complete skull is of a juvenile, further discoveries are needed to confirm the identification of the species.

Another early site in Western Europe is Isernia la Pineta in Italy, dated to more than 700,000 years ago (Peretto 2006). In the Sett. I t.3a level, a dense occupation layer of stone tools and animal bones was found covering an area of 24 square metres. Over 1,000 stone tools were discovered, mostly simple flakes made on poor-quality stone. The animal bones include the remains of bears, elephants, rhinos, bison, and deer.

■ The Acheulian Problem

In East Asia, chopper and flake tools characterize most Lower Paleolithic sites. Paradoxically, the earliest date for an Acheulian industry anywhere outside of Africa is at the site of **Bose** in China (Yamei et al. 2000). Bose is also the only site in China where handaxes have been uncovered. The artifacts at Bose are found in a river terrace in a stratigraphic unit that varies between 25 and 100 centimetres in thickness.

oxygen isotope curve The record of fluctuations in global climate during the Pleistocene.

▲▲ **Gran Dolina, Atapuerca** A cave in Spain where stone tools and hominin remains dated to 800,000 years ago were found. These artifacts are the oldest reliable evidence of human occupation of Western Europe.

▲▲ **Bose** A site in southern China that produced a stone tool industry that includes handaxes dated to 800,000 years ago.

FIGURE 4.3 Handaxe (left) and flake tool (right) from the Lower Paleolithic site of Cagny-l'Epinette, France.

Cagny-l'Epinette
0   5 cm
Level I1

Argon dating of tektites (small fragments of glass formed by meteor impacts) found with the tools has dated the site to 800,000 years ago. As with volcanic ash and lava, argon dating determines when the glass formed.

Other than Bose, the earliest well-dated Acheulian site outside of Africa is **Gesher Benot Ya'akov**, Israel, located to the north of the Sea of Galilee in the northern extension of the East African Rift Valley. Dated to 780,000 years ago, Gesher Benot Ya'akov is similar to African Acheulian sites. Bifaces are made on very large flakes, and handaxes and cleavers are common. The excavations at Gesher Benot Ya'akov have also produced limited evidence for the use of fire and for cracking of nuts.

It is beginning only 500,000 years ago that Acheulian sites became common across Europe, the Middle East, and on into the Indian subcontinent—the geographic region known as Eurasia. There is regional variation in the **Eurasian Acheulian**, but taken as a whole, these industries show some significant contrast with the African Acheulian. Cleavers are almost completely absent from the Eurasian Acheulian, and handaxes are the major type of biface.

Another characteristic of the Eurasian Acheulian is that the handaxes were often part of a tool kit that also included retouched flakes—flakes that were modified after being struck off the core. The characteristic type of flake tool is the sidescraper, in which one or two edges of the flake have been regularized and strengthened by retouching (see Figure 4.3).

Boxgrove, located in West Sussex in southern England, is among the earliest known Acheulian sites in Europe and one of the most extensively excavated (see Figure 4.4). On the basis of the animal species represented in the faunal assemblage, the site is dated to 500,000 years ago (Roberts et al. 1999). The hominin occupation of Boxgrove appears to have been close to the shore of a small lake near the sea. The stone tools include the debris from handaxe manufacture, which, when refit, provides a detailed picture of the process involved in making these tools. The handaxes found at Boxgrove were shaped with both hard and soft hammers.

▲▲ **Gesher Benot Ya'akov** An Acheulian site in Israel dating to 780,000 years ago that has produced limited evidence for the use of fire and for cracking of nuts.

Eurasian Acheulian A stone tool industry found on sites throughout the Middle East and Europe beginning 500,000 years ago. The handaxe is the characteristic tool of this industry.

▲▲ **Boxgrove** One of the oldest known Acheulian sites in Europe; located in England and dated to 500,000 years ago.

FIGURE 4.4 Excavation at Boxgrove. Notice how artifacts are left in place as they are exposed, providing a clear view of a broad horizontal surface.

Experiments in which an experienced butcher was given a replicated handaxe to use showed that these tools would have served very well to skin and butcher carcasses. Animal bones from the site, including the bones of a large horse, have traces of tool cut marks, and whether or not these animals were hunted, hominins did have early access to the carcasses. No evidence for the use of fire or of a base camp has been found at Boxgrove.

Not all sites in Europe dating later than 500,000 years ago have produced handaxes. The **Clactonian** is an industry in England of simple flake tools contemporary with the Acheulian. Some have argued that Clactonian sites are simply Acheulian handaxe manufacturing sites from which the finished products are absent. This idea has been refuted, and it is now clear that the Clactonian is distinct from the Acheulian. In Eastern Europe, a number of Lower Paleolithic sites have produced flake tool industries. Vértesszölös is a particularly rich site located in Hungary dated to 350,000 years ago. The stone tools at Vértesszölös are choppers and retouched flakes.

The variation in Lower Paleolithic industries is modest compared with that found in later periods, but is nonetheless real. The patterns of variation that do exist confound some of our expectations and prove difficult to explain. One would expect that all groups would rapidly adopt the Acheulian technology. However, this was clearly not the case. The site of Bose has produced the oldest known handaxes outside of Africa. However, handaxe manufacture never became widespread among early hominins in East Asia. In Europe, Acheulian industries appeared only 500,000 years ago, hundreds of thousands of years after the first arrival of hominins. Even after the widespread appearance of handaxes in Europe and Western Asia, there were industries, such as the Clactonian, that did not involve handaxe manufacture.

One approach to this problem is to explain variation in the Lower Paleolithic as the result of ecological factors. Geoffrey Pope (1989) has proposed that the absence of handaxes in East Asia tracks the limits of the distribution of bamboo and that hominins in the region made many of their tools from bamboo. Ethnoarchaeological

Clactonian A simple flake tool industry contemporary with the Acheulian in England.

research with the Kuchung ethnic group in Yunan province, China, has shown that a wide range of bamboo tools could be fashioned with simple choppers and flakes. Ecological factors might also account for the differences between the African Acheulian and the Eurasian Acheulian. The African Acheulian is found in an area where large volcanic boulders are readily available, unlike the Eurasian Acheulian. Perhaps the availability of types of stone accounts for the regional differences.

Another possibility is that different industries are evidence of distinct groups and that one can use the archaeological industries to track not just one hominin dispersal out of Africa but rather several waves. Eudald Carbonell has argued that the initial dispersal was of Oldowan people pushed out of Africa by more successful Acheulian groups (Carbonell et al. 1999). In his opinion, this hypothesis would account for the absence of handaxes in the earliest hominin sites outside of Africa. Carbonell sees the widespread presence of Acheulian industries across Eurasia beginning 500,000 years ago as evidence of yet another wave of migration out of Africa.

FIGURE 4.5 Historic photo of the site of Zhoukoudian at the time of the discovery of a *Homo erectus* fossil.

The stone tool industries might also reflect social factors such as group size. Steven Mithen (1994) has pointed out the importance of learning in stone tool manufacture. Elaborate stone tool manufacture involves the transmission of skills and knowledge across generations. Perhaps the size and density of the social group influenced the amount of learning that took place and thus affected the elaboration of technology. For Mithen, the elaborate technologies of the Acheulian indicate a high degree of social learning. He suggests that the context for such intensified learning was large groups of hominins living in glacial open environments with a high risk from predators and an unpredictable availability of food resources. According to this model, the far less elaborate Clactonian industries were produced by small groups of hominins living in an interglacial wooded environment with a low risk from predators and an evenly distributed availability of food resources.

Beyond Stone Tools

The picture of Lower Paleolithic culture is limited by the nature of the available evidence. A number of unique discoveries provide tantalizing hints of the complexity of Lower Paleolithic culture.

Zhoukoudian is a series of caves in Longgu-shan, or Dragon Bone Hill, outside of Beijing (Peking), China (see Figure 4.5). Since excavations began at the cave known as Locality 1 in the early 1920s, the remains of more than forty *Homo erectus* individuals and over 100,000 stone tools, all choppers and flakes, have been recovered. The hominins from Zhoukoudian, also known as Peking man, are at the centre of one of the unsolved mysteries of archaeology. After Japan attacked Pearl Harbor in World War II, an attempt was made to get the fossils out of Peking, which was under Japanese occupation. In the confusion of war, the fossils were lost, and no trace of them has ever reappeared. Fortunately, accurate casts of most of the fossils were saved.

Zhoukoudian A series of caves in Longgu-shan, or Dragon Bone Hill, outside of Beijing (Peking), China, where the remains of more than forty *Homo erectus* individuals and over 100,000 stone choppers and flakes were recovered.

Locality 1 at Zhoukoudian is an absolutely massive site. The scale of the early excavations was more like a mining operation than what we expect from a modern archaeological project. The total depth of the deposits at Locality 1 is 48 metres, which has been divided into seventeen layers. The dating of the site is

Davidson Black and Zhoukoudian

Davidson Black was born in Toronto in 1884 and grew up exploring the lakes of northern Ontario. Black received a medical degree from the University of Toronto, but his interests soon took him far from Canada in the pursuit of evidence of the early stages of human evolution. In 1919, he took a position as a professor in the anatomy department of the newly established Peking Union Medical College and began to plot out an expedition in search of human ancestors in central Asia. His interest was soon drawn to the site of Zhokoudian, located 50 kilometres south-west of Beijing. At Zhoukoudian, Swedish geologist Johan Gunnar Anderson had found rich fossil deposits. Anderson

brought Black in to publish an article about two human teeth recovered from the site, and from that point until his death in 1934, Zhoukoudian was the focus of Black's research. His crowning achievement came in 1929 when the Chinese archaeologist Pei Wenzhong uncovered the skull of a *Homo erectus*. Black then turned to the difficult of task of extracting the fossil from the matrix that encased it. He writes in one of his letters that "the work of unmasking the villain or of extracting *Sinanthropus* [the species name Black gave to this fossil] from his clinging hard matrix progresses slowly . . . I wish you would see the halo of dust after 15 minutes of grinding with a dental carborundum point" (Van Oosterzee

2000, 119). After his death, Black was remembered not only for the importance of his discoveries at Zhoukoudian but also for the way he treated his Chinese colleagues. In remembering Black, Ding Wenjiang wrote that "Black was a conservative, but in his dealings with his Chinese colleagues he altogether forgot their nationality or race, because he realized that science was above such artificial and accidental things" (Lanpo and Weiwenn 1990, 249). ◆

REFERENCES: Jia Lanpo and Huang Weiwen. (1990). *The Story of Peking Man: From Archaeology to Mystery.* Oxford: Oxford University Press.

Penny van Oosterzee. (2000). *Dragon Bones: The Story of Peking Man.* Cambridge, MA: Perseus Publishing.

FIGURE 4.6 Horizontal exposure of hearths at the site of Beeches Pit. The hearths are visible as clearly delineated areas of black sediment.

▲▲ **Beeches Pit** A site in England dating to 400,000 years ago that has produced compelling evidence for the use of fire in the Lower Paleolithic.

extremely complex; however, most studies agree that the hominin occupation occurred between 500,000 and 300,000 years ago. Recent dating of Zhoukoudian by the newly developed cosmogenic burial age dating method suggests that the site might actually be as much as 750,000 years old (Shen et al. 2009).

Locality 1 at Zhoukoudian has long been thought to provide the earliest evidence for the use of fire. The most important evidence comes from Layer 10, which has been described as an ash layer. However, recent research has demonstrated that there is no ash in Layer 10 and that what had been identified as ash is actually organic material brought in by a river that ran through the cave (Goldberg et al. 2001). Similar conclusions have been reached concerning the evidence of burning in Layer 4. The only evidence suggestive of the controlled use of fire by hominins at Zhoukoudian Locality 1 is the occurrence of burnt bones together with stone tools. Although evidence of fire has been identified at the Acheulian site of Gesher Benot Ya'akov in Israel, in general terms the use of fire during the Lower Paleolithic was rare. The most compelling evidence for the use of fire in the Lower Paleolithic comes from the site of Beeches Pit in England, which is dated to 400,000 years ago (Preece et al. 2006). At **Beeches Pit**, there are clearly discrete areas where a concentration of charred bones and stone tools was found (see Figure 4.6). However, the possibility of

FIGURE 4.7 Harrmut Thieme with the 400,000-year-old wooden spear he discovered at the site of Schöningen, Germany. Notice the horse skull to the right of the spear.

natural fire cannot be completely ruled out, since burnt lizard and rat bones were found along with the bones of large mammals. There is nonetheless strong support for controlled use of fire by the hominins occupying the site. The evidence of fire is found only in strata in which artifacts are present, and it is restricted to small, shallow depressions.

Excavations in a coal mine at **Schöningen**, Germany, have uncovered three spruce spears together with a rich collection of stone tools and animal bones dated to 400,000 years ago (Thieme 1997). The unique context of this site allowed for the preservation of these wooden artifacts (see Figure 4.7). The spears vary between 1.8 and 2.2 metres in length and between 29 and 47 millimetres in diameter. Another piece, which is pointed on both ends (as opposed to the spears, which are pointed at only one end), is 0.8 metres long. The spears are well made and balanced, but do not appear to have had a stone tip or any decoration. The excavator interprets them as projectiles.

FIGURE 4.8 The Berekhat Ram figurine. The white bar is a scale of 1 cm. The groove running around the top part of the stone appears to be artificial.

There is very little evidence of either artwork or ritual behaviour in Lower Paleolithic contexts. Two exceptions to this generalization deserve particular mention. The first is a small pebble of volcanic rock found at the Lower Paleolithic site of Berekhat Ram, Golan Heights (see Figure 4.8). The excavator of Berekhat Ram discerned signs of work on this stone and identified it as a representation of a human female. Because the site is more than 230,000 years old, the stone is possibly the earliest evidence of human representation. Subsequent research has confirmed that the pebble was indeed worked by the incision of a single line. Whether the intention was to create a figurine remains unclear (d'Errico and Nowell 2000).

The only significant evidence for special treatment of the dead during the Lower Paleolithic comes from a cave at Atapuerca known as Sima de los Huesos, which is dated to 300,000 years ago. In this pit, the complete remains of

▲▲ **Schöningen** The location in Germany where 400,000-year-old wooden spears were discovered.

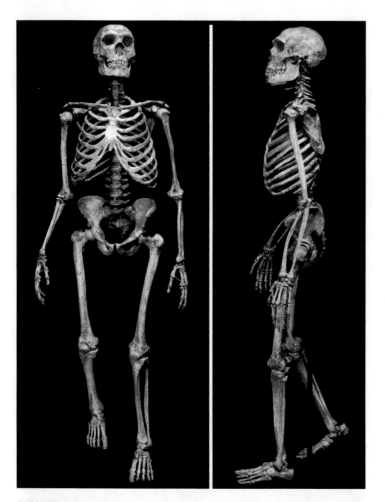

FIGURE 4.9 A reconstructed Neanderthal. No complete Neanderthal fossils have been found, so this model was constructed by combining elements from a number of different fossils. Notice that the skull is long and the face juts forward. There is no chin, the rib cage is broad, and the pelvis is somewhat different from that of modern humans.

twenty-seven hominin individuals were recovered (Carbonell et al. 2003). Only one stone tool, a well-made quartz handaxe, has been found in the cave. There is no evidence of human occupation of Sima de los Huesos, nor is there evidence that it was an accessible cave. It appears to have been a crevice in the rock, in which the inhabitants were cave bears and other carnivores. The excavators argue that the hominins were not brought to the cave by carnivores and that the cave was not a natural crevice into which they fell. Rather, they interpret Sima de los Huesos as a place where corpses were placed as part of a funerary ritual, and they construe the handaxe to be a funerary offering. They suggest that the large number of corpses reflects a burial of the victims of an ecological crisis. There is evidence of carnivore gnawing on almost half of the human bones. These gnaw marks include the actions of a small fox-sized animal and a larger lion-sized animal. There is no evidence that the corpses were buried.

4.3 Neanderthals

All living humans are members of the species *Homo sapiens*, also known as modern humans. Neanderthals are at once similar to modern humans and yet highly distinctive (Figure 4.9). The significance of the similarities and differences between Neanderthals and our own species is the focus of intense debate. Some scientists argue that the similarities are so strong that Neanderthals must be merely a subspecies—*Homo sapiens neanderthalensis*—of our own. Others argue that despite the similarities, the differences warrant the creation of a distinct species—*Homo neanderthalensis*—for the Neanderthals. Table 4.1 lists some important attributes of Neanderthals.

The similarities between modern humans and Neanderthals are rooted in their shared ancestry. Unfortunately, there is some controversy surrounding the identification of the last common ancestor of modern humans and Neanderthals. Three scenarios (shown in Figure 4.10) have been posed for the evolution of Neanderthals:

1. Neanderthals and modern humans each evolved separately from populations of *Homo erectus*, possibly through local intermediate species.

TABLE 4.1

GENUS OR SPECIES	DATE	BRAIN SIZE	CHARACTERISTICS	DISTRIBUTION
Homo neanderthalensis or *Homo sapiens neanderthalensis*	175,000–30,000 years ago	1,200–1,700 cc	Muscular and adapted to the cold.	Europe and the Middle East

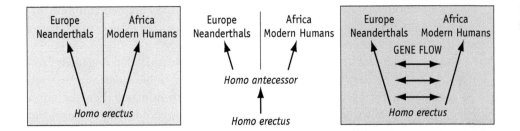

FIGURE 4.10 Three scenarios for the evolution of Neanderthals.

According to this scenario, the evolution of Neanderthals and modern humans took place in parallel, in separate geographic areas. Evidence for the evolution of modern humans in Africa will be discussed in the next chapter. Neanderthals, a species (or subspecies) adapted to cold climates, evolved in Europe.

2. The common ancestor of modern humans and Neanderthals was a distinct species that itself evolved from *Homo erectus* and lived between 700,000 and 300,000 years ago. One candidate for this critical intermediate position is *Homo antecessor*, whose fossils have been found at Atapuerca Gran Dolina TD-6.

3. Neanderthals and modern humans did not evolve in isolation; rather, there was a constant exchange of genetic material, or gene flow, between the two populations. This possibility cannot be ruled out; however, some degree of isolation must have existed in order for Neanderthals to evolve some of their characteristic skeletal traits. According to this model, Neanderthals and modern humans are members of a single species.

The distinctiveness of a Neanderthal skeleton is easy to identify. The skull is elongated compared with the skull of a modern human, with an occipital bun at the back and a large, projecting nose in front. The forehead is sloping and the chin almost absent. As in *Homo erectus*, there is a brow ridge over the eyes; however, in Neanderthals, this ridge is double arched. The skull is not as thick as that of *Homo erectus* but is still thicker than the norm among living humans. The molars of Neanderthals were large, and the front teeth show marks of wear, indicating the regular use of the incisors as tools in preparing food or gripping hides. The Neanderthal body is stocky and similar in proportion to modern humans adapted to cold climates. Particularly notable are a broad rib cage and bowed long bones. The muscle insertions are well developed, and the bones are generally robust. Although Neanderthals were completely bipedal, the way they walked was slightly different from that of modern humans.

The overall impression one forms of Neanderthals is that they were very strong and well adapted to cold climates. Among the features tied to a cold-weather adaptation are the projecting face and large nose. These features distinguish Neanderthals from both *Homo erectus* and modern humans. Studies of fossil remains of Neanderthal children indicate that many of the characteristic Neanderthal features developed quite early in childhood.

The brains of Neanderthals were within the size range of those of modern humans, between 1,200 and 1,700 cubic centimetres. This is considerably larger than the brain of *Homo erectus*. If Neanderthals and modern humans each evolved independently from *Homo erectus*, then the increase in brain size took place as a parallel process in the two lineages. Alternatively, the large brains of Neanderthals and

FIGURE 4.11 The Neanderthal hyoid bone from Kebara. The hyoid bone is found in the larynx and connects to the muscles used in producing speech. The Kebara hyoid is identical to the hyoid bone found in modern humans. The width of the Kebara hyoid is 4.5 cm.

modern humans could be derived from a large-brained common ancestor such as *Homo antecessor*. Or the parallel evolution of larger brains could be the product of gene flow.

The evolution of the brain in the Neanderthal lineage is critical to assessing Neanderthal behaviour. If Neanderthals evolved larger brains independently from modern humans, then there is a possibility that, despite being the same size, modern human and Neanderthal brains are significantly different in organization and cognitive capacity. The idea that Neanderthals might have differed cognitively from modern humans has intrigued many researchers. One proposal is that Neanderthals lacked the cognitive capacity for language, as well as the anatomical apparatus to produce speech. Much of this argument is based on the shape of the Neanderthal cranium base, which is flat in comparison to the flexed morphology of modern human skulls. But because the soft tissue of the larynx is not preserved in the fossil record, it is difficult to make conclusive statements about Neanderthals' ability to speak. The only skeletal element incorporated into the musculature of the larynx is a very small bone called the hyoid. The discovery of the complete hyoid of a Neanderthal at the site of Kebara Cave in Israel has produced no evidence supporting the argument that Neanderthals were physically incapable of speech (Arensburg 1989). The Kebara hyoid is identical to modern human hyoids, an unlikely coincidence if the morphology of the Neanderthal larynx had been significantly different (see Figure 4.11).

■ Neanderthal Genetics

In 1999, scientists announced that they had succeeded in extracting and sequencing mitochondrial DNA from a Neanderthal fossil (Krings et al. 1999). The results of this test, performed on the Neander Valley fossil from Germany, have since been replicated on a fossil from the site of Mezmaiskaya Cave in the Caucasus Mountain region of Eastern Europe (see Figure 4.12 on the next page).

The sequences of Neanderthal DNA that have been recovered are significantly different from those of living humans. This suggests that the divergence between the Neanderthal lineage and the modern human lineage dates back approximately 450,000 years, a date, however, that comes with a large margin of error, limiting the divergence to a period of 400,000 years between 320,000 and 740,000 years before the present. The degree of difference between Neanderthal and modern human DNA is less than the difference separating the two living species of chimpanzees (*Pan troglodytes* and *Pan paniscus*) but exceeds the variation between subspecies of chimpanzees. The genetic evidence suggests that Neanderthals, whether one chooses to label them a species or subspecies, evolved separately from the modern human lineage for a considerable period of time.

Nuclear DNA from a Neanderthal specimen from the site of Vindija Cave, Croatia, has now been extensively sequenced by two research teams (Green et al. 2006; Noonan et al. 2006). One team was able to sequence 62,250 base pairs of the Neanderthal genome and derived a date of 700,000 years ago for the last common ancestor of Neanderthals and modern humans. The other team sequenced over one million base pairs and arrived at a date of 500,000 years ago for the split between the modern human and Neanderthal lineages. In 2008, the complete mitochondrial DNA sequence for the Vindija Neanderthal was published (Green et al. 2008).

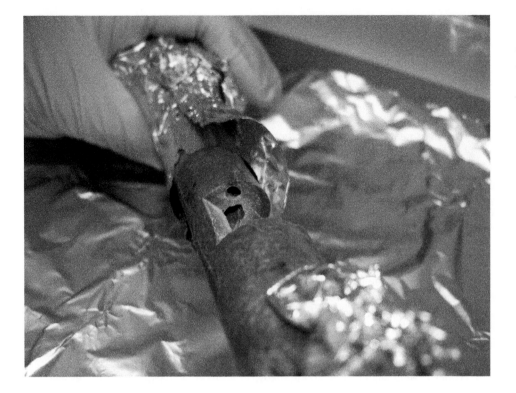

FIGURE 4.12 Sampling of a Neanderthal bone for DNA analysis. Great care must be taken to avoid contamination by modern DNA.

The comparison of this sequence with modern human mitochondrial DNA confirms the early date for the divergence of the Neanderthal and modern human lineages at roughly 650,000 years ago. The mitochondrial DNA sequence also suggests that the population size of Neanderthals was small.

Chronology and Ecology

The oldest fossil that can be clearly classified as a Neanderthal was discovered at **Biache-Saint-Vaast** in northern France. Biache has been dated to 175,000 years ago by means of thermoluminescence. A possible older date has been proposed for a Neanderthal fossil, found at the Ehringsdorf site in eastern Germany, which has been dated between 200,000 and 250,000 years ago. The Biache and Ehringsdorf fossils suggest that Neanderthals first appeared in Europe in the latter part of interglacial Oxygen Isotope Stage 7.

The most recent date for a Neanderthal fossil is roughly 30,000 years ago, from sites such as the **Mezmaiskaya Cave**, the source of one of the Neanderthal fossils from which DNA was successfully extracted. Neanderthals thus lived through two complete glacial cycles, beginning with interglacial Oxygen Isotope Stage 7 and ending with glacial Oxygen Isotope Stage 3. Neanderthals survived through rapidly changing climatic conditions, including the deep glacial advances of Oxygen Isotope Stage 6 and the very warm conditions of the early part of interglacial Oxygen Isotope Stage 5.

Neanderthal fossils have been found across a wide area stretching from Western Europe to Central Asia. The southern limit of the distribution of Neanderthal fossils is in the Middle East. No Neanderthal fossils have been found in either Africa or East Asia. Neanderthal fossils and archaeological remains have been found in a wide range of ecological zones, including open temperate grasslands in northern Europe and Mediterranean-climate woodlands in the Middle East.

Biache-Saint-Vaast The site in France where the oldest known fossil of a Neanderthal, dated to 175,000 years ago, was found.

Mezmaiskaya Cave The location that has produced the most recent Neanderthal fossil, dated to 30,000 years ago.

Religion and Evolution

The struggle between evolution and religion predates the publication of Charles Darwin's *On the Origin of Species*. Paralyzed by fear of the implications of his ideas and of the reception they would receive, Darwin delayed the publication of his theory for years (Desmond and Moore 1992). Many of the archaeologists who first took up the study of human evolution during the late nineteenth century were motivated by an intense antipathy to religion. Perhaps the most outspoken was the French prehistorian Gabriel de Mortillet, who viewed religion as a brake on the progress of humanity.

It is curious that, in the early twentieth century, prehistoric archaeology came to be dominated by a group of Jesuit priests. These priests recognized the power of evolutionary theory and enthusiastically engaged in pioneering research in all aspects of archaeology and paleontology. The most active archaeologist in this group was the Abbé Henri Breuil, who pioneered the study of Paleolithic cave art. The Jesuit prehistorians also attempted to reconcile evolutionary theory with Catholic theology. Pierre Teilhard de Chardin developed an elaborate interpretation of evolution as a process directed by divine intervention and tending toward the unity of humanity. De Chardin was "rewarded" for his creativity by a lifetime church ban on the publication of his writings.

In the United States, evolution has played a particularly central role in drawing the line between church and state. The celebrated Scopes "monkey trial" pitted Clarence Darrow in defence of the teaching of evolution against William Jennings Bryan (Larson 1997). At issue in this case was the violation of a Tennessee law against the teaching of evolution in a public school by a schoolteacher named John Scopes. The Scopes trial became the "trial of the century" and inspired the play and movie *Inherit the Wind*. The fight between Darrow and Bryan resonates to this day in court cases about the teaching of creationism and intelligent design in public schools. Courts have decided that both creationism and intelligent design are religious doctrine rather than science, and therefore should not be taught in public schools. However, one would have to be extraordinarily naïve to think that the issue will not reappear in U.S. courts and legislative bodies.

Why has evolution attracted such conflict? After all, it is one among many scientific theories. Even within biology, other influential theories, such as the role of DNA in inheritance, have not produced similar controversy. We can trace this question back to Charles Darwin. Why did he delay publishing his breakthrough? These are difficult and profound questions that go to the very core of the nature of science and the meaning of religious belief. The power of evolutionary theory is that it provides a framework for understanding the development of the natural world without recourse to a deity. Until Darwin published his book, there was no convincing way of explaining the diversity of life on earth without relying on divine intervention. Darwin set out a way to look at the natural world that does not require a God. For people who draw on faith as a cornerstone of their lives, this can clearly be an unsettling concept, and the passion of the resulting debate is understandable.

As an archaeologist, I do not feel a need to struggle with these issues on a daily basis. I do not find that studying human evolution removes all meaning from the world. On the contrary; I find that the theory of evolution is a key to unlocking the complexity of the world around us. Recognizing that variability is produced by history is a fundamentally enriching insight. ●

FIGURE 4.13

Abbé Henri Breuil was a pioneering prehistoric archaeologist and a Jesuit priest.

4.4 Aspects of Neanderthal Culture and Adaptation

Neanderthals are often portrayed as loutish brutes, and the word *Neanderthal* has become an insult indicating a lack of intelligence or culture. Our fascination with Neanderthals might be the result of their status as both similar and different from living humans. Archaeological research presents a subtle picture of Neanderthal culture and adaptations. The archaeological period during which Neanderthals occupied Europe and the Middle East is known as the **Middle Paleolithic**.

■ Stone Tools

Neanderthals only rarely made handaxes. After having been a central part of the hominin tool kit for over a million years, handaxes rapidly disappeared from the archaeological record around 200,000 years ago. Rather than fashioning bifacial tools from cobbles or very large flakes, Neanderthals made tools by retouching the edges of flakes. The flakes used by Neanderthals as tools were not made haphazardly. The dominant approach to tool manufacture during the Middle Paleolithic is known as **prepared-core technology**, a technique in which the person making the tools carefully shaped the core to control the form of the flakes produced (see Figure 4.14).

Within the narrow range of Neanderthal stone tool technology, there is surprising diversity. With some important exceptions, the Lower Paleolithic is characterized as showing a great deal of uniformity across broad geographical areas and long time scales. This is not the case for the stone tool industries made by Neanderthals which show a great deal of variation, both in the location and nature of the retouching and in the shape of the flakes on which the tools were made. The study of variation in Middle Paleolithic stone tools has played a critical role in developing archaeological methods of artifact analysis. Understanding these tools is key to understanding Neanderthal adaptation, culture, and cognition.

FRANÇOIS BORDES AND NEANDERTHAL ETHNICITY. In the early twentieth century, excavations of Neanderthal sites in Europe were undertaken on a massive scale. Layers were described on the basis of particularly characteristic artifacts that

Middle Paleolithic The archaeological period during which Neanderthals occupied Europe.

prepared-core technology The dominant approach to tool manufacture during the Middle Paleolithic; a technique in which the person making the tools carefully shaped the core to control the form of the flakes produced.

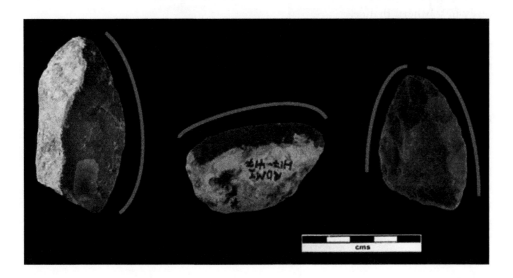

FIGURE 4.14 The typology of Middle Paleolithic retouched flakes is determined by the location and shape of retouched edges. Single convex sidescraper (left), transversal sidescraper (centre), convergent double sidescraper (right).

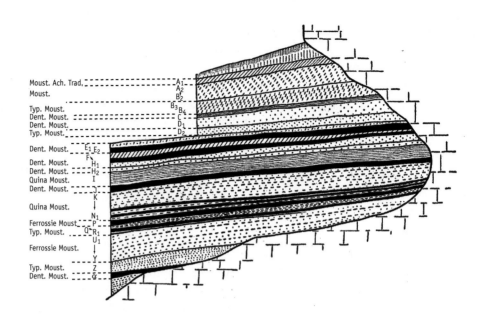

FIGURE 4.15 The stratigraphic sequence from Combe Grenal, France. Sixty-two occupation levels were identified, allowing François Bordes to examine patterns of change in archaeological industries through time. The labels on the left refer to the type of industry identified within each layer. How would you describe the sequence of archaeological industries in this figure?

became known as "fossil directors." In most cases, the bulk of the material recovered was simply discarded as irrelevant. This approach to the excavation of Middle Paleolithic sites changed drastically due to the pioneering efforts of the French prehistorian François Bordes, who worked to improve excavation methods and to create a more fine-tuned stratigraphic division of sites. In his excavations at the sites of Combe Grenal and Pech de l'Azé, he divided the stratigraphic sequence into dozens of well-defined levels (Bordes 1972) (see Figure 4.15). He was also dissatisfied with the characterization of the archaeological content of a layer on the basis of so small a number of tools as the fossil directors. By creating a detailed list of tool types (a typology) and counting how many of each type was found in a particular level, Bordes was able to quantify the totality of the tools found in that level.

On the basis of his excavations and quantitative studies, Bordes identified a series of distinct types of Middle Paleolithic industries. He found that in southern France these industries did not form a chronological sequence; rather, within a single site, they were found in alternating levels. Bordes interpreted the Middle Paleolithic industries as the product of distinct ethnic groups. He maintained that the stratigraphic evidence showed that these different groups lived contemporaneously in southern France.

THE BINFORD–BORDES DEBATE. Attacking Bordes's interpretation was a temptation Lewis Binford could not resist (Binford 1983). Binford had spent time in France with Bordes while his wife, Sally, worked on analyzing the stone tools from her excavations of a Middle Paleolithic site in Israel. Both Binfords had enormous respect for Bordes's analysis, but found his interpretation fundamentally flawed. Binford could not accept that variation in the types of tools found on sites was the result of ethnicity during the Middle Paleolithic. He argued that it was far more plausible that the tools found in a level reflected the activities that took place there. Different tools would be used, depending on the purpose of the site, whether for the preparation of hides, for butchery, or, as Bordes joked back, for peeling carrots. For Binford, the idea of Neanderthal ethnicity was an illusion built of Bordes's biases.

DISSENTING VOICES. As Binford and Bordes squared off, the study of Middle Paleolithic stone tool variability became an archaeological cause célèbre pitting the "traditional" European archaeologists against the brash American "New Archaeologists." Ultimately, it became a classic debate over the relative importance of culture and biological adaptation in archaeology. However, a number of studies emerged that undermined some of the central arguments of both Binford and Bordes.

Paul Mellars (1996) studied the sequences from southern France and reached the conclusion that the variants Bordes identified are, for the most part, found in a chronological sequence. Contrary to Bordes, Mellars did not find evidence that these variants were contemporaneous. Bordes's vision of neighbouring ethnic groups is not supported by these data. Binford's picture of sites reflecting particular activity areas suffers as well, unless one imagines that a "hide-working period" was followed by a "butchery period."

Philip Chase (1986) studied the sequence of animal remains from the site of Combe Grenal. His studies failed to identify any relationship between the types of animals found or the way the bones had been processed and the type of industry. Chase's analysis further undermines Binford's position.

THE FRISON EFFECT. The debate between Binford and Bordes centred on the shared premise that the typology developed by Bordes was valid. On this shared basis, the two researchers went on to argue whether variation in the types of tools found was the result of ethnicity or site function. Bordes's typology is a list of tools based on subtle variations on the locations of retouch. The main type of tool is the sidescraper, which is simply a flake with retouch along the side. Sidescrapers are subdivided into flakes with retouch on one edge (simple sidescrapers), flakes with retouch on two edges (double sidescrapers), and flakes with retouch on two edges that meet (convergent sidescapers), as shown in the photo on page 105. These categories of tools are then further subdivided according to the shape of the edge.

To Bordes, tool types were fixed entities representing the goal of their manufacture. In the 1980s, American archaeologist Harold Dibble developed an elegant critique of the Bordes typology (Dibble 1987). Dibble pointed out that stone tools have a lifetime of use, or use-life, that includes resharpening. This quality of stone tool technology is known as the **Frison effect**. During its use-life, a single piece might pass through several forms as it undergoes resharpening. Dibble argued that this is exactly what happened with sidescrapers during the Middle Paleolithic. The types of tools that Bordes saw as desired end products were actually stages in a process of a tool's use-life. A flake could begin as a single scraper, become a double scraper, and then become a convergent scraper as it passed through successive stages of resharpening. Or, as shown in Figure 4.16, a simple sidescraper can be transformed into a transversal sidescraper.

Frison effect Due to resharpening, the process through which the shape of stone tools changes during their use-life.

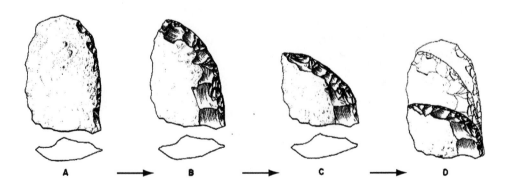

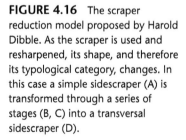

FIGURE 4.16 The scraper reduction model proposed by Harold Dibble. As the scraper is used and resharpened, its shape, and therefore its typological category, changes. In this case a simple sidescraper (A) is transformed through a series of stages (B, C) into a transversal sidescraper (D).

Levallois method A particular prepared-core technology used during the Middle Paleolithic that can often be recognized on the basis of tortoise-shaped cores.

Dibble argued that Bordes was wrong in his view of Neanderthal society, saying that, as Binford had argued, ethnicity was an illusion. Perhaps all variability could be accounted for by the degree to which tools were exhausted. In place of Binford's site function model, Dibble proposed that variability in Middle Paleolithic stone tool industries could be explained on the basis of access to raw material and the degree of mobility of the inhabitants of the site. The farther the sites were from sources of raw material, the more the scrapers would be retouched. The more mobile a group of hunter–gatherers, the more likely the members of the group would be to maintain their tool kit, and, in turn, the more likely an increase in the number of pieces intensively retouched.

THE *CHAÎNE OPÉRATOIRE*. Dibble put the argument against Neanderthal ethnicity on new and more solid ground. By going to the root and challenging the very basis of Bordes's method, he managed to cast doubt on the entire theory. The French riposte came rapidly. The basis of the counterattack was the idea of the *chaîne opératoire*, developed by ethnographer and archaeologist André Leroi-Gourhan (see Toolbox on page 110). The *chaîne opératoire* looks beyond the use-history of a tool to its entire life history, beginning with the gathering of raw material and ending with the spent tool finally being discarded. Leroi-Gourhan emphasized that human tool manufacture is a combination of knowledge and skill. This idea seemed intuitively true to a group of French prehistorians, who began making stone tools experimentally. To arrive at the types of flakes found on Neanderthal sites, one has to know what one is doing. The same, then, must have been true of Neanderthals. But what did they know?

The answer to this question crystallized in the study of stone tools from the site of Biache-Saint-Vaast carried out by Eric Boëda (1995). It was clear that the stone tools at Biache-Saint-Vaast were produced by a prepared-core method called the **Levallois method**, recognizable from its characteristic products. The flakes produced by this method are very large and regular and usually have quite a sharp cutting edge (see Figure 4.17). The cores are asymmetrical and bifacial and

FIGURE 4.17 Experimental Levallois core (left) and flake (right). The surface of the core has been carefully shaped to allow the removal of a large, sharp-edged flake.

bear a striking resemblance to a tortoise flipped on its back. Because of this similarity, Levallois cores are often known as "tortoise-shaped cores." Like Dibble, Boëda was interested in getting at the process behind these types of tools, but for him the process was one of manufacture rather than resharpening. During the study of the Biache-Saint-Vaast stone tools, Boëda realized that to arrive at Levallois-type flakes and cores, the stone tool knappers have to respect a series of rules throughout the process. These rules are flexible, much like a strategy one might use in playing pool, and allow the knapper to respond to accidents or flaws in the material. The rules are abstract spatial concepts, such as treating the block as asymmetrical and bifacial.

As Boëda and his colleagues applied this insight to Middle Paleolithic sites across Europe and the Middle East, it became apparent that there is indeed Neanderthal ethnicity, but not in the way Bordes had thought. The methods used in making flakes and the resulting types of flakes vary significantly across time and space. Researchers now realize that there is much greater diversity in the way Neanderthals made stone tools than they had imagined. One important example is a group of sites in northern Europe that have produced evidence for the manufacture of elongated flake tools known as blades (Conard 1990). Nowadays, *Neanderthal ethnicity* refers to strongly held traditions in the way stone tools are manufactured. These traditions require that knowledge and skill be transmitted between generations by learning.

SUMMING UP THE STONES. Dibble and Boëda have pushed the study of Middle Paleolithic stone tools into an entirely new realm, one in which the focus of study is a process rather than a finished object. The stone tool analyst becomes more like an ethologist watching behaviour than an art historian appreciating objects. This is not to imply that consensus reigns. Ironically, the debate between Dibble and Boëda is every bit as intense as the debate between Binford and Bordes. However, it is likely that both archaeologists have seized on a critical piece of the puzzle. Boëda has demonstrated that Neanderthal stone tool manufacture was highly sophisticated learned behaviour. At the same time, Dibble has alerted us to the critical importance of raw material and mobility in identifying which tools will be found on a site.

◼ Hunting

Some authors, notably Binford, have questioned whether Neanderthals were hunters. However, the discovery of a series of sites at which archaeological material is associated with a large number of animal carcasses leaves little doubt that Neanderthals were capable of hunting large game. Whether they also relied on scavenging remains an open question.

The site of **La Cotte de St. Brelade** is today located on the Jersey Islands in the English Channel. When the site was occupied during glacial Oxygen Isotope Stage 6, the Jersey Islands were connected to continental Europe due to lower sea levels. Excavations uncovered the remains of at least twenty mammoths and five woolly rhinos at the foot of a steep rock face (Scott 1986). These animals were deliberately led to stampede over the cliff face and fall to their deaths, where Neanderthal occupants butchered them.

Four Middle Paleolithic sites in southern France have produced evidence of specialized hunting of bovids, both aurochs and steppe bison. At Mauran, a 25-square-metre excavation produced a minimum number of individuals (MNI) count of at least 136 bison. The excavators do not think that this was a mass kill site, but rather a seasonal occupation where animals were hunted and butchered.

▲▲ **La Cotte de St. Brelade** The location on the Jersey Islands where evidence of Neanderthals hunting mammoths by stampeding them off a cliff was found.

TOOLBOX

Chaîne Opératoire and the Levallois Method

Driving a car, baking a cake, and playing music are all activities that involve combining knowledge and skill to produce a sequence of actions. Archaeologists have seized on this basic observation to produce a novel perspective on the artifacts uncovered on excavations. By looking at the sequences of actions involved in making and using these artifacts, it is possible to gain insight into the knowledge and skill of the people behind them. The idea of a *chaîne opératoire* or operational sequence is a critical element of this approach. The goal is ultimately to go beyond describing artifacts and sequences of manufacture to get at the social dynamics of technology (Dobres 2000). How did people learn the skills that made them members of society? The way that Neanderthals made stone tools has been a particular focus of archaeologists using the *chaîne opératoire.*

Neanderthal stone tool production involved a great deal more than simply banging one rock against another. Neanderthals did use percussion methods to make stone tools. However, the process of removing flakes from cores was carefully organized, with the form of the flakes produced controlled by the knapper. It is useful to think of flint knapping as similar to a game of pool. In both pool and knapping, it is necessary to have a strategy, and this strategy involves controlling angles. In pool, it is the angles between the balls on the table and the angles between those balls and the pockets. In making stone tools, the control of angles allows the knapper to remove flakes of a desired shape and size. Of course, in both knapping and pool, it is also necessary to have the skill to put a plan into action! Although Neanderthals used a number of strategies to produce flakes,

the most characteristic was the Levallois method. This method can be recognized by the shape of the cores, which resemble a tortoise flipped on its back, and by the presence of flakes that are sharp-edged around their entire circumference. Recently, archaeologists have come to understand the strategy that underlies the Levallois method. In this method, the knapper conceives of the core as two surfaces that meet at a plane of intersection. The surfaces are hierarchically related, with each playing a different function. The upper surface is the one from which the desired flakes are struck, while the lower surface pro-vides the platform that receives the hammer blows for the removal of these flakes. The knapper controls the shape of the Levallois flakes by shaping the convexity of the upper surface. By following these rules, a skilled knapper, whether a Neanderthal or an archaeologist, can control the form of flakes produced, from the initial use of the core until it is too small to be worked. There is tremendous flexibility within the Levallois method, and the shapes of the flakes produced can include points, large oval flakes, or long, thin flakes, depending on how the knapper shapes the upper surface. ●

FIGURE 4.18
The French archaeologist Jacques Tixier making stone tools. Tixier is among the pioneers of experimental archaeology.

The dating of Mauran is the subject of some controversy; however, a date of roughly 75,000 years ago, in Oxygen Isotope Stage 5, appears most likely.

There is no evidence of highly developed hunting equipment during the Middle Paleolithic. From the discovery of the wooden spear at the Lower Paleolithic site of Schöningen, we can assume that such tools were used, although they are rarely preserved. Stone tools that could have been used as spear tips are found in small numbers on most Middle Paleolithic sites in Europe. In the Middle East, such pieces are more common, and use–wear analysis of pointed Levallois flakes from the site of Kebara Cave in Israel supports the identification of these flakes as spear tips (Shea et al. 2001).

Graphic proof that Neanderthals used stone spearpoints in hunting has been found at the Middle Paleolithic site of Umm el Tlel in Syria (Boëda et al. 1999). Umm el Tlel is an open-air site with fifty-seven levels of Middle Paleolithic occupation and excellent preservation of animal bones. The site has not been precisely dated, but it is over 50,000 years old. At Umm el Tlel, a fragment of a Levallois point was found embedded in the cervical vertebra (neck bone) of a wild ass (see Figure 4.19). The point had clearly entered the bone while the animal was alive, and the blow most likely immobilized it. The excavators have demonstrated that the spearpoint had to have entered the animal with considerable force and was more likely to have been thrown than thrust.

Despite the clear evidence of Neanderthal hunting, it appears the technology used in this activity was fairly basic. The only methods available to Neanderthals were hunting with handheld and perhaps thrown spears, and communal hunting by driving animals over a cliff, as occurred at La Cotte de St. Brelade. Some have argued that the high incidence of trauma, such as healed broken bones, found on Neanderthal skeletons was the result of hunting with minimal technology. One study found that the incidence of trauma among Neanderthals agrees well with the pattern found among rodeo riders (Berger and Trinkaus 1995).

Rare evidence of exploitation of fish, shellfish, and other marine resources by Neanderthals comes from a series of sites on the coast of Gibraltar (Stringer et al. 2008). At Vanguard Cave in Units C and D, dated by radiocarbon to 42,000 years ago, a hearth was found with approximately 150 mussel shells along with seal and dolphin bones. Two of the seal bones have clear cut marks. Bones of terrestrial mammals, including deer and boar, were also found in this context, indicating a very broad diet for the Neanderthal occupants of the site.

STABLE-ISOTOPE ANALYSIS. The evidence for Neanderthal hunting is overwhelming but it provides little information about the role of meat in the diet.

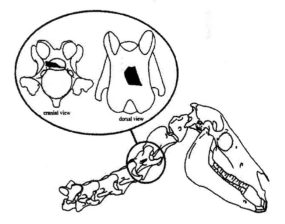

FIGURE 4.19 A fragment of a Levallois point embedded in the vertebra of a wild ass from the site of Umm el Tlel, Syria. The upper picture shows an overview; the middle view is a detail; the bottom is a diagram showing where the Levallois point entered the animal.

Studies of the bone chemistry of Neanderthal fossils from Belgium, France, and Croatia suggest that Neanderthals were essentially meat eaters. In ecological terms, these studies have demonstrated that Neanderthals were at the top of the food chain, or at a high trophic level. The chemical signature of Neanderthal bones matches that of predators such as lions and wolves (Bocherens et al. 2001).

Chemical evidence of the nature of the diet is based on the relative proportions of isotopes that build up in bone collagen during life. Collagen is the protein that produces the structure of bone. The amount of ^{15}N in bone collagen increases between the food and the consumer. As one rises within the food chain, the amount of ^{15}N increases. Analyses of Neanderthal fossils from three sites in Belgium and one in Croatia show that the ^{15}N found in the bones of Neanderthals is equaled only by the ^{15}N found in the bones of predators.

A similar study of a Neanderthal fossil from the site of St. Césaire, France, examined the ratios of strontium to calcium and barium to calcium. These ratios are lower the higher one moves in the food chain. The low ratios of strontium to calcium and barium to calcium found in the St. Césaire fossil suggest that 97 percent of the diet of this individual consisted of meat (Balter et al. 2002).

■ Site Organization and the Use of Fire

The evidence from animal bones and from the chemical analysis of Neanderthal fossils demonstrates that Neanderthals were hunters. Neanderthal sites include specialized kill sites, such as Mauran, but most appear to fit well with Glynn Isaac's concept of a base camp (see Chapter 3). These sites are sheltered locations to which meat and other resources would have been brought back for consumption. Many of the Neanderthals' base camp sites are located in caves, which serve as excellent depositional contexts with well-preserved archaeological remains. Many Neanderthal sites show evidence of intensive occupation and a deep accumulation of archaeological layers. Microscopic analysis of the sediments found in Middle Paleolithic cave sites shows that, although some of the fill is made up of sediments blown into the cave, a large proportion of the deposits, including charcoal, bone fragments, and fragments of stone tools, are the products of human activities.

Although alignments of stones are occasionally reported, there is very little evidence for any kind of construction at Neanderthal sites. A possible exception is a circle of large mammoth bones found at the site of Moldova in the Ukraine, a configuration that has been interpreted as the remains of a hut. The careful horizontal excavation of cave sites has begun to show that there is spatial organization to Neanderthal habitations. **Kebara Cave**, Israel, is a Neanderthal cave site dating to approximately 50,000 years ago (Bar-Yosef et al. 1992). The horizontal excavation of the central part of the cave indicates that the main living surface was relatively clean, while the sides of the cave were refuse areas into which bones were tossed. A feature found in the central area appears to have been a pit used for the collection of discarded material.

The most significant features found at Kebara cave were hearths. In horizontal excavation, these hearths were poorly defined, and no stones were used to delimit a fireplace. Vertical excavation of the site produced a section that is striped black and white. Microscopic analyses of these deposits show that they are the remains of numerous simple fires. The black layers are charcoal, the white layers ash. Similar evidence of an extensive use of fire is found on most Neanderthal sites. In addition to burnt sediments, burnt flint and bone are also very common.

▲▲ Kebara Cave A site in Israel where excavations have produced important evidence about the nature of Neanderthal occupation of caves, as well as one of the most complete skeletons of a Neanderthal.

TOOLBOX

Geoarchaeology and Micromorphology

Geoarchaeology is the interdisciplinary field of study that brings the methods of the geological sciences to bear on archaeological research. From a geoarchaeological perspective one sees familiar archaeological phenomena in a completely different way. Understanding the geology of a survey region is the first step in identifying localities where archaeological deposits are preserved and visible. Geoarchaeologists also play a fundamental role in identifying the sources for the raw materials used to make artifacts, including rocks for stone tools, clays for pottery, and ores for metal artifacts.

Soil micromorphology is a method used by geoarchaeologists to conduct a detailed examination of the deposits that make up an archaeological site. Micromorphologists begin their research by carefully removing a block of sediment from a stratigraphic profile. The block is encased in plaster or tape for transport to a laboratory, where it is placed in a vacuum chamber and impregnated with silicon. Once the silicon has hardened, a thin slice can be taken from the sample for examination under a microscope. Micromorphologists have shown that a single depositional unit is in fact made up of a very large number of discrete events. The power of micromorphology is that it can reveal how a feature formed. For example, the process can identify rodent activity and the multiple events involved in resurfacing floors. In Paleolithic archaeology, micromorphology is a valuable tool for identifying the often ephemeral traces of occupation left by hunter–gatherers. At Kebara Cave in Israel, micromorphology has demonstrated that the stratigraphy of the Middle Paleolithic occupation consists of hundreds of individual hearths built up one on top of another. Micromorphological analysis at Kebara Cave has also shown that a high percentage of the sediments are anthropogenic—microscopic pieces of bone, charcoal, and stone tools brought in by the Neanderthals who occupied the site. ●

REFERENCE: Paul Goldberg and Richard Macphail. (2006). *Practical and Theoretical Geoarchaeology*. Malden, MA: Blackwell.

FIGURE 4.20 Micromorphology thin section taken from the hearth deposits of Kebara Cave. The black areas are charcoal, and the white streaks are the remains of ash.

Discovering the Past: Understanding the Neanderthal Way of Life

BY ARIANE BURKE, UNIVERSITÉ DE MONTRÉAL

As a palaeoanthropologist, I study early hominis. My research focuses on understanding the Neanderthal way of life. Our closest relatives among the hominins, Neanderthals existed from about 300,000 years ago until just over 30,000 years ago. Physically dissimilar to us in some ways and remarkably like us in others, the Neanderthals ranged from western Europe to central Asia, living in regions uninhabited by modern humans until comparatively recently. They left behind an archaeological record that gives us few clues as to the reasons for their disappearance—but the spread of modern human populations into northern Eurasia, coinciding with the onset of full glacial conditions (Marine Isotope Stage 2), are likely factors in their extinction.

I am currently conducting an archaeological survey of the Sado river basin in Alentejo province (Portugal). From a European perspective, the Iberian Peninsula is an interesting region to study given its geographical proximity to Africa. Theoretically, hominins could have migrated from Africa into western Europe by crossing the straits of Gibraltar into Iberia—a comparatively short, albeit dangerous, sea crossing. The dis-covery of the earliest known western European hominins at Gran Dolina (Atapuerca, Spain) is seen by some researchers as indirect support for a hypothesis of Palaeolithic dispersals across the straits of Gibraltar. However, there is conspicuously little direct proof of either population exchange or cultural contact between Iberian and North African populations during the Palaeolithic.

Another curious feature of the Palaeolithic record of the Iberian Peninsula is that Neanderthal populations persisted there until comparatively recently—well after the time modern humans, bearing Aurignacian technology, had established themselves everywhere else in Europe. The Iberian Peninsula is emerging as a key region for the study of the dynamics of population replacement during the Late Pleistocene; for this reason, I am conducting basic fieldwork in Portugal in an effort to help build our inventory of Middle Palaeolithic sites in southern Iberia.

The target area for the survey is the Sado basin (Baixo Alentejo). The Sado basin is a tertiary basin some 7,640 km^2 in area, with an average altitude of 200–250 metres above sea level. Much of the landscape in the Sado basin is open and readily surveyed. Pine plantations are common in the north of the survey area, replaced by extensive olive plantations and grainfields in the south. Over the course of the first three years of the project, we have randomly surveyed river terraces of Miocene, Plio-Pleistocene, and Pleistocene age, and systematically surveyed small bodies of water ("lagõas") that have formed in the paleogenic deposits in the southern part of the region as well as primary raw material sources.

Survey teams consist of students from Portuguese and Canadian universities and seasoned archaeologists who work in groups of three to five, walking parallel transects approximately 5 metres apart, equipped with WAAS-enabled GPS units. We automatically record tracks and individually record archaeological finds as waypoints before collecting them. We upload the GPS data to a laptop at the end of each day and use MapSource to post-process the information. We retain tracks and waypoints, recording the distances covered by each operator and the location of archaeological materials. We then save these data in a format compatible with ArcGIS 9.2 before uploading them to the GIS. Finally, we merge the

Neanderthal base camps were apparently modest encampments that included central living areas with hearths and peripheral areas that were used as dumps. There is no evidence that the hearths were maintained or constructed. One significant complication in the study of Neanderthal cave sites is that the caves were shared (although not at the same time) by Neanderthals, hyenas, and, in some cases, cave bears. Distinguishing which aspects of the bone assemblage are the results of Neanderthal activity is critical.

■ Treatment of the Dead

The discovery of intact Neanderthal skeletons in cave sites rapidly led archaeologists to conclude that Neanderthals buried their dead, in turn leading to speculation that

data by survey area and project them onto digitally stored topographic maps to visually check the day's work. This ensures that we can calculate survey intensity and coverage, as well as the number and location of artifacts and their relative density.

Preliminary results of the project indicate that the Sado basin was definitely occupied by Neanderthals. Most of the lithic material recovered points to a Middle Palaeolithic occupation of the region. Artifacts are primarily made of jasper and quartz; initially present as veins in bedrock, these raw materials are well represented in the Sado basin in the form of cobbles in secondary deposits. It seems likely that these secondary deposits were being exploited by Palaeolithic people. Primary deposits of jasper have also been identified throughout the study region and are being systematically surveyed. A Levallois chipping station located near a jasper vein indicates that Neanderthal people may have been aware of the location of these primary sources.

We have identified Middle Palaeolithic sites and localities in a variety of contexts, including river terraces, jasper sources, and the margins of several small lakes. Lithic densities are low, but material has been recovered from almost all of the areas surveyed, indicating fairly generalized use of the landscape. The next step in the project will be to complete a geomorphological model for the target region and correlate it with the distribution of surface finds to design the second phase of the survey.

Eventually, we hope to model land-use strategies over time during the Middle and Upper Palaeolithic in the survey region, so that we can use comparisons to reveal clues about the disappearance of Neanderthals in southern Iberia. ▲

FIGURE 4.21   Survey team at work.

the Neanderthals had a concept of an afterlife. Although in many cases the evidence for Neanderthal burial can be questioned (Gargett 1989), in a number of instances it is clear that the corpse was placed into a pit dug into the ground. Particularly clear evidence was found at Kebara Cave, where the outline of the burial pit could be traced stratigraphically. Moreover, if Neanderthals were not burying their dead, it is hard to understand why complete skeletons are recovered with no evidence of disturbance by scavengers.

At Kebara Cave, the burial pit is shallow and there is no evidence of any ritual beyond placing the body in the pit. More extravagant claims, however, have been made about a number of other sites. One such claim asserts that a Neanderthal at Shanidar Cave, Iraq, was buried with flowers (Leroi-Gourhan 1975). The claim is

FIGURE 4.22 The Amud Neanderthal child with an associated deer maxilla.

based on an analysis of pollen recovered from soil collected near the skeleton. However, significant questions remain about the association of the soil with the skeleton and the source of the pollen.

One of the few sites to have produced detailed evidence of an object deliberately buried with a Neanderthal is **Amud Cave**, Israel (Hovers et al. 2000). At Amud Cave, a Neanderthal infant was found in a natural niche in the side of the cave, together with the upper jaw (maxilla) of a red deer resting against the child's pelvis (see Figure 4.22). The excavators carefully considered the possibility that the bone was beside the infant simply by chance. After all, the child was found in a site full of animal bones and stone tools. However, the excavators concluded that such a scenario was undermined by the fact that this maxilla was the only such specimen found on the site, despite the fact that deer bones were common. They thought it an extremely unlikely coincidence that a unique specimen would appear in a clear burial context and concluded that the maxilla had been placed with the infant deliberately. The excavators did not speculate on the meaning of this gesture.

On the basis of the evidence from sites such as Kebara Cave and Amud Cave, it appears that Neanderthals did at times bury their dead in small pits, perhaps placing objects in the pits with the deceased. However, such a reverent approach to the dead is not always found on Neanderthal sites. Analyses of the Neanderthal skeletal remains from the sites of Moula-Guercy, France, and Krapina, Croatia, show clear evidence of cannibalism (see Figure 4.23 on page 117). The Moula-Guercy Neanderthal remains had been treated like all other animal bones. Evidence of butchery includes cut marks from defleshing and percussion marks from smashing the bones to obtain marrow (Defleur et al. 1999).

■ Artwork

There is currently no known artwork from Neanderthal archaeological sites. Occasionally, archaeologists have claimed to have found bones with signs of incisions. However, in every case it has been shown that the incisions were the result of gnawing by carnivores or some other natural process. One of the most spectacular recent claims was about a cave bear bone with two holes in it found at the site of Divje Babe I Cave in Slovenia. The claim was that the bone had been fashioned to be a musical instrument, perhaps a flute. However, a comparison of the bone in question with others from a natural accumulation of cave bear bones shows that similar holes can occur as the result of gnawing by carnivores. Thus, it is unlikely that the piece was actually manufactured by Neanderthals.

There is evidence that Neanderthals used mineral colours. On a number of Neanderthal sites, small blocks of red ochre and black manganese are found in archaeological contexts. Some of these pieces show clear signs of scraping by a stone tool. The function of these colourants remains an enigma, as no painted objects have ever been found. Some scientists have speculated that the Neanderthals would have painted their bodies or even practised tattooing.

■ Neanderthal Society

If Glynn Isaac's model is correct, then the existence of Neanderthal base camps suggests that Neanderthals, like modern hunter–gatherers, lived in societies

▲▲ **Amud Cave** The location where a Neanderthal child was found buried with the upper jaw of a red deer.

characterized by sharing. Certainly, there is no evidence from Neanderthal sites of any markers of status or wealth. There is also almost no evidence at all, with the exception of the possible grave offering at Amud, of any kind of ritual object.

Understanding the structure of Neanderthal societies remains difficult. Although some evidence of reverence toward the dead exists in the form of burial, there are also clear cases of cannibalism. We can say little about gender roles in Neanderthal societies or about how a social hierarchy was established. The studies of stone tool manufacture do show that technical knowledge was passed between generations and that there is a persistence through time in local traditions of tool manufacture. Whether this translates into ethnicity is questionable. We know of no objects with which Neanderthals could have displayed their group identity. Whether the colourants found on Neanderthal sites were used for such a purpose is a matter of speculation.

There is no clear basis for determining Neanderthal group size; however, the overall sense is that, given the small size of most sites, the groups occupying them must have been relatively small as well. What is striking is that while many sites are quite small, they show signs of intensive activity. In cave sites, this activity led to the buildup of deep stratigraphic deposits. One possibility is that Neanderthals were far more sedentary than modern human hunter–gatherers. Perhaps the reason the cave sites show such a buildup of sediments is that they were inhabited continuously. Such a pattern of occupation would be in sharp contrast to the high-mobility strategies practised by recent hunter–gatherer groups.

Looking at the remains of small animals from the site of Hayonim Cave, Israel, Mary Stiner came up with an ingenious method of exploring Neanderthal group size and mobility (Stiner et al. 1999). Stiner found that Neanderthals at Hayonim Cave ate certain tortoises that were easy to collect, but that matured slowly. Surprisingly, she found that the tortoises consumed were quite large and did not exhibit the reduction in size that would take place with heavy exploitation. On the basis of her observations, Stiner suggests that Neanderthal populations were "exceptionally small and that [they]. . . did not spend much time foraging in any one vicinity" (Stiner et al. 1999, 193). If there had been large populations or permanent settlements, one would expect to see more of an impact on the tortoises. Stiner's results appear to contradict the picture of Neanderthals as quasi-sedentary hunter–gatherers, showing them instead as highly mobile hunter–gatherers living at an extremely low population density.

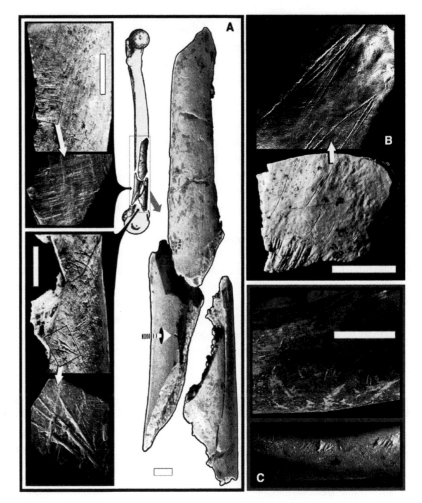

FIGURE 4.23 Evidence for Neanderthal cannabalism from the site of Moula-Guercy, France. A: Cut marks and percussion marks on a femur, indicating that the bone was defleshed before being smashed on an anvil for access to marrow. B: Cut marks on a skull fragment. C: Cut marks on a juvenile Neanderthal jaw (above) and a red deer jaw (below), showing similarities in butchery. Scale bars equal 1 centimetre.

SUMMARY

- Global climate during the Pleistocene fluctuated between glacial and interglacial episodes. The fluctuations are recorded in the Oxygen Isotope Curve.
- The earliest evidence of human occupation of Western Europe is the TD-6 Level of the Gran Dolina site at Atapuerca, which is dated to 800,000 years ago.
- The Eurasian Acheulian is found across Europe, the Middle East, and the Indian subcontinent beginning 500,000 years ago. With the exception of Bose, China, there is little evidence of Acheulian sites east of India.
- There is little evidence of artwork or human burial during the Lower Paleolithic.
- Neanderthals share many features with modern humans, including a large brain size. There are also distinctive Neanderthal features, many of which are adaptations to cold weather.
- The pattern of similarities and differences between modern humans and Neanderthals has led to debate over the evolutionary relationship between the two groups. The main question is whether there was gene flow between populations of modern humans in Africa and populations of Neanderthals in Europe or whether the two populations were two distinct species that evolved in isolation from *Homo erectus* or an intermediary species.
- Neanderthals occupied sites over a wide range of ecological settings, including fully glacial and interglacial Europe.
- There is clear evidence that Neanderthals hunted large animals. Stable-isotope analysis indicates that meat was a major component of the Neanderthal diet.
- Neanderthal sites have no constructed features; however, evidence of the intensive use of fire is often found.
- Analysis of variability in Middle Paleolithic stone tool assemblages have produced a wide range of interpretations.
- Neanderthals appear to have buried their dead in some cases and practised cannibalism in others. At one site, there is evidence that a Neanderthal child was buried with the jaw of a red deer.
- There is no evidence of Neanderthal (Middle Paleolithic) artwork.

KEY TERMS

Amud Cave, 116
Beeches Pit, 98
Biache-Saint-Vaast, 103
Bose, 94
Boxgrove, 95
Clactonian, 96
Eurasian Acheulian, 95
Frison effect, 107
Gesher Benot Ya'akov, 95
Gran Dolina, Atapuerca, 94

Kebara Cave, 112
La Cotte de St. Brelade, 109
Levallois method, 108
Mezmaiskaya Cave, 103
Middle Paleolithic, 105
Oxygen Isotope Curve, 94
Pleistocene, 92
prepared-core technology, 105
Schöningen, 99
Zhoukoudian, 97

REVIEW QUESTIONS

1. What are the three theories of Neanderthal phylogeny? Which view does the DNA evidence from Neanderthal fossils support?

2. How do the results of archaeological research affect our understanding of Neanderthals?

3. Why are Middle Paleolithic stone tools the subject of intense debate among archaeologists?

CANADIAN ARCHAEOLOGISTS

- Michael Bisson, professor in the Department of Anthropology at McGill University has published extensively on the archaeology of Neanderthals and early modern humans. His current field research is on the Middle Paleolithic in northern Jordan.
http://www.mcgill.ca/anthropology/faculty/fulltime/michael_bisson/

- Ariane Burke, professor in the Department of Anthropology at the Université de Montréal, specializes in the archaeology of Neanderthals. She studies the faunal remains from Middle Paleolithic sites, including research projects in France and the Crimea. She now directs a field survey project in Portugal.
http://myprofile.cos.com/burkea89

- April Nowell, professor in the Department of Anthropology at the University of Victoria, has published widely on the evolution of cognitive capacity in the hominin lineage, including the edited volume *In the Mind's Eye: Multidisciplinary Approaches to the Evolution of Human Cognition* (International Monographs in Prehistory, 2001).
http://anthropology.uvic.ca/people/faculty/nowell.php

- Lucy Wilson is a professor of Geology at the University of New Brunswick (Saint John) with expertise in the sourcing of the raw materials used in stone tool manufacture. She has applied this expertise to the study of the way Neanderthal populations in southern France moved around the landscape. She has also carried out similar studies on prehistoric sites in the Maritimes.
http://www.unbsj.ca/sase/biology/gradstudies/geoarchaeology.htm

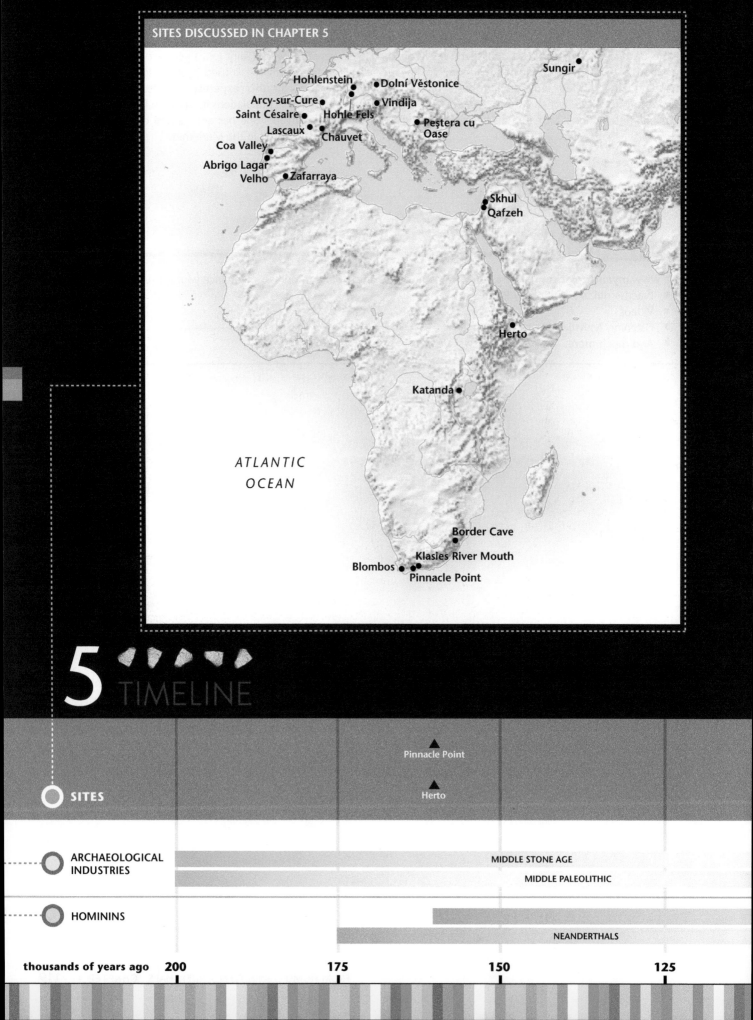

SITES DISCUSSED IN CHAPTER 5

Sungir

Hohlenstein
Dolní Věstonice
Arcy-sur-Cure
Vindija
Saint Césaire
Hohle Fels
Lascaux
Chauvet
Peştera cu Oase
Coa Valley
Abrigo Lagar
Velho
Zafarraya
Skhul
Qafzeh

Herto

Katanda

ATLANTIC
OCEAN

Border Cave
Klasies River Mouth
Blombos
Pinnacle Point

5 TIMELINE

SITES

Pinnacle Point

Herto

ARCHAEOLOGICAL
INDUSTRIES

MIDDLE STONE AGE

MIDDLE PALEOLITHIC

HOMININS

NEANDERTHALS

thousands of years ago   200   175   150   125

THE ORIGIN OF MODERN HUMANS

Modern humans first appeared in Africa between 200,000 and 100,000 years ago and replaced Neanderthals in Europe between 40,000 and 27,000 years ago. The arrival of modern humans in Europe was marked by a dramatic change in material culture known as the Middle to Upper Paleolithic Transition.

After reading this chapter, you should understand:

- The chronological and archaeological relationiship between Neanderthals and modern humans in the Middle East.

- The major characteristics of the Middle Stone Age.

- The three main models for the replacement of Neanderthals by modern humans.

- The major characteristics of the Upper Paleolithic.

The view from Klasies River Mouth, South Africa.

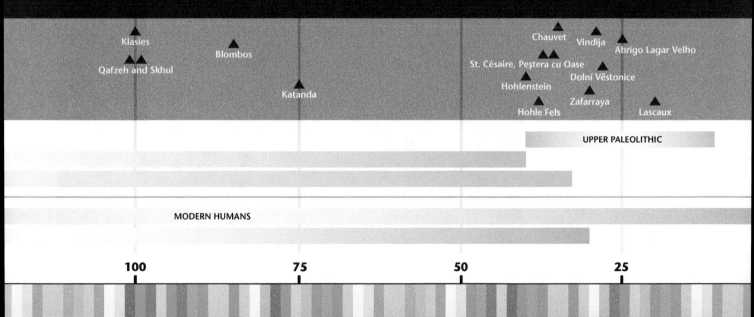

Klasies

Qafzeh and Skhul

Blombos

Katanda

Chauvet   Vindija

Abrigo Lagar Velho

St. Césaire, Peştera cu Oase

Dolní Věstonice

Hohlenstein

Zafarraya

Hohle Fels

Lascaux

UPPER PALEOLITHIC

MODERN HUMANS

100   75   50   25

modern humans Members of the species *Homo sapiens*, which includes all living humans.

Homo sapiens The species name for modern humans.

A visit to Lascaux Cave in southwestern France begins with a descent into inky blackness. Visitors, limited to a small number in order to preserve the cave, are asked to dip their feet into a pan filled with disinfectant and are then ushered through a door into a chamber shrouded in darkness, where they wait until the guide is ready. A switch is thrown, and in the dazzle of newly erupting light, all eyes are drawn upward to gaze in awe at scenes of massive bulls painted onto the cave walls 15,000 years ago. The wonder of Lascaux Cave is so powerful that it stuns even the most jaded (see Figure 5.1). One feels an instinctive connection to the people who shared our drive to represent the world—to make art of our experience. How did humanity move from the age of *Homo erectus* and Neanderthals to the explosion of creativity found on the walls of Lascaux Cave? This question has both inspired and vexed archaeologists for close to a century as they have struggled to understand the origin of modern humans and the fate of Neanderthals.

We begin this chapter with an examination of the biological definition of modern humans. We then move to Africa to trace the earliest evidence for modern human fossils and explore what archaeology can tell us about these earliest members of our species. Next, we pause to consider the relationship between modern humans and Neanderthals in the Middle East before continuing on to Europe and the momentous question of the last Neanderthals. We will then be in a position to consider the revolution in human culture that led to the painted cave of Lascaux.

5.1 What Is a Modern Human?

The term **modern human** refers to all members of the biological species ***Homo sapiens***, including all living humans. On both genetic and anatomical grounds, some authors argue that the similarity among human populations requires that all humans be included under a single subspecies, *Homo sapiens sapiens*. Studies of the genetic diversity of living humans indicate a very low degree of species diversity. Most of the genetic variation within living humans is found within members of a single population rather than between populations. The low genetic variation within modern humans reflects a relatively recent common ancestry.

FIGURE 5.1 A panoramic view of Lascaux Cave, France.

Characteristics of the skull that distinguish modern humans from earlier species include a large brain (1200–1700 cc), a globular braincase, a vertical forehead, reduced brow ridges, and a pronounced chin. Teeth tend to be smaller. Modern human bodies have a reduced body mass, a narrow trunk, and a unique pelvic shape. There is, of course, considerable variability among living humans, both as individuals and as populations; however, the anatomical traits that define *Homo sapiens* are characteristic of all living human populations.

5.2 Early Modern Humans in Africa

Modern humans first appeared in Africa between 200,000 and 100,000 years ago, during Oxygen Isotope Stages 6–3. The oldest known fossils clearly ascribed to *Homo sapiens* were discovered in the Middle Awash region of Ethiopia (White et al. 2003). At the **Herto** site, an adult skull, a partial juvenile skull, and a fragmentary adult skull were found eroding out of a level argon dated between 160,000 and 154,000 years ago (see Figure 5.2). The complete skull has a large brain, 1,450 cubic centimetres, and lacks any of the specialized traits that characterize Neanderthals. The skull has been placed within its own subspecies, *Homo sapiens idaltu*, because it retains some traits from *Homo erectus* not found among later modern humans.

Fragments of fossils that are clearly modern humans have also been found in South Africa at the sites of **Klasies River Mouth** and **Border Cave** (Deacon and Deacon 1999). In both cases, the fossils are dated to between 70,000 and 120,000 years ago. The collection of fossils from Klasies River Mouth includes bits of a skull, a jaw, an arm, and a foot. The morphology of all these fossils fits within the range for modern humans.

■ The African Middle Stone Age

The Acheulian industries in Africa were replaced between 300,000 and 200,000 years ago by a group of industries known as the **Middle Stone Age**. The Middle Stone Age, which ended roughly 40,000 years ago, is the archaeological context for the earliest modern humans.

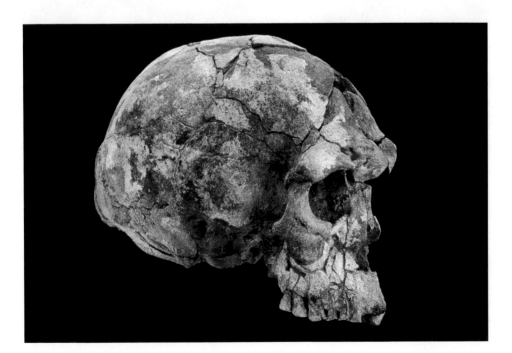

▲▲ Herto A site in Ethiopia where the oldest known fossil of a modern human was discovered, dating to between 160,000 and 154,000 years ago.

▲▲ Klasies River Mouth A Middle Age site in South Africa that has produced remains of modern humans and that offers evidence of hunting and the intensive use of fire.

▲▲ Border Cave One of the South African sites where fossils of modern humans dated to between 120,000 and 70,000 years ago were discovered.

Middle Stone Age The archaeological period of the earliest modern humans in Africa. The Middle Stone Age began between 300,000 and 200,000 years ago and ended around 40,000 years ago.

FIGURE 5.2 The Herto fossil. The significant features demonstrating that this is a modern human include the rounded form of the skull and the absence of forward projection in the face.

Aterian A North African stone tool industry distinguished by the presence of points with a pronounced tang—a small projection located at the base of the point and used to secure the point to a spear handle.

Sangoan/Lupemban A Middle Stone Age industry found in Central and East Africa. Characterized by very crude heavy-duty tools, the Sangoan/Lupemban might be indicative of an adaptation to a heavily wooded environment.

Howiesons Poort A Middle Stone Age industry found in southern Africa that is characterized by small crescent-shaped stone tools.

Katanda A Middle Stone Age site in the Democratic Republic of Congo where bone harpoons have been found.

STONE TOOLS. The technology of stone tool manufacture in the Middle Stone Age in Africa has many similarities to that of the European Middle Paleolithic. For example, it is now recognized that the Levallois method was widely used in Africa during the Middle Stone Age. However, when one looks at the African continent as a whole, it becomes evident that the Middle Stone Age includes a greater degree of variation than is found in the Middle Paleolithic. Also, types of tools are found in the Middle Stone Age that are absent from the Middle Paleolithic.

Across Africa, a number of distinct Middle Stone Age industries have been identified (McBrearty and Brooks 2000). The **Aterian** is a North African stone tool industry distinguished by the presence of points with a pronounced tang—a small projection located at the base of the point and used to secure the point to a spear or handle. Aterian tools also include finely made bifacial tools that served as knives or hunting points.

The **Sangoan/Lupemban** is a Middle Stone Age industry found in Central and East Africa. Characterized by very crude heavy-duty tools, the Sangoan/Lupemban might be indicative of an adaptation to a heavily wooded environment.

The **Howiesons Poort** is an industry that has been identified in South Africa. Among the sites on which Howiesons Poort tools have been discovered is Klasies River Mouth. The tools found on Howiesons Poort sites include very small crescent-shaped implements known as microliths, which would have been used as part of a complex tool made by putting together a number of pieces (see Figure 5.3). The most likely function of these tools is as an element of spears or arrows.

BONE TOOLS. Katanda is a site located on cliffs overlooking the Semliki River in the Democratic Republic of Congo (Yellen et al. 1995). Dating of the site has been complicated; however, all methods agree on a date that is earlier than 75,000 years ago, and the stone tools are characteristic of the Middle Stone Age (Brooks et al. 1995). The excavations at Katanda uncovered ten remarkable barbed bone points, along with

FIGURE 5.3 Experimental hafting of Howiesons Poort microliths. Spears tipped with these types of points would have been very effective hunting tools.

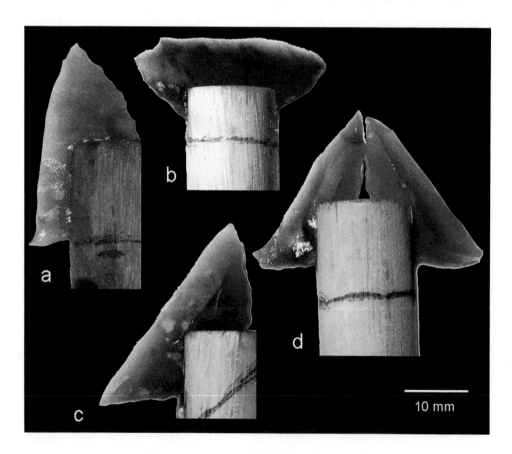

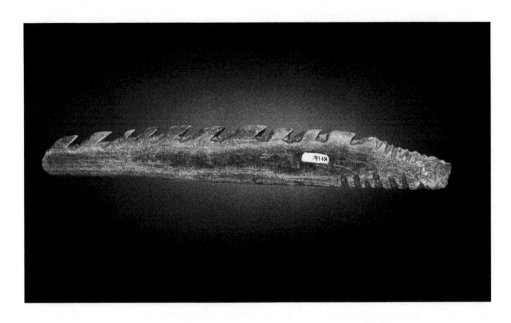

FIGURE 5.4 Bone tool from the Middle Stone Age site of Katanda. This tool has a series of barbs and incisions that appear to have been used to connect it to a haft. The length of this tool is 13 cm.

a smaller number of unbarbed bone points and one piece identified as a bone knife (see Figure 5.4). These are the oldest tools of the kind known in the world. Although barbed points are often used on harpoons, the excavators believe that the grooves on the base of the points suggest that they were mounted on spears.

Bone points have also been found in Middle Stone Age sites in South Africa. At the site of Blombos Cave, located at the southern tip of Africa, twenty-one bone tools were found, including two points and a number of awls (Henshilwood and Sealy 1997). The Middle Stone Age levels at Blombos Cave have been dated to 77,000 years ago by thermoluminescence.

ADAPTATION. The remains of large game are found on Middle Stone Age sites, where it appears that hunting took place. At Klasies River Mouth, a stone tool was found embedded in the vertebrae of a bovid. Middle Stone Age sites, including Klasies River Mouth, also show evidence of the kind of intensive use of fire documented at Kebara Cave and other Neanderthal sites.

At Klasies River Mouth and a number of other Middle Stone Age sites, large quantities of shellfish were found, along with seal bones. In contrast, the use of marine resources is rare on Neanderthal sites. At a site on the Buri peninsula on the coast of the Red Sea in Eritrea, Middle Stone Age tools were found embedded in a coral reef deposit (Walter et al. 2000). Clearly, those who wielded these tools were people living at the edge of the sea, and it is likely that they were exploiting shellfish and other marine resources. Katanda has produced impressive evidence of fishing. Among the faunal remains recovered were many bones of large catfish weighing over 35 kg. At the site of **Pinnacle Point** on the coast of South Africa there is evidence that mollusks were part of the diet as early as 160,000 years ago (Marean et al. 2007). The excavators suggest a link between this expansion of hominin diet and the harsh conditions of glacial Oxygen Isotope Stage 6. Research by Julio Mercader at the site of Ngalue, Mozambique, has produced evidence for the use of plant foods, including sorghum, during the Middle Stone Age (Mercader 2009). Mercader recovered starch grains on stone tools found in the Middle Stone Age levels at Ngalue suggesting that these tools were used to collect plants.

ART. In 1999 and 2000, two pieces of ochre with incised designs were found at **Blombos Cave**, South Africa, in a Middle Stone Age level dated to 77,000 years ago (Henshilwood et al. 2002). Ochre is a soft, red, iron-rich rock often used as a

Pinnacle Point A site on the southern coast of South Africa that has produced evidence that mollusks were part of the diet of modern humans as early as 160,000 years ago.

Blombos Cave A site in South Africa where pieces of ochre with incised decoration were found in a Middle Stone Age level dated to 77,000 years ago.

The Strange Case of the Grimaldi Figurines

MICHAEL S. BISSON, MCGILL UNIVERSITY

Little did I know that when an artist asked me to identify some sculptures he had purchased in a Montreal antique store, it would set me on a journey through one of the most mysterious and colourful episodes in nineteenth-century archaeology. Yet in winter 1993, I sat in shocked amazement as the man handed me a small sculpture of a pregnant unclothed woman, carved from ivory and obviously extremely old. The piece was similar to the many European Upper Paleolithic female figurines, inappropriately referred to as "Venus," that are generally thought to be from the Gravettian period, between about 26,000 and 23,000 years ago. There were more to come, five in all, each beautifully preserved. He also brought Upper Paleolithic stone tools, mounted on display cards signed in the elegant handwriting of a M. Louis Jullien. That evening I called Randall White, an expert on Paleolithic art, who years earlier had warned me that some missing Paleolithic sculptures might be in Montreal. The artist traced the original owners of the figurines, two granddaughters of Louis Jullien, and found two additional sculptures still in their possession. With the generous permission of the owners, White and I studied and authenticated the seven figurines. They turned out

to be from the Grimaldi Caves in Italy, and were the long-missing half of the largest assemblage of Upper Paleolithic female sculptures ever discovered in Western Europe.

Jullien was an antiquities dealer during the late nineteenth century, when the distinctions between dealers and amateur and professional archaeologists were blurred, excavations were often crude quarrying operations, record-keeping was rudimentary or nonexistent, and personal rivalries often caused fierce competition for access to the "best" sites. In 1883 and 1884, Jullien purchased a concession to dig in the Barma Grande, one of six caves on the Italian-French border that were among the richest Upper Paleolithic sites then known.

He partnered with the founder of a local museum but quit the site in a dispute over the ownership of a burial he had discovered. His letters indicate that he then began clandestine nocturnal digging in the Grotte du Prince, a large neighbouring cave owned by Albert Grimaldi I, the prince of Monaco. During these excavations, Jullien obtained a total of fifteen small stone and ivory sculptures. He sold one, the "Yellow Steatite Figurine," to the French National Museum of Antiquities (M.A.N.) in 1896, and it became the first Paleolithic female image known to science.

Although at least three sculptures came from his authorized excavations, Jullien was very secretive about the source of the others. Near the turn of the century, he sold six figurines to a French archaeologist and moved to Montreal, keeping the existence of his others a secret. His son sold one figurine to Harvard University, but after Louis Jullien's death in 1928, the remaining seven stayed hidden until 1993.

White and I were thus faced with the classic problem of trying to understand an important archaeological collection for which there was almost no reliable contextual information. We studied 379 stone tools collected by Jullien in the Barma Grande and bought by McGill University and the Peabody Museum, but almost none were marked in terms of depth below surface, a problem since the archaeological deposits were over 8 metres thick! Typologically, those collections suggest that most of the Barma Grande sequence corresponded to the Arenian and Epigravettian technological traditions, the Italian equivalents of the French Solutrean and Magdalenian, but some Barma Grande collections in Europe show that Mousterian, Aurignacian, and Gravettian components were also present. Given the lack of records, and the fact that many of Jullien's artifacts were sold to

pigment. More than 8,000 pieces of ochre, many with traces of use, have been found in the Middle Stone Age levels at Blombos Cave.

As shown in Figure 5.6 (see page 128), the pieces of incised ochre are small—between 5 and 7 centimetres long. The incisions are a set of hatched lines on one face of the piece. These modest artifacts are the earliest evidence in the archaeological record of a hominin marking a pattern. Incisions have been found on thirteen other pieces of ochre at Blombos in levels dating back as far as 100,000 years ago (Henshilwood et al. 2009). These remaining pieces are either fragments or lacking in clear patterns.

tourists, we will never know the exact makeup of the site.

Dating the figurines has also been a problem. It has been long assumed that most Upper Paleolithic female sculptures were Gravettian, and there was a Gravettian component in the Barma Grande. This was recently confirmed by a radiocarbon date of 25,000 years ago from a human skeleton found by a later digger near the base of the Upper Paleolithic deposits at the back of the cave. However, one of Jullien's letters provided depth measurements for two of the figurines, including the "Yellow Steatite" and the one that seems typically "Gravettian" in form. That figurine came from 4.2 to 4.8 m below the surface, and another from above that. Since a skeleton thought to be Gravettian was found by Jullien at 8.43 m below the surface, then the figurine was at least 3.5 m above it and thus from substantially later in time. Our radiocarbon dates for animal bones that Jullien had labelled 8 m and 6 to 6.5 m below surface were between 17,000 and 19,500 years old. In my opinion, most if not all the Grimaldi figurines are less than 20,000 years old, although some European colleagues strenuously disagree.

Understanding the meaning of Paleolithic art is notoriously difficult. The fifteen Grimaldi figurines are highly varied in both form and raw material, although most do share some fundamental characteristics. First, they are very small, with an average length of under 6 centimetres. Of the twelve full-body statuettes, all could have been suspended (six were perforated for that purpose) and were probably personal property worn on the body. Ten of the eleven complete specimens are female, nine of which are depicted as pregnant, and eight show a dilated vulva or an emerging baby. Their primary referent is probably the early stages of childbirth, a particularly dangerous moment for both baby and mother. Although proof will never be possible, I suspect that these figurines were produced by female shamans or midwives who employed them as amulets not for fertility but to ensure the health and safety of mothers during delivery. In Ice Age societies, the survival of a productive adult was probably more important than any individual child.

The Grimaldi figurines are an early example of the irreparable harm caused by the commercial artifact trade and how much information can be lost when archaeologists fail to record the context of their finds. Hopefully a century from now, future archaeologists will not have as much trouble working with the collections we make today. ▲

FIGURE 5.5 The "Yellow Steatite Figurine."

But what are these objects? The Blombos Cave artifacts have received considerable attention as the earliest evidence of human artwork or symbolic behaviour. *Symbolic behaviour* suggests that these artifacts are meant to represent something, while *artwork* implies that the incisions to the artifacts were made with an aesthetic goal in mind. This is a lot of baggage for a series of lines scratched into small pieces of ochre. Untangling the significance of the simple pattern of lines found at Blombos Cave remains one of the most difficult challenges facing Paleolithic archaeologists. Pieces similar to the Blombos ochre have been found at the site of Klein Kliphuis, South Africa, which is tentatively dated between 80,000 and 50,000 years ago

FIGURE 5.6 One of the incised pieces of ochre from Blombos. This photograph shows all of the sides of this piece. The incised pattern is limited to one narrow face (third from the top).

1 cm

(McKay and Welz 2008). At Pinnacle Point, pieces of ground ochre have been found in the level dated to 160,000 years ago, although the incisions on these pieces lack the clear patterns shown in the ones from Blombos (Marean et al. 2007). Taken together, these discoveries place the Blombos incised ochre in a broader context but do not resolve the questions surrounding these artifacts.

A collection of pierced shells was also found at Blombos Cave. Pierced objects have been reported from a number of Aterian sites in North Africa, and a number of late Middle Stone Age sites are reported to have included beads. A particularly interesting discovery is a painted slab with the depiction of an animal, found in the Apollo 11 Cave in Namibia. The slab is reported to come from a Middle Stone Age context, but the date provided is between 26,000 and 28,000 years ago, which raises some questions about this attribution.

■ Comparing the Middle Stone Age and the Middle Paleolithic

A comparison of the Middle Stone Age archaeological record left by modern humans in Africa with the Middle Paleolithic record left by Neanderthals in Europe points to both similarities and differences. As regards the similarities, in both cases (1) stone tools were made mostly by using a prepared core technology, (2) there is variability between stone tool industries, and (3) evidence supports both hunting and the intensive use of fire. One difference is that the amount of variability in the Middle Stone Age stone tool industries is greater than that of their Middle Paleolithic counterparts. Another is that in the Middle Stone Age there are elaborate bone tools, as well as clear evidence of fishing and collecting shellfish, two elements that are rare in the Middle Paleolithic. Finally, there is modest evidence of artwork in the Middle Stone Age, while such evidence is absent in the Middle Paleolithic.

The significance of the differences between the Middle Stone Age and the Middle Paleolithic remains elusive. Why didn't Neanderthals make bone tools? Carving a point out of bone appears no more complicated than chipping a point from flint. And what is the meaning of the shellfish and fish remains found on Middle Stone Age sites? Why didn't Neanderthals exploit similar resources wherever they were available in Europe? The Blombos incised ochre is clearly important, but do these small pieces with their simple abstract design truly mark the entrance of humanity into the realm of symbolism?

5.3 Early Modern Humans in the Middle East

The Middle East is the crossroads of the continents, lying at the geographic intersection of Europe, Asia, and Africa. As a result, the Middle East plays a critical role in research on the origin of modern humans. Middle Stone Age modern humans in Africa were contemporaneous with European Middle Paleolithic Neanderthals.

The critical problem is determining what happened in the region where these two populations might have overlapped and coexisted.

Excavations at **Qafzeh Cave**, located in the hills of northern Israel just outside of Nazareth, uncovered a number of skeletons in Middle Paleolithic levels (Vandermeersch 1981). Although, from their context, one might expect that these bones would be the skeletons of Neanderthals, as was the case at other Middle Paleolithic sites in the region, the Qafzeh skeletons are modern humans. A similar discovery was made at **Skhul Cave** on the Mediterranean coast. The Skhul and Qafzeh discoveries raise several critical questions. The first question is whether there are characteristics that distinguish the archaeological remains found on these sites from the remains found on Neanderthal sites. The second question is what the chronological relationship is between Neanderthals and modern humans.

■ The Archaeological Record

Surprisingly, there is little that distinguishes the archaeological material found at Qafzeh and Skhul from the remains found on Neanderthal sites in the Middle East—sites such as Kebara Cave, Tabun Cave, and Amud Cave in Israel; Shanidar Cave in Iraq; and Dederiyeh Cave in Syria. Both Neanderthals and modern humans made stone tools typical of the Middle Paleolithic, often using the Levallois method. Neither group produced bone tools or very much in the way of art; the only exception is a piece of flint with an incised pattern found at Qafzeh cave. Both groups buried their dead in shallow pits with little in the way of burial goods. The discovery of a deer maxilla with a Neanderthal child at Amud is paralleled by the placement of a deer antler in a burial of a modern human at Qafzeh and a boar jaw found with a modern human buried at Skhul. Both groups lived in small sites where evidence indicates the extensive use of fire.

■ Chronology

Although the Middle Paleolithic cave sites in the Middle East all have deep stratigraphic sequences, none have produced fossils of both modern humans and Neanderthals. Thus, the chronological relationship between Neanderthals and modern humans in the region cannot be determined on the basis of stratigraphy. Until the 1980s, there was no method for dating the sites, and the general sense was that the Neanderthal sites must be early ones, and that Skhul and Qafzeh, with their modern human fossils, must be more recent. Many paleoanthropologists believed that modern humans likely had evolved from Neanderthals; therefore, Neanderthal sites must be earlier than modern human sites. With the development of electron spin resonance and thermoluminescence dating methods in the 1980s, it finally became possible to date the Middle Paleolithic cave sites (see Toolbox on page 130). The results came as a shock: Skhul and Qafzeh date from between 120,000 and 80,000 years ago, while most of the Neanderthal sites produced dates that cluster in the range between 60,000 and 50,000 years ago (Valladas et al. 1988).

■ Assessing the Middle Eastern Pattern

The Middle Paleolithic of the Middle East confounds our expectation of the relationship between Neanderthals and modern humans. There is no obvious difference in the behaviour and technology of modern humans and Neanderthals living in the Middle East during the period between Oxygen Isotope Stages 5 and 3. As far as the current state of our knowledge goes, all that separates the behaviour of these two species during that period is a single incised piece of flint. But what is even more puzzling is that the fossils of modern humans are actually older than those of Neanderthals.

The Middle Eastern sequence provides clear evidence that Neanderthals were not a primitive precursor of modern humans, but rather a population that evolved parallel to them. Geographically, the Middle East is located between the European

▲▲ **Qafzeh Cave** One of the sites in Israel where modern human skeletons were found in a Middle Paleolithic context.

▲▲ **Skhul Cave** One of the Middle Paleolithic sites in Israel where modern human skeletons have been found.

TOOLBOX

Luminescence Dating

Luminescence dating methods are critical for the study of the later stages of human evolution. The luminescence methods that are most widely used are thermoluminescence (TL), electron spin resonance (ESR), and optically stimulated luminescence. Thermoluminescence dates burnt stone tools made of flint, electron spin resonance dates animal teeth, and optically stimulated luminescence (OSL) dates either quartz or feldspar grains in sediments.

All minerals consist of atoms and molecules arranged in a three-dimensional lattice known as a crystal. Inevitably, flaws arise within the structure of a crystal. These flaws serve as traps that accumulate electrons over time. The rate at which electrons are trapped is a function of the natural background radiation. The rate at which electrons are accumulated in a year is known as the annual dose rate and is specific to a given locality. Thus, every time one uses a luminescence dating method, the annual dose rate at the precise location of the find must be measured. The annual dose rate can be measured with a tool called a dosimeter.

When a sample of a mineral is heated, the trapped light energy, or luminescence, is driven out of the crystals. The amount of this energy can be measured precisely. The measure of the trapped luminescence is known as the accumulated dose. If one knows the accumulated dose and the annual dose rate, it is fairly simple to divide the accumulated dose rate by the annual dose rate to determine how long the mineral has been accumulating light energy.

The problem is that crystals begin trapping energy the moment they are formed. Thus, as with argon dating, the critical factor is finding a mechanism that zeroes the clock at exactly the point in time one is interested in dating.

Thermoluminescence dating of flint is based on the observation that heating flint to between 400 and 600 degrees centigrade effectively drives off the accumulated energy, thus resetting the clock to zero. After the rock is heated to a temperature in that range, the crystals again begin to accumulate energy at the annual dose rate. When one finds a stone tool that was burnt, the equation accumulated dose rate divided by the annual dose rate will provide a measure of the date when the tool was burnt. If one is confident that the burning took place at the time the site was inhabited, usually as the result of the tool falling into a fire, then the foregoing equation yields a date for the occupation of the site. Fortunately, beginning in the Middle Stone Age and the Middle Paleolithic, burnt stone tools are common on archaeological sites.

Thermoluminescence can also be used for more recent periods to date the manufacture of pottery. The principle in the dating of pottery is that firing a ceramic vessel effectively zeroes the clock. Thermoluminescence dating of pottery has been particularly useful in detecting forged artifacts.

---

range of the Neanderthals and the African range of early modern humans. In ecological terms, the range of Neanderthals was centred in Eurasia, the range of modern humans in Africa. In periods when the Neanderthal range expanded, Neanderthal remains are found in the Middle East. When the modern human range expanded out of Africa, fossils of modern humans are found in the Middle East. There is no evidence that the modern human range expanded into Europe earlier than 60,000 years ago. However, around 40,000 years ago, Neanderthals became extinct in the Middle East as part of a process that swept modern humans into Europe.

5.4 The Arrival of Modern Humans in Europe and the Fate of the Neanderthals

Extinction is an integral element of evolution. However, when extinction strikes a member of the hominin lineage, we often struggle to understand what happened. Nowhere is this problem more acute than in the case of the Neanderthals, who disappeared from Europe between 40,000 and 27,000 years ago and were replaced by populations of modern humans. The **Upper Paleolithic** is the archaeological period that corresponds to the first occupation of Europe by modern humans.

Upper Paleolithic The archaeological period that saw the earliest occupation of Europe by modern humans.

Optically stimulated luminescence works on the same principles as thermoluminescence. Among the grains that make up most sediments are crystals of quartz and feldspar. It has been observed that exposure of these grains to sunlight effectively drives out the trapped light energy and zeroes the clock. Thus, the relationship accumulated dose rate divided by the annual dose rate produces a date for when the sediments were last exposed to the sun, thereby effectively dating the time the site was buried.

Electron spin resonance works on the same principles as thermoluminescence and optically stimulated luminescence. The main application of electron spin resonance is dating the enamel layer of teeth. Tooth enamel is made up of the mineral hydroxyapatite. Because mineral crystals form during the life of the animal, the accumulation of light energy begins when the animal is alive. The beauty of this method is that there is no need to reset the clock to zero, because the accumulation of light energy begins only at the point in time one is attempting to date. Electron spin resonance can be used on teeth covering the entire range of hominin evolution. ●

REFERENCE: R. E. Taylor and Martin J. Aitken, eds. (1997). *Chronometric Dating in Archaeology*. New York: Plenum Press.

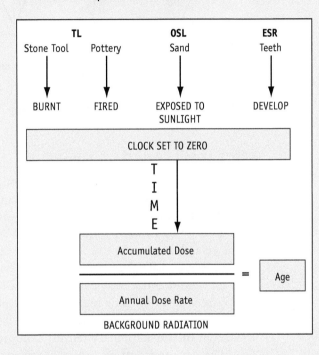

FIGURE 5.7
Luminescence dating method works on the principle of measuring the accumulated dose and dividing this by the annual dose rate to arrive at an age determination.

The **Middle to Upper Paleolithic transition** is marked by a dramatic change to material culture. Three major theories relate to the replacement of Neanderthals by modern humans in Europe (see Figure 5.8).

The *out of Africa hypothesis* argues that Neanderthal populations in Europe were replaced by invading populations of modern humans during the period between 40,000 and 30,000 years ago. The archaeological transition is the direct result of this replacement. Neanderthals were a distinct species that evolved parallel to modern humans and then became extinct.

The *hybridization hypothesis* proposes a middle ground by acknowledging the evidence for an influx of modern humans into Europe, but not accepting extinction of the Neanderthals as a result of that influx. Rather than becoming extinct, Neanderthals "disappeared" as a result of substantial interbreeding with modern humans. The archaeological transition is seen as the result of interaction between Neanderthals and modern humans.

The *multiregional hypothesis* is rooted in the idea that beginning with the first spread of *Homo erectus* out of Africa, there was continuous gene flow between populations. Therefore, positing Neanderthals as a discrete, isolated species is an artificial rendering of their lineage. Neanderthals evolved locally into modern humans as the result of a continuous gene flow between European and African populations. The

Middle to Upper Paleolithic transition The archaeological period that saw the appearance of modern humans in Europe. It includes the development of new types of stone and bone tools and the dramatic appearance of a wide range of symbolic artifacts.

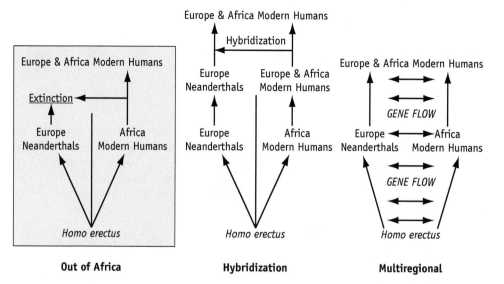

FIGURE 5.8 Three scenarios for the fate of the Neanderthals.

Out of Africa

Hybridization

Multiregional

multiregional hypothesis sees the Middle to Upper Paleolithic transition not as a local European phenomenon but rather as part of a global process in the evolution of modern humans.

■ The Fossil Record

The fossil evidence appears to increasingly support the out of Africa position. Early fossils of modern humans have now been found in Africa at Klasies River Mouth and Herto. In Europe, there is no tendency toward modern human traits within late Neanderthal populations. The skeleton of a Neanderthal discovered at **St. Césaire** in France and dated to 36,000 years ago by thermoluminescence is in every sense a classic Neanderthal (Day 1986). The earliest well-dated modern human remains from Europe are those of a jawbone found in **Peştera cu Oase Cave** in Romania (Trinkaus et al. 2003). This mandible was collected by spelunkers among the scattered bones of cave bears. The mandible itself has been dated to 36,000 years ago by accelerator mass spectrometry (AMS) radiocarbon dating.

The persistence of Neanderthal traits poses an immense problem for proponents of the multiregional hypothesis. This evidence is not problematic for proponents of the hybridization hypothesis, who expect Neanderthal traits to have persisted until there was an influx of modern humans. The hybrid hypothesis predicts that after the influx of modern humans there would be skeletons that show a mixture of Neanderthal and modern human traits. Such hybrid skeletons would be evidence of Neanderthal and modern human interbreeding.

The difficulty with the hybrid hypothesis is that there is little agreement about how to identify a hybrid skeleton. A particularly important case is the skeleton of a child discovered in Portugal at the site of **Abrigo Lagar Velho** (Duarte et al. 1999). Dating to 24,500 years ago, the skeleton was found with Upper Paleolithic tools. The analysis of the skeleton led a group of paleoanthropologists to conclude that it presents "a mosaic of European early modern human and Neanderthal features. . . . This mosaic indicates a mixture between regional Neanderthals and early modern humans" (Duarte et al. 2003, 7604). However, this assessment was rapidly contested by two paleoanthropologists who concluded that "this is simply a chunky . . . child, a descendant of the modern invaders who had evicted the Neanderthals" (Tattersall and Schwartz 2003, 7119). Part of the difficulty with the Abrigo Lagar Velho skeleton is that it is a child. However, the fact that paleoanthropologists studying the skeleton have taken contrasting positions suggests that there is still a fundamental lack of agreement on how to identify hybridization between Neanderthals and modern humans.

▲▲ **St. Césaire** A site in France where a Neanderthal was found dating to 36,000 years ago.

▲▲ **Peştera cu Oase Cave** The site in Romania where the oldest modern human remains in Europe, dating to 36,000 years ago, were found.

▲▲ **Abrigo Lagar Velho** A site in Portugal where the skeleton of a modern human child dating to 24,500 years ago was discovered. The discovery is thought by some to support the hybridization model.

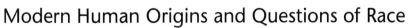

ARCHAEOLOGY in the world

Modern Human Origins and Questions of Race

There is a degree of irony to the fact that Darwin's engagement in the struggle to end slavery was an important factor leading him to develop his theory of evolution (Desmond and Moore 2009). Darwin's writings on variation had the potential to strike a fatal blow to racism. Unfortunately, this element of Darwin's work was often suppressed, and perceived splits within the human lineage formed the basis for labelling races as either more or less "evolved." Evolutionary theory was also used to support programs of eugenics, in which people viewed as showing "degenerate" traits were discouraged from having children or even, in extreme cases, sterilized. Ernst Hooton, a professor at Harvard University in the 1930s, argued that criminals were degenerate evolutionary throwbacks. He wrote "a biological purge is the essential prerequisite for a social and spiritual salvation . . . We must stop trying to cure malignant biological growths with patent sociological nostrums. The emergency demands a surgical operation" (Hooton 1937, 295). This chilling language presages the role that racial theory played in Nazi policies of extermination during the Second World War (Proctor 1988).

In the aftermath of the Second World War the anthropological community turned strongly against the concept of race. Subsequent research on living populations has emphasized the essential unity of the human species (Lewontin 1982). Nonetheless, race remains a powerful and volatile issue in contemporary society. It is against this backdrop that the "out of Africa" model emerged in the late 1980s, providing both archaeological and genetic evidence of a very recent common ancestry for all living humans. As the media picked up on the story, it often placed a highlight on the discovery's social implications.

Some archaeologists and biological anthropologists were concerned by the tone of discussions of modern human origins. Proponents of the multiregional model found themselves targeted as racists or felt that the scientific debate was being judged on political rather than scientific merits (Wolpoff 1997). Others argued that the entire discussion of modern human origins tended to adopt a racist tone by viewing human variation in terms of "types" (Lieberman and Jackson 1995).

When we study human origins we explore who we are by going back in time. It is almost inevitable there will be a political dimension to some aspects of this research. The question is how we deal with areas where research touches on issues that also have an ethical or moral dimension. ●

FIGURE 5.9 Charles Knight's classic painting of the Paleolithic artist at work. What assumptions did Knight make about the people who painted in these caves?

■ Genetic Evidence

Another important line of evidence in the debate over the fate of the Neanderthals comes from studies of the genetic diversity of living humans. The analysis of DNA from Neanderthal fossils was discussed in the last chapter. The analysis of the DNA of living humans offers strong evidence in support of the out of Africa hypothesis (Cann 2002). These studies work in a fashion similar to the genetic analysis of the split between the lineages of great apes and humans. Most studies look at mitochondrial DNA, which is inherited exclusively from the mother. Analyses of the mitochondrial DNA of living humans concur in identifying Africa as the place of origin of all living humans and a recent dispersal of humans out of Africa.

A study published in 2000 based on the comparison of the complete DNA sequences of fifty-three individuals from diverse origins places the date for the spread of humans out of Africa within the last 100,000 years (Ingman et al. 2000).

Studies of the Y chromosome add important information about the male lineage. The results of these studies agree with the results of the analysis of mitochondrial DNA in identifying Africa as the region of origin for all living humans and a date for the dispersal of humans from Africa within the last 100,000 years.

The use of genetic evidence to reconstruct the later stages of human evolution is a relatively new undertaking. Several geneticists have strongly criticized the use of such evidence to support the out of Africa model (Underhill et al. 2000). Much of their criticism focuses on the statistical methods used to analyze the degree of gene flow between populations. Alan Templeton concluded a critique of the genetic evidence by stating that gene flow was common among populations and that population expansions (such as the spread of modern humans out of Africa) resulted in "interbreeding, not replacement" (Templeton 2002, 45).

■ Archaeological Evidence

The fossil evidence and genetic evidence combine to strongly support the out of Africa model. Proponents of the multiregional hypothesis are faced with the difficulty of explaining both the existence of classic Neanderthals, such as those at St. Césaire, dating to less than 40,000 years ago, and the genetic evidence from studies of both mitochondrial and Y chromosome DNA. The fossil evidence poses less of a difficulty for the hybridization hypothesis, although the genetic studies remain problematic. When we turn to the archaeological record, the balance shifts somewhat and questions emerge for the out of Africa model.

Before examining the archaeological data, it is important to consider the nature of archaeological evidence. In a famous debate with a French colleague, Sally Binford made the pertinent observation that "stone tools don't mate." This is a rather obvious point, but one that is nonetheless critical. The fossil record and the genetic evidence reflect patterns of mating and biological reproduction. The transmission of culture takes place not through a process of cell replication, but through learning. Archaeology can inform us about interaction, but not about interbreeding.

European archaeologists have had a strong tendency to see the transition from the Middle to Upper Paleolithic as a local process. Several archaeological industries have been identified as transitional between the Middle and Upper Paleolithic. In Eastern Europe, the transitional industry is known as the **Szeletian** and is characterized by bifacial points. The **Ulluzian** is a transitional industry in Italy in which arched-backed knives and some bone points are found.

The best-documented transitional industry is the **Châtelperronian**, found in France and northern Spain. The exact date of the Châtelperronian is the subject of debate; however, it clearly falls between 40,000 and 35,000 years ago. Châtelperronian stone tools are characterized by a type of knife known as a Châtelperronian point. Otherwise, the stone tools are similar to those found at Middle Paleolithic sites.

At the site of **Arcy-sur-Cure** in northern France, excavators discovered a rich collection of ornaments and bone tools in a Châtelperronian level (White 1992). The ornaments include grooved and perforated canine teeth from fox, wolf, bear, hyena, and deer species, and grooved and perforated incisors from bovid, horse, marmot, bear, and reindeer species (see Figure 5.10). There are also small ivory beads. The bone tools include 142 items, including points, awls, and pins. The site of Quinçay is the only other Châtelperronian industry in which ornaments have been found.

Szeletian An archaeological industry found in Eastern Europe during the transition between the Middle Paleolithic and Upper Paleolithic. Bifacially retouched tools are characteristic of the Szeletian.

Ulluzian An archaeological industry found in Italy during the transition between the Middle Paleolithic and Upper Paleolithic. Arched-backed knives are characteristic of the Ulluzian.

Châtelperronian An archaeological industry found in France and northern Spain identified as transitional between the Middle Paleolithic and Upper Paleolithic.

▲▲ **Arcy-sur-Cure** A site in northern France where excavators discovered a rich collection of ornaments, bone tools, and Châtelperronian stone tools.

All available evidence indicates that the Châtelperronian industry was produced by Neanderthals. The St. Césaire Neanderthal previously discussed was found in a Châtelperronian level. Identification of the Neanderthals as the hominin responsible for the Châtelperronian is supported by the discovery of several teeth identified as Neanderthal in the Châtelperronian levels of Arcy-sur-Cure.

There is considerable debate over the interpretation of the Châtelperronian industry. Critical to this debate is the chronological position of the Châtelperronian in relation to the earliest Upper Paleolithic industry, known as the Aurignacian. In all but two sites, the **Aurignacian** is found stratigraphically above the Châtelperronian. In the two exceptions, a Châtelperronian level is sandwiched between Aurignacian levels. This situation, described as the interstratification of Châtelperronian and Aurignacian levels, suggests that these two cultures lived at the same time in France and northern Spain.

If Neanderthals and modern humans lived in the same region at the same time, then the possibility of interaction exists. Some archaeologists suggest that the ornaments found at Arcy-sur-Cure are evidence of this interaction. They also suggest that these ornaments were made by Neanderthals copying the behaviour of modern humans. Others go further and propose the possibility of exchange between Neanderthals and modern humans. Such a scenario would make the hybridization hypothesis plausible.

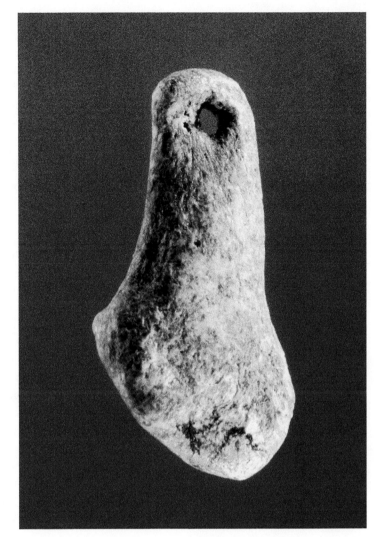

FIGURE 5.10 Châtelperronian bone bead manufactured from a reindeer metapodial from Arcy-sur-Cure, France.

Although the available dates for the Châtelperronian and the earliest Upper Paleolithic imply that these two industries overlap in time, there is room to critique those dates. A group of European archaeologists has suggested that the Châtelperronian was an independent development within Neanderthal societies that predated the arrival of modern humans in France (d'Errico et al. 1998). If this is correct, then there would not have been any sustained interactions between the two populations. These authors stress that the Châtelperronian is evidence of the culture of Neanderthals, not the influence of modern humans on Neanderthals. However, it is not clear why Neanderthals would have adopted these behaviours independently immediately before being replaced by modern humans. Why would we not see similar artifacts in earlier periods?

▪ The Last Neanderthals

The case of the Châtelperronian industry suggests that in some areas Neanderthals were not rapidly replaced by incoming hordes of modern humans, but rather that these two populations might have coexisted for considerable lengths of time. In other areas, it appears that Neanderthals continued to live as they had, with no evidence of interaction with or replacement by modern humans for very long periods. These areas are what biologists call refugia—isolated areas where no widespread evolutionary

Aurignacian The earliest Upper Paleolithic period. Aurignacian industries have been found on sites across Europe and the Middle East.

▲▲ **Zafarraya Cave** A site in Spain where the discovery of Neanderthal remains dated between 33,000 and 27,000 years ago suggests that, at least in this area, Neanderthals survived long after the arrival of modern humans in Europe.

▲▲ **Vindija Cave** A site in Croatia where the discovery of Neanderthal remains have been dated to 29,000 years ago.

change has occurred. Two refugia that have been identified are the Iberian Peninsula (Spain and Portugal) south of the Ebro River, and Croatia. In these areas, Neanderthals appear to have survived in isolation from modern humans for a considerable length of time. In Spain, the site of **Zafarraya Cave** has produced Neanderthal remains and a Middle Paleolithic industry dated between 33,000 and 27,000 years ago (Hublin et al. 1995). In Croatia, two Neanderthal fossils from the site of **Vindija Cave** have been directly dated to 29,000 years ago by AMS radiocarbon (Smith et al. 1999).

■ Summing Up the Evidence

Of the three models describing the fate of the Neanderthals, the multiregional hypothesis appears least likely. The absence of any trend toward modern human morphology among late Neanderthals and the genetic evidence based on both mitochondrial DNA and Y chromosome DNA argue against a local evolution of Neanderthals into modern humans.

The fossil and genetic evidence offers strong support for the out of Africa model. Clearly, modern humans evolved in Africa long before they appeared in Europe. The fossils found with the early Upper Paleolithic industries are distinctly modern humans and could not have evolved from local Neanderthals. The genetic evidence supports Africa as the region of origin for all living humans and also supports a dispersal of modern humans after 100,000 years ago.

The archaeological evidence presents a more nuanced picture that might offer support for the hybridization theory. The arrival of modern humans was a dramatic event, but it did not signal the immediate disappearance of Neanderthals. In some areas, transitional industries such as the Châtelperronian developed that might provide evidence for interaction between Neanderthals and modern humans over a long period of time. In Spain and in Croatia, refugia areas have been identified where Neanderthals survived for thousands of years after the first arrival of modern humans in Europe. The archaeological evidence suggests that the arrival of modern humans in Europe did not spell the instant demise of Neanderthals.

5.5 The Upper Paleolithic

The first modern human hunter–gatherer societies that lived in Europe are known collectively as the Upper Paleolithic. The Upper Paleolithic is dramatically different from the preceding Middle Paleolithic.

■ Chronology

The stone tool industries of the Upper Paleolithic show a clear pattern of change through time (see Table 5.1). For Western Europe, the broad chronological framework is well developed. The earliest Upper Paleolithic industry is the Aurignacian,

TABLE 5.1

INDUSTRY	DATE	CHARACTERISTICS
Aurignacian	40,000–26,000 years ago	Bladelets and split-based bone points
Gravettian	26,000–23,000 years ago	Small hunting points
Solutrean	23,000–20,000 years ago	Bifacial points
Magdalenian	20,000–11,000 years ago	Bone harpoons

dated to between 40,000 and 26,000 years ago. Aurignacian sites are found throughout Europe, and later-stage Aurignacian sites are also found in the Middle East. The characteristic tools of the Aurignacian are microliths known as Dufour bladelets, which would have been used as elements in complex tools, and a characteristic bone point known as a split-based point.

The **Gravettian** dates to between 26,000 and 23,000 years ago and is found across much of Europe. The characteristic tools of the Gravettian are small hunting points. The following period, the Solutrean, dates between 23,000 and 20,000 years ago. The latter dates correspond to Oxygen Isotope Stage 2 and the height of the Last Glacial Maximum. The Solutrean is limited mostly to France and Spain and is characterized by the presence of beautifully thin bifacial points—pieces that have been thinned by removing flakes from each face, not by striking the rock, but by applying pressure with an antler to push off remarkably delicate flakes.

The final industry of the Upper Paleolithic is the Magdalenian, which dates to between 20,000 and 11,000 years ago. The characteristic artifacts of the Magdalenian are a vast array of bone tools, including harpoons.

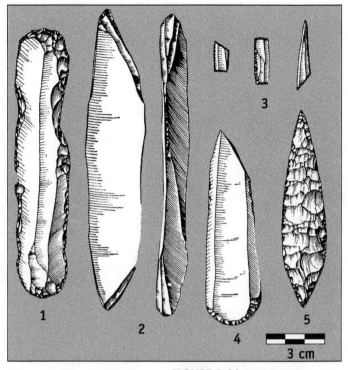

FIGURE 5.11 Stone tools characteristic of the Upper Paleolithic. All of these pieces are blades as their length is twice their width. 1. Endscraper with retouch creating a rounded end. 2. Burin with elongated flakes known as spalls removed along the edge creating a pointed working end. On this piece there are burins on both ends of the tool. 3. Retouched bladelets. These very small tools were used for projectile points or cutting tools. 4. A multiple tool with a burin at one end and an endscraper at the other end. 5. Bifacial point characteristic of the Solutrean period.

■ Stone and Bone Tools

The Upper Paleolithic industries include microliths and bone tools, unknown in the repertoire of the Middle Paleolithic. It is interesting that both of these types of tools are known from the Middle Stone Age of Africa—bone tools from Katanda and Blombos and microliths from the Howiesons Poort.

In the Upper Paleolithic, many tools were made on blades, defined as flakes (pieces detached from a core) that are twice as long as they are wide (see Figure 5.11). The dominant types of tools are endscrapers, which are blades that have been retouched at the end, and burins—flakes or blades off of which a flake, known as a burin spall, has been removed along one edge. The removal of a burin spall produces a sharp-angled bit at the end of the tool, which has been likened to the burin tools used in engraving.

Perhaps the most striking aspect of Upper Paleolithic stone and bone tool industries is the presence of sophisticated points used as light projectiles. By the Gravettian industry, there is clear evidence that an atlatl, or spear thrower, was in use. An atlatl is a hooked piece of bone, ivory, or wood used to launch a light spear.

A number of archaeologists have studied the movement of the raw materials used in stone tool manufacture. During the Upper Paleolithic, raw materials, including the famous "chocolate flint" found in Poland, were moved across long distances. This pattern is interpreted as evidence of long-distance trade networks.

The bone tool industry encompasses a wide range of items, including hunting tools. In the later part of the Upper Paleolithic, there is also evidence of a well-developed tool kit for sewing, including fine bone needles (see Figure 5.12 on the next page).

Gravettian The second major Upper Paleolithic archaeological period in Europe.

FIGURE 5.12 Bone tools from the site of La Madelaine, France, dating to the Magdalenian period. Notice that the tools include harpoons used for either hunting or fishing as well as awls and a sewing needle.

■ Human Burials

Human burials are absent from the Aurignacian. Beginning in the Gravettian, burials of individuals or groups are found with rich ornamentation. Some of these burials raise questions about the extent of inequality in Upper Paleolithic societies. At Sungir in Russia, for example, two children were found buried in a context dated to 24,000 years ago (Formicola and Buzhilova 2004). The children were buried in a large, shallow grave and covered with red ochre. The wealth of artifacts found in these burials includes thousands of ivory beads (probably the remains of beaded clothes), long mammoth-tusk spears, ivory daggers, pierced fox canines, antler rods, bracelets, ivory carvings of animals, disc-shaped pendants, and ivory pins.

At the site of Dolní Věstonice in Moravia, a triple burial was discovered in a context dated to 28,000 years ago (Bahn 2002). The three individuals, all young adults between seventeen and twenty years old, face south and are positioned in a striking tableau. The central skeleton is the most gracile and is most likely female. She lies on her back and her pelvic area is covered in red ochre. To her left, a heavily built male was buried lying face down, with his head turned away from the central figure and his hand apparently clasping hers. His head had been smashed. To the woman's right, a second male was buried with his hands positioned on her pelvis. A large piece of wood had skewered his body through to his sacrum. Burial offerings included wolf- and fox-tooth pendants and small ivory beads. The excavator proposed that the triple burial reproduces the failed birth of a child, the male figure on the right being a medicine man attempting to aid in the delivery and the man on the left attempting to provide comfort.

In the Sungir burial, a tremendous wealth of objects is buried with young children who would not have had a chance to accumulate such wealth through their own efforts. The practice suggests that some individuals in that society were born into positions of high status. At Dolní Věstonice, the triple burial raises the question of the connection between the three young people and why they were afforded such extraordinary treatment.

Detailed analysis of the skeletal remains has uncovered a surprising link between the two sites. Both the woman from Dolní Věstonice and one of the children from Sungir show evidence of pathology. The Sungir child's skeleton displays a marked bowing and shortening of the femur, while the skeleton of the woman from Dolní Věstonice exhibits deformities to her skull and her torso. Taken together, these discoveries suggest that individuals with visible pathologies might have held a particular status in some Upper Paleolithic societies.

TOOLBOX

Use–Wear Analysis

Figuring out how a particular stone tool was used is not as easy as it may seem. Archaeologists have developed a method known as use–wear analysis by means of which they infer the function of a tool on the basis of microscopic traces of wear left on its edge. There are two approaches to use–wear analysis: Low-power use–wear analysis documents damage to the edge of the tool that is visible below 70-power magnification. High-power use–wear analysis examines polishes that form on the surfaces near the edge of the tool. These polishes are usually visible only at very high magnification or under a scanning electron microscope.

Use–wear analysis hinges on experiments that provide the analyst with a reference collection. The analyst uses a stone tool for a particular task, such as scraping a hide or butchering a carcass, and the wear observed on the tool can then serve as a key to understanding the wear patterns found on an archaeological sample.

One of the most compelling use–wear studies was an analysis of Solutrean points carried out by the French archaeologists Jean-Michel Geneste and Hugues Plisson. The strength of this study is that it combined multiple lines of evidence to reach the conclusion that these delicately made tools were the tips of projectiles used for hunting. The first step of the study was to produce replicas of Solutrean points and use them for a variety of tasks, including shooting at a target with a longbow, a spear thrower, and a crossbow. The crossbow was particularly valuable, allowing for control of the speed of the arrow. Points were also used for a variety of other tasks, such as cutting and butchery. The patterns of breakage and wear found on the experimental tools were then compared with the assemblage of shouldered points found at the site of Combe Saunière in southwestern France. The comparison of the experimental and archaeological tools enabled the archaeologists to identify the way the tools were used by Solutrean hunters. ●

REFERENCE: Jean-Michel Geneste and Hugues Plisson. (1993). Hunting technologies and human behavior: Lithic analysis of Solutrean shouldered points. In *Before Lascaux: The Complex Record of the Early Upper Paleolithic*, edited by Heidi Knecht, Anne Pike-Tay, and Randall White. Boca Raton, Florida: CRC Press.

FIGURE 5.13 Experimental use of stone tools provides a reference for interpreting the traces of wear found on archaeological tools.

■ Artwork

The hallmark of the Upper Paleolithic is the dramatic appearance of a wide range of art objects. This richness of the repertoire of symbolic artifacts is in sharp contrast to the almost total absence of such artifacts at Middle Paleolithic sites.

MOBILIARY ART. The earliest Upper Paleolithic artwork is found in the Aurignacian levels of sites in southern Germany dated between 40,000 and 36,000 years ago. The most spectacular discovery is a representation of a lion–headed man found at the site

FIGURE 5.14 The Hohlenstein ivory figure of a human with a lion's head dating to the Aurignacian period. The height of this figure is 28 cm.

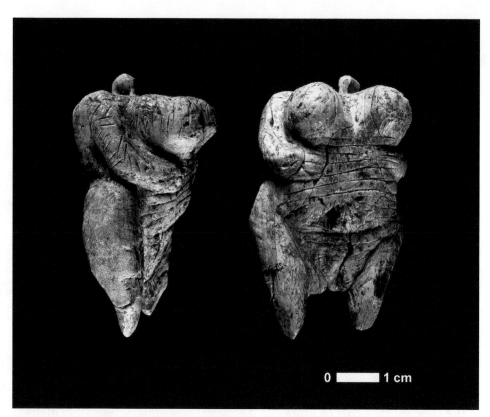

0 ▭▭▭ 1 cm

FIGURE 5.15 Front and side views of the recently discovered female figurine from the Aurignacian levels of Hohle Fels. Are there points of similarity between this figure and that of the lion-headed man found at Hohlenstein (Figure 5.14)? How does the Hohle Fels figurine compare to the Gravettian Venus figurine (shown in Figure 5.16), which is from a later time period?

▲▲ **Hohlenstein** A site in Germany where a lion-headed figure was found in levels with an Aurignacian industry.

▲▲ **Hohle Fels** A site in Germany where bone flutes and a female figurine have been discovered in levels dating to the Aurignacian.

Venus figurines Portable art objects that are found with the Gravettian industry and that depict the female body.

of **Hohlenstein** (see Figure 5.14). What is particularly striking about this piece of artwork is that it is a depiction, not simply of the world as it is, but of the world of imagination. Similar carvings of animals and human figures are found at Vogelherd and Geissenklösterle, also located in southern Germany (Conard 2003). Recent excavations at the neighbouring site of **Hohle Fels** has produced one of the most intriguing pieces of mobiliary art from the Early Aurignacian (Conard 2009). This nearly complete figure of a woman is less than 10 centimetres high (see Figure 5.15). The figure lacks a head, but there is a ring above the shoulders that has been polished, suggesting that the figure may have been suspended as a pendant. The figure has large breasts, and although the carving is quite crude, the genitals are depicted in detail, as are the five fingers on each hand. The entire surface of the figure is covered with patterns of lines, reminiscent of patterns found on animal figures from neighbouring sites. The legs are short and pointed. The figure was found in several fragments at the base of over 1 metre of deposits dating to the Aurignacian that were in the process of a meticulous excavation. A large suite of radiocarbon dates from this level produced a range of dates but the most likely age for this figure is between 40,000 and 35,000 years ago.

Portable art objects such as those from Vogelherd and Hohlenstein are found throughout the Upper Paleolithic. Gravettian period objects that have become known as Venus figurines are found in sites across Europe (see Figure 5.16). The **Venus figurines** vary from a highly abstract to a more detailed representation of

FIGURE 5.16 A Venus figurine dating to the Gravettian period from the site of Dolní Věstonice. The schematic representation of the face, large breasts, and hips, and the absence of feet are features found on many Venus figurines. The height of this figure is 11 cm.

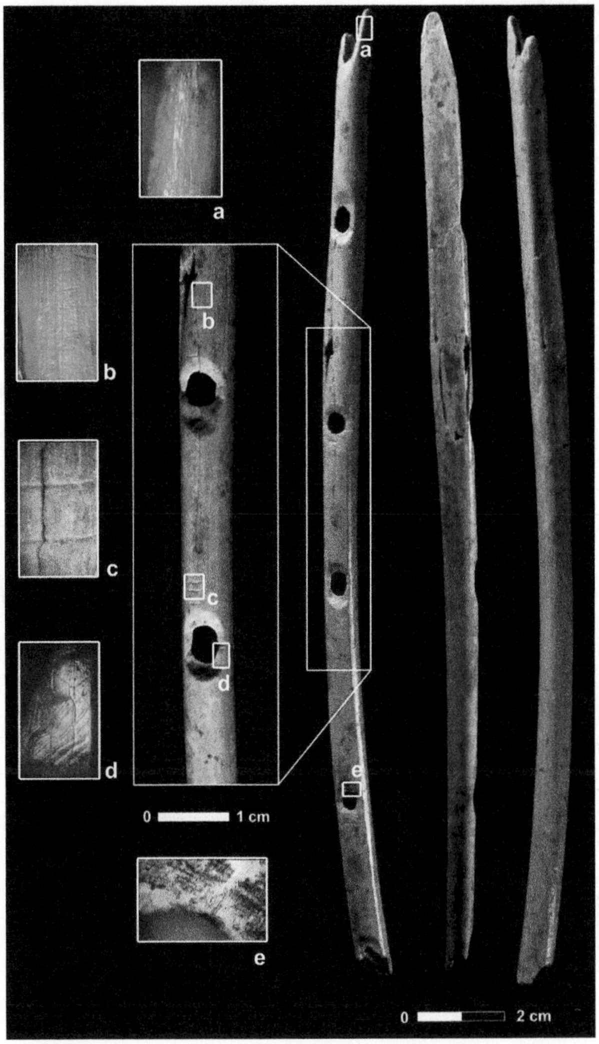

FIGURE 5.17 A well-preserved flute found in the Aurignacian levels of Hohle Fels. The boxes provide detailed views of the marks left when shaping the flute and the finger holes. Note the two parallel lines in box c. These markings might have been used to determine the placement of the finger holes.

the female body. The faces are rarely depicted in any detail and in many cases are simply blank. The feet are always absent and in some cases have been deliberately broken off. The meaning and function of these pieces are the subject of a great deal of speculation.

Bone flutes are known from the Gravettian levels of the cave of Isturitz in southern France. It is interesting that two of these flutes are made of vulture bones. One flute was also recovered from the Aurignacian levels at Isturitz and fragments have been found in the Aurignacian of Geissenklösterle (d'Errico et al. 2003). The most dramatic evidence for music in the early stages of the Upper Paleolithic comes from the excavations of the Aurignacian levels at Hohle Fels, Germany—the same site that has recently produced the earliest Upper Paleolithic sculpture of a woman (Conard et al. 2009). Like the Isturitz flutes, the flute from Hohle Fels, shown in Figure 5.17, was produced from the radius of a large vulture. With a wing span of over 2 metres,

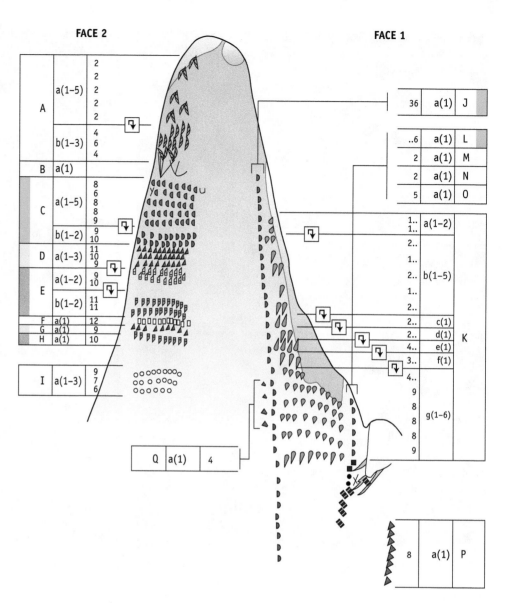

FIGURE 5.18 Diagram of the La Marche antler. This piece is one of the most elaborate examples of Upper Paleolithic art with a complex array of lines that might have served as a form of notation. The results of analysis by Francesco d'Errico demontrate that these marks were made in groups using a series of different tools. Capital letters indicate groups of marks made by the same tool. Small letters and arrows show where the antler was turned.

FACE 2

FACE 1

vultures have large hollow bones well suited for making flutes. The flute has five holes, and two V-shaped notches have been carved into one end, evidently to serve as the mouthpiece. There are thin markings around each of the holes, clearly to indicate where they were to be placed. The meticulous excavation procedures at Hohle Fels assure that the context of the flute at the base of the Aurignacian sequence is secure.

Some of the Upper Paleolithic mobile art is carved onto tools. Particularly notable are Magdalenian atlatls with fine engravings. Some pieces are decorated not only with depictions of animals, but also with arrays of dots and lines. Alexander Marshack has argued that these pieces were lunar calendars (Marshack 1972). However, detailed analyses carried out by Francesco d'Errico do not support the identification of these pieces as lunar calendars but do support the idea that the incisions were not simply decorative (d'Errico 1995) (see Figure 5.18). D'Errico concludes that the marks were used to store information but does not speculate as to what that information might have been.

CAVE ART. The spectacular paintings discovered at Lascaux Cave in France and other sites such as Altamira in Spain are both awe-inspiring and enigmatic. The paintings were made by people who penetrated below the surface of the earth with only crude oil lamps for light. These people covered the walls of caves with sensitive depictions of the animal world, often using the irregular features of the cave to accentuate aspects of the animals' bodies. They also left stencils of their hands on the cave walls, outlined by colourants they spat out of their mouths. In these handprints, fingers are often missing, most likely because they were deliberately held clenched by the artist. Not only did these people paint the caves, but they also incised the outlines of animals, often overlaying image over image in a dizzying mat of lines. Oddly, depictions of human figures are extremely rare in caves. Most of the paintings are of animals; abstract forms such as grids and dots are also found.

The earliest known painted cave is also one of the most recently discovered. **Chauvet Cave**, shown in Figure 5.19, was a chance discovery made by amateur spelunkers (Clottes 2003). Imagine their shock when they looked around by the light of their torches and saw walls covered with panthers, battling rhinos, aurochs, and bears. The colourants used at Chauvet have been AMS-radiocarbon dated to between 38,000 and 33,000 years old. The tradition of cave painting continues throughout the Upper Paleolithic. Both Lascaux and Altamira, which are among the most famous painted caves, date to the Magdalenian period.

Archaeologists have struggled to arrive at an understanding of the paintings in Upper Paleolithic caves. This is one of the most difficult tasks an archaeologist can undertake, because the goal is to recover the lost meaning of the paintings. Oscar Moro Abadía has pointed out that that our perception of Paleolithic art is "largely based on the projection of the concepts which structure our 'modern system of art' to the past" (Moro Abadía 2010, 120-121). This bias adds to the difficulty of understanding Paleolithic art.

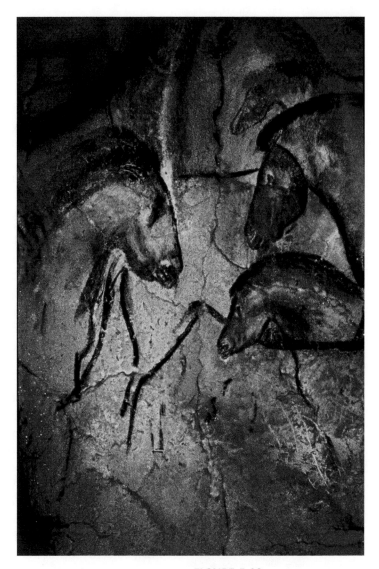

FIGURE 5.19 These beautiful paintings of horses from Chauvet Cave show the subtlety and expressiveness of Paleolithic cave art.

Hunting Magic. One possibility is that the paintings were elements of magic associated with hunting. Perhaps they were a form of sympathetic magic, whereby the hunter would first create an image of the animal and then be able to succeed in the hunt. Perhaps such magic even had a rational aspect: The paintings might have been plans for hunts or records of successful hunts. Proponents of the hunting magic hypothesis point to images of objects piercing the bodies of animals and to various geometric forms that can be interpreted as traps or pens.

Fertility Magic. Another explanation emphasizes aspects of the cave paintings related to fertility. Some of the arguments for this position are quite far-fetched and even suggest that many of the animals appear pregnant. Nonetheless, representations of females and of geometric forms resembling the vulva are found in the caves. Moreover, the female figure is frequently represented in mobiliary art, such as the Venus figurines of the Gravettian period.

Shamans and Trances. Both the hunting magic and fertility hypotheses emphasize the potential role of cave paintings as elements of magical practice. The conception of magic in these explanations is that it helps people arrive at an end or

▲▲ **Chauvet Cave** The earliest known painted cave, dated to between 38,000 and 33,000 years ago. It is located in France.

addresses their anxiety about the outcome of an unpredictable undertaking. Another approach to magic stresses the individual mystical experience of the sorcerer or shaman, who acts as an intermediary between humans and the supernatural realm. A number of archaeologists link the practice of cave paintings to shamanism and trances. The existence of images of humans transforming into animals, such as the lion-headed man figurine from Hohlenstein, suggests that shamans may have played a role in Paleolithic society. Certainly, the very act of entering caves to create a painted world suggests that cave painting had a powerful spiritual component. However, whether one can explain the paintings as direct representations of what shamans visualized while in a trance or under the influence of hallucinogens remains open to question.

Mythogram. The theories just discussed view the painted cave as the accumulation of numerous unconnected events. People went down into caves to practise magic or to experience a trance. A rather different perspective is proposed by archaeologists who see the cave as a structured whole. From this perspective, the caves, in their entirety, are to be read as a "mythogram" expressing a sophisticated metaphysical system. Such a hypothesis raises a number of questions. Why would people create a mythogram in a deeply buried cave? Why are the images overlain, sometimes many times over? Nonetheless, there is value to approaching caves as a whole entity that expresses fundamental ideas held by the group. André Leroi-Gourhan developed an elaborate conception of the caves as expressing basic structural oppositions in the worldview of Paleolithic societies. It is not surprising that Leroi-Gourhan saw the fundamental opposition as that between male and female. He argued that the depictions on the caves were laid out to express this gender opposition, with certain animals associated with women and others with men.

Artwork made on objects that cannot be transported is not limited to the insides of caves. In the Côa Valley, Portugal, incised drawings of animals on exposed slabs of rock have been dated to the Upper Paleolithic (Zilhao 1998). Luckily, these unique drawings were discovered before the completion of a dam in the valley. Intense lobbying by the archaeological community led the Portuguese government to halt construction of the dam and create a park in the Côa Valley.

BODY ORNAMENTATION. Bone beads, pierced animal teeth, and pierced shells are found throughout the Upper Paleolithic. It is assumed that these objects were worn as necklaces or attached to clothing. Studies of impressions found on burnt clay at the site of Dolní Věstonice have identified woven textiles and basketry made from plant fibers. In an innovative study, Olga Soffer has identified depictions of headgear and other clothing on the Gravettian Venus figurines (Soffer et al. 2000). A rather unusual line of evidence links the development of clothing with the spread of modern humans (Kittler et al. 2003). Human body lice evolved from head lice and are adapted to living in clothing. A genetic analysis of human lice places the origin of body lice at around 70,000 years ago and indicates that body lice probably first evolved in Africa. Kittler and colleagues suggest this data indicates that clothing was a surprisingly recent innovation. However, it remains unclear whether body lice are adapted to any type of clothing, including hides, or if they are specifically adapted to textiles.

■ Site Structure

A number of open-air Upper Paleolithic sites have produced evidence of huts. Often, the existence of huts is inferred from the distribution of artifacts. At Mezherich in the Ukraine, a large circular mass of mammoth bones has been interpreted as the remains of a structure. Extensive horizontal excavations of open-air Magdalenian sites in the

Paris Basin have allowed archaeologists to reconstruct the locations of tents that have left no physical trace. The distribution of animal bones and artifacts makes it possible to determine where the walls of tents once stood. In a particularly innovative study, data on the spatial distribution of artifacts and a large number of refit cores at the site of Etiolles have been combined to produce a picture of the organization of stone tool manufacture. This study demonstrated that the most experienced knappers worked on the best materials in close proximity to a central hearth, while less expert knappers worked on lower-quality flint at the edges of the habitation (Pigeot 1987). At the site of Pincevent, James Enloe was able to use refit animal bones to track the sharing of meat between habitations (Enloe 1992).

Although some Upper Paleolithic sites are quite large, there is no evidence that any of them included more than two or three structures at any given time. Margaret Conkey has interpreted some late Upper Paleolithic sites as aggregation sites where hunter–gatherer groups from a large territory would come together for a brief time (Conkey 1980).

Subsistence

There is clear evidence that the Upper Paleolithic inhabitants of Europe were hunters. There is also limited evidence of fishing, particularly in the later part of the Upper Paleolithic. Upper Paleolithic hunters often focused on herd animals, including reindeer. Unfortunately, we know little about how plant resources were utilized during this period. Based on an analysis of the fauna from the site of St. Césaire, France, Eugène Morin finds evidence that the early Upper Paleolithic was a period of climatic stress that led to a reduction in the diversity of mammals available to hunt (Morin 2008). Morin suggests that the resulting reliance on reindeer would have led to a contraction in the size of human populations in the region.

Some archaeologists see evidence that some Upper Paleolithic societies engaged in the management or control of animals. One possibility is that some groups mapped their own mobility onto the seasonal movements of a particular herd of animals; evidence of this practice is found among modern Lapp reindeer herders (Ingold 1980). There is very limited evidence to support the argument that humans controlled animals during the Upper Paleolithic in a way which anticipates their domestication. One of the most controversial pieces of evidence is an incised rock from the site of La Marche (Bahn 1978). As with many Upper Paleolithic engraved plaques, this piece is covered in a dense network of overlapping lines, so the actual depiction must be extracted by the archaeologist. The La Marche plaque clearly shows the head of a horse with a diagonal line crossing the muzzle (see Figure 5.20). Paul Bahn has suggested that what is shown is a horse wearing a halter. Randall White has sharply disputed this interpretation, pointing out that similar lines are found on Magdalenian depictions of bison (White 1989). White similarly disputes the validity of the evidence in support of the view that Upper Paleolithic hunters mapped their movements onto those of particular herds.

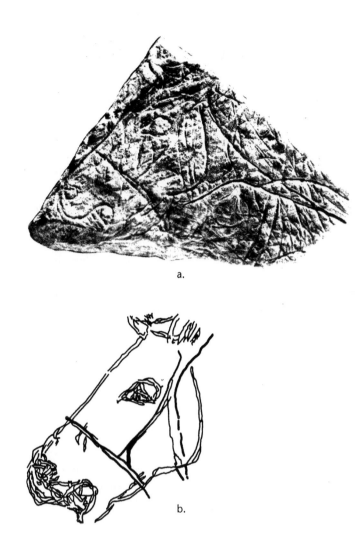

a.

b.

FIGURE 5.20 The engraved picture of a horse head from La Marche with possible evidence of a harness. A picture of the slab (a) shows the complexity of the piece. The drawing of the horse with a harness (b) was pulled out of the overlapping scenes engraved on the rock.

5.6 Explaining the Upper Paleolithic

The richness and diversity of Upper Paleolithic material culture stands in stark contrast to that of the Middle Paleolithic. It seems obvious that this contrast must have something to do with the replacement of Neanderthals by modern humans in Europe. Many of the characteristics of the European Upper Paleolithic are anticipated by the Middle Stone Age of Africa. For example, the use of bone tools and microlithic stone tools is found in the Middle Stone Age. The discoveries at Blombos Cave demonstrate that art was not completely absent from this period.

Nonetheless, nothing in the Middle Stone Age record prepares us for the cave paintings and portable art of the European Upper Paleolithic. Perhaps there has simply not been enough excavation on Middle Stone Age sites. This certainly is a possibility. New discoveries in Africa have had a tendency to bring major surprises. However, given what we know today, archaeologists are forced to grapple with the problems posed by the Upper Paleolithic: Why did this industry appear when it did? Why did modern humans replace Neanderthals?

Because of the discoveries at Herto, Klasies River Mouth, Qafzeh, and Skhul, it is not possible to say that something about modern humans inevitably produces complex material culture. In Africa, modern humans produced Middle Stone Age industries for close to 100,000 years. In the Middle East, modern humans produced Middle Paleolithic industries for close to 50,000 years. Richard Klein has developed a bold explanation for this pattern: Klein suggests that around 50,000 years ago, there was a genetic mutation within modern human populations living in Africa. This mutation did not lead to a change in the morphology of the skeleton or the size of the brain, but it did cause changes in the organization of the brain, giving the people the cognitive capacity for language. Armed with this new capacity, the affected population experienced explosive growth and expansion. Modern humans replaced Neanderthals because modern humans had the cognitive capacity for language. Modern humans made symbolic artifacts because humans who use language will inevitably make such objects.

FIGURE 5.21 Later Stone Age rock art from Wildebeest Kuil, South Africa. (http://www.museumsnc.co.az/wildebeestkuil.htm)

One of the strengths of Klein's proposal is that he sees the Upper Paleolithic as part of a global transformation of human culture. He links the Upper Paleolithic with the emergence of the African Later Stone Age, which also saw an increase in the use of clearly symbolic objects (see Figure 5.21), and with the colonization of Australia and the Americas.

Klein's scenario is plausible, but difficult to prove. How does one identify a mutation that had no effect on skeletal form? How do we know that the modern humans at Herto did not have language? One of the major challenges facing Paleolithic archaeologists is to devise alternative hypotheses for the replacement of Neanderthals by modern humans and for the dramatic innovations found in the Upper Paleolithic.

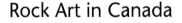
Rock Art in Canada

Rock art sites have been found across Canada and include engravings in Kejimkujik National Park in Nova Scotia, along the Milk River in Alberta, and at a number of sites in British Columbia. In some places, rock art is threatened by flooding due to hydroelectric dams, requiring careful documentation and monitoring. This is the case with the rock paintings along the Churchill River in Manitoba, some of which have been submerged by the Churchill River Diversion Project.

One of the most spectacular rock art sites in Canada is located in the Petroglyphs Provincial Park north of Peterborough, Ontario. Over 900 carvings, including human figures, boats, sun discs, and animals, were incised into the crystalline limestone between A.D. 900 and 1400. The carvings are attributed to the Algonquin, and the figures are clearly consistent with Algonquin cosmology. At first glance, they appear to be distributed haphazardly across the rock face, but closer examination shows that the carvings are oriented along the sloping surface of the rock in alignment with crevices in the rock surface (Vastokas and Vastokas 1973). The crevices not only structure the organization of the carvings but in many cases are incorporated into the carvings themselves. As a result, a powerful connection is made between the human act of carving and the natural surface of the rock. ◆

FIGURE 5.22 The Peterborough petroglyphs

SUMMARY

- The earliest modern human fossil was found at the site of Herto, Ethiopia, and was dated to between 160,000 and 154,000 years ago.
- The Middle Stone Age is characterized by (1) a wide diversity of stone tool industries produced by using prepared core technologies, (2) evidence of sophisticated bone tools, (3) hunting and the use of fish and shellfish, and (4) modest evidence of artwork.
- Modern humans are found at the sites of Skhul and Qafzeh, Israel, in layers with a Middle Paleolithic industry dating between 120,000 and 80,000 years ago. This date is earlier than that of the Neanderthal sites in the Middle East.
- The three theories of the relationship between modern humans and Neanderthals are the multiregional hypothesis, the out of Africa hypothesis, and the hybridization hypothesis.
- The earliest modern human fossil in Europe dates to 36,000 years ago, while the most recent Neanderthal fossil dates to between 33,000 and 27,000 years ago.
- The Middle to Upper Paleolithic transition corresponds to the appearance of modern humans in Europe and includes the development of new types of stone and bone tools and the dramatic appearance of a wide range of symbolic artifacts.
- One explanation for the Middle to Upper Paleolithic transition and the replacement of Neanderthals by modern humans is that modern humans were unique in possessing the cognitive capacity for language.

KEY TERMS

Abrigo Lagar Velho, 132
Arcy-sur-Cure, 134
Aterian, 124
Aurignacian, 135

Blombos Cave, 125
Border Cave, 123
Châtelperronian, 134
Chauvet Cave, 143

REVIEW QUESTIONS

1. What is the significance of the discoveries made at the Qafzeh and Skhul Caves?
2. How does the Middle Stone Age archaeological record compare with the Middle Paleolithic archaeological record?
3. Why is the modern human skeleton discovered at Abrigo Lagar Velho thought to be significant?
4. How does Klein explain the replacement of modern humans by Neanderthals and the Middle to Upper Paleolithic transition? What are the strengths and weaknesses of his hypothesis? Can you think of any alternatives?

CANADIAN ARCHAEOLOGISTS

- Oscar Moro Abadía, professor in the Department of Anthropology at Memorial University, combines research on Paleolithic art with an interest in the history of archaeology.
  http://www.mun.ca/archaeology/faculty/omoro.php

- Alicia Hawkins, professor in the Department of Anthropology at Laurentian University, has carried out field research on the prehistory of the desert oases in Egypt and at the Birimi Site in Ghana. She has written extensively on the archaeology of the Aterian in the Western Desert of Egypt.
  http://ahawkins.laurentian.ca/

- Eugene Morin, professor in the Department of Anthropology at Trent University, focuses on forager ecology and social evolution in the Old World and in Eastern North America. He has carried out an analysis of the animal bones from the early Upper Paleolithic site of St. Césaire, France.
  http://www.trentu.ca/anthropology/morin.php

- Randall White received his Ph.D. from the University of Toronto and is currently a professor in the Department of Anthropology at New York University. He is a leading authority on the study of Paleolithic Art and his publications include *Prehistoric Art: The Symbolic Journey of Humankind* (Harry Abrams, 2003). He has recently been excavating the Aurignacian site of Castanet in southwestern France.
  http://www.nyu.edu/gsas/dept/anthro/programs/csho/pmwiki.php/Home/RandallWhite

- Pamela Willoughby, professor in the Department of Anthropology at the University of Alberta, has carried out extensive fieldwork on Middle Stone Age sites in Tanzania. She recently published *The Evolution of Modern Humans in Africa: A Comprehensive Guide* (AltaMira Press, 2007).
  www.arts.ualberta.ca/~pwilloug/

PEARSON **myanthrokit**™

Visit **www.myanthrokit.com**, where you will find a variety of tools and resources to enhance your learning, including:
- Practise quizzes with Study Plans
- Videos
- Listening Activities
- And much more!

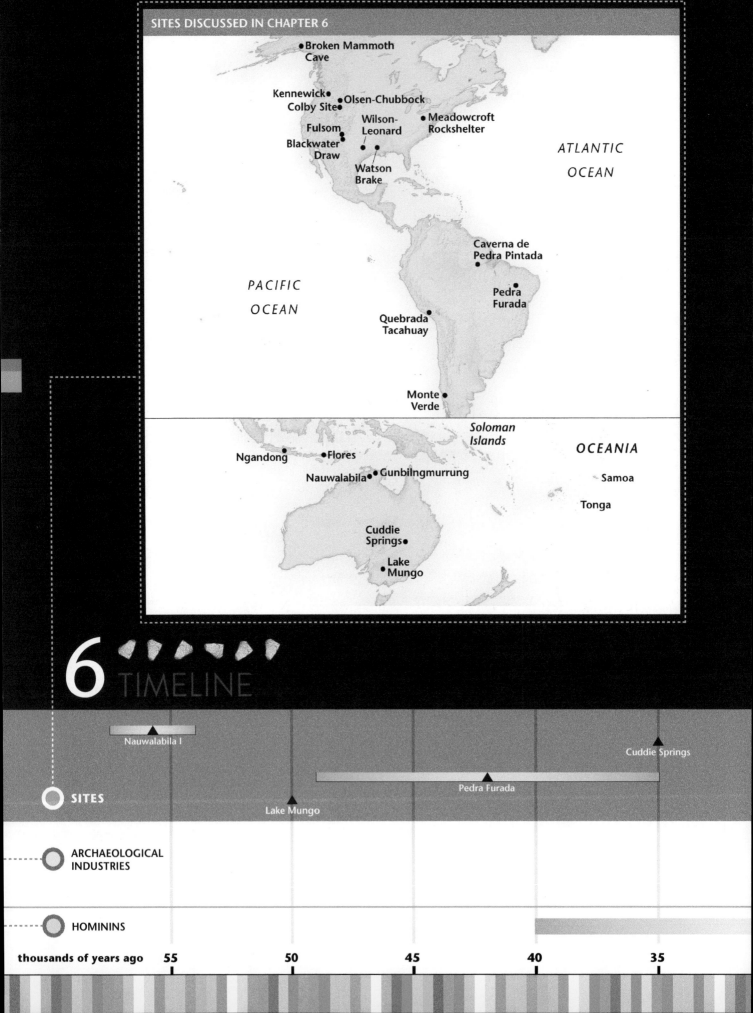

SITES DISCUSSED IN CHAPTER 6

- Broken Mammoth Cave
- Kennewick
- Colby Site
- Olsen-Chubbock
- Wilson-Leonard
- Meadowcroft Rockshelter
- Fulsom
- Blackwater Draw
- Watson Brake

ATLANTIC OCEAN

PACIFIC OCEAN

- Caverna de Pedra Pintada
- Pedra Furada
- Quebrada Tacahuay
- Monte Verde

Soloman Islands

OCEANIA

- Ngandong
- Flores
- Nauwalabila
- Gunbilngmurrung
- Samoa
- Tonga
- Cuddie Springs
- Lake Mungo

6 TIMELINE

Nauwalabila I

Cuddie Springs

Pedra Furada

SITES

ARCHAEOLOGICAL INDUSTRIES

HOMININS

Lake Mungo

thousands of years ago 55   50   45   40   35

THE PEOPLING OF AUSTRALIA AND THE NEW WORLD

The dispersal of modern humans is a global process reaching across Australia and the Americas.
After reading this chapter, you should understand:

- The debates over the timing of the initial occupation of Australia and the Americas.

- The migration routes followed by the first humans moving into Australia and the Americas.

- The relationship between human occupation of Australia and the Americas and the extinction of megafauna.

Australian rock art site.

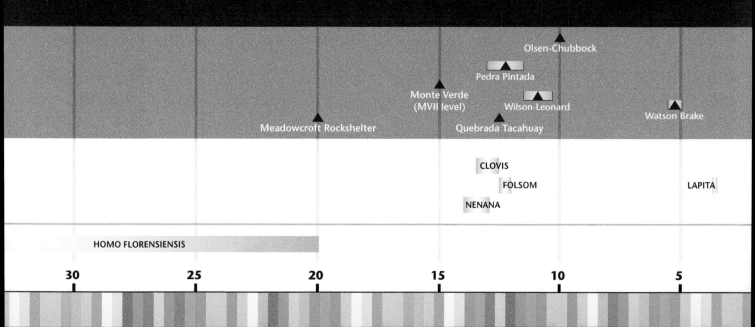

Olsen-Chubbock

Pedra Pintada

Monte Verde
(MVII level)

Wilson-Leonard

Watson Brake

Meadowcroft Rockshelter

Quebrada Tacahuay

CLOVIS

FOLSOM

LAPITA

NENANA

HOMO FLORENSIENSIS

30   25   20   15   10   5

FIGURE 6.1 Folsom point with associated bones from Folsom, New Mexico.

George McJunkin was a quintessential scientific outsider. An African American rancher born into slavery, McJunkin became an avid amateur scientist with wide-ranging interests, including astronomy, archaeology, and fossil bones (Douglas 1997). In 1908, while fixing a fence after a storm, McJunkin noticed bones eroding out of a gully near Folsom, New Mexico. It was only in 1926, however, four years after McJunkin died, that Jesse Figgins of the Denver Museum of Natural History began excavations at Folsom. In his first season excavating there, Figgins found a distinctive spearpoint together with bison fossils. This spearpoint was thin and finely worked, with a long channel, or flute, running from the base toward the tip (see Figure 6.1). Figgins' discovery was met with skepticism, but doubt evaporated in 1927 when another spearpoint was found lodged between the ribs of a bison skeleton. The discoveries at Folsom proved that humans had been in North America for at least 10,000 years. Finding a spearpoint embedded in the remains of a large animal also suggested that early occupants of the Americas were specialized big-game hunters.

In this chapter, we focus on the debates surrounding the initial human occupation of Australia and the Americas. The only hominins known from these continents are *Homo sapiens*. Migration routes into both Australia and the Americas led through East Asia, so it is important to review the current understanding of modern human origins in that area first. With this background, it is possible to move on to consider the timing of the occupation of Australia and the likely migration routes. We also consider the significance of the recent discovery of a new species belonging to the genus *Homo* on the island of Flores in Indonesia. Beyond tracking when and how people first arrived in Australia, we examine the role of humans in the extinction of megafauna on the continent and the evidence for the development of cave painting in the Australian context. We then move on to the debates concerning the timing and migration routes taken by the first people to arrive in the Americas. Here, too, we consider the role of humans in megafauna extinctions.

The question of when people first arrived in Australia and the Americas is the subject of intense scientific controversy. It is important to recognize that it is also a subject of great sensitivity to indigenous people. The archaeological debate is framed entirely on the basis of scientific inquiry, which is often in conflict with native beliefs. The question of when people first arrived can conflict with native convictions that their people have been in a place since creation. Bridging these disparate worldviews requires care and respect. Although archeologists have only recently begun dealing with this conflict, they have already made great strides. The development of postprocessual archaeology, which acknowledges alternative narratives and viewpoints, provides room for dialogue and constructive disagreement. Of course, issues such as the treatment of human remains that indigenous groups claim as ancestral require particular care.

6.1 Modern Humans in East Asia

Populations of *Homo erectus* had arrived on the Indonesian island of Java perhaps as early as 1.8 million years ago, and by 1.6 million years ago they were well established in China. However, what happened to East Asian populations of *Homo erectus* while modern humans were evolving in Africa and Neanderthals were evolving in Europe remains unclear. On the one hand, some paleoanthropologists argue, as part of the multiregional hypothesis, that there was a local East Asian evolution of modern humans from *Homo erectus* parallel with the evolution of modern humans in Africa. On the other hand, proponents of the out of Africa hypothesis argue vehemently that in East Asia populations of *Homo erectus* persisted until they were replaced by modern humans from Africa. Both sides of the debate recognize that they are relying on inadequate data.

One critical piece of evidence has emerged from the dating of *Homo erectus* fossils from the island of Java. Electron spin resonance and uranium series dating of animal teeth found with *Homo erectus* fossils at the site of **Ngandong** have produced dates that range between 46,000 and 27,000 years ago (Swisher et al. 1996). If this range is correct, it indicates that populations of *Homo erectus* remained in East Asia far later than anywhere else in the world. This evidence offers strong support for the out of Africa hypothesis. However, these dates are not universally accepted, as some scientists doubt that the animal teeth were actually found in the same deposits as the hominin fossils.

The questions concerning the fate of *Homo erectus* and the initial appearance of modern humans in East Asia provide a rather uncertain backdrop to the debates surrounding the peopling of Australia and the New World (North and South America). The Paleolithic of East Asia is a critical area of research that is likely to see dramatic developments in coming years.

6.2 Australia

During periods of glacial advance and low sea level, Australia, Tasmania, and New Guinea were connected in a landmass known as **Sahul**. A similar landmass known as **Sunda** connected much of Southeast Asia, including Vietnam, Malaysia, the Philippines, and much of Indonesia. As shown in Figure 6.2 on the next page, Sunda and Sahul are separated by a string of islands known as Wallacea, where the channels between the islands are too deep to have been dry land at any time for the past 50 million years. The **Wallace Line** that runs through Wallacea separates the unique animals and plants of Australia from the animal and plant communities of Southeast Asia. In order to reach Australia, humans had to cross the Wallace Line by sea.

The discovery of stone tools on the island of Flores in Wallacea suggests that *Homo erectus* was able to cross bodies of water. The levels in which stone tools are found are dated to between 900,000 and 800,000 years ago, when *Homo erectus* was the only hominin in Southeast Asia. Some authors have argued that the evidence from Flores demonstrates that *Homo erectus* was able to make and use watercraft. However, *Homo erectus* was not the only mammal species to arrive in Flores between 900,000 and 800,000 years ago. At the same time, a species of large elephant (*Stegadon*) and a species of large rat also made their first appearance on the island. These animals could not have arrived by a land bridge connecting Flores to the Sunda, as it is clear that no such land bridge ever existed. It is suggested that a combination of low sea level and favourable currents enabled such animals to reach Flores. It is quite likely that *Homo erectus* could have arrived through similar circumstances.

Continued excavations on Flores at the site of Liang Bua have stunned the scientific community with the discovery of tiny hominins so unique that they have been given their own species name: *Homo floresiensis* (Brown et al. 2004). The hominin remains date to the period between 38,000 and 18,000 years ago (Morwood et al. 2004). The body of *Homo floresiensis* is quite small, and its brain is 380 cubic centimetres, about the size of a grapefruit, which is below the range of any other member of genus *Homo*. It appears likely that the unique characteristics of *Homo floresiensis* are the result of the long-term isolation of a population of *Homo erectus* on the island of Flores for hundreds of thousands of years. There is a general tendency for isolated island populations to evolve into species with reduced body size

▲▲ **Ngandong** Site on the island of Java where the most recent known fossil of *Homo erectus* was found, dating to between 46,000 and 27,000 years ago.

▲▲ **Sahul** The landmass that encompassed Australia, Tasmania, and New Guinea during periods of low sea level.

▲▲ **Sunda** The landmass that connected much of Southeast Asia during periods of low sea level.

▲▲ **Wallace Line** The line that runs through Wallacea and separates the unique animals and plants of Australia from the animal and plant communities of Southeast Asia.

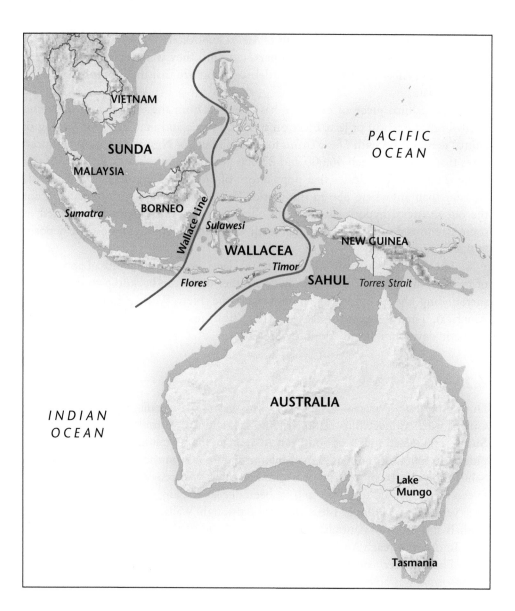

FIGURE 6.2 Map of the landmasses of Sunda and Sahul that existed during periods of low sea level. The areas exposed by low sea levels are indicated in purple.

(Van den Bergh et al. 2001). The discovery of *Homo floresiensis* raises many tantalizing issues, including the reasons for the eventual extinction of this species and the nature of their interactions with the first modern humans to arrive on the island. Some paleoanthropologists remain unconvinced that *Homo floresiensis* is a distinct species, arguing that the fossils discovered are modern humans with a pathology known as microcephaly that results in a small brain (Martin et al. 2006).

The stone tool industry from Liang Bua associated with *Homo floresiensis* is, like the human fossils themselves, somewhat odd and difficult to characterize (Moore et al. 2009). The methods of manufacture are very simple, and the retouched tools are not highly standardized. What is somewhat surprising is that there is a tendency to use flakes as cores. This is a technology used in the Acheulian of Africa to produce large bifacial tools, but on Flores the flakes produced are quite small. The stone tools are associated with faunal remains dominated by the bones of pygmy elephants and Komodo dragons (see Figure 6.3). Figure 6.4 shows that there are clear cut marks on the elephant bones. It is likely that the Komodo dragons, fierce predators, were vulnerable to hunting when they were inactive either due to nighttime cold or high midday temperatures (Van den Bergh et al. 2009).

There is no evidence that *Homo erectus* ever crossed Wallacea into Sahul. Nor is there evidence of an influx of mammals across the Wallace Line into Sahul at any time during the Pleistocene, as is found on Flores. Two possible routes for crossing Wallacea into Sahul have been identified. The northern route follows a string of small islands between the Indonesian island of Sulawesi and western New Guinea, known today as Irian Jaya. The southern route follows a series of small islands between Java and Timor, then a sea crossing between Timor and northern Australia. Both routes require sea voyages of greater than 10 kilometres and the settlement of a series of islands. Although the southern route is the most direct, it would have required a sea voyage of approximately 90 kilometres.

■ Dating the Earliest Human Occupation

A series of sites in Australia is now well dated to between 60,000 and 50,000 years ago. Thus, the arrival of humans in Australia predates the arrival of modern humans in Europe by at least 10,000 years.

FIGURE 6.4 Cut marks on elephant bones from Liang Bua, Flores.

The site of **Nauwalabila I**, located in Arnhem Land in Northern Australia, is a rock shelter with 3 metres of archaeological deposits (Bird et al. 2002). The deepest levels have been dated by thermoluminescence and optically stimulated luminescence to between 60,000 and 53,000 years ago. Unfortunately, attempts to radiocarbon date these levels have failed. The archaeological remains from the lowest levels are mostly flake stone tools, including a thick retouched scraper. Two pieces that apparently served as grinding stones were also found.

Lake Mungo is one of a series of dried-out lakes known as the Willandra Lakes, located in southern Australia near the city of Canberra (Bowler et al. 2003). Two human burials and numerous stone tools have been discovered eroding out of the Lower Mungo Unit along the edge of the dried-out lake bed. The deposits in which these skeletons were found have been dated to 40,000 years ago by optically stimulated luminescence. The earliest stone tools at Lake Mungo have been dated to between 50,000 and 46,000 years ago. The stone tools found at Lake Mungo are simple flake tools and cores similar to those found at Nauwalabila I. A number of hearths were found, and the animal bones that were recovered include a large number of fish remains.

The evidence for human occupation of Australia before 60,000 years is scant. The Jinmium Cave site in Arnhem Land has produced thermoluminescence dates of 116,000 years ago for deposits with archaeological material (Spooner 1998). However, these dates have been contested and are not widely accepted. Current data suggest that human occupation of Australia began roughly 60,000 years ago and that the spread of humans across the continent was fairly rapid. The Lake Mungo dates indicate that humans had spread to southern Australia within 10,000 years of their initial arrival on the continent.

The current understanding of the timing of the first arrival of modern humans in Australia suggests that by 60,000 years ago they were capable of sea voyages and had already spread far beyond Africa. Some archaeologists remain skeptical about these dates and question how modern humans could have arrived in Australia before reaching Europe (O'Connell and Allen 1998). For others, the early Australian dates offer support for the multiregional hypothesis. Such an early date for modern humans in Australia might support the idea that they evolved locally in East Asia. Yet another possibility is that there were multiple dispersals of modern humans out of Africa. The modern human populations that arrived in Australia might have followed the same coastal route used by *Homo erectus* to get to Java. We are left wondering about the voyagers who set off across the seas to arrive in Australia. What kind of boats did they use? What compelled them to take this voyage into an unknown land?

■ Megafauna Extinction

Throughout the world, there was widespread extinction of animal species at the end of the Pleistocene Ice Age. Particularly hard hit were large animals, collectively known as **megafauna**. Some have suggested that the extinction of megafauna was largely the result of hunting by modern humans; others argue that a more broadly based ecological explanation is needed.

The unique animal communities of Sahul fit the pattern of widespread extinction toward the end of the Pleistocene. Twenty-three of twenty-four genera of Australian land animals with a body weight greater than 45 kilograms became extinct at the end of the Pleistocene (see Figure 6.5). These large animals included marsupials such as the rhinoceros-sized kangaroo *Procoptodon*, mammals, and a large flightless bird, *Genyornis newtoni*. The date of the extinction of these species is the subject of debate. The dating of 700 *Genyornis newtoni* eggshells indicates that this species

▲▲ **Nauwalabila I** The site that offers the earliest secure evidence of human occupation of Australia, dating between 60,000 and 53,000 years ago.

▲▲ **Lake Mungo** One in a series of dried-out lakes located in southern Australia where evidence of human occupation dates to between 50,000 and 46,000 years ago.

megafauna Species of large animals that became extinct in many areas of the world, including the Americas and Australia, toward the end of the Pleistocene.

FIGURE 6.5 In an odd juxtaposition, a herd of sheep graze around a model reconstruction of an extinct giant marsupial.

disappeared suddenly around 50,000 years ago (Miller et al. 1999). A project dating paleontological sites indicates that the large placental and mammalian animals became extinct around 46,000 years ago (Roberts et al. 2001). This study was restricted to sites in which articulated animal bones were found (i.e., a part of the skeleton was found with bones in their proper anatomical positions). When focusing on articulated skeletons, there is a high degree of confidence that the bones are in their original geological context and that dating the sediments provides an accurate date for the bones. Some sites have produced unarticulated bones of megafauna in contexts dated considerably later in time. One of the most important of these sites is Cuddie Springs in southeastern Australia (Field et al. 2001). At Cuddie Springs, stone tools were found together with the bones of extinct megafauna in layers dated to between 36,000 and 27,000 years ago. There is some question as to whether these bones are in their original place of deposition, and it has not yet been possible to date the bones directly.

The preponderance of the data suggests that the extinction of Australian megafauna was an event that took place across the continent between 50,000 and 40,000 years ago. Thus, the event took place within 10,000 to 15,000 years of the first arrival of humans on the continent. It is difficult to explain why an extinction took place at this time. Although there was a major climatic change in Oxygen Isotope Stage 2 (the Last Glacial Maximum) around 20,000 to 15,000 years ago, the extinction appears to have preceded the change by more than 20,000 years.

The fact that the megafauna extinction took place during the first 10,000 years after the first arrival of humans in Australia suggests that human activity caused the extinction. However, evidence for hunting of megafauna by humans is practically nonexistent. Cuddie Springs is one of the few sites to produce an association of stone tools and the bones of extinct animals. There is no evidence from stone tools that the first inhabitants of Australia had highly sophisticated hunting weapons. Harpoons and spear-throwers developed only much later in Australian prehistory.

There is little evidence that the first inhabitants of Australia hunted large game or had a highly developed tool kit for hunting. It is therefore extremely unlikely that these people hunted the megafauna to the point of extinction. Some archaeologists have suggested that human activity altered the ecology of Australia in a manner that disrupted the highly specialized adaptations of the megafauna. One possible factor

FIGURE 6.6 Rock art from the site of Ubirr, Kakadu National Park, Australia. This figure gives a good sense of the range of equipment carried by aboriginal Australian hunter–gatherers.

would have been human use of fire in hunting. Rhys Jones has described the aboriginal use of fire in Australia as **fire-stick farming**. Early European travellers in Australia describe the active use of fire by aboriginal societies. For example, in 1848 Thomas Mitchell wrote, "Fire is necessary to burn the grass and form those open forests in which we find the large forest-kangaroo; the native applies that fire to the grass in certain seasons; in order that a young green crop may subsequently spring up, and so attract and enable him to kill and take the kangaroo with nets" (in Lourandos 1997, 97). If the first inhabitants of Australia used a similar strategy, then, over a period of 10,000 years, it might have resulted in the alteration of the ecology to the point where the megafaunal species became extinct.

■ Rock Art

Among archaeologists, Australia is known as a continent in which a hunter–gatherer way of life persisted until contact with Europeans. This characterization of Australia does little to express the diversity and richness of aboriginal societies. Ethnographers often point to the nonmaterial aspects of aboriginal Australian culture, particularly the highly developed mythological and ritual traditions. Aspects of aboriginal mythologies have found expression in the spectacular artwork painted on thousands of rock shelters across the continent; Figure 6.6 shows an example of rock art. Many of these sites were painted recently or are still revisited and painted today. Archaeological research has begun to provide evidence that this practice is of great antiquity.

Rock art in Australia takes many forms (Chaloupka 1993). One particularly interesting form is that of drawings made by applying beeswax to a rock-shelter wall. At the site of **Gunbilngmurrung** in western Arnhem Land, a beeswax figure of a turtle has been radiocarbon dated to 4,000 years ago (Watchman and Jones 2002). The turtle is drawn in "X-ray style," with some of the internal bone structure depicted. As at most Australian rock art sites, paintings at Gunbilngmurrung are found one on top of another. The beeswax turtle clearly lies above six older sets of figures drawn with red ochre that appear to be more than 4,000 years old.

In an ingenious application of optically stimulated luminescence dating, archaeologists have managed to date mud wasp nests overlying paintings on rock shelters in Arnhem Land. In one cave, a nest overlying a mulberry-coloured human figure was dated to 16,400 years ago. The human figure itself overlies a hand stencil that must be of even greater antiquity (Roberts et al. 1997).

■ Voyaging On

The spread of people across the islands of Micronesia and Polynesia (see Figure 6.7) began at least 35,000 years ago. Some of the earliest islands settled would have been visible from New Guinea. But by 29,000 years ago, there is evidence of voyagers occupying New Britain Island, which is not visible from either New Guinea or a previously occupied island. There is clear evidence from 20,000 years ago onward of human occupation across the Solomon Islands and the Bismarck Archipelago, a massive area that is more than 1,000 kilometres in length. Settlement of these islands was not the result of a one-time chance voyage. Obsidian from sources in New Britain is

fire-stick farming A term used by Rhys Jones to describe the aboriginal use of fire in Australia.

▲▲ **Gunbilngmurrung** A site in Australia where a beeswax figure of a turtle was found, radiocarbon dated to 4,000 years ago.

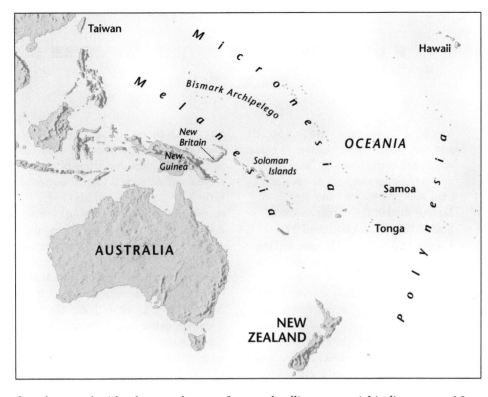

found across the islands, as are bones of a tree-dwelling marsupial indigenous to New Guinea, which provides evidence of sustained trade between islands. Although it is clear that these societies had mastered seafaring, there is not yet evidence for people venturing farther out into Melanesia until 3,500 years ago, when the **Lapita** culture spread across the region. The Lapita brought with them a new way of life that included a distinctive style of pottery (shown in Figure 6.8), large village settlements, and subsistence based on farming and fishing. Both archaeological and linguistic evidence

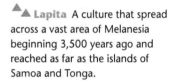 **Lapita** A culture that spread across a vast area of Melanesia beginning 3,500 years ago and reached as far as the islands of Samoa and Tonga.

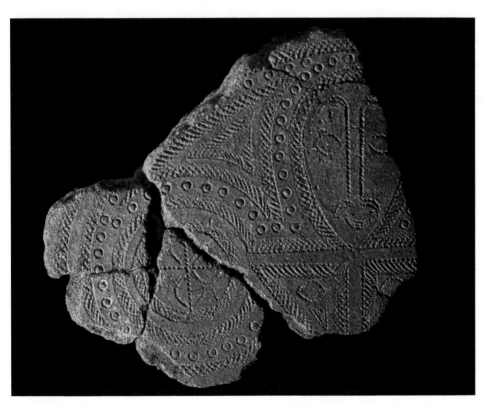

FIGURE 6.8 Fragment of Lapita pottery from the Solomon Islands. The incorporation of a human figure into the design is unusual for Lapita pottery.

Experimental Archaeology

Voyaging across the sea figures prominently in Polynesian oral history; however, many anthropologists have viewed these voyages as myths rather than stories based on actual experience. There is good reason for skepticism. Hawaiian oral history speaks of repeated trips between Hawaii and an ancestral land that appears to be Tahiti. Is such a voyage conceivable in a canoe without a compass? The trip from Hawaii to Tahiti covers over 3,620 kilometres of open sea, but the actual distance is quite a bit farther, since it is necessary to curve eastward against the trade winds and currents that flow across the course. Archaeologists came to view the ancient Polynesians as hapless sailors blown off course until they reached fortuitous landfall.

A set of experiments has led to a reversal of opinion about the voyaging of ancient Polynesians and the veracity of Polynesian oral history. The first experiment was a computer simulation. In 1973, Michael Levison and colleagues used a computer model of Pacific Ocean currents and wind speeds to run over 100,000 simulations of what would happen to a vessel drifting away from various Polynesian islands. They found that while hitting an island by drifting from east to west was possible, drifting from west to east and hitting an island was virtually impossible. These results cast doubt on the claim made by Thor Heyerdahl, based on his voyages on the raft Kon-Tiki, that Polynesia was settled by drifting sailors from South America. Perhaps most significantly, the computer simulation showed that out of 16,000 trials from various Polynesian islands, none reached Hawaii. The implication is that Hawaii was reached by sailors who set their course intentionally.

In 1976, to push the experiment a step farther, Ben Finney and colleagues formed the Polynesian Voyaging Society and built a double-hull canoe. The goal was to sail from Hawaii to Tahiti using only traditional methods of navigation. Mau Piailug, a master navigator from Satawal Atoll in the Caroline Islands, guided the canoe, christened the *Hokuile,* to a successful landfall in Tahiti. Since that time, the *Hokuile* has continued to voyage across the Pacific. The experiment successfully showed that controlled voyaging across Polynesia using traditional methods was possible, and has sparked a rebirth of pride and interest among Polynesian and Hawaiian communities in their legacy of sea voyaging. The project has also led to a complex "dialogue developing between indigenous peoples in search of their own past and anthropologists seeking to reconstruct ancient practices" (Finney 1991, 398).

Finney's research is an example of an application of experimental archaeology, which allows archaeologists to test ideas about the past in a controlled setting. The range and scope of experimental archaeology is vast. At Butser Farm in England, researchers have recreated a working Bronze Age farm. In a very different setting, archaeologists working in engineering laboratories have tested the fracture mechanics that underlie stone tool manufacture. At the root of all these activities is the spirit of the inquiry, an effort to explore the dynamics of the past by carrying out experiments in the present. Experimental archaeology is closely associated with ethnoarchaeology, taphonomic analysis, and other aspects of archaeological methodology that use studies set in the present as a source of insight into the dynamics that formed the archaeological record. ●

For more information on the Polynesian Voyaging Society see http://pvs.kcc.hawaii.edu/index.html.

FIGURE 6.9 The canoes of the Polynesian Voyaging Society have provided insight into the archaeology of the Pacific Islands. These vessels have also served as a powerful means for local people to explore their history and identity.

place the origins of the Lapita people in Taiwan and the islands of Southeast Asia. The Lapita migration eventually covered an area 7,240 kilometres across, reaching eastward as far as Samoa and Tonga. What drove these voyagers not only to discover but also to settle new lands? It does not appear that population pressure can account for this expansion. It would be virtually impossible for population growth rates to even keep up with, let alone fuel, the rapid rate of colonization. An intriguing idea is that Lapita social structure was the underlying cause for their migration. Patrick Kirsch suggests that the Lapita had very strict rules of inheritance that heavily favoured the firstborn. Kirsch writes that "in such societies, junior siblings frequently adopt a strategy of seeking new lands to settle where they can found their own 'house' and lineage, assuring their own offspring access to quality resources" (Kirsch 1997, 65). Similar social dynamics, along with developments in the technologies of seafaring, might have also underlain the final stage of expansions into Eastern Polynesia (including Hawaii) and New Zealand. Further research is needed to refine the chronology for the initial occupation of these islands, but the oldest dates are currently between 1,000 and 1,500 years ago, which suggests that there was a significant hiatus between the Lapita expansion across to Samoa and Tonga and the complete colonization of the Polynesian islands.

6.3 The New World

Despite decades of intensive research, the timing of the first arrival of humans in the New World (North and South America) remains the topic of heated debate. There are three models for human occupation of the Americas. The **Clovis first model**, long dominant among North American archaeologists, views the Clovis culture, dated to between 13,500 and 12,500 years ago, as the initial human occupation of the Americas. Recently, a large number of archaeologists have come to support the **pre-Clovis model**, according to which the initial human occupation of the New World dates back earlier than 13,500 years ago. The **early arrival model**, which argues for human presence in the New World by 30,000 years ago, is a minority position.

■ Clovis First

In 1932, archaeologists excavating in **Blackwater Draw** near the town of Clovis, New Mexico, discovered the remains of bison in a level with Folsom points. Below this level, evidence of an earlier occupation was found. In this earlier level, spearpoints were found that were slightly different from the Folsom points. Clovis points, as these earlier forms came to be known, are fluted like the Folsom points, but the resulting channel does not extend the entire length of the point. Figure 6.10 shows two Clovis points. At Blackwater Draw, Clovis points were found together with mammoth and horse bones.

Clovis points have subsequently been found on a large number of sites across North America. These discoveries have led many archaeologists to conclude that the remains found at Clovis are characteristic of the earliest human occupation of the Americas.

CLOVIS CULTURE AND CHRONOLOGY. The definition of **Clovis culture** is based largely on the form of spearpoints. In the midcontinental United States and eastern Canada, Clovis points are absent, but similar pieces known as Gainey points are found on many sites. Besides spearpoints, other stone tools found on Clovis

FIGURE 6.10 Clovis points from the Lehner and Naco sites in Arizona. The point on the left is 9.7 cm long; the point on the right is 7.2 cm long. Both have been carefully shaped by bifacial flaking and have small flutes at their base.

Clovis first model Clovis culture, dated to 13,500 to 12,500 years ago, is the first human occupation in the Americas.

pre-Clovis model Human occupation of the Americas predates 13,500 years ago.

early arrival model Human occupation of the Americas began as early as 30,000 to 40,000 years ago.

▲▲ Blackwater Draw A site near Clovis, New Mexico, where spearpoints were found in levels below Folsom points.

Clovis culture The period many North American archaeologists view as the initial human occupation of the Americas, dated to between 13,500 and 12,500 years ago.

FIGURE 6.11 Engraved stones from the Gault site, Texas, are among the only incised artifacts found on Clovis sites.

sites include blades and multifunctional tools made on flakes. Apart from these stone tools, few cultural remains are found. Built features are not known, and the main features identified are hearths. A deep feature found in the Clovis levels at Blackwater Draw has been identified as a well that might have been excavated in response to drought conditions (Haynes et al. 1999).

The main type of bone tool found on Clovis sites is a rod-shaped object probably used as part of the haft of a spearpoint. A worked bone discovered at the Murray Spring site in Arizona is described as a shaft wrench because of the hole bored in one end. This is the only such object known from a Clovis site; engraved or incised objects are rare. At the Gault site in Texas, limestone slabs with geometric decorations have been found (see Figure 6.11), but it is not clear that they are from the Clovis level (Haynes 2002). The discovery of Clovis tools at a red-ochre mining site known as Powars II in Platte County, Wyoming, suggests that colourants might have been used during the period (Stafford et al. 2003).

The chronological range for Clovis sites is between 13,500 and 12,500 calendar years ago. The dates 11,500–10,500 B.P. are often given for the Clovis period; however, these are uncalibrated radiocarbon dates.

MIGRATION ROUTES. When global sea levels dropped during periods of glacial advance, the Bering Strait that separates Siberia from Alaska became dry land. The resulting land bridge that connected Asia to North America is part of the region known as **Beringia**. It is likely that the first inhabitants of the New World crossed into North America across this land bridge. The area of Beringia includes eastern Siberia, Alaska, and parts of the Yukon, as well as the land that today is submerged under the Bering Strait. Beringia was not covered by glaciers, but was a steppe landscape with a rich cover of sage and grass that supported extensive populations of mammals, including mammoth, horse, and bison. Figure 6.12 illustrates the changes in sea level in Beringia between 21,000 and 10,000 years ago.

The continental ice sheets that covered much of Canada during the last period of glacial advance (the Wisconsin glaciation, or Oxygen Isotope Stage 2) consisted of the Cordilleran glacier in the west and the more massive Laurentide glacier in the east. Proponents of the Clovis first model have argued that toward the end of the last glaciation a gap existed between the Cordilleran and Laurentide glaciers. This gap formed an **ice-free corridor** that funnelled people down from Alaska to the Great Plains, from where they spread rapidly across North America. Recent research has cast doubt on whether such an ice-free corridor existed in time to serve as a migration route for the Clovis people (Mandryk et al. 2001). However, the discovery of the partial frozen carcass of a now extinct species of bison at Tsiigehtchic in the Northwest Territories casts a tantalizing new light on the ice-free corridor (Zazula et al. 2009). This rare specimen has been dated to approximately 12,000 years ago indicating that by this time the ice sheets had begun to retreat and the ice-free corridor was populated by bison.

The Archaeological Evidence. If, indeed, the Clovis people moved into Alaska from Siberia and then migrated rapidly down an ice-free corridor, one would

▲▲ **Beringia** A land bridge that connected Asia and North America during periods of low sea level.

ice-free corridor A potential migration route for populations expanding out of Beringia, running between the Cordilleran and Laurentide ice sheets.

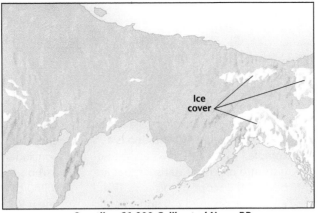

FIGURE 6.12 Maps showing changes of sea level in Beringia between 21,000 and 10,000 years ago.

Ice cover

Coastline 21,000 Calibrated Years BP

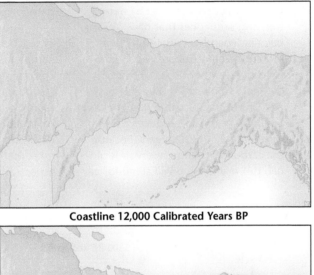

Coastline 12,000 Calibrated Years BP

Coastline 10,000 Calibrated Years BP

expect to find a well-developed tradition of fluted points in Siberia and Alaska before 13,500 years ago, the date of the earliest Clovis sites.

The earliest well-dated site in Beringia is Broken Mammoth Cave in central Alaska (Yesner 2001). The stone tools at this site are characteristic of the **Nenana** culture, which dates to between 14,000 and 12,800 years ago. Nenana stone tools include small, bifacially flaked triangular points and knives. Among bone and ivory tools are an eyed needle and points. The preservation of animal remains at Broken Mammoth Cave is excellent. A wide range of species is found, including large game (bison and elk), carnivores (bear, wolf, and fox), small game (squirrel, hare, marmot, and otter), and birds (goose, duck, and ptarmigan). Stone tools

Nenana The earliest culture in Beringia, dating to between 14,000 and 12,800 years ago.

Radiocarbon Calibration

In Chapter 1, the basic principles of radiocarbon dating were introduced. The essential facts are that the ratio of carbon-14 to nonradioactive carbon is the same throughout the carbon exchange reservoir, which includes the atmosphere, oceans, and biosphere, and that carbon-14 decays at a constant rate. W.F. Libby, who discovered radiocarbon dating, believed that the carbon ratio was not only constant throughout the earth, but was also constant through time. He has been proven wrong. Most dramatically, modern burning of fossil fuels and atomic weapons testing have increased the amount of carbon-14 in the reservoir. Also, detailed analyses of tree-ring-dated samples indicate that there have been significant fluctuations in the concentration of carbon-14 over the past 50,000 years. Apart from contributions from burning fossil fuels and testing atomic weapons, there is a gradual trend of reduction in the concentration of carbon-14 over time. Overlying this decline is an extraordinarily complex pattern of fluctuations, known as "wiggles." The long-term trend is thought to be related to a reduction in the strength of the earth's magnetic field, while the wiggles appear to be related to solar activity.

Because the ratio of carbon-14 to nonradioactive carbon is not stable over time, radiocarbon years do not map directly onto calendar years. If we think of the decay of radiocarbon as a stopwatch that begins at the death of an organism, the problem is that the starting line is set by the concentration of radiocarbon and this starting line has been redrawn over and over again.

How have archaeologists dealt with this complication? Calibration is a complex issue that draws archaeologists into realms of statistics that are beyond the scope of this text. The essential tools used to connect radiocarbon time with calendar time are calibration curves created by dating tree-ring sequences that have already been independently dated by dendrochronology (Chapter 9). Calibration curves present the radiocarbon date for samples of known calendar age. For example, a tree ring known to be 6,900 years old produces a radiocarbon date of 6,000 years. Because the carbon exchange reservoir is global, this relationship will stand for all organisms that died in that particular calendar year. Conversely, one can conclude that a sample with a radiocarbon age of 6,000 years is actually 6,900 calendar years old. The calendar age is known as the calibrated date. All dates in this book are calibrated dates.

It is important to emphasize that in practice, calibration is extremely complex, largely because of the aforementioned wiggles, which often result in a single radiocarbon age corresponding to more than one calendar age on the calibration curve. Resolving these conflicts is among the most mathematically challenging aspects of archaeology. ●

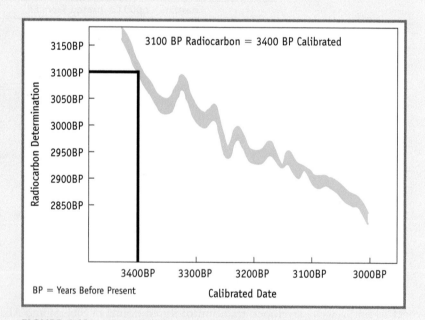

FIGURE 6.13 Radiocarbon calibration diagram. To arrive at a corrected radiocarbon date, draw a horizontal line from a radiocarbon determination on the y-axis to the point where it intersects with the calibration curve (the wiggly blue line). Draw a vertical line from this point down to the x-axis to arrive at the calibrated date. How do the wiggles on the calibration curve complicate finding a calibrated date?

similar to those uncovered at Broken Mammoth Cave are found at the site of Ushki on the Siberian side of the Bering Strait. At neither site is there evidence for fluted points. In subsequent periods, the stone tools of Siberia and Alaska are characterized by the production of very small microblades. This toolmaking tradition did not spread into areas to the south of the coast of British Columbia. Fluted points are found in Alaska; however, most do not come from sites that have been dated. It seems that the appearance of fluted points in this area is considerably later than the Clovis.

■ Pre-Clovis

In the years following the discoveries made at Folsom and Blackwater Draw, many claims have been made for sites predating the earliest Clovis occupation. Among the sites that have produced evidence supporting a pre-Clovis occupation of the New World are Meadowcroft Rockshelter, Pennsylvania; Monte Verde, Chile; Pedra Pintada, Brazil; and Quebrada Tacahuay, Peru. The pre-Clovis hypothesis is also supported by reconstructions of a possible migration route along the Pacific Coast.

MEADOWCROFT ROCKSHELTER. One of the most compelling claims for pre-Clovis occupation of North America comes from excavations of the **Meadowcroft Rockshelter** in western Pennsylvania. Excavations have uncovered eleven natural levels in the shelter. Stratum IIa, near the base of the sequence, has produced a series of radiocarbon dates ranging between 23,000 and 15,500 years ago in association with stone tools. These dates have been disputed by archaeologists who claim that the carbon used in dating the site has been contaminated by "old" carbon carried by groundwater from coal beds in the surrounding bedrock.

MONTE VERDE. The site of **Monte Verde**, excavated by Tom Dillehay, is on the banks of Chinchihuapi Creek in southern Chile (Dillehay 1989). Located near the southern tip of South America, this site would seem to be an unlikely spot to find the earliest occupation of the New World. However, the discoveries made at Monte Verde pose the most serious threat to the Clovis first hypothesis. The archaeological layer at Monte Verde, which the excavators designate as the MVII level, has produced a series of radiocarbon dates that give an average of 15,000 years ago, at least 1,500 years older than Clovis. The MVII level is overlain by a level of peat dated to between 14,000 and 12,500 years ago.

Much of the debate concerning Monte Verde is due to the extremely unusual nature of the site (see Figure 6.14 on the next page). The preservation of organic remains is extraordinary. Not only were the bones of animals found, but there are even traces of meat. Among the artifacts are a small number of stone tools, including projectile points. The bulk of the artifacts, however, are made of organic material, including rope and wood. Much of the evidence for human occupation comes from the discovery of objects (e.g., plant remains and unmodified stones) that the excavators argue were transported to the site by humans. The excavators have also identified the remains of huts built of organic materials. Perhaps the most unusual evidence found at Monte Verde is the trace of a human footprint.

The clearly dated MVII horizon presents a significant challenge to the Clovis first model. It is not surprising, particularly given Monte Verde's unexpected location and the unusual nature of its artifacts, that Dillehay's announcement of

Meadowcroft Rockshelter A site in Pennsylvania where evidence was found supporting pre-Clovis occupation of the New World.

Monte Verde A site in Chile where evidence of human occupation 15,000 years ago supports the argument that Clovis culture does not represent the first occupation of the Americas.

FIGURE 6.14 Foundations of a wood structure at Monte Verde, Chile. Some archaeologists have questioned whether these are actually the remnants of human habitations.

FIGURE 6.15 Stratigraphic profile and radiocarbon dates from Pedra Pintada. The diagram shows the stratigraphic context of the radiocarbon samples. Note that the dates shown are uncalibrated radiocarbon dates and are therefore later than the dates of the occupation of the site given in the text. Why do you think the excavators ran so many radiocarbon samples?

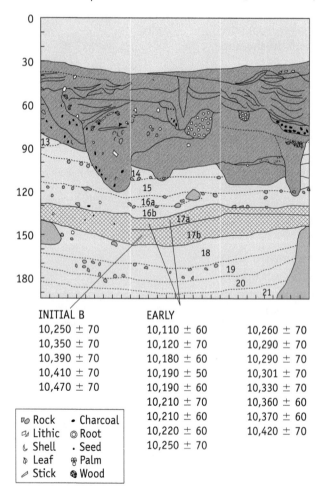

INITIAL B	EARLY	
10,250 ± 70	10,110 ± 60	10,260 ± 70
10,350 ± 70	10,120 ± 70	10,290 ± 70
10,390 ± 70	10,180 ± 60	10,290 ± 70
10,410 ± 70	10,190 ± 50	10,301 ± 70
10,470 ± 70	10,190 ± 60	10,330 ± 70
	10,210 ± 70	10,360 ± 60
	10,210 ± 60	10,370 ± 60
	10,220 ± 60	10,420 ± 70
	10,250 ± 70	

⬳ Rock	· Charcoal
⌇ Lithic	◎ Root
ↄ Shell	· Seed
◌ Leaf	⚘ Palm
✐ Stick	❀ Wood

the site's discovery was met with considerable skepticism (Fiedel 1999). Doubts were raised concerning the site's stratigraphy and the validity of the artifacts. In 1997, a prominent group of prehistorians visited Monte Verde and formed a commission to judge the validity of Dillehay's claim (Meltzer et al. 1997). Although they were not able to see the actual site, which had been destroyed by road construction, they were able to see all of the artifacts, detailed excavation records, and the regional geology. At the end of the trip, the commission published an article stating that Dillehay's identification of Monte Verde as a site of human occupation dating to 15,000 years ago was valid. The commission's report was met with criticism and even hostility, and one member of the commission recanted his support for Dillehay. In subsequent attacks, many important questions have been raised about Dillehay's interpretation of Monte Verde. However, the existence of strong evidence that humans were in southern Chile 15,000 years ago has given new life to the idea that perhaps Clovis does not represent the initial occupation of the New World.

CAVERNA DE PEDRA PINTADA. At present, Monte Verde remains the only site in South America that has produced widely accepted evidence for pre-Clovis occupation of the Americas. However, other discoveries in South America also cast doubt on the Clovis first model. Working in the Brazilian Amazon, Anna Roosevelt excavated the cave of **Pedra Pintada**, located in the Monte Alegre region of the Lower Amazon (Roosevelt 1996), a region rich in caves, many of which bear traces of decoration. Pedra Pintada has a stratigraphic sequence 2.25 metres in depth from the surface to bedrock. Figure 6.15 shows the stratigraphy of Pedra Pintada, along with associated radiocarbon dates. Fifty-six burnt remains of seeds were dated from layers 16 and 17, near the base of the deposits (see Figure 6.16). The dates obtained range between 13,000 and 11,500 years ago. This occupation is thus roughly contemporary with Clovis.

The stone tools from the early levels at Pedra Pintada include triangular bifacial points, as well as tools made on flakes, as shown in Figure 6.17. Hundreds of lumps of red pigment were found in layers 16 and 17, but it was not possible to determine whether the paintings on the cave walls date to the same early period. The preservation of plant remains on the site is excellent, and there is evidence that the early occupants of the cave ate a wide range of plant foods, including fruits, palm, and Brazil nuts. The most abundant animal bones were fish, of both small and large species. There were also the remains of large and small land mammals.

The discoveries at Pedra Pintada demonstrate that either at the same time or slightly after the Clovis occupation of North America, people lived in the Brazilian tropical rain forest, subsisting not on megafauna, but on a wide range of resources, including plants and fish. Unlike Monte Verde, Pedra Pintada does not claim to be earlier than Clovis. However, the results of this excavation cast doubts on a simple model for the initial occupation of the New World by Clovis hunters. Roosevelt concludes that the initial occupation of the Americas was more complex than the Clovis first model recognizes and that Clovis was "only one of several regional traditions" (Roosevelt 1996, 381).

QUEBRADA TACAHUAY. Further support for Roosevelt's argument comes from excavations at Quebrada Tacahuay, near the coast of Peru (Keefer et al. 1998). Limited excavations at this site have produced a small number of stone tools from a level dated between 12,700 and 12,500 years ago. These stone tools were found together with a large collection of animal bones in the remnants of hearths. The dominant faunal species are seabirds and marine fish. The dominant species of fish is the anchovy, which, due to its small size, suggests the use of nets. Some remains of marine mollusks were also found. Evidence of cut marks and burning were discovered on the bird bones, and there is some evidence for burning on the fish remains. The discoveries at Quebrada Tacahuay indicate that people in Peru were hunting seabirds and fishing, possibly with the use of netting, roughly contemporaneously with Clovis occupation of North America.

COASTAL MIGRATION. One obvious objection to Monte Verde is that it seems implausible that people coming from Siberia would reach Chile before arriving in the Great Plains, particularly if the ice-free corridor between the Cordilleran and Laurentide glaciers was the only route connecting Beringia with areas to the south. The discovery at Monte Verde suggests that decades of intensive research in North America have missed evidence of thousands of years of human occupation.

In the 1970s, K.R. Fladmark advanced a model of human migration into the Americas along the west coast rather than through an ice-free corridor (Fladmark 1979). This model has recently gained widespread attention. One attraction of a **coastal migration** is that it would make an early occupation of Chile more plausible. If the first occupants of the New World were adapted to coastal environments, they might have moved relatively rapidly down the coasts of North and South America. With geologists increasingly casting doubt as to whether an ice-free corridor was ever a viable migration route, interest in coastal migrations has grown.

Still, there are objections to a coastal route for human occupation of the New World. In parts of Alaska, there may have been glaciers blocking the coast, so that travel would have required the use of boats. Moreover, there is no evidence to date of any early sites on the West Coast from Alaska to California.

▲▲ **Pedra Pintada** A site in the Brazilian Amazon that demonstrates that there were groups contemporary with the Clovis that were living in South America in a rain-forest environment.

FIGURE 6.16 Carbonized seeds of tropical forest trees from Pedra Pintada, Brazil.

FIGURE 6.17 Stone tools from Pedra Pintada, Brazil.

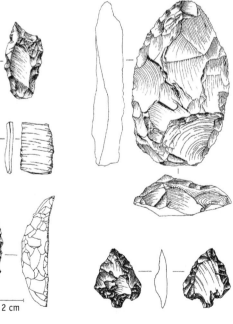

Repatriation of Indigenous Burial Remains

On January 9,1877, at least eighty-three Northern Cheyenne were massacred by U.S. government troops near Fort Robinson, Nebraska. Remains of seventeen of the Northern Cheyenne, including those of a three-year-old child, were collected for study by the U.S. Army Medical Examiner and were subsequently transferred to the Smithsonian National Museum of Natural History. Over one hundred years later, on October 9, 1993, the bones from the Fort Robinson massacre were returned to the Northern Cheyenne for reburial (Thornton 2002).

In 1996, a human skeleton was discovered washing out of the bank of the Columbia River near the town of Kennewick, Washington. When a flint arrow was found embedded in the pelvis, it became clear that this was not a normal forensics case. Radiocarbon dating of the bones showed that Kennewick Man was 9,200 years old, one of the earliest known human remains in the Americas. The Army Corps of Engineers, which controls the land where the skeleton was found, decided to repatriate the bones to the Confederated Tribes of the Umatilla Indian Reservation for reburial. Outraged

archaeologists filed suit in federal court to block the reburial and allow for scientific study of the skeleton. How, the archaeologists asked, could the Umatilla claim direct descent from an individual who lived over 9,000 years ago? How could the loss of such a valuable scientific specimen possibly be justified? As of 2005, the archaeologists have prevailed in court, but it is unlikely that this is the final word on the disposition of Kennewick Man.

Few would dispute the right of the Northern Cheyenne to bury their dead, but at the same time many find the reburial of ancient skeletons such as that of Kennewick Man to be a tragic loss of knowledge. The scope of the problem cannot be overstated; estimates place the number of aboriginal human remains in North American institutions at between 100,000 and 200,000 individuals (Isaac 2002). Indigenous communities insist that the scientists must understand the pain and destruction caused by the excavation and collection of the remains of their ancestors. But the archaeological and scientific communities, of course, have a tremendous stake in this dispute. Claims for the reburial of human remains and restrictions

on the study of skeletons strike at the core of the archaeological enterprise.

The dispute over repatriation is ultimately a political issue, and the U.S. government has crafted an impressive mechanism for regulating competing claims. A measure known as the Native American Graves Protection and Repatriation Act (NAGPRA) was voted into law in 1990. Senator John McCain eloquently expressed the need for NAGPRA, stating that "the subject of repatriation is charged with high emotions in both the Native American community and the museum community. I believe this bill represents a true compromise" (quoted in McKeown 2002).

NAGPRA applies to all federal agencies and all museums that receive federal funds. The basis of the law is the right of Indian tribes and Native Hawaiian organizations to request the repatriation of burial remains, funerary offerings, sacred objects, and objects of cultural patrimony. There are also provisions requiring consultations with Indian tribes and Native Hawaiians concerning the disposition of human and cultural remains discovered on federal lands.

Reconstructing the contours of the West Coast of North America during the end of the Wisconsin glaciation is complex. On the one hand, the drop in sea level due to the formation of glaciers led to the exposure of extensive areas of the continental shelf. On the other hand, in the northwestern coast, the weight of the glaciers actually lowered the landmass in places, causing sea levels to be higher than they would otherwise be. Recent studies suggest that despite the weight of the glaciers, the sea level during the end of the Wisconsin glaciation was considerably lower than it is today. The exposed coastal region was rich in natural resources and largely free of glaciers. The difficulty is that if there was a migration along the coast, most of the relevant archaeological sites would be submerged today.

In summarizing a coastal migration model, E.J. Dixon proposes that any "human colonization of the Americas suggested by the most current data [consists of] coastal migration with inland movement and settlement within broad environmental zones . . . that extend from north to south throughout the Americas" (Dixon

coastal migration The route some archaeologists say was used by the earliest people in the Americas to move out of Beringia instead of moving through an ice-free corridor.

The implementation of NAGPRA is often complex. Although cases such as Kennewick Man have led to intense disputes between indigenous groups and archaeologists, such acrimony has proven to be the exception rather than the rule. The general consensus is that the impact of NAGPRA has been positive. The clear legal language provides a framework for archaeologists to redress historic wrongs. Many archaeologists have found that the implementation of NAGPRA has led to a new level of engagement between themselves and indigenous communities.

In the Canadian context, the repatriation of aboriginal cultural property and burials is not the subject of a unified legislative act. The history of the relationship between archaeologists and aboriginal communities in Canada is complex and, in many cases, painful (Jacknis 1996). Repatriation in Canada is largely addressed through private negotiations between institutions and aboriginal communities (Bell and Paterson 1999). Many institutions, including the Canadian Museum of Civilization, have developed detailed policies on repatriation (www.civilization.ca/cmc/repat/

repat00e.html). In some areas of the country, provincial legislation also addresses these issues (see www.iigr.ca/pdf/documents/892_First_Nations_Sacred_Cer.pdf for Alberta legislation).

A notable case in the emerging relationship between archaeologists and aboriginal communities in Canada is that of Kwäday Dän Ts'ìnchí (Long-Ago Person Found), the frozen corpse of a man dating to 500 years ago found in northern British Columbia. In this case, a committee including representatives of the Champagne and Aishihuk First

Nations on whose traditional lands the body was found oversees research on samples taken from the Kwäday Dän Ts'ìnchí (www.tsa.gov.bc.ca/archaeology/kwaday_dän_ts'inchi/index.htm). The remains were cremated and the ashes ceremonially scattered in 2001.

REFERENCE: Cressida Fforde, Jane Hubert, and Paul Turnbull. (2002). "The Dead and Their Possessions: Repatriation in Principle, Policy, and Practice," in *One World Archaeology*, vol. 43. London: Routledge.

FIGURE 6.18 Onondagas prepare ancestral remains for reburial in Jamesville, New York.

2001, 292). Like Roosevelt, Dixon sees the initial occupation of the Americas as a complex process of groups of people adapting to different environments. Unlike the traditional model, which sees people moving through an ice-free corridor before being "dumped" onto the Great Plains, Dixon sees a process of people migrating along the coast and branching off to inhabit inland regions they encountered along the way. Clovis would simply be one of these branches.

■ Early Arrival Model

The pre-Clovis model differs significantly from the Clovis first model in the precise timing of the initial occupation of the New World and the migration routes used to reach the areas south of the glaciers. However, both models agree that human occupation of the Americas took place during the later stages of the last period of glacial advance (the Wisconsin glaciation, or Oxygen Isotope Stage 2). Thus, the consensus of the archaeological community is that, with the exception of Antarctica, the Americas were the last continents to be occupied by humans. Whether these people followed a coastal route or an ice-free corridor, their voyage breached one of the last true frontiers.

A small number of archaeologists argue that the initial human occupation of the Americas was actually much earlier. Proponents of an early arrival model place the first appearance of humans in the Americas as early as 50,000 years ago, in Oxygen Isotope Stage 3. One impediment to this model is that human occupation of Beringia at that early date was extremely limited. Recent discoveries in Siberia have begun to push back the date for the initial occupation of western Beringia. The Yana River site, dated to 30,000 years ago, is the earliest evidence for human occupation of eastern Siberia.

Archaeologists working in the Old Crow Basin in the Yukon claimed to have found evidence of human activity dating as far back as 40,000 years ago. However, direct radiocarbon dating of a number of bone tools from the basin has shown that they are actually less than 3,000 years old (Nelson et al. 1986). Currently, it is claimed that two bones found in contexts dating to 40,000 years ago at Old Crow show evidence of being cut by a stone tool, and a number of bones are held to have been flaked by humans (Morlan 2003). Neither of these claims is widely accepted, and there is as yet no clear evidence for human occupation of western Beringia (Alaska and the Yukon) before the end of the last glacial advance.

A number of claims have been made for evidence of early human occupation of South America. At Monte Verde, Dillehay found objects that might be tools in level MV I, which is below level MV II. MV I is dated to 33,000 years ago. The evidence of artifacts from that level has not been widely accepted, and Dillehay himself expresses some reservations about this claim.

The boldest claim for early human occupation of the Americas comes from the excavators of the site of **Pedra Furada** in Brazil (Guidon et al. 1996). Excavations in the rock shelter at the site uncovered burnt patches associated with pieces identified as stone tools. Radiocarbon dating placed the earliest levels at Pedra Furada between 48,000 and 35,000 years ago. The excavators argue that the burnt patches are evidence of controlled use of fire by humans. Critics have countered that these patches are equally consistent with natural bush fires. The major point of contention is whether the pieces identified as stone tools are actually the result of human manufacture. Most of the tools are quartzite cobbles that have been very simply chipped and whose source is a geological deposit found at the top of the cliff, 100 metres directly above the site. The actual sediment of the site is made up of cobbles and soil that plunged down from the top of the cliff over the course of millennia, probably during periods of heavy rainfall.

David Meltzer, James Adovasio, and Tom Dillehay have suggested that the chipping found on the stones recovered at Pedra Furada is the result, not of human activity, but of the impact of the cobbles as they fell down the cliff and were smashed on the ground (Meltzer et al. 1994). The researchers suggest that the cobbles are "geofacts"—objects created by geological forces—rather than artifacts made by humans. The excavators Fabio Parenti, Michel Fontugue, and Claude Guérin have reacted with outrage to this suggestion, stating that the patterns of chipping found at Pedra Furada are too complex to have been created by a natural process. Resolving the question of whether humans were involved in the burnt features and stone tools found at Pedra Furada is of critical importance. However, it seems unlikely that a site with the geological characteristics of Pedra Furada will ever be able to provide the kind of unambiguous proof of human occupation needed for there to be widespread acceptance of the early arrival model.

▲▲ **Pedra Furada** A site in Brazil where highly controversial evidence of human occupation, dating between 48,000 and 35,000 years ago, was found.

Mawlukhotepun—Working Together

SUSAN BLAIR, UNIVERSITY OF NEW BRUNSWICK

Karen Perley and I met on a bright sunny day in late August 1996 near the banks of the Jemseg River in central New Brunswick. Our meeting place was an old farmer's field next to the river, overgrown with alders and wildflowers and alive with grasshoppers, frogs, and snakes. The provincial Department of Transportation had plans to begin clearing this area for the new TransCanada highway within the year. This rerouting of the highway was long overdue and would replace the narrow, winding, windblown road along the banks of the Saint John River with a broad, four-lane, modern highway.

Under our feet, we were told, was an archaeological site.

I was a recently graduated archaeologist, and Karen was an educator, grandmother, and traditional person from Tobique First Nation. With us were Patrick Polchies of Kingsclear First Nation, provincial archaeologist Dr. Chris Turnbull, and highway engineers. We were being given an opportunity to participate in what grew to be the largest archaeological salvage ever undertaken in Atlantic Canada. Over the next eight months, we struggled through a Maritime winter, devising ground thawing units that were laid in succession in long, tunnel-like tents. As we excavated, we realized that the deposits that we had thought would be localized, shallow, recent, and disturbed were in all ways more complicated. Furthermore, a precipitous construction schedule left us little time to excavate, let alone adequately consult and communicate with the descendants of the creators of the site, the Wolastoqiyik. We hired First Nations crew and crew leaders and established advisory committees and processes of notification. Nonetheless, throughout the fall there was growing concern in First Nation communities

and protest about the project and the appropriateness of archaeology itself. There were also unfounded rumours that we were excavating burials.

My archaeological training had only partially prepared me for this experience. I had learned to think critically about science and the role of authority in the process of exploring about the past, but I had little idea of how I could transpose these concepts into practice. How should I balance the role of project leader with a reflexive theoretical stance?

Karen guided me through these challenges by refocusing me on the specific and immediate challenges of communication and practice. Our oblong test units looked like burial plots. Our practice of marking artifacts with clear polish and ink was being viewed as an assault on the objects themselves. Elders needed to feel welcomed and comfortable.

Karen brought us to her community and culture and taught us basic principles to guide our work. *Mawlukhotepun*—"working together"—reflected the true spirit of collaboration and partnership between equals. *Kcit'mitahoswagon*—"respect"—governed not only our interactions with individuals, but our relationship to their culture, history, and ideas.

Weci apaciayawik—"so that it will come back"—firmly rooted the idea that we must return something for everything gained from our work. In a profound way, these teachings led me to reconsider my role as team leader, technical expert, and archaeologist. Working together meant relinquishing authority and control. Respect meant hearing instead of telling. Commitment to archaeology meant an obligation to living and breathing people and their communities. In Karen's words, "archaeology should not be only about the past and the dead but should also represent the present and the living. When you include First Nations perspectives in science, you

FIGURE 6.19 The Jemseg Crossing site in New Brunswick where excavations led to the emergence of cooperation and efforts at mutual understanding between archaeologists and members of the local First Nations communities.

breathe life into it, you give it a voice, you give it Spirit. Their knowledge provides a window through which to see what was happening in their past."

Ten years on, the Jemseg Crossing project remains for many of us a transformative experience. We finished the project, though not as we had intended. We continued our work with written assurances that the project would not impact on burials. We found living floors, hearths, pottery, and stone tools, evidence of food preparation and storage, eating, socializing, and toolmaking extending over thousands of years. At the same time, we built bonds of friendship and mutual respect.

Near the end of the project we found a small, basin-shaped pit, quite unlike anything else we had seen. Although it did not contain artifacts, it was coated with red ochre, a mineral commonly used in burials in the northeast. Despite comparative archaeological and ethnographic research, chemical testing, and radiometric analysis, I was unable to determine that it categorically was not a burial, and so, on April 14, 1997, the planned route of the highway was shifted southwest, bypassing the site entirely. ▲

■ The Solutrean Hypothesis

The lack of evidence of antecedents of the distinctive Clovis points in Siberia and Alaska casts some doubt on the Clovis first model. Added to this doubt are the aforementioned questions raised about the viability of an ice-free corridor as a migration route connecting Beringia with the regions to the south of the Cordilleran and Laurentide glaciers. According to the **Solutrean hypothesis**, proposed by Dennis Stanford and Bruce Bradley, the origin of the Clovis people was not Siberia, but rather Western Europe (Stanford and Bradley 2000). This is a very unlikely scenario, as it would require a lengthy crossing of the North Atlantic. Stanford and Bradley point to similarities in the fine bifacial flaking of spearpoints in the Clovis of North America and in the Solutrean period of the Upper Paleolithic of Spain and France. Their proposal, however, does not explain why these similarities could not be the result of parallel invention. As has been pointed out by Lawrence Straus, there are considerable differences between Solutrean and Clovis points, notably a lack of fluting in the Solutrean (Straus 2000). Moreover, the Solutrean industry ends around 5,000 years before the beginning of the Clovis.

■ The Skeletal Evidence

Only a small number of human skeletal remains have been recovered from sites in the Americas that are older than 9,000 years. No significant human remains have been found from either Clovis or pre-Clovis contexts. All of the human skeletal remains found in the Americas can be assigned unambiguously to *Homo sapiens*.

The small number of human skeletal remains that have been found in contexts slightly later than Clovis have recently become the focus of controversy. On the basis of analyses of the shape of the skulls of these individuals and comparisons with the shape of the skulls of modern populations, some scientists have argued that they are distinct from modern populations of Native Americans. The description of a skeleton discovered in **Kennewick**, Washington, as Caucasoid has led to an intense dispute in which the critical issue is ownership and control of the skeleton. The intensity of the political debate has clouded the question of what the recovered human remains tell us about the initial human occupation of the Americas.

On balance, it appears that at present, the skeletal material is too sparse to contribute significantly to models about the initial phases of occupation. There is little evidence to challenge the consensus view that the origin of the initial groups occupying the Americas was broadly Eurasian. Such a perspective does not contradict the identification of Beringia as the migration route. Several studies suggest that the skeletal evidence is consistent with multiple waves of migration into the Americas, some of which might have been relatively recent. However, this claim remains tentative (Swedlund and Anderson 2003).

■ Clovis Adaptations and Megafauna Extinction

The discovery of spearpoints together with the remains of now-extinct megafauna at both Folsom and Blackwater Draw suggested that the earliest inhabitants of the New World were specialist big-game hunters (see Figure 6.20). It is clear from a number of sites beyond Blackwater Draw that Clovis people were able to hunt very large animals, including elephants. The Colby site in Wyoming has produced a number of mammoth bones with clear evidence that they were hunted and possibly that the meat was stored for later consumption. Because the widespread extinction of megafauna in the Americas correlates with the Clovis period, it would seem obvious that the large animals must have been killed off by Clovis hunters. Seventeen

FIGURE 6.20 One possible cause for the extinction of North American megafauna is hunting by humans. In this painting, hunters armed with spears and spear-throwers stalk a mammoth mired in a bog.

genera of North and South American megafauna, including elephants (mastodons and mammoths), horses, and camels, became extinct between 13,250 and 12,900 years ago. Other species, such as ground sloths, become extinct slightly later.

Although Clovis people hunted large animals, and many of these became extinct soon after the earliest Clovis sites were established, some archaeologists doubt whether overhunting was the cause of widespread extinction of megafauna. In examining the archaeological record, Donald Grayson and David Meltzer found that only fourteen sites show clear evidence of Clovis hunting of megafauna (Grayson and Meltzer 2002). In every case, the hunted animals were elephants, either mastodons or mammoths. In most cases, the remains of only one or two animals were found, a pattern similar to that found in Australia, where the case for human overkill of megafauna is lacking a "smoking spear."

Another point of contention is whether Clovis hunters specialized exclusively in hunting large game. A number of sites have produced evidence of hunting of smaller game, (see Canadian Research). Clovis people were clearly superbly equipped hunters capable of killing very large animals. The question that remains unresolved is whether this killing resulted in the widespread extinction of megafauna.

A novel proposal links the extinction of megafauna with an extraterrestrial impact event. No impact crater has been identified, but there is evidence in levels overlying Clovis sites of features such as nanodiamonds and traces of iridium that are linked to impact by meteors or other extraterrestial materials (Firestone et al. 2007). One possibility is that a massive impact caused widespread burning and sudden climatic change, which in turn caused the extinction of megafauna. The end of the Clovis is correlated with the onset of the Younger Dryas cold event, which in North America is characterized by "black mat" layers that might be evidence of widespread burning. The possibility that the extinction of megafauna

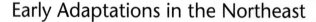

Early Adaptations in the Northeast

Numerous sites belonging to the Gainey Complex, an eastern North American culture contemporary with the Clovis culture, have been found across Eastern Canada from Ontario to the Maritimes. Some sites are quite large. The Debert site in Nova Scotia covers an area of over 9 hectares and has produced over 4,000 artifacts. However, the preservation of animal bones is extremely rare on these early sites, leaving many questions about human adaptation during the Gainey complex. Thus, the discovery of thirteen animal bones at the Udora site in south-central Ontario has taken on unusual importance. The Udora site consists of a series of concentrations of stone tools collected from the surface and from excavation. Excavation Area A contained a dense concentration of lithic material mixed with fragments of calcined bone—remnants of bones that have survived heating to a temperature above 400°C—in an area of approximately 1 metre square at the base of the ploughzone. Although they survive relatively well, calcined bones are very prone to fracture. Apart from the dense concentration of artifacts and bone fragments, this lithic layer was invisible, since there was no associated change in soil colour.

The thirteen bones include three that are either caribou or deer, three hoof bones of caribou, five bones of hare (either snowshoe or arctic hare), and one bone fragment of arctic fox. This combination of species suggests that the region was a tundra or parkland environment. As well, the representation of species, including small and medium-sized animals, suggests a far more diversified diet than the megafauna that some have proposed for the Clovis period. Unfortunately, the evidence is too scant to determine whether the earliest inhabitants of the Northeast specialized in caribou hunting. ◆

REFERENCE: Peter Storck and Arthur Spiess. (1994). The significance of new faunal identifications attributed to an Early Paleoindian (Gainey Complex) occupation at the Udora site, Ontario, Canada. *American Antiquity* 59(1): 121–142.

was caused by a catastrophic event is intriguing, but there is some reason for caution. One problem is that the type of evidence of extraterrestrial impact found in the layers overlying Clovis sites could be "the result of constant and certainly noncatastrophic rain of sand-sized micrometeorites into Earth's atmosphere" (Pinter and Ishman 2008). There are three further problems: The available evidence suggests the disappearance of megafauna was gradual rather than catastrophic; there is no indication of a decrease in human population size at the end of the Clovis; and the "black mat" layers are formed by a higher water table rather than by burning (Haynes 2008; Buchanan et al. 2008).

■ Beyond Clovis

Due to the complexities of radiocarbon calibration, it is difficult to mark the precise timing of the transition from the Clovis to the Folsom (approximate dates for the Folsom are 12,500 to 12,000 years ago). However, the data seem to support a rather abrupt end to the Clovis, followed directly by the onset of the Folsom. Most archaeologists stress the continuities that link the Clovis and Folsom, along with a series of other regional cultures referred to collectively as the Paleoindian time period. Despite these continuities, there are shifts in later Paleoindian adaptation and technology, including increased evidence for mass kill sites and for hunting of small game, as well as changes in the technology of projectile point production. The Paleoindian time period is followed by the Archaic. We will return to the Archaic in Chapter 8 in the context of discussion of the origins of agriculture, but a brief consideration of recent discoveries in Texas, Florida, and Louisiana will provide a sense of the importance of this period.

LATE PALEOINDIAN AND ARCHAIC SUBSISTENCE AND TECHNOLOGY. In the late Paleoindian, there is clear evidence for mass kill sites. At the Olsen–Chubbock site in Colorado, Joe Ben Wheat excavated a continuous bed of bison bones lying in a small arroyo, or dry stream bed (Figure 6.21). The hunters had stampeded the animals into this narrow gorge, killing almost 200. Many of these animals show evidence of systematic butchery; however, the sheer mass of the kill resulted in the hunters leaving some carcasses untouched—particularly those buried in the pileup. Most of the artifacts recovered at the Olsen–Chubbock site are points. The form of the points indicate that the site belongs to the Cody Complex, which dates to approximately 10,000 years ago. It is interesting that despite the clear evidence for bison kill sites, the species did not become extinct.

Late Paleoindian technology shows an impressive development of the tools used for hunting. Folsom points are among the most sophisticated stone tools ever made. In the first step of their manufacture, the knapper thinned the point by applying pressure along the edges with the tip of an antler, forcing off wafer-thin flakes. This process, known as pressure flaking, requires a high degree of skill and takes a significant effort to complete. Once the point was exquisitely thinned, one step remained before it was ready. The knapper took the point and drove a long, thin flake off the base. The point was then flipped and the same procedure repeated on the other side. The result was a shallow channel, or flute, running from the base of the point to near the tip on both faces. One aspect of the process that has puzzled archaeologists is exactly how the flute was produced. Some experimental archaeologists have suggested that a lever-type device was used in fluting the point.

An even more puzzling issue is why the flute was made to travel the entire length of the point. Consider that before the flute was produced, a major effort had been expended in carefully thinning the point with pressure flaking. All of this work was put at risk not once, but twice, as the point was subjected to the pressure required to produce the flutes. On archaeological sites, points broken during the process of fluting are common. Why take this risk with artifacts that were already suitable for use as hunting points?

A number of answers have been proposed to solve the riddle of the Folsom flute. One obvious possibility is that the flute was designed to fit a specific type of haft. Perhaps the points were designed to fit into a socket at the end of a spear shaft. Another functional explanation is that the flutes enhanced the ability of the point to penetrate an animal. However, some archaeologists question functional explanations for fluting and stress possible symbolic significance of the fluting as part of hunting rituals. None of these explanations accounts for the seeming inefficiency of investing so much energy in producing a hunting tool. One novel explanation advanced recently by Stanley Ahler and Phil Geib (2002) is that the goal of fluting was to produce a tool that could be continually resharpened as the tip was damaged during hunting. According to Ahler and Geib's theory, the investment of both effort and risk in fluting a Folsom point was balanced by the gain in efficiency from a point that could be continually resharpened (see Figure 6.22).

A chance discovery in the moutains of Wyoming has provided a unique glimpse into other strategies used by late Paleoindian hunters (Grayson et al. 1986). In the Absaroka Mountains east of Yellowstone National Park, hikers came across a folded net that had been preserved by overlying deposits of packrat feces. Radiocarbon dating has determined that this net is roughly contemporary with the Olsen–Chubbock site, dating to the Late Paleoindian, 10,000 years ago. The precise dimensions of the net cannot be determined but it is about 1.5 metres long and half a metre high. The effort involved in making the net is impressive, requiring over 2,000 metres of juniper cordage. The net was probably used to hunt mountain sheep that are found in the Absaroka Mountains. The mesh is too large for it to have been used in hunting smaller animals such as rabbits.

FIGURE 6.21 Excavation of a bison mass kill at the Olsen–Chubbock site, Colorado.

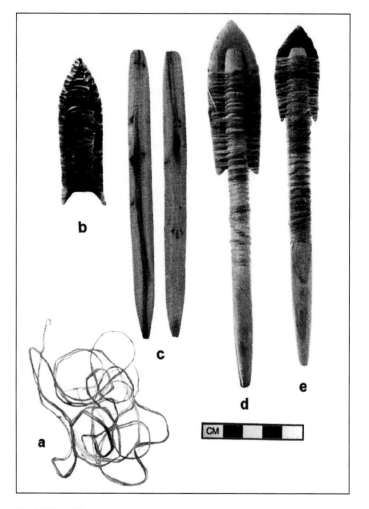

FIGURE 6.22 According to Ahler and Geib, twine (a) was used to bind a Folsom point (b) between the two halves of a split wood shaft (c) to create a stone pointed weapon (d). Through the use-life of the tool the point would become shorter as it was resharpened (e).

THE PALEOINDIAN TO ARCHAIC TRANSITION. Already in the late 1950s, Gordon Willey and Philip Phillips (1958) proposed a series of criteria that distinguish the Archaic from the Paleoindian periods. Adaptations shifted toward an increased reliance on small animal and plant foods. Technologies for food processing, including grinding stones and stones used for cooking, also develop. Sites indicate reduced mobility, and there is systematic burial of the dead. Typologically the Archaic is identified by stemmed, corner-notched, or side-notched projectile points. Archaic points have a clearly defined tang at the base that indicates a change in the way they were attached to the shaft of projectiles (spears, darts, or arrows). This list of traits is useful for distinguishing between the Paleoindian and Archaic, but leaves open the question of the nature and causes of the transition. Recent research in Texas has shed new light on the nature of the transition. The **Wilson-Leonard site** is located 65 kilometres north of Austin on a tributary of the Brazos River (Bousman et al. 2002). Excavations at this site have produced a stratigraphic sequence in which an Archaic level, known as the Wilson component, lies between two Paleoindian occupations (see Figures 6.23 and 6.24). The sequence has a large number of radiocarbon dates that place the Archaic occupation between 11,500 and 10,250 years ago. The faunal remains indicate that these were generalized hunters who focused on rabbit, hare, turtle, deer, and occasional bison. Unlike other Archaic sites in the region, the Wilson-Leonard site produced few ground stone tools or other

▲▲ **Wilson-Leonard site** A site in Texas with a stratigraphic sequence that includes both Paleoindian and Archaic occupations.

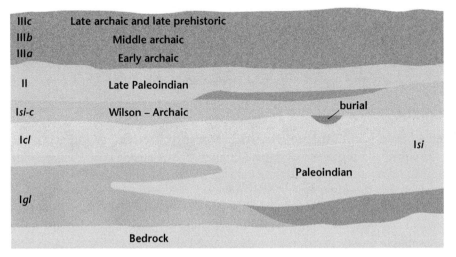

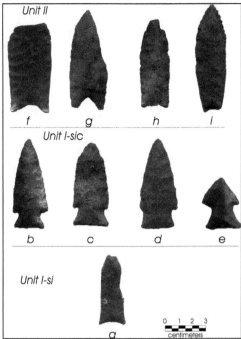

FIGURE 6.23 Stratigraphy of the Wilson-Leonard site. Note that the Wilson component (Unit Isi-c) is located stratigraphically above the bone bed (Unit Isi) and below the Late Paleoindian (Unite II). Based on this stratigraphic profile, why is the burial thought to date to the Wilson occupation?

FIGURE 6.24 Projectile points from the Wilson-Leonard site. Notice the difference between the Paleoindian points with concave bases (Unit I-si and Unit II) and the stemmed points characteristic of the Archaic (Unit I si-c).

evidence for the processing of plant foods. One burial was found in the Archaic occupation. The excavations at Wilson–Leonard demonstrate that the transition from the Paleoindian to the Archaic was a lengthy process and that Archaic and Paleoindian groups overlapped chronologically. These discoveries point to the need for further research into this important element of the prehistory of North America.

COPPER TOOLS. In the Great Lakes region, the appearance of copper artifacts in a tradition known as the Old Copper Complex, dated between 6,000 and 3,000 years ago, is a striking aspect of the Middle and Late Archaic period. Nuggets of copper known as native copper were used to form plates or blanks by hammering, flattening, and folding (Ehrhardt 2009). Heat might have been used to anneal or soften the metal for hammering, but the metal was not smelted (see Toolbox on p. 404–405 for more information on metallurgy). One of the most impressive collections of Archaic copper artifacts comes from the **Allumettes Island site** in the Ottawa River on the Ontario–Quebec border, dated between 5,500 and 5,000 years ago (Clermont et al. 2003, Ellis et al. 2009). At the Allumettes site, over 1,000 copper artifacts have been recovered, including points, barbs, awls, fishhooks, and needles, along with a small number of beads and a single pendant. The copper found at the Allumettes site has been traced to rich deposits in the Lake Superior Basin, over 1,000 kilometres from the site. It remains unclear whether copper was valued during the Archaic strictly for its functional properties or whether these tools also were symbolic markers of status.

MOUND BUILDING. We will return to the topic of Archaic monumental construction when we examine the site of Poverty Point, Louisiana, in Chapter 8. Recent research has demonstrated that the practice of mound construction has deep routes in the Archaic. The site of **Watson Brake** is a series of mounds and ridges constructed on the floodplain of the Ouachita River in Louisiana (Saunders et al. 1997). A combination of radiocarbon and luminescence dating securely places this site in the Middle Archaic between 5,400 and 5,000 years ago. Building on the discoveries at Watson Brake, archaeologists have begun to turn their attention from a narrow focus on those aspects of the Archaic related

▲▲ **Allumettes Island site** A site on the Ontario–Quebec border where a large number of copper tools have been recovered, dating to the Archaic period.

▲▲ **Watson Brake** A series of mounds in Louisiana built between 5,400 and 5,000 years ago that provide the earliest evidence of monumental construction in eastern North America.

Dorset A Paleo-Eskimo culture characterized by small winter village sites consisting of large rectangular structures.

to subsistence toward an examination of the social forces within Archaic society. As Kenneth Sassaman has written, "The next generation of researchers must jettison the received wisdom of their forebears who, in canonizing the Archaic as the antecedent to 'complex' society, perpetuated the myth that little of interest took place. Clearly this was not the case" (Sassaman 2005, 102).

■ The Arctic

The initial occupation of the Americas does not appear to have spread across the Arctic, since this region was not deglaciated until approximately 6,000 years ago. The initial human occupation of the Arctic took place between 5,000 and 4,000 years ago, perhaps when small groups from Alaska followed rich resources such as herds of muskoxen (McGhee 1996). These societies, known as Paleo-Eskimo, lacked the float harpoons and dog sleds that were essential to later Inuit adaptations. Excavations at the Qeqertasussuk site in Greenland have produced rare Paleo-Eskimo objects from wood and string made from whale baleen. The material recovered at Qeqertasussuk includes remnants of a kayak, bows and arrows, and harpoons used in seal hunting (Grønnow 1996). Paleo-Eskimo subsistence was based on the hunting of caribou, muskoxen, and sea mammals that could be reached from the edge of the sea ice.

A vivid picture of early Paleo-Eskimo life in the high Arctic has been found on sites discovered at Independence Fjord in northern Greenland, occupied between 4,500 and 4,000 years ago (Knuth 1967). In this remote area, small populations were able to survive by hunting herds of muskoxen using bows and arrows, supplemented by a summer diet that included migratory birds, hares, eggs, and occasional seals. They lived in large rectangular houses built of turf, many of which retain a central hearth (Figure 6.25). Excavation found the hearths to be full of charcoal, ash, and muskoxen bones. No remains of stone lamps were found, so the central hearth must have provided light and heat. Similar sites have also been found in the Canadian Arctic.

Around 2,500 years ago, changes in Paleo-Eskimo societies culminated in the appearance of the **Dorset** culture across much of the Arctic (Figure 6.26). These societies had much in common with earlier Paleo-Eskimo societies but began to construct small winter villages of large rectangular houses built of turf and insulated with snow. These shifts reflect significant changes both in adaptation and social organization

FIGURE 6.25 A Dwelling from the Early Dorset period near Cambridge Bay with a central hearth.

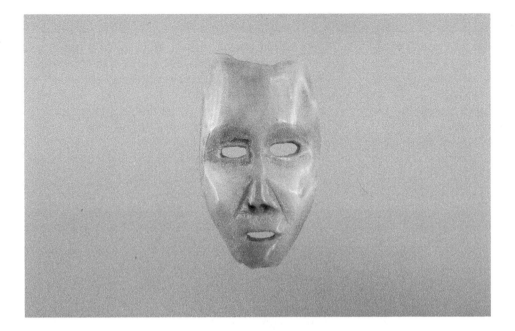

FIGURE 6.26 Miniature human mask carved from ivory discovered at the early Dorset site of Tyara on the south shore of Hudson Strait.

that developed in response to a period of highly unstable climate conditions (McGhee 1996). The Dorset used oil lamps to heat their houses. The use of oil lamps was made possible by a shift in hunting from an emphasis on muskoxen and caribou to marine mammals that are rich in fat, such as seal and walrus. Dorset houses were dug slightly into the ground, resulting in excellent preservation and a spectacularly rich archaeological record. The Dorset hunted land mammals using communal drives, and the bow and arrow appears to have been absent from their technological repertoire.

The ancestors of contemporary Inuit were populations known as the **Thule,** who spread across the Arctic from Alaska approximately 1,000 years ago (Dumond 1987). Inuit oral history speaks of the Tunit, probably the last of the Dorset Paleo-Eskimo cultures. Oral histories describe the Tunit as people who made the land habitable by building drives for caribou hunting and fish weirs for catching char. The Thule arrived with new technologies, including dog sleds and the ability to hunt bowhead whale, beluga, and large numbers of walruses.

Recently, researchers have sequenced the genome of a man who lived in Greenland 4,000 years ago, casting new light on the origin of the earliest occupants of the Arctic (Rasmussen et al. 2010). This scientific feat was performed on strands of human hair recovered from a site locked in permafrost. The results indicate that this person has no genetic relationship to either modern Native Americans or modern Inuit. He does share a close genetic similarity to inhabitants of the Arctic regions of East Asia. This discovery strongly supports the argument that the initial migration into the Arctic was from Siberia. The lack of a genetic match between this individual and modern Inuit fits well with the archaeological evidence for the replacement of the Dorset by the Thule.

The archaeology of the Arctic is an emerging field that has greatly expanded our understanding of hunter–gatherer ways of life and raised many questions about the processes that lead to culture change and migration. The emergence of the Dorset culture appears to be linked to a period of cold climate that made hunting of sea mammals off the edge of the sea ice increasingly effective, while the arrival of the Thule coincides with a warming trend that would have offered advantages to hunters equipped with kayaks and float harpoons.

Thule The archaeological culture ancestral to contemporary Inuit.

SUMMARY

- Human migration to Australia required the crossing of the Wallace Line by boat.
- The earliest evidence of human occupation in Australia is dated between 60,000 and 53,000 years ago.
- The extinction of Australian megafauna appears to have taken place approximately 46,000 years ago.
- Human occupation of the Americas followed the Beringia land bridge, which was exposed during periods of low sea level.

- There is considerable debate as to whether the Clovis culture represents the initial occupation of the Americas or whether there was an earlier migration, represented by sites such as Monte Verde.
- The first people to arrive in the Americas migrated south from Beringia either through an ice-free corridor or along a coastal migration route.
- The extinction of American megafauna took place around 13,000 years ago.

KEY TERMS

Allumettes Island site, 177
Beringia, 162
Blackwater Draw, 161
Clovis culture, 161
Clovis first model, 161
coastal migration, 167
Dorset, 178
early arrival model, 161
fire-stick farming, 158
Gunbilngmurrung, 158
ice-free corridor, 162
Kennewick, 172
Lake Mungo, 156
Lapita, 159
Meadowcroft Rockshelter, 165

megafauna, 156
Monte Verde, 165
Nauwalabila I, 156
Nenana, 163
Ngandong, 153
Pedra Furada, 170
Pedra Pintada, 166
pre-Clovis model, 161
Sahul, 153
Solutrean hypothesis, 172
Sunda, 153
Thule, 179
Wallace Line, 153
Watson Brake, 177
Wilson-Leonard site, 176

REVIEW QUESTIONS

1. How and when did people first arrive in Australia? What is the importance of Lake Mungo in understanding the spread of humans in Australia?
2. Was the process of megafauna extinction similar in Australia and the Americas?
3. What is the significance of Monte Verde to debates about the initial occupation of the Americas? What additional information is brought by the excavations at Caverna de Pedra Pintada?
4. What are the alternative migration routes for the initial occupation of the Americas?

CANADIAN ARCHAEOLOGISTS

- Sue Blair, is a professor in the Department of Anthropology at the University of New Brunswick, specializing in the archaeology of the Maritimes. She is engaged in a long-term collaboration with Metepenagiag Heritage Park to explore the archaeological heritage of Metepenagiag Mi'kmaq Nation. Her research projects focus on pre-contact technology, including copper working, and stone tool, pottery, and textile manufacturing.
  http://www.unb.ca/fredericton/arts/departments/anthropology/people/sblair.html

- Christopher Ellis is a professor in the Department of Anthropology at the University of Western Ontario. His research focuses on the Paleoindian and Archaic archaeology of Ontario. His publications include a number of site reports and *The Archaeology of Southern Ontario to A.D. 1650*, co-edited with N. Ferris and published by the London Chapter of the Ontario Archaeological Society in 1990.
  http://anthropology.uwo.ca/cje/ellis.html

- Daryl Fedje is a coastal archaeologist with Parks Canada. His research on reconstructing changes in sea level provides important data for debates on the route taken by the earliest people arriving in the Americas.
  http://www.sfu.museum/journey/05p_secondary/transcripts/fedje.php

- Max Friesen is a professor in the Department of Anthropology at the University of Toronto. He is a specialist in zooarchaeology and Arctic archaeology. He currently directs the Iqaluktuuq Archaeology Project.

  http://www.anthropology.utoronto.ca/people/faculty-1/faculty-profiles/max-friesen

- B.A. Nicholson, professor of archaeology in the Department of Native Studies at Brandon University, is the director of the SCAPE (Study of Cultural Adaptations in the Prairie Ecozone) Project, a multidisciplinary project examining past human-environmental interactions within the Canadian Prairies ecozone.

  http://www2.brandonu.ca/nicholson/

- Paul Taçon, trained at the University of Waterloo and Trent University before receiving his Ph.D. from the Australian National University, is an anthropologist, archaeologist, and photographer who specializes in collaborative research involving creative artists, scientists, and indigenous people. He has published widely on Australian rock art and is currently a professor at Griffith University in Australia.

  http://www3.griffith.edu.au/01/griffithprofiles/content_profile.php?id=7332313933333031

PEARSON
myanthrokit™

Visit **www.myanthrokit.com**, where you will find a variety of tools and resources to enhance your learning, including:
- Practise quizzes with Study Plans
- Videos
- Listening Activities
- And much more!

PART THREE

PERSPECTIVES ON AGRICULTURE

The development of agriculture involved a profound reorientation in the way humans relate to plants and animals, along with equally significant changes in human society and technology. Because the transition to agriculture took place independently in several distinct regions, we can take a comparative approach to the origins of agriculture in order to gain a broad understanding of this process. In doing so, we learn that the shift to an agricultural way of life often spanned a period of several thousands of years and that the details of the process differ significantly among regions.

The development of agriculture has been linked to a trend toward the separation of humanity from nature. Recent perspectives on the domestication of plants and animals challenge this assumption. After reading this introduction, you should understand:

- The ideas of Lewis Henry Morgan and V. Gordon Childe about the origin of agriculture.

- The challenge to these ideas posed in the writing of David Rindos, Tim Ingold, and Marshall Sahlins.

- The major components of the Neolithic Revolution.

Introduction: Definitions of Agriculture

Almost the entire evolutionary history of genus *Homo* has taken place within a hunting-and-gathering context. It was only 15,000 years ago that societies of modern humans in different areas of the world began to shift to an agricultural way of life. The transition from hunter–gatherer societies to agricultural societies is one of the most profound and significant events in prehistory. Early anthropologists and archaeologists saw the development of agriculture as the natural result of an inherent human tendency to move toward more advanced ways of life. Today, most archaeologists reject both the association between agriculture and progress and the use of progress to explain changes in prehistory. We are left with the challenge of discovering the diverse pathways that societies around the world took toward agriculture and to grapple with the question of what caused those societies to change.

■ Early Perspectives

> *Mankind are the only beings who may be said to have gained an absolute control over the production of food. (Morgan 1877, 24)*

The pioneering American anthropologist **Lewis Henry Morgan** wrote that through the invention of agriculture, humans placed themselves outside of the world of nature and moved toward "human supremacy on the earth" (Rindos 1984, 9). In his book *Ancient Society*, published in 1877, Morgan labelled the transition to agriculture as the shift from a period of "savagery" to one of "barbarism." Among the defining aspects of barbarism, he included the invention of pottery, the domestication of animals and plants, and the construction of buildings out of mud brick. In his writing on barbarism, Morgan emphasized that the transition to agriculture was a stage in the progress of humanity.

> *The escape from the impasse of savagery was an economic and scientific revolution that made the participants active partners with nature instead of parasites on nature. (Childe 1942, 55)*

In the 1940s, V. Gordon Childe synthesized the existing archaeological information to reformulate Morgan's ideas about the origin of agriculture. He coined the term the **Neolithic Revolution**. For Childe, the most important result of the Neolithic Revolution was the ability to actively control food production. This led to an increase in the food supply, which in turn supported an increase in population, resulting in the development of settled villages.

The concepts developed by Morgan and Childe remain essential to the study of prehistory. Few archaeologists question the revolutionary effects the development of agriculture had on human society, and understanding the Neolithic Revolution remains central to the study of prehistory. However, although Morgan's and Childe's contributions are widely recognized, most of their specific ideas about the nature of the shift to agriculture are the subject of debate and criticism.

■ Humanity and Nature in the Shift to Agriculture

Both Morgan and Childe viewed the development of agriculture as a shift in the relationship between humanity and the natural world. Morgan believed that "barbaric" society had set itself in a position of supremacy above nature. Childe saw Neolithic societies as "active partners with nature" rather than "parasites on nature." Both Childe and Morgan seem to imply that humans consciously removed themselves

Lewis Henry Morgan
A nineteenth-century American anthropologist who viewed the transition to agriculture as marking the boundary between the period of "savagery" and the period of "barbarism."

Neolithic Revolution The term V. Gordon Childe used to describe the transition to agriculture as an event that affected every aspect of human society.

from nature by inventing agriculture. Today, such a concept is contested by archaeologists and anthropologists working from a wide range of perspectives.

> *The idea that we as a culture, a nation, or a species are in conscious control of our environment and thus of our destiny is one part truth, one part rhetoric, and two parts wishful thinking. (Rindos 1984, 6)*

For **David Rindos**, the development of agriculture was a coevolutionary process involving a symbiotic relationship between plant and animal species in which each species contributes to the other's support. Symbiotic relationships with plants and animals are not unique to humans, and are widespread in the natural world. For example, there is a symbiotic relationship between ants and acacia trees. The ants live in the acacias, harvesting the trees' sugars and leaves while feeding on insects that would otherwise destroy the trees. If the ants are removed, other insects attack the trees which then rapidly die. The relationship is a symbiotic one in which the ants receive nutrients and shelter and the acacias receive protection from harmful insects. Nobody would argue that this biological process involves a conscious decision on the part of either the ants or the trees. Rindos argued that the domestication of plants by humans was a similar coevolutionary process.

Rindos's view on the origins of agriculture was based on biological theory. Working from a different perspective, anthropologist **Tim Ingold** (2000) has also argued against agriculture as the removal of humans from nature. Ingold begins by looking at the way modern hunter–gatherer societies see the world. He finds that these people do not make the kinds of distinctions between the natural and human worlds that are so critical to Childe and Morgan's account. Ingold sees the domestication of animals as a shift from a world where relationships are based on trust to one where they are based on domination. The relationship between hunter–gatherers and animals is based on trust in a powerful natural world that will provide for people in return for human respect and propitiation (see Figure III.1). Social relations between humans are made on the same basis of trust, because there is no essential distinction between the human and animal worlds. A hallmark characteristic of hunter–gatherer social relations is sharing based on trust.

David Rindos An archaeologist who saw agriculture as the result of a coevolutionary process involving a symbiotic relationship between plant and animal species.

Tim Ingold An anthropologist who views the shift from hunting to agriculture as a shift from trust to domination.

For Ingold, the shift from hunting to agriculture involves a move from trust to domination that pervades all aspects of human life. Thus, in agricultural societies, animals are dependents of humans. Animals no longer present themselves; instead, the herdsman makes life-and-death decisions about them. Similar concepts of domination and control pervade the social life of humans with the development of owned property and social hierarchy. But Ingold stresses that the shift from trust to domination does not involve a separation of humanity from nature as envisioned by Morgan and Childe. Rather, the development of agriculture involves a "change in the terms of engagement." Not until the recent development of industrialized agriculture did animals become merely objects of human control.

Agriculture and Progress

> *There is also a Zen road to affluence . . . That human material wants are finite and few, and technical means unchanging but on the whole adequate. . . . That, I think, describes the hunter. (Sahlins 1972, 2)*

Today it is quite jarring to read Morgan and Childe describe hunter–gatherer societies as savages. The term clearly embodies a value judgment, as does the term *barbaric* for farming societies. Both characterizations are repugnant to contemporary anthropologists, who see them as dehumanizing (Figure III.2). Moreover, the entire notion of linking the transition to farming to the idea of progress has become extremely problematic. In a clever turn of phrase, anthropologist **Marshall Sahlins** (1972) has called hunter–gatherers the "original affluent society." Through a careful comparison of ethnographic studies of hunter–gatherer and farming communities, Sahlins has shown that, contrary to our expectations, hunter–gatherers spend less time working for their food than agriculturalists. Hunter–gatherers actually have far more leisure time than farmers. In a similar vein, on the basis of a study of human skeletal remains from prehistoric sites, Marc Cohen (1977) has demonstrated that early agriculturalists were not as healthy as hunter–gatherers. Because of increased crowding in permanent villages, agricultural societies were vulnerable to outbreaks of disease. Also, their health suffered from a decrease in the quality of their diet. As a result of studies such as these, many archaeologists question whether the development of agriculture was the result of people choosing or inventing a "better" way of life.

Searching for Explanations

If agriculture is not inherently advantageous, why did it develop? Kent Flannery once crystallized the difficulty of answering this question, saying, "If you asked me 'Why did agriculture begin?' I'm not sure what I'd give you as a cause" (quoted in

FIGURE III.2 San hunter–gatherers in the Kalahari, Botswana. How does this picture compare to the image you have of hunter–gatherers?

Marshall Sahlins An anthropologist who described hunter–gatherers as the "original affluent society."

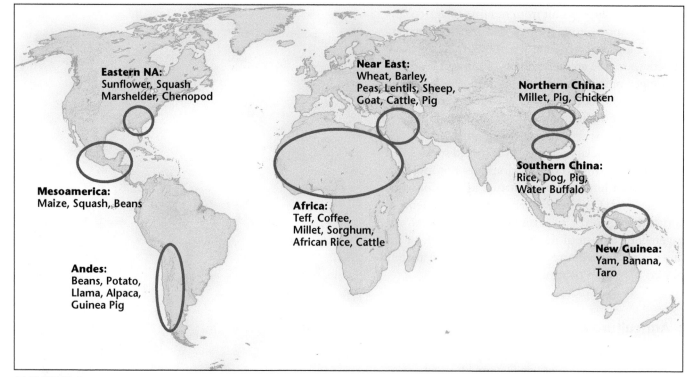

FIGURE III.3   Map of the major centres of domestication.

Hayden 1990, 31). In the chapters that follow, we will pursue the trail of empirical evidence that archaeologists have uncovered and continue to uncover. Central to the study of agricultural origins is the recognition that plants and animals have been domesticated independently in numerous locations. The major centres for the independent domestication of indigenous plants and animals were the Middle East, south China, north China, Africa, the Andes, and central Mexico (see Figure III.3). Other regions where there was limited independent domestication of plants include eastern North America and New Guinea. Because agriculture developed independently in at least six regions, archaeologists can explore whether there were regularities in its unfolding.

Archaeologists make a distinction between areas where agriculture developed independently and areas into which agriculture spread. The spread of agriculture is increasingly recognized as a process that is as complex and worthy of study as the original domestication of plants and animals. The origin of agriculture is a complex topic that involves both empirical and theoretical components. The essential theoretical issue that faces archaeologists is how to approach the origins of agriculture as a process. How and why did societies across the globe shift from a hunter–gatherer way of life to living in settled village farming communities?

One approach to this question has been to look for an external trigger that played a role in the shift to agriculture. One obvious candidate for such a trigger is climate change. Another factor that might have triggered the shift to agriculture is an increase in population. Research by **Ester Boserup** suggests that population growth might actually be an underlying cause, rather than an effect, of agriculture. Boserup's (1965) studies suggest that subsistence systems—the ways people get their food—tend to be the result of population pressures.

A major breakthrough in the study of agricultural origins has been the recognition that it is unlikely that searching for a single external trigger will

Ester Boserup An economist whose research suggests that increased population size might have been the cause of the shift to agriculture.

produce a satisfying explanation. Following an approach based on systems theory, archaeologists have shifted to developing models of how the interaction between a number of factors might have led to the adoption of agriculture (Bender 1975). For example, Lewis Binford (1968) examined the interaction between increasing population size and fluctuating climatic conditions. A particularly intriguing model developed by Brian Hayden focuses on the interaction between surplus food and social organization. Hayden begins by arguing that not all hunter–gatherer societies are the same. *Generalized hunter–gatherers* rely on scarce or unpredictable resources and, as a result, live at low population densities. In such societies, competition over food resources will be detrimental to the group and therefore maladaptive. *Complex hunter–gatherers* use more reliable and abundant resources (such as salmon, cod, insects, rodents, grass seeds, and nuts) and therefore can live at higher population densities. Because overexploitation of these resources is practically impossible, competition can develop and will largely take the form of feasting events. It is the "competition between individuals using food resources to wage their competitive battles," says Hayden, that "provides the motive and the means for the development of food production. . . . Aspiring accumulators can be expected to exert all their ingenuity to bribe, coerce, cajole, and con other members of the community into supporting competitive feasts and producing as many delicacies or other high-quality foods as possible for feasts" (Hayden 1990, 35–36).

An interesting aspect of Hayden's model is that it builds on changes in hunter–gatherer adaptations, which then interact with social factors to push societies toward agriculture. In every case study that we examine in the coming chapters, we will see that increasing complexity in hunter–gatherer adaptations precedes the shift to agriculture. Such societies of hunter–gatherers are often labelled "Archaic" in the Americas and "Epipaleolithic" or "Mesolithic" in other parts of the world. Kent Flannery has emphasized that a common characteristic of these societies is that they relied on a **broad spectrum adaptation** that included a wide range of plant and animal foods. (Flannery 1973).

In examining the case studies in the coming chapters, no particular model for the origins of agriculture is adopted. We will find much support for Barbara Bender's conclusion that "there is no single hypothesis that will explain the shift to food production in different parts of the world" (Bender 1975, 215). There is considerable variation in the pathways different societies took in adopting farming. Agriculture can be viewed as a broad phenomenon that can be broken into three components.

1. *Domestication.* A relationship between humans, on the one hand, and plants and animals, on the other.
2. *Technology.* The tools used for daily tasks.
3. *Community.* The development of a constructed landscape.

Domestication refers to a relationship between humans, plants, and animals in which the humans play an integral role in the protection and reproduction of the plant or animal species. As Rindos (1984) makes clear, domestication is not necessarily the result of conscious manipulation of plants and animals by humans. Archaeologically, a plant or animal is identified as domestic based on changes in the shape or size (morphology) of its remains, compared with the morphology of the wild ancestors (progenitors) of the same plants or animals. Plants or animals are also identified as domesticated when they are found outside their expected geographic distribution.

broad spectrum adaptation
Exploitation of a wide range of plant animal resources characteristic of many hunter–gatherer societies that preceded the shift to agriculture.

domestication The relationship between humans, on the one hand, and plants and animals, on the other, in which the humans play an integral role in the protection and reproduction of plants and animals.

FIGURE III.4 A farmer harvesting maize. This picture shows the close relationship between the farmer and plants in traditional agricultural systems.

With animals, domestication can sometimes be identified on the basis of the ratio of the sexes of an animal by age. Generally, an overrepresentation of young male animals is indicative of domestication. Figures III.4 and III.5 give a sense of the variability that exists in the cultivation of domesticated crops.

Technology refers to the tools used for daily tasks, including farming, food processing, and food storage. Among the technological innovations that are often linked to agriculture are pottery, ground stone axes, and sickles.

Community refers to more than just physical changes to the landscape through the construction of villages. The community aspect of agricultural origins also refers to a change in the way people view the landscape and the way ownership of the land is conceived. Agriculture involves important shifts in social organization, leadership, and the relationship between kin groups and property. The shift to agricultural society also had significant effects on cosmology—the way people saw themselves in relation to supernatural forces. The historic photograph of the Walpi Pueblo in Figure III.6 gives a sense of the size and organization characteristic of farming villages.

■ Agriculture and Progress Revisited

Progress has been rejected as an *explanation* for why agricultural societies came into being; however, there does seem to be an element of progress, or at least directionality, built into our conception of the origins of agriculture as a process. For example, Hayden (1990) discusses a shift from generalized hunter–gatherers, to complex hunter–gatherers, to farmers. Flannery (1973) emphasizes broad-spectrum adaptations as a precondition for agriculture.

FIGURE III.5 Manually harvesting rice in China. How does this picture compare to the maize harvest in Figure III.4?

FIGURE III.6 Historic photograph of the Walpi Pueblo, Arizona.

Systems theory, as presented in Chapter 2, should not allow for such a "ratchet effect." The feedback loop between your furnace and your thermostat is a self-regulating system that has no direction; it simply adjusts to changes in temperature. The directionality inherent in the shift to agriculture poses a significant theoretical challenge. A similar challenge plagues evolutionary biologists struggling to explain how evolution can have direction without recourse to models that view progress as explaining evolution (Nitecki 1988). Several concepts from evolutionary biology are useful to our study of agricultural origins. The first is that directionality and progress are distinct. Stephen Jay Gould (1988) has argued that directionality is the essential element of any historical process. Notably, Gould states that "history must be more than a string of isolated, if distinctive, events strung together one after the other" (Gould 1988, 333). The essence of historical processes is that they unfold in time. Our task in examining case studies of agricultural origins is not only to look at how various aspects of agriculture are related, but also to understand the *process* of agricultural origins. We will be interested in both the tempo of this process (e.g., was it a revolution, as Childe proposed?) and the relationships among events.

In one of the classic articles of evolutionary biology, Gould and his colleague Richard Lewontin used the essentially historical nature of evolutionary processes to launch an attack on what they called the "Panglossian paradigm" (Gould and Lewontin 1979). Doctor Pangloss is a character from a satire by Voltaire who elaborates ridiculous explanations of how everything in the world is for the best. Gould and Lewontin argue that evolutionary biologists think much as Dr. Pangloss does, explaining every aspect of organisms as the best possible adaptation. To counter the Panglossian paradigm, Lewontin and Gould use an illustration from architecture. At the cathedral of San Marco in Venice, small triangular spaces between arches are used for a perfectly fitted

technology The tools used for daily tasks, including farming, food processing, and food storage.

community The term applied to the changes in society and settlement patterns in the transition to an agricultural way of life. This includes not only physical changes to the landscape through the construction of villages and monuments, but also a change in the way people viewed the landscape and the way the ownership of the land was conceived.

FIGURE III.7 In this photograph of the interior of the cathedral of San Marco an angel fills the space created by a spandrel.

painted scene (see Figure III.7). One might think that these triangular spaces were built for the needs of the painter, but that is not the case. The spaces, known by the architectural term *spandrels*, are created by the intersection of two rounded arches that meet at a right angle. The critical point is that the paintings in the spandrels are adapted to an existing structure. It is useful to keep Dr. Pangloss and the spandrels of San Marco firmly in mind as we move through the world of agricultural origins. We are looking at the way changes built on preexisting conditions, just as the painters of the cathedral took advantage of spaces that were structurally essential to the building; thus, we must be wary of explaining every aspect of society as adaptive.

In the next three chapters, we will explore a series of case studies in the shift to agriculture. The focus will be on examining the relationships among domestication, technology, and community, as well as the role of external triggers, including climate changes and increases in population. The picture that emerges is one of tremendous diversity in the way agricultural societies developed. Agriculture came into being because of the actions of people, and the changes unleashed by the process shook the foundations of the world in which those people lived. The shift from hunter–gatherer societies profoundly affected every aspect of human life, from the diversity of the ecosystem to the way people experienced the supernatural. Living as we do in a rapidly changing world, we are in a good position to have some empathy and insight into such an experience. The development of agriculture is a process with immediate relevance to the upheavals that we experience today. The origins of agriculture point to the essential link between aspects of experience we often treat as distinct. Social change, technological innovation, ecological impact, and religious experience are all inextricably linked in a process that produced a truly revolutionary change in human societies. From thousands of years away, we look back at this process and try to piece together the evidence that survives. What was it like to be part of the generations that experienced the Neolithic Revolution? What role did individuals play in effecting the large-scale changes they lived through? Similar questions might be asked about our own experience living in a world of change.

SUMMARY

- To many early archaeologists and anthropologists, including Lewis Henry Morgan and V. Gordon Childe, the origin of agriculture involved the separation of humanity from nature.
- More recently, anthropologists and archaeologists working from a diversity of perspectives have challenged the traditional understanding of the origins of agriculture.
- Ester Boserup has proposed that the development of agriculture was a response to an increase in population.

- Childe labeled the development of agriculture the Neolithic Revolution, one that includes changes in three major aspects of human society and adaptation: domestication, technology, and community (the process of settling down).
- Plants and animals have been domesticated independently in numerous locations.

KEY TERMS

broad spectrum adaptation, 187
community, 188
David Rindos, 184
domestication, 187
Ester Boserup, 186

Lewis Henry Morgan, 183
Marshall Sahlins, 185
Neolithic Revolution, 183
technology, 188
Tim Ingold, 184

REVIEW QUESTIONS

1. Why are contemporary archaeologists and anthropologists critical of Morgan's and Childe's conception of the origin of agriculture?
2. How do Rindos's ideas about the origins of agriculture differ from Ingold's?

3. Why did Childe choose to describe the origin of agriculture as the Neolithic Revolution?

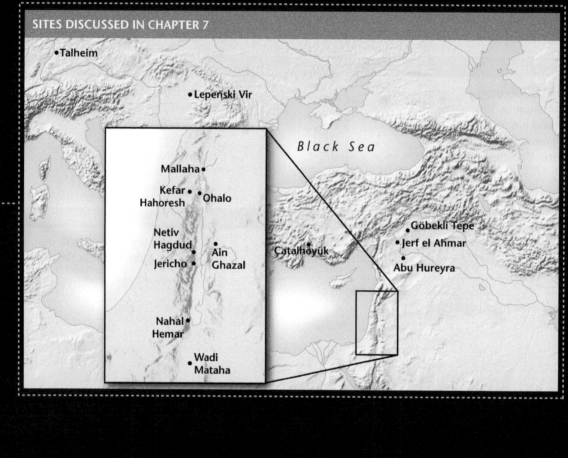

SITES DISCUSSED IN CHAPTER 7

•Talheim

•Lepenski Vir

Black Sea

Mallaha•

Kefar •
Hahoresh • Ohalo

Netiv
Hagdud •
Jericho • • Ain
Ghazal

Nahal•
Hemar

Wadi •
Mataha

Çatalhöyük

Göbekli Tepe
• Jerf el Ahmar
Abu Hureyra

7
TIMELINE

SITES

▲
Ohalo

**ARCHAEOLOGICAL
INDUSTRIES**

KEBARAN AND GEOMETRIC KEBARAN

thousands of years ago   **25**   **20**

TOWERS, VILLAGES, AND LONGHOUSES

In the Middle East, the domestication of plants and animals
took place within the context of large villages.
After reading this chapter, you should understand:

- The emergence of settled villages
  in the Middle East.

- The domestication of plants and
  animals in the Middle East.

- The relationship between
  domestication, villages, and
  technology in the development
  of agriculture in the Middle East.

- The questions surrounding the spread
  of agriculture to Europe.

Excavation of the plaster figures at the Neolithic site
of Ain Ghazal, Jordan.

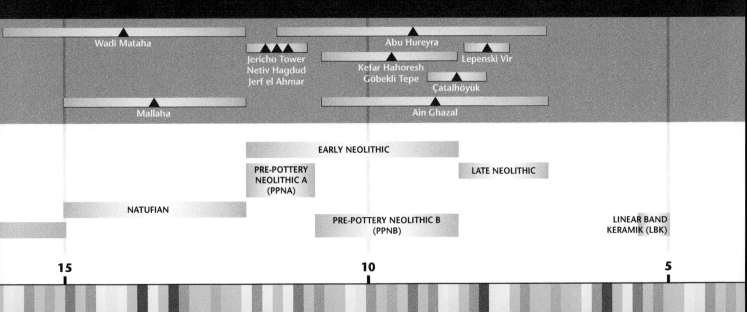

Wadi Mataha

Jericho Tower
Netiv Hagdud
Jerf el Ahmar

Abu Hureyra

Lepenski Vir

Kefar Hahoresh
Göbekli Tepe

Çatalhöyük

Mallaha

Ain Ghazal

EARLY NEOLITHIC

PRE-POTTERY
NEOLITHIC A
(PPNA)

LATE NEOLITHIC

NATUFIAN

PRE-POTTERY NEOLITHIC B
(PPNB)

LINEAR BAND
KERAMIK (LBK)

15

10

5

FIGURE 7.1 Photograph of the Jericho tower during excavation. Notice the opening in the top of the tower that leads to a stairway.

The ancient mound, or *tel*, of Jericho is a powerful lure to archaeologists. The famous walls of Jericho, toppled in the biblical book of Joshua, are exactly the type of concrete evidence archaeologists should easily be able to identify and recover. The British archaeologist Kathleen Kenyon sank massive trenches through the tel of Jericho, documenting the stratigraphic sequence and revealing the history of the site. Surprisingly, Kenyon recovered no evidence of a settlement dating to the biblical period. Why these remains are absent is unclear. Perhaps the story of Joshua is more myth than reality. Or maybe the settlement of Jericho described in the book of Joshua was in a different, as yet undiscovered, location.

As Kenyon penetrated the deepest archaeological deposits at Jericho, she uncovered a wall and a tower that astounded the archaeological community (see Figure 7.1). These constructions were far older than Joshua; in fact, they were the oldest known monumental architecture ever discovered. The tower and wall at Jericho were built 12,000 years ago, during the Early Neolithic period.

The tower of Jericho is only one of a string of discoveries that have shed dramatic light on the origins of agriculture in the Middle East. In this chapter, we examine the shift from hunter–gatherer to agricultural societies in the Middle East. The domestication of plants and animals in this region took place within the context of large and dense villages. The adoption of agriculture resulted in a transformation of all aspects of life. These profound changes affected not only social relations between people, but also the way people conceived of the supernatural. In the last section of the chapter, we explore the spread of domesticated plants and animals into Europe.

7.1 Setting the Scene

The Middle East includes a wide range of climates. A ribbon of Mediterranean climate extends today from Israel and Jordan in the south, up into Turkey, Syria, and Lebanon in the north, and stretches to the east into northern Iraq and western Iran. Together, these regions form an area known as the **Fertile Crescent**, characterized by dry summers and winter rains with enough precipitation to support vegetation ranging from woodlands to open-park woodlands. Along with trees such as oak and pine, large stands of wild cereals, including wheat, barley, and rye, dot the countryside. To the south and the east of the Fertile Crescent, the Mediterranean open-park woodlands grade into steppe environments that in turn grade into true deserts.

The archaeological record clearly shows that the shift to an agricultural way of life in the Middle East was a process rather than a revolution. The transition to agriculture can be traced through a number of stages (see Table 7.1):

1. During the Kebaran and Geometric Kebaran periods, hunter–gatherers living in the region subsisted on a wide range of plant and animal resources.

Fertile Crescent A ribbon of Mediterranean climate that arcs across the Middle East. It is characterized by dry summers and winter rains with enough precipitation to support vegetation ranging from woodlands to open-park woodlands.

TABLE 7.1

STAGE	PERIOD	DATE (YEARS AGO)
1	Kebaran and Geometric Kebaran	25,000–15,000
2	Natufian	15,000–12,000
3	Early Neolithic	12,000–8,500
4	Late Neolithic	8,500–7,000

Political Borders and Archaeology

Politics and archaeology frequently intersect in the Middle East. Sites like Masada, where a group of Jewish rebels made a futile last stand against the Roman army, have become powerful symbols for the modern state of Israel (Zrubavel 1995). As Palestinians reach for statehood, archaeology has also been an important tool for exploring identity and asserting a presence that has often been overlooked or even suppressed. In Jordan, archaeology has had strong sponsorship from the royal family. The Syrian government has used travelling exhibits of archaeological finds as an opportunity to expand the narrow perspectives Americans hold about their country.

Prehistoric archaeology, including the study of the origins of agriculture, has relatively little political significance. But this does not mean that prehistoric archaeology has escaped the influence of politics. Steven Rosen (1991) has shown that national borders have had a major influence on the reconstruction of the prehistory of the region, even though these boundaries were irrelevant for ancient hunter–gatherer and early farming communities. The modern borders heavily affect the limits of where archaeologists work and even where they can visit. A UN diplomat tells of having breakfast in Tel Aviv, Israel; lunch in Amman, Jordan; and dinner in Damascus, Syria; before getting back to Tel Aviv after dinner. All of this travel was possible thanks to a diplomatic passport. However, an Israeli archaeologist who has lived in Israel his whole life is unable to visit Syria, and a Syrian archaeologist who has lived her whole life in Syria is unable to visit Israel. The result is a lack of communication and a fragmentation of the archaeological record. There are cultural groupings in the Epipaleolithic that closely map onto national borders. These are modern impositions on a prehistoric landscape, filters that distort our view of the past.

The signing of a peace agreement between Israel and Jordan has eased travel between these two countries, but ongoing tensions and outbreaks of violence have kept interaction to a minimum. Nonetheless, the increased ease of travel has led to an improved understanding of the connections between Israel and Jordan in prehistory. The influence of national borders on our view of prehistory is not unique to the Middle East; it is simply heightened and thus more visible in this politically sensitive region. Prehistoric archaeologists have a natural interest in open borders. In many ways, the emphasis on understanding local archaeological developments from a global perspective, which is the core of prehistoric archaeology, is a very useful counterbalance to tendencies to use archaeology to promote nationalist agendas. One hopes that in the future prehistoric archaeologists might contribute to building bridges across our fragmented modern landscape (Scham and Yahya 2003).

FIGURE 7.2 The site of Gesher/'Jesir al-Majami, a bridge spanning the Jordan River that dates back to the Roman period, is a focus of the PUSH project. The PUSH project works to promote dialogue and cultural understanding of shared heritage between Israelis, Jordanians, and Palestinians. See www.pushproject.org.

Reproduced with the permission of PUSH project.

There is no evidence of domesticated plants or animals during those periods, and the remains of brush huts are the only evidence of architecture.

2. During the Natufian period, constructed architecture and increased elaboration of material culture appear. There is no evidence that agriculture had yet become widespread.

3. In the Early Neolithic period, people lived in villages and began to farm a range of cereals and pulses (lentils and peas). Subsequently, they also began to domesticate goats.

4. During the Late Neolithic period, the earliest pottery manufacture appears. In most areas, the sites of this period are smaller and less densely packed than those of the end of the Early Neolithic. Sheep, goat, cattle, and pig were fully domesticated.

7.2 Stage 1: Kebaran and Geometric Kebaran

Most sites dating to the Kebaran and Geometric Kebaran periods are small hunter–gatherer encampments with few remains other than stone tools and animal bones. The recent discovery of **Ohalo**, a Kebaran site with excellent preservation of organic remains, has shed new light on that period.

■ Technology

Sites belonging to the Kebaran and Geometric Kebaran are easily identified on the basis of their characteristic stone tools (Goring-Morris and Belfer-Cohen 1998). The tools from these periods are made mostly on small blades known as bladelets. In the Geometric Kebaran, bladelets are often shaped into geometric forms such as triangles and rectangles.

■ Settlements

Most sites from the Kebaran and Geometric Kebaran periods are the remains of small camps left by highly mobile hunter–gatherers who did not live all year round in one location. Ohalo, in northern Israel, has provided a unique glimpse of a Kebaran occupation site (Nadel 2002). Soon after it was abandoned, the encampment at Ohalo was submerged beneath the waters of the Sea of Galilee. Because the deposits were not exposed to air, the preservation of organic remains is extraordinary. A recent period of drought led to an unprecedented lowering of lake levels that exposed the site. Archaeologists were able to open up a horizontal 2,000-square-metre area at Ohalo and unearth the remains of six brush huts that could be traced as shallow oval depressions in the ground between 3 and 4.5 metres in length.

The artifacts recovered at Ohalo include a large collection of stone tools dominated by retouched bladelets. Tools were also made of bone, mostly in the form of awls. The only personal ornaments recovered were shell beads that had been transported from the Mediterranean Sea coast. An adult male was buried near the huts at Ohalo. The skeleton was found lying on its side in a semiflexed position. No burial items were found with the skeleton; however, the excavator believes that a stone circle found near the burial might have some ritual significance.

Burials from the Kebaran and Geometric Kebaran sites are rare. A puzzling Geometric Kebaran burial was excavated at the site of Wadi Mataha in southern Jordan (see Figure 7.3). Wadi Mataha was a very small campsite during that period, so the discovery of a somewhat elaborate burial feature was a surprise (Stock et al. 2005). The individual at Wadi Mataha was a young adult male buried with his face pointed down and his arms and legs "hogtied" behind his back. A stone bowl with the bottom broken out was found with the human remains, as was a long flint blade. The man's

FIGURE 7.3 The excavation of the Wadi Mataha burial. At this stage of the excavation, the body's legs have been removed. Note how the shoulder bones (scapula) are overlapping. What does this tell us about the way the body was buried?

▲▲ **Ohalo** A Kebaran site in northern Israel with excellent preservation of organic remains.

The Author on His Fieldwork at Wadi Mataha

The Nabateans were some of the greatest architects of the ancient world. They carved massive tombs out of the sandstone outcrops around Petra in southern Jordan and also built palaces, theatres, and an entire city in this now desolate region. Petra is starkly beautiful. The Nabatean monuments combine the geological beauty of the sandstone with the grandeur of monumental architecture. The Nabateans sculpted the landscape to gather every drop of water to support agriculture, but after the collapse of their kingdom, the irrigation system fell into disrepair and subsequent soil erosion has left much of the bedrock exposed and the land incapable of supporting large-scale agriculture.

Umm Sayhun, the Bedouin village overlooking Petra is a very modest village, mostly small square houses with dusty yards and the occasional animal roaming the streets. Many of the houses appear unfinished, with rebars left poking out of the flat roofs. When I worked at Petra, we lived in Dakhlala's house, a relatively grand and massive structure at the edge of town. Dakhlala was responsible for a good amount of the reconstructive stone masonry in Petra, and he had adorned his own house with some of the simple geometric patterns found on the ancient sandstone monuments.

I had come to Petra with Joel Janetski of Brigham Young University via a rather roundabout route. Joel is a specialist in early agricultural societies of Utah and learned from a colleague who worked on the Nabateans of Petra that there

might be an interesting prehistoric site tucked in this 2,000-year old city. Joel needed a specialist in Near Eastern prehistory, and that is how I landed at Dakhlala's house.

We were looking for the Natufians, who lived in this area more than 10,000 years before the Nabateans. We worked on a slope of a tributary of the Wadi Mataha (which gave the name to the site) that was littered with the artifacts characteristic of the Natufians. But would we discover anything more than a scatter of surface finds? Our first full

season after Joel's initial test of the site yielded a windfall of finds, including the walls of a Natufian structure and the Geometric Kebaran burial described on page 196. We returned for two more seasons, which expanded our coverage and confirmed that we did in fact have the earliest architectural remains in southern Jordan. We are still hard at work on the analysis of the material we recovered during our excavations. This is perhaps the greatest challenge in archaeology—not making the discoveries, but finishing the publication. ▲

FIGURE 7.4 Excavation of one of the Natufian structures at Wadi Mataha. The floors of the structures were poorly defined so it was necessary to map every artifact and piece of fallen rock.

---

skull had been broken open sometime soon after death, leaving a large hole slightly above the forehead.

On the basis of the discoveries at Ohalo and Wadi Mataha, it is very difficult to understand the spiritual world of the people of the Kebaran and Geometric Kebaran periods. The burial at Ohalo, located within the camp, would fit with a burial ritual that serves to form a spiritual link between a group and its place of habitation. The situation at Wadi Mataha is quite different, and it is difficult not to

FIGURE 7.5 Small, crescent-shaped lunates are the characteristic tools found on Natufian sites. How might such small tools have been used?

see the burial as a violent event. Art objects from either period are rare; the only known examples are two crudely incised pebbles.

■ Domestication

There is no evidence of either animal or plant domestication during the Kebaran or Geometric Kebaran period. The people at Ohalo lived near the edge of a lake with access to a wide range of resources. The plant remains recovered are wild grasses—including wild barley and wild wheat—fruits, nuts, and water plants. The most common mammal bones are gazelles, but the remains of deer, wild pig, wild goat, hare, red fox, and wildcat are also found. From a single hut, nearly 10,000 fish bones, mostly of carp and cichlids, were found. The remains of over 77 species of birds, including grebes, ducks, geese, quail, and birds of prey, were also found at Ohalo.

7.3 Stage 2: The Natufian

The **Natufian** societies of the Middle East constructed the earliest stone buildings in this area of the world and developed an impressive range of art objects and personal ornaments. However, there is no evidence that the Natufians domesticated any plants or animals. The Natufian settlements at sites such as **Mallaha** were small villages with up to a dozen structures.

We are still far from understanding the causes underlying the innovations found in the Natufian period. It is possible that an increase in population led to an increase in the size and complexity of settlements, but even if this was the case, we are left to question the reasons for an increase in population. Toward the end of the Natufian, coinciding with a period of climatic stress known as the Younger Dryas, there was a reduction in the size and number of Natufian settlements.

■ Technology

The technology of the Natufian shows a great deal of continuity with that of preceding periods. The stone tools continue to be made on small bladelets. The characteristic shape of tools in the Natufian is a crescent-shaped bladelet known as a **lunate** (Bar-Yosef and Valla 1991). It is assumed that, like the bladelet tools of the preceding periods, lunates served as elements in hunting tools or as parts of tools made up of many small pieces (see Figure 7.5). At the site of Wadi Hammeh in Jordan, a series of bladelets was found mounted in a bone haft of what appears to be a knife or a sickle (Edwards 1991). Some lunates show a type of lustre known as sickle polish, which forms only when stone tools are used to harvest grasses.

The Natufians were the first people in the Middle East to invest a great deal of energy in the manufacture of ground stone tools. Among such tools found on Natufian sites are mortars, pestles, and grooved stones known as shaft straighteners (see Figure 7.6) decorated with a simple meander pattern. In some cases, the tools have been found far from the source of the stone, indicating that they were traded across long distances.

Natufian Societies in the Middle East that practised a broad-spectrum subsistence strategy that relied on a wide range of resources.

▲▲ **Mallaha** A Natufian site in northern Israel with the remains of oval stone structures.

lunate Tiny crescent-shaped stone tool characteristic of the Natufian.

Younger Dryas A period of global climatic stress that had a significant impact on Natufian society.

Long-distance trade is also indicated by the abundance of Red Sea and Mediterranean Sea shells and shell beads found on Natufian sites, which are often quite distant from the sea.

Settlements

The transition to village life began during the Natufian. Structures consist of undressed stones piled to form walls that are often preserved to a height of up to 1 metre. The structures are oval or open semicircles. The floors of the structures are covered with refuse, including stone tools and debris and animal bones (see Figure 7.7). It is hard to imagine these surfaces being used as houses for families, although it is not clear what other function they might have had. It is usually suggested that the stone walls would have supported a superstructure made of wood and brush.

The size of Natufian sites ranges from large villages, such as Mallaha or Wadi Hammeh, with up to a dozen structures, to much smaller sites. There is considerable debate as to whether these sites were occupied year-round.

During the later part of the Natufian, there is a marked reduction both in the number and in the size of the sites. The contraction in Natufian settlements is correlated with a brief period of climatic stress known as the **Younger Dryas**, a global event often characterized as a "little Ice Age." Recent research suggests that the onset of the Younger Dryas was extremely rapid and that major shifts in climate would have taken place within a single generation. In the Middle East, the effect of the Younger Dryas was to reduce the areas suitable for human occupation. From the change in the size and density of the settlements, it is clear that the Younger Dryas had a significant effect on Natufian society.

Burials are commonly found on Natufian sites, often under the floors of houses. In some cases, in a practice that is elaborated in the subsequent Neolithic periods,

FIGURE 7.6 Fragment of a ground stone artifact known as a shaft straightener from the site of Wadi Mataha. Note the groove in the upper surface and the incised decoration around the base.

FIGURE 7.7 Excavation of a large Natufian structure at the site of Mallaha, Israel. The excavators sit on planks so as not to disturb the floor of the structure that is covered with debris. In addition to the circular wall of the structure several postholes lined with stones are visible.

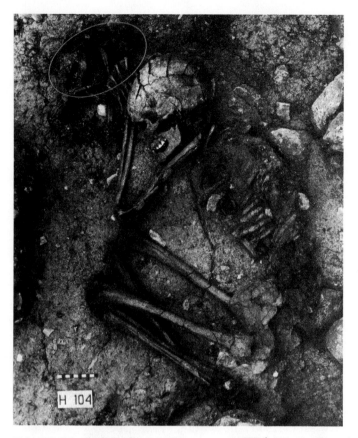

FIGURE 7.8 Burial of a dog, indicated by the red circle, together with a human from the Natufian site of Mallaha. Archaeologists have interpreted this burial as evidence that dogs were domesticated during the Natufian period.

the skull has been removed prior to burial. Objects found in some Natufian burials include shell necklaces and head coverings.

■ Domestication

Unfortunately, it has rarely been possible to recover plant remains from Natufian sites. An important exception is the site of **Abu Hureyra**, located on the Upper Euphrates River in Syria. Abu Hureyra is a site with multiple levels of occupation that span the sequence from the Natufian through the Neolithic. Excavations in the earliest levels at Abu Hureyra uncovered a culture parallel to the Natufian, but with subtle differences. For example, the houses at Abu Hureyra were sunken pits rather than built walls. An ambitious program of flotation for burnt seeds at Abu Hureyra was richly rewarded with a spectacular assemblage of botanical remains. The analysis of the recovered seeds indicates that the people living at Abu Hureyra, like the people at Ohalo, exploited a wide range of plants. Such a broad-spectrum strategy is not surprising, as it is an effective way for hunter–gatherers to minimize the risk that any particular resource will be temporarily scarce. The plant species do not show clear evidence of having been domesticated.

With some exceptions, the animal bones found on Natufian sites are dominated by gazelle bones. At Abu Hureyra, 80 percent of the bones identified were from gazelle. At the same time, Natufians continued to hunt a wide range of animals, including wild sheep, goats, and cattle. At sites such as Mallaha, which is located near a marsh, birds were hunted as well.

The Natufians did not domesticate any herd animals. (Gazelles have actually never been completely domesticated.) Interestingly, there is evidence that Natufians had domesticated, or at least tamed, dogs. At two sites—Hayonim Terrace and Mallaha—dog skeletons were found buried with human remains (see Figure 7.8). These burials signify that dogs were brought into human society. There is also some indication that the snouts of dogs found on Natufian sites are smaller than the snouts of wild dogs (Dayan 1994). This change in morphology is consistent with the early stages of domestication.

7.4 Stage 3: The Early Neolithic

The Early Neolithic is divided into two major periods: the Pre-Pottery Neolithic A, which dates between 12,000 and 10,800 years ago, and the Pre-Pottery Neolithic B, which dates between 10,800 and 8,500 years ago. The beginning of the Pre-Pottery Neolithic A corresponds with the end of the Younger Dryas event, while the Pre-Pottery Neolithic B corresponds to a period of improved climate.

■ Technology

For archaeologists, the major marker that distinguishes the Early Neolithic from the Natufian is a gradual shift away from tools made on bladelets to a tool kit made on blades with a particular emphasis on arrowheads (see Figure 7.9). By the Pre-Pottery Neolithic B, arrowheads were made on skillfully manufactured blades. Blades are also

▲▲ **Abu Hureyra** A site on the Euphrates River in Syria that was occupied during the Natufian and the Neolithic periods.

CANADIAN research

Settlement Archaeology in the Wadi Ziqlab, Jordan Place

Archaeologists working in the Neolithic of the Middle East are often drawn to excavate large village sites. These sites are relatively easy to locate and excavation is likely to produce a rich assemblage of material remains. However, an emphasis on large sites might create a bias in our understanding of how people actually lived during this time period. The Late Neolithic poses a particular problem, as there are very few large village sites dating to this period. Ted Banning, an archaeologist at the University of Toronto, developed a long-term project of intensive survey in the Wadi Ziqlab in northern Jordan to produce a more balanced picture of Neolithic settlement patterns. One of the successes of this project has been the discovery and excavation of Tabaqat el-Buma, a small hamlet dating mainly to the Late Neolithic. At this site, excavations uncovered a series of structures that appear to be the remains of a community consisting of a small number of households. Banning suggests that small, dispersed communities like the one at Tabaqat el-Buma might actually be the characteristic of the majority of the settlements in the Late Neolithic, replacing the nucleated large village communities of the Early Neolithic. ◆

REFERENCE: E.B. Banning. (1998). "The Neolithic period: Triumphs of architecture, agriculture, and art," in *Near Eastern Archaeology*, 61(4): 188–237.

---

used for sickles, as is indicated by the frequent presence of sickle polish. Ground stone axes and adzes suitable for working wood or clearing trees are an important addition to the Early Neolithic tool kit. Grinding stones used for processing grain are also found in extremely large quantities on Early Neolithic sites.

The use of plaster is highly developed during the Pre-Pottery Neolithic B period. Manufacturing plaster involves burning large quantities of limestone. Plaster was used to line the floors of houses and for ritual purposes that will be described shortly. In some cases, plaster was used to build simple basins and bowls.

■ Settlements

During the Pre-Pottery Neolithic A, the size of settlements increased and the first evidence of communal structures appeared. Houses continued to be circular, but settlements were larger than Natufian ones. At the site of **Netiv Hagdud** in the Jordan Valley, the remains of at least three houses were found in an excavation covering 500 square metres, less than 10 percent of the total area of the settlement (Bar-Yosef et al. 1991). Although population sizes are difficult to estimate, it seems likely that Netiv Hagdud housed somewhere between twenty and thirty families. Beyond the size of the settlement, there are other contrasts between Netiv Hagdud and large Natufian sites such as Mallaha. A rapid accumulation of sediments on Early Neolithic sites points to the extensive use of mud brick architecture. At Netiv Hagdud, there was a buildup of close to 4 metres of sediment over a period of two to three hundred years. The floors of the structures on Early Neolithic sites are well maintained, and debris tends to be concentrated in refuse pits. Storage pits, which are rare on Natufian sites, are common at Netiv Hagdud and other Early Neolithic sites.

FIGURE 7.9 Early Neolithic arrowheads and blades. Note the skillful pressure flaking on the tangs of the light-coloured pieces on the left side of the photo.

FIGURE 7.10 View of the site of Jerf el Ahmar showing houses surrounding a central circular structure.

The appearance of communal structures is the most striking aspect of the Pre-Pottery Neolithic A. The most spectacular of these structures is the tower discovered in the Pre-Pottery Neolithic A levels at Jericho. The 9-metre-high tower is made of undressed stones and mud brick and is attached to the inside of a massive wall. A staircase built inside the tower runs from the base to a hole in the flat platform at the top. The **Jericho tower** is the earliest known large-scale piece of architecture in the Middle East. Estimates for the time taken to build the tower and the attached wall range between 10,000 and 15,000 working days (Bar-Yosef 1986). Kenyon (1981) interpreted the tower as part of a defensive wall, which she thought ran around the Neolithic village. Because only a small portion of the Neolithic site was excavated, there is no way of knowing whether the bit of wall found attached to the tower does in fact run around the site. In any case, it seems extremely unlikely that the tower could have served a military purpose, as it is built on the inside of the wall. The interpretation of the tower is made more difficult by the fact that twelve skeletons were found at the base of the staircase. The skeletons were inserted when the staircase began to collapse. Among the suggestions for the purpose of the tower are (1) that the tower and the wall served for flood protection, and (2) that the entire installation had a cultic function, as its construction and use appear to have been a community effort.

Excavations on Pre-Pottery Neolithic A sites in Syria have also uncovered evidence of communal structures. At the site of **Jerf el Ahmar**, on the Upper Euphrates River in Syria, the excavators found that although the Pre-Pottery Neolithic A houses appear to be located somewhat randomly across the site, there is a sense of community planning, with groups of houses distributed around a central structure (Stordeur 2000). As Figure 7.10 shows, this central structure is larger than the others and is built into the ground rather than on its surface. These semi-subterranean buildings are round, with a large central room surrounded by a series of small cubicles. The excavators suggest that the buildings played a central communal role in the small Early Neolithic village at Jerf el Ahmar. In one case, the skeleton of an individual lying splayed on his back with his head removed was found in the central chamber of a semi-subterranean house. Soon after this person died, the building was destroyed and burnt. The discoveries at Jericho and Jerf el Ahmar indicate that the organization of Pre-Pottery Neolithic A society allowed the community to act as a group. It is intriguing that much of the evidence of community-level activity is found in structures with ritual functions associated with evidence of violence. We are left to question the role that ritual and violence played in knitting these early communities together.

During the Pre-Pottery Neolithic B period, there was a shift from round houses to rectangular ones and the size of settlements increased significantly. The shift to rectangular houses allowed sites to be more densely packed than they had been in the Pre-Pottery Neolithic A. The villages of the Pre-Pottery Neolithic B are quite large and often show a high degree of planning. Excavators estimate that in the Early Neolithic levels of Abu Hureyra there were up to 1,440 houses with a population of about 5,000 people (Moore 2000). As seen in Figure 7.11, the houses in the areas

▲▲ **Netiv Hagdud** A Pre-Pottery Neolithic A site in the Jordan Valley that was a village of between 20 and 30 houses.

Jericho tower A 9-metre-high structure made of undressed stone and mud brick dating to the Pre-Pottery Neolithic A.

▲▲ **Jerf el Ahmar** A Pre-Pottery Neolithic A site on the Euphrates River in Syria with the remains of communal structures.

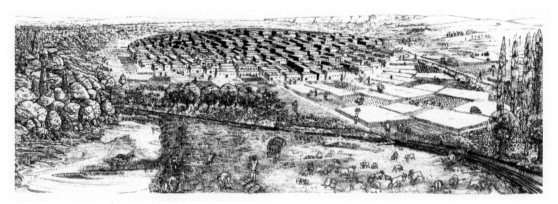

FIGURE 7.11 Reconstruction of the Pre-Pottery Neolithic B village at Abu Hureyra, Syria. This picture shows the extent to which the landscape of the early Neolithic was shaped by human construction and activity.

excavated were closely packed together and had a regular orientation. There is no evidence that the site was protected by a defensive wall.

Estimates for the size of Abu Hureyra place it at the high end of Early Neolithic sites in the Middle East. However, sites that could have easily housed hundreds or even thousands of people are common. Excavations at the site of Badja in southern Jordan have shown that houses during the later part of the Early Neolithic were two or even three stories high (Gebel et al. 1997). At Badja, the size of the settlement was limited by its rather precarious setting on cliffs above a deep gully. It appears that people responded to this limitation by crowding their houses closely together and building upwards. Why people chose to live in such an inaccessible setting is an intriguing question.

During the Pre-Pottery Neolithic B, people lived in dense villages where their social life and interactions were constrained within a grid of houses. Life in these villages also required institutional structures to maintain social order. Hunter–gatherer societies, which are highly mobile, can resolve disputes simply by breaking into smaller groups, or "fissioning." The people living in villages like Abu Hureyra would not have had this option. Moreover, life in a densely packed village would have led to inevitable tensions over issues of inheritance and property rights. Discovering how Early Neolithic societies resolved these conflicts is a challenging archaeological problem, but one that is essential to resolve.

It is somewhat surprising that there is no real evidence for a social hierarchy in early Neolithic villages. Most houses look more or less the same, as do most burials. There is no sense that the regular layout of the sites reflects the decisions of a central authority.

▪ Ritual

Jacques Cauvin has eloquently called the Early Neolithic period the "birth of the gods," and a staggering array of symbolic artifacts has been found on Early Neolithic sites. Ritual objects appear to have operated at many levels, including everyday household objects and objects of display found in sacred precincts or temples. Within both houses and temples there was also a domain of bodies and objects built into walls and buried under floors. It seems clear that as they walked the streets of their villages, these people negotiated not only a world of constructed architecture, but also a world charged with deities, both visible and hidden. The archaeological evidence for Early Neolithic ritual activity can be broken down into three broad categories (based on ideas in Verhoeven 2002 and Naveh 2003): hidden, displayed, and daily life.

HIDDEN RITUALS. Many of the ritual objects found on Early Neolithic sites are hidden away in pits or under floors. The most striking hidden objects are **plastered skulls**.

plastered skulls Human skulls on which a plaster face has been modelled; found buried beneath floors on sites dating to the Pre-Pottery Neolithic B period.

Harris Matrix

Any process that has led to the accumulation of material on an archaeological site is considered to be a depositional event. Because deposition on archaeological sites is not continuous, archaeologists can define depositional units. What makes the concept of depositional units confusing is that these units can be of many types, including walls, floors, and the fill of pits. The job of the archaeological stratigrapher is to place these units into a matrix of relationships. Many archaeologists use a formal system called a Harris matrix to represent the network of relationships between depositional units (Harris 1989). Much of the challenge of stratigraphy comes from the fact that we do not actually observe the creation of the site. Instead, we observe changes in the composition and colour of deposits as we excavate. The excavator's art is to determine whether a change in colour or soil texture represents a new depositional unit.

Building a Harris matrix is based on identifying one of three possible relationships between depositional units.

1. Units can have no stratigraphic connection. For example, if there is a floor on the inside of a wall and a road on the outside, there is no direct stratigraphic relationship between the road and the floor.

2. Units can be in superposition. For example, if a wall is built over the remains of another wall, then the two units are in superposition.

3. Units can be correlated as parts of what was originally part of a single feature. For example, if there was a large pit house that was cut in half by the excavation of a foundation trench for a wall, then the two halves of the pit (which would be identified in the field as two separate depositional units) would be correlated as part of a single feature.

On the basis of these three types of relationships, it is possible to build a formal matrix expressing the stratigraphic relationships between all of the depositional units on a site.

The life of a mud brick house provides a useful example of the range of processes that result in depositonal units.

The following is a list of depositional units that might be found in such a house:

1. The wall built into the foundation trench.

2. The fill placed between the edges of the trench and the base of the wall.

3. A pile of dirt excavated from the foundation trench and dumped in a pile outside of the house.

4. The material incorporated into the dirt floor of the house during the life of the building.

5. A pile of garbage built up against the outside wall of the house.

6. The mud bricks that have collapsed after the abandonment of the house.

7. Garbage that accumulated in the remains of the house after its abandonment.

It is possible to put all of the units of the abandoned mud brick house in a sequence, except for the garbage pile outside the house and the dirt pile from the digging of the foundation trench. It is possible to say that the garbage pile appeared later than the wall. However, because there is no stratigraphic connection between the inside and the outside of the house, it is not possible to determine the stratigraphic relationship between the pile outside the house and any of the features on the inside. The dirt pile from the digging of the foundation trench is in no stratigraphic relationship with any of the other depositional features. ●

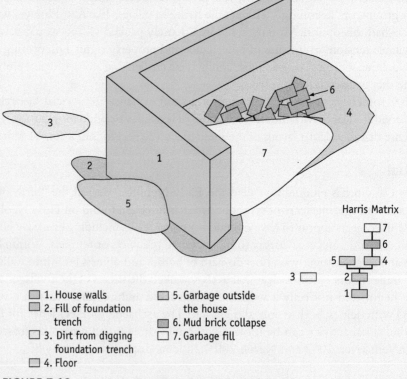

Legend:
- 1. House walls
- 2. Fill of foundation trench
- 3. Dirt from digging foundation trench
- 4. Floor
- 5. Garbage outside the house
- 6. Mud brick collapse
- 7. Garbage fill

FIGURE 7.12 Diagram and Harris matrix of a mud brick house.

The removal of skulls from human skeletons is found as far back as the Natufian. On Pre-Pottery Neolithic B sites, excavators have discovered skulls on which a plaster face has been modelled. Both plastered and unplastered skulls are found below the floors of houses or in small caches.

An analysis of one of the skulls from the site of Kefar Hahoresh has provided a particularly detailed picture of the process of creating a plastered skull (Goren et al. 2001). In most cases, the mandible or jawbone was removed before the face was modelled. The first stage was to plug up the recesses in the skull, including the eye sockets and nasal passages. The face was then modelled onto the skull but the position of the features was adjusted upwards. Thus, the eyes were built up on the forehead, the nose over the eye sockets, and the mouth over the nasal passage. As a result, the faces of the plastered skulls have an oddly shortened appearance. The analysis of the Kefar Hahoresh skull has shown that the process of modelling a plaster skull took place in several stages and included a range of types of plaster as well as other materials (see Figure 7.13).

Careful stratigraphic analysis has indicated that in some cases plastered skulls were removed from their hiding places below the floors of houses and then carefully redeposited. Some archaeologists argue that this practice was an aspect of ancestor worship and that it was through reverence for the ancestor that Early Neolithic societies maintained cohesion. However, a number of sites appear to challenge this interpretation. At Kefar Hahoresh, much of the excavated area is taken up by a dense deposit of human skeletal remains, hardly consistent with a normal habitation site. The excavator of Kefar Hahoresh has argued that it was a ritual site serving to bring together various communities in the region.

At the site of Ain Ghazal in Jordan, a collection of plaster figures—one of which is shown in Figure 7.14—was discovered in two pits (Rollefson 2000). How these figures relate to the Pre-Pottery Neolithic B plastered skulls is an enigma. Another puzzling site is a small cave known as Nahal Hemar, located in a remote region south of the Dead Sea (Bar-Yosef 1985). In this cave, a wide range of artifacts was found, such as beads, bone tools, and arrowheads. Due to the dry conditions, textiles, including the remains of a cap and a bag, were recovered, along with a painted stone mask and a skull on which the face was not decorated, but a net pattern had been applied to the cranium. What the function of this collection of artifacts was and, perhaps more importantly, how they got to where they were found are two questions that remain difficult to answer.

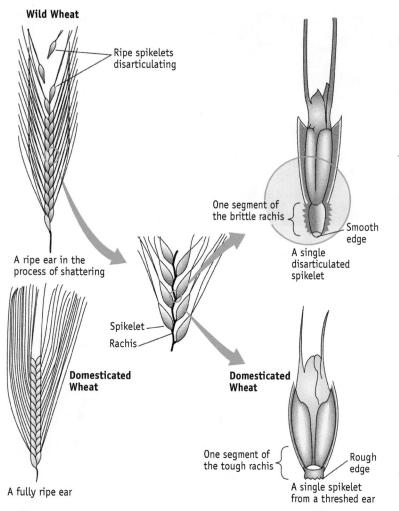

Wild Wheat

Ripe spikelets
disarticulating

A ripe ear in the
process of shattering

Domesticated
Wheat

A fully ripe ear

Spikelet

Rachis

One segment of
the brittle rachis

Smooth
edge

A single
disarticulated
spikelet

Domesticated
Wheat

One segment of
the tough rachis

Rough
edge

A single spikelet
from a threshed ear

FIGURE 7.15 Domesticated cereals such as wheat and barley develop a tough rachis that holds seeds to the plant until threshing after harvest. Wild cereals have a brittle rachis that allows for easy dispersal of the seeds.

rachis The part of a cereal plant that holds the seed to the stalk and keeps the seed on the plant until it is harvested.

At the site of Badja in southern Jordan, the excavator has found a series of unused axes carefully hidden within the walls of a house. The excavator suggests that these beautifully crafted hidden objects would have had a magical function.

DISPLAY RITUALS. The Pre-Pottery Neolithic A tower of Jericho and the central structure at Jerf el Ahmar were meant to be seen. It seems quite likely that, regardless of their practical functions, these structures also stood as visible symbols of the community. During the Pre-Pottery Neolithic B, visibly special buildings are found on a number of sites.

At the site of Göbekli Tepe, on the Euphrates River in eastern Turkey, a series of buildings has been found built around monumental t-shaped pillars quarried as a single block from the bedrock. Some of these pillars are carved with either human or animal figures (Schmidt 2001). At the nearby site of Navali Çori, a series of large stone sculptures has been uncovered that includes depictions of humans, birds, snakes, and birds combined with humans. Most of these sculptures come from a structure identified as a temple.

The majority of the display items found in the Pre-Pottery Neolithic B would not have been visible from any great distance. They are thus quite different from the Jericho tower. Many authors have argued that the context for display in the Pre-Pottery Neolithic B was within temples or sacred precincts. This is a very important point, because it suggests that access to visible signs of divinity was controlled. Perhaps the elite of Early Neolithic society was a ritual elite.

In some cases, there is evidence for the display of skulls, objects that are normally found in hidden contexts. At the site of Çayanu in eastern Turkey, the remains of 450 individuals have been recovered from a single structure known as the skull room, mostly from pits (Schirmer 1990). However, forty-nine burnt skulls were also found in contexts which suggest that they fell off shelves when the building was burnt.

RITUALS OF DAILY LIFE. On several Early Neolithic sites, a large number of simple clay figurines have been found. Although some archaeologists suggest that the statuettes were children's toys, it appears more likely that they had symbolic meaning. These objects are usually found distributed among houses, together with domestic debris.

■ Domestication

Excavations at the Pre-Pottery Neolithic A site of Netiv Hagdud recovered the remains of barley with a tough **rachis**—the part of the plant that holds the seed to the stalk. In wild grains, the rachis is brittle and shatters easily, allowing seeds to disperse. For agriculturalists, it is desirable to have a plant with a tough rachis so that the seed remains on the plant until it is harvested. A plant with a tough rachis is truly domesticated in that it depends on human intervention for successful reproduction. Figure 7.15 illustrates the differences between a brittle rachis and a tough one.

Although the discovery at Netiv Hagdud was interpreted at first as evidence of domesticated plants in the Pre-Pottery Neolithic A, it now appears that this conclusion is not warranted (Bar-Yosef et al. 1991). Within wild populations of barley, a small percentage of plants have a tough rachis, so the small number of remains of apparently domesticated barley found at Netiv Hagdud could have been collected from wild stands along with a wide range of wild plants.

Harvesting of grains did take place during the Pre-Pottery Neolithic A, as is attested by botanical remains, grinding stones, and sickles. However, it does not appear that these plants were farmed. The wild forms of plants, including wheat and barley, were harvested, but there is no indication that seeds were stored and planted. In accordance with the criterion developed by Rindos (see page 184), cereals exploited during the Pre-Pottery Neolithic A were not domesticated, in the sense that the plants did not depend on their relationship with humans for protection or reproduction. There is no evidence of domesticated animals other than dogs during the Pre-Pottery Neolithic A. Gazelles remained the main species hunted, together with a wide range of other animals, including fish and birds.

A series of dried figs recovered from the Pre-Pottery Neolithic A site of Gilgal, located in the Jordan Valley near Netiv Hagdud, provides the earliest compelling evidence of plant domestication in the Middle East (Kislev et al. 2006). Figure 7.16 shows a scanning electron microscope photo of one of the figs. These figs, like modern domesticated ones, are not capable of reproduction without human intervention. Although this intervention is simple, involving merely the cutting and planting of branches, it clearly meets the definition of domestication.

Farming developed across the Middle East during the Pre-Pottery Neolithic B. A wide range of domesticated crops is found, including cereals (emmer wheat, einkorn wheat, and barley), pulses (lentil and pea), and legumes (bitter vetch and chickpea). The domesticated grains show an increase in the size of individual grains and a shift to a tough rachis.

Animal domestication developed somewhat later than plant domestication. The later part of the Pre-Pottery Neolithic B shows evidence of the domestication of sheep and goats. Sheep were domesticated in the northern mountainous regions of Turkey, Iraq, or Iran, their natural habitation zone. Establishing the location and timing for the domestication of goats is quite complex, as wild goats are found across the entire region of the Middle East. By the end of the Pre-Pottery Neolithic B, pigs and cattle were domesticated. The evidence for domesticated animals in this phase includes a reduction in animal sizes, an overrepresentation of the bones of young males, and the discovery of animals such as sheep outside of their natural range. The domestication of sheep and goats appears to have followed a fall-off in gazelle populations.

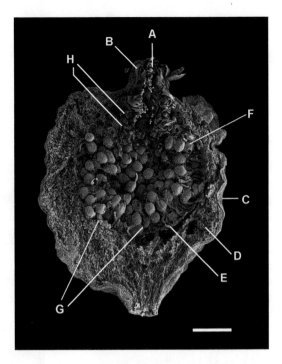

FIGURE 7.16 A scanning electron microscope photo of a fig from Gilgal. The letters indicate features that show that the fig was not wild. Notably, the droplets (E) are empty, unlike wild figs, which show evidence of wasp activity.

7.5 Stage 4: Late Neolithic

At the end of the Pre-Pottery Neolithic B, there is a sharp reduction in the number of large village sites across most of the Middle East. Some archaeologists argue that the collapse of the Early Neolithic settlement system was the result of ecological degradation caused by deforestation. At the same time that the settlement system collapsed, there were significant changes in technology, including the introduction of pottery, and in the production of symbolic artifacts.

Paleoethnobotany

Paleoethnobotanists grasp at the most ephemeral of archaeological remains. Paleoethnobotany is defined as "the study of past cultures by an examination of human populations' interactions with the plant world" (Popper and Hastorf 1988, 1). In rare cases, plant remains are exquisitely preserved. Dry climates, such as the highland caves of Mexico, can preserve the desiccated remains of plants that would otherwise rapidly disintegrate. By contrast, waterlogged conditions, including bogs and deposits sealed under water, can preserve botanical remains because of the absence of oxygen. An example of such anaerobic preservation is the remains of brush huts at the site of Ohalo, Israel, which was sealed below the waters of the Sea of Galilee.

All botanical remains that can be seen without magnification are known as macrobotanicals. Most macrobotanicals are not preserved. An important exception is the charred remains of burnt seeds, plant parts, and wood found on the majority of archaeological sites. The problem for paleoethnobotanists is that these tiny fragile specimens are usually found dispersed across the site, closely bound in the soil matrix. Trying to recover such plant remains is a literal case of grasping at straws. To get around this problem, paleoethnobotanists have developed a recovery method known as flotation. The basic principle behind flotation is simple: Burnt macrobotanical remains will float in water, whereas the soil matrix will sink; therefore, if soil is vigorously mixed with water, the macrobotanicals will float free of the soil matrix. The paleoethnobotanists can then skim off the charred seeds, stalks, and wood for analysis.

Paleoethnobotanists have developed elaborate floatation machines that allow large amounts of soil to be processed. After macrobotanicals are skimmed off, they need to be carefully dried and then laboriously sorted. Paleoethnobotanists can identify species of seeds and other plant parts and can also usually distinguish between domesticated and wild plants. By looking at where different types of plant remains are found, paleoethnobotanists can also contribute to understanding the spatial organization of activities on a site—for example, identifying areas where food was prepared. ●

FIGURE 7.17 Using flotation to recover charred plant remains at the site of Jerf el Ahmar, Syria.

FIGURE 7.18 Charred barley seeds recovered from the site of Tel Kerma.

▪ Technology

Pottery manufacture developed in the Middle East during the Late Neolithic. Among the vessels that have been found are small bowls and jars, as well as pots used for cooking. There is significant variation in the forms of vessels and in the way they are decorated in different regions and within different periods (see Figure 7.19). Two of the main methods of decoration were burnishing the clay to produce a polished surface and using red pigments in painted designs. All pots were built by hand without the use of a potter's wheel and were fired at a low temperature. At the same time that pottery was developed, the wide-scale production of plaster was abandoned.

There was also a significant shift in stone tool manufacture during the Late Neolithic. The skillful production of blades disappeared and arrowheads became rare. Most stone tools found on Late Neolithic sites are expedient tools made on locally available materials with a minimal investment of energy. Sickle blades remain common and often have a serrated edge created by a series of notches.

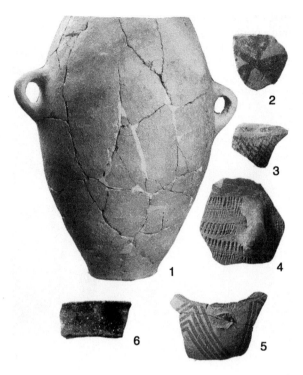

FIGURE 7.19 Neolithic ceramics. 1. Unpainted jar. 2–5. Sherds of vessels with red painted decoration. Note the incised decoration on 4. 6. Sherd of a black burnished vessel.

▪ Settlement and Ritual

The end of the Pre-Pottery Neolithic saw a decline in the number and size of sites. By the end of this period, which is often labelled Pre-Pottery Neolithic C, most of the large sites in Israel, Jordan, Syria, and eastern Turkey were abandoned. The Late Neolithic in these areas is characterized by a limited number of large sites and small dispersed hamlets. The large sites differ from those of Pre-Pottery Neolithic B in that they are not densely packed with structures.

The seeming collapse of the Pre-Pottery Neolithic B settlement system presents a challenge for archaeological interpretation. One possibility is that the collapse was the result of a human-induced ecological crisis. The large populations concentrated in Pre-Pottery Neolithic B villages along with their herds of domesticated animals might have degraded their environments to the point where such population densities could no longer be supported. One important culprit in this scenario is the large-scale production of plaster, which could have led to extensive deforestation.

An alternative perspective sees the end of the Pre-Pottery Neolithic B settlement system not as a collapse, but rather as a shift toward a way of life focused on the grazing of herds of domesticated animals. The dispersed settlement system found in the Late Neolithic might reflect a population that had shifted to living scattered across the landscape rather than huddled in large villages.

The symbolic system of the Early Neolithic seems to have collapsed along with the settlement system by the time of the Late Neolithic. Among the most striking symbolic artifacts of the Late Neolithic are small figurines that tend to be of stylized humans rather than animals. Skull removal and ornamentation is not found on Late Neolithic sites.

In central and western Turkey, there is a continuity in dense village settlement through the Late Neolithic. It is during this period that the settlement of **Çatalhöyük** developed on the Konya Plain of central Turkey. Excavations at the site have revealed a densely occupied settlement dating between 9,000 and 8,000 years ago (Mellaart 1967, Cessford 2001). The excavations at Çatalhöyük uncovered a series of rooms richly decorated with frescoes depicting scenes of leopards, bulls, and goddesses, as well

▲▲ **Çatalhöyük** A Late Neolithic site in Turkey that includes rooms decorated with elaborate frescoes.

FIGURE 7.20 Fresco painted onto a plaster wall at the site of Çatalhöyük. How would you describe the interaction between the human figures and the large bull at the centre?

as geometric designs. A particularly striking image found in these rooms is that of vultures, at times depicted circling around headless human figures. Figure 7.20 shows a fresco from Çatalhöyük that depicts a large bull surrounded by human figures. Bulls' heads and other figures were often modelled in relief, and bulls' horns were set into the plaster bulls' heads. Arrangements of bulls' horns were also found on benches running through the rooms, and human burials were commonly found beneath the benches.

James Mellaart, the first excavator of the site, interpreted the decorated rooms at Çatalhöyük as shrines or temples. This interpretation is consistent with that of Pre-Pottery Neolithic B structures from sites such as Göbekli Tepe and Navali Çori. However, of the 139 rooms Mellaart excavated, more than 40 were interpreted as shrines. It appears that ritual spaces at Çatalhöyük were widely distributed. Alternatively, it could be that the structures Mellaart interpreted as shrines were actually houses and that ritual and elaborate symbolism were an integral part of daily activity rather than something set apart.

The actual interpretation of the symbolism found at Çatalhöyük has provided rich grounds for speculation. The discovery of a significant number of goddess figurines at the site has drawn the attention of archaeologists who argue that Neolithic society was focused on a goddess cult. Çatalhöyük has attracted the attention of Ian Hodder, who has reopened excavations at the site in order to gain a broader contextual understanding of the ritual activity and symbolism.

■ Domestication

During the Late Neolithic, there is a continuous decline in the role of hunting for subsistence. Evidence of the domestication of animals during the Late Neolithic includes changes in the shape of horns in goats. A recent study has found that even at Çatalhöyük, despite the heavy symbolic emphasis on bulls, the main source of meat was domestic goats. It is interesting that the earliest pottery is not linked to evidence for the use of cattle for their milk (Greenfield 2010). One theory had been that early ceramics were used to collect and process milk, but analysis of residues in Neolithic ceramic vessels has failed to find traces of dairy products (Gregg et al. 2009). Late Neolithic societies also continue to rely on the full range of plants domesticated during the Early Neolithic.

7.6 Assessing the Neolithic Revolution

The evidence from the Middle East demonstrates that there is a great deal of value in Childe's concept of a Neolithic Revolution. By the end of the Pre-Pottery Neolithic B, every aspect of life in the Middle East had been transformed as a result of the adoption of a village farming way of life. However, the shift to agriculture in the Middle East was not a sudden process, as predicted by Childe. Rather, the beginning of the shift dates back to the Natufian period with the construction of small settlements, which then grew during the Pre-Pottery Neolithic A phase of the Early Neolithic, when there is evidence of community planning and monumental architecture. The people who lived during this phase had begun to rely heavily on cereals, but had not domesticated either plants or animals. Plant and animal domestication began in the Pre-Pottery Neolithic B phase of the Early Neolithic, together with an increase in the size and density of settlements. Pottery was introduced only in the Late Neolithic, when there was a *decrease* in the size and density of settlements in much of the region.

The Middle East affords important insights into the reasons for the adoption of agriculture. There is some evidence that the climatic stress of the Younger Dryas corresponding to the end of the Natufian and the beginning of the Pre-Pottery Neolithic A was a trigger in the development of villages. Most strikingly, agriculture developed as a consequence of people living in villages. In other words, villages preceded agriculture in the Middle East.

7.7 The Spread of Agriculture to Europe

In classic fictional mysteries, all of the clues are exposed, but the pattern stubbornly refuses to emerge. The spread of agriculture from the Middle East is as obvious and elusive as any work of fiction. The facts are clear. The origins of European domesticated plants and animals can be traced to the Middle East. There is no evidence of indigenous domestication of plants and animals. Instead, the spread of the Middle Eastern domesticates can be tracked as they move across Europe in what some archaeologists characterize as a "Wave of Advance" (Renfrew 1990). By 8,500 years ago, domesticated plants and animals had begun to spread into southeastern Europe. Around 7,500 years ago, farming spread into central and western Europe. By 6,000 years ago, people in most of western Europe, including southern Scandinavia, Britain, and Ireland, were practising agriculture.

The clarity of the pattern has led many archaeologists to claim that a massive movement of populations explains the spread of agriculture into Europe. According to this perspective, incoming farmers gradually replaced the hunter–gatherer societies of Europe. The driving force behind the expansion is thought to be the population increase associated with farming. One fascinating line of research links the expansion of populations of farmers into Europe with the spread of the Indo–European language family. Indo–European languages include all the European romance languages, such as French, Portuguese, Italian, and Spanish; the Germanic languages, such as English, German, and Dutch; the Slavic languages, such as Russian, Polish, and Czech; Asian languages such as Farsi, Hindi, and Bengali; several Baltic and Balkan languages, such as Latvian, Lithuanian, and Albanian; and a number of more dispersed languages, such as Sanskrit and the ancient language Hittite, spoken in the area that is now Turkey. The **language dispersal hypothesis**, as this idea has come to be known, views the spread of agriculture as the movement of people carrying with them an entire way of life, including farming, religion, and language (Renfrew 1990).

language dispersal hypothesis The theory that the spread of agriculture across Europe was the result of the migration of farmers who spoke Indo-European languages.

The language dispersal hypothesis is a bold concept, reminiscent of the out of Africa hypothesis discussed in Chapter 5. Farming is linked with people and language. The spread of agriculture into Europe involves the replacement of hunter–gatherers by farmers. In this model, the hunter–gatherers emerge as passive and defenceless in the face of the gradual wave of advancing farmers.

However, there is increasing evidence that the millennia leading up to the shift to agriculture saw dramatic shifts in European hunter–gatherer societies that preceded the arrival of farming. These societies, collectively labelled as Mesolithic, practised a broad-spectrum adaptation similar to that found in the Natufian of the Middle East (Perlès 2001). In the Mesolithic levels of the Franchthi Cave, Greece, occupied around 11,000 years ago, there is evidence that the occupants hunted red deer, cattle, and pigs and also collected land snails and shellfish. Wild plants, including pistachios, almonds, pears, wild oats, and wild barley, were also collected. There is also evidence of long-distance sea travel. Obsidian was brought to the site from the island of Melos, a 100-kilometre sea voyage from the mainland. Tuna are also found in large quantities, indicating offshore fishing.

Paleoenvironmental studies along the coast of England are producing strong evidence that Mesolithic hunter–gatherers used fire to shape their landscape (Brown 2005). Charcoal is ubiquitous in sediment profiles dating to the period of Mesolithic occupation. The prevalence of charcoal cannot be explained on the basis of natural phenomena such as lightning strikes. Similar use of fire by Australian hunter–gatherers is known as fire-stick farming (see discussion on page 158). Burning would have increased the fodder available to wild animals, which could then be hunted, and would also have increased the availability of wild plants for collecting. The evidence of burning by Mesolithic hunter–gatherers in England muddies the clarity of the division between hunter–gatherers and farmers. Clearly, the hunter–gatherers in what is now England were capable of actively manipulating aspects of their environment.

The most impressive Mesolithic site is **Lepenski Vir**, located next to a whirlpool in the Iron Gates gorges of the Danube River in Serbia. Lepenski Vir consists of a series of trapezoid-shaped structures associated with a large number of burials and sculptures that mix human and fish attributes (see Figure 7.21). Untangling the relationship between sculptures, burials, and other household features such as hearths remains a major challenge (Srejovic 1972; Boric 2005). The Danube would have been a rich source of fish, particularly sturgeon, and it is not surprising that the faunal remains from the earliest levels are dominated by fish bones. In the final stages of occupation, there appears to have been a shift to increased reliance on hunting deer. The dates for the occupation of Lepenski Vir range between 8,400 and 7,600 years ago. These dates overlap with the time of the arrival of Neolithic agriculturalists, indicating that in the later phases of the village the Mesolithic hunter–gatherers of Lepenski Vir lived alongside farming communities.

The complexity of Mesolithic hunter–gatherer societies has led some archaeologists to argue that these societies adopted domesticated plants and animals (Whittle 1996). The spread of agriculture is not seen as the result of the migration of populations from the Middle East. Rather, there was a continuity of local communities that experienced a gradual but dramatic shift in every aspect of their lives.

On the one hand, there is clear evidence that domesticated plants and animals spread into Europe from the Middle East. However, there is also little doubt that the Mesolithic societies were capable of adopting these plants and animals into their broad-spectrum adaptations. The resulting clash of ideas about the origins of agriculture in Europe—advancing populations of farmers or innovating societies of

Lepenski Vir An impressive Mesolithic site along the Danube River in Serbia where structures, burials, and sculptures were found.

FIGURE 7.21 Fish-like sculpture from the Mesolithic site of Lepenski Vir.

hunter–gatherers—is most clearly expressed in diverging interpretations of the farming communities that emerged around 7,200 years ago in central and western Europe known as the **Linear Band Keramik**, or LBK, culture. LBK societies cultivated Middle Eastern plants and herded Middle Eastern animals, but they lived in communities unlike any found in the Middle East. LBK villages consist of longhouses built of massive timbers, as illustrated in Figure 7.22. The houses reached up to 30 metres in length. Clearly, the large size of these houses must reflect the nature of the households that lived in them. It is hard to escape the conclusion that during the LBK period extended kinship groups lived together. LBK houses are evidence of far more than simply changes in technology or construction.

LBK culture is highly uniform across its entire distribution and appears to have spread across Europe very rapidly (Dolukhanov et al. 2005). James Connolly and his colleagues have pointed out that LBK farmers planted a limited range of crops in comparison to Neolithic farmers in southeastern Europe and the Middle East (Connolly et al. 2008). They argue that the best explanation for this pattern is an adaptive response to the climate of central Europe and possibly cultural preferences. Those who view agriculture as the expansion of populations point to these features and argue that the LBK is best explained as the result of people moving with their way of life. However, the novelty of LBK community structure suggests that it might in fact represent a local innovation, rather than an idea that came with new groups of people.

There is a compromise position that views the shift to agriculture in Europe as the interaction between incoming populations and innovative hunter–gatherers. This perspective raises the question of the nature of the interaction between farmers and hunter–gatherers in Europe. There is some evidence of trade and exchange between LBK and Mesolithic groups. There are also some indications of violent interaction. The most graphic evidence comes from the LBK site of **Talheim** in southern Germany. At Talheim, a large pit was found with the remains of eleven men, seven women, and sixteen children. Blows to the head had killed twenty of these people, and two adults had been shot in the head by arrows. Who were the people found at Talheim? Why were they killed? How does this discovery fit with the emerging picture of the spread of agriculture into Europe? It is interesting that a detailed

Linear Band Keramik The term referring to the earliest farming communities that emerged around 7,200 years ago in central and western Europe culture; also referred to as LBK culture.

▲▲ **Talheim** An LBK site in Germany where a pit containing a mass grave was discovered.

FIGURE 7.22 Reconstruction of a Linear Band Keramik village. How does this compare to the reconstruction of Neolithic Abu Hureyra in Figure 7.11 on page 203?

analysis of skeletons from the site of Lepenski Vir, where a community of Mesolithic hunter–gatherers lived alongside farming communities, did not find significant evidence of interpersonal violence (Roksandic et al. 2005).

■ Summing Up the Evidence

The basic facts of the spread of agriculture through Europe are clear, but their significance remains the subject of debate and research. Did populations of farmers sweep across Europe and bring new crops and a new way of life with them? Or did Mesolithic hunter–gatherers adopt domesticated plants and animals to forge a new way of life? Finding the human agents behind large-scale events such as the origins of agriculture is often a challenging undertaking. There is clearly a rupture at the beginning of the Neolithic in Europe. The problem is determining whether this rupture is the result of new people arriving or of a dramatic reorganization of local societies and economies.

SUMMARY

- There is no evidence for the domestication of plants or animals during the Kebaran and Geometric Kebaran periods.
- Excavation of the waterlogged site of Ohalo in the Sea of Galilee has revealed the remains of a series of brush huts.
- The characteristic stone tool of the Natufian period is the lunate, a small crescent-shaped bladelet. Some lunates have sickle polish. Other characteristic Natufian artifacts include decorated ground stone artifacts and shell beads.
- Natufian sites include the remains of circular stone-built structures and burials.
- There is no evidence of the domestication of plants from the Natufian period. Dogs were the only animal domesticated during the period.
- During the Early Neolithic, large settled villages developed. Some of these sites show evidence of large communal structures, such as the tower at Jericho and the semi-subterranean buildings at Jerf el Ahmar.

- Numerous ritual objects, including plastered human skulls, are found on Early Neolithic sites.
- Plant domestication developed sometime in the Early Neolithic during the Pre-Pottery Neolithic B period. Among the plants domesticated were wheat, barley, lentils, peas, bitter vetch, and chickpeas.
- The domestication of sheep and goats developed during the Early Neolithic, after the domestication of plants.
- The earliest pottery is found in the Late Neolithic.
- There was a reduction in the number of large village sites across much of the Middle East during the Late Neolithic.
- In contrast to the general pattern, the site of Çatalhöyük in Turkey developed into a major centre during the Late Neolithic period.
- The origin of agriculture in Europe is based on the adoption of Middle Eastern domesticated plants and animals.
- There is considerable debate over the mechanisms underlying the adoption of agriculture in Europe.

KEY TERMS

REVIEW QUESTIONS

1. Can the development of agriculture in the Middle East be described as a "Neolithic Revolution"?
2. In what ways does the Natufian period differ from the preceding Kebaran and Geometric Kebaran periods?
3. What is the evidence and significance of ritual behaviour during the Early Neolithic?
4. What are the opposing views of how agriculture came to be adopted in Europe? Why is the LBK significant to this debate?

CANADIAN ARCHAEOLOGISTS

- Tristan Carter, professor in the Department of Anthropology at McMaster University, is a member of the Çatalhöyük project specializing in the study of stone tools. He is also involved in research projects in Turkey and on the island of Crete.
  http://www.anthropology.mcmaster.ca/faculty-1/stringy

- Haskel Greenfield, professor in the Department of Anthropology at the University of Manitoba, is a zooarchaeologist who has worked on projects in eastern Europe, North America, the Near East, and South Africa. His publications include *The Secondary Products Revolution in Macedonia,* co-authored with Kent Fowler (British Archaeological Reports, 2005).
  http://home.cc.umanitoba.ca/~greenf/

- Ian Kuijt was trained at the University of Lethbridge and Simon Fraser University before receiving his Ph.D. from Harvard University. He has published widely on community structure in the Neolithic village societies of the Middle East and has directed excavations at the sites of Dhra' in Jordan.

He is currently a professor in the Department of Anthropology at the University of Notre Dame.
www.nd.edu/~ikuijt/

- Mirjana Roksandic, professor in the Department of Anthropology at the University of Winnipeg, is a biological anthropologist whose research includes a focus on mortuary practices and evidence of violence in prehistory. She has carried out reanalysis of the skeletal remains from the site of Lepenski Vir in Serbia.
  http://uwwebpro.uwinnipeg.ca/faculty/anthropology/pages/roksandic/main.html

- Andrzej Weber, professor of anthropology at the University of Alberta, is the director of the Baikal Archaeology Project. This interdisciplinary project examines the prehistoric sites and cemeteries of the Lake Baikal region of Siberia, Russia.
  http://www.anthropology.ualberta.ca/People/Academic%20Faculty/WeberAndrzej.aspx

PEARSON
myanthrokit™

Visit **www.myanthrokit.com**, where you will find a variety of tools and resources to enhance your learning, including:
- Practise quizzes with Study Plans
- Videos
- Listening Activities
- And much more!

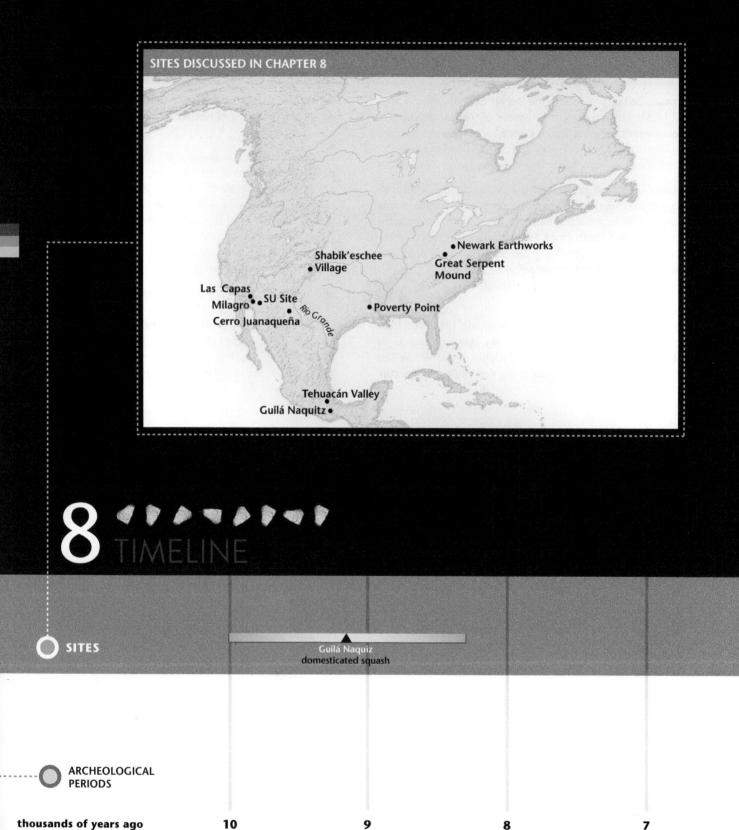

SITES DISCUSSED IN CHAPTER 8

- Newark Earthworks
- Shabik'eschee Village
- Great Serpent Mound
- Las Capas
- SU Site
- Milagro
- Cerro Juanaqueña
- Río Grande
- Poverty Point
- Tehuacán Valley
- Guilá Naquitz

8 TIMELINE

SITES

Guilá Naquiz
domesticated squash

ARCHEOLOGICAL
PERIODS

thousands of years ago   10   9   8   7

MOUNDS AND MAIZE

Maize was domesticated in Mesoamerica and was subsequently
adopted by societies throughout the Americas.
After reading this chapter, you should understand:

- The archaeological record of the
  domestication of maize, beans,
  and squash in Mesoamerica.

- The impact of the adoption of maize
  agriculture on the Archaic societies
  of the southwestern United States
  and northern Mexico.

- The complex interaction between the
  indigenous domestication of plants
  and the adoption of maize in eastern
  North America.

- The context of the mound construction
  of the Adena and Hopewell cultures.

Drawing of the Algonquian village of Secotan made
by John White in 1585.

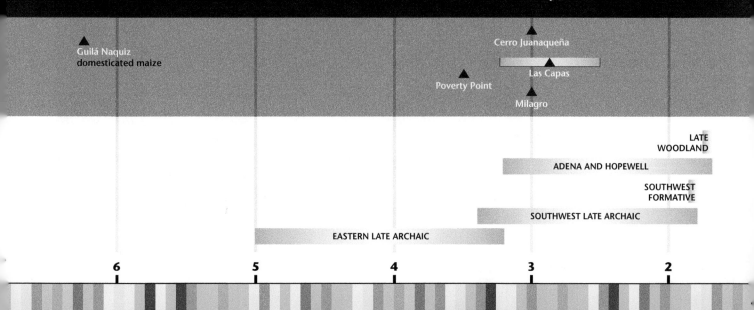

As European settlers spread westward across North America, they encountered the remains of massive artificial earthworks (Silverberg 1986). These monuments of a remote and mysterious past fired the imagination of colonial Americans. The earthworks were astonishing in their size and density. One mound at Miamisburg, Ohio, was 20 metres high and 200 metres in circumference. In the Ohio River Valley alone, there were 10,000 mounds. The earthworks were found in a wide array of forms, including flat-topped mounds, conical mounds, and enclosures. Some of the earthworks, such as the Wisconsin effigy mounds, included human and animal forms. In Figure 8.1, we see the Great Serpent Mound in Adams County, Ohio, which has the figure of an undulating snake with a curled tail stretching over 200 metres along a hill overlooking Brush Creek (Squier and Davis 1848). At the open mouth of the snake is an oval mound.

In the nineteenth century, the belief was widespread that the earthworks of eastern North America were the remains of a mysterious race of mound builders with no relation to modern Native Americans (Silverberg 1986). The mound builders were often portrayed as "civilized" in contrast to the perceived "savagery" of modern Native Americans. Theories of the origins of the mound builders ranged from the Vikings to the Lost Tribes of Israel. The fate of the mound builders was imagined as either migration to Mexico or defeat in bloody battle. The idea of a race of mound builders is now thoroughly discredited. Rather than searching for lost tribes, archaeologists today seek to trace the economic and social context of mound building among early agricultural societies.

It is difficult to organize the origins of agriculture in Mesoamerica and North America into a clear set of stages. The picture that emerges from recent research is of regional variation in the pathways taken in the shift to an agricultural way of life. In this chapter, we begin in Mesoamerica before moving to the American Southwest and then to eastern North America. Mesoamerica has been studied primarily as the area where major food crops, including maize, squash, and beans, were domesticated. The

FIGURE 8.1 The Great Serpent Mound, Ohio.

development of new dating methods has radically altered the chronology for the domestication of these plants. Although we know quite a bit about the timing of crop domestication, many questions linger. Currently, we know little about the social context of domestication in Mesoamerica.

The uptake of maize agriculture in the American Southwest was geographically variable. In some areas, large villages with features such as terrace walls and irrigation canals appeared at the same time as the first domesticated maize. However, in other parts of the Southwest, the impact of maize agriculture was minimal. In explaining this variation, archaeologists working in the American Southwest have emphasized the ecological variability of the region and have developed models based on optimal foraging theory.

In eastern North America, we trace a complex situation involving the local domestication of plants, followed by the addition of maize to an already established farming way of life. Archaeologists in eastern North America have struggled to explain the early and pervasive appearance of earthen mounds long before the appearance of large villages. In grappling with the social meaning of these monuments, archaeologists have drawn on a variety of theoretical frameworks, including agency theory.

We end the chapter by following a debate among archaeologists working in eastern North America over the question of who actually domesticated plants. The context for this debate is feminist archaeology, but the questions raised go to the very core of the origins of agriculture.

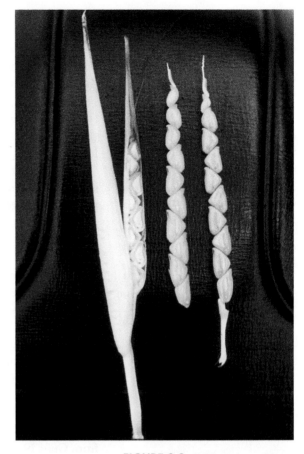

FIGURE 8.2 Wild teosinte with two rows of small triangular seeds.

8.1 Plant Domestication in Mesoamerica

The Pueblo societies of the American Southwest express the centrality of maize or corn to both their subsistence and their spiritual life with the simple phrase "Corn is our mother" (Ford 1994). Maize plays a similar central role in many indigenous farming communities throughout the Americas. Archaeologists and botanists have traced the origins of maize back to **teosinte**, a wild grass found in the highlands of Mexico. Teosinte produces two rows of small triangular-shaped seeds encased in a thick glume (see Figure 8.2). Maize seeds are usually several times larger than teosinte seeds and grow in four or more rows (Harlan 1995). Teosinte also differs from corn in that the rachis, the part of the plant that holds the seeds, is brittle, so the seeds disperse at maturity.

The identification of teosinte as the wild ancestor of maize has been the subject of debate. However, the genetic relation between the two plants is now well established. It is even possible that the shift from the one to the other took place rapidly (Eubanks 2001). Genetic analysis of modern populations of maize suggests that there was a single centre of domestication for this crop, probably located in the highlands of Mexico (Matsuoka et al. 2002).

Archaeological research on the origins of agriculture in Mesoamerica has focused on the excavation of dry caves in the highlands of Mexico, where plant remains are well preserved. The picture that has emerged from the cave excavations is that plants, including maize, squash, and beans, were domesticated in Mexico by groups of mobile hunter–gatherers. The domestication of plants appears to have had little effect on these societies beyond providing an additional resource for subsistence. However, it is possible that the archaeological emphasis on highland caves has biased our understanding of the impact of agriculture.

teosinte A wild grass found in the highlands of Mexico; the wild ancestor of maize.

▲▲ **Tehuacán Valley** A valley in the Mexican highlands where excavations by Richard MacNeish recovered some of the earliest evidence of domesticated plants in Mesoamerica.

▲▲ **Guilá Naquitz** A site in Oaxaca, Mexico, that has produced the earliest evidence of domesticated plants in Mesoamerica.

accelerator mass spectrometry (AMS) radiocarbon dating A refined method of radiocarbon dating that makes it possible to date very small samples, including plant remains.

Excavations by Richard MacNeish in a series of caves in the Tamaulipas Mountains and in the **Tehuacán Valley**, and by Kent Flannery at the cave site of **Guilá Naquitz** in the Oaxaca Valley, have produced a long record of occupation by prehistoric hunter–gatherers who gradually incorporated domesticated plants into their subsistence base. The highland valleys of Tehuacán (1,000–1,500 metres above sea level) and Oaxaca (2,000 metres above sea level) might not be the actual location where any of the Mesoamerican crop species were initially domesticated (Piperno and Flannery 2001). The sites were chosen for excavation because of their long sequences of occupation and excellent preservation of plant remains.

The identifiable plant remains excavated at the highland dry cave sites are too small to be dated directly with conventional radiocarbon dating methods. However, it was possible to date other organic remains, such as wood charcoal, and to build an absolute chronology of the stratigraphic sequence. The age of identifiable plant remains was then determined based on the level in which they were recovered.

The stratigraphic sequences at Guilá Naquiz and the Tehuacán Valley sites are relatively shallow and compacted. At Guilá Naquiz, five levels were identified. The top of the sequence is Zone A, a 20-centimetre-thick level dated to a little over 1,000 years ago. Below Zone A is a series of levels labelled Zone B–Zone E, which date between 12,700 and 7,800 years ago. The entire thickness of Zone B–Zone E is approximately 60 centimetres, covering a period of over 4,000 years (Flannery 1986). When one considers that plant remains are often extremely small and deposits shallow, it is perhaps not surprising that the stratigraphic method of dating plant remains from dry caves has turned out not to be dependable.

The development of **accelerator mass spectrometry (AMS) radiocarbon dating** has made it possible to date identifiable plant remains. When plant remains from Guilá Naquiz and the Tehuacán Valley are directly dated using AMS radiocarbon dating, the ages obtained are often different (in most cases, younger) from what is expected based on the age of the level from which the sample was recovered.

On the basis of AMS radiocarbon dating, squash has been identified as the earliest plant to be domesticated in Mexico. The type of squash domesticated in Mesoamerica, *Curcubita pepo*, is the ancestor of the vast array of squash we eat today, including pumpkin, zucchini, and acorn, marrow, and spaghetti squash. Squash seeds recovered from Zones C and B at Guilá Naquiz have been directly dated to between 10,000 and 8,300 years ago (Smith 1997). The seeds are larger than those of wild squash. The thickness and colour of the rind also distinguish the domesticated variety from the wild one. It is only in Zone B, which dates to around 8,000 years ago, that there is an increase in the thickness of the squash rinds and a change in colour from green to orange (see Figure 8.3). On the basis of these results, it appears

FIGURE 8.3 Fragments of early domesticated squash from Guilá Naquiz, Mexico. (A) Fragment of the stalk; (B) fragment of the rind that retains its orange colour; (C) a seed.

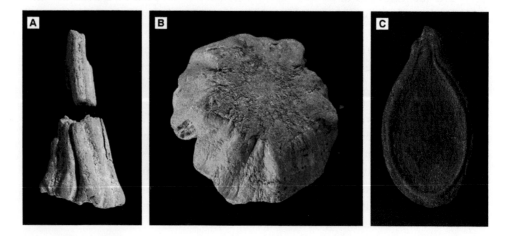

TOOLBOX

AMS Radiocarbon Dating

In previous chapters, the basic methods of radiocarbon dating and calibration were introduced. The principles of radiocarbon dating are that (1) the ratio between radioactive carbon-14 and stable carbon atoms is constant throughout the carbon exchange reservoir, which includes the atmosphere, the oceans, and the biosphere; and (2) carbon-14 decays at a known rate. When an organism dies, it is removed from the carbon exchange reservoir and the concentration of carbon-14 in the remains of the organism decreases at a fixed rate. By measuring the concentration of radiocarbon in a sample, it is possible to calculate the time since the death of the organism. Calibration becomes necessary because the concentration of carbon-14 in the global carbon reservoir fluctuates over time.

But how is the concentration of carbon-14 measured? The initial method was to measure the radio-activity of a sample as an indirect measure of its carbon-14 concentration. The problem with this method is that the concentration of carbon-14 in the carbon reservoir is very low. Therefore, in order to measure the carbon-14, large samples are needed. Thus, there was a limitation on the type of samples that could be dated. Also, very old samples in which most of the carbon-14 had already decayed could not be dated.

Accelerator mass spectrometry (AMS) radiocarbon dating is a solution to this problem. AMS radiocarbon dating combines ingenuity and power to directly count the carbon isotopes in a sample. The first step in developing AMS radiocarbon dating draws on the following principle of physics: When an electrically charged particle travels through a magnetic field, it follows a curved path, and the amount of curvature is related to the mass of the particle. Specifically, the lower the mass, the greater the curvature. Using this method, a scientist should be able to take a sample of (radioactive) carbon-14 mixed with nonradioactive carbon-13 and carbon-12 isotopes (which are lighter than carbon-14), sort them into separate streams, and literally count their atoms. However, to count the small number of carbon-14 atoms, tremendous energy is needed, so an atomic accelerator is used to blast the carbon-14 atoms through the system at an acceleration of 8 million volts.

The impact of AMS radiocarbon dating has been almost as dramatic as the initial impact of radiocarbon dating. It is now possible to directly date small samples, including seeds and residues. Samples can be dated more quickly than with conventional methods, and in some cases it is possible to date very old samples in which the surviving concentration of carbon-14 is extremely low. ●

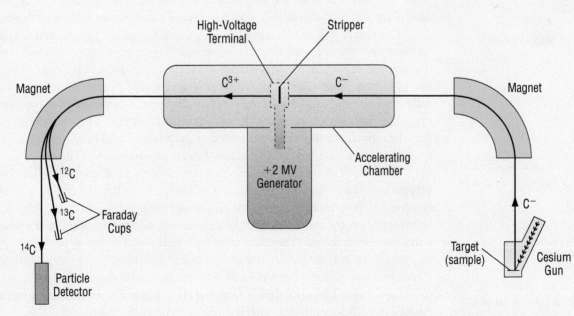

FIGURE 8.4 Diagram of an accelerator used for AMS radiocarbon dating. Note how different isotopes of carbon are separated at the end of the line.

that the domestication of squash was a prolonged process that began 10,000 years ago with selection for larger seeds. Over the next 2,000 years, farmers selected for an increase in the thickness of the rind and a change in its colour.

The oldest directly dated maize was also found at Guilá Naquiz. The stratigraphic context for these maize samples is an ephemeral occupation between Zone A and Zone B. Two fragments of maize cobs from this context were directly dated to 6,250 years ago. The maize from Guilá Naquiz has a tough rachis and is thus clearly domesticated. It is interesting that one cob has two rows, like teosinte, while the other has four rows, as is found in most maize.

The earliest maize from the Tehuacán Valley, directly dated to 5,500 years ago, is of the four-row variety. The long sequence from the Tehuacán Valley sites illustrates a gradual increase through time in the size of the cobs and the number of kernels. John Smalley and Michael Blake have suggested that maize was initially domesticated for the sugar that can be recovered from the stalk, rather than for the kernals. They suggest that the sugar might have been used for making alcoholic beverages (Smalley and Blake 2003). Following this line of argument, the domestication of maize must be understood in its social context.

Studies of modern domesticated beans suggest that both common beans and lima beans were domesticated independently in the Andes and Mesoamerica (Smith 1995). The oldest direct date on a domesticated bean from Mexico is approximately 2,500 years ago, for a single bean from Coxcatlán Cave in the Tehuacán Valley. It is likely that beans were domesticated at a far earlier date, possibly at the same time as maize.

Turkeys were the only animals domesticated in Mesoamerica. It is unclear when the domestication of turkeys took place.

8.2 Maize Agriculture in the American Southwest

Domesticated maize was grown in the highlands of Mexico by 6,250 years ago. Maize and squash agriculture spread to northern Mexico and the southwestern United States during the Southwestern Late Archaic period (ca. 3,400 years ago) (Cordell 1997). The initial impact of maize and squash agriculture varied across the region. In some areas there is evidence of increased sedentism, while in others it appears that agriculture did not substantially alter the lives of Late Archaic hunter–gatherers.

On a steep hill overlooking the Río Casas Grandes in northwest Chihuahua, Mexico, near the New Mexico border, archaeologists have found dramatic evidence that some Late Archaic farmers shifted to village life (Hard and Roney 1998). At the site of **Cerro Juanaqueña**, archaeologists have traced over 8 kilometres of terrace walls and one hundred rock rings. Although the construction of these features is simple, it represents a considerable investment of energy. The excavators estimate that the construction of the walls found at the site involved moving 20,000 tones of rock and soil, which would have taken sixteen person-years of labour.

Excavation of three of the stone circles at Cerro Juanaqueña has failed to yield evidence of their function. Excavation of the terraces has yielded a wide array of domestic debris, including ground stone and chipped stone tools, ashy soil, and burnt and unburnt animal bones. On one terrace, postholes outlining the remains of a structure were found. The excavators believe that the function of the terraces was to provide a level surface for the construction of houses. Four maize kernels from Cerro Juanaqueña have been directly AMS radiocarbon dated to an average date of 3,070 years ago. The arrowheads found at the site are forms belonging to the Late Archaic, which is consistent with the radiocarbon dates.

Although a small amount of maize has been found in excavations at Cerro Juanaqueña, seeds from wild plants, including chenopodium, gourds, and grasses,

▲▲ **Cerro Juanaqueña** An early agricultural site in northern Mexico with extensive evidence of terracing and other stone built features.

dominate the plant remains found on the site. The faunal remains indicate that animals such as jackrabbit, cottontail rabbit, mule deer, and pronghorn antelope were hunted. There is no evidence of significant fishing, despite the proximity of the site to the Río Casas Grandes. Almost 600 grinding slabs and basins have been found, indicating that grinding seeds or grain was a very important activity at the site. The only pottery found is from later occupations limited to two small areas of the site. Three additional large Late Archaic sites have been reported in the vicinity of Cerro Juanaqueña.

Moving to the northeast from Cerro Juanaqueña, archaeologists have found that people living in the Jornada Mogollon region along the Río Grande did not significantly engage in agriculture until A.D. 1000. There is a 2,000-year gap in the onset of agriculture over a distance of less than 100 kilometres between the Río Casas Grandes, where Cerro Juanaqueña is located, and the Jornada Mogollon region. Robert Hard and John Roney explain this pattern in terms of **optimal foraging theory** (Hard and Roney 2005). According to this theory, humans act on the basis of rational self-interest to maximize efficiency in collecting and processing resources. Hard and Roney argue that in the Río Casas Grandes region, maize agriculture offered a higher rate of return than many low-ranked resources that were exploited during the Late Archaic, such as grama grass and dropseed grass. These grasses are described as low-ranked resources because they offer little return of energy for the input of energy required to collect and process them. The Jornada region has lower rainfall than the Río Casas Grandes, resulting in low returns and high risk for maize agriculture. At the same time, the availability of shrubs such as mesquite and saltbush, as well as other plants, offered resources with higher rates of return. Optimal foraging explains the early uptake of maize agriculture at Cerro Juanaqueña as the result of rational decision making based on the available resources. The delay in the development of maize agriculture in the Jornada region was the result of similar rational decisions, reflecting differences in local ecology.

Maize agriculture associated with large settlements is also found in the area around Tucson, Arizona. At the **Milagro** site, the Late Archaic people lived in pit houses and appear to have stored maize in bell-shaped pits. The plant remains recovered at Milagro include domesticated maize, along with wild plants such as amaranth, chenopod, and grass seeds. The faunal remains recovered at the site include jackrabbit and possibly deer. Two radiocarbon dates place the occupation of Milagro at 2,950 years ago.

Large-scale cultural resource management projects outside Tucson have produced spectacular insights into the agricultural settlements of the Late Archaic period (Mabry 2005). Terrace walls associated with maize remains have been excavated at the Tumamoc Hill site. At the **Las Capas** site, a sequence of canals was discovered dating to between 3,250 and 2,500 years ago (Figure 8.5). The canals carried water at least 2 kilometres from the Santa Cruz River to irrigated fields. These features indicate that the adoption of maize agriculture in this region involved a significant investment of labour. Some of the sites excavated in the area around Tucson include over one hundred

optimal foraging theory
A theory based on the assumption that the choices people make reflect rational self-interest in maximizing efficiency when collecting and processing resources.

▲▲ **Milagro** An early agricultural village located outside Tucson, Arizona.

▲▲ **Las Capas** A site near Tucson, Arizona, where an Archaic village and canal system have been discovered.

Irrigation Ditch

FIGURE 8.5 Stratigraphic profile at the Las Capas site showing the section of an irrigation ditch. The ditch is visible as a concave feature in the dark sediments at the base of the profile.

FIGURE 8.6 View of the Las Capas site near Tucson, Arizona. The site is located on the median strip of a highway.

pit houses (although not all of these were occupied simultaneously), as well as large communal structures. Figure 8.6 shows a view of the structures excavated at the Las Capas site.

Maize agriculture spread to the higher altitudes of the Mogollon Highlands and the Colorado Plateau at roughly the same time as the occupation of Milagro and Cerro Juanaqueña. In these regions, the adoption of agriculture did not result in the development of villages (Plog 1997). However, the storage areas, garbage pits, and remains of fireplaces found in the excavation of cave sites indicate that the use of caves intensified with the adoption of agriculture (Cordell 1997).

Because of the dry conditions in the highland caves, the remains of basketry and other organic materials are superbly preserved. A particularly rich collection of organic remains was recovered at White Dog Cave, Arizona, named for one of the mummified dog burials found at the site (Kidder and Guernsey 1915; Cordell 1997). The organic artifacts recovered at White Dog Cave include a net made of fine fibre string that is over 200 metres long and 1 metre wide and a range of baskets decorated in woven or painted designs.

A number of human burials were also excavated at White Dog Cave. Women were buried with necklaces of beads made of stones, shells, and seeds. Men were buried without clothes, while women were buried in loose-fitting aprons made of soft fibre. Both men and women were buried wearing sandals made of yucca fibre, and with robes made of animal skins. Babies were found wrapped in soft rabbit-skin blankets and diapers made from juniper bark. Mobile cradles for infants were also found at the site.

■ The Formative Period

Although some pottery, including figurines from Milagro and Las Capas and vessel fragments from Las Capas, has been found on Late Archaic sites, the widespread introduction of pottery into the American Southwest occurred around 1,800 years ago at the beginning of the Formative period. It is interesting that the introduction of pottery overlaps with the introduction of domesticated beans in this region. By this time, sites with architecture in the form of pit houses are common across the Southwest. These houses were usually square or rectangular and were excavated as much as 1 to 2 metres below the surface (Plog 1997). The superstructure was usually built of wooden beams, brush, and soil.

Turkeys appear to have been domesticated in the Southwest during the Formative period. Recent genetic analysis of turkey bones recovered from archaeological sites suggests that turkey domestication in the Southwest and in Mesoamerica were separate events (Speller et al. 2010).

The number of houses found on Formative-period sites varies from one or two to as many as twenty-five to thirty-five. Although storage pits are common on most sites, their placement varies (Plog 1997). The Shabik'eschee Village site in Chaco Canyon, New Mexico, is an unusually large one where the remains of sixty pit houses have been excavated. There is some question whether the entire site was occupied at any one time (Wills and Windes 1989). A large number of carefully constructed storage pits were found at Shabik'eschee, all located outside the houses.

The SU site in central New Mexico is a large Formative-period settlement with forty pit houses. At this site, the storage pits are located inside the houses. The contrast between the location of storage pits in Shabik'eschee Village and the SU site has been interpreted as reflecting differences in the ownership of food stores. The placement of pits outside houses suggests communal ownership; the placement of pits inside suggests household ownership.

At both Shabik'eschee Village and the SU site, unusual structures were found that appear to have played a communal function. At Shabik'eschee Village, one structure was five times the size of other pit houses and was surrounded by a bench. At the SU site, one structure was unusually large and lacked the internal storage pits found in other structures.

Regional variation in the impact of maize agriculture in the American Southwest continued into the Formative period. In Utah, the Fremont culture, dated between A.D. 700 and A.D. 1200, challenges archaeologists to explain the variations in adaptation after the introduction of maize agriculture. What is particularly striking about the Fremont is "the diversity it presents in the importance of maize farming relative to hunting and gathering" (Barlow 2002, 68). Renee Barlow has analyzed the yield of maize agriculture practised by modern Guatemalans using traditional methods and has concluded that intensive agriculture produces little food in return for the energy expended in growing, collecting, and processing the plants. Less formal methods of maize agriculture, in which fields rotate frequently, produce a lower total yield, but a greater yield per unit of energy expended. On the basis of optimal foraging theory, Barlow suggests that Fremont farmers adapted the intensity of their reliance on maize agriculture to the availability of other, higher-ranked food resources. When resources such as game or pine nuts were available, maize would be exploited using only low-yield methods, which require a low investment of energy. When highly ranked resources were scarce, intensive maize agriculture became worth the energy investment. The variation in the Fremont reflects the variation in rational choices made by people living in different ecological settings.

■ Summing Up the Evidence

New discoveries have established the onset of intensive maize agriculture in northern Mexico and the American Southwest during the Late Archaic period, approximately 3,000 years ago. Agricultural societies lived in large villages and built large-scale features, including terraces and canals. However, the uptake of maize agriculture was not uniform across the region during the Late Archaic, and the pattern continues into the Formative period. In responding to the challenge of understanding this diversity, archaeologists have turned to optimal foraging theory to explain the variation in adaptation as a rational response to differing ecological conditions.

TOOLBOX

Hand-Built Pottery

The pottery produced by the native societies of the American Southwest is the antithesis of modern mass-produced ceramics. The first step in producing hand-built pottery is to mine the clay and mix it with water. In some cases, inclusions such as sand, straw, or even crushed sherds of broken pots are added to the clay paste. Forming a vessel often begins by making a shallow bowl from a ball of clay. The walls of the vessel are then built up with either coils or slabs of clay. Next, a paddle may be used to smooth and sometimes thin the walls of the vessel. Afterwards, the vessel is left to partially dry before surface decoration is added. Many fine-ware pots are dipped in a slip—a slurry of fine-grained clay, often mixed with iron-rich clay. A slip mixed with minerals can also be used to paint designs on pots. Pots can be polished by burnishing the semi-dry surface with a smooth stone that compresses the clay particles. After the surface of the vessel has been treated with slip, paint, or burnishing, the pot is again left to dry. Once completely dry, pots are stacked and heated in an open fire or in a kiln. If the fire is smothered and the pots are heated without access to oxygen, the surface will be black. If the fire is allowed to burn freely, the iron in the clay will oxidize and the surface will be red.

Over the centuries during which Southwestern potters have hand-built clay vessels, they have used these basic processes to produce a wide array of shapes and surface treatments. Many such vessels raise hand-built pottery to a fine art. The Mimbres potters created beautiful bowls with simple yet powerful scenes painted in black against a white background. More recently, Pueblo potters have explored the range of surface treatments that can be achieved by combining burnishing with carefully controlled firing. Maria Martinez of the San Ildefonso Pueblo is among the most celebrated modern ceramic artists. Her creations include vessels with patterns formed by setting highly polished designs against a matte unpolished background. Many of these vessels are a deep black colour, which is achieved by smothering the pot while it is firing. ●

FIGURE 8.7 A Mimbres bowl from New Mexico.

The AMS radiocarbon dating of maize from the highland caves of Oaxaca and the Tehuacán Valley has shown that the time between the domestication of maize and its spread to northern Mexico and the American Southwest is shorter than had previously been thought. Some archaeologists have argued that the spread of maize agriculture was the result of the movement of populations of farmers northward (Matson 2003). This is a controversial proposal, however, one that is difficult to assess on the basis of the available data.

8.3 Eastern North America

The development of agriculture in eastern North America involved both the domestication of a wide range of local plants and the adoption of maize. The initial domestication of plants in this area took place during the Eastern Late Archaic period, (5,000 to 3,200 years ago). (For discussion of other aspects of the Archaic period see Chapter 6). The intensification of agriculture and the first appearance

FIGURE 8.8 A. A pot made by Maria Martinez. The following photographs show the process she used to make this type of vessel. B. Preparing the clay. Notice the pots drying in the background. C. Using coils of clay to build up the vessel walls. D. Smoothing the vessel walls. E. Burnishing a pot with a smooth stone. F. Removing finished pots from the fire.

(top left): Maria Montoya and Julian Martinez (San Ildefonso Pueblo, native American, ca 1887-1980; 1879-1943). "Jar" c. 1939. Blackware. 11? x 13 in. (dia.). The National Museum of Women in the Arts, Washington, DC. Gift of Wallace and Wilhelmina Holladay.

of maize in the region occurred during the florescence of the Adena and Hopewell traditions of the Early and Middle Woodland period (3,200 to 1,700 years ago). However, maize played a minor role in people's diet, and settlements remained small and dispersed for almost a thousand years after the plant was first adopted in eastern North America. Intensive maize agriculture and large settled villages became established only at the beginning of the Late Woodland period.

■ The Indigenous Domestication of Plants

A wide range of plants, including squash, chenopod, marsh elder, and sunflower, was domesticated by the Late Archaic hunter–gatherer groups of eastern North America (Smith and Cowan 2003). The domestication of squash in the region was independent of the earlier domestication of the plant in Mexico. Chenopodium was independently domesticated in South America, Mexico, and eastern North America.

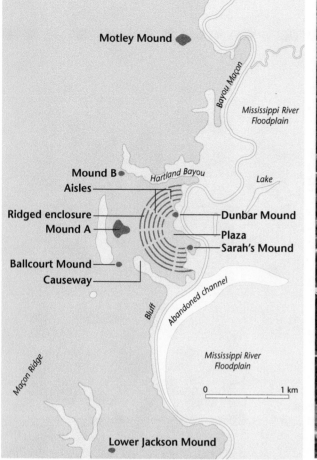

FIGURE 8.9 Plan of Poverty Point.

FIGURE 8.10 Oblique aerial view showing the semicircular rings at Poverty Point, Louisiana.

Along with the presence of domesticated plants, the Eastern Late Archaic is characterized by an increasingly narrow subsistence base, particularly in areas with rich supplies of shellfish. Large accumulations of discarded shells are found on sites known as **shell middens**. Some of these sites, such as the Indian Knoll site on the Green River in Kentucky, are quite large. At the Indian Knoll site, thousands of burials were recovered, along with the traces of structures built of posts (Brose et al. 1985).

Crude ceramic vessels first appeared in eastern North America 5,000 years ago in the Stalling Island culture of the Savannah River Valley, Georgia. The material culture of the Late Archaic also includes a wide range of ceremonial objects and ornaments. There is evidence of trade in various minerals, including galena (lead), hematite (iron oxide), jasper, native copper, and slate, over very long distances.

The Late Archaic **Poverty Point** site in Louisiana is a massive planned construction that raises many questions about subsistence and social organization during that period. The site consists of a series of six concentric embankments 2 metres high and over 20 metres across that form a semicircle more than 1 kilometre wide (Figure 8.9). Aerial photography (Figure 8.10) and GIS analysis (Figure 8.11) provide a sense of how this site fits within the landscape. Along with the embankments there are a series of massive mounds, some of which appear to be in the shape of birds.

The purpose of the embankments remains unclear. If they were house platforms, then Poverty Point was an extremely large, exquisitely planned village. However, plowing has largely removed any evidence that might have remained of houses.

shell middens Sites built up with large accumulations of discarded shells.

▲▲ **Poverty Point** A Late Archaic site in Louisiana with a series of six concentric embankments.

The density and diversity of cultural materials found on Poverty Point support the identification of the site as a village. Most of the finds are objects of daily life: net sinkers for fishing, stone tools for hunting animals and gathering plants, soapstone and pottery vessels, and more. But the most compelling evidence that Poverty Point was a village comes from the extensive deposits of refuse. As Jon Gibson summarizes the situation, "Claims that Poverty Point was a vacant ceremonial centre are simply not tenable given the extensive midden and its secular-looking trash" (Gibson 2000, 105).

Stones for tool manufacture are not available in the area around Poverty Point. It is therefore not surprising that stone tools were brought onto the site from non-local sources. However, the quantity of material and the distance to the sources are astounding. It has been estimated that 70 tonnes of stone were brought onto the site. The distance of the site from the sources of the material makes this figure even more staggering: Burlington chert and galena (lead) ore were brought from quarries near St. Louis, 725 kilometres from Poverty Point; hematite, crystal quartz, slate, volcanic rocks, and other minerals came from the Ouachita Mountains in Arkansas, 240 kilometres away; other types of chert came from Kentucky, 585 kilometres away; and soapstone came from Alabama and Georgia, 645 kilometres from Poverty Point. These distances are those of the most direct route; if people were travelling by river, then the figures would be roughly doubled.

The stones were brought to Poverty Point either as finished tools or as pieces that had been roughed out. Cherts were used for hunting points, hoes, and knives; hard minerals were used to make net sinkers for fishing; and soapstone was used for cooking vessels. In most cases, archaeologists expect to trace a "down the line" pattern for trade items, meaning that the quantity of a given item will decrease as the distance from the source increases. Generally, this rule works for the Late Archaic, but Poverty Point stands out from the pattern. There is something about the activities that took place at that site that led to the deposition of enormous quantities of artifacts at a great distance from their source.

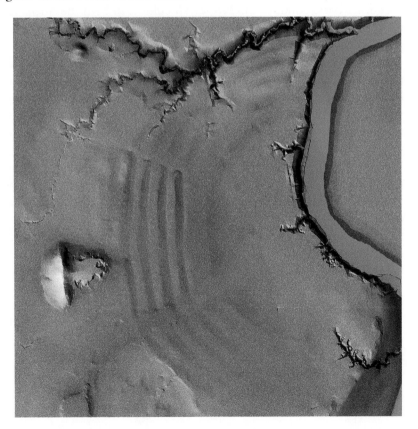

FIGURE 8.11 Perspective map of Poverty Point created using GIS software.

One possible explanation for what took place at Poverty Point can be found by returning to Hayden's model for the origins of agriculture, which stresses the importance of competitive feasts. Perhaps Poverty Point was not a large village, but rather the focal point of feasting events, drawing in people from a very wide region—people who were not otherwise living together in village communities. Is it possible that in the Late Archaic of eastern North America monumental construction preceded large settled villages? The same issue will emerge when we turn to the monuments of the Hopewell. The essential question is whether the early farming communities of eastern North America could have found an alternative pathway to creating farming communities—a pathway that relied on the construction of massive earthworks instead of large villages.

Although the Late Archaic was clearly a period of significant change in the societies of eastern North America, the impact of domesticated plants on subsistence was minimal. Collecting wild plant foods and hunting wild animals continued to form the basis of subsistence. One source of evidence relevant to the role of domesticated plants in the diet is the human fecal remains, or coprolites, found on archaeological sites. Although coprolites are certainly not the most glamorous aspect of archaeological research, studying them provides a unique insight into the human diet. Studies of coprolites from two sites in Kentucky dated to 3,400 years ago demonstrate a great deal of variability in the diet (Gremillion 1996). In some samples domesticated plants were dominant, whereas in others they were a smaller component. These findings suggest that cultivated crops played a variable role in the diet during the initial period of plant domestication.

■ The Adena and Hopewell

Most of the mounds in Ohio and surrounding areas date to the Early and Middle Woodland period between 3,200 and 1,700 years ago (Gremillion 2003). In the Ohio River Valley, the Early Woodland corresponds to the **Adena** culture and the Middle Woodland corresponds to the **Hopewell** culture. In both the Adena and Hopewell, there is evidence of elaborate burial practices, including the construction of mounds, and extensive trade networks. Figure 8.12 shows an example of Hopewell art. The distribution of similar burial mounds extends along the St. Lawrence River as far east as New Brunswick (Wright 1994). At the Augustine Mound, located on the Metepenagiag reserve in New Brunswick, thousands of copper beads were found with a series of burials (Turnbull 1976). The presence of copper resulted in the remarkable preservation of textiles including twined and plaited fabric, basketry, and matting, wrapped textiles, braids, and cordage.

Careful excavations of Hopewell mounds have shown that some were erected over structures built of bent poles (Brown 1979). Multiple human remains were placed in these structures before they were filled in and covered by a mound of earth. In some cases, bodies were laid out to decompose before burial, and the bones were either left in their original position or gathered together into bundles after decomposition. In other cases, the bodies were cremated in ceramic basins or placed in pits dug into the floors of the structures. There is also evidence that in some cases burials were excavated into mounds, while in others new structures for burial or cremation were built on top of mounds and were subsequently covered over by a secondary mound (Brose et al. 1985).

Hopewell material culture includes impressive art objects made of copper, mica, and polished stone. Expertly crafted objects that were traded over long distances are found in many Hopewell burials. It is likely that objects such as hard stone pipes in the form of animals and large plaques made of sheets of mica were produced by craft specialists. Such discoveries suggest that elite members of these societies controlled a network of trade in prestige objects.

Adena A period of intensive mound building in the Ohio River Valley; it corresponds to the Early Woodland culture.

Hopewell A period of intensive mound building in the Ohio River Valley; it corresponds to the Middle Woodland culture.

FIGURE 8.12 A bird claw cut from a sheet of mica. This is a masterpiece of Hopewell art.

In his classic work on eastern North American prehistory, James Griffin suggested that the Hopewell lived in villages near the massive earthworks (Griffin 1967). Griffin had in mind not only the mounds, but also the earthen enclosures found at sites such as the Liberty Earthworks near Chillicothe, Ohio. At the Liberty site, there are two circular enclosures, one over 200 metres in diameter and the other over 500 metres, as well as a square enclosure covering 11 hectares (Squier and Davis 1848). However, materials collected from the farm that now includes the Liberty Earthworks have not yielded any remains of a large village until the late Middle Woodland period, toward the end of the Hopewell culture (Coughlin and Seeman 1997).

There is evidence that some of the earthworks were occupied. The massive Newark Earthworks, shown in Figure 8.13 in a map from 1848, have largely been engulfed by the city of Newark, Ohio. The construction of a new highway that goes through the earthworks led to a salvage project in which the remains of two Hopewell houses were identified, together with evidence of domestic activities (Lepper and Yerkes 1997). Despite this evidence, some archaeologists have suggested that, rather than residing in large villages, the Hopewell lived dispersed across the landscape in small farmsteads (Dancey and Pacheco 1997). According to this model, known as the **vacant centre pattern**, the earthworks served as the symbolic and ceremonial core of a community that lived across a wide area.

Christopher Carr and Troy Case have challenged archaeologists to think about the Hopewell phenomenon from an agency perspective. Adopting such a perspective requires that we shift our focus from the community as a whole to the individuals who make it up. However, the conception of the individual is not the rational calculator of optimal foraging theory, but rather a person negotiating his or her place in the world within the context of overlapping structures of power. On the basis of careful analysis of the iconography of Hopewell figurines, Carr and Case argue that there were different types of leaders in Hopewell society, including both shamans and others with more secular sources of power. Carr and Case raise the possibility that, rather than a series of households held together by a ceremonial core in the form of a particular earthwork, what actually existed was a situation in which each individual might have connections to multiple earthworks.

vacant centre pattern The model that sees the Hopewell earthworks as the empty core of a dispersed settlement system.

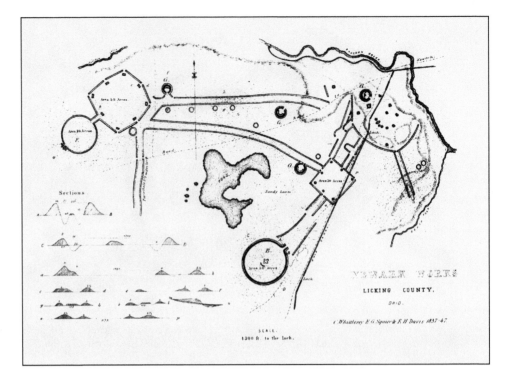

FIGURE 8.13 Map of the Newark Earthworks, Ohio, published by E.G. Squier and E.H. Davis in 1848. Squier and Davis's drawings are a critical resource, since many of the features they record have subsequently been destroyed.

Given both the widespread modern destruction of the earthworks and their massive scale, it remains difficult to determine whether they were the locations of large villages. Adding to the difficulty of assessing the nature of Hopewell settlements is the low archaeological visibility of many Hopewell habitation sites. Because of the massive buildup of riverborne alluvial sediments in the Ohio River Valley, Hopewell sites located in the valley are deeply buried and not easily discovered by archaeologists (Stafford and Creasman 2002).

Early and Middle Woodland subsistence included the cultivation of indigenously domesticated plants (Smith 1995). The earliest direct AMS radiocarbon dates of maize in eastern North America are between 2,000 and 1,800 years ago, from three Middle Woodland sites in Tennessee, Illinois, and Ohio. However, maize remains rare and does not appear to have played a major role in the diet. Throughout the Woodland period, hunting and collecting wild plants continued to be key elements of subsistence alongside the cultivation of domesticated plants.

■ Intensification of Maize Agriculture

At the end of the Middle Woodland period, around 1,700 years ago, the extensive trade networks of the Hopewell culture and the construction of massive earthworks came to an end. At the same time, there was an increase in the number of large settled villages. By the beginning of the Late Woodland, maize is found as far north as Ontario (Crawford et al. 1997). An analysis of residues adhering to the inside of ceramic vessels from sites in the Boreal Forest of western Ontario and Manitoba has identified microscopic remains of maize, including pollen and phytolith, as early as 1,500 years ago (Boyd and Surette 2010; for information about phytoliths and starch grains see the Toolbox on p. 249). Although maize was cultivated throughout much of eastern North America by 1,700 years ago, the **isotope analysis** of human skeletal remains provides strong evidence that maize did not come to play a major role in the diet until around 1,000 years ago. The bone chemistry of humans and animals is determined largely by their diet. Because of this, the chemistry of bones can be used as a

isotope analysis The study of diet through the chemical signature of bones; particularly effective in tracing the spread of maize agriculture.

Who Owns the Past?

Who owns the past? This is a rather vague question, but for archaeologists it takes on a very concrete meaning. For example, the Metropolitan Museum recently returned the Euphronios vase, a 2,500-year-old Greek vessel with exquisite paintings of mythological scenes, to Italy because it was resolved that the vase had been illegally acquired. In this case, the Metropolitan Museum's claim of property rights to an artifact was found to be legally faulty; therefore the object was returned to the Italian government, whose claims to property rights were supported by international law.

But should laws of property rights always determine who owns archaeological artifacts or sites? What happens when property rights clash with other claims to ownership and access? This question is particularly pertinent in North America,

where property rights are highly prized. The Newark Earthworks provide an illustration of this problem. Squier and Davis documented the Newark Earthworks in 1848 in their study of Ohio Valley mounds. In 1853, the local agricultural society purchased the northwestern part of the earthworks, and in 1891 the land was sold to the City of Newark for State Encampment Grounds. The state militia used the Encampment Grounds for a number of years before the land was leased to its current tenants, the Moundbuilders Country Club. In 1933 the deed to the property was transferred to the Ohio Historical Society.

It is quite incredible that one of the most impressive monuments in the Americas is today a golf course. Two events have brought renewed attention to the earthworks. The first was an unsuccessful attempt by the country

club to build a new clubhouse that would have damaged the mounds. The second was the identification of a lunar orientation for the octagon-shaped enclosure. The archaeologist Chris Scarre has included the Newark Enclosures among his seventy wonders of the ancient world (Scarre 1999). But for the club manager, it is the right of the club to limit access to this site because the club holds the lease (Maag 2005).

As with many significant archaeological sites, the planning for the long-term conservation of the Newark Earthworks is an extremely delicate undertaking. The Ohio Historical Society has set out a management plan for the site that does include removing the golf course. In the meantime, procedures have been put in place to provide at least limited access to visitors wishing to experience this spectacular site. ●

FIGURE 8.14 The return of the Euphronios vase to Italy.

FIGURE 8.15 The golf course on the Newark Earthworks.

source of data for reconstructing diet. However, identifying diets using bone chemistry is successful only if the consumers ate foods that had a particular chemical signature. One type of chemical signature is the relative frequency of two isotopes of the same element. Fortunately for the study of maize agriculture, the ratio of carbon-13 (^{13}C) to carbon-12 (^{12}C) varies in plants with different photosynthetic pathways. The ratio of carbon-13 to carbon-12 is expressed as the value $\delta^{13}C$, which is the deviation from an international standard. Trees, bushes, and

The Princess Point Complex

Archaeologists around the world debate the question of how agricultural systems spread. In southern Ontario, there is no question that maize arrived from the south, but the mystery of *how* it arrived remains unsolved. On one hand, Dean Snow (1995) argues that Iroquois-speaking groups brought maize agriculture and a village way of life to Ontario around A.D. 900. He suggests that the Iroquois homeland is in Pennsylvania. Gary Crawford and David Smith (1996), archaeologists at the University of Toronto at Mississauga, have brought compelling arguments against this migration model. The crux of the debate is the Princess Point complex, which dates to A.D. 650–900. Snow argues that the Princess Point consisted of Algonkin-speaking groups of hunter–gatherers that preceded the arrival of agriculture. However, Crawford and Smith have discovered extensive remains of maize from Princess Point sites and directly dated kernels to as early as A.D. 540. Thus, maize arrived in Ontario during the Princess Point. Moreover, Smith has shown that innovations in pottery manufacture thought to have begun only in A.D. 900 actually began in the Princess Point. Most intriguing is the suggestion that a degree of sedentism might have already developed during the Princess Point. Crawford and Smith paint a picture of the gradual adoption of agriculture by local groups of hunter–gatherers while leaving open the possibility that migration might also have played an important role in the spread of agriculture into southern Ontario. ◆

REFERENCES: Dean Snow. (1995). Migration in prehistory: The northern Iroquoian Case. *American Antiquity* 60: 59–79.

Gary Crawford and David Smith. (1996). Migration in prehistory: Princess Point and the northern Iroquoian case. *American Antiquity* 61: 782–790.

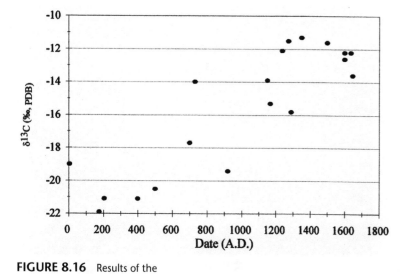

FIGURE 8.16 Results of the carbon isotope analysis of human skeletal remains from Ontario. Note the elevation of δ carbon-13 (measured on the y-axis) around A.D. 1200 (time measured on the x-axis) indicating a shift to heavy dietary reliance on maize.

shrubs (C_3 plants) have a low ratio of carbon-13 to carbon-12. Grasses from the tropics and subtropics, including maize, sorghum, and sugar cane (C_4 plants), have a high ratio. The only C_4 plant that contributed to the diet of the people of the Woodland period in eastern North America is maize. By analyzing the $\delta^{13}C$ value for Woodland-period skeletal remains, it is possible to determine the role that maize played in those people's diets. The shift to a high $\delta^{13}C$ value in human skeletal remains takes place only during the period around 1,000 years ago, approximately 700 years after the initial introduction of maize into eastern North America (see Figure 8.16). This finding indicates that there was a considerable length of time between the first planting of maize in eastern North America and the adoption of this plant as an essential food source.

■ The People Behind the Transition

Archaeologists studying the development of agriculture have a tendency to forget to include people in the process. The dating of the initial domestication of various crops and the description of archaeological sites provide an essential framework for understanding the transition to agriculture; however, it is necessary to go beyond this framework to consider what led people to adopt a radically new way of life.

Patty Jo Watson and Mary Kennedy have linked the seeming invisibility of people in the origins of agriculture to gender bias in our conception of the past.

According to Watson and Kennedy, in the anthropological literature "men are strong, dominant protectors who hunt animals; women are weaker, passive, hampered by their reproductive responsibilities, and hence, consigned to plant gathering" (Watson and Kennedy 1991, 256).

Watson and Kennedy have identified strategies that have been used by archaeologists to maintain gender bias in their explanations of the origin of agriculture. The first strategy is to view its development as a passive process that simply happened as the result of the unconscious ecological consequences of human actions. Bruce Smith's coevolutionary model for the indigenous domestication of plants in eastern North America is an example of such an approach. According to Smith, climate change led to an increased permanence of human settlements in eastern North America. This shift to more permanent settlements led to gradual ecological changes that resulted in the emergence of domesticated plants over a period of several thousand years.

Smith outlines five major stages in the process. In the first stage, the garbage heaps around long-term human occupations provided an excellent ecological niche for weedy plants that thrived on the availability of sunlight and fertile soil. In these contexts, seeds that sprouted and grew quickly had a selective advantage. Seeds that sprout and grow quickly would be large and have a thin coat. In the second stage, people tolerated edible plants and removed useless or harmful ones. In the third stage, people began to encourage and systematically harvest useful plants while carefully weeding out useless ones. In the fourth stage, seeds of the useful plants were planted deliberately every year. In the fifth stage, plants that were clearly morphologically domesticated emerged.

Smith's model for plant domestication sets this process within a well-constructed ecological framework. The model fits with the kind of evolutionary approaches advanced by Rindos. However, Watson and Kennedy argue that "the built-in mechanisms adduced [in the model] carry plants and people smoothly and imperceptibly . . . with little or no effort on anyone's part. The plants virtually domesticate themselves" (Watson and Kennedy 1981, 262). The formulation "women = plants = passive" is maintained.

Whereas Smith views domestication of plants as a passive process, Guy Prentice has proposed that domestication might have been the result of intentional actions by individuals. Prentice argues that the introduction of domesticated squash into eastern North America was carried out by male shamans who would have used gourds as rattles or ritual containers. Prentice writes of the shaman, "He would have the greatest knowledge of plants" (Prentice 1986, 113). Here, the domestication of plants is seen as an active process, and, tellingly, the agent is explicitly male.

As a counterbalance to existing models for the role of women in the development of agriculture, Watson and Kennedy propose a model for the adoption of maize in eastern North America that emphasizes the active role of female gardeners. The introduction of maize, which is a tropical grass, into the northern latitudes of North America is an impressive event. The spread of maize into northern latitudes involved a transition from midwestern twelve-row maize to a variety known, due to the smaller number of rows per cob, as eastern eight-row, or Northern Flint, maize. Watson and Kennedy propose that the women in eastern North America, who already had extensive experience growing indigenous cultivated plants, actively experimented with the midwestern twelve-row maize to develop a variety that was better suited to the soils and climates of their region. The result was the development and spread of eastern eight-row maize. According to this proposal, then, the adoption of maize agriculture in eastern North America was an achievement of the active intervention of women.

"Towns They Have None": In Search of New England's Mobile Farmers

ELIZABETH S. CHILTON, UNIVERSITY OF MASSACHUSETTS, AMHERST

I am an associate professor and chair of the Department of Anthropology at the University of Massachusetts at Amherst. I returned to UMass in 2001, after spending five years at Harvard University as an assistant, and then associate professor of anthropology.

When I began my graduate studies at UMass Amherst, I was very interested in the Late Woodland (A.D. 1000 to A.D. 1600) and Contact (A.D. 1600 to A.D. 1700) periods in the Massachusetts portion of the Connecticut River Valley in the western part of the state. In particular, archaeologists had long been looking for large Late Woodland-period villages. On the basis of previous experience with research on the neighbouring Iroquoian tribes, archaeologists expected to find large sedentary villages as a result of the adoption of maize horticulture around A.D. 1000. Nevertheless, when I came to UMass in 1988, no large Late Woodland villages had yet been found in the region.

In 1989, a local farmer reported that he had found a large number of ceramics on a forested hill surrounded by a floodplain in the valley of the Deerfield River, a major tributary of the Connecticut River. Subsequent excavation at the Pine Hill site in 1989, 1991, 1993, 1995, and 1997 as part of the UMass Amherst Archaeological Field School revealed that this was, indeed, an important Late Woodland site. We uncovered fragments of more than 300 Late Woodland-period vessels, a large number of lithic artifacts, and 22 large pit features, which likely served for food storage and/or refuse disposal. Radiocarbon dates firmly placed most of the activity at the site during the Late Woodland period.

Despite the fact that we had excavated quite a few of these Late Woodland pit features and had identified food remains (e.g., small and large mammal bones, charred nutshells and seeds), until 1995 we had not found a single kernel of maize. This surprised us, since elsewhere in New England maize had been dated to the start of the Late Woodland period. One day at the site, a student was excavating the plow zone from a 2 × 2 metre test unit and suddenly said, "Hey Elizabeth, I found a weird blueberry thing." I looked at it and immediately recognized it as a charred maize kernel! Later that summer, we discovered the first pit feature on that site to yield maize kernels, approximately 200 in all! Still, 200 maize kernels are equivalent to only about one cob of Northern Flint, eight-row maize (Chilton et al. 2000). We have many more nutshells and small animal bones than maize kernels.

I had done some work in Belize after graduating from SUNY Albany in 1986. Now, digging conditions on this site were quite gruelling, despite the fact that we were in Massachusetts. There was standing water in an oxbow near the Deerfield site; therefore, the mosquitoes were far more intense than any pest that I encountered in Belize. We were bitten through our clothes, on our lips and eyelids, and on our fingers.

■ Summing Up the Evidence

The transition to agriculture in Mesoamerica and North America was a complex process. In the southwestern United States, maize agriculture was either adopted by groups of Archaic hunter–gatherers, who appear to have had no previous experience with domesticated plants, or possibly spread by populations of farmers moving in from the south. The impact of the adoption of agriculture on these societies varied. In some cases, notably at Cerro Juanaqueña and the sites around Tucson, large villages developed, while in other areas people continued to live in temporary camps. This regional variability continued into the Formative period. Archaeologists have tried to explain the pattern that developed in terms of optimal foraging theory.

In eastern North America, hunter–gatherer groups had domesticated a number of plant species long before the introduction of maize agriculture. Intensively occupied sites are already found in the Late Archaic and, in the case of the Poverty Point site, had reached an impressive size and degree of planning. In the Early and Middle

On top of that, we did not have ready access to restrooms, and there was a fair bit of poison ivy. The digging itself was quite easy, the soils are sandy from the postglacial lake deposits. But digging in a forested environment provides its own challenges, in the form of tree roots and rodent activity.

After several years of excavating the Pine Hill site, and after conducting a detailed analysis of the attributes of the ceramics for my dissertation, we came to the conclusion that it was a Late Woodland-period site that was repeatedly occupied on a seasonal basis, primarily in the late summer to early fall (Chilton 1999, 2002). This conclusion dovetails nicely with archaeological evidence from throughout the Connecticut River Valley, which suggests that, although New England peoples had adopted maize by A.D. 1000, it did not significantly alter their seasonal mobility, nor did it significantly change their diet. Archaeological evidence indicates that maize may have become more

FIGURE 8.17 Pine Hill site, UMass Amherst Archaeological Field School, 1993 (Elizabeth Chilton, shown left).

important across New England around A.D. 1300. Nevertheless, year-round villages like those of the Iroquois have not been found in New England. Instead, New England peoples offer us a clear example of mobile farming. ▲

Woodland Adena and Hopewell cultures, massive earthworks were constructed and there is evidence for specialized craft manufacture and long-distance trade in high status items. However, the nature of the settlement systems remains poorly understood. The possibility remains that in eastern North America monumental architecture preceded settled villages. The initial introduction of maize at the end of the Middle Woodland period had little impact on the diet. Studies of bone chemistry indicate that it took approximately 700 years before maize came to play a major role in the diet.

The spread of agriculture is as complex a process as the initial domestication of plants and animals. It is clear from the study of North America that local societies adapted agriculture into their lives in different ways. Rarely did the initial introduction of agriculture have an immediate transformative effect on those societies. As discussed in the last chapter, research in other areas, such as Europe, where agriculture was introduced rather than developed indigenously, similarly points to the active role played by the indigenous societies of hunter–gatherers in the adoption of this practice.

- The wild ancestor of maize is teosinte, a wild grass found in the highlands of Mexico.
- The three major crops domesticated in Mesoamerica are maize, squash, and beans. Turkeys are the only animals domesticated in the region.
- Evidence for the initial domestication of plants in Mesoamerica comes mostly from excavations of highland caves in the Tehuacán and Oaxaca Valleys.
- The earliest domesticated squash dates between 10,000 and 8,300 years ago. The earliest domesticated maize dates to 6,250 years ago.
- Cerro Juanaqueña, in northern Mexico, is a large Archaic-period site with evidence of extensive terrace walls and maize agriculture.
- Archaic-period villages with evidence of maize agriculture have been found at the Milagro and Las Capas sites in Arizona.
- Archaic-period sites in the Mogollon highlands and the Colorado Plateau have also produced evidence of domesticated maize. However, there is no evidence of Archaic-period villages in these areas.
- Pottery first appeared widely in the American Southwest during the Formative period around 1,800 years ago.
- Among the plants that were domesticated indigenously in eastern North America were squash, chenopod, marsh elder, and sunflower. This domestication took place between 5,000 and 3,500 years ago.
- Extensive earthworks were built in Ohio and surrounding areas during the Early Woodland (Adena culture) and Middle Woodland (Hopewell culture) periods.
- The earliest maize in eastern North America dates to the Middle Woodland period. However, there is evidence that maize did not play a major role in the diet until about 700 years after its introduction.

KEY TERMS

Adena, 230
accelerator mass spectrometry (AMS)
    radiocarbon dating, 220
Cerro Juanaqueña, 222
Guilá Naquitz, 220
Hopewell, 230
isotope analysis, 232
Las Capas, 223

Milagro, 223
optimal foraging theory, 223
Poverty Point, 228
shell middens, 228
Tehuacán Valley, 220
teosinte, 219
vacant centre pattern, 231

REVIEW QUESTIONS

1. What is known about the initial domestication of squash and maize?
2. What impact did the spread of maize have on Southwest Archaic societies? Was the effect the same throughout the region?
3. What was the social and economic context surrounding the construction of the Adena and Hopewell mounds?
4. What is the basis for Watson and Kennedy's critique of models for the origin of agriculture in eastern North America? What model do they propose?

CANADIAN ARCHAEOLOGISTS

- Michael Blake, professor in the Department of Anthropology at the University of British Columbia, has carried out fieldwork in the Soconusco region of Chiapas, Mexico, on some of the earliest village societies in the region. He also has a long-term project concentrated on the village site of Scowlitz in the Fraser River Valley of British Columbia.
  http://www.anth.ubc.ca/people/anthropology-faculty/michael-blake.html

- Matthew Boyd, professor in the Department of Anthropology at Lakehead University, studies past ecosystem processes and human-environment interactions in northern (especially boreal) North America. His recent research focuses on the role of rice and wild rice in diet using a range of methods including analysis of residues on ceramic vessels.
  http://anthropology.lakeheadu.ca/?display=page&pageid=34

- Andrea Freeman is a professor in the Departments of Archaeology, Geography, and Geology at the University of Calgary. She is a geoarchaeologist with a wide range of interests, including the retreat of ice in western Canada in relation to human settlement in the region. She has also published extensively on the transition from foraging to farming in the American Southwest.

  www.ucalgary.ca/%7Efreeman/index.htm

- Anne Katzenberg is a professor in the Department of Archaeology at the University of Calgary. Her research focuses on the study of skeletal remains including paleopathology, paleonutrition, and stable isotope analysis.

  http://arky.ucalgary.ca/profiles/m-anne-katzenberg

- David Smith is a professor in the Department of Anthropology at the University of Toronto at Mississauga whose research focuses on the development of agriculture in southwestern Ontario. He has also carried out studies of stylistic change in Northeast Woodland ceramics.

  www.utm.utoronto.ca/~w3dsmith/dsmith.html

- Dongya Yang is a professor in the Department of Anthropology and director of the Ancient DNA Facility at Simon Fraser University. His research explores the dynamic interactions between humans, animal and plants through analyses at a molecular level.

  http://www.sfu.ca/~donyang/Indexresearch.html

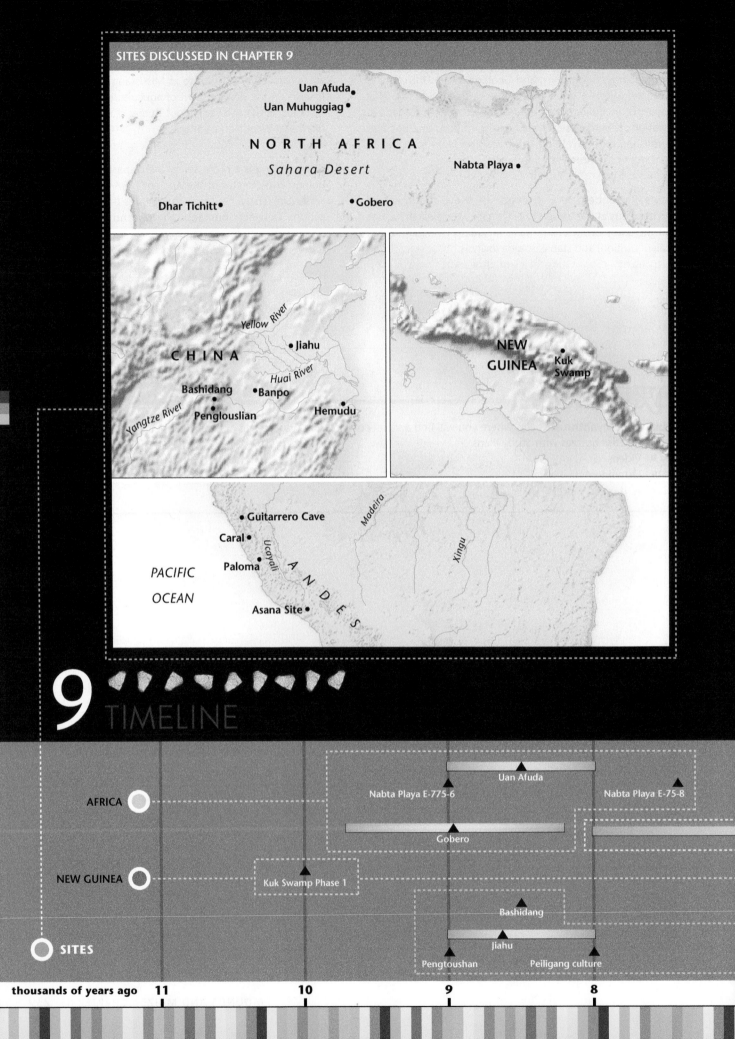

SITES DISCUSSED IN CHAPTER 9

Uan Afuda

Uan Muhuggiag

NORTH AFRICA
Sahara Desert

Nabta Playa

Dhar Tichitt

Gobero

Yellow River

CHINA

Jiahu

Huai River

Bashidang
Banpo

Yangtze River

Penglouslian

Hemudu

NEW
GUINEA

Kuk
Swamp

Guitarrero Cave

Madeira

Caral

Ucayali

Paloma

A N D E S

Xingu

PACIFIC

OCEAN

Asana Site

9 TIMELINE

thousands of years ago   11   10   9   8

AFRICA

Nabta Playa E-775-6   Uan Afuda   Nabta Playa E-75-8

Gobero

NEW GUINEA

Kuk Swamp Phase 1

Bashidang

SITES

Jiahu

Pengtoushan   Peiligang culture

A FEAST OF DIVERSITY

By comparing case studies, it is possible to learn whether the shift to agriculture always followed a single path. This chapter examines the origins of agriculture in Africa, New Guinea, the Andes, and East Asia. After reading this chapter, you should understand:

- The role of pastoralism and the timing for the introduction of pottery in Africa.

- The nature and significance of the archaeological site at Kuk Swamp, New Guinea.

- The relationship between the origin of village life and domestication in the Andes.

- The evidence from the two centres of domestication in China.

A field of quinoa growing in the Andean highlands.

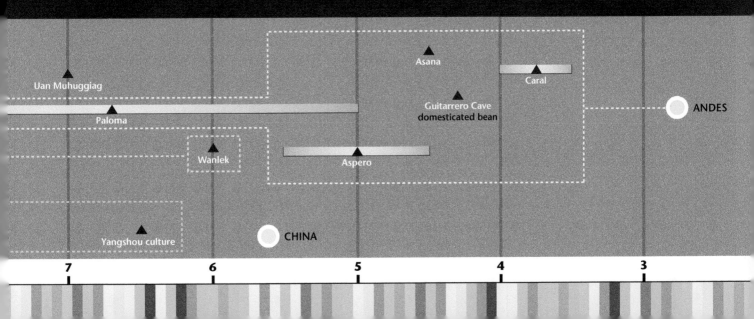

Uan Muhuggiag

Paloma

Asana

Caral

Guitarrero Cave
domesticated bean

ANDES

Wanlek

Aspero

Yangshou culture

CHINA

7   6   5   4   3

A visit to the supermarket is also a trip around the world. In the produce section, we find corn and squash, plants domesticated in Mesoamerica; the bakery section is filled with breads baked from wheat, domesticated in the Middle East; at the butcher, we find the meat of cattle and pig (as well as the occasional sheep and goat), also domesticated in the Middle East; and down the aisle, we find sunflower seed oil, a crop first domesticated in eastern North America. As we wander through the aisles, we also come across foods such as potatoes, yams, rice, and coffee, which point to other centres of domestication.

In this chapter, we briefly examine four additional case studies in the origins of agriculture:

- In Africa, pastoral societies based on domesticated animals developed without plant domestication.

- In New Guinea, domestication focused on plants that could be grown by transplanting suckers, cuttings, or shoots, rather than by planting seeds.

- In the Andes, there is a contrast between the domestication of plants and animals by mobile societies living in the highlands and village societies living on the coast, which depended heavily on marine resources. When agriculture was adopted on the coast, the main focus was a nonfood crop: cotton.

- The early agricultural societies of China might yield the strongest support available for Childe's concept of the origins of agriculture as a rapid and revolutionary event. However, this picture might be the result of limitations of the archaeological record, rather than a reflection of the actual historical process. Resolving the question is an exciting and active area of research.

When we broaden our focus, what emerges is a great deal of flexibility in the sequence of events leading to the shift from hunting and gathering to farming. As we fill our shopping carts in the supermarket, we are not only sampling the global diversity of agricultural crops, but also enjoying the fruits of a cornucopia of social transformation.

9.1 Africa

The development of agriculture in Africa involved the indigenous domestication of plants and possibly animals, as well as the adoption of domesticated plants and animals from the Middle East. There are three major regions in Africa where plants were indigenously domesticated.

- In Ethiopia and Eritrea in northeast Africa, a wide range of plants was domesticated, including grains such as teff and finger millet, which are essential to the local diet (D'Andrea et al. 1999). A local domesticate that has had a more global impact is coffee. Unfortunately, the timing and process of the domestication of all these plants is poorly understood.

- In central Africa, two critical cereals—pearl millet and sorghum—were domesticated. It is most likely that pearl millet was first domesticated in the Sahara, but the location where sorghum was first domesticated is not known.

- In west Africa, African rice (*Oryza glaberrina*) was domesticated (Linares 2002).

In addition to these indigenously domesticated plants, African agricultural systems incorporated domesticated plants introduced from the Middle East, including wheat, barley, and lentils. Among the domesticated animals introduced to Africa from the Middle East were sheep and goats. However, there is considerable debate over the origin of domesticated cattle on the continent. Although there is some genetic evidence supporting the argument that cattle were independently domesticated in Africa, the preponderance of evidence is that the animals were introduced from the Middle East.

The **Sahara Desert** is the most dominant feature of the North African landscape today. The current arid environment in the Sahara developed only within the last 4,000 to 5,000 years. Between 14,000 and 4,500 years ago, there was considerably more rainfall in the Sahara, allowing for extensive human occupation (Muzzolini 1993).

■ Villages of Hunter–Gatherers

During the period of increased rainfall in the Sahara, small villages of hunter–gatherers developed across northern Africa. The sites resemble the Natufian societies of the Middle East in several ways—their size, the nature of the structures, the exploitation of a wide range of resources, and the use of grinding stones. However, there are also significant differences between the African sites and the Natufian. The most striking difference is that pottery is commonly found on the African sites. In the Middle East, pottery was developed only during the Late Neolithic. Another feature found on African sites that is lacking from the Natufian is a large number of storage pits.

One of the most complete pictures of an early village of hunter–gatherers in North Africa comes from excavations at **Nabta Playa** in the Egyptian Western Desert (Wendorf and Schild 1998). This area is barren today, but when it was occupied, it was a small lake surrounded by grasslands. Site E-75-6 was a village of fifteen square or circular huts built in two rows that was occupied 9,000 years ago. Storage pits are found next to the remains of each structure. Pottery, in the form of small jars with impressed designs, is also present, although it is rare. A large range of plant remains has been recovered from this site, where the inhabitants focused particularly on the collection of wild sorghum.

Excavations at the cave site of **Uan Afuda** in Libya have given a unique perspective on the preagricultural societies of the Sahara. Uan Afuda was occupied between 9,000 and 8,000 years ago. The spectacular preservation on the site has allowed the excavators to recover wooden artifacts, basketry, and a rich array of charcoal and seeds. The botanical remains at the site indicate that the people living there exploited a wide range of resources. One of the most interesting discoveries was a 10-centimetre-deep bed of animal dung and plant remains found in the back of the cave. Analysis of the dung indicates that it is from wild barbary sheep, a North African species that was never domesticated. The excavators argue that such an accumulation of dung does not form from sheep visiting a cave site. It appears that the early occupants of Uan Afuda were keeping wild sheep in a pen at the back of the cave. This discovery suggests that although these people had not domesticated sheep, they were practising a form of animal management by capturing live animals and keeping them corralled in a cave.

Excavations at the site of **Gobero**, in the southern Sahara in Niger, have uncovered a cemetery and associated evidence of habitation dating to 9,700 to 8,200 years ago (Sereno et al. 2008). The site was located on a peninsula in a large lake, and fish appear to have made up a large part of the diet (see Figure 9.1). Artifacts recovered include barbed bone points, bladelets, and pottery (see Figure 9.2). Due to an increasingly arid climate, the site was abandoned a little over 8,000 years ago.

■ Pastoralists

In much of North Africa, domesticated animals were introduced before domesticated plants. Domesticated cattle, sheep, and goats appear to have been incorporated into mobile hunter–gatherer societies (see Figure 9.4 on page 246). Mobile societies with an economy focused on maintaining herds of domesticated animals are known as **pastoral societies** (Holl 1998).

Based on excavations at Nabta Playa, Fred Wendorf and his colleagues have argued that cattle might have been domesticated independently in Egypt as early as 10,000 years ago. This theory has not been widely accepted. However, it is clear that by 8,000 years ago, domesticated cattle, sheep, and goats had been introduced into

▲▲ **Sahara Desert** The most dominant feature of the North African landscape today. Between 14,000 and 4,500 years ago, there was increased rainfall in the area, allowing for human occupation.

▲▲ **Nabta Playa** An area in the Egyptian Western Desert that was the location of a series of early agricultural and preagricultural sites located along the edge of a lake.

▲▲ **Uan Afuda** A preagricultural site in the Sahara that yielded evidence that wild sheep were kept in pens in the back of a cave.

▲▲ **Gobero** A site in the Sahara alongside an ancient lake where a hunter–gatherer occupation dating between 9,700 and 8,200 years ago has been discovered.

pastoral societies Mobile societies with an economy based on herds of domesticated animals.

FIGURE 9.1 The field camp for excavations at the Gobero site is visible in the distance. Between 9,700 and 8,200 years ago this barren desert was the site of a hunter–gatherer village at the edge of a lake.

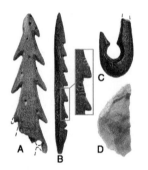

FIGURE 9.2 Artifacts from the Gobero site. A–B: Barbed bone points. C: Bone hook. D: Crescent-shaped microlith.

societies that still did not exploit domesticated plants. Site E-75-8 at Nabta Playa has produced vivid evidence of the reliance on cattle roughly 7,500 years ago. At this site, a series of cattle burials was found under piles of stones known as tumuli (Wendorf and Schild 1998). At Site 270 in the Dakhleh Oasis in the Egyptian desert, Mary McDonald has documented a settlement of 200 hut circles dating to 7,000 years ago (McDonald 1998). The animal bones from Site 270 include wild animals such as gazelle and hartebeest along with domesticated goats and possibly cattle. A large stone ring found near Site 270 has been identified as a possible animal pen.

The earliest evidence of domesticated animals in the Central Sahara, at the site of Uan Muhuggiag, is dated to 7,000 years ago (Holl 1998). As with Nabta Playa, there is no evidence of domesticated plants. The site of Gobero was reoccupied 7,200 years ago as climate conditions improved. By 6,000 years ago the occupants added a small component of domesticated cattle to their subsistence base, although they continued to rely heavily on fishing.

■ The First Farmers

Unfortunately, the development of village farming communities in Africa is poorly understood. In Egypt, the earliest evidence for domesticated plants dates to approximately 7,000 years ago. Wilma Wetterstrom has suggested that these resources were at first adopted by hunter–gatherers to provide a "backup" for brief periods of drought or low Nile floods. Once domesticated plants were introduced, large villages developed rapidly in the rich environment of the Nile Valley.

In western Africa, the earliest evidence of plant domestication is the imprint of domesticated millet grains found in the village sites of the Dhar Tichitt region of Mauritania around 3,500 years ago. Sorghum appears to have been introduced at a somewhat later date.

■ Summing Up the Evidence

There is a great deal that we still need to learn about the origins of agriculture in Africa. However, even given the preliminary nature of the archaeological record, we can observe some interesting patterns. Pottery was introduced at the beginning of the sequence in Africa, whereas it is found only in the Late Neolithic in the Middle East.

Ethiopian Farmers Yesterday and Today

CATHERINE D'ANDREA, SIMON FRASER UNIVERSITY

People often ask, "Why would you go to Ethiopia to do archaeology? Don't Ethiopians have more pressing issues to deal with, like drought and food shortages?" The short answer is yes, there are more significant developmental priorities, but in fact cultural resource management is a high priority for Ethiopia and many other developing nations because they are often more vulnerable to the loss of precious cultural heritage. It's true that Ethiopia is actively working on improving infrastructural and agricultural sectors of its economy, but heritage preservation is also of major importance, and the country's potential to develop a tourism industry holds great promise.

I became interested in developing an archaeological survey project after completing five years of ethnoarchaeological research on traditional farming societies in northern Ethiopia. This work involved documenting several aspects of traditional lifeways—including non-mechanized crop processing, cooking, and house construction—to be used as guides to understanding the archaeological record.

As I read more about the late prehistoric archaeology of Ethiopia, I noticed that much of the research has focused on the ancient capital cities of Yeha and Aksum, which were important urban centres of two ancient Ethiopian polities, the pre-Aksumite and Aksumite kingdoms (800 B.C. to A.D. 700). We know a fair amount about the origin and development of these societies, which were major trading partners for the Romans, but what was the contribution of rural populations to the origin and development of these ancient kingdoms? We decided to try to answer this question by developing a survey project in a region of eastern Tigrai known as Gulo-Makeda.

Conducting a ground survey in a country like Ethiopia is quite physically demanding. Located in the East African Highlands, the landscape has a spectacular rugged, rocky, mountainous topography. Some of our survey transects were over 3,000 metres above sea level. Although our surveyors are in excellent physical condition, we are not trained rock-climbers, so we have to be aware of our limitations. We continually combat physical fatigue, as well as thirst and heat (not to mention clashes with cactus patches, wayward bulls, and misplaced military ordinance) while hauling several kilos of stone tools and ceramic artifacts in our backpacks. Our work takes us to rural areas sometimes far away from main roads, and we tend to attract the attention of curious individuals, especially children, who immediately offer to help us collect artifacts. Because of their intimate familiarity with their environment, the children know exactly what we are looking for, and quickly spot the differences between ancient and modern pottery fragments. Meeting and working with villagers has been one of the most rewarding and interesting aspects of our fieldwork, as well as a lesson in hospitality. We are frequently invited to visit peoples' homes, where we are invariably offered food and drink, even if there is only one piece of bread in the house. People also perform a coffee ceremony—a uniquely Ethiopian tradition in which fresh coffee beans are roasted and pounded in front of us.

Our foot surveys and GPR (Ground-Penetrating Radar) work indicate that, far from being a rural hinterland, Gulo-Makeda was a significant regional centre that had large-scale buildings and artifacts indicating the presence of local elites who may have been involved in international trade. Many of the larger sites were likely chosen for settlement because of their proximity to water runoff sources and their location along major trade routes running between the cities of Yeha and Aksum and the Red Sea coast. Gulo-Makeda was an especially significant region during the Classic Aksumite period (A.D. 150 to 350). We are now eagerly planning to test some of what we have learned from surveys by conducting excavations at several sites in Gulo-Makeda. ▲

FIGURE 9.3
Attracting the attention of curious individuals, especially children, while collecting artifacts (mostly stone tools and potsherds) from a 10 x 10 metre controlled collection unit at an archaeological site in eastern Tigrai, Ethiopia.

FIGURE 9.4 Rock art painted by pastoralists in the Sahara showing cattle being herded. Can you make any observations about herd structure or social organization based on this image?

Pastoral societies in Africa developed thousands of years before fully agricultural villages did. In Africa, as in the Middle East, small villages predate the domestication of plants and animals. The evidence for a particular focus on wild sorghum at Nabta Playa and the penning of wild sheep at Uan Afuda is particularly intriguing.

9.2 New Guinea

During glacial periods, New Guinea, Australia, and Tasmania formed a single land mass known as Sahul. Today, New Guinea is a large island divided into the independent country of Papua New Guinea in the east and the Indonesian province of Irian Jaya in the west. The New Guinea highlands run the length of the island at an elevation between 1,300 and 2,500 metres.

Ethnographers studying the modern agricultural societies of New Guinea have emphasized the centrality of pigs and sweet potatoes, not only for subsistence, but also in developing a social hierarchy (see Figure 9.5). The exchange of pigs is an essential element of political power. Sweet potatoes are an important part of the diet of pigs; therefore, accumulating sweet potatoes is an essential element in gaining political power (Golson and Gardner 1990). Surprisingly, neither sweet potatoes nor pigs were domesticated indigenously in New Guinea, and both were introduced fairly recently. Sweet potatoes were domesticated in South America and were probably introduced

Ethnoarchaeology of Baking in Highland Ethiopia

The archaeology of agricultural systems requires that archaeologists extend their attention to the methods used to prepare foods. Working in modern villages in the Ethiopian highlands, Dyan Lyons from the University of Calgary and Catherine D'Andrea from Simon Fraser University have explored the baking methods used to prepare tef, an indigenous cereal. They found that the primary method used to bake the pancake bread was on a clay griddle known as a *mogogo*. One implication is that the presence of griddle fragments on archaeological sites is likely indirect evidence of tef cultivation. They also found that the fact that different cereal grains were prepared in different ways might have led to a bias in the archaeological record. For example, in baking pancake bread on a mogogo, few whole grains fall into the oven to be charred. By contrast, wheat, barley, chickpea, and sorghum are prepared by roasting entire grains, resulting in many grains being charred. Because charred seeds are more likely to be preserved and recovered, tef might be less archaeologically visible than wheat, barley, chickpea, and sorghum.

Lyons and D'Andrea also raised the question of why griddles, as opposed to other kinds of baking, were used in the highlands of Ethiopia. Part of the answer is clearly related to the characteristics of tef, which does not have the gluten needed to bake into a loaf of bread. However, even when barley and wheat are used in preparing bread, the method involves baking on a griddle. Lyons and D'Andrea suggest that part of the answer relates to the resistance of women, who carried out all aspects of bread preparation, to take on new methods of baking that would require additional labour. ◆

REFERENCE: Diane Lyons and A. Catherine D'Andrea. (2003). Griddles, ovens and agricultural origins: An ethnoarchaeological study of bread baking in Highland Ethiopia. *American Anthropologist* 105(3): 515–530.

into New Guinea after they were brought to the Philippines by Spanish sailors sometime in the sixteenth century (Gichuki et al. 2003). The timing of the introduction of domesticated pigs to New Guinea is poorly understood.

Recent genetic research indicates that a wide number of plant species were domesticated indigenously in New Guinea. These crops include yams, bananas, taro, and possibly sugarcane (LeBot 1999). None of these crops are cereals, and traditional agricultural processes in New Guinea involve transplanting suckers, cuttings, or shoots, rather than planting seeds.

FIGURE 9.5 Sweet-potato farming in New Guinea. In modern societies in New Guinea, sweet potatoes play an important role in social hierarchy.

▲▲ **Kuk Swamp** A site in highland New Guinea that has produced early evidence of agriculture.

■ Clearing Forests and Draining Swamps

The earliest evidence of human occupation of New Guinea is found at coastal sites on the Huon peninsula, dated to 40,000 years ago (Groube et al. 1986). The earliest occupation of the highlands is found at the sites of Kosipe and Yuku, which are dated to approximately 30,000 years ago (Bulmer 1976). Animal bones recovered from these sites indicate that a wide range of animals was hunted. There is no evidence of domesticated plants or animals. The exact date for the introduction of ground stone tools in the highlands is unclear; however, polished axes dating to 10,000 years ago are found on a number of sites.

Most of the archaeological sites in the highlands are cave sites. However, at Wanlek, the remains of a 6,000-year-old village, including remains of circular houses and a large central structure, were excavated. The artifacts recovered at Wanlek include polished stone axes, but no pottery. On archaeological sites in the highlands, no pottery is found that dates to earlier than 800 years ago.

The main evidence for the development of agriculture in highland New Guinea comes from the excavation of ancient field systems at the **Kuk Swamp** in the Wahgi Valley (Denham et al. 2003). The major features found at Kuk Swamp are drainage canals, pits, and earth mounds (see Figure 9.6). These features are the result of efforts to drain the swamp and create beds for planting crops. The age of the features at Kuk Swamp is based on radiocarbon dating of wood charcoal found in the fills of channels. Canals from the earliest phase at Kuk Swamp, radiocarbon dated to approximately 10,000 years ago, are limited in size and extent. In the second phase, dated to 6,500 years ago, there are regularly distributed earth mounds and channels across the site. In the third phase, dated to 4,000 years ago, a network of drainage ditches was excavated through the site. Subsequently, the network of channels became denser and more regular. Around 3,000 years ago, the maintenance of agricultural fields at Kuk Swamp appears to have come to an end.

Starch grains on stone tools from the first two occupations have been identified as taro, which does not grow naturally in the highlands and therefore must have been planted at Kuk Swamp. There is also evidence of banana cultivation beginning

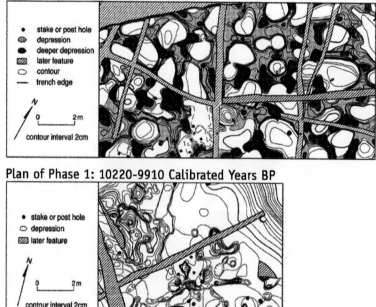

Plan of Phase 2: 6950–6440 Calibrated Years BP

- • stake or post hole
- ⊙ depression
- ● deeper depression
- ▨ later feature
- ◯ contour
- — trench edge

N
0 ____ 2m
contour interval 2cm

Plan of Phase 1: 10220–9910 Calibrated Years BP

- • stake or post hole
- ◯ depression
- ▨ later feature

N
0 ____ 2m
contour interval 2cm

FIGURE 9.6 Maps showing the development of agricultural ditches and mounds at Kuk Swamp, New Guinea.

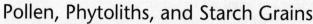

Pollen, Phytoliths, and Starch Grains

Paleoethnobotanists are not limited to the macrobotanical remains recovered through flotation. In their efforts to understand human interactions with plants, paleoethnobotanists also draw on microbotanicals, the preserved microscopic remains of plant material.

Pollen grains, produced by the male reproductive organs of plants and trees, can be used to reconstruct past climate conditions. Pollen is best preserved in freshwater lakes and ponds, where the grains are embedded in the continuous buildup of sediments on the lake bottom. The continuous sequences recovered from these contexts allow botanists to track changes in the makeup of plant communities over time. One major change that can be tracked is the shifting ratio between pollen from trees and pollen from grasses. By looking at changes in this relationship, it is possible to determine periods when local ecology shifted from woodlands to open grasslands. Often, pollen can also be recovered from archaeological sites, providing a window into the ecological setting.

Phytoliths are silica structures that build up along plant cell walls. The source of the silica is groundwater that is pulled into the plant during its life. The form of the phytolith is shaped by the morphology of the plant; as a result, it is possible to identify types of plants on the basis of their phytoliths. Commonly preserved on archaeological sites, phytoliths can be used to reconstruct the ecological setting of a site. Sometimes phytoliths are found adhering to artifacts, and in these cases the phytoliths can provide an insight into how a tool was used.

Paleoethnobotanists have begun to explore starch grains found adhering to artifacts. In some cases, the grains have been shown to be remarkably resilient, surviving for thousands of years. In a research project in Mozambique, Julio Mercader has recovered starch grains of sorghum from stone tools that are between 40,000 and 100,000 years old (Mercader 2009). Starch grain analysis has the potential to provide critical data about how tools were used. In one instance, the analysis of starch grains on pottery vessels recovered in Egypt allowed archaeologists to trace the process of beer production. ●

REFERENCE: Dena F. Dincauze. (2000). *Environmental Archaeology: Principles and Practices.* Cambridge, U.K.: Cambridge University Press.

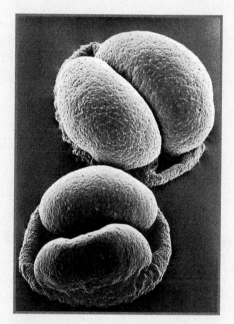

FIGURE 9.7 Scanning electron microscope photograph of pine pollen.

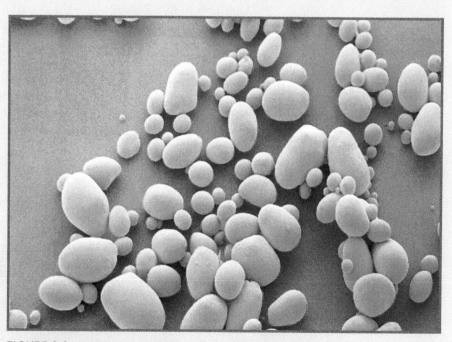

FIGURE 9.8 Scanning electron microscope photograph of potato starch grains.

around 6,500 years ago. Phytoliths of bananas are found throughout the Kuk Swamp sequence. Phytoliths are mineral structures that build up on plant tissue. In the early phase of the occupation of Kuk Swamp, the presence of banana phytoliths is expected, because wild banana trees would have grown in the forest environment that was found in the region at that time. However, around 6,500 years ago, the environment around Kuk Swamp changed to grassland, in which a high percentage of banana phytoliths would not occur without human intervention. Therefore, the presence of large quantities of banana phytoliths in the swamp deposits after 6,500 years ago is evidence that people were planting banana trees. Features similar to those found at Kuk Swamp have been found on other sites, such as Kana, which is also located in the Wahgi Valley (Muke and Mandui 2003). However, as there is very little evidence from the excavation of village sites from these early periods in highland New Guinea, there is little basis for reconstructing the social context of early agriculture. It appears that the transition to agriculture in New Guinea was quite gradual and that only plants were involved. New Guinea is unique in that no cereal crops were domesticated. The development of ground stone tool technology appears to be related to agriculture; however, pottery was introduced quite late and did not have any role in early agricultural systems.

9.3 The Andes

The Andes is the second-highest mountain chain in the world, with peaks reaching close to 7,000 metres above sea level. The Andean highlands can be divided into four zones based on altitude (Quilter 1989) (see Figure 9.9). In the Quechua zone, between 2,300 and 3,500 metres above sea level, corn grows well. In the Suni zone, between 3,500 and 4,000 metres, a range of crops indigenous to the Andes are grown. The most important of these crops are a cereal called quinoa and root crops, including potatoes, oca, and olluco. The Puna zone, between 4,000 and 4,800 metres, is an open grassland used for grazing llamas and alpacas. The high peaks of the Cordillera zone, above 4,800 metres, are not exploited for agriculture. To the east, the Andean highlands drop off rapidly into the Amazon rain forest, the archaeology of which, unfortunately, remains poorly understood (Raymond 1988).

To the west, the Andes descend gradually to the Pacific coast. The coastal region is a barren desert bisected by numerous rivers running down from the mountains (Burger 1992). Agriculture is limited to the river valleys. The desert is also broken by llomas—patches nurtured by mist from coastal fog where dense vegetation grows during the winter. The coast itself is remarkably rich in marine resources, including small fish such as anchovies, large fish, ocean birds, marine mammals, and

FIGURE 9.9 Diagram showing major ecological zones in the Andes.

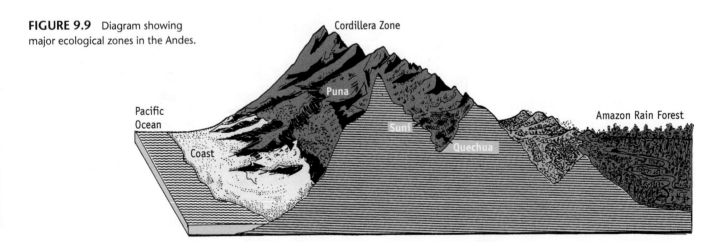

shellfish such as clams and mussels. The wealth of resources along the Andean coast is due to the **Humboldt Current**, which sweeps cool waters up the coast of South America, bringing nutrients to the surface.

■ Domestication in the Andean Highlands

Excavations at **Guitarrero Cave** in the Andean highlands of Peru uncovered domesticated beans, which subsequently were dated to approximately 10,000 years ago (Smith 1980). But it was not the beans themselves that were dated; rather, it was charcoal recovered from the same level as the beans. When one of the beans was dated directly with AMS radiocarbon, it turned out to be only 4,300 years old (Kaplan and Lynch 1999). Apparently, the beans came from a higher level in the stratigraphic sequence at Guitarrero Cave and were perhaps moved by burrowing animals.

The redating of the beans from Guitarrero Cave has thrown all early dates for domesticated plants in the Andean highlands into question. At Panaulauca Cave, a small number of quinoa seeds have been found in layers dating to between 5,700 and 4,500 years ago (Smith 1995). Until these seeds are dated directly, the timing for the domestication of quinoa remains open to question. The earliest evidence for domesticated potatoes from sites on the Peruvian coast dates to between 4,000 and 3,000 years ago (see Figure 9.10). It is unlikely that these are the earliest domesticated potatoes, as the coast is not the region where wild forms of potatoes grow. An added problem is that distinguishing domesticated quinoa and potatoes from wild forms is difficult. With quinoa, a thin seed coat means the grain is domesticated.

Humboldt Current A current that brings cool waters from the south up along the Andean coast, accounting for the remarkable wealth of marine resources in the area.

▲▲ **Guitarrero Cave** Site in the Andean highlands of Peru where excavations uncovered the earliest evidence of domesticated beans dating to 4,300 years ago.

FIGURE 9.10 Illustration of Inca farmers digging up potatoes, from a Spanish sixteenth-century document. The domestication of potatoes in the Andes dates back at least 3,000 years.

FIGURE 9.11 A herd of llamas in the highlands of Peru.

llamas Camelid animals domesticated in the Andean highlands; *guanacos* are the ancestral species of llamas.

alpacas Camelid animals domesticated in the Andean highlands; *vicuñas* are the ancestral species of alpacas.

With potatoes, the shape and size of the starch grains are used to distinguish between wild and domesticated forms.

The domestication of **llamas** (Figure 9.11) and **alpacas** in the Andean highlands is fairly well documented (Lavallée 2000). Both animals are camelids. The ancestral species of llamas are *guanacos*; the wild ancestors of alpacas are *vicuñas*. It is difficult to distinguish between domesticated and wild camelids on the basis of the shape and size of their bones. However, at a number of cave sites in the Andean highlands, the percentage of camelids relative to deer increases steadily throughout the period between 10,000 and 5,000 years ago, a trend that appears to indicate a gradual shift toward camelid domestication. Beginning around 7,000 years ago, the number of very young camelids increased sharply. This pattern is interpreted as the result of disease, which struck closely packed herds of domesticated animals. Another line of evidence for domestication is found at the Asana site near Lake Titicaca. In a level dated to 4,500 years ago, chemical analysis of the soils indicated that there had been a high concentration of dung in an area surrounded by postholes. The excavators interpret this feature as the remains of a corral for domesticated camelids. The other domesticated animal in the Andes is the guinea pig. Little is known about when guinea pigs were first domesticated, but it appears to have been considerably later than camelids.

No village sites from these early periods have been excavated in the Andean highlands. Currently, it appears that the domestication of plants and animals took place in the context of mobile hunter–gatherer societies.

■ Coastal Villages

By 8,000 years ago, small settled villages had developed in the lloma fog meadows on the Peruvian coast (Pineda 1988). The inhabitants of these villages were hunter–gatherers who relied heavily on the rich coastal marine resources.

The village of **Paloma**, which was inhabited intermittently between 8,000 and 5,000 years ago, provides a broad view of one of these early preagricultural villages (Quilter 1989). Houses were built of reeds and grasses over a structure of wooden poles. The total population of the villages is unclear, but it appears to have been in the range of ten families at any given time. A large number of burials were

▲▲ Paloma A preagricultural village site on the coast of Peru.

excavated at Paloma, mostly in pits dug into the floors of houses, with grave offerings placed near the skeleton. An analysis of the burials demonstrated an overall uniformity in the treatment of the dead, although males tended to be buried toward the centre of houses, suggesting that they might have had a higher status than females.

The Paloma site provides a vivid demonstration of the centrality of marine resources to these early village communities. Analysis of the faunal remains from the site showed that 98 percent of the individuals recovered were marine animals and shellfish (Reitz 1988). The dominant species were anchovies. Only a small number of land mammal remains were found; these include spider monkeys, camelids, and deer.

The skeletal remains also afford evidence of the intensive exploitation of marine resources at Paloma. Eight skeletons were found with auditory exostoses, a growth in the inner ear caused by spending long periods in cold water. Burial 159 at Paloma presents particularly graphic evidence of the relation these people had with the sea. Burial 159 is a young man in excellent health, except for a missing leg (see Figure 9.12). This man was buried in an elaborate cane structure tied with cord along with a number of burial offerings. A series of cut marks was found on the man's pelvis, indicating "the likelihood that his leg was removed by a shark" (Quilter 1989, 59).

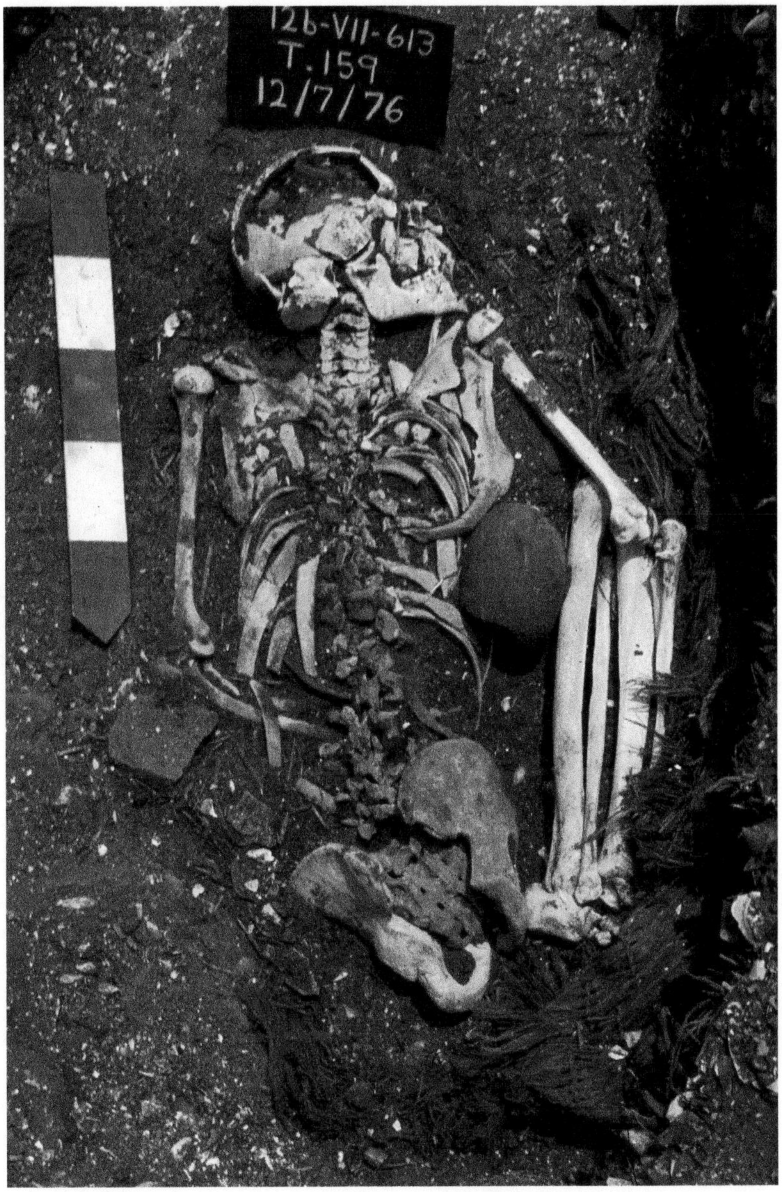

A wide range of plant resources from the llomas, including seeds, fruits, and tubers, was exploited by the people living at Paloma. The only clearly domesticated plants were cultivated gourds. Beans and squash might have been cultivated, but there is no evidence that they played a significant role in the diet.

FIGURE 9.12 Burial 159 from the Paloma site, Peru. The left leg is missing and the pelvis shows marks consistent with attack by a shark.

■ The Cotton Preceramic

Approximately 5,700 years ago, large sites with monumental architecture began to appear on the coast of Peru. These belong to a period called the **Cotton Preceramic,** in recognition of the prevalence of cotton seeds and the absence of pottery. The sites from the Cotton Preceramic reach up to 58 hectares at El Paraíso and 65 hectares at Caral (Quilter et al. 1991; Solis et al. 2001). At the site of Aspero, a large flat-topped pyramid known as Huaca de los Ídolos is dated between 5,500 and 4,500 years ago. At Caral, there are six large artificial mounds, the largest of which measures 160 metres by 150 metres and is 18 metres high, dated between 4,000 and 3,500 years ago (Solis et al. 2001). Figure 9.13 on the next page shows one view of the Caral site.

Cotton Preceramic The period beginning 5,700 years ago when sites with monumental architecture flourished on the coast of Peru.

FIGURE 9.13 A Cotton
Preceramic mound at the Caral site.

There has been considerable debate concerning the economic basis of the large Cotton Preceramic sites. Because the site of Aspero is located on the coast, it has been suggested that these sites were based on fishing and collecting marine resources, rather than on agriculture. Subsequent studies have shown that, in fact, the bulk of the diet of Cotton Preceramic sites consisted of fish and shellfish. Even at the site of Caral, located 23 kilometres from the coast, almost all of the faunal remains recovered were of clams, mussels, anchovies, and sardines (Solis et al. 2001). However, at both Caral and the coastal site of El Paraíso, a wide range of domesticated plants, including gourds, squash, chili pepper, and beans, as well as the tubers achira and jicama, were grown. The dominant crop species was cotton, which was used for making nets and textiles.

■ The Role of El Niño

The Humboldt Current, which brings cool waters from the south up along the Andean coast, is responsible for the wealth of marine resources that allowed villages such as Paloma to thrive without agriculture. The large centres of the Cotton Preceramic also relied heavily on the rich marine resources brought by the Humboldt Current. **El Niño** is a severe reversal of the Humboldt Current that occurs every twenty-five to forty years. When major El Niño events strike, there is a massive decline in fish and shellfish populations on the coast, as well as torrential rains on the shore, which cause massive flooding and mudslides (Burger 1992). It is hard to imagine how villages like Paloma would have survived such events.

Studies of the shellfish found on archaeological sites have led scientists to argue that El Niño events began only around 6,000 years ago (Sandweiss et al. 2001). According to this model, El Niño events between 6,000 and 3,000 years ago were less frequent than they are today. The onset of El Niño appears to correlate with the beginning of the Cotton Preceramic. It is possible that the climatic uncertainty of the arrival of El Niño played a role in pushing the development of large centres with a partial reliance on agriculture.

El Niño A severe reversal of the Humboldt Current that causes a massive decline in marine resources along the Andean coast.

Summing Up the Evidence

The domestication of plants and animals in the highlands of the Andes appears to have had little impact on the way people lived. Early agricultural sites are either small cave sites or open-air ones, with little evidence of architecture. However, the absence of early agricultural villages in the highlands might be the result of a bias in the types of sites that have been excavated. Archaeologists have focused largely on dry cave sites with well-preserved organic remains.

On the coast, settled villages preceded the adoption of agriculture. These villages were small collections of huts showing little evidence of social inequality. The adoption of domesticated plants took place on the coast in the context of increased settlement size and the emergence of monumental architecture. Because of the availability of rich coastal marine resources, agriculture played only a minor role in the subsistence of Cotton Preceramic settlements. The dominant crop was cotton, used for making fishing nets and textiles. The adoption of agriculture on the Andean coast might have been a reaction to the climatic uncertainty introduced by the onset of El Niño.

9.4 East Asia

The two most significant plants domesticated in East Asia are **rice** and **millet**. Today, rice feeds half of the world's population. The wild ancestor of rice is the species *Oryza rufipogon*, and all domesticated Asian rice belongs to the species *Oryza sativa*. (Note that this species is distinct from African rice and from the plant we call wild rice.) *Oryza rufipogon*, the wild ancestor of rice, was a plant that thrived in seasonally flooded areas. The earliest stages of domestication might have involved the construction of temporary dams to expand the lands that were seasonally inundated (Smith 1995).

One strain of rice, *Oryza sativa japonica*, was domesticated in southern China in the **Yangtze and Huai River Valleys**. Other plants domesticated in southern China include water caltrop and fox nut, both of which grow, like rice, in inundated fields. Among the domesticated animals in southern China are dogs, pigs, and water buffalo. Genetic evidence suggests that another strain of rice, *Oryza sativa indica*, was independently domesticated in the region between India and Thailand (Londo et al. 2006). There is not yet any archaeological evidence for rice domestication from this region.

Two types of millet—broomcorn and foxtail millet—were both domesticated in northern China in the region around the **Yellow River Valley**. Both species of millet are highly drought-resistant cereals. Animals domesticated in northern China include pigs and, possibly, chickens.

Early Pottery

By 10,000 years ago, societies of hunter–gatherers across East Asia were utilizing a wide range of wild resources and living in permanent or semipermanent settlements. Many of these groups produced pottery (see Figure 9.14). The **Jomon** societies of Japan, dated to between 13,000 and 2,500 years ago, produced elaborate pottery and lived in villages that included as many as fifty pit houses (Imamura 1996). The subsistence of the Jomon was based on hunting and gathering, with a particular emphasis on fish and

rice A major cereal crop domesticated in southern China in the Yangtze and Huai River Valleys.

millet A cereal crop domesticated in northern China in the region around the Yellow River Valley.

▲▲ **Yangtze and Huai River Valleys** The area of southern China where rice was domesticated.

▲▲ **Yellow River Valley** The area in northern China where millet was domesticated.

Jomon Japanese preagricultural societies that lived in large villages and produced elaborate pottery.

FIGURE 9.14 Jomon pottery from Japan.

Jar, with string decor. Japan, Neolithic. Mid Jomon period (2500-1600 BCE). ca. 2000 BCE. Terracotta, 37.5 x 31.2 cm. Inv.: MA3355. Photo: P. Pleynet. Musee des Arts Asiatiques-Guimet, Paris, France. © Reunion des Musees Nationaux/Art Resource, NY.

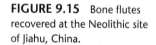 **Pengtoushan** A site in southern China that has produced some of the earliest evidence of domesticated rice dating to approximately 9,000 years ago.

shellfish. Rice and millet agriculture was introduced into Japan only during the Late Jomon period, around 3,000 years ago (D'Andrea et al. 1995).

In the Yangtze Valley, pottery has been discovered at a number of sites dating to earlier than 10,000 years ago (Higham and Lu 1998). The people who produced this pottery subsisted on wild plants and animals. It is interesting that wild rice was among the plants they collected. Because the excavated sites from this period are mostly caves, it is not possible to say whether these people lived in large settlements like those found during the Jomon period in Japan.

In northern China, little is known about preagricultural societies. The reason for this paucity of knowledge is a massive buildup of windblown sediments known as loess, which has buried sites from these periods deep underground.

■ The First Farmers

The earliest evidence of rice farming is found on village sites in the Yangzte and Huai River Valleys. The site of **Pengtoushan** is a village dated to approximately 9,000 years ago that has produced evidence of domesticated rice (Higham and Lu 1998). The excavations at Pengtoushan recovered traces of houses surrounded by a protective ditch. The neighbouring site of Bashidang has also produced a large quantity of charred rice (Pei 1998). Bashidang appears to have been occupied slightly after Pengtoushan. The village at Bashidang covered an area of 30,000 square metres. A wide range of wild animal bones were recovered at Bashidang, indicating that hunting continued to be important for subsistence.

In the Huai River region, the village site of Jiahu, occupied between 9,000 and 8,000 years ago, covered an area of roughly 55,000 square metres (Zhang et al. 1999). Excavations have uncovered a total of forty-five houses, storage pits, and graves. As at Bashidang, a range of wild animals was hunted. Figure 9.15 shows the six complete flutes made from the long bones of red-crowned crane found at Jiahu. These flutes

FIGURE 9.15 Bone flutes recovered at the Neolithic site of Jiahu, China.

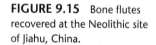

TOOLBOX

Residue Analysis

When animals are exploited for milk and wool, they are more than just a source of meat. Andrew Sherratt has argued that the exploitation of domesticated animals for secondary products such as milk and wool transformed the economy of early farming societies. Herds of animals became a walking source of wealth.

But how can we tell whether an animal was milked? One approach is to look for evidence of dairying in the population structure of the herd. If dairying was economically significant, one would expect a culling of young males. However, this approach provides evidence that is at best indirect. In 2003, a group of biochemists published dramatic results of a new method that allowed them to identify the biochemical traces of milk residues on pottery sherds from the Neolithic in Britain (Copley et al. 2003). These results provide direct evidence that milk was an important aspect of the early farming communities of Britain.

The milk residues found in this study are lipids that have survived for approximately 6,000 years. The first stage of analysis is to get the lipids out of the pot sherd. Sherds are cleaned thoroughly, and then a sample weighing 2 grams

is ground to a powder and soaked in a solvent in an ultrasonic bath. Next, the solvent, which now contains the lipids, is evaporated, leaving the lipids behind. The chemical composition of the lipids is determined with a mass spectrometer. The critical step in developing this method was finding a signature that would distinguish between adipose (body) fat and milk fat. Fortunately, such a marker, based on differences in ratios of carbon isotopes, was found.

Biochemical methods have also been used to identify the processing of plants. In one notable study, a chemical analysis of pottery sherds from the Neolithic site of Jiahu, China, found evidence of a fermented beverage made of rice, honey, and fruit (McGovern et al. 1994). ●

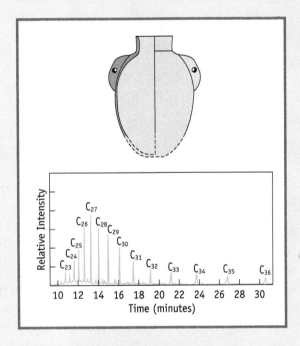

FIGURE 9.16 Neolithic storage jar from the site of Jiahu, China, with the result of a mass spectrometry analysis of the chemical composition of the residues found inside the vessel.

are so well preserved that a musician was able to use one of them to play a Chinese folk song, "The Chinese Small Cabbage." The excavators point out that in ancient China music was a part of nature and was associated with government.

Until recently, the initial stages of millet farming were thought to date to approximately 8,000 years ago in what is known as the Peiligang culture. But research at the site of **Cishan**, located in northern China, has now pushed back the date for the initial domestication of millet to roughly 10,000 years ago, based on direct accelerator mass spectrometry (AMS) radiocarbon dating of plant remains (Lu et al. 2009). Cishan was a village at least 400 metres square that was occupied for over 3,000 years. Gary Crawford has emphasized the significance of the discoveries at Cishan as the earliest evidence of "a significant degree of food production in China" (Crawford 2009, 7272).

Cishan A site in northern China that has yielded dates of 10,000 years ago for domesticated millet

Yangshao culture A Neolithic
.culture in northern China that is
particularly well represented in
the village site of Banpo.

▲▲ **Banpo** A large farming village
located in the Yellow River
Valley (China) dating to the
Yangshou culture.

▲▲ **Hemudu** A well-preserved rice-
farming village in southern China.

■ The Development of Farming Societies

The Peiligang culture of the Yellow River developed into the Yangshao culture 6,500 years ago (Debaine-Francfort 1999). The **Yangshao culture** is particularly well represented at **Banpo**, a village site that consisted of both round semisubter-ranean houses and rectangular houses built on ground level. A range of wild plants and animals, including fish, fruits, and nuts, was exploited. Millet was fully domesticated, as were dogs and pigs. The repertoire of pottery vessels found at Banpo is particularly impressive and includes vessels with elaborate painted dec-orations (see Figure 9.17). Research on the spread of agriculture into the Korean peninsula is still in early stages. Working on botanical remains from sites in South Gyeongsang Province, Gary Crawford and Gyoung-Ah Lee were able to push

FIGURE 9.17 Pottery vessels found *in situ* on the floor of a hut structure at the Banpo village site, China.

back the earliest date for domesticated mil-let in Korea to 5,300 years ago (Crawford and Lee 2003). Rice, soybeans, and wheat first appeared in Korea over a thousand years later. The introduction of domesticated plants in Korea, apparently from northern China, slightly predates the spread of agri-culture to Japan.

In southern China, the **Hemudu** site provides a picture of a village based on rice cultivation contemporaneous with Banpo (Smith 1995). The excavations at Hemudu have uncovered 4 metres of superbly pre-served archaeological deposits. The houses at Hemudu were skillfully built of wood and raised on piles above the waters of a river or pond that existed on the spot. Because the site is waterlogged, the wooden houses are well preserved. Enormous quantities of domesticated rice, along with the bones of domesticated dogs, pigs, and water buffalo, were also recovered at Hemudu.

Chinese archaeologists have been particularly interested in understanding the social life of early farming villages (Pearson and Underhill 1987). As a result, many of the early village excavations are on a very large scale. The tendency in China is to view early agricultural societies as matrilineal clans organized around maternal lineages. Over time, these societies are seen as having evolved into patrilineal property-owning families. The logic behind this theory is that women played a decisive role in raising and tending plants and would therefore have wielded power in early agricultural societies. Attempts have been made to use the distri-bution of burial practices within village sites to gain a fuller understanding of their social organization. One of the burial fea-tures that has been emphasized is that young girls found in Yangshao cemeteries were richly adorned.

Archaeology and the Environment

Archaeology is the only discipline capable of providing empirical evidence about the long-term environmental effects of human actions. In recent years archaeologists have documented the impact of climate change on ancient civilizations (deMenocal 2001) and cases of environmental degradation linked to overexploitation of resources. Global warming has placed the environment at the top of the international political agenda. Yet archaeologists are rarely active voices in environmental policy debates. Peter Mitchell (2008) has raised the question of what archaeologists should be doing in response to the urgency of environmental issues, particularly global warming. He argues that archaeologists should be focusing on research that can provide substantive data relevant to contemporary concerns about the environment.

But what exactly is the archaeological perspective on the environment? Archaeologists tend to emphasize that culture and environment are closely linked. Moreover, archaeologists tend to be cautious about the concept of pristine environments, stressing that even landscapes that appear untouched have been shaped by human activity. Karl Butzer writes that "contemporary ecosystems are the product of millennia of co-evolution between environmental components and human activities . . . ecological issues are sufficiently complex to demand a new and greatly expanded medium of interdisciplinary interaction and collaboration. Archaeol-ogy should, indeed must, be a major player" (Butzer 1996, 142).

Frances Hayashida (2005) warns the archaeological community to expect their data and interpretations to be misrepresented in the political arena. Hayashida identifies three dangers:

1. Archaeological interpretations will be used to depict indigenous practices as ecologically detrimental.

2. The recognition that few landscapes are truly pristine can be used to excuse modern destruction.

3. Modern development might be justified as mimicking natural processes or ancient practices.

But Hyashida ends this list of potential hazards with a call to action: "Only by taking active roles can we shape how our research results are interpreted in public discourse and applied to policy outcomes" (Hayashida 2005, 57). The time when archaeologists sit on the sidelines of debates about the environment appears to be coming to a close.

FIGURE 9.18 This terraced landscape on the island of Sifnos in the Cyclades, Greece, illustrates the co-evolution of the environment and human activities.

■ Summing Up the Evidence

In China, as in Africa, pottery manufacture predates the development of agriculture. Hunter–gatherers living in large settlements with constructed houses are found in Japan, as they are in both the Middle East and Africa. Although the earliest stages of agriculture in China are poorly understood, it appears that the domestication of both plants and animals happened at the same time. As in the Middle East, the adoption of agriculture was accompanied by an increase in the size of sites. In China, domestication took place independently in two centres, with rice domesticated in the south and millet in the north. The overlap in domesticated animal species suggests that there was some connection between these two centres of domestication.

The earliest agricultural sites in China are large sedentary villages. The excavations at Pengtoushan, Bashigan, and Jiahu have uncovered the remains of large settlements with some evidence of defensive ditches. If these sites were inhabited soon after the initial domestication of rice, then southern China would provide a case in which domestication is linked directly with the formation of large villages. However, research on the preceding periods is in its early stages, so the validity of this conclusion remains open to question.

9.5 Questioning the Neolithic

Julian Thomas has written, of the origins of agriculture, that it was a "messy and fragmented series of developments, and any attempt to define a particular set of attributes as constituting the Neolithic will be arbitrary in the extreme" (Thomas 1999, 13). The evidence in this chapter supports the view presented by Thomas and contrasts sharply with Childe's view of the Neolithic Revolution as a sudden transformation of human society that took place in much the same way around the globe.

In all regions, the transition to agriculture was a gradual process. This fact has led Bruce Smith (2001) to argue that it is necessary to consider a territory "in between" hunting and gathering, on the one hand, and farming on the other. The route taken in traversing this intermediate territory was extremely varied. Settled villages preceded agriculture in the Near East, Africa, and the Andean coast, but, apparently, not in New Guinea, the Andean highlands, or Mesoamerica. Pottery can develop very early in the process, as it did in Africa and China, or very late, as it did in the Middle East, New Guinea, the Andes, and Mesoamerica. Plants can be domesticated before animals (Middle East, New Guinea), after animals (Africa and the Andes), at the same time as animals (China), or animals might play a very minor role (Mesoamerica).

The development of agriculture is a complex process involving changes in the biology of plants and animals, human subsistence strategies, human social organization, and the way people think about their place in the world. Perhaps it should not come as a surprise that this transition can follow many trajectories, depending on the plant and animal species involved, the characteristics of the local environment, and the particularities of cultural practices. In a sense, the diversity found in the archaeological record forces us to recognize the need for multiple perspectives on the origins of agriculture.

SUMMARY

- Indigenous plant domestication in Africa took place in three major regions: Ethiopia and Eritrea, central Africa, and west Africa.
- At Nabta Playa, a village of circular huts with storage pits and pottery vessels is dated to 9,000 years ago.
- Pottery developed in North Africa before the domestication of plants and animals.
- Domesticated animals were introduced into North Africa by pastoral societies before the adoption of domesticated plants.

- Yams, bananas, and taro were domesticated indigenously in New Guinea.
- The main evidence for the development of agriculture in New Guinea comes from the excavation of ancient field systems at the Kuk Swamp site. There is evidence of artificial drainage systems at Kuk Swamp beginning 10,000 years ago.
- Because of the Humboldt Current, the Andean coast is extraordinarily rich in marine resources.

- Domesticated beans from Guitarrero Cave, Peru, have been directly dated to 4,300 years ago. The earliest evidence for domesticated potatoes is between 4,000 and 3,200 years ago.
- There is evidence for the domestication of llamas and alpacas beginning 6,000 years ago.
- By 8,000 years ago, small villages relying on marine resources had developed along the Andean coast.
- During the Cotton Preceramic, large sites, including monumental mounds, were built on the Andean coast. Among the domesticated crops from these sites were gourds, squash, and beans. The most significant crop was cotton.

- Rice was domesticated in southern China in the Yangtze and Huai River Valleys. The Pengtoushan site has produced the earliest evidence of domesticated rice.
- Millet was domesticated in northern China in the region around the Yellow River.
- The Jomon societies of Japan were hunter–gatherers who lived in small villages and made pottery.
- The Banpo site in northern China and the Hemudu site in southern China are large villages with extensive evidence of both plant and animal domestication.

KEY TERMS

REVIEW QUESTIONS

1. Do any aspects of the pattern of domestication in the Middle East fit in with the case studies in this chapter?
2. In what ways was the origin of agriculture in New Guinea unique?
3. What does Bruce Smith mean by a territory "in between hunting and gathering, on the one hand, and farming on the other"? What are some examples of such "in-between" societies?
4. What generalizations can be made about pottery and the origins of agriculture?

CANADIAN ARCHAEOLOGISTS

- Joanna Casey was trained at Simon Fraser University and the University of Toronto. She is now a professor in the Department of Anthropology at the University of South Carolina, specializing in the archaeology of northern Ghana. She directs a project based at the Birimi site, which includes a large component from the Later Stone Age Kintampo Complex dating to 3,000–4,000 years ago.
  www.cas.sc.edu/ANTH/Faculty/Caseyj/index.htm

- Gary Crawford, professor in the Department of Anthropology at the University of Toronto in Mississauga, is a specialist in archaeological botany and has published extensively on plant remains recovered from archaeological sites in Ontario, Wisconsin, and Kentucky. He has also carried out research in East Asia on the Jomon societies of Japan and more recently in the lower Yellow River Valley in China.
  www.profgarycrawford.ca/

- Catherine D'Andrea, professor in the Department of Archaeology at Simon Fraser University, is a specialist in the study of ancient agricultural systems through analysis of plant remains. She has published extensively on the ethnoarchaeology and archaeology of agricultural systems in East Africa, including research in the Ethiopian Highlands and in the Nile Valley region of Sudan.
  http://www.sfu.ca/archaeology/faculty/dandrea/index.html

- Gyoung-Ah Lee, professor in the Department of Anthropology at the University of Oregon, received her Ph.D. from the University of Toronto, where she worked on the origins of agriculture in Korea. Her research includes studies of ancient agriculture in Korea, China, and Ontario.
  http://www.uoregon.edu/~anthro/index.php?p=People&s=Faculty&sub=Arch

- Mary McDonald, professor in the Department of Archaeology at the University of Calgary, has carried out fieldwork on late prehistoric sites in the Dhakleh Oasis in the Western Desert of Egypt.
  http://arky.ucalgary.ca/profiles/mary-mcdonald?dir=68

Visit **www.myanthrokit.com**, where you will find a variety of tools and resources to enhance your learning, including:

- Practise quizzes with Study Plans
- Videos
- Listening Activities
- And much more!

PART FOUR

THE DEVELOPMENT OF SOCIAL COMPLEXITY

In the previous section, we examined the shift to an agricultural way of life. In this final section, we visit different societies in many parts of the world and consider the increasing inequality among members of these societies that developed as they grew larger. Power and access to resources came to be controlled by a smaller segment of the population, leading to the emergence of state societies. After reading this introduction you should understand:

- Fried and Service's categories for the forms of social organization.

- Childe's ten criteria that define urban societies.

- Explanations for the emergence of social complexity.

Introduction: Defining Social Complexity

In the modern world, institutionalized power is a basic fact of life. With the exception of a small number of disputed territories, the deep oceans, and Antarctica, the entire globe is carved up into sovereign entities in which a central government holds authority. The way this authority is exercised and its limits vary considerably; however, the existence of centralized authority is a global phenomenon that shapes the world we live in (Figure IV.1).

Centralized government or authority is a relatively recent development in human society. Gaining an understanding of how these institutions came into being is one of the central themes of archaeological research. Through much of the early history of archaeology, the origin of central authority was couched within the broader framework of the progress of humanity. Lewis Henry Morgan and V. Gordon Childe considered what was often called the origin of civilization to have been the inevitable next step in the upward movement of humanity following on the origins of agriculture. From such a perspective, the source of central authority explains itself: People would naturally aspire to live within more advanced and highly developed societies.

Today, most archaeologists have a more subtle understanding of the development of politically complex human societies. Although it is recognized that centralized authority was essential in order for people to live in large urban centres and for significant developments to occur in culture and technology, there is also a clear sense of the costs of such authority. Political complexity is inevitably linked with increased social inequality and limitations on personal autonomy. While early archaeologists might have questioned what allowed societies to "advance" to civilization, archaeologists today are more likely to ask about the forces that pushed societies toward increasing social inequality. The critical issue underlying much contemporary research is how centralized authority gained legitimacy. An authority has **legitimacy** when its right to power is accepted. One question is: To what degree was the legitimacy of authority the result of consensus or coercion? In a system grounded in consensus, members of society believe in the rights of the centralized authority; in a system based on coercion, people are forced to accept this authority. In most cases, legitimacy is the result of a combination of consensus and coercion.

FIGURE IV.1 The Canadian-American border between Maine and Quebec.

■ Categorizing Political Complexity

A number of anthropologists have developed schemes for categorizing the types of social organization found in societies around the world. These schemes provide an essential framework for guiding research endeavours dealing with the development of political complexity. The goal of such schemes is not to encompass the tremendous variation that characterizes human societies, but rather to provide a model of commonalities in the way that political complexity develops.

Morton H. Fried (1967) defined four types of societies: egalitarian, ranked, stratified, and state. In **egalitarian societies**, the only differences in status between members are based on their skill at subsistence activities (such as hunting), their age, and their gender. A person's status is determined by a combination of these factors.

legitimacy A quality or status achieved when the right of a centralized authority to have power is accepted. Legitimacy can be based on consensus or on coercion.

egalitarian society A society in which the only differences in status are based on skill, age, and gender.

ranked society A society in which there is a hierarchy of prestige not linked to age, gender, or ability.

stratified society A society in which access to key resources is linked to prestige.

states Societies in which power is organized on a supra-kin basis or by a bureaucracy that uses force.

urban society A society in which people live in large cities. V. Gordon Childe developed ten criteria defining an urban society.

Production in egalitarian societies takes place within households, with each one carrying out more or less the same tasks. Exchange tends to be casual and based on reciprocity.

In an egalitarian society, there are as many positions of prestige as there are people to fill them. In a **ranked society**, there are fewer positions of prestige than there are people to fill them, and there is a hierarchy of prestige that is not linked to age, gender, or ability. The basis for prestige is often a simple attribute, such as birth order. In such a society, the firstborn son might have higher prestige than his siblings. Although there is a hierarchy in a ranked society, there is no real political power or exploitation. The role of a person occupying a high-status position is to collect, not to expropriate; to redistribute, rather than consume.

In ranked societies, there are individuals with high prestige but little real power. These "big men" or "chiefs" serve as the focal point of a system of collecting and redistributing resources, but they do not expropriate or consume more than their neighbours who have lower prestige. By contrast, in a **stratified society**, all people do not have equal access to key resources; rather, access is tightly linked to prestige: People of high prestige have unimpeded access to these resources, while people of low prestige encounter impediments. In stratified societies, as in ranked societies, the number of high-prestige positions is limited on the basis of criteria other than age, gender, and ability. Because of the unequal access to key resources, including food and shelter, stratified societies are characterized by a growth of exploitation, which can take the form of demands on labour, institutional slavery, or more complex systems based on a division of labour among groups of specialists. Organization is based, not only on the household and kin group, but also on communities of people drawn from different households and kin groups.

Fried defined **states** as societies in which power is organized on a supra-kin basis (Fried 1967). The essential task of the state is to use its power to maintain the social hierarchy that has escaped from its grounding in the kin group. Characteristics of state societies include population control through the fixing of boundaries, the development of a legal system, the maintenance of military and police forces, taxation, and conscription. For Fried, the evolution of political complexity is a gradual process in which the basic unit of organization shifts from the family and kin group to large "supra-kin" communities. This process also sees increasing control of access to key resources and an increase in centralized political power.

A similar scheme developed by Elman Service (1971) divides societies into bands, tribes, chiefdoms, and states. Service's definition of *band* and *tribe societies* corresponds roughly to Fried's egalitarian and ranked societies. For Service, chiefdoms are societies characterized by an intermediate level of social complexity, where centralized leadership is based on heredity. However, leaders in these societies have little ability to use force to maintain order, relying on religious authority as their source of power (Service 1975). State societies are sharply different from chiefdoms in that government and law are backed by force. Service summarizes his view of the state as a society integrated by a bureaucracy that uses force (Service 1971, 167). The state has a legitimate monopoly over the use of force. This does not mean that state societies are inherently violent. Rather, it is through the monopolization and controlled use of force that the rulers of state societies are able to maintain peaceful order among a large population. The role of force is to allow the bureaucratic elite to integrate society.

Both Fried and Service see the development of political complexity as the movement of authority from the kin group to a government that is not based on kinship. Fried tends to emphasize the emergence of inequality as high status becomes increasingly concentrated in the hands of a smaller number of people (see

Figure IV.2 for an example of the way that high status can be indicated). Service highlights the emergence in state societies of a control over the legitimate use of force.

■ Defining Cities

V. Gordon Childe chose to sidestep the search for the early state by shifting the emphasis from political institutions to the cities that characterize **urban society**. In the modern world, urban centres are characterized by high population density as well as a high degree of planning (Figure IV.3). Childe developed ten criteria that archaeologists could use to identify urban societies in the archaeological record: urban centres, surplus production and storage, taxes to a deity or king, monumental architecture, a ruling class, writing systems, exact and predictive sciences, sophisticated art styles, foreign trade, and specialist craftsmen. In the same way that he saw the origins of agriculture as the Neolithic Revolution, Childe saw the development of state societies as the Urban Revolution. Once again, all aspects of human life were transformed by interlocking changes in economy and society.

The advantage of Childe's criteria is that they are likely to leave visible traces in the archaeological record. However, a number of these criteria are poorly defined. For example, how big does a settlement have to be to count as an urban centre? Furthermore, Childe did not make it clear why these criteria are relevant, other than the fact that they are archaeologically visible. One solution to this problem is to define the urban centre in terms of its place in a regional settlement system. Henry Wright and Gregory Johnson (1975) have emphasized that, in urban societies, there is a hierarchy with at least three different levels of settlement size. This hierarchy is significant because it reflects a differentiated administrative structure. In a clever turn of phrase, Norman Yoffee (2005) points out that the birth of the city was also the origin of the countryside. The movement of people and power into cities inevitably restructured the lives of people living in towns and villages.

■ A Comparative Approach to State Formation

Inequality is an essential element of all human societies. Even in those societies which Fried describes as egalitarian, there are differences in status based on skill, age, and gender. The categories developed by Fried and Service are useful tools, but they should not trick us into believing that the emergence of inequality followed a single trajectory in all societies. For example, the societies of the northwest coast of North America offer a fundamental challenge to our expectation that the emergence of political complexity builds on the economy of a village farming way of life. The societies of the northwest coast,

FIGURE IV.2 Maori women from New Zealand. Their high status is indicated by their feather cloaks and jade pendants.

FIGURE IV.3 Midtown Manhattan. This picture illustrates the density and organization that characterize modern urban centres.

FIGURE IV.4 Northwest coast village near Bella Coola, British Columbia.

complex hunter–gatherers with a subsistence base that included a broad range of marine and terrestrial resources, lived in villages (see Figure IV.4) and had a complex social hierarchy that included the institution of slavery. Perhaps any attempt to shoehorn societies into a category such as a chiefdom or a state is misguided. One could argue that it would be better to study social complexity as a continuum or, alternatively, to focus on the internal logic of each individual society.

There certainly are dangers to taking a comparative approach to the emergence of political complexity. While recognizing these dangers, Bruce Trigger has written an eloquent defense of comparative studies: "The most important issue confronting the social sciences is the extent to which human behavior is shaped by factors that operate cross-culturally as opposed to factors that are unique to particular cultures . . . . Given the biological similarities and the cultural diversity of human beings, how differently are they likely to behave under analogous circumstances? The answer to this question is crucial to understanding human behavior and cultural change and shaping the future course of human development" (Trigger 2003, 3). Adopting a comparative approach allows archaeologists to explore the regularities associated with the formation of states, regardless of the context in which that formation occurs, and at the same time to appreciate the unique features of the process in particular regions.

State societies can be divided into primary states, which form without external influence from neighbouring state societies, and secondary states, which form under the influence of neighbouring state societies. As with the origins of agriculture, the transition to state societies is a process that took place independently in a number of regions. Increasingly, archaeologists are paying close attention not only to the processes leading to the formation of states, but also to those that cause them to collapse (Diamond 2005).

In some cases, states began aggressive campaigns of expansion, resulting in the formation of empires (Alcock et al. 2001). **Empires** are political entities that bring together a diverse and heterogeneous group of societies under a single ruler. Often, empires rely on the brutal use of military power to achieve domination. This power is vividly depicted in the sculpture of the temples of the Assyrians (Figure IV.5), who expanded out of Mesopotamia to control a large part of the Middle East. Empires also require the development of methods of communication to allow for the rapid transmission of information. Communication enables the core of the empire to control events far from the centre. The inequality between a core region and peripheral ones is characteristic of empires. The flow of goods and resources moves from the periphery to the core, usually in the form of tribute.

The archaeology of empires requires research covering an immense geographic area. One of the most interesting aspects of this study is exploring how the core maintained control and domination over the periphery. Archaeologists must look at sites at the core and at the periphery, while paying attention to the two linchpins of the empire: communication and force. Excavations and surveys of roads and military camps are a common part of the archaeology of empires.

empires Political entities that bring together a diverse and heterogeneous group of societies under a single ruler.

■ Ecology and Society

Karl Wittfogel proposed a theory of early state formation that emphasized the importance of large-scale irrigation processes. Wittfogel (1957) argued that the need to organize large groups of workers to build and maintain irrigation canals allowed the formation of a hierarchical form of government he labelled "oriental despotism."

Wittfogel's model is an example of a prime-mover model—one in which a single factor is seen as the cause of a phenomenon. In this case, the organization of large-scale agriculture leads to the formation of a centralized bureaucratic government. Robert Carneiro (1970) has proposed a model of state formation that considers the interaction among geography, population increase, and violence. Carneiro emphasizes that early state societies tend to develop in circumscribed areas—that is, areas surrounded by natural barriers or frontiers with neighbouring groups. A population increase in a circumscribed area leads to increasing pressure for resources, which, in turn, will lead to increased violence between communities. Carneiro argues that it is within the context of this competitive violence that power will become increasingly centralized. Unlike Wittfogel's model, the "circumscription model" proposed by Carneiro suggests that it is the interaction among multiple factors that leads to the development of state societies.

FIGURE IV.5 Relief showing the Assyrian attack of the town of Lachish.

■ The Source of Power

Exploring early state societies is essentially a search for the roots of power—the glue that held these large-scale, highly differentiated societies together. How did some people gain the ability to control the actions of others? The critical characteristic of power in state societies is that it comes to reside in institutions as well as developing around charismatic individuals.

A number of archaeologists have suggested that the control of information was a major element in the formation of state societies. The rise of a centralized bureaucracy rested on the ability to gather, control, and record information. The development of specialized craft production involved the transmission of elaborate technical skill and knowledge among a small group of people. The development of writing systems and mathematical knowledge gave the centralized government the ability to control resources and people.

Theories of the origin of the state tend to focus on factors drawn from Western economics. Access to resources, control of labour, population size, competition, access to information, and bureaucracy are among the factors that are often stressed as underlying the power of the centralized government of early states. Another approach is to ask how the people themselves saw the world in which they lived. From this perspective, it is likely that part of the power of rulers flowed from their possession of unique symbols of power and an intimate connection to the gods. The power of special objects, be they banners, thrones, or scepters, to invoke fear, awe, or loyalty is a force that must be kept in mind when trying to understand how centralized bureaucracies came to have legitimacy in the eyes of their subjects (Figure IV.6 on the next page).

FIGURE IV.6 Modern symbols of power. Queen Elizabeth II and Prince Philip open Parliament.

In the coming chapters, we will explore the emergence of state societies from a comparative perspective. We will begin with five societies that afford clear evidence of a complex social organization without the institutionalization of power that is characteristic of state societies. From this foundation, we will move on to examine early states in chapters organized geographically. Our own experience living in a world structured by complex local and global political interrelationships serves as the backdrop to all of these case studies. We are essentially examining how the world we inhabit came into being.

SUMMARY

- Archaeologists today see the development of political complexity as a process that requires explanation and cannot be viewed as the natural result of progress. Political complexity is linked with increased social inequality and limitations on personal autonomy.
- An authority has legitimacy when its right to power is accepted. Legitimacy can be based on coercion or consensus (or both).
- Morton Fried developed a system of classifying human societies into egalitarian, ranked, stratified, and state societies. For Fried, state societies are defined as the organization of society on a "supra-kin" basis.
- Elman Service divides human societies into bands, tribes, chiefdoms, and states. For Service, state societies are defined

as a system that implements bureaucratic government by force.
- Gordon Childe developed a definition of urban societies based on ten criteria.
- Karl Wittfogel explained the emergence of states as a response to the need to organize large groups of workers for public-works projects.
- Robert Carneiro argued that states developed in circumscribed settings as a response to the warfare generated by population growth.
- Empires are political entities that bring together a diverse group of societies under a single ruler.

KEY TERMS

egalitarian society, 265
empires, 268
legitimacy, 265
ranked society, 266
states, 266
stratified society, 266
urban society, 267

REVIEW QUESTIONS

1. How does Fried's system for classifying societies differ from Service's?
2. Why is it important for archaeologists working on state societies not to focus exclusively on the excavation of tombs and palaces?
3. How do Wittfogel and Carneiro explain the development of state societies? Why is such an explanation needed?

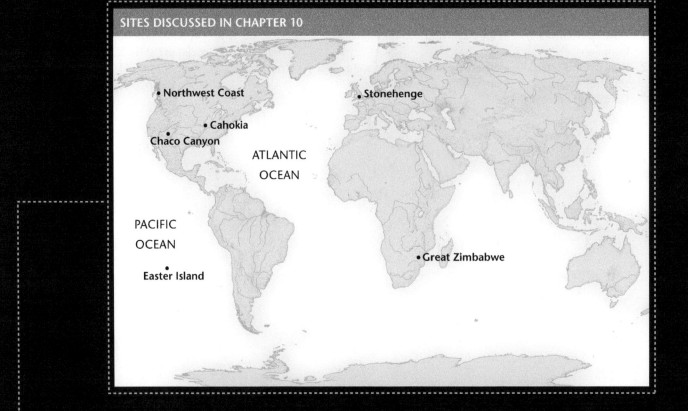

SITES DISCUSSED IN CHAPTER 10

• Northwest Coast   • Stonehenge
• Cahokia
Chaco Canyon

ATLANTIC
OCEAN

PACIFIC
OCEAN

• Great Zimbabwe

• Easter Island

10 TIMELINE

AFRICA SITES

NORTH AMERICAN SITES

LOCARNO BEACH PHASE

GREAT BRITAIN SITES

Durrington Walls

Amesbury Archer

PHASES

STONEHENGE PHASE 2
BURIALS AND TIMBER

STONEHENGE PHASE 1
EARTHWORK CIRCLE

STONEHENGE PHASE 3
STONE MONUMENT

thousands of years ago   5   4   3

COMPLEXITY WITHOUT THE STATE

Some of the most impressive archaeological sites in the world were produced by societies that Morton Fried would describe as ranked or stratified and Elman Service would describe as chiefdoms. After reading this chapter, you should understand:

- The development of Stonehenge and the social and economic context surrounding the construction of this monument.

- The evidence for the function and political organization of Pueblo Bonito and Cahokia.

- The current theories of the organization of the society of Great Zimbabwe.

Stonehenge viewed from above.

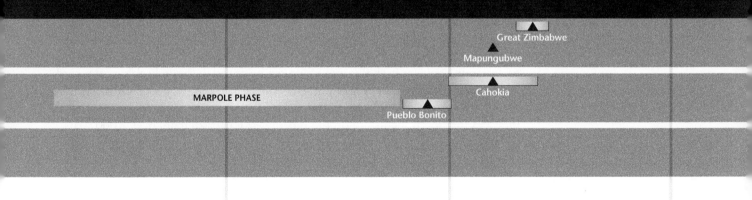

Great Zimbabwe

Mapungubwe

MARPOLE PHASE

Cahokia

Pueblo Bonito

FIGURE 10.1 Partly finished Moai statues on Easter Island.

E aster Island is a speck of land thousands of kilometres from any other inhabited island. The monumental stone heads known as Moai that dot the island embody the enigma which is at the heart of this chapter (see Figure 10.1). Easter Island has never had large cities or even large populations. The island has no particular material wealth, and its inhabitants were not in contact with any of its neighbours until Europeans reached there in 1722. So how—and perhaps more importantly, why—did the people of Easter Island construct these massive monuments? What motivated them to quarry the rock laboriously, drag the massive stones across the island, and set them up on elaborate platforms? Archaeological research on Easter Island has gone a long way toward providing an answer to these questions. Competing leaders erected the Moai during periods of prosperity. Competition between chiefs fuelled a cycle of construction of monuments. Some archaeologists argue that in the fragile island ecology of Easter Island this competitive cycle had disastrous consequences, resulting in deforestation and the decimation of resources (Flenley and Bahn 2003). During the subsequent period of ecological distress, the construction of Moai ceased and appears to have been replaced by increased levels of violence.

Societies that have developed a degree of political complexity but lack a fully developed state bureaucracy often produce archaeological sites that strike us as enigmatic or even mysterious. These sites are frequently characterized by elaborate and well-planned construction yet yield little evidence of a ruling elite. We begin this chapter by examining the archaeological record of social complexity of the Northwest Coast. We then move on to examine the archaeological record of Stonehenge, Chaco Canyon, Cahokia, and Great Zimbabwe. These four sites are the ruins of structures built by societies that Fried would define as ranked or stratified and Service would describe as chiefdoms. None produce evidence of the centralized bureaucracy that characterizes the state. In this chapter we explore these spectacular sites in order to gain insight into the social life of pre-state complex societies.

10.1 Northwest Coast

Central to most hunter–gatherer societies is egalitarian social organization and an ethos of sharing. However, the Tlingit, Haida, Tsimshian, Kwakiutl, Nuu-chah-nulth (Nootka), and Coast Salish societies of the Northwest Coast stand in sharp contrast to this pattern. These were societies of hunter–gatherers whose subsistence was based largely on fishing, particularly salmon, and collecting shellfish. Northwest Coast societies, divided into nobles, commoners, and slaves, lived in settlements of large houses built of wooden planks. Sharing was central to these societies, but it took the form of competitive sharing through feasts known as **potlatches**. Archaeologists struggle to determine how far back this way of life can be traced in the archaeological record. Was social complexity a result of colonial contact and the fur trade? Or did it have far deeper roots? Although the record is far from complete, archaeological research indicates that social inequality on the Northwest Coast stretches over 2,000 years.

■ The Ethnographic Record

A potlatch was a feast as well as a battle. The phrase "fighting with property" expresses the ferocity of these events, which often escalated into the destruction of valued objects such as copper and the burning of fish oil (Codere 1950, 92). In describing the

potlatch A competitive feast described in ethnographic accounts of Northwest Coast society.

▲▲ **Ozette site** A site in Washington state where rapid burial led to the superb preservation of artifacts made from organic materials, including baskets, bows, and arrows.

motivation behind these events, anthropologist Franz Boas wrote: "It is not as much the possession of wealth as the ability to give great festivals which makes wealth a desirable object" (Boas 1895, 74). Competitive giving, sometimes culminating in destruction, was the way to achieve status.

Ethnographic accounts of the Northwest Coast all concur on the importance of status in these societies. It is clear that people living in Northwest Coast societies were classified as nobles, commoners, or slaves (Matson and Coupland 1995). Nobles were the heads of households who controlled resources and directed the ceremonial activities of their household. Commoners comprised the largest group. Although they did not control resources, they did have a degree of freedom. Slaves, on the other hand, were property. Their lives were in the hands of their masters. Usually acquired through raids, slaves had no status and could be sold or even put to death at the will of their owners. Leland Donald argues that slavery was an essential element of Northwest Coast society, providing the labour needed for the accumulation of surpluses, which then became the basis of competitive feasting (Donald 1997). The sculpture shown in Figure 10.2 gives a visual representation of the role of status in Northwest Coast society.

Although we know that Northwest Coast society was clearly far from egalitarian, there is less certainty about the extent of the power of the nobles. It appears that the power of a lineage leader was primarily to be the highest-ranking member of his household. Within a village, households were ranked so that the leader of the highest-ranking household was the village leader. Although these village leaders might have been referred to as chiefs, it does not appear that a single chief had control over a region. The village was the highest level of social organization. One exception is found in the Tsimshian, who did develop a regionally based chiefdom during the colonial period (Martindale 2003).

FIGURE 10.2 Carving showing a chief being carried by a slave. This sculpture vividly depicts the inequality characteristic of Northwest Coast social organization.

■ The Archaeological Record

Surplus, status, competitive feasting, and warfare were the interlocking components of social complexity in the hunter–gatherer societies of the Northwest Coast. Finding evidence for the origins and development of social complexity is a central challenge for archaeologists working in the region. The challenge is made all the more difficult by the nature of the material culture of the Northwest Coast. Most of the artifacts made by these societies, including their houses, boats, nets, baskets, weapons, and ritual objects, were made of wood and bark. These organic materials have survived poorly on archaeological sites.

Occasional exceptional discoveries of sites with preserved wood and bark objects reveal the extent of the resulting bias in the archaeological record. At the **Ozette site** on the northern end of the Olympic Peninsula in Washington state, four houses built between 1600 and 1720 were buried by mudslides, resulting in superb preservation. Not only were the wooden planks of the houses preserved, but also decorative objects such as the whale saddle shown in Figure 10.3, baskets, and whaling tools. The number of organic versus inorganic remains found in these houses is sobering. Organic weapons include 1,534 arrow shafts, 5,189 wooden arrow points,

FIGURE 10.3 Whale saddle from the Ozette site embedded with over 700 sea otter teeth.

Doing Archaeology where the Mountains, the Sea, and History Meet

BY FARID RAHEMTULLA, UNIVERSITY OF NORTHERN BRITISH COLUMBIA

As a student at the University of Toronto some years ago, I was interested in the archaeology of human origins. I spent a couple of summers participating in a field school and then volunteered on archaeological projects, all in East Africa. The following summer, I was somewhat sad because I could not return to Africa due to lack of funds. At the time, Professor Gary Coupland was organizing a research excavation in Prince Rupert, on the north coast of British Columbia, and he asked me if I was interested in being part of the crew. I must have agreed, because the next thing I remember is driving a van full of people some 5,000 kilometres across Canada!

Although I had travelled through British Columbia previously and had some background knowledge of the archaeology of the Pacific Northwest Coast, nothing could have prepared me for what I was about to experience. The first thing almost everyone notices is the natural beauty of the coast. Snow-capped mountains covered with dense rain forest rise from the water, and ocean mists add a dramatic sense of mystery. Wildlife is abundant everywhere, from dolphins, orcas, and numerous types of fish in the oceans, to grizzly and black bears on land, to majestic eagles soaring the skies. It truly is like being inside a postcard.

We spent that summer excavating an ancient village in Prince Rupert harbour with remnants of large plank houses and midden areas dating to about 2,400 years ago. It was my first real exposure to the archaeology of the Northwest Coast, and I was hooked. I finally understood why anthropologists and archaeologists are so interested in this part of the world. That and other experiences eventually led to a change in my primary focus of research from Africa to the Northwest Coast, and I pursued my Ph.D. studies at Simon Fraser University (SFU).

At SFU, my research focused on the site of Namu, located on the central coast of British Columbia in what is now the Great Bear Rainforest. The area around Namu is the ancient homeland of the Heiltsuk First Nation, who still reside here and continue to practise their traditions. Namu is a very significant archaeological site for many reasons, one of the most important of which is its antiquity. Several excavations at the site have revealed a chronology that begins at roughly 10,000 years ago and continues into the modern period. In other words, the peoples of this area have used the site continuously for at least 10,000 years. There are very few archaeological sites in the Americas that extend over such a long time period.

My first opportunity to work in the area was as a teaching assistant in the SFU archaeology field school under the direction of Roy Carlson. As in most parts of the coast, the scenery around

and 115 wooden bows (Croes 2003, 58). In contrast, only seven stone arrow points were recovered. Thus, the archaeological record on most sites preserves only a fraction of the total material culture used by prehistoric societies on the Northwest Coast. As a result, archaeologists are forced to search for evidence of inequality from the limited materials that survive. This includes identifying the accumulation of surplus, linking evidence for personal adornment to the display of social hierarchy, analyzing the distribution of artifacts within and between households, and documenting defensive structures related to warfare.

▪ Surplus

The Northwest Coast offers a wealth of marine resources, including marine mammals, fish, and shellfish. However, the challenge to hunter–gatherers living off these resources is that although they are plentiful, they are also seasonal. The greatest resource is salmon, an anadromous fish born in fresh water that migrates to the sea, where it spends most of its life. Toward the end of their life cycle, salmon return to fresh water, where they spawn and die. The scale of salmon runs is staggering. The annual run on the Columbia River is estimated at 8 to 25 million fish (Ames and

Namu is spectacular, and it is sometimes easy to forget its remoteness. The only way to reach it is by boat or floatplane, as there are no roads. All of our efforts that season were directed at excavating a midden area named the "Rivermouth Trench" due to its proximity to the Namu River. The depth of the midden is an amazing 4.2 metres. This is also the oldest part of the site. The upper two-thirds of the midden consists of shellfish remains, as well as fish, bird, and mammal bones, and stone and bone tools. Toward the bottom, organic preservation is poor, and stone tools dominate the archaeological materials. It was very exciting to think that as we excavated further, we were going back in time all the way to 10,000 years!

Perhaps one of the most gratifying aspects of doing archaeology on the coast is the people. At Namu, we work side by side with Heiltsuk community members and learn about their culture and history. It is important to understand the relevance of Namu to the Heiltsuk; their oral histories reveal the strong spiritual connection they have to the site as part of their ancestral heritage. In a sense, this contextualizes what we do as archaeologists; it serves as a reminder that we are working on people's histories, not just artifacts and radiocarbon dates. This kind of cooperative research has truly enhanced archaeology, and has made it even more exciting to work where the mountains, the sea, and history meet. ▲

FIGURE 10.4 Excavation of the Rivermouth Trench, Namu.

Maschner 1999, 115). If hunter–gatherers were capable of smoking and storing salmon, this fish would become a staple of their diet throughout the year. As a number of archaeologists have pointed out, storage of salmon also represented a source of wealth that provided the resources necessary for the status found in ethnographic Northwest Coast societies. The demand for a large labour force to process fish for storage might also have led to the emergence of slavery. Archaeologists have recently emphasized aspects of Northwest Coast resources beyond salmon. This research points to the importance of a wide range of plant foods, particularly berries, in Northwest Coast subsistence (Lepofsky and Lyons 2003). At the sites of Psacelay and Ginakangeek, excavation of lenses with densely packed seed remains yielded elderberry seeds estimated to represent 190 to 475 kilograms of fruit (Martindale and Jurakic 2004).

As shown in Figure 10.5 salmon storage is well documented ethnographically; however identifying salmon storage in the archaeological record requires some ingenuity. Just because a large number of salmon bones are found on a site does not mean that salmon was stored. Such a pattern could be the result of a seasonal encampment where people lived off salmon for a very brief period of time without preparing it for storage. The most compelling evidence for the storage of salmon is the

FIGURE 10.5 Lily Jackson, a Gitksan woman, next to split salmon hanging from a drying rack. This photograph was taken in 1920.

frequency of salmon cranial bones found in the assemblage. In ethnographically known cases, heads were removed before the bodies of the fish were smoked for storage. The heads may have been boiled for grease and then discarded. Thus, if an archaeological site has a low frequency of cranial bones but a large overall number of salmon remains, it is good evidence that salmon was stored on the site. However, the fragility of salmon crania must be taken into account when assessing such data to make sure that any pattern seen is not the result of taphonomic processes. The earliest widely accepted evidence for large-scale storage of salmon comes from the Locarno Beach Phase, dated to between 3,500 and 2,500 years ago. A series of sites from this time period from the area around Seattle and Vancouver have produced very low numbers of salmon cranial bones. Claims for earlier storage of salmon have been made but are not yet conclusive (Cannon 2006). In some areas, salmon was replaced by other species as the basis for storage economies. There is evidence of whale hunting among the Nuu-chah-nulth (Nootka) on the west coast of Vancouver Island (Monks 2003).

■ Displaying Status

It is interesting that the archaeological evidence for salmon storage precedes the evidence for differences in social status. Thus, the evidence to date supports the models that regard status as building on the opportunities to accumulate wealth and the demands to mobilize labour that develop with the storage of salmon. Nonetheless, there is reason for caution. Status is often very hard to detect in the archaeological record.

A number of lines of evidence point to the emergence of inherited status during the **Marpole Phase**, dated between 2,400 and 1,100 years ago in the Gulf of Georgia. The clearest evidence for status comes from burial contexts. The burial of young people together with precious artifacts during the Marpole Phase suggests that differences in status were not the result of achievement but rather evidence of inherited status (Matson and Coupland 1995, 203). Analysis of skeletal remains has allowed archaeologists to discover the ways that people altered their bodies to display status. During historical periods, **labrets** (large plugs, such as the pieces shown in Figure 10.6) placed below the lip or on the side of the mouth,

Marpole Phase The period when inherited status appears to have developed on the Northwest Coast, 2,400–2,100 years ago.

labrets Large plugs placed below the lip or on the side of the mouth that were worn by people on the Northwest Coast as markers of status.

FIGURE 10.6 Labrets from the Northwest Coast.

were worn on the Northwest Coast. Status was indicated by the size of the labret. In the archaeological record, the use of labrets can be determined when the artifacts are found or through characteristic "labret wear" found on teeth (Cybulski 1993). Labret wear has been dated to as early as 6,000 years ago on a skeleton found at the site of Namu. At the Pender Canal site, dated to the Lucarno Phase, a limited number of individuals, both male and female, have been found with labret wear. It is interesting that several individuals were also buried with grave goods, including carved horn spoons, at this site. Despite this evidence, there is general agreement that labret wear during this phase is not clear evidence of inherited status (Matson and Coupland 1995, 183).

Labret wear has not been found on skeletal remains from the Marpole Phase, but there is evidence for cranial deformation. Cranial deformation involves wrapping an infant's head in a cradleboard to change the appearance of the skull. This practice does not result in any harm to the developing child, but does cause clearly visible change in the shape of the head. In historical periods, cranial deformation on the Northwest Coast was associated with high status. What makes evidence of cranial deformation of particular interest to archaeologists is that it indicates that an individual was born into a particular status in society. The skull must be wrapped at a very young age in order to create an appearance that becomes a lifelong badge of a person's standing in society. In contrast, labrets can be adopted later in life and thus may be a sign of achieved rather than inherited status.

Figurative art on the Northwest Coast dates at least as far back as the Lucarno Phase but the earliest widespread evidence for the types of artwork characteristic of Northwest Coast cultures appeared during the Marpole Phase. Art objects include bone clubs, stone bowls, pendants, and toggles with representations of animals, humans, and geometric forms (Figure 10.7). At the Esilao site on the Fraser River, the charred remains of a decorated wooden box were recovered, with geometric designs reminiscent of those found on sites of the historic period. The relationship between Marpole Phase artwork and emerging social complexity remains unclear.

■ Household Archaeology

Another line of evidence in the archaeology of social structure is the analysis of differences between the households that made up Northwest Coast villages. The McNichol Creek site was a village located near Prince Rupert, British Columbia, dated

FIGURE 10.7 Marpole Phase soapstone bowl from Vancouver Island

between 2,000 and 1,500 years ago (Coupland et al. 2003). The site, measuring approximately 100 by 150 metres, consists of a large midden deposit of broken shells, bones, artifacts, and burials running behind a main residential area. The residential area consisted of fifteen houses arranged in two rows, as shown in Figure 10.8. Excavation of three houses showed clear differences in their contents and size. One of the houses, House O, was very large, with over 100 square metres of floor space. At its centre was a large square hearth, perhaps used for feasting. Sixty-five artifacts were recovered, including a labret, two adze blades made of nephrite, and chert and obsidian flakes. The other houses were much smaller, around 60 square metres in size. House D had two small hearths. Artifacts recovered include tooth pendants, one chert flake, and one nephrite fragment. House E was similar to House D in size but had only a single hearth. Recovered artifacts include ground slate points from what might have been a manufacturing area for slate tools. The differences between House D and House O are also apparent in the animal bones found (the faunal remains from House E have yet to be published). In House D, 75 percent of the identifiable specimens (NISP) were fish and 25 percent were mammals, while at House O the percentages are almost the reverse: 67 percent mammal (deer, otter, dog, beaver, turtle, and harbour seal) and 33 percent fish. Based on this data, the excavators argue that House O was an elite household while Houses D and E reflected a commoner status. Looking at the distribution of the artifacts in House O, most were found in the back, which appears to match the ethnographically known pattern of where a chief's quarters were usually located, toward the back of a house. Slaves lived toward the front.

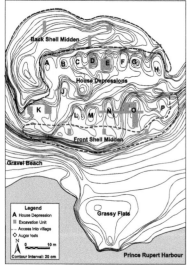

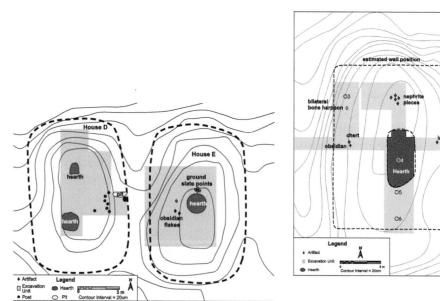

FIGURE 10.8 Plans of the site of McNichol Creek, British Columbia. The plan on the left shows an overview of the site with a series of houses laid out along two parallel rows. The plan in the middle shows the layout of low status Houses D and E. The plan on the right shows the high status House O. Shaded areas indicate the limits of excavated units.

The World's Longest-Lived Corporate Group

The site of Keatley Creek, located in British Columbia on an interior plateau about 300 kilometres from the coast, has provided a unique perspective on the social organization of hunter–gatherers. Excavations by Brian Hayden of Simon Fraser University uncovered the remains of a series of large housepit structures. Hayden interprets these structures as the houses of multifamily groups he refers to as "residential corporate groups." Radiocarbon dating of stratified deposits inside the houses indicates that these structures were in use for a period of approximately 1,500 years, from 2,600 to 1,000 years ago. Based on the common understanding of hunter–gatherer societies, we might expect that the long use-life of these structures was the result of intermittent occupations by unrelated groups. We would not expect each structure to have remained the home of a particular residential corporate group over many generations. However, an analysis of the rock types (raw material) used in stone tool manufacture suggests that contrary to these expectations, residential corporate groups persisted for 1,500 years at Keatley Creek. Comparing the raw materials used in three different housepit structures, Hayden and colleagues found that the types of raw materials varied between houses but remained consistent within a structure throughout the stratigraphic sequence. This pattern appears to indicate that throughout the occupation of a structure, a resident group had vested rights to areas in the surrounding landscape as well as to resources, including stone tool raw material and probably food resources in the same vicinity. ◆

REFERENCE: Brian Hayden, Edward Bakewell, and Rob Gargett. (1996). The world's longest-lived corporate group: Lithic analysis reveals prehistoric social organization near Lillooet, British Columbia. *American Antiquity* 61: 34–356.

The social institution of slavery on the Northwest Coast was tightly linked to raiding and warfare. Slaves were the captives taken during conflict. In historical periods, raiding parties would number in the hundreds and could travel nearly 1,000 kilometres from their homes on raiding expeditions (Ames and Maschner 1999, 198). The tools of war included bows and arrows made of wood; daggers made of whalebone, copper, chipped stone, or slate; spears; clubs; and armour made of wooden slats. Unfortunately, little of this material survives in the archaeological record. A skeleton dated to 4,200 years ago found at Namu had a bone point embedded in his back, providing early evidence for violence. Signs of trauma are common in the skeletons recovered from burial sites, including fractures to the forearms and occasionally decapitation or depressed skull fractures. However, such violence is not necessarily the result of warfare, as high levels of violence might have taken place within communities.

Defensive fortifications offer more compelling evidence that raiding parties were active. David Schaepe (2006) found rock fortifications along the Fraser River Canyon, British Columbia. These stone walls and platforms would have controlled movement up the river and access to settlements from the river. Local oral history recounts that they were constructed as protection from raiders arriving in canoes. Available evidence suggests that these defensive features predate European contact and might be 1,000 years old.

▪ Summing Up the Evidence

The Northwest Coast demonstrates that generalizations about hunter–gatherer social organization must be made with caution. Although the subsistence base of these societies did not include a significant agricultural component, their social organization had a clear hierarchy that included slaves, commoners, and nobles. The archaeology of the Northwest Coast demonstrates the difficulty of identifying social complexity based on the archaeological record. Particularly in areas where much of material culture was made of perishable goods, it is essential to pay close attention to subtle clues of differences in status among members of society.

FIGURE 10.9 Sketch of Stonehenge by the British artist John Constable. How did Constable choose to represent this monument?

▲▲ **Stonehenge** A ring of massive standing stones on the Salisbury Plain, England, that was constructed beginning in the Early Neolithic and ending in the Early Bronze Age.

10.2 Stonehenge

Stonehenge, a ring of massive standing stones on the Salisbury Plain in southern England, has been the subject of contemplation and wonder for centuries (see Figure 10.9). William Wordsworth wrote about the site in a poem:

> Pile of Stone-henge! so proud to hint yet keep
>
> Thy secrets, thou that lov'st to stand and hear
>
> The Plain resounding to the whirlwind's sweep,
>
> Inmate of lonesome Nature's endless year;

The construction of Stonehenge has been variously attributed to Romans, Druids, Danes, and Greeks (Castleden 1993). For some, Stonehenge is the product of mystical forces or "earth mysteries" (Chippindale et al. 1990). Archaeological research has demonstrated that Stonehenge is not a single monument, but rather the site of a sequence of monuments built over a period of more than 1,000 years. Research on the region surrounding Stonehenge has documented an entire landscape upon which monuments were constructed. As a result, Stonehenge can now be grounded within a long process of development and within a broad regional context. Still, the wealth of archaeological research at Stonehenge and in the surrounding region has not dispelled all the enigmas. Understanding the social and economic organization of the people who built Stonehenge still poses significant challenges.

■ The Development of Stonehenge

Archaeological research at Stonehenge has demonstrated that the site developed through a series of stages beginning in the Late Neolithic (5,000 years ago) and ending in the Early Bronze Age (3,500 years ago) (Souden 1997; Cleal et al. 1995). Understanding Stonehenge requires an understanding of the long process through which the site came into being. Figure 10.10 illustrates the major stages of construction of Stonehenge.

PHASE 1: THE EARTHWORK CIRCLE. The first monument at Stonehenge was a round ditch excavated to enclose an area 110 metres in diameter. Slight embankments

Phase 1: The Earthwork Circle.

Phase 2: Burials and a Timber Structure.

Phase 3a: The Bluestones.

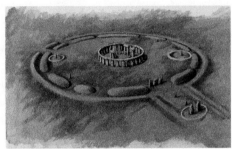

Phase 3b: Sarsen Circle and Trilithons.

FIGURE 10.10 The major stages in the development of Stonehenge.

were built up on both the inside and outside of the ditch. Wooden posts were erected in a ring of holes known as the Aubrey holes, which were dug along the inside of the ditch. Animal bones, including a cattle jaw and an ox skull dating to Phase 1, were found buried in the ditch. Phase 1 dates to the Late Neolithic, roughly 5,000 years ago.

PHASE 2: BURIALS AND A TIMBER STRUCTURE. During Phase 2, the ditch and the Aubrey holes were largely filled in. Human remains dating to Phase 2, including remains from cremated burials, are found in the fill of both the ditch and some of the Aubrey holes. A structure of standing timber posts was constructed near the centre of the monument. Phase 2 dates to the Late Neolithic, between 5,000 and 4,500 years ago. The recent reappraisal of the site (Parker Pearson et al. 2009) suggests that most of the burials actually date to Phase 1.

PHASE 3: STONE MONUMENT. The monumental standing stones that are the most impressive aspect of Stonehenge were erected in a series of six subphases during the Early Bronze Age between 4,500 and 3,500 years ago.

Phase 3a: The Bluestones. The **bluestones**, shown in Figure 10.11, were set up in either a circular or semicircular formation at the centre of the monument in a series of holes known as the Q and R holes. The bluestones, which stand between 2 and 2.5 metres high, are not the most impressive stones at the site, but they do raise many questions. The geological source of these stones is not in the vicinity of Stonehenge; it lies in the Preseli Mountains in Wales, over 240 kilometres away. Moving these stones from Wales to the Salisbury Plain would have required an enormous effort. Some archaeologists have argued that the bluestones had been transported to southern England by glacial activity during the Pleistocene. However, it remains possible that the stones were transported from Wales as part of the construction of Stonehenge. Why these particular stones would have had a value to justify such an effort remains an open question. Recent research suggests that the

bluestones A ring of standing stones at the centre of Stonehenge. The source of the stones is over 240 kilometres from Stonehenge.

FIGURE 10.11 The bluestones are the smaller standing stones in the inner circle surrounded by the far larger sarsen stones.

Sarsen Circle A circle of massive upright sandstone blocks capped with lintels set up in the central area of Stonehenge.

trilithons Three pairs of upright sandstone blocks capped with lintels at Stonehenge located within the Sarsen Circle.

bluestones might have been brought to Stonehenge as early as the first construction phase (Parker Pearson et al. 2009).

Phase 3b: Sarsen Circle and Trilithons. The **Sarsen Circle**, constructed of massive blocks, was set up in the central area of the site. The blocks were of sarsen stone, a very hard sandstone found 30 kilometres from Stonehenge. In a staggering triumph of engineering, the circle of sarsen stones was capped by lintels made of solid blocks. These lintels and their supporting stones were fit together with carved joints. Inside the Sarsen Circle, another set of sarsen monoliths known as the **trilithons** were set up in a horseshoe arrangement oriented toward the northeast. The trilithons were set up in five pairs, each capped by a lintel. The trilithons are truly massive, reaching a maximum height of 7 metres.

Phases 3c–f: Rearranging Bluestones and Digging Holes. The construction of the Sarsen Circle and the trilithons was the most intensive phase at Stonehenge. There followed a series of three phases in which the bluestones were reorganized and a series of holes was dug in concentric circles around the site. In the final configuration, one set of bluestones was set up in the shape of a horseshoe on the inside of the trilithons and another was erected between the trilithons and the Sarsen Circle. Two concentric rings of pits were excavated around the outside of the monument.

■ A Constructed Landscape

Stonehenge was not an isolated monument. Numerous different types of earthen mounds and enclosures were built on the Salisbury Plain during the Late Neolithic and the Early Bronze Age (see Figure 10.12). One of the most impressive features is the Avenue, a path bounded by ditches and embankments that runs for over a kilometre between the Avon River and Stonehenge. Although the function of the Avenue appears to have been to guide people toward Stonehenge, other features on the site have a less clear purpose. The most massive of these is the Cursus, a slightly raised earthen platform that runs for almost 3 kilometres in an east–west alignment. The entire landscape of the Salisbury Plain was sculpted by these massive earthen constructions (Thomas 1991). New excavations at the Cursus have shown that this feature might actually predate the first phase of construction at Stonehenge (Thomas et al. 2009).

The Context of Stonehenge

Stone monuments constructed during the Late Neolithic and Early Bronze Age are found in many parts of western Europe. However, even within this context, Stonehenge stands out as a marvel of engineering and a true enigma. What was its function within the lives of the people who built it? Many have argued that the monument is aligned to allow for the prediction of celestial events. It seems beyond question that it was a construction of religious significance. Almost no domestic remains have been discovered during excavations at the site. Moreover, in the region as a whole, domestic remains are limited to small pits with artifacts and refuse and the faint traces of houses built of wooden posts (Hunter and Ralston 1999). The people who built Stonehenge were agriculturalists who raised wheat and grazed cattle. There is botanical evidence that in the Late Neolithic the Salisbury Plain became an increasingly open landscape used mostly for grazing. Recent excavations at the site of **Durrington Walls**, located 2.8 kilometres from Stonehenge, have revealed the exciting discovery of a series of houses that appear to be part of a village dating to the Late Neolithic (Parker Pearson et al. 2005).

The construction of Stonehenge required the ability to organize a large group of people for work beyond their basic subsistence activities. This labour force had to be coordinated and guided by clear planning. The accomplishment of transporting and erecting the 7-metre-high trilithons and then capping them with a lintel stone is quite impressive. These feats of engineering and organization were achieved by people who did not live under a state bureaucracy. The leaders who directed these projects are invisible to us today. Their authority would have rested not on an absolute control based on force, but rather on the "soft power" that comes from the redistribution of surplus goods and the status that comes from holding an inherited position in society.

Colin Renfrew (1984) has argued that Stonehenge was built by people living in chiefdoms and that the increasing scale of the monument over time reflects the increasing size of territories controlled by a single chief. Renfrew recognizes that a critical weakness in his argument is the absence of "direct evidence among the artifacts found for personal ranking, as indicated by distinctive dress, ornament, or possessions" (Renfrew 1984, 243). However, in 2002, archaeologists working on a rescue excavation before a housing development was to be constructed found a pair of burials that fulfill Renfrew's prediction: The people who built Stonehenge did include elites marked by ornaments and possessions.

The **Amesbury Archer**, as the main burial came to be known, was found 4.8 kilometres from Stonehenge (see Figure 10.13). He lived during the Early Bronze Age, corresponding to Phase 3 in the construction of Stonehenge. A recent program of radiocarbon dating indicates that the Amesbury Archer lived during

FIGURE 10.12 Map of Stonehenge landscape.

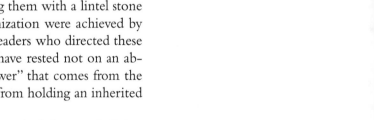

▲▲ **Durrington Walls** A site on the Avon River near Stonehenge with three monumental timber circles and evidence of occupation.

Amesbury Archer A burial with a range of elite burial goods found near Stonehenge.

Phase 3c-f, after the Sarsen Circle and trilithons had been erected (Parker Pearson et al. 2007). Objects found with the burial include two slate wrist-guards, a bone pin, two copper knives, five pots, boar tusks, a cache of flints, arrowheads, a shale belt ring, and two gold earrings. No other burial with a similar wealth of grave goods has been discovered from this period. Nearby, a second burial was found of an individual with more modest grave goods that include gold earrings. The goods found with these two burials are precisely the kind of display items that Renfrew would expect in the burials of the leaders of a chiefdom. However, the Amesbury Archer also raises questions. Isotopic analyses of the skeletal remains indicate that the Archer grew up, not in the vicinity of Stonehenge, but rather far off in the Alps. Why did he move such a long distance? How did he gain status in a society he was not born into?

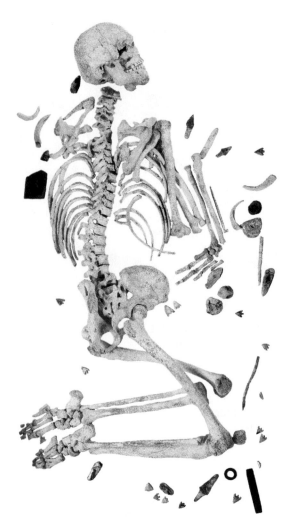

FIGURE 10.13 The Amesbury Archer with associated grave goods.

What Did Stonehenge Mean?

It might seem that there must be an explanation for Stonehenge, that it is a mystery waiting to be unlocked. There is no lack of explanations for the monument; they range from the construction of a "prehistoric observatory" to fantasies of a Druid sanctuary (Chippendale et al. 1990). Certainly, there is some truth behind these ideas: Stonehenge must have had a ritual function, and many aspects of the arrangement of the standing stones correspond to celestial orientations. However, Barbara Bender (1992) has criticized such explanations as attempts to "freeze" the past that lack a sense of an ongoing historical process. Bender's critique is particularly relevant to the site of Stonehenge, a monument that came into being as part of a process lasting over 1,500 years. According to Julian Thomas, "Stonehenge never had a meaning" (Thomas 1996, 62). Over more than eighty generations, Stonehenge became the landscape within which people lived. The essential explanation of the monument is that it does not have a single explanation; rather, it must be understood as the long-term unfolding of a society's relationship to the landscape.

But can we say *anything* about what Stonehenge meant? Determining the meaning of ancient monuments is treacherous terrain, since we are essentially trying to gain insight into prehistoric beliefs. Ian Hodder has placed Stonehenge within the broader context of monument building in the Neolithic of western Europe. He sees the emergence of large monuments as part of the expansion of the household to include a larger group of people spread over a wider area. For Hodder (1990), Stonehenge is one of many monuments that recreate the household at the level of a regional landscape. Bender (1992) takes a somewhat different approach, seeing the scale of construction at Stonehenge and the surrounding area producing a fusion of nature and culture. Over the generations, the constructions at Stonehenge became elements of a developing landscape, where the lines between nature and culture were blurred. One intriguing idea is that, for Stonehenge and the surrounding earthworks, such as the Avenue, the act of producing and experiencing the landscape was as important as the enduring monument. Bender points to the digging and refilling of holes and the way the earthworks would have channelled peoples' movements. She also suggests that the shaping of the landscape might have expressed and strengthened conceptions of gender and power in society.

FIGURE 10.14 Excavation of a series of postholes at the site of Durrington Walls marking the fence that surrounded a house visible as a faint square outline. The red earth is the hearth or fireplace that was in the centre of the house.

Mike Parker Pearson and Ramilisonina (1998) have developed an interpretation of Stonehenge that builds on recent research at the site of Durrington Walls (see Figure 10.14). Like Stonehenge, Durrington Walls sits on the Avon River, but in every other respect these sites are opposites. At Durrington Walls there is evidence of occupation, including houses, while at Stonehenge no domestic debris has been recovered. Durrington Walls has three monumental circles, but these were built of timber rather than standing stones. Radiocarbon dating now shows that Durrington Walls and Phase 3b at Stonehenge, the period of the construction of the trilithons and Sarsen Circle, are contemporary. Parker Pearson and Ramilisonina have suggested a connection between the two sites, saying that Durrington Walls was the land of the living while Stonehenge was the domain of the ancestors. At Stonehenge, the wood circle at Durrington Walls was transformed into stone, a material that represented the builders' ancestors. If Parker Pearson and Ramilisonina's interpretation is correct, it might explain why the builders of the Sarsen Circle used mortise and tenon as well as tongue-and-groove joints to fit the lintels onto the upright stones. These are techniques used in woodworking and their use at Stonehenge is puzzling. Perhaps the explanation of this feature is symbolic rather than technological—perhaps Stonehenge was built as a stone replica of a wooden structure. Parker Pearson and Ramilisonina believe that Stonehenge would have stood empty after its construction, that "its inhabitants were the spirits of the ancestors" (Parker Pearson and Ramilisonina 1998, 319).

■ Summing Up the Evidence

Archaeological research has demonstrated that Stonehenge came into being over a period of more than 1,500 years. It is therefore very unlikely that the site has a single meaning or explanation. The source of power underlying the construction of the site did not rest on control based on force, as is often found in state societies. The Amesbury Archer provides the first direct evidence of the elites of Early Bronze Age society in the region. Although the cultural context of Stonehenge remains enigmatic, the new excavations at Durrington Walls have opened up a promising new line of research on the cultural landscape of Stonehenge.

FIGURE 10.15 Satellite image of Chaco Canyon.

10.3 Pueblo Bonito, Chaco Canyon

Beginning around A.D. 700, there is evidence for an increased level of social complexity across the American Southwest (Plog 1997). In the arid deserts of southern Arizona, sites with platform mounds and ball courts have been attributed to the Hohokam culture. The largest Hohokam site is Snaketown, located in the Phoenix Basin. At the height of its development in the eleventh century, Snaketown had a population of 300 to 600 people and two large ball courts. The Hohokam developed large-scale irrigation projects to pull water from the Salt and Gila rivers to agricultural fields.

The ancestral Puebloan cultures flourished in what is now the Four Corners region where Arizona, New Mexico, Utah, and Colorado meet. Beginning around A.D. 800, **Chaco Canyon** in the San Juan Basin of New Mexico became the centre of a regional settlement network and the site of the construction of spectacular multistoried structures known as **Great Houses**. Understanding the organization of Chaco society and the function of the Chaco Great Houses is one of the most exciting challenges in the study of the prehistory of North America.

The current environment of Chaco Canyon "does not exactly correspond to most people's concept of Eden" (Sebastian 1992, 9). Chaco Canyon covers an area 30 kilometres long and between 0.5 and 1 kilometre wide and is between 90 and 180 metres deep. Rainfall, vegetation, surface water, and game are all sparse (see Figure 10.15). The inhabitants of the canyon responded to this challenging environment by developing dams and canals to control runoff water from torrential summer rains.

▲▲ **Chaco Canyon** A canyon in New Mexico that became the centre of a regional settlement network and the site of the construction of large multistoried structures, known as Great Houses, beginning around A.D. 800.

Great Houses Large multistoried structures located at Chaco Canyon, New Mexico, that became the centre of a regional settlement network beginning around A.D. 800.

FIGURE 10.16 Aerial view of Pueblo Bonito. This photograph shows the semicircular plan of the site with a central plaza divided by a wall and flanked by rooms and circular kivas.

■ The Development of Pueblo Bonito

Pueblo Bonito, a massive multistory complex of 650 rooms covering almost 1 hectare, is the largest Great House in Chaco Canyon (see Figure 10.16). The rooms are arranged in a semicircle enclosing a central plaza, which is divided roughly in half by a wall running in a north–south direction (see Figure 10.17). The rooms that make up the Great House include a large number of subterranean circular chambers known as **kivas**, structures that have religious significance in modern Pueblo villages.

Archaeological research at Pueblo Bonito has demonstrated that the massive Great House was built up over centuries (Windes 2003). The excellent preservation of wooden beams in the dry environment of Chaco Canyon has allowed archaeologists to use dendrochronology, or tree-ring dating, to develop a tight sequence of events. The construction of Pueblo Bonito began around 1,200 years ago (A.D. 800) and the complex reached its full size over the next 200 to 300 years (A.D. 1000 to A.D. 1100). Subsequently, there was a reduction in the extent of occupation, and building activity slowed before the site was abandoned about 750 years ago (A.D. 1250).

▲▲ Pueblo Bonito A massive 650-room complex, the largest Great House in Chaco Canyon.

kivas Subterranean circular chambers found on sites in the American Southwest.

FIGURE 10.17 Reconstruction of Pueblo Bonito drawn in 1878. How did the artist view the site?

■ The Function of Pueblo Bonito

Archaeologists working at Pueblo Bonito have struggled to determine the function of this impressive site (Neitzel 2003). The construction of a complex of hundreds of rooms suggests that the site was a very large settlement and population estimates for the site have ranged as high as 1,200 people. However, excavations have uncovered a surprisingly small number of fireplaces and few remains of domestic activities. These observations, along with the layout of the site and the large number of kivas, have led some to argue that Pueblo Bonito was essentially a ceremonial centre and that it rarely had a population of much more than 100.

Two large mounds of cultural debris and earth reaching 6 metres in height and located in front of the plaza are an important source of information on the function of Pueblo Bonito (Cameron 2002). Similar mounds, known as berms, are a common feature of Great Houses from the Chaco period. A unique feature of the Pueblo Bonito berms is that they were plastered, so they could have served as a platform for ceremonies. Excavation of the berms here and at other sites has produced massive quantities of ceramics. The types of vessels found suggest that they are the refuse of ceremonial feasting rather than of normal daily activities.

The function of Pueblo Bonito might have changed over time (Neitzel 2003). Its initial occupation conforms to the size and organization of a residential site. It is possible that between A.D. 800 and A.D. 1000 it was the residence of an elite group. With the expansion around A.D. 1000, the focus of the site shifted toward ceremonial function. Of course, it is possible that throughout its occupation Pueblo Bonito served as both an elite residence and a ceremonial centre; it appears that at A.D. 1000, the balance of activity shifted toward the ceremonial aspect. The connection between an elite residence and a ceremonial centre indicates that the elite's power was at least partly the result of their special role in religious ceremonies.

■ Evidence for Elites

The sheer scale of the construction at Pueblo Bonito suggests some form of political leadership. To get a sense of the size of the undertaking, consider that over 200,000 trees were used to make the floors and roofs of the Great House. One estimate places the amount of labour involved in its construction at 800,000 person hours (Metcalf 2003).

Archaeological evidence for social inequality at Pueblo Bonito is restricted largely to the finds made in two small rooms at the north end. Although a number of rooms at the site included burial remains, those at Room 33 are unique (Akins 2003). Here, the disarticulated remains of sixteen individuals were found above a wooden plank floor. Below the floor, two male burials were found together with lavish offerings. Altogether, the burial offerings found in Room 33 included over 50,000 pieces of turquoise in the form of beads, pendants, and mosaic inlays. Such a concentration of turquoise is unknown in any contemporary context. Not far away, in Room 38, a rich deposit of beads, pendants, and mosaic pieces made of jet, a hard black stone, was discovered (see Figure 10.18). Although no human burials were found in Room 38, it also contained fourteen skeletons of macaws, colourful birds native to the Gulf Coast of Mexico.

FIGURE 10.18 Jet stone frog with inlaid turquoise from Room 38 at Pueblo Bonito.

TOOLBOX

Remote Sensing

Methods of remote sensing, including aerial and satellite photography, play a critical role in discovering sites and orienting exploration. Satellite imagery can cover large geographical regions. In recent years, methods of satellite imagery have come to rely heavily on sensors that detect features invisible to the human eye. Radar imaging from satellites is able to detect large-scale buried features. In research in the eastern Sahara desert, archaeologists have used space shuttle radar images to trace the remains of buried river systems associated with Paleolithic sites. Some sensors can detect minute variations in the surface temperature of the earth, thus providing an index of the characteristics of the soil. In Chaco Canyon, New Mexico, a Thermal Infrared Multispectral Scanner (TIMS) flown by NASA was used to detect a road system dated to between A.D. 900 and A.D. 1000 (www.ghcc.msfc.nasa.gov/archeology/chaco.html).

Photography from aircraft or balloons can reveal buried features, raised mounds, or wall systems. Most aerial photographs used by archaeologists are taken at an oblique angle to further enhance the visibility of features. Aerial photographs are particularly useful in giving a view of an area that would be too large to excavate. Photographs of ancient cities often reveal the complete urban plan, including roads and fortification walls. Aerial photographs have even been used successfully in making the outlines of ancient field systems visible to archaeologists. In a small number of cases, aerial photography has revealed construction on a scale that is too large to be seen from the ground. The most spectacular of these types of construction are the Nazca Lines in Peru, which consist of representations of animals made by clearing paths on the desert floor. The form of these alignments is visible only from the air. ●

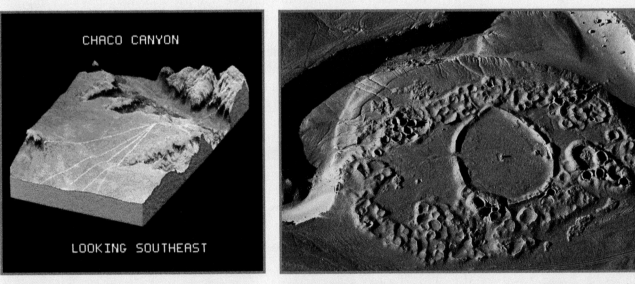

FIGURE 10.19 Photograph taken by NASA using a Thermal Infrared Multispectral Scanner (TIMS) showing roads radiating out from Chaco Canyon.

FIGURE 10.20 Aerial photograph of Guatacondo in the Atacama Desert of Chile, A.D. 200 to A.D. 500. Notice how structures that have not been excavated are visible in this photograph.

The discoveries in Rooms 33 and 38 at Pueblo Bonito make it clear that wealth was not equally distributed among members of society. It is interesting that turquoise, jet, and macaws were traded over very long distances. The concentration of large quantities of these objects in two rooms suggests that the elite of Pueblo Bonito society exercised some degree of control over trade networks.

■ The Chacoan Network

The large number of trade items found in Rooms 33 and 38 at Pueblo Bonito indicate that the site was part of a larger network. Within Chaco Canyon, archaeologists have identified a system of roads connecting the Great Houses. Research using satellite imagery has provided clear evidence that the system of roads stretched far beyond the limits of the canyon (www.ghcc.msfc.nasa.gov/archeology/chaco.html). A series of photographs taken by NASA with a Thermal Infrared Multispectral Scanner (TIMS) detected over 200 miles of roads radiating out from Chaco Canyon.

The road system links Chaco Canyon with sites covering a large part of what is today the Four Corners region of the American Southwest. Sites in this region tend to share similarities in architecture which, together with the road system, suggest that they were linked into what has been called the **Chacoan Network**. Although Chaco Canyon was clearly the centre of this network, there is no evidence that the people living there had control over the outlying settlements. However, more than just high-status trade items such as turquoise, jet, and macaws flowed into the Great Houses at Chaco. It has long been recognized that much of the pottery recovered at Chaco Canyon was not produced locally, but was brought to the site from outlying areas in the Chacoan Network. A study of maize kernels suggests that some of the food consumed at Chaco Canyon was not grown locally. By looking at the isotopes of the element strontium in maize kernels found at Chaco Canyon, researchers have shown that at least some of the maize was grown in areas over 80 kilometres away (Benson et al. 2003).

The riddle of the Chacoan Network is, What made it run? What compelled people to bring food and pottery into Chaco Canyon from surrounding areas? What gave the people living at Pueblo Bonito the ability to control large quantities of high-status trade items? One possibility is that these items were brought to Chaco Canyon as taxes collected by a central authority backed by the threat of force. The problem with such a scenario is that there is no evidence of such an authority or even of very large populations in Chaco Canyon. Another possibility is that the power of the people living at Chaco Canyon was the result of the centrality of the canyon in the ritual and religious life of the people living within the greater Chacoan Network. The flow of goods into Chaco Canyon might have been the result of cycles of ceremonial feasting in which large groups of people congregated in the canyon for very brief periods, bringing from their homes food and utensils that were then discarded in the refuse piles such as the berm in front of Pueblo Bonito.

■ The Rise and Fall of Chaco Canyon

The location of the elaborate structures like Pueblo Bonito in the highly arid environment of Chaco Canyon has led archaeologists to look for a connection between fluctuations in climate and the rise and fall of the Great Houses. The relationship between climate and the end of the occupation of these houses is clear and direct (Sebastian 1992). A devastating drought beginning in A.D. 1130 made continuing intensive occupation untenable. As a result, construction of the Great Houses came to an end and occupation was abandoned. By the time the drought had ended, the Chacoan Network had collapsed and Chaco Canyon never regained its central role.

The link between climate and the rise of Chaco Canyon is more complex than the connection between climate and the end of its occupation. A number of archaeologists have suggested that the Chacoan Network developed as a means of buffering risk in an uncertain environment. Given the low rainfall in the region around Chaco Canyon, there was always a risk of local crop failure. If each group lived in isolation,

TOOLBOX

Dendrochronology

Almost all archaeological dating methods provide a date with a margin of error. Dendrochronology, or tree-ring dating, is the only method capable of absolute precision. Dendrochronologists use the annual rings laid down by trees as they grow to build a clock that today reaches back 10,000 years. How does this clock work? The principles are simple. Each year, as trees grow, they add on a single ring of new wood immediately under the bark. These annual rings are clearly visible in sections cut through a tree trunk. As the rings accumulate, they form a pattern that we can think of as the tree's fingerprint.

The ring pattern of a tree is a record of the fluctuating climatic conditions experienced as it grew. Within the same climatic region, trees of the same species experience similar growth conditions. This uniformity allows dendrochronologists to match up the ring patterns from different trees. Ultimately, by overlapping the ring patterns of trees stretching back in time, it is possible to build up a long-term chronology. The first tree used is a living one, anchoring the chronology in the present. The beginning of the growth of this tree might overlap with a beam found in a historic house, allowing the chronology to be pushed back. This historic beam might be found to overlap with the ring pattern of a tree recovered from an ancient bog, pushing the chronology still further back in time. Once a chronology has been built up, any new piece of wood can be precisely dated by finding the closest match between its ring pattern and the fluctuating pattern found in the long-term chronology.

Dendrochronology has played a critical role in dating the prehistory of the American Southwest. The method has also provided the essential scale for calibrating radiocarbon dates. Although dendrochronology does achieve absolute precision, this does not mean that archaeologists do not need to be very careful in using the data obtained.

The ring pattern of a tree can be fit into a long-term chronology to anchor its growth and death precisely in time. However, archaeologists need to be certain that the wood from the tree was used soon after its death. If, for example, wood was salvaged from an old building, the dates provided by dendrochronologists could be far older than the date of the archaeological occupation. As with all dating methods, knowledge of the context in which the sample is found is critical. ●

REFERENCE: M.G.L. Baillie. (1995). *A Slice Through Time: Dendrochronology and Precision Dating.* London: Batsford.

FIGURE 10.21
Dendrochronologist measuring tree rings in the cross-section of the trunk of a Douglas fir.

then crop failure would lead to starvation. However, if groups were linked through a network in which exchange regularly took place, any group that experienced a failure of its crops could trade for food with other members of the network whose crops had not failed. The existence of a network for the redistribution of food and other goods thus acted as a buffer between the uncertain environment and local communities.

Lynne Sebastian (1992) has argued that this explanation for the rise of Chaco Canyon is wrong. She points out that the Great Houses were built during a period with relatively high rainfall. Why would a buffering mechanism develop when climate pressures were reduced? As an alternative, Sebastian suggests that during the periods beginning around A.D. 1000, there was an increase in annual rainfall, which allowed for an agricultural surplus. The accumulation of surpluses in the hands of local elites led to a cycle of competition. The elaborate construction at Pueblo Bonito and the concentration of rare trade goods such as turquoise and jet are expressions of this competition. For Sebastian, it is the existence of an agricultural surplus, rather than the threat of agricultural failure, that led to the spectacular developments in Chaco Canyon.

■ Summing Up the Evidence

The Great Houses of Chaco Canyon were the hub of an extensive Chacoan Network. Whether this network was a buffer against stress or the result of surplus production remains the subject of debate. Excavations at Pueblo Bonito have demonstrated that there was a considerable concentration of wealth in the hands of an elite. This wealth included trade goods drawn from a very large area. At the same time, excavations indicate that the Great Houses were not densely settled towns, but rather ceremonial centres that were probably permanently occupied only by a small group. Given the effort expended in the construction of the Great Houses, the concentration of wealth in burials, and the evidence for the influx of goods to Chaco Canyon from the Chacoan Network, it is clear that the leaders of this society were extremely powerful. However, there is no evidence that their power rested on the monopolization of force. One possibility is that the power of the leaders flowed from the centrality of Chaco Canyon in ritual and ceremony.

10.4 Cahokia

Two hundred years ago, while travelling along the Mississippi River near what is now St. Louis, Missouri, the explorer Henry Brackenridge encountered the great mound at **Cahokia** and was led to exclaim, "What a stupendous pile of earth!" (Brackenridge 1814). The principal mound at Cahokia is spectacular. **Monk's Mound**, as it has come to be known, rises over 30 metres high in a series of four terraces, covers an area of more than 60,000 square metres, and contains over 600,000 cubic metres of earth (see Figure 10.22).

▲▲ Cahokia A large settlement dating to the Mississippian Period located just outside of St. Louis, Missouri.

Monk's Mound A massive earthen pyramid occupying the core of the ancient settlement of Cahokia.

FIGURE 10.22 Aerial view looking from the back of Monk's Mound, Cahokia, across the Grand Plaza.

Exploring the area around Cahokia, Brackenridge found that the "great number of mounds, and the astonishing quantity of human bones . . . announce that this valley was at one period filled with habitations and villages" (Brackenridge 1814, 271). The site at Cahokia is the largest known settlement of the Mississippian Period in eastern North America (A.D. 1000 to A.D. 1400). Archaeologists now understand Monk's Mound to be the centre of an enormous site covering roughly 4.5 kilometres. At a very brisk pace, it takes about an hour to walk across the site.

Grand Plaza An artificially cleared and levelled area at the core of Cahokia located just to the south of Monk's Mound.

■ The Layout of the Site

Cahokia is located in the floodplain of the Mississippi River near St. Louis. This area, known as the American Bottom, is rich in meandering stream channels, wetlands, and swamps. Monk's Mound is located to the south of Cahokia Creek, forming the northern limit of a large flat area known as the **Grand Plaza**, which was cleared and levelled to create an open area at the core of the site. Smaller mounds bound the eastern, southern, and western edges of the Grand Plaza (see Figure 10.23). Both geophysical survey and excavation have demonstrated that a wooden wall known as a palisade surrounded the Grand Plaza and mounds.

The settlement at Cahokia consisted of a series of small clusters, with the Grand Plaza and the mounds of "Downtown Cahokia" at the centre. It is likely that swamps and wetlands broke up the landscape. Unfortunately, the size of the site and the poor preservation of domestic structures make it difficult to determine the density and distribution of houses. As a result, estimates of the population of Cahokia range anywhere from 4,000 to 40,000 (Milner 1998). Although Cahokia was a large population centre, it is not clear that the term city or metropolis accurately describes it. More likely, the site was a series of dispersed living areas centred on the monumental core of Monk's Mound and the Grand Plaza.

■ Evidence of Inequality

Understanding the political organization of Cahokia poses an enormous challenge. Clearly, there was some mechanism in society that made it possible to construct a mound on a scale unparalleled anywhere else in eastern North America. Just as clearly,

FIGURE 10.23 Map of Cahokia.

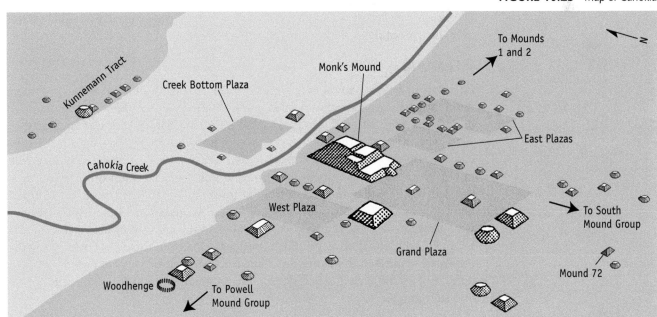

FIGURE 10.24 The main burial at Mound 72 at Cahokia, laid out on a bed of 20,000 shell beads in the shape of a bird.

Mound 72 A mound at Cahokia where excavation uncovered an individual buried on a bird-shaped platform made of shells, as well as mass burials of apparently sacrificial victims.

a large number of people, whether in the thousands or tens of thousands, lived at the site. For some archaeologists, Cahokia was a chiefdom on the verge of becoming a state (Young and Fowler 2000). From this perspective, Cahokia's elite ruled not only over the site itself, but also over the surrounding settlements in the American Bottom (Pauketat 2004). Others argue that Cahokia's elite were simply the most powerful among many competing chiefdoms and that their power was limited.

The most vivid evidence of social inequality within Cahokia society comes from the excavation of **Mound 72**, located to the south of "Downtown Cahokia." Mound 72 is relatively unimpressive; what brought it to the attention of archaeologists is the fact that it is aligned directly with the western edge of Monk's Mound. Students excavating the mound were surprised to come across a cache of hundreds of complete arrowheads (Young and Fowler 2000). As they continued excavating, they found that the arrowheads were part of an elaborate burial complex. The central figure was a man laid face up on a bird-shaped platform made of over 20,000 cut shell beads (see Figure 10.24). A number of other people were buried alongside this individual, together with a rich array of goods, including hundreds of arrowheads and polished granite discs. Other discoveries at Mound 72 suggest the possibility that victims were killed to accompany the main burial. In one area, the bodies of four men were laid out with their arms overlapping those of the others. All four skeletons were missing their heads and hands. In a nearby pit, the skeletons of over fifty young women were found. The discoveries made at Mound 72 indicate that wealth was concentrated in the hands of a small number of people within the community living at Cahokia. Twenty thousand shell beads and hundreds of arrowheads represent an enormous amount of skilled workmanship. The mass burials of young women and the series of headless and handless buried males raise the possibility that the elite of Cahokia had control not only over material wealth, but also over the lives of their subjects.

■ Feasting

Excavations below Mound 51, located to the east of the Grand Plaza, provide a different perspective on the social life of Cahokia that complements the dramatic discoveries from Mound 72 (Pauketat et al. 2002). Mound 51 was excavated in 1961 when it was in the process of being destroyed by residents of a nearby subdivision. Below the mound, archaeologists found a well-stratified sequence rich in botanical and faunal remains and pottery. This material is not ordinary residential debris, but rather the refuse from large-scale feasting that took place in the Grand Plaza. The quantity of material found suggests that these feasting events were massive. The excavators have extrapolated the amount of material in the pit by multiplying the density of objects per cubic metre in the excavated unit by the estimated volume of the entire pit. They calculate that there were over 18,000 ceramic vessels, more than 5,000 deer, and over a half-million tobacco seeds within one stratigraphic zone.

The excavations below Mound 51 indicate that the Grand Plaza at Cahokia was the site of massive feasting events. The number of people who could have fit within the palisades has been estimated at 30,000 (Dalan 2003). The Grand Plaza appears to have served as the site of communal feasts involving people from Cahokia and the surrounding region. If so, the power of the elite of Cahokia might have stemmed from their ability to organize large numbers of people through feasting events rather than through a bureaucracy exercising the threat of force. One interesting possibility is that the Grand Plaza served as the setting for sporting events. The polished granite discs found in Mound 72 fit with ethnographic descriptions of a game known as chunkey, played with discs that were rolled along a line and struck with thrown spears (Young and Fowler 2000).

Two discoveries in the Mound 51 excavations cast light on the religious system of Cahokia. The most common bird bones were those of swan and prairie chickens. Both species are rarely found in excavations of sites contemporary with Cahokia. In Mound 72, the burial of the main individual on a shell platform in the shape of a bird also suggests that birds had particular significance in Cahokia society. This interpretation is supported by the discovery, during excavations in Monk's Mound, of a small sandstone plaque depicting a birdman, shown in Figure 10.25.

The excavations at Mound 51 also produced a significant amount of red cedar branchlets and cypress wood chips. It has been suggested that both of these types of wood had ritual significance. Large poles of red cedar, including an enigmatic ring of poles known as "woodhenge," were used at Cahokia in special buildings.

FIGURE 10.25 Tablet of the "birdman" found at Cahokia.

■ Summing Up the Evidence

The elites of Cahokia were able to mobilize large numbers of people. The bulk of Monk's Mound and the expanse of the Grand Plaza are evidence of large-scale work parties. The burial goods in Mound 72 are the product of a great deal of effort by skilled artisans. The remains found below Mound 51 indicate that there were feasting events in the Grand Plaza involving thousands or even tens of thousands of people. The political force that made this organization possible remains unclear. Was it the "soft power" of the chief, or did the elites of Cahokia also have recourse to the controlled use of force that characterizes the state? Many archaeologists see Cahokia as a society on the verge of forming a state. Unlike the societies that built Stonehenge and Pueblo Bonito, the people who built the monuments at Cahokia lived in a large, densely populated centre. The sacrificial victims in Mound 72 also seem to indicate a degree of power that goes a long way toward the kind of authority found in the hands of the rulers of state societies.

10.5 Great Zimbabwe

When early European explorers visited **Great Zimbabwe**, they were convinced that they had found the palace of the Queen of Sheba. It has taken decades of archaeological research to firmly discredit such fantasies that "sustain a 'colonial' interest in denying the local people a claim in their history" (Pikirayi 2001, 24). Great Zimbabwe is now understood as evidence of local development of political complexity in southeast Africa during the period between A.D. 1300 and A.D. 1450 (see Figure 10.26).

▲▲ **Great Zimbabwe** A large settlement in modern Zimbabwe that includes the remains of impressive stone enclosures and was built between A.D. 1300 and A.D. 1400.

FIGURE 10.26 View of Great
Zimbabwe from the Hill Complex
across to the Great Enclosure.

FIGURE 10.27 One of the bird
sculptures from Great Zimbabwe.

dhaka A mixture of clay and gravel
that was used for building huts
at Great Zimbabwe.

■ The Layout of the Site

Great Zimbabwe is located in the modern state of Zimbabwe. The region around
Great Zimbabwe is agriculturally productive and capable of supporting large herds
of cattle. Great Zimbabwe also sits within an area rich in mineral resources, particularly gold.

The architecture of Great Zimbabwe consists of large enclosures surrounded by
walls standing up to 10 metres high, built of carefully dressed granite blocks. Circular huts built of a mixture of clay and gravel known as **dhaka** were constructed inside the enclosures. Unfortunately, early excavations at the site focused on the search
for evidence of the supposed foreign origin of the builders, resulting in the destruction of much of the archaeological sequence of the dhaka structures built within the
enclosures. Careful excavations of some of the remaining deposits have shown that
the structures were frequently rebuilt, leading to the rapid buildup of deposits that
reach a depth of 5 metres.

Great Zimbabwe stretches across two hills and an intervening valley. The earliest occupation of the site was on the northern hill, known as the Hill Complex,
which consists of a large enclosure on the western end and a series of smaller enclosures to the east. The western enclosure is roughly 50 metres across. It is estimated
that there was space for around twenty dhaka huts within the enclosure. The eastern enclosure in the Hill Complex appears to have had a ritual function. A series of
tall, monolithic stones carved with the figures of birds and crocodiles was found in
this area (see Figure 10.27).

When the site expanded, a new enclosure, known as the Great Enclosure, was
built on the southern hill. The Great Enclosure is approximately 100 metres across
and could have contained over forty dhaka huts. The most striking architectural
feature of the Great Enclosure is a conical stone tower 5 metres in diameter
and 10 metres in height (see Figure 10.28). Probes into the tower proved that it
is solid.

The enclosures running down the sides of the hills and into the valley are
smaller and more modest in construction than the Hill Complex and the Great
Enclosure. It is estimated that they could each have contained about 10 dhaka huts.

FIGURE 10.28 The tower in the Great Enclosure at Great Zimbabwe. Note that during occupation the enclosure was filled with dhaka huts.

■ The Organization of Great Zimbabwe Society

There is no evidence that the walls of the enclosures at Great Zimbabwe served a defensive function. There is no source of water within the Hill Complex, and there is no sign that the walls were damaged in a conflict. The walls appear to have been built to screen the activities of elites from the view of people outside the enclosure. Moreover the enclosure walls on the Hill Complex and the Great Enclosure would have been visible from a distance. In some cases, this visibility was enhanced by mounting monolithic stones on top of the walls.

Many questions remain to be answered about Great Zimbabwe. As with Cahokia, there is considerable controversy over the size of the population. Low estimates put Great Zimbabwe's population between 1,000 and 2,500 people, while others claim it was between 11,000 and 18,000.

The degree to which the elite of Great Zimbabwe had control over the rest of society and the extent to which they ruled over the surrounding region are unclear. More trade items, including glazed pottery from Iran and China and glass beads from Syria, are found here than at any other site in the region. These artifacts indicate that the elite of Great Zimbabwe played a critical role in the trade networks that stretched from the gold mines of southern Africa as far as China.

The evidence from the site of **Mapungubwe** in northeastern South Africa puts Great Zimbabwe into a broader perspective and suggests that the rise of social complexity in this region was not simply the result of the role of developing trade networks (Huffman 2009). Mapungubwe provides the earliest evidence for the type of large enclosures found at Great Zimbabwe (see Figure 10.30 on page 301). Around A.D. 1220, a large community moved to Mapungubwe from a settlement known as K2, about a kilometre away. By A.D. 1250, these people had begun to build stonewalled enclosures around the elite living quarters, a pattern not found at K2. Archaeological evidence for rain-making rituals is found on sites in the hills around Mapungubwe. The ruler built an enclosure at the top of the hill at Mapungubwe, directly overlying

▲▲ **Mapungubwe** A predecessor to Great Zimbabwe; located in South Africa, it features an elite residence situated within a walled compound.

The Trade in African Antiquities

The systematic looting of archaeological sites in Africa has been described as a "horror in the making" (Schmidt and McIntosh 1996). Nowhere is this problem worse than in Mali, around the ancient urban centre of Jenne-Jeno, where sites are plundered for their terracotta and metal artifacts. The destruction of the cultural heritage of Mali is fuelled by a lucrative market for antiquities in Europe and North America. Collectors are willing to pay very high prices for sculptures and other precious artifacts that serve as marks of prestige and wealth. But for archaeologists, the plunder of archaeological sites results in the irreparable loss of all contextual information. These objects, ripped from their context, lose much of their historical value.

In 1970, UNESCO passed a historic legal convention to stem the illegal trade in antiquities (http://portal.unesco.org/en/ev.php-URL_ID=13039&URL_DO=DO_TOPIC&URL_SECTION=201.html). This convention seeks to bar the import and export of cultural property without authorization from the country of origin. The burden of responsibility for stopping the looting of sites lies not only with local authorities, but also with the governments of countries into which the antiquities are transported.

The scale of the illegal trade in antiquities places a heavy ethical burden of responsibility on archaeologists. Their expertise is often sought out by collectors and dealers who want to authenticate objects in their possession. Archaeologists are tempted to cooperate, not only out of financial self-interest, but also from a desire to see objects that otherwise will disappear into the hands of collectors without documentation. Increasingly, archaeologists have come to understand that it is important to resist this temptation (Schmidt and McIntosh 1996).

Stemming the trade in antiquities is imperative. The antiquities market has developed sophisticated methods for moving artifacts around the world in violation of the UNESCO convention. International policing agencies such as Interpol are increasingly involved in trying to track and recover looted artifacts.

How do archaeologists fit into this complex situation? One part of the answer is that archaeologists must work to raise awareness of cultural heritage as a fundamental human right. ●

REFERENCE: Peter R. Schmidt and Roderick J. McIntosh (Eds.) (1996). *Plundering Africa's Past*. Bloomington, Indiana: Indiana University Press.

FIGURE 10.29 Rare example of a terracotta figurine recovered from controlled archaeological excavations at the site of Jenne-Jeno. Because the provenience of this artifact is known, it provides important information on the chronology and society of Jenne-Jeno. This information is lost for similar artifacts that have been looted from the site.

FIGURE 10.30 The main hill at Mapungubwe where the ruler constructed his enclosure over a site used for rainmaking rituals.

a rain-making location. At the same time the surrounding hills ceased to be used for rain-making ceremonies. It appears that, as the power of the rulers increased, they expropriated the powers of rain-making, becoming ritual as well as political leaders. It is likely that the placement of the Hill Complex at Great Zimbabwe reflects a similar association between the ruler and rain-making.

■ Summing Up the Evidence

Great Zimbabwe emerged as an important node in a far-flung trade network that tied the gold mines of Africa with markets as distant as China. The elite of Great Zimbabwe lived within great enclosures that screened their lives from the rest of society and sent a visible message of their power and standing. By considering the evidence from the site of Mapungubwe it is possible to suggest that there was also a sacred aspect to the power of the rulers of Great Zimbabwe that was associated with rain-making ceremonies.

10.6 Comparative Perspectives

A comparison of the Northwest Coast, Stonehenge, Pueblo Bonito, Cahokia, and Great Zimbabwe brings out the diversity of societies that Fried would define as ranked or stratified and Service would describe as chiefdoms. The Northwest Coast had a highly stratified coastal culture. Stonehenge was built by people who lived in small, dispersed hamlets that have left little archaeological traces. Pueblo Bonito and the other Great Houses in Chaco Canyon were at the core of a settlement network that stretched across a wide region of what is today the American Southwest. Both Cahokia and Great Zimbabwe were large population centres inhabited by thousands, if not tens of thousands.

These case studies also bring out the difficulty of understanding the political organization of non-state complex societies. The prestige of the elites is clear in most cases. At Pueblo Bonito and Cahokia, the burial of individuals with large quantities of goods presents a vivid picture of social inequality. At Great Zimbabwe, the height of the walls of the enclosures projects the power of the elite, as well as their separation from the rest of society. The monumental nature of these four sites also leaves no doubt about the ability of the elites to organize labour on a massive scale. However, the source of the power of the elites remains less clear. The critical question is whether the elites had control based on the use of force or whether they managed society by other means, such as religious authority or the organization of ceremonies and feasting. The enigma of the Northwest Coast, Stonehenge, Pueblo Bonito, Cahokia, and Great Zimbabwe is a not only a question of engineering, but also one of social organization. One ultimately asks how and why a group of people came together to create these structures. In each case, this is a question that will continue to motivate archaeological research well into the future.

SUMMARY

- Ethnographic evidence indicates that there was a social hierarchy within Northwest Coast societies that included three levels of status: nobles, commoners, and slaves.
- Archaeological evidence demonstrates the emergence of inherited status on the Northwest Coast during the Marpole phase, dated to between 2,400 and 1,100 years ago in the Gulf of Georgia
- Stonehenge is located on the Salisbury Plain in southern England. This impressive monument was built up in stages beginning in the Late Neolithic and ending in the Early Bronze Age.
- Stonehenge was part of a landscape marked by many monumental constructions, including earthen mounds and enclosures.
- Excavations at Durrington Walls have uncovered the remains of a settlement near Stonehenge.
- The Amesbury Archer burial provides rare evidence for elite status contemporary with the later stages of the construction of Stonehenge.
- Beginning around A.D. 800, Chaco Canyon, New Mexico, became the centre of a regional network and the site of the construction of multistoried structures known as Great Houses.
- Pueblo Bonito is the largest of the Chaco Canyon Great Houses, with 650 rooms covering almost 2 acres.

- Population estimates for Pueblo Bonito range between 100 and 1,200 people. It is possible that the site's primary function was as a ceremonial centre and that only a small number of people lived there permanently.
- A small number of rooms in Pueblo Bonito have a concentration of high-prestige items.
- Chaco Canyon was connected by roads to a network of sites known as the Chacoan Network, which covered a large part of the Four Corners region of what is today the American Southwest.
- Cahokia is the largest known settlement dating to the Mississippian Period (A.D. 1000 to A.D. 1400) in eastern North America.
- Monk's Mound is a massive structure that lies at the core of Cahokia, overlooking a large open area known as the Grand Plaza.
- Excavations at Cahokia have uncovered evidence of human sacrifice and material wealth in a burial mound, and the remains of large-scale feasting near the Grand Plaza.
- Great Zimbabwe was a large settlement built between A.D. 1300 and A.D. 1450.
- Large enclosures that appear to have housed the elite of Great Zimbabwe are located on hills on the east and west ends of the site. The power of the elite of Great Zimbabwe was derived from their control over long-distance trade routes.

KEY TERMS

Amesbury Archer, 285
bluestones, 283
Cahokia, 294
Chaco Canyon, 288
Chacoan Network, 292
dhaka, 298
Durrington Walls, 285
Grand Plaza, 295
Great Houses, 268
Great Zimbabwe, 297
kivas, 289

labrets, 278
Mapungubwe, 299
Marpole Phase, 278
Monk's Mound, 294
Mound 72, 296
Ozette site, 275
potlatch, 274
Pueblo Bonito, 289
Sarsen Circle, 284
Stonehenge, 282
trilithons, 284

1. What is the archaelogical evidence for the emergence of social inequality on the Northwest Coast?
2. How did Stonehenge fit into the surrounding landscape? Is it associated with a large settlement or other monuments?
3. What similarities and differences are there between Pueblo Bonito and Cahokia?
4. What evidence is there that part of the power of elites in the complex societies discussed in this chapter rested on their control over trade routes? What other sources of power emerge from these case studies?

CANADIAN ARCHAEOLOGISTS

- Aubrey Cannon, professor in the Department of Anthropology at McMaster University, is involved in fisheries archaeology research on the Northwest Coast and Tonga. He also has carried out research on on Victorian gravestones and prehistoric mortuary practices.
  http://www.anthropology.mcmaster.ca/faculty-1/cannona

- Gary Coupland is a professor in the Department of Anthropology at the University of Toronto. His excavations in British Columbia include the site of McNichol Creek. He is the co-author with R.G. Matson of *Prehistory of the Northwest Coast* (Academic Press, 1994).
  http://anthropology.utoronto.ca/people/faculty-1/faculty-profiles/gary-coupland

- Brian Hayden, professor in the Department of Anthropology at Simon Fraser University, is a leading authority in the study of the origins of agriculture and the development of social complexity. He has carried out long-term fieldwork at the site of Keatley Creek in British Columbia. His recent publications include *Shamans, Sorcerers, and Saints: The Prehistory of Religion* (Smithsonian Institution Press, 2003).
  http://www.sfu.ca/archaeology-old/dept/fac_bio/hayden/

- Andrew Martindale, professor in the Department of Anthropology at the University of British Columbia, is an archaeologist working on the Northwest Coast. His recent fieldwork focuses on cultural change among the Tsimshian people of northwestern Canada during the contact era and a multidisciplinary study of the Dundas Islands.
  http://www.anth.ubc.ca/people/anthropology-faculty/andrew-martindale.html

- Marit Munson is a professor in the Department of Anthropology at Trent University. Her research focuses on art and issues of gender, identity, and group relations in the American Southwest. She has published on rock art in the southwest and on the imagery found on Mimbres period pottery.
  http://www.trentu.ca/anthropology/munson.php

- Farid Rahemtulla, professor in the Department of Anthropology at the University of Northern British Columbia, carries out research on the central coast of British Columbia, including investigation of changes in stone tool technology at the site of Namu.
  http://www.unbc.ca/anthropology/faculty.html#FaridRahemtulla

PEARSON
myanthrokit™

Visit **www.myanthrokit.com**, where you will find a variety of tools and resources to enhance your learning, including:
- Practise quizzes with Study Plans
- Videos
- Listening Activities
- And much more!

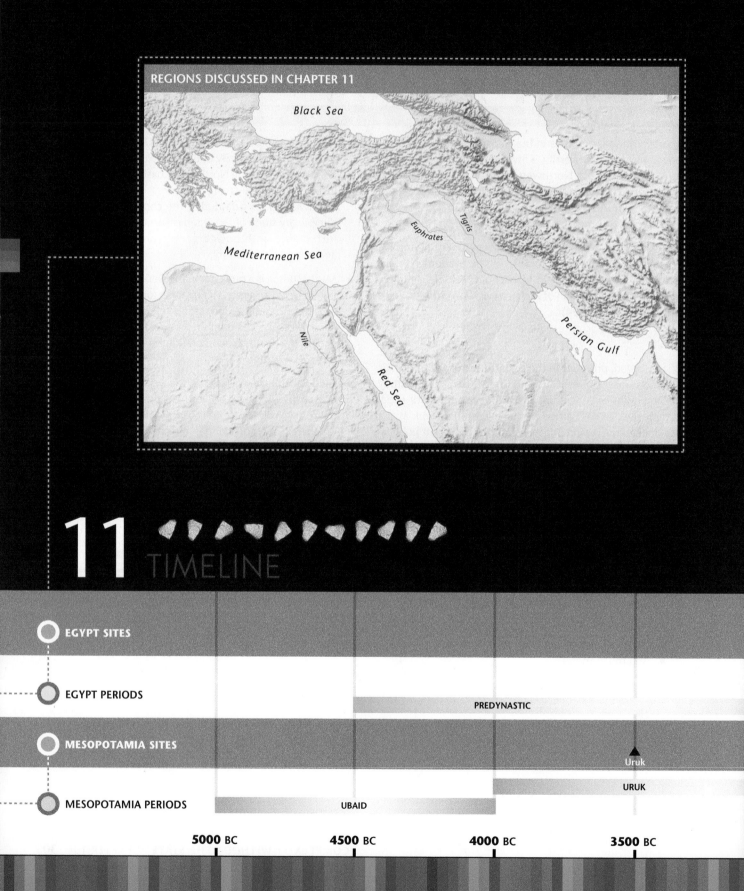

REGIONS DISCUSSED IN CHAPTER 11

Black Sea

Mediterranean Sea

Euphrates

Tigris

Nile

Red Sea

Persian Gulf

11 TIMELINE

EGYPT SITES						
EGYPT PERIODS				PREDYNASTIC		
MESOPOTAMIA SITES						Uruk
MESOPOTAMIA PERIODS			UBAID			URUK

5000 BC **4500** BC **4000** BC **3500** BC

CITIES AND PYRAMIDS:
EARLY STATES OF MESOPOTAMIA AND EGYPT

The early state societies of Mesopotamia and Egypt provide a study in contrasts. In Mesopotamia cities were at the centre of the state, while in Egypt monumental mortuary complexes were critical to the emergence of social complexity. After reading this chapter you should understand:

- The evidence for urbanization in early Mesopotamia.
- The development of royal mortuary complexes in ancient Egypt.
- The nature of bureaucracy and social inequality in both Egypt and Mesopotamia.

Statue of Mycerinus found at Giza.

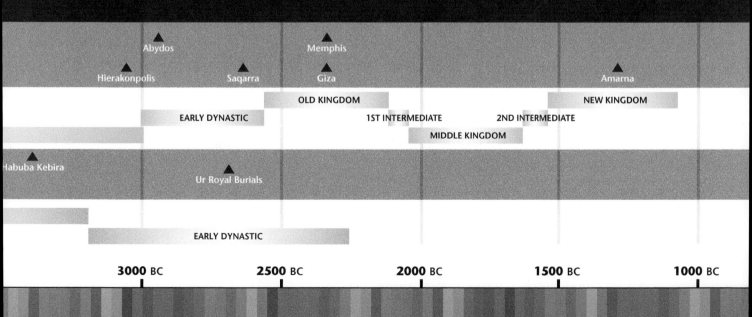

Abydos

Memphis

Hierakonpolis

Saqarra

Giza

Amarna

OLD KINGDOM

NEW KINGDOM

EARLY DYNASTIC

1ST INTERMEDIATE

2ND INTERMEDIATE

MIDDLE KINGDOM

Habuba Kebira

Ur Royal Burials

EARLY DYNASTIC

| 3000 BC | 2500 BC | 2000 BC | 1500 BC | 1000 BC |

FIGURE 11.1 Cuneiform tablet of the *Epic of Gilgamesh*. Although the epic is set in the Uruk period, all known copies come from later contexts. The text was preserved partly because it was used as an exercise for students learning cuneiform writing.

© Copyright The British Museum.

The *Epic of Gilgamesh* is a poem recounting the exploits of the king of the city of Uruk, located in ancient Mesopotamia (see Figure 11.1). Gilgamesh is a partly historical and partly mythical figure whose adventures carry him through a world of both gods and humans. The core of the tale is Gilgamesh's search for the source of eternal life, which is triggered by his grief over the death of his companion, Enkidu. Gilgamesh's quest takes him to Utnapishtim, the survivor of the great flood, who gives him a plant that grants immortality. Gilgamesh tragically loses this plant and is left to struggle with his own mortality. It is telling that in this story the king of a great city is left to struggle with the inevitability of death; Gilgamesh is a human king. The epic is also the story of the friendship between two very different characters. Gilgamesh embodies the power of the city, while Enkidu is a wild man, a man living outside of civilization.

Did Uruk need Gilgamesh? Did Gilgamesh need Uruk? Or did both hero and city emerge as one? Many archaeologists argue that cities require the organization provided by state bureaucracy. In large population centres, roads need planning, laws need enforcement, and violence must be controlled. Some people claim that state bureaucracy developed only in response to the organizational challenges of urban life.

In this chapter, we begin in Gilgamesh's homeland, Mesopotamia, which saw the emergence of the world's first state societies. We then move on to ancient Egypt, where the spectacular mortuary complexes of the pyramids provide the clearest evidence for emerging social complexity. We conclude by briefly considering the archaeological record of early state formation in Africa beyond the Nile Valley, with particular focus on the site of Jenne-Jenno in Mali.

11.1 Mesopotamia

Mesopotamia, meaning the land between the two rivers, covers the region along the course of the Tigris and the Euphrates (see Figure 11.2). The heartland of Mesopotamia is in southern Iraq, where two rivers flow into the Arabian Gulf. However, Mesopotamia also extends to the north into Syria and Turkey and to the east into Iran. Archaeologists working in Mesopotamia have recovered a rich and complex archaeological record, as well as documents that include the earliest written epics and legal systems in the world (Hallo and Simpson 1971). The earliest stages of state formation appear to have been focused in southern Mesopotamia, also known as Sumer.

■ The Physical Setting

The **Tigris and Euphrates rivers** flow through a geological depression formed where the Arabian Shield ploughs into and under the Asian Shield. This powerful geological process has pushed up the Zagros Mountain chain that runs along the eastern edge of the Tigris floodplain. As they flow through the area defined by the geological depression, the Tigris and Euphrates deposit their load of waterborne silts on the valley floor.

▲▲ **Mesopotamia** A region along the course of the Tigris and Euphrates Rivers centred in modern Iraq.

▲▲ **Tigris and Euphrates rivers** Two large rivers that were the focus for the development of Mesopotamian civilization.

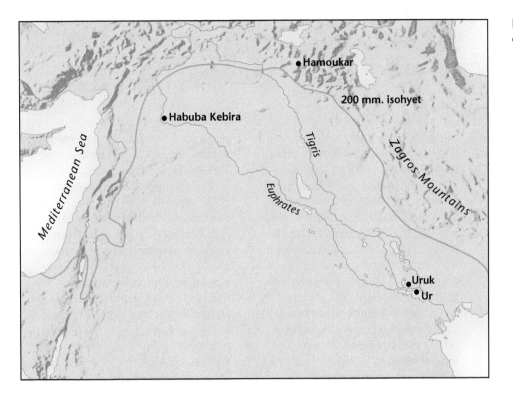

FIGURE 11.2 Map of Mesopotamia.

There are three important consequences of the geological position of Mesopotamia. The first is that many early sites are deeply buried by the deposit of river silts. As a result, little is known about the Paleolithic and Neolithic periods of the Tigris and Euphrates River Valley. The second consequence is that there are no mineral resources in southern Mesopotamia. The only locally available building materials are reeds from marshes and the ubiquitous mud (see Figure 11.3). The third consequence of the geological situation of the Tigris and Euphrates rivers is that the soils of Mesopotamia are extremely fertile. This fertility is in sharp contrast to the desert regions along the western edge of the Euphrates River floodplain.

In southern Mesopotamia, crops can be grown only with irrigation, which draws water from the rivers out onto agricultural fields. Dry farming, which depends on rainfall, is possible only in areas with over 200 mm of rain per year. The 200-mm isohyet (a line on a map that connects areas of equal rainfall) defining the limit of the dry farming region runs through northern Iraq and Syria.

Many of the early cities of southern Mesopotamia today lie in what appears to be a desert wasteland. Archaeological surveys, along with aerial photographs, have shown that when these sites were occupied, they lay either within or at the edges of extensive marshlands. However, as the Euphrates River shifted course, ancient cities were left isolated far from the river channel. The degraded state of the modern landscape

FIGURE 11.3 Photograph of marsh settlements in southern Iraq. The setting of many of the early cities of southern Mesopotamia resembled this marsh.

The Fate of Iraq's Antiquities

The devastation of the Iraq Museum in the days following the U.S.-led invasion of Iraq was a traumatic event. Pictures of looted storerooms and display cases provoked fears that the cultural heritage of Iraq had been irreparably damaged. The exact extent of the loss and the precise sequence of events is still being determined years later. It is likely that the repercussions of this tragedy will shape the field of archaeology for decades to come.

Before trying to assess the implications of the events in Iraq, it is important to give some details about what happened to the Iraq Museum. Press stories have varied enormously and much remains unknown. However, Matthew Bogdanos, the U.S. Marine charged with investigating the events, has presented a useful timeline and parameters of the looting. U.S. forces entered the area around the museum on Tuesday, April 8, 2003, three days after first reaching Baghdad. At that point, the museum became a battleground as Iraqi troops took up positions in it and the staff was forced to leave. With two exceptions, U.S. troops refrained from shelling the museum, and damage from military operations was minimal. The museum staff returned on April 12, and after that time no further looting took place. U.S. forces entered the museum on April 16. The looting appears to have taken place between April 8 and April 12. There were three separate episodes. In the public galleries, forty objects were stolen; the looters were organized and careful in their choices. In the aboveground storage rooms, there was extensive looting, apparently

carried out by a disorganized mob. The number of objects stolen from these storage rooms is hard to calculate but is in the thousands. In the basement, a collection of small valuable objects, including thousands of cylinder seals, were stolen. This appears to have been an inside job, and the objects chosen were both valuable and easy to transport. Close to 10,000 objects were taken from the basement storage.

Colonel Bogdanos, together with Italian and Iraqi colleagues, set up a project that combined amnesty and seizure, resulting in the return of close to 2,000 objects, mostly from the aboveground storage and the gallery. The objects returned include many of the most famous pieces, including the Warka Vase. Sadly, the devastation of Iraq's antiquities goes beyond the

museum: There are extensive reports of large-scale looting of archaeological sites and regional museums.

The events in Iraq highlight the political significance of archaeological remains and force archaeologists to reconsider the degree to which they can sequester themselves from current events. Archaeologists are left with a number of troubling questions. Perhaps the most important is what role archaeologists play in the international antiquities market and how they can help fight against the growing market for illegal objects. Although the looting in Iraq was carried out locally, the devastation of the museum ultimately points to a network of dealers who are able to move antiquities across international borders and into the hands of collectors. ●

FIGURE 11.4 U.S. tank stationed in front of the Baghdad Museum.

is also the result of the farming practices of the early inhabitants of the cities, which caused salt to be concentrated in soils near the surface. As a result of this process of salination, crops can no longer be grown in the fields that once supported great cities.

■ Chronology

Most Paleolithic and Neolithic sites in southern Mesopotamia are inaccessible to archaeologists because they are deeply buried by the accumulation of river silts. The earliest well-represented period in southern Mesopotamia is the Ubaid, between 5000 B.C. and 4000 B.C. The first urban sites appeared in the subsequent **Uruk period**, between 4000 B.C. and 3200 B.C. The Uruk is followed by the **Early Dynastic period**, during which a series of city-states developed in southern Mesopotamia. The rulers of these city-states are known from written documents recovered on archaeological sites. The Early Dynastic period drew to a close when Sargon of Akkad unified southern Mesopotamia under his rule in 2350 B.C.

■ Uruk

The site of **Uruk** in southern Iraq is the oldest known city in the world. It grew from the unification of two towns dating to the Ubaid period built along opposite banks of a channel of the Euphrates River. During the Uruk period, the city grew to cover an area of 2.5 square kilometres and had an estimated population between 20,000 and 40,000 (Nissen 2002). Surveys in the area around Uruk show that the city was by far the largest site in a landscape densely settled with smaller towns and villages.

Excavations at Uruk have focused on the two massive temple precincts located in the centre of the city, where a sequence of temple structures stretching back to the Ubaid period has been uncovered. The city of Uruk grew around these central temple precincts. The temples were built of limestone and bitumen, both of which would have been imported from outside of southern Mesopotamia. Many of the temple structures were built on platforms, evidently the precursor of the stepped pyramid or **ziggurat** that is at the centre of Mesopotamian temple precincts from later periods (see Figure 11.5). The structures were often elaborately decorated. One method of decoration was the use of coloured clay cones inserted into mud brick walls to form a mosaic.

Unfortunately, we know little about the organization of the city of Uruk outside of the temple area. From excavations at other sites, we know that houses were usually built around a central courtyard and were sometimes grouped together into large enclosures (Postgate 1994, 91). It is likely that these were the houses of extended families. Surprisingly, few palace structures have been found from early cities in southern Mesopotamia. Extensive surveys around Uruk have provided some information about the regional setting of this city. On the basis of these surveys, it

Uruk period The period between 4000 and 3200 B.C. during which the first cities in Mesopotamia were developed.

Early Dynastic period The period that follows the Uruk period, during which southern Mesopotamia was home to a series of city states.

▲▲ **Uruk** The oldest known city in the world, located in southern Iraq.

ziggurat Stepped pyramid found in many Mesopotamian temple precincts.

FIGURE 11.5 The ziggurat at Ur. This massive brick structure acted as the support for a temple.

bevel-rim bowls Small undecorated vessels made of coarse clay that are ubiquitous on Uruk-period sites.

appears that the growth of the urban centre took place at the expense of rural villages. By the Early Dynastic period, there was a sharp drop-off in the number of village sites, suggesting that a migration occurred from these to the urban centre.

■ Government

Mesopotamian society revolved around three sources of authority: the temple, the palace, and the city council. The temple was a permanent installation at the heart of the city, and the deity to which the temple was dedicated was a basic element of the city's identity. The temple compounds were quite large; they included land and fulfilled economic functions (see Figure 11.6). Excavations of temple complexes have uncovered the remains of both workshops and storage rooms.

During the Uruk and Early Dynastic periods, the relationship between the palace and the temple was complex and remains poorly understood. It is possible that the chief priest of the temple was the ruler of the city. The duties of the king, or *ensi*, included maintenance of the temple and military leadership of the city. Kingship was not determined strictly by descent, and there is evidence that the king was selected by a city council. Unfortunately, little is known about the powers of this council.

During the Early Dynastic period, there were over thirty independent cities in southern Mesopotamia. Although they cooperated on military and economic ventures, there were also rivalries and not all rulers were equal.

The Code of Hammurabi, which dates to the period around 1800 B.C., is the most extensive of a series of early Mesopotamian legal documents. The laws set out in this code cover a wide range of domains, including penalties for perjury, robbery, and murder; the regulations surrounding adoption, marriage, and the ownership of slaves; and more mundane issues, such as the cost of hiring an ox or an ass. From the Code of Hammurabi, it appears that the king had jurisdiction over the regulation of commercial activities, punishment for violent acts, and aspects of family life.

■ Surplus and Specialization

The growth of the cities of Mesopotamia was based on the production of agricultural surplus. This surplus depended on irrigation agriculture, which required the organization of large work crews to build and maintain canals. Already by the Uruk period, there were people who specialized in various aspects of craft production. One of the most interesting artifacts found on Uruk sites is also one of the most modest. Bevel-rim bowls are small, undecorated vessels made of a very coarse clay fabric (see Figure 11.7). Both complete and broken shards of bevel-rim bowls are found in enormous quantities on Uruk-period sites. It is possible that these bowls were simply the Styrofoam cups of the Uruk period, cheap and easy-to-manufacture containers that were rapidly discarded. However, archaeologists have puzzled over their function and particularly the regularity of their size. Why would such simple vessels be consistently made the same size?

One proposal is that **bevel-rim bowls** were vessels in which grain rations were distributed to workers. The standardized size would then reflect the basic ration for a day of work. If this proposal is correct, it implies that the rulers had tight control over the distribution of agricultural surplus to workers. Some archaeologists have pointed out that the shape of the bowls is not appropriate for carrying around a ration of grain. Imagine thousands of labourers carefully trying to avoid spilling any grain from their bowls as they carried their rations home. An alternative is that these vessels were used as moulds for baking bread. If this is the case, then the bevel-rim

FIGURE 11.6 The Warka vase showing a procession of offerings being brought to the temple.

FIGURE 11.7 A drawing of a bevel-rim bowl, the Styrofoam cup of the Uruk world.

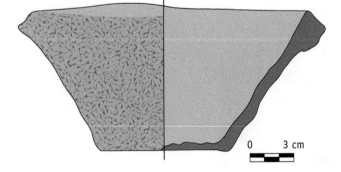

0   3 cm

bowls indicate that baking in the Uruk period was carried out by specialists who produced bread in very large quantities, perhaps to be paid out as a ration for work.

■ Inequality

Mesopotamian society included kings, priests, craft specialists, merchants, labourers, and slaves. There were clear disparities in wealth and privilege among the various members of society. It appears that clothing and hairstyle were often used to mark status. The king in the Uruk period is often shown wearing a flat hat and a netted skirt. Slaves are described as bearing a distinguishing mark known as an *apputum*, which might have been a particular hairstyle.

In the 1920s, Leonard Wooley, shown in Figure 11.8, excavated a cemetery at the site of Ur that provides a vivid picture of the wealth and power of the rulers of an Early Dynastic city (Zettler et al. 1998). The cemetery includes hundreds of burials, most of which are simple interments of individuals with a few pottery vessels. The chambers known as the **Royal Tombs at Ur** present a startling contrast. These tombs contain staggering deposits of wealth, including tools, jewellery, musical instruments, and vessels made from a wide range of metals (gold, silver, copper, and electrum) and precious stones (lapis lazuli, carnelian, steatite, and calcite). These materials were brought to Ur from considerable distances: Lapis lazuli comes from Afghanistan, carnelian from Pakistan. The Royal Tombs are associated with chambers that Wooley called death pits; they contained the skeletons of men and women together with the remains of oxen attached to carts (see Figure 11.9). These people and animals appear to have been slaughtered as part of the burial ritual. Many of the skeletons are still adorned with lavish jewellery and ornaments; many clutch weapons in their hands. Among the most famous objects is the headdress of one of the main figures, which consists of leaves made of thinly hammered gold (see Figure 11.10). Other impressive artifacts include a series of lyres inlayed with elaborate scenes and a sculpture of a ram peering out from behind some branches.

FIGURE 11.8 Photo of Wooley excavating at the site of Ur.

▲▲ **Royal Tombs at Ur** Tombs dating to the Early Dynastic period in which the dead were buried with a spectacular array of precious artifacts and sacrificial victims.

FIGURE 11.9 Reconstruction of the death pit at Ur just before the attendants and animals were killed. ©The Trustees of the British Museum/Art Resource, NY.

FIGURE 11.10 Queen Puabi's
headdress from the Royal Tombs
at Ur.

Queen Puabi's headdress from the Royal Tombs
at Ur, Iraq, Image #150028, reprinted by
permission of University of Pennsylvania
Museum.

It is probable that the rich burial goods and the sacrificial victims found in
the Royal Tombs were meant to accompany the deceased to the afterlife; perhaps
the goods were used to provide offerings to the gods. The woman buried with an
elaborate headdress appears to be a queen by the name of Puabi. Another tomb is
thought to have been the burial chamber of a king.

The Royal Tombs illustrate the wealth concentrated in the hands of the king
and his close family. This wealth included access to large quantities of precious materials imported from a wide geographical region outside of the areas directly controlled by the Mesopotamian state. How did the king come to be the focal point
of such an extensive trade network? One possibility is that he controlled the production of textiles in Mesopotamia. The surplus textiles produced were traded for
the precious material that the king used as the expression of his power.

The king not only controlled the flow of precious materials, but was able to spon-
sor the highly skilled artisans who produced the spectacular objects found in the burials. The sacrificial victims point to another facet of the ruler's power: the ability to
control the life and death of his subjects. It is hard not to conclude from the Ur burials that Mesopotamian rulers had immense power. The riddle remains why so much
wealth was buried with the dead. Such a squandering of resources seems at odds with
the accumulation of power found in Mesopotamian kingship. Why sacrifice not only
people, but also prestigious objects? One possibility is that the destruction of wealth fuelled the continuing effort to accumulate more of it; this effort was the key to the ruler's
power. This power might have been based, not simply on a wealth of goods, but on the

ability to maintain a system of trade, tribute, and specialized craft production that continuously created wealth. While studying the monumental architecture of this time period, Bruce Trigger focused on the role of energy in human society. He argued that in most contexts, human societies are organized to be energetically efficient. However, monumental architecture and the Ur burials flagrantly break this rule. Trigger concluded that "the most basic way that power can be symbolically reinforced is through the conspicuous consumption of energy" (Trigger 1990, 128).

Perhaps it is wrong to look at the Royal Tombs from only an economic perspective. Looking back to the *Epic of Gilgamesh*, we see that despite his power as the ruler of Uruk, Gilgamesh struggled with his own mortality. It seems likely that the elaborate rituals of the Ur Royal Tombs tapped into the same desire for immortality.

FIGURE 11.11 Early cuneiform tablet. The dots and semicircles are numbers, and most individual compartments refer to a quantity of a commodity. The signs are still visibly pictographic, some depicting bowls or jars. Note the compartment in the lower right-hand corner that includes a series of signs with no numbers. What do you think this could refer to?

■ The Development of Writing

The origins of some of the symbols used by Mesopotamian scribes have been traced to clay tokens found on Neolithic sites in the Zagros Mountains. The **cuneiform** writing system in Mesopotamia first developed during the Uruk period (see Figure 11.11). Mesopotamian scribes wrote on clay tablets, using a stylus to impress the signs into the wet clay (Walker 1987). The cuneiform writing system originated as a pictographic script in which each picture represented a term or concept. By the Early Dynastic, the symbols were increasingly stylized and were used to represent syllables. The cuneiform script was used to write in several different languages. During the Uruk and Early Dynastic periods, the main written language was Sumerian. During later periods the cuneiform script was also used to write texts in Akkadian, a Semitic language related to modern Arabic and Hebrew, and Hittite, an Indo-European language.

Mesopotamian scribes also developed elaborate methods for making seals. The seals were carved in hard stone, which could then be pressed onto clay or mud to mark ownership by a person or group. An important function of seals was to ensure that, once closed, a room or vessel remained undisturbed. These early precursors of our tamper-proof lids were frequently applied to clay plugs sealing vessels and closures on doors. **Cylinder seals** first appear in the Uruk period (see Figure 11.12). They were made by carving a scene onto cylinders of stone. The cylinder seal was then rolled

cuneiform A writing system in which signs were impressed in wet clay. Cuneiform was used to write a range of languages, including Sumerian and Akkadian.

cylinder seals One of the methods developed by Mesopotamian scribes to mark ownership.

FIGURE 11.12 Cylinder seal. The original seal is shown on the left. The right side shows the impression produced when the seal is rolled across soft clay.
Picture Desk, Inc./Kobal Collection.

FIGURE 11.13 Bullae are clay envelopes that enclose small tokens like those shown on the right. The surface of the bulla was marked with seals before the clay dried.

across fresh clay or mud, leaving behind an impression. The carving of cylinder seals quickly became a highly developed art. Working on a miniature scale, Mesopotamian seal carvers illustrated vivid scenes from daily life and mythology.

The earliest cuneiform documents were developed to record ownership and economic transactions, not unlike our receipts and contracts. On sites dating to early in the Uruk period, hollow clay balls filled with small clay tokens are found. The surface of the clay balls, known as bullae (singular: *bulla*), is covered with impressions from seals and marks recording numbers (see Figure 11.13). In at least one case, the number on the bulla is known to correspond to the number of tokens in the interior.

Bullae were a concrete method of recording a transaction. Each object is represented by an actual token, and the tokens are enclosed in a clay "envelope" that was then sealed. The earliest written documents, which date to the end of the Uruk period, mirror the function of the bulla, but discard the need for the concrete tokens. If bullae are one level of abstraction from reality—the sealed tokens representing real objects—the earliest written documents take this abstraction one step further to replace the tokens with marks in clay. The development of syllabic script extended the economic functions that texts could fulfill still further. One of the most interesting types of documents from the Early Dynastic period is the kuduru texts that record transactions involving the exchange of land for goods such as bread, oil, beer, cloth, and silver. The kuduru make it clear that land was privately owned in Early Dynastic Mesopotamia and give insight into the relative values of commodities. The economy of early Mesopotamian cities included the wealth of the king and the temple, as well as private wealth. Written documents played an essential role in the operation of this complex system of ownership and exchange.

Over the course of over 2,000 years, the use of the cuneiform writing system was expanded to include texts as varied as epics, histories, dictionaries, and mathematical treatises, as well as letters, treaties, and accounts.

■ Warfare and Expansion

From the wealth and power displayed in the Royal Tombs of Ur, one might assume that early Mesopotamian cities were highly militaristic societies. Archaeology and texts combine to suggest that although warfare between cities was common, the extent of the violence was quite limited. Cities were walled, and the texts often speak of wars between them. Perhaps even more telling are cylinder seals from the Uruk period depicting bound prisoners. However, the tools of war were limited, and the conflicts described in the texts appear to be more a display of power than battles resulting in massive numbers of casualties. The main tools of war were axes, spears, arrows, and carts drawn by asses or oxen. The earliest mention of a standing army comes from the time of Sargon, when there is mention of an army of over 5,000 soldiers. In later periods, the power of the Mesopotamian military expanded significantly, allowing for far-ranging campaigns of conquest in foreign lands.

Given the apparently limited extent of military might during the Uruk and Early Dynastic periods, the discovery of Uruk colonies far from southern Iraq has come as a surprise. The most completely excavated Uruk colony is the site of **Habuba Kebira**, located on the upper reaches of the Euphrates River in northern Syria (see Figure 11.14) (Algaze 1993). Habuba Kebira was occupied only during the Uruk period, and there has been very little subsequent accumulation of sediments. As a result, archaeologists have been able to open up a large horizontal excavation, uncovering an almost complete plan of the settlement. The site of Habuba Kebira is a walled town of densely packed houses running for about half a kilometre along the banks of the Euphrates. All of the artifacts found on the site are made in the styles found in the Uruk heartland in southern Iraq. Bullae with Uruk seal impressions and a temple in classic Uruk style have also been found on the site. There is very little evidence of artifacts made in the styles of the surrounding local communities. Habuba Kebira and similar sites present a challenging enigma. They are clearly evidence of the expansion of people out from the Uruk heartland, but there is no evidence that the expansion was a military one. Some archaeologists have argued that Habuba Kebira was a trading post or a settlement built to protect trade routes for critical mineral resources coming from northern Syria and Turkey. However, it remains unclear whether the people coming from southern Iraq actually dominated and controlled these exchange routes or whether there was a more subtle relationship between the people coming from the southern cities and local groups.

Recent excavations at the site of Hamoukar in Syria, directed by Clemens Reichel, provide some of the first evidence that the Uruk expansion involved violent conflict (see http://oi.uchicago.edu/research/projects/ham/). The main occupation of Hamoukar is contemporary with the Uruk period. But the occupation at Hamoukar is characterized by a local material culture that is clearly distinct from the Uruk material culture of southern Mesopotamia. In Area B, a large structure was found that had been destroyed by fire, and among the artifacts there were several thousand clay sling bullets. Although the identification of these artifacts as weapons was first greeted with skepticism, it is now clear that these are in fact projectiles that were launched from slings. Recent analysis has found that many were squashed on impact, indicating that these were fired before they had fully dried—perhaps to restock spent supplies in the heat of battle. Some of the bullets even bear the imprint of the cloth sling. Reichel envisions a deadly volley of sling bullets which might have been followed by house-to-house combat and the burning of the city.

Ongoing excavation at Hamoukar is continuing to raise new and interesting questions. Expansion in Area B has revealed that the burning was limited to the single large structure. Does this mean that the warfare was localized in its impact, rather than destroying the entire city? Excavation off the side of the mound has identified an occupation that, like Habuba Kebira, is characterized by southern Mesopotamian Uruk material culture. The connection of this Uruk presence and the evidence for warfare goes to the heart of the questions surrounding the Uruk expansion.

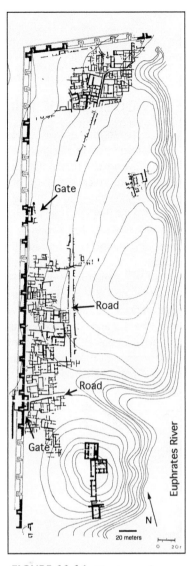

FIGURE 11.14 The town of Habuba Kebira, Syria. The Euphrates runs along the east side of the site; the other sides were fortified by a city wall. Notice the major road running north–south through the site and the crossroad running from the city gate.

▲▲ **Habuba Kebira** An Uruk colony located on the upper reaches of the Euphrates River in northern Syria.

▲▲ **Hamoukar** A site in northern Syria that has produced evidence of violent conflict that might relate to the Uruk expansion.

3D Modelling of Tell 'Acharneh, Syria

Archaeologists usually choose between focusing on either plan views showing the horizontal aspect of their excavation or drawings of stratigraphic profiles showing its vertical aspect (see p. 16). Michel Fortin, an archaeologist at Laval University, has begun to experiment with methods of representing the excavation of an archaeological site as a virtual three-dimensional model. Fortin is excavating the site of Tell 'Acharneh, a large artificial mound located in western Syria. The size and complexity of this site, with archaeological levels covering over 4,000 years of occupation, from the Early Bronze Age to the Crusaders and the Ottoman Period, make it an ideal candidate for 3D modelling. For this project, Fortin has collaborated with colleagues from the Department of Geomatics at Laval University. The process begins in the field, where spatial data on features is captured using a high-precision GPS surveying system. The challenge is to find a way to treat the masses of data collected in the field. Fortin's solution is to bring together two different types of software—GIS software used to treat large quantities of spatial data (see p. 10) and CAD software often used by architects to create three-dimensional models of buildings.

The initial results of the experiments at Tell 'Acharneh are very promising. The software produces highly accurate representations of archaeological features that compare well to field photographs. The resulting models allow archaeologists to examine the relationship between depositional units in three dimensions and gain a clear understanding of the relationships between them. In the long term, these methods promise to facilitate both the planning of excavations and the interpretation of results. It is even possible that these experiments will lead to new methods for publishing the results of excavations. ◆

REFERENCE: L.-M. Losier, J. Pouliot, and M. Fortin. (2007). 3D geometrical modeling of excavation units at the archaeological site of Tell 'Acharneh (Syria). *Journal of Archaeological Science* 34: 272–288.

■ Summing Up the Evidence

The development of state societies in southern Mesopotamia is closely linked with the emergence of large urban centres. The Royal Tombs at Ur give a sense of the extensive power of the ruler of the early Mesopotamian cities. The rapid expansion of Uruk-period settlements into northern Mesopotamia provides an indication of the dynamism of these early cities. Much of the power of the cities and their rulers can be linked to economic factors, the organization of large-scale irrigation systems, and the control of surplus production of textiles. The development of the cuneiform writing system served the need of this economy to control and regulate trade and ownership. However, the growth of the Mesopotamian cities was not simply the product of economic forces. In fact, the core around which the city grew was not the palace, but the temple precinct. Still, in ancient Mesopotamia the boundary between the temple and the palace is difficult to draw. Ultimately, the strength of the early Mesopotamian state seems to flow from a blending of the power of the temple and that of the palace.

11.2 Egypt

The splendor of the temples and tombs of ancient Egypt have long evoked wonder and mystery. Some people have even been led to mystical interpretations of ancient Egypt, seeing monuments such as the pyramids at Giza as evidence of supernatural or extraterrestrial activity. Archaeological research has uncovered a very different perspective. As scientists unearth potsherds and domestic remains and trace the processes by which monuments were constructed, a picture of the intensely human aspect emerges. Ancient Egypt is not the product of otherworldly forces. The monuments that amaze us are the result of human effort and imagination on an enormous scale. Perhaps the most awesome feature of the pyramids is not their sheer size, but

FIGURE 11.15 Map of Egypt.

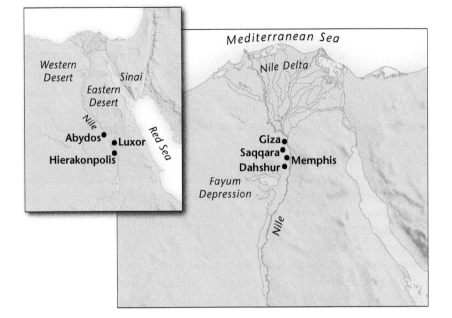

rather the chisel marks left on the stones over 4,000 years ago. These marks open up the real mysteries of the pyramids: How were people motivated to undertake such a venture? How were they organized? How were they fed? These questions lead to the core of the issues surrounding the origin of the state.

■ The Setting

The Nile descends out of the highlands of Ethiopia to cut a dramatic swath through the deserts of the Sudan and Egypt (see Figure 11.15). Until the construction of the Aswan Dam in the 1960s, the annual flooding of the Nile deposited rich alluvial silts across the valley floor. The contrast between the lush vegetation of the **Nile Valley** and the surrounding desert is stark (see Figure 11.16). One can

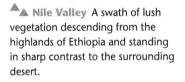 **▲ Nile Valley** A swath of lush vegetation descending from the highlands of Ethiopia and standing in sharp contrast to the surrounding desert.

FIGURE 11.16 The lush Nile Valley contrasts sharply with the surrounding desert.

FIGURE 11.17 The Narmer Palette shows Narmer wearing the crowns of Upper and Lower Egypt. How is the power of Narmer shown through this artifact?

▲▲ **Upper Egypt** The southern Egyptian Nile River Valley ending in a series of cataracts, or rapids, in the area around the modern border between Egypt and Sudan.

▲▲ **Lower Egypt** The northern part of the Egyptian Nile River Valley, including the Nile Delta.

Narmer Palette Artifact discovered at the site of the Hierakonpolis; its two sides show the unification of Upper and Lower Egypt under King Narmer.

literally place one foot in agricultural fields and the other in desert sand. Egypt is thus an extreme case of circumscription in which the limits of inhabitable land are clearly defined.

Egypt is divided into **Upper Egypt** in the south and **Lower Egypt** in the north. To the north of Cairo, the Nile Valley spreads into several branches, forming the Delta region as it flows toward the Mediterranean Sea. To the south, the limit of Upper Egypt is defined by a series of cataracts or rapids in the area around the modern border between Egypt and Sudan. Aside from the Nile Valley and the Delta, the major inhabitable areas in Egypt are a number of small oases in the Western Desert and the Fayum Depression located just south of Cairo.

The unusual geography of Egypt played a major role in defining the nature of ancient Egyptian society. Because the area was protected by deserts to the east and west and cataracts to the south, the threat of foreign invasion was minor. Almost all human settlement was located along the Nile Valley. The Nile served as a means of transportation, allowing for the easy movement of people and goods north and south along the river. The annual flooding of the Nile served to replenish the soil, so the problems of salination found in southern Mesopotamia are not endemic to Egypt. The richness of the flood also meant that massive irrigation projects were not necessary. The Nile Valley, like Mesopotamia, is completely lacking in mineral resources. However, the surrounding deserts contain sources of metals, including copper and gold, and building materials—including limestone, alabaster, and granite—that the Egyptians exploited heavily.

■ Chronology

The shift toward state society in Egypt began during the Predynastic period, whose political organization remains poorly understood. However, it appears that by the late Predynastic period three kingdoms had formed along the Nile Valley. The earliest evidence for the unification of Egypt under a single ruler is a slab of carved slate known as the **Narmer Palette**, discovered at the site of Hierakonpolis in Upper Egypt.

The Narmer Palette shows scenes of conquest by a king named Narmer (see Figure 11.17). The rule of Narmer marks the end of the Predynastic period and the beginning of the Early Dynastic. Significantly, on one side of the palette Narmer is shown wearing the white conical crown of Upper Egypt, while on the other he is shown wearing the red crown of Lower Egypt. The depiction of Narmer with these two crowns indicates that he ruled the entire Nile Valley.

The chronology of Egyptian kings is known from documents and monuments. The classical historian Manetho (300 B.C.) devised the system of grouping kings into dynasties. Egyptian dynastic history, outlined in Figure 11.18, can be divided into three cycles of integration and collapse (Hallo and Simpson 1971). During periods of integration (Early Dynastic/Old Kingdom, Middle Kingdom, New Kingdom), Egypt was controlled by a single centralized authority. During periods of collapse (First Intermediate, Second Intermediate, Third Intermediate), competing centres of authority emerged and competing dynasties, with control over only a part of the country, ruled simultaneously.

A constant dynamic in Egyptian dynastic history is a struggle for dominance between Upper and Lower Egypt. The **First Dynasty** was based in **Hierakonpolis** and **Abydos** in Upper Egypt. In the Second Dynasty the site of the royal cemetery shifted to Saqqara in Lower Egypt. During the Old Kingdom, kingship was firmly

PERIOD	DATES	DYNASTY	MAJOR SITES
Predynastic	4500 B.C.–3000 B.C.		
Early Dynastic	3000 B.C.–2575 B.C.	1–3	Hierakonpolis, Abydos, Saqqara
Old Kingdom	2575 B.C.–2134 B.C.	4–8	Giza, Memphis
First Intermediate	2134 B.C.–2040 B.C.	9–11	
Middle Kingdom	2040 B.C.–1640 B.C.	12–14	
Second Intermediate	1640 B.C.–1532 B.C.	15–17	
New Kingdom	1532 B.C.–1070 B.C.	18–20	Thebes, Amarna
Third Intermediate	1070 B.C.–712 B.C.	21–25	

FIGURE 11.18 Chronology of ancient Egypt.

Source: Lehner 1997.

established at Memphis in Lower Egypt. In the New Kingdom, the centre of power shifted to Luxor in Upper Egypt.

Although Egypt was relatively well protected from foreign invasion, incursions from the north and south did take place, particularly during the periods of collapse. During the Middle and New Kingdoms, Egypt embarked on ambitious military campaigns in the north, ultimately coming into conflict with Mesopotamian powers. During those same kingdoms, Egypt also came to play an active role in trade networks connecting the lands of the eastern Mediterranean and the Aegean.

■ Government and Writing

The ultimate source of the power of the Egyptian king was his identification as a divinity. The king in Egypt was the human incarnation of the falcon god Horus, the paramount god in the Egyptian pantheon. Upon his death, the king became the incarnation of the god Osiris, the god of the dead. The king also had a special relationship to the sun god Ra; however, the way this relationship was expressed varies among documents.

The power of the king was tightly linked to the critical Egyptian concept of *ma'at*, which combines the virtues of balance and justice. In Egyptian thought, chaos and disorder were viewed as catastrophic, and the role of the king was to ensure the preservation of *ma'at*. The breakdown of centralized rule during periods of collapse is described in Egyptian documents as a calamity. Katja Goebs has pointed out that for the Egyptians the concept of *ma'at* also had a cosmic dimension (Goebs 2009). The king was seen as fighting off *isfet*, the force of chaos embodied by the snake-demon Apophis, which threatened the equilibrium of the cosmos.

It is quite a distance from the lofty concepts of divine kingship and *ma'at* to the more mundane business of organizing a large kingdom. It is clear, for example, that the divine status of the ruler did not prevent palace intrigue and, in some cases, even murder. The king controlled the state through the agency of armies of scribes (Kemp 1991). During the harvesting and processing of cereals, scribes intervened at every stage to measure output and deter theft. The yield of the harvest was measured in the field, during transport, and at delivery. The quantities of bread and beer produced from grain were carefully measured before being distributed as rations.

First Dynasty The dynasty based in Hierakonpolis and Abydos in Upper Egypt.

▲▲ **Hierakonpolis** Along with Abydos, one of the two centres of Egypt during the late Predynastic period and the First Dynasty.

▲▲ **Abydos** The site of the royal cemetery of Egypt during the First and Second Dynasties.

ma'at A concept that combines the virtues of balance and justice; it was of central importance to Egyptian society.

A picture of the role of the scribe is found on the bottom register of a scene painted in an Old Kingdom tomb from Saqqara. Egyptian tombs were often painted with detailed depictions of daily life meant to magically provide for the deceased in the afterlife. The Tomb of Ty at Saqqara gives particularly detailed pictures of a bakery/brewery. In the bottom register, a line of scribes is shown at work. Scribes are depicted as an integral element of the operation of a bakery (see Figure 11.19). An individual to the left of the scene depicted here is shown being brought to the scribes for discipline.

There is a clear sense that in ancient Egypt the extended family remained an essential social unit. Some even go as far as to suggest that the conception of kingship was based on an extension of the household. A study of graffiti left by workers on blocks in the Giza pyramids affords a unique insight into the organization of labour in the Old Kingdom (Roth 1991). Workers were organized into large labour groups, perhaps by clan or extended family. This evidence challenges the idea that the state represents a rupture with social organization based on kinship.

The Egyptian bureaucracy often operated by breaking tasks into equivalent parts. This practice is preserved in an unfinished chamber located below the pyramid of Cheops at Giza. The chamber is reached by descending a long passageway that stretches deep below bedrock. For reasons that are not clear, this chamber was abandoned in the midst of quarrying and was never completed. Walking around, one can follow the hammer blows of the workers as they laboured to hollow out the subterranean room. One can see that the chamber has been divided in half and then in half again, with two sets of two teams working in parallel. This simple organizational tactic appears to have been widely used by Egyptians to organize large-scale construction projects.

The hieroglyphic writing used by Egyptian scribes is based on a combination of logograms (signs that represent a whole word), phonograms (signs that represent sounds), and determinatives (signs that indicate the exact meaning of a word). Documents were written in ink on paper made of papyrus, a reed native to the

Nile Valley. Unfortunately, few of these documents survive from early periods. Because hieroglyphics were not suited for rapid writing of administrative documents, an alternative script, known as hieratic, was developed by the Fourth Dynasty. Hieroglyphics remained in use primarily for inscribing monuments.

■ The Pyramids

The pyramids of Old Kingdom Egypt are among the most impressive monuments ever built. These spectacular structures were constructed on the desert fringe far from major settlements. The pyramids were temples to the deceased king, who was the incarnation of the god Osiris. Veneration of the king required both the preservation of his corpse and provision for his needs in the afterlife. The mortuary temples of Egypt were not the core around which the city developed, but were rather a distinct centre of power.

THE DEVELOPMENT OF MORTUARY ARCHITECTURE. The development of royal mortuary architecture in Egypt has its roots in the Predynastic period. By the Early Dynastic period, elaborate royal burial structures were built at the site of Abydos. The first pyramid was the stepped pyramid at Saqqara, built in the Third Dynasty. This structure was soon followed by the construction of true pyramids, culminating in the Great Pyramid at Giza.

Hierakonpolis and Abydos. The earliest structure identified as a royal tomb is Tomb 100 from the site of Hierakonpolis, which dates to the end of the Predynastic period. Tomb 100 is a mud-brick structure with crude wall paintings that include depictions of a figure smiting an enemy. It is interesting that the wall paintings of Tomb 100 include depictions of two boats, possibly reflecting the beliefs that led later kings to bury boats next to their tombs (see Figure 11.22).

During the First and Second Dynasty, the royal burial ground moved to the desert cemetery of Abydos (Kemp 1991). The tombs at Abydos are simple brick chambers built into pits dug into the ground. Above the burial chamber, a square mud-brick enclosure was erected and then filled in with earth and gravel. A pair of stone markers inscribed with the name of the king was placed in front of the tomb, and a separate small temple was built close to the valley floor. Recent excavations of the burial enclosures related to King Aha at Abydos have made some surprising discoveries. The burial enclosure appears to have been purposefully destroyed shortly after construction. Outside the enclosure, a number of subsidiary burials have been excavated that appear to provide evidence of human and animal sacrifice to accompany the deceased king to the afterlife (O'Connor 2009). Archaeologists have also recently uncovered an enigmatic fleet of buried boats at Abydos.

Saqqara and Dahshur. By the Third Dynasty, the royal burial site had shifted to **Saqqara**, located outside of Cairo. The first pyramid is the stepped pyramid constructed by **King Djoser** of the Third Dynasty (Lehner 1997). At Saqqara, an enclosure wall surrounds a large open-air courtyard in the middle of which stands the stepped pyramid (see Figure 11.23). The royal tomb is located in a granite vault in an elaborate network of chambers branching off from a central shaft below the pyramid. The pyramid itself was built in a series of stages. It appears to have been originally conceived as a simple, if massive, filled enclosure like those found at Abydos. Only after building was underway did the project evolve into the construction of a pyramid.

Three engravings found in the Djoser complex depict the Sed festival, an event during which the king would run a course in an important ritual of renewal. The

▲▲ **Saqqara** The location of the stepped pyramid, the earliest pyramid constructed in Egypt. In later periods, Saqqara continued to be used as a sacred burial area.

King Djoser The Third Dynasty Egyptian king who constructed the first pyramid, located at Saqqara.

TOOLBOX

Tracking Trade Routes

Tracking trade routes is essential to understanding how politically complex societies interact with their neighbours. Archaeologists can trace trade routes on the basis of the physical properties of artifacts. For example, on Egyptian sites dating to the New Kingdom, pottery vessels from Cyprus and the Aegean can easily be identified on the basis of their distinctive shape and surface finish. However, in many cases it is necessary to employ more complex methods to identify the source of archaeological artifacts.

For objects made of clay, petrographic analysis is often used to identify the place where the artifact was produced. Petrography is a branch of geology that focuses on the identification of minerals and rocks on the basis of their physical properties. Archaeological petrographers identify the minerals that have been added to clay during its manufacture. Petrographic analysis involves taking a very thin slice from a piece of pottery and polishing it until it is so thin that light can travel through it. This thin section is then studied under a petrographic microscope, which allows light to pass through the sample. By combining evidence of size, colour, and the way light is refracted through the thin section, the petrographer can identify the mineral component of the pottery vessel. By referring the mineral composition of the specimen to geological maps, he or she will often be able to determine where a pot was manufactured.

Petrographic analysis has been applied to the study of diplomatic letters discovered in the New Kingdom Egyptian city of Amarna (Goren et al. 2004). Although found in Egypt, these documents were written on clay tablets in Akkadian, the language of Mesopotamia, using cuneiform script. During the New Kingdom, cuneiform was used as the medium for diplomatic

FIGURE 11.20
One of the Amarna letters. Although written in cuneiform, these are letters between the Egyptian ruler and vassal states to the north.
Picture Desk, Inc./Kobal Collection. The Art Archive/Musée du Louvre/Dagli orti.

king's performance was essential to maintaining order in the world. The architecture of the Djoser complex actually replicates in stone the course that the living king would have run during the Sed festival. It is notable that because of the high enclosure walls, this symbolic ritual ground was hidden from view. Although the portion of the stepped pyramid visible beyond the enclosure would have been impressive, the fundamental characteristic of the Djoser pyramid complex is that it encloses and hides sacred space.

The first true pyramid was built by King Snefru of the Fourth Dynasty at the site of Dahshur, just south of Saqqara. Snefru actually attempted this construction three times before succeeding in building a true pyramid. The first attempt, at the site of Meidum, appears to have collapsed during construction. Snefru then moved to Dahshur, where

communication. The letters are from neighbouring kings seeking alliances with Egypt. Unfortunately, some information about the geographical location of the kings sending the letters is unclear. A petrographic analysis project treated these tablets as clay artifacts and managed to link some of the tablets to the places they were made on the basis of the mineral component of the clay.

Based on their analysis of pottery from the site of Tell Hadidi, Syria, Robert Mason and Elisabeth Cooper point out that petrography also provides information about the techniques used in ceramic manufacture because in many cases potters purposefully add mineral inclusions to the clay (Mason and Cooper 199). Based on the variation they find in the mineral inclusions in the Tell Hadidi potsherds Mason and Cooper are able to identify the products for different workshops.

Neutron activation analysis is another method for finding the source of ceramic artifacts. Rather than looking at the mineralogy of materials added to the clay, neutron activation focuses on the chemical characteristics of the clay itself. With the help of a nuclear reactor, it is possible to create a profile of the rare elements that are present at very low levels in the clay. This profile can serve as a chemical fingerprint for the clay a pot was made from that can be matched with the fingerprint of known geological clay sources. Neutron activation analysis was used to trace a unique pot, known as the "Dolphin Vase" and found on the Middle Kingdom Egyptian site of Lisht, back to its place of manufacture near the modern city of Gaza (McGovern et al. 1994). Rare element analysis can also be carried out with instrumentation known as an inductively coupled plasma mass spectrometer or ICP-MS. ●

FIGURE 11.21 Petrographic thin section of a pottery vessel from Jordan. The white speckled masses are pieces of calcite.

he built the bent pyramid that began at a very steep slope of approximately 60 degrees (Lehner 1997). Midway through construction, the slope was decreased to approximately 44 degrees, resulting in a pyramid with a pronounced "bend." The final pyramid built by Snefru was the Red Pyramid, a true pyramid 105 metres high.

Giza. Pyramid building reached its apex with the Fourth Dynasty kings—**Cheops, Cepheren**, and **Mycerinus**—who built their pyramids at Giza. Subsequent dynasties put far less effort into the construction of monumental pyramids, although the tradition persisted well into the Middle Kingdom. The Giza pyramids are very different in conception from the Djoser pyramid complex. At Giza, there is no enclosure wall hiding the sacred ground. The Giza pyramids are one element of a

▲▲ Giza The site of the pyramids of Cheops, Cepheren, and Mycerinus— monuments representing the apex of pyramid construction in Old Kingdom Egypt.

Cheops A Fourth Dynasty Egyptian king who constructed the first and largest pyramid ever built at Giza.

FIGURE 11.22 The painted wall of Tomb 100 at Hierakonpolis. Can you find any scenes like those on the Narmer Palette?

Cepheren A Fourth Dynasty Egyptian king who constructed a pyramid at Giza that was slightly smaller than the one constructed by Cheops. The great Sphinx is located alongside the Cepheren Valley Temple.

Mycerinus The last Fourth Dynasty Egyptian king to build a pyramid at Giza; it was smaller than the other pyramids and at least partially sheathed in polished granite.

complex made up of four parts (see Figure 11.24). The first element is the valley temple, constructed near the Nile Valley. The second element is a massive causeway connecting the valley temple to the desert plateau on which the pyramids were built. This causeway is also connected to the third element of the complex, the mortuary temple, which is built up against the pyramid. The final and most visible element of the complex is the pyramid itself. The three royal pyramids at Giza are surrounded by subsidiary structures including secondary pyramids, massive fields of bench-shaped "mastaba" tombs of nobility, and long pits in which boats were buried.

The pyramid of Cheops, the first constructed at Giza, is also the largest ever built. The pyramid of Cheops rises to a height of 146 metres and contains an estimated 2,300,000 blocks of stone (see Figure 11.25). This monumental building task appears to have been accomplished during a reign that lasted thirty-two years. Ironically, the only royal statue that remains of Cheops is a crude stone figure less than 8 centimetres high. Originally, the Cheops pyramid was sheathed in a casing of fine polished limestone. It is hard to imagine the effect this massive gleaming edifice would have had, emerging from the flat, dull landscape of the desert plateau. The burial chamber of the Cheops pyramid is hidden within the body of the pyramid at the top of a massive ramp. The actual burial chamber is constructed of massive granite monoliths transported from Upper Egypt. Standing in the burial chamber today, one is struck by the complete absence of ornamentation. The body of the king, presumably wrapped in a shroud, was laid to rest in a sarcophagus embedded in the floor of the burial chamber. The sarcophagus was then enclosed in the massive granite walls of the chamber, which itself is buried deep within the pyramid structure.

FIGURE 11.23 Aerial photo of the Djoser complex. The pyramid complex is contained within an enclosure wall.

FIGURE 11.24 Aerial photograph of the Giza pyramids.

Key:
1. Cheops pyramid
2. Cheops mortuary temple
3. Cheops causeway
4. Cepheren pyramid
5. Cepheren mortuary temple
6. Cepheren causeway
7. Cepheren valley temple
8. The Great Sphinx
9. Mycerinus pyramid
10. Mycerinus mortuary temple
11. Mycerinus causway
12. Mycerinus valley temple
13. Mastaba fields
14. Lehner excavation area

The Cepheren pyramid is slightly smaller than the Cheops pyramid. Some of the original casing stones are still preserved on the upper part of the Cepheren pyramid, providing an idea of what these monuments looked like when they were first constructed. Cepheren's image is well preserved in a series of powerful sculptures discovered in his pyramid's valley temple. One of the most famous features at Giza is the Great Sphinx, the figure of a cat with a human head, carved into the bedrock of a small hill adjoining the Cepheren valley temple (see Figure 11.26).

Mycerinus was the last king to build a pyramid at Giza. His effort was more modest than those of his predecessors. The most impressive aspect of the Mycerinus pyramid, which is only 65 metres high, is the fact that it was at least partially sheathed in polished granite. Some of the most beautiful Old Kingdom sculptures are figures of Mycerinus that were recovered from this valley temple. These figures convey the sense of quiet power that is the hallmark of Old Kingdom art.

THE PYRAMIDS AND THE STATE. The stepped pyramid of Djoser at Saqqara is cloaked in an enclosure wall. The great power of the pyramid complex was visible only to those allowed into the enclosure. The conception of the pyramid complex

FIGURE 11.25 View of Cepheren (left) and Cheops (right) pyramids from the south.

FIGURE 11.26 The Great Sphinx was carved from a small limestone hill. The layers of rock vary in hardness, resulting in uneven weathering of the Sphinx's body.

first developed by Snefru at Meidum and Dahshur and then brought to full fruition at Giza is radically different. At these sites, the complex sits on sacred ground, but the monumental pyramids are an inescapable presence visible to all. The Giza pyramids project the power of the king and make the power of the state an inescapably real part of the landscape. However, even at Giza, not all is visible: The king's body is wrapped in a shroud and placed in a stone sarcophagus in a chamber hidden in the mass of the pyramid.

The pyramid complexes made visible the power of the king while cloaking his body in mystery. At the same time, the construction of the pyramids was an undertaking of such immensity that it became a substantial aspect of what the state did. One of the most fascinating questions in archaeology is how the early Egyptian state was able to mobilize the labour to build these spectacular monuments.

To build the Giza pyramids, the Egyptians exploited limestone quarried from the edge of the Giza plateau itself. However, some of the stone had to be transported a greater distance. The facing stone was usually a finer grained limestone from the opposite bank of the Nile, while the granite used for the Mycerinus pyramid and the Cheops burial chamber came from distant quarries in Upper Egypt. Research by Leanne Mallory-Greenough and colleagues has identified the source of the black basalt that was used for the paving stones in the Cheops mortuary temple (Mallory-Greenough et al. 2000). Using chemical analysis, they were able to match samples of basalt from Giza with the rocks from a quarry in the Fayum.

Beginning in the 1980s, excavations to the south of the Great Sphinx have begun to pick up traces of the massive organization of labour involved in constructing the pyramids (see From the Field, p. 328). The discovery of breweries and bakeries to the south of the pyramid complex suggests that at least some of the workers were paid in the form of food rations. The organization required in building the pyramids involved not only labour for constructing the structures, but also people to produce food for the labour force.

■ The City

The Egyptian king ruled over the entire Nile Valley. Egypt was a territorial state rather than a city-state. The fundamental expression of the state was the unification of Egypt embodied by the figure of the king wearing the crowns of Upper and Lower Egypt. The monumental core of the early Egyptian state was not embedded in an urban centre.

The largest settlements known from the Early Dynastic and Old Kingdom periods are best characterized as large towns rather than cities. However, it is possible that the picture of Egypt as a state without cities is partly the result of the limitations of archaeological recovery. At many sites, the Early Dynastic and Old Kingdom levels are far below the water table and cannot be reached by excavation. This is true of Memphis, the Old Kingdom capital of Egypt, where excavations have not been able to penetrate below the New Kingdom occupation.

AMARNA. A unique picture of an Egyptian city is preserved at the New Kingdom site of **Amarna** in Upper Egypt (Kemp 1991). Amarna was founded as a new capital city by the heretic king **Akhenaten** (1363 B.C. to 1347 B.C.). Akhenaten put in place a reform of Egyptian religion, discarding much of the traditional pantheon and focusing on the visible disc of the sun, known by the Egyptians as Aten. In addition to instituting religious reform and founding a new capital, Akhenaten developed a new art style in which he and his queen, Nefertiti, were depicted with oddly elongated features.

After Akhenaten's death, his religious reforms were rejected, his monuments smashed, and his city at Amarna abandoned. Because Amarna was not subsequently reoccupied, it has provided archaeologists an opportunity to map extensive horizontal exposures of a fortified city stretching for over a kilometre along a major ceremonial road. Excavations of workshops, houses, and bakeries have provided unique insights into life in an Egyptian city. The question that lingers is whether cities like Amarna existed during earlier periods of Egyptian dynastic history or whether urban centres developed only during the New Kingdom.

■ Summing Up the Evidence

The Egyptian state challenges the expectations archaeologists have formed of state societies. The most obvious challenge is that there is at present no evidence that the early Egyptian state was an urban society. No cities are known from the Old Kingdom. Indeed, not only are cities absent, but the focal point of the state was the construction of massive funerary monuments that were set out in the desert margins. However, there is also a more subtle challenge: What we know about social organization suggests that in Egypt, kinship continued to play an important role long after the formation of the state.

The pyramids of Giza lead us to question the source of the legitimacy of this early state society. These monuments are spectacular feats of engineering, organization, and sheer human effort. We have begun to gain an understanding of how the labour was organized, but the question remains how these people were motivated to participate in such an undertaking. Is it possible that the state was powerful enough to coerce such a massive labour force? There is no evidence to

Amarna A city built by the heretic king Akhenaten and abandoned after his reign. Excavation of this city has provided a unique horizontal exposure of an Egyptian urban centre.

Akhenaten A religious reformer who built the city of Amarna.

The Author on His Fieldwork Excavating at Giza

In 1988 I stood on the Giza Plateau in Egypt to try to help answer a fundamental question: Where did the workers who built the pyramids live? We hoped that by looking at the Plateau as an archaeological landscape we might be able to unlock the answer to questions about the organization of the society that built these monuments. I was at the site thanks to Mark Lehner. Mark had spent years working at Giza before returning to the States for graduate school. He enlisted me, along with a group of other graduate students, to join him on his new project, and we of course jumped at the opportunity.

Mark drew on his intimate knowledge from over a decade of experience at Giza and tried to figure out where on the crowded Giza Plateau there might be space for a settlement. The first location we studied was a bowl-shaped depression to the south of the pyramids. Examination of this area quickly showed that it had never been inhabited. Mark then turned to a second area behind the Cepheren pyra-

mid, where the archaeologist Flinders Petrie in the late nineteenth century had found a series of large rectangular rooms or galleries. Our excavations, directed by Nick Conard, uncovered the same galleries found by Petrie and showed that this was a truly massive structure, longer than a football field. However, there was no sign of habitation in the rooms—only scant traces of manufacturing. It appears that the spaces were storerooms and workshops.

Mark then turned to a third area near the shallow depression where he had begun his search. Here, a massive wall separated the sacred space of the plateau from the area beyond. One of my most vivid memories is watching as more than forty men came over this monumental wall, ready to work. I knew little Arabic and there was very little basis for the considerable trust Mark had placed in me to supervise them. We quickly got to work, burning off scrub and measuring out excavation units. We soon began to pick up the traces of occupation, particularly

vessels used for brewing beer and baking bread. By the end of the second season, we had uncovered a bakery, and our Egyptian colleagues, led by Zahi Hawass, had found a large burial ground.

My responsibilities alternated between excavation and work in the storerooms, which were located in the middle of the Mastaba field. We were inundated by potsherds and struggled to keep up with the sorting and cataloguing of the finds. We worked with inspectors from the Egyptian Antiquities Organization, who taught me a great deal about pottery—and also about how I was perceived as an American. One day, after we had been working together long enough for them to know me fairly well, I was trying to explain to them how the television show "Dallas" gave an unrealistic view of the United States and its people, after all they knew me and I was nothing like that. Their response was to emphatically insist that I was exactly like one of the characters from the show!

support such a hypothesis, although, undoubtedly, not everybody participated willingly. There is good reason to think that the people's belief in the king as the actual incarnation of divinity essential for the maintenance of *ma'at* played a key role in the creation of the Egyptian state. It is hard not to conclude that the people who built the pyramids at Giza did so, at least in part, because they believed that they were building the tomb of a living deity.

11.3 Africa Beyond the Nile Valley

The development of African states was not restricted to the Egyptian Nile Valley. However, the formation of indigenous African states remains poorly understood (Connah 1987). In the Sudan, a series of complex societies developed along the Nile in what is known as Nubia. In the Ethiopian highlands, an impressive kingdom developed around the city of Axum, which flourished during the first millennium A.D.,

What I found striking about working at Giza was the focus that Mark was able to keep on understanding the Plateau as a complete entity. I learned that a successful project requires a clear goal and that one cannot simply hope to get direction from what one digs up. Once the bakery was excavated, Mark was faced with a problem: He could continue to dig, structure by structure; but using traditional archaeological methods, he would never get an idea of the area as a whole. So he launched a bold campaign of horizontal excavation, stripping the overlying sands from a massive area with the help of heavy equipment. These excavations are still in progress, but already the traces of a palace and workshop complex have been uncovered. These traces provide a picture of the royal establishment at Giza and the workshops that would have produced the food to supply a large workforce.

But where was the workers' village? One possibility is that such a village lies below the modern town Nazlet el

Seman, which borders the excavated areas. However, as Mark and his team continue stripping the overlying sands from areas beyond the palace complex, the remains of modest irregular structures have begun to appear. Perhaps they have finally found the elusive traces of the pyramid builders. (For more on the Giza Plateau Mapping Project, see www.aeraweb.org.) ▲

FIGURE 11.27 Excavation of a bakery in the area south of the Giza pyramids.

contemporary with the Roman Empire. Axum is famous for its standing stones carved in the shape of multistory buildings (see Figure 11.29). The tallest of these monuments, carved from a single block of stone, rises 21 metres. Along the East African coast, stretching from Somalia in the north to Mozambique in the south, a series of cities developed along the Indian Ocean contemporary with medieval Europe. These cities were active in extensive trade networks connecting southern Africa with the Middle East and Asia.

When European explorers reached the coast of west Africa, they found well-established cities. One of the most impressive was Benin, in what is today Nigeria. Benin is celebrated for its remarkable brass plaques, many of which have been acquired by Western museums. Some have questioned whether cities such as Benin developed indigenously in west Africa or whether they emerged as the result of an external stimulus, first from Islamic North Africa and then from Europe.

Excavations at the site of **Jenne-Jeno**, located in the Middle Niger Valley in Mali, have demonstrated that urban centres in west Africa predate extensive

▲▲ **Jenne-Jeno** The site of an urban centre in Mali, West Africa, that predates extensive external contact.

Archaeology and Genetics

Rapid advances in biotechnology have begun to have a significant impact on archaeology. As discussed in Chapter 4, genetic research has already had an impact on our understanding of human evolution, particularly the phylogenetic relationship between Neanderthals and Modern Humans (see pp. 133–134). When geneticists turn to more recent samples, the risk of contamination from modern DNA becomes acute. To overcome this challenge, careful protocols have been developed to minimize the risk of contamination and to provide researchers with tools to detect when contamination has taken place.

One of the most impressive genetic studies to emerge is the sequencing of nearly the entire genomic sequence of a man who lived in Greenland 4,000 years ago from a single hair recovered on an archaeological site locked in permafrost (Rasmussen et al., 2010). This study is far more than a demonstration of technical wizardry. The genome of this person sheds light on the earliest human occupation of the Arctic and resolves questions that have challenged archaeologists for decades. It can now be said with a high degree of certainty that the initial occupants of the Arctic came from Siberia rather than from within North America. Moreover, this discovery offers strong evidence that the modern Inuit populations of the North American Arctic and Greenland are the descendants of a second wave of human migration.

Another fascinating application of genetics is a study of a series of Egyptian mummies thought to be members of the family of Tutankhamun (Hawass et al., 2010). Although the tomb of Tutankhamun was found intact, many questions about this New Kingdom ruler remain. Great care was taken in the genetic analysis to avoid contamination, including repeating the study in two separate labs and testing the genetic markers from the mummies against the genetic markers of the scientists. The analysis determined that Tutankhamun's father, the heretic king Akhenaten, and Tutankamun's mother were brother and sister. The identification of inbreeding within Tutankhamun's lineage accounts for the presence of a genetic walking impairment, a condition known as Köhler disease II, that was detected in a radiological analysis of his mummy. This genetic disease was likely a contributing factor to Tutankhamun's death at a young age. It is interesting that the radiological examination of Tutankhamun and the members of his lineage did not find any evidence of the genetic disorder known as Marfan syndrome. Marfan syndrome produces a feminine physique and some archaeologists have suggested that the unusual art style characteristic of Akhenaten's reign was actually an accurate representation of a person with this condition. We now know that in fact the representations of Akhenaten are not a realistic depiction of his physique. The genetic analysis of Tutankhamun's mummy also recovered evidence of malaria, a subject we will return to in the Toolbox on Archaeology and Disease in Chapter 14, p. 412. ●

REFERENCES: Rasmussen, M. et al. (2010). Ancient human genome sequence of an extinct Palaeo-Eskimo. *Nature* 463: 757–762.

Hawass, Z. et al. (2010). Ancestry and pathology in King Tutankhamun's family. *JAMA* 303(7): 638–647.

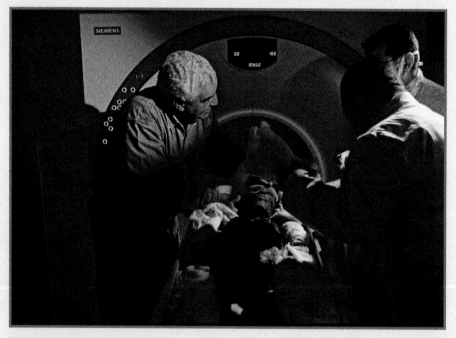

FIGURE 11.28 Preparing the mummy of Tutankhamun for a CT scan. The combination of radiographic and genetic analysis of this mummy has produced new insight into the genealogy and health of the rulers of New Kingdom Egypt.

external contacts (McIntosh and McIntosh 1993). The city of Jenne is known from historical sources as an important trade centre for caravans coming from Timbuktu to the north. The region around Jenne is very fertile and the river is rich in a wide array of fish. Jenne-Jeno is a site 3 kilometres from modern Jenne. The mound at Jenne-Jeno rises 8 metres and covers over 330,000 square metres. Excavations have uncovered three major phases of occupation beginning around 250 B.C. and lasting through A.D. 800. By A.D. 300, the entire area of the site appears to have been densely inhabited. Population estimates for the site range from 7,000 to 16,000. There is considerable evidence of local iron smelting and other specialized craft activity. The city was surrounded by a mud-brick wall; however, there is no evidence that the houses were laid out along a regular grid. Surveys in the region around Jenne-Jeno have shown that the area was dotted with a range of sites of different sizes.

FIGURE 11.29 One of the monumental stelae at Axum, Ethiopia.

Only a small area of Jenne-Jeno has been excavated, making it difficult to come to any conclusion about the social organization of the city. The excavators of the site, Susan Keech McIntosh and Roderick McIntosh, have found no evidence of either a clearly defined elite or a special elite area of the site. Roderick McIntosh has developed a picture of Jenne-Jeno as a city ruled by overlapping sources of authority, rather than the centralized authority found in other early state societies (McIntosh 1998).

SUMMARY

- Mesopotamia covers the area along the course of the Tigris and Euphrates rivers, a region where large-scale agriculture is possible only with irrigation.
- Urban sites appear in Mesopotamia during the Uruk period, 4000 B.C. to 3200 B.C. These cities were developed around temple precincts dating back to the earlier Ubaid period.
- The cuneiform writing system developed in Mesopotamia to record economic information. Cuneiform came to be used for a wide variety of texts, including epics and legal codes.
- The Royal Tombs at Ur demonstrate the power and wealth of early Mesopotamian kings.
- There is little evidence of extensive warfare in early Mesopotamia; however, Uruk sites such as Habuba Kebira did develop far to the north on the Euphrates River.
- The Nile Valley, a highly fertile agricultural land bounded by desert, is divided into Upper Egypt in the south and Lower Egypt in the north.
- The shift toward complex societies in Egypt began during the Predynastic period. Egyptian dynastic history can be divided into three cycles of integration and collapse.

- The Egyptian king was the human incarnation of the god Horus and was responsible for preserving *ma'at*—balance and justice.
- Scribes played a critical role in maintaining the organization of Egyptian society.
- The earliest Royal Tombs are found at Hierakonpolis and Abydos. The stepped pyramid constructed by Djoser at Saqqara was the first Egyptian pyramid.
- The first true pyramid was constructed by Snefru at Dahshur. Pyramid building reached its apex in the three pyramids at Giza constructed during the Fourth Dynasty.
- No cities are known from the Old Kingdom of Egypt. The most completely documented Egyptian city is the site of Amarna, built by the heretic New Kingdom king Akhenaten.
- The site of Jenne-Jeno in the Middle Niger Valley was a large city occupied between 250 B.C. and A.D. 800.

KEY TERMS

REVIEW QUESTIONS

1. Why are the Royal Tombs at Ur significant for understanding early Mesopotamian society?
2. What was the role of writing in early Mesopotamia and Old Kingdom Egypt?
3. What can we learn about the process of state formation by comparing Mesopotamia and Egypt?

CANADIAN ARCHAEOLOGISTS

- Elisabeth Cooper, professor in the Department of Classical, Near Eastern, and Religious Studies at the University of British Columbia, is a specialist in Mesopotamian archaeology. Along with fieldwork in Syria her research includes petrographic analysis of pottery.
  http://www.cnrs.ubc.ca/index.php?id=3490

- Michel Fortin, professor in the Department of Archaeology at Laval University, is the director of the excavation at the Bronze and Iron Age site of Tell 'Acharneh in Syria, which appears to be the site of the ancient city of Tunip mentioned in the Amarna letters.
  www.acharneh.hst.ulaval.ca/english/framelnter.asp

- Katja Goebs, professor in the Department of Near and Middle Eastern Civilizations at the University of Toronto, is an Egyptologist with interests in religion and funerary texts.
  http://www.utoronto.ca/nmc/faculty/goebscv.htm

- Timothy Harrison, professor in the Department of Near and Middle Eastern Civilizations at the University of Toronto, is the director of the Tayinet Archaeological Project in Turkey and the Tell Madaba Archaeological Project in Jordan. Both projects explore the development of urban societies in the region during the Bronze Age.
  http://www.utoronto.ca/nmc/faculty/harrisoncv.htm

- Clemens Reichel, curator at the Royal Ontario Museum and professor in the Department of Near and Middle Eastern Civilizations at the University of Toronto, is director of the excavations at the site of Hamoukar, Syria. This project is shedding new light on the Uruk expansion.
  http://www.rom.on.ca/collections/curators/reichel.php

PEARSON
myanthrokit™

Visit **www.myanthrokit.com**, where you will find a variety of tools and resources to enhance your learning, including:
- Practise quizzes with Study Plans
- Videos
- Listening Activities
- And much more!

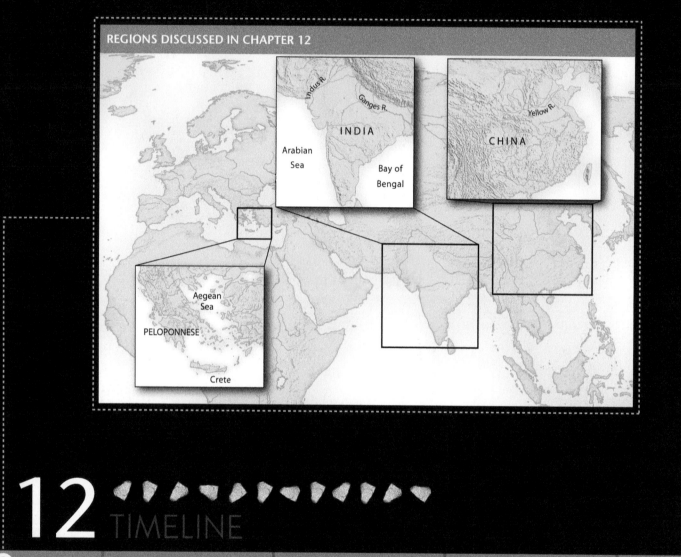

REGIONS DISCUSSED IN CHAPTER 12

Indus R.

Ganges R.

INDIA

Arabian
Sea

Bay of
Bengal

Yellow R.

CHINA

Aegean
Sea

PELOPONNESE

Crete

12 TIMELINE

CHINESE SITES			
CHINESE PERIODS		EARLY LONGSHAN	
INDUS SITES			
INDUS PERIODS		PRE-HARAPPAN	
AEGEAN SITES			
AEGEAN PERIODS			

4000 BC   **3500** BC   **3000** BC   **2500** BC

ENIGMAS AND DIVERSITY:
EARLY STATES IN EUROPE AND ASIA

The early state societies of the Aegean, the Indus Valley, and China challenge our understanding of the archaeology of social complexity. After reading this chapter you should understand:

- The basic characteristics of Minoan and Mycenaean society, including questions about interactions between polities.

- The archaeological evidence for urbanism and the questions regarding social inequality in the Harappan civilization.

- The evidence from surveys and excavation for the emergence of state societies in China.

Figure of an archer from the Xian Tomb.

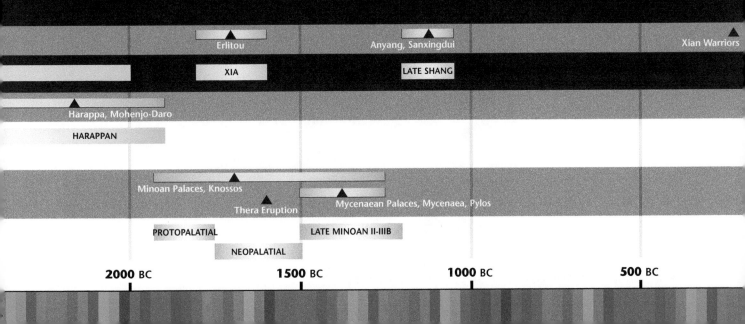

Erlitou

XIA

Anyang, Sanxingdui

LATE SHANG

Xian Warriors

Harappa, Mohenjo-Daro

HARAPPAN

Minoan Palaces, Knossos

Thera Eruption

Mycenaean Palaces, Mycenaea, Pylos

PROTOPALATIAL

LATE MINOAN II-IIIB

NEOPALATIAL

2000 BC   **1500** BC   **1000** BC   **500** BC

Sometime around 221 B.C., Ying Zheng, the First Emperor of Qin, began to assemble an army unlike any the world had ever seen. This army—over 7,000 men with bronze swords, halberds, daggers, axes, crossbows and bows, 130 chariots, and close to 700 horses—was not meant for the world of the living. Ying Zheng's army is made of clay, beautifully sculpted life-sized models of soldiers set in formation to stand guard against the enemies the emperor would face after his death, perhaps the spirits of the armies he had massacred in wars of conquest (Figure 12.1). A chance discovery in 1974 near the city of Xian led to archaeological excavations that have brought to light the First Emperor's army, much of it still standing intact after more than 2,000 years. In the Royal Tombs of Ur and the pyramids of Giza we have already seen the efforts of rulers to continue their dominance in the afterlife. The paradox at the core of the Epic of Gilgamesh—that power among the living does not conquer death—would have been familiar to the First Emperor, who is said to have searched in vain for a secret source of immortality. The terracotta army, row after row of intricately carved yet mute figures, is among the most spectacular archaeological sites in the world. The tomb of the First Emperor is an ultimate expression of the power of administration in which "the realm of the future became peopled by officials, servants and armies, unlike the afterlife populated by gods and spirits described by so many of the world's religions" (Rawson 2007, 145). In the terracotta army of Xian we see the extension of the institutions of social complexity into the realm of the afterworld on a monumental scale.

In this chapter we will trace the early stages of state formation in the Aegean, the Indus Valley, and China. In the Aegean we will examine the palaces of the Minoans of Crete and the Mycenaeans of mainland Greece. A particular focus will be the interaction between small-scale political entities and how these interactions might lead to the development of states. The Indus Valley presents a fascinating quandary, a clearly urban society without clearly visible elite. In China we will examine the large urban centre of Anyang but also look at recent archaeological research, much of it based on intensive surveys, that is leading to a nuanced picture

FIGURE 12.1 The Emperor's army at Xian.

of state formation in China. It is important to remember that the well-ordered soldiers of the terracotta army, each with a distinctive hairstyle indicating status and ethnicity, is—despite the realism of the individuals depicted—ultimately a fiction. Where the rulers of states and empires might have seen order and discipline, the reality was often far more complex. Similarly archaeologists have learned that although models for the social structure of early states and theories of state formation are essential, the archaeological reality will continuously challenge our expectations.

△△ Knossos A site excavated by Arthur Evans that is the largest Minoan settlement.

Minoan A Bronze Age society located on the island of Crete.

Mycenaean A Bronze Age society that developed on the Peloponnese Peninsula and in central Greece.

Lion Gate An important example of Mycenaean defensive architecture.

12.1 The Aegean

On a spring day in 1900, Arthur Evans stood on the hill of **Knossos** on the island of Crete and began the excavations that were to transform our knowledge of ancient Greece. Greek mythology told the story of King Minos of Crete and the terrible secrets of his labyrinth, where the minotaur, a man-eating monster who was half-man and half-bull, lived imprisoned in the twisted complex built by Daedalus. Perhaps Evans imagined Daedalus and his son flying away from Knossos on wings made of wax and feathers before Icarus, flying too close to the sun, melted his wings and plunged to his death.

Evans's excavations at Knossos uncovered a large palace adorned with frescoes showing incredible scenes of bull-leaping festivals, helping to raise the curtain on a previously unknown civilization—the **Minoan** culture of Crete. Over a century after Evans sank his first pit at Knossos, fundamental questions remain about the organization of Minoan society, as well as about the relationship of the Minoans with their neighbours in the Aegean, particularly the **Mycenaeans** of the Peloponnese Peninsula and central Greece.

■ Setting and Chronology

The homeland of the Minoan culture was the island of Crete, while Mycenaean societies developed on the Peloponnese Peninsula in southern Greece and to the north in central Greece (see Figure 12.3). The islands of the Cyclades also played an important role in the development of these societies, as did the area of western Turkey known as Asia Minor. Both the Peloponnese Peninsula and Crete are characterized by a varied topography with high mountain peaks and small open plains.

Although the earliest occupation of many Minoan and Mycenaean sites dates back to the Neolithic, the Bronze Age was the period during which complex social institutions developed. The emergence of centralized power structures began in Crete around 1900 B.C. during the Protopalatial and Neopalatial periods. It was 500 years until similar institutions developed among the Mycenaens around 1500 B.C. After this time, during a period known as the Late Minoan II–IIIB, there is evidence in Crete for strong Mycenaean influence on Minoan society.

■ Comparing Palaces

Archaeologists have tended to paint a picture of the Minoans and Mycenaeans as polar opposites, with the Minoans playing the role of peace-loving flower-worshipers and the Mycenaeans cast as aggressive warriors. It is true that while the Minoans appear to have left their settlements exposed, the Mycenaeans often surrounded their citadels with massive fortification walls, including the monumental **Lion Gate** at

TOOLBOX

Underwater Archaeology

The most important thing about underwater archaeology is that it is archaeology. Much of the motivation that leads people to underwater sites is the search for treasure, often gold bullion that went down with ships lost at sea. The distinction between treasure hunting and archaeology is the respect archaeologists have for the careful recording of the context of discoveries. Underwater archaeologists use many of the same techniques as archaeologists working on land, including survey, mapping, and stratigraphic excavation, although the tools used often differ. On underwater sites, lighting and photography are a challenge, as are seemingly simple procedures like maintaining a grid. Artifacts recovered from underwater sites must also often undergo a complex process of conservation when they are transferred to dry conditions. On the other hand, underwater archaeologists can use tools not available to other archaeologists, including sonar for detecting site location and an airlift or dredge to pull away deposits. An additional ad-vantage of underwater archaeology is that, due to the anaerobic environment, wood and other perishable materials are often preserved.

There is a wide range of underwater archaeological sites, including harbours and submerged settlements, but it is shipwrecks that have pushed the development of the field. Shipwrecks provide essential information about seafaring technology and maritime trade. Since shipwrecks are a powerful draw to treasure and adventure-seekers, underwater archaeologists often have to battle to preserve this unique archaeological legacy.

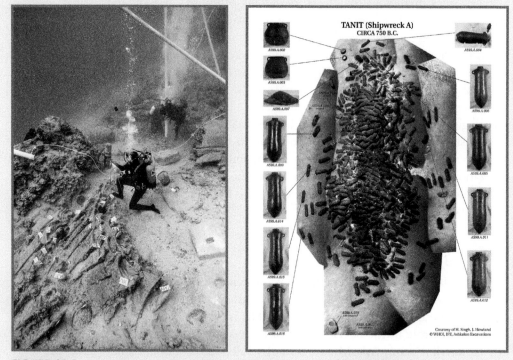

FIGURE 12.2 (a) Excavation of the shipwreck of the site of Ulu Burun, Turkey. Notice how the divers are carefully mapping the site, in this case a cargo of copper ingots. (b) Mosaic of the *Tanit* shipwreck dating to 750 B.C., found off the coast of Israel at a depth of 400 metres.

early state modules Colin Renfrew's term to describe autonomous political units.

peer polity interaction Colin Renfrew's term to describe the full range of exchanges taking place between autonomous socio-political units.

Mycenaea (see Figure 12.4). However, the picture of the Minoans and Mycenaeans as archetypical opposites does little to help us understand why these societies differed and obscures their similarities.

Minoan and Mycenaean society consisted of a series of autonomous political units. Colin Renfrew (1986) refers to such units as **early state modules**. The interaction between early state modules, or what Renfrew calls **peer polity interaction**, has the potential to fuel the development of social complexity, since change within each polity has an effect on its neighbour. John Cherry (1986) has argued that the development of the Minoan states fits very well with the model

Shipwreck archaeology has also pushed the application of new technologies from three-dimensional imaging of the ocean floor to the use of submersibles and underwater vehicles to gain access to wrecks at depths beyond the reach of conventionally equipped divers (Ballard 2008).

One of the greatest discoveries made by underwater archaeologists is the wreck of a ship dated to the Egyptian New Kingdom at the site of Ulu Burun, off the southern coast of Turkey (Bass 1986). Excavations at Ulu Burun have recovered a rich assemblage of trade items, including copper, tin, and glass ingots, storage jars containing traces of organic products, and more exotic items such as gold and ivory. More recently, the remains of two ships, given the names *Tanit* and *Elissa* dating to the eighth century B.C. were identified on the seabed 33 nautical miles off the coast of Israel at a depth of 400 metres (Ballard et al. 2002). Using a remotely operated vehicle, it was possible not only to document the shipwrecks but also to retrieve representative artifacts. It is important to emphasize that the archaeological team took extreme care not to damage the shipwrecks and that the provenience of all artifacts was carefully recorded. The results show that both

vessels sailed from the coast of Lebanon to either Egypt or Carthage in North Africa carrying a cargo of roughly 10 tonnes of wine each. The wine was transported in highly standardized storage vessels known as amphora that had been sealed against leakage with resin. Traces of tartaric acid, an organic acid found in grapes, were found in chemical analysis of the interior of these vessels.

Among the accomplishments of Canadian underwater archaeology, one highlight is the recovery of the *Hamilton* and the *Scourge,* two merchant ships that were refit for military service by the United States during the War of 1812. These ships sank in a storm just after midnight on August 8, 1812, in Lake Ontario. In 1973, the wrecks of the *Hamilton* and the *Scourge* were detected using sidescanning radar lying at a depth of 90 metres near Hamilton. Subsequent research using remotely operated vehicles has documented the spectacular preservation of these vessels. The conditions in the Great Lakes are ideal for the preservation of organic materials including shipwrecks, although the recent proliferation of zebra mussels—an invasive species that attaches to wood— poses a very serious threat to this unique heritage (Binnie et al. 2000).

Another exciting new discovery in Canadian archaeology is the tentative identification of the wreck of the *Tonquin*, a boat in the service of the Pacific Fur Company that sank off the coast of Vancouver Island in 1811 after a struggle with warriors from the Tla-o-qui-aht First Nation (Robinson and Griffiths 2005). In 2003, fishermen raised an anchor that had snagged some crab traps in the Templar channel. Close examination showed that this anchor was made using materials and techniques characteristic of the early nineteenth century. Adding to the interest was the discovery of trade beads encrusted in iron concretions adhering to the anchor. Further research on the seabed has led to the recovery of more beads, as well as wooden artifacts that appear to be a net gauge. Regardless whether this turns out to be the remains of the *Tonquin* itself or another early trade vessel, the discovery indicates the potential of underwater archaeology to contribute to our understanding of the history of European contact with the communities of the west coast. ●

REFERENCE: Amanda Bowens (Ed.) 2009. *Underwater Archaeology: The NAS Guide to Principles and Practice.* Malden, MA: Blackwell.

For information on the *Hamilton* and the *Scourge*, see http://www.hamilton-scourge.hamilton.ca/.

of peer polity interaction; however, recently a number of archaeologists have questioned whether the hierarchical organization characteristic of state society actually existed on Minoan Crete. The concept of **heterarchy** has been advanced as a better framework for understanding the organization of Minoan society. Carole Crumley defines heterarchy as "the relation of elements to one another when they are unranked or when they possess the potential for being ranked in a number of different ways" (Crumely 1995, 3). She illustrates the concept of heterarchy by pointing out that oak trees and symphonies are both highly structured, and yet neither is hierarchically organized. In the context of Minoan Crete, the concept

heterarchy The relationship of elements to one another when they are not ranked.

FIGURE 12.3 Map of the Bronze Age Aegean.

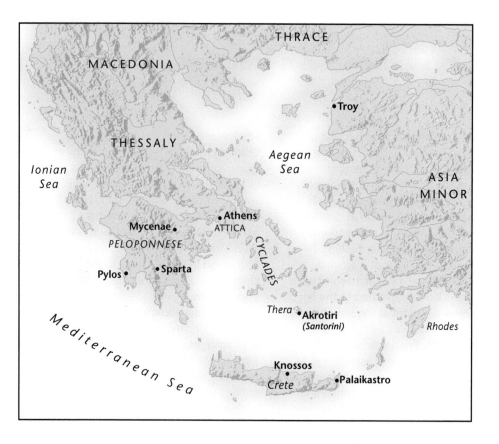

FIGURE 12.4 A historic photograph of the Lion Gate at Mycenaea gives a sense of the scale of the fortification walls surrounding Mycenaean citadels.

Deutches Arch. Inst. Lion's Gate - Athens. Deutsches Archaologisches Institut, Athens, D-DAI-ATH-Mykene 63.

of heterarchy means that complex social organization may be developed in the absence of a clearly defined ranking of members of society.

For the island communities of Crete, Mainland Greece, and the Cyclades, the interactions between polities raise questions about how to analyze such interactions. Studying the Aegean between 2000 and 1600 B.C., Carl Knappett and colleagues have used mathematics to explore the network of relationships that connected these sites (Knappett et al. 2008). Knappett's approach opens up the possibility of exploring how changes in nature of connections between individual sites might have an effect on the network as a whole.

The core of both Minoan and Mycenaean states was the palace. Minoan palaces are massive and elaborate constructions that might have been the inspiration for the myth of the labyrinth (see Figure 12.5). The centre of the palace and the heart of its function is the central court. Bull games, feasting, dancing, and other public events are thought to have taken place in these open spaces, buried deep within the palace structure. Estimates for the number of people who would have participated in these rituals range between 1,500 and 5,000.

The core of the Mycenaean state was also the palace. The most completely preserved example of a Mycenaean palace was excavated at the site of Pylos. Here the centre of

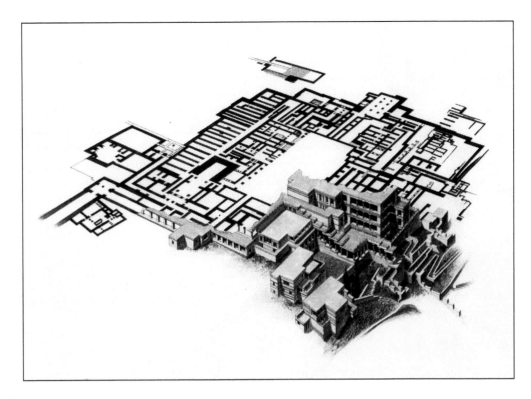

the structure is a large room known as a **megaron**, with a central hearth and four central pillars (see Figure 12.6). An open court for public gatherings, on a smaller scale than the central courts in Minoan palaces, was located in front of the megaron. Both the Minoan and the Mycenaean palaces were lavishly painted. One striking difference between these palaces is the presence of elaborate funerary ritual on Mycenaean sites and the absence of large tombs on Minoan sites like Knossos.

megaron A large hall located at the centre of the Mycenaean palace.

The palaces were more than simply the setting for spectacle. They were also the seat of the administration of the Aegean early state societies. This pairing of spectacle and administration is very interesting. It also lends support to the kind of dynamics Renfrew and Cherry discuss as characteristic of peer polity interaction, which include competition, emulation, symbolic entertainment, and exchange. Until the middle of the Neopalatial period, the only documents that survive from Crete are in scripts—Linear A and Cretan hieroglyphics—which have not been deciphered. The Mycenaean script, **Linear B**, was used to write a form of the Greek language that has been deciphered, providing insight into the function of the Minoan and Mycenaean palaces. Linear B was subsequently adopted on Crete as well; in fact, it is possible that it was first developed by Mycenaeans living in Crete.

FIGURE 12.6 Reconstruction of Pylos megaron.

FIGURE 12.7 One of the storage rooms at Knossos with large ceramic storage vessels known as pithoi.

The title of the ruler in the Linear B tablets is the **wanax**, but little detail is given on the powers of this position. What is apparent is that the wanax controlled vast quantities of resources. In the Linear B tablets from Knossos there is mention of 800 tonnes of harvested wheat and 80,000 to 100,000 sheep that would have been valued primarily for their wool (Killen 2007, 115). These very large quantities fit with the archaeological data from the excavation of the palace storerooms at Knossos, which found both large storage vessels known as pithoi and built storage facilities (see Figure 12.7). Beyond simply housing commodities, there is evidence from both texts and archaeology that the palaces also played an important role as workshops for the production of goods, including fine textiles.

The palaces of the Late Bronze Age Aegean controlled the production of basic commodities, housed the manufacture of finished goods, and hosted large-scale spectacles and feasts. However, the palaces were part of a broader cultural landscape. Estimates for the population of Minoan and Mycenaean settlements are difficult to determine with a high degree of accuracy. Current estimates place the population of Knossos at around 15,000. Knossos was the largest settlement in Crete, so this can be taken as a maximum size for a Minoan town.

Archaeological research in the Aegean includes a heavy emphasis on the use of survey to gain an understanding of the countryside beyond the palace and surrounding settlement. For example, survey in the Pediada region, a rich agricultural area to the south of Knossos, has found an increase in settlement density in the period contemporary with the full development of the palace (Panagiotakis 2004). During this period, settlements with Knossos-style luxury products are found lining the communication routes to Knossos. The survey results suggest that this region was drawn into the provisioning of agricultural commodities for the palace at Knossos. The mechanisms that connected the palaces to their hinterland were varied. In some cases, during the Late Minoan II–IIIB periods, the Linear B texts refer to taxes while in other cases they refer to land owned by the palace.

■ Violence and Warfare

Determining the actual nature of conflict in ancient societies is often difficult and requires a thorough understanding of the technology of warfare. For the Bronze Age Aegean, there is evidence of both military conflict as well as ritualized contests, including the boxing matches and bullfights depicted in palace frescos (see Figures 12.9 and 12.10). Experimental archaeology has provided new insight into the fighting capacity of Late Bronze Age Aegean swords and in turn a new perspective on the structure of Minoan and Mycenaean society. These swords tend to be 50 centimetres or longer, straight, with a central midrib and sharp edges. Archaeologists have studied the typology of these artifacts but have rarely asked what it would be like to wield them as weapons. This is the question that Barry Molloy (2008) examined in his experimental study. He began by developing his own skills through two years of martial arts training with swords; he then carried out a series of tests using replicas of archaeological weapons. A great deal of skill was needed to effectively use these swords, and there was a risk of breakage during combat if the weapon was misused. To work effectively, the sword must be drawn in a whip-like motion at the same time the blow is delivered. Tests on linen, leather, and metal armour showed that only thrusting attacks penetrated the first two, while the swords were unable to penetrate the metal

Linear B A script used to write the Mycenaean language; texts in Linear B are a major source of information about the organization of Aegean society.

wanax The title of the ruler in Linear B texts.

TOOLBOX

Space Syntax

Buildings are both objects we build and places we inhabit. Architecture blurs the line between artifact and landscape. Archaeologists have many ways to study architectural remains. One approach is to look at the activities that took place within a structure by analyzing the distribution of artifacts or the microstratigraphy of floor deposits (Steadman 1996). From this perspective, how we use space determines its nature.

A different, complementary perspective explores how architectural space can shape social life. The Minoan and Mycenaean palaces provide excellent examples of elaborate structures that constrain and shape action. The presence of large open spaces at the core of these structures not only reflects the social organization of the palace but in many ways also makes the social structure possible.

Space syntax is a methodology for studying the configuration of architectural space. It was first developed by architects and city planners, but is increasingly used by archaeologists (Cutting 2003). Space syntax can be applied at any level, from a single structure to a complete settlement. The methodology works with floor plans or city plans, and abstracts from these a graph representing the relationship between spaces (Bafna 2003). At least in the first stage of analysis, the size of the rooms and other qualities of these spaces are put aside to focus on the access between spaces. Figure 12.8 provides an illustration of the use of space syntax analysis to create a graph for a simple structure with eight rooms. The plan on the left shows the layout of these rooms; the dotted lines indicate the links between spaces. The numbers indicate the "depth" of the space, or the extent to which it is linked to other spaces. The number 4 signals connection to only one other space and is the maximum possible depth, essentially a dead end. The number 3 indicates two links, one of which is a dead end; the number 2 signifies two links to spaces that lead on to other rooms; and the number 1 stands for the lowest measure of depth, a highly integrated space. On the right is a "justified access graph" showing the relationship of these spaces. The isolation of the one dead-end space is very apparent in this graph, as is the presence of two widely accessible spaces within the structure. The fundamental idea of space syntax analysis is that these characteristics would shape the nature of social relations that took place within this structure. By reducing architectural space to a graph, patterns emerge that might otherwise be obscured, and comparisons between types of architecture become possible.

Peter Dawson has applied space syntax analysis to ethnographic and ethnohistoric descriptions of snow houses built by Central Eskimo groups in the Canadian Arctic (Dawson 2002). This project found a relationship between the integration of space in snow houses and kinship structure. These results provide a potential method for connecting the architectural remains documented on archeological sites with less tangible aspects of society, such as kinship. ●

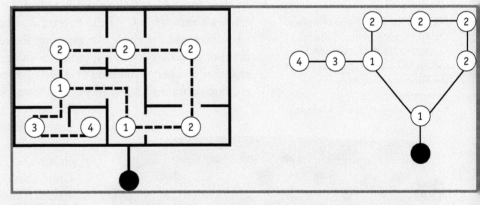

FIGURE 12.8 Space syntax.

armour. Tests of the swords on recently slaughtered pigs gave a sense of how the blades would have cut into unprotected flesh during battle. Molloy concludes that

> only very effectively executed strikes would inflict serious injury, such as severing tendons or arteries. . . . Other less effective strikes would nonetheless cut the flesh, resulting in loss of blood, wearing down combatants over a longer duration of fighting. The combat skills of the prehistoric warriors needed to have been sufficiently developed to allow these strikes to be executed repeatedly in a single combat event with limited risk to the weapon itself (Molloy 2008, 126).

FIGURE 12.9 Bullfight fresco from Knossos.

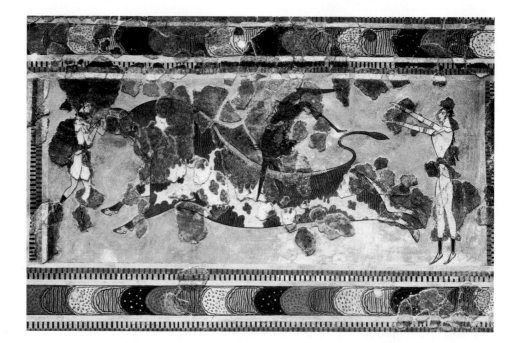

▲▲ **Akrotiri** A Bronze Age town on the island of Thera that was buried by a catastrophic volcanic eruption.

▲▲ **Thera** A Cycladic island that was devastated by a major volcanic eruption during the Bronze Age.

FIGURE 12.10 A row of warriors shown on a Mycenaean pottery vessel. Notice the weapons that include shields and spears as well as the elaborate uniforms worn by the warriors.

National Archeological Museum, Athens/Art Resource, NY.

These results indicate that warfare in Minoan and Mycenaean society would be a test of skills and that the combatants would have a fair chance of surviving violent encounters. The sense of controlled violence in combat, and the training that it would have required, adds a vivid feel of what lay behind peer polity interactions in the Late Bronze Age Aegean.

■ The Eruption of Santorini and Its Impact

At the site of **Akrotiri** on the island of **Thera**, (also known as Santorini) visitors can walk through a Cycladic Bronze Age town that has been preserved under the ash deposited by the volcanic eruption that devastated the island. A large-scale program of radiocarbon dating indicates an age slightly earlier than 1600 B.C. for the eruption of Thera (Manning et al. 2006). However, an argument based on the stratigraphic context of Minoan pottery found in Egypt leads another group to argue for an age of 1500 B.C. The excavations at Akrotiri provide a unique picture of life in a Late Bronze Age Cycladic town and also give important evidence about the expansion of Minoan influence from Crete into the Cycladic islands. The frescoes recovered at Akrotiri are both beautiful and informative. One set of paintings gives an unparalleled view of Minoan ships, and includes possible evidence of conflict at sea (see Figure 12.11). However, Thera has sparked a debate that reaches far beyond Akrotiri and is fundamental to the archaeology of Minoan Crete. There is no question that the eruption of Thera was a massive event, but archaeologists differ greatly in their opinions of its impact on the palaces and towns of Crete. For some, the volcanic eruption was merely a loud noise that the inhabitants of Crete would have heard from a distance. Others see the eruption as ushering in a

FIGURE 12.11 Ship fresco from Akrotiri.

rapid decline in the power of the Minoan elites. About a century after the eruption of Thera there was an increase in Mycenaean influence on Crete, and Knossos appears to have emerged as a paramount centre for the entire island. But was Thera a causal factor in these changes? If so, where are the archaeological indications for massive destruction caused by the eruption? And, why is there a hiatus of a century between the volcanic eruption and its impact?

Geoarchaeological research at the site of Palaiakastro on the eastern coast of Crete has produced evidence that the eruption of Thera might have caused a massive tsunami that would have led to widespread destruction, at least on the eastern coast (Bruins et al. 2008). At Palaiakastro, volcanic ash reworked by water was found in buildings well away from today's shoreline. Chemical tests confirm that the source of this ash is the Thera eruption. In exposed sections along the coastline, deposits of cultural material such as ceramics, building stones, and animal bones are found at 1.5 metres above sea level. Based on the geoarchaeological data, it is suggested that, as a result of the eruption of Thera, a tsunami wave as high as 9 metres hit the eastern coast of Crete. If true, this would indicate that the eruption had a catastrophic impact on the people living at Palaiakastro and other towns along the eastern coast of Crete. However, to date there is little evidence for a tsunami on other coastal Minoan sites.

Even if this evidence of a tsunami holds up, it does not completely explain the impact of the Thera eruption on Minoan society, as there is no widespread evidence for upheaval across Crete until approximately one hundred years after the volcanic eruption. One possibility is that the eruption led to the destruction of Minoan naval forces, leaving the island vulnerable to attack by Mycenaeans. Another possibility revolves around the source of authority of the rulers of Minoan Crete. If the Thera eruption did lead to calamity, this could have shaken people's faith in their leaders' ability to provide safety and stability (Driessen and Macdonald 1997). The result of such a crisis might have been a gradual shift to a more bureaucratically centralized way of life.

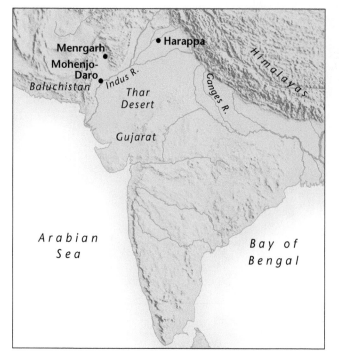

FIGURE 12.12 Map of the Indus Valley.

■ **Summing Up the Evidence**

The development of social complexity in Minoan and Mycenaean Greece might have been the result of peer polity interactions between multiple early state modules. However, archaeologists are increasingly questioning whether the model of a hierarchical state fits with the evidence from Minoan Crete. For both Minoans and Mycenaeans, the palace was the core of the state. These massive complexes served both as large-scale storage facilities, the seat of administration, and the site of public spectacle. The nature of violence and warfare, particularly among the undefended Minoan centres, is an intriguing question. Experimental study of swords suggests that combat was highly skilled and perhaps not always lethal. One of the major questions facing archaeologists working in the region is the impact of the eruption of Thera. This debate includes both empirical questions, such as the validity of the evidence for a tsunami, and more interpretive questions that examine how such a disaster would influence the nature of Minoan social organization.

12.2 The Indus Valley

The Harappan civilization developed along the Indus Valley in modern-day Pakistan at approximately the same time that the Great Pyramids were built in Egypt (see Figure 12.12). The defining characteristic of this civilization is the presence of well-planned cities, notably the urban centres of Harappa and Mohenjo-Daro. However, monumental architecture is virtually absent from the Indus Valley, as is any evidence for the elaboration of the power of the ruler through intricate mortuary rituals. The Harappan civilization remains wrapped in enigma and mystery. The rulers remain largely faceless and nameless, and perhaps most intriguing, the Harappan script remains one of the few undeciphered ancient languages.

■ **The Setting and Chronology**

The Indus River descends from the highlands of the Himalaya Mountains and winds through 3,000 kilometres of modern Pakistan before flowing into the Arabian Sea. The Indus is among the most powerful rivers in the world, with twice the annual flow of the Nile and three times the combined flow of the Tigris and the Euphrates (Jarrige 1989). The Indus is also an unpredictable river that frequently changes its course. During the time of the Harappan civilization, the Ghaggar-Hakra River, which is now dry, flowed to east of the Indus.

The rich agricultural lands of the **Indus Valley** are bounded on the west by the highlands of Baluchistan and on the northwest by the highlands of Afghanistan. To the east, the Indus Valley is bounded by the Great Thar desert. The Harappan civilization extended across the entire Indus Valley, covering an area of almost half a million square miles. In the southeast, Harappan sites are found along the coastal regions of Kutch and Gujarat (Allchin and Allchin 1982). Trade networks connected the Harappan civilization by sea to the Arabian Peninsula and Mesopotamia and overland into Iran and Afghanistan. Carnelian beads made in the Indus Valley are among the treasures discovered in the Royal Tombs at Ur. The Indus Valley has been identified as the land of Melluha, mentioned in Mesopotamian texts as an important trading partner.

▲▲ **Indus Valley** An area extending along the course of the Indus River that covers much of modern Pakistan and the Kutch and Gujarat provinces of India.

Excavations at the site of Mehrgarh in the Baluchistan foothills to the west of the Indus Valley have produced important information on the Neolithic and later prehistoric societies of the region (Jarrige 1989). The agriculture of Mehrgarh was based on plants and animals first domesticated in the Middle East, including wheat, barley, sheep, goats, and cattle. These plants and animals continued to form the basis of agriculture during the Harappan period. In Level IIa at Mehrgarh, which dates to around 5500 B.C., buildings consisting of a series of square cells have been excavated. The excavators interpret these structures as silos for storing surplus crops.

The earliest evidence for extensive settlement of the Indus Valley comes from the Pre-Harappan period between 3300 B.C. and 2600 B.C. Sites dating to this period include large towns surrounded by fortification walls. It is unclear whether these walls were for defence from human invaders or for protection against river floods and erosion. During the Pre-Harappan period, there was an increase in the uniformity of material culture across the Indus Valley.

The **Harappan period** lasted for 700 years, from 2600 B.C. to 1900 B.C. The beginning of this period is marked by the expansion of a small number of sites into major urban centres. The material culture of the Harappan period is extremely uniform across the entire Indus Valley. The end of the period is the subject of considerable debate. Some archaeologists believe that invading forces—perhaps even the Aryan invaders described in the sacred Hindu texts of the Rig-Veda—destroyed the Harappan people. The main evidence for this interpretation consists of groups of skeletons found in the final levels of Mohenjo-Daro. In one staircase, thirteen skeletons of adults and children were found, while in another area the sprawled skeletons of three men, one woman, and a child were discovered (Agrawal 1985). A recent re-analysis of the skeletons from Mohenjo-Daro suggests that these people may have died from an outbreak of malaria, rather than as the victims of a conquering army (Bahn 2002). Many archaeologists today emphasize that the decline of the Indus civilization was a gradual process (Kenoyer 1998). Following the collapse of the Harappan civilization there was a decline in the size of sites in the Indus Valley and an increased diversity of material culture within the region. When large urban centres were reestablished in the Indian subcontinent over a century later, they were built along the Ganges river system in India.

Harappan period The period between 2600 B.C. and 1900 B.C. during which urban centres developed in the Indus Valley.

■ The City

In the 1850s, British railway engineers began construction of a railway link between Lahore and Multan in what was then the Punjab province of the British Empire (Kenoyer 1998). Searching for material for the railway beds, these engineers seized on the idea of using crushed brick rubble from mounds they found along the path of the railroad. Archaeologists were both powerless to stop the destruction and puzzled by the absence of Buddhist-period remains from the mounds. It took over fifty years for archaeologists to understand that these sites were the remains of a previously unknown civilization (Marshall 1928).

Harappan cities have a number of common features. Houses and other structures are laid along a regular grid of streets that run through the city (see the reconstruction in Figure 12.13). The most striking aspect of Harappan cities is the sense of order and the emphasis on hygiene. Elaborate drains are found leading from the houses to covered

FIGURE 12.13 Reconstruction of the city of Harappa. A large street with a central drain runs from the gate through the city.

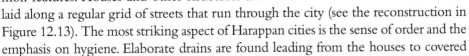

FIGURE 12.14 The Great Bath at Mohenjo-Daro, Pakistan.

channels that run through the streets and out of the city (Jansen 1989). Water was supplied by wells lined with fired bricks, and structures were built of fired bricks of a uniform size. The normal brick size was 28 × 14 × 7 centimetres (Allchin and Allchin 1982). Most of the Harrapan settlements were small villages. Only five cities greater than 80 hectares are known. The largest Harappan cities were the sites of **Harappa** and **Mohenjo-Daro**.

Both Harappa and Mohenjo-Daro were built on a series of walled mounds. Most archaeologists believe that the cities consisted of an elite area on a high mound or citadel at the western side, overlooking a lower town where the non-elite members of society lived. Excavations along the edge of the high mound at Mohenjo-Daro suggest that the citadel buildings were constructed on a massive mud-brick platform. Although the mounds that make up Harappa and Mohenjo-Daro had walls, it is not clear whether they were designed for military defence. There is no evidence of warfare at either site, with the possible exception of the skeletons of Mohenjo-Daro.

At Mohenjo-Daro and Harappa, excavations uncovered large buildings that have been interpreted as granaries. At Harappa, the "granary" is a building measuring 40 × 50 metres, constructed on a mud-brick foundation. It consists of a series of two rows of six rooms built along a central passage. At Mohenjo-Daro, the "granary" is a building measuring 50 × 27 metres. The foundation is divided into twenty-seven square blocks (Kenoyer 1998). There is no evidence to decisively support the identification of these structures as granaries. However, the edifices are clearly the remains of large public buildings of some kind.

The most impressive structure found on a Harappan site is the **Great Bath** of Mohenjo-Daro (see Figure 12.14). At the centre of the Great Bath is a 12 × 7 metre wide, 3-metre-deep, brick-lined basin sealed with gypsum mortar and asphalt and surrounded by an impressive pillared gallery. A flight of stairs at both ends leads to the bottom of the basin. A large well found in an adjoining room was the source of water for filling the Great Bath. Archaeologists have developed a wide array of interpretations of this structure, ranging from a site of sacred rituals of cleanliness to a nice place to cool off on a hot summer day.

■ Writing

The **Harappan script** is known mostly from small carved stone sealings used to mark vessels and bundles (Kenoyer 1998). Other inscribed objects include flat pieces of copper, a gold pendant, a bronze axe, and small incised tablets. The writing is limited to a small number of characters per inscription. Although over 400 different signs have been identified, the longest-known inscription has a series of twenty-six signs. Given the large number of symbols, it appears likely that the writing system was either logographic (signs representing words) or ideographic (signs representing concepts). To date, the Harappan script has not been deciphered (see Figure 12.15).

The unreadable inscriptions on the Harappan seals leave many unanswered questions. Are the inscriptions the names of the owners of the seals? Or perhaps the names of deities with whom the owner was identified? The questions increase when

Harappa One of the two major urban centres of the Harappan period.

Mohenjo-Daro One of the two major urban centres of the Harappan period.

Great Bath An impressive structure built around a rectangular basin at the site of Mohenjo-Daro. It is one of the few monumental structures found on a Harappan site.

Harappan script A script that has not yet been deciphered and is known mostly from small carved stone sealings used to mark vessels and bundles.

CANADIAN research

Material Signs of Status in the Harappan

In contemporary society, the use of material objects as markers of status is pervasive. Cars, houses, clothing, and jewellery all send out clear signals of social position. The same processes are evident in early complex societies, where the elite and emerging middle class strived to mark out their position in society. The gold ornaments of Ur are a good example of such unambiguous markers of elite status.

However, in the Indus Valley, markers of high or even middle-class status are hard to find in the cities of the Harappan civilization. Heather Miller, an archaeologist at the University of Toronto at Mississauga, has explored the technology of bead production in the Indus Valley to gain an understanding of how material objects were

used in the context of this early state society. Beads are an ideal focus because they are very common on Harappan sites and because bead necklaces have the potential to be visible status markers. Miller's results are fairly complex. She found some differentiation in red coloured beads that might indicate a hierarchy of value: from beads made of stone, which would have likely had a high value, to similar beads made from artificial materials that appear to be imitations of the more valuable stone ones. However, when she turned to the analysis of white and blue beads, she found very different results. Here there were no high-status variants made from stone, and there was no observable difference that might have reflected social markers.

Miller suggests that the white and blue beads might have been used to reinforce the solidarity of Harappan civilization rather than to reinforce the differentiation among social classes. She also emphasizes the nature of the technological process involved in producing these beads. Particularly for pieces made of talc-faience, the process involves transforming a dull, soft material into a hard, shiny, finished product through firing at a high temperature. Miller suggests that the value of this material came from the cultural value attached to the transformational process of manufacture. ◆

REFERENCE: Heather Miller. (2007). *Archaeological Approaches to Technology*. New York: Academic/Elsevier.

we consider the depictions on the seals. The most common scene is of a bull, an elephant, or a rhinoceros, often shown standing in front of what appears to be an incense burner. But more fantastic creatures, including unicorns, three-headed animals, and what appears to be a horned tiger, are also found. The most enigmatic seals show what appear to be deities. One type of deity appears as a three-headed horned person sitting in a lotus position. In a more complex scene, a figure wearing a crescent-shaped headdress is in front of a kneeling form and a bull. Below this scene is a procession of what appears to be people wearing bangles and headdresses.

The seals afford evidence of a complex administrative system. Carefully standardized stone weights offer further evidence for control over the flow of goods. These weights are usually plain cubes of rock carefully carved to adhere to a strict standard.

FIGURE 12.15 The script on these seals from the Indus Valley has not been deciphered, and the significance of the scenes shown remains an enigma.

FIGURE 12.16 Sculpture of the "priest king" found at Mohenjo-Daro. Notice the diadems on his head and arm and the elaborate pattern on his cloak. These might be indicative of his high status in Harappan society. Height 17.5 cm.

■ Government

The people of the Harappan civilization lived in highly organized cities with a bureaucracy that used a writing system, seals, and weights. The influence of this bureaucracy was so pervasive that even bricks were made to a standard size. The power of the Harappan state is vividly expressed by its construction and maintenance of an urban sewage system unparalleled among other early state societies. Although the vitality of the Harappan state is evident, the structure of the state remains obscure. The identity of the elite, the basis of their claim to power, and their relation to other sectors of society remain largely unknown.

The Harappan elite appear not to have lived very differently from other members of society or to have expressed their power by constructing monuments or burying their dead with pomp and splendor. Only a handful of sculptures that can be considered depictions of royalty have been found on Harappan sites. The most impressive is a small steatite sculpture known as the "priest king," (see Figure 12.16). This sculpture depicts a bearded man wearing a headband with a circular ornament at the centre of his forehead and a similar ornament on a bracelet around his right forearm. He is dressed in a cloth adorned with a geometric pattern.

■ Summing Up the Evidence

The cities of the Harappan civilization remain deeply puzzling. These large population centres were exquisitely organized down to the minute details of their sewage channels and standardized building materials. This degree of planning is unparalleled in the ancient world. Yet the leaders remain almost invisible. There are elite areas in the large cities of Mohenjo-Daro and Harappa, but impressive burials and palaces are noticeably absent. The only monumental architecture of note is, of all things, a bath! Were the Harappan cities based on an egalitarian form of social organization different from that of any other known early state societies? If not, was it perhaps an ethos of equality that in fact cloaked a very real social inequality? Ultimately, we are left to wonder about the identity of the person sculpted so powerfully into the figure of the "priest king." Was this the ruler of the city? If so, what was his power and on what was it based?

12.3 China

Chinese archaeologists stress the continuity of Chinese culture going as far back in time as the Neolithic. As a result, the culture history of China is highly developed, as is the study of particular types of artifacts. Until recently, the ideological demands of the modern Chinese state have often limited the ability of Chinese archaeologists to think freely about the processes of state formation. Political tensions, as well as the difficulty of mastering the Chinese language and culture history, have often stood in the way of interaction between Chinese archaeologists and their international colleagues. In recent years there has been a gradual shift, and a new generation of Chinese archaeologists shows a real interest in developments in archaeological method and theory. At the same time, a number of international teams have been working in China to explore the process of state formation, often through archaeological survey. As a result, the picture of state formation in China is in flux, with new questions emerging and archaeologists struggling to keep pace with the flow of new data.

■ Anyang and Late Shang China

According to Chinese historical texts, three powerful dynasties—the Hsia, the Shang, and the Zhou—emerged in northern China during the period between 2000 B.C. and 500 B.C. The oldest archaeological site that can be securely correlated with the historical documents is the impressive site of Anyang, the capital of the Late Shang Dynasty (1200 B.C. to 1045 B.C.; see Figure 12.17).

Anyang was discovered when inscribed bones began to appear on the antiquities market and their source was tracked to a small village in northern China. Intensive excavations at the site recovered the remains of an immense city. The inscribed bones that first led archaeologists to the site are **oracle bones**, used by the Shang kings to predict the outcomes of events ranging from battles to the weather (see Figure 12.18). The king posed a question to his ancestors in a special ceremony. This involved applying a heat source to specially prepared hollows on the back of the bone to produce cracks on the front. These cracks were then interpreted by the king to determine the course of future events. Beginning in the Late Shang period, the question posed, the divination, and the eventual outcome were carefully inscribed on the bone. In total, over 150,000 inscribed oracle bones have been recovered, providing a unique perspective on the lives of the rulers of the **Shang Dynasty** and the earliest record of systematic writing from China (Keightley 2000).

In later periods, historical records and economic transactions were recorded on silk and bamboo slips; however, none of these documents have survived from the Shang period. The other source of inscriptions from Anyang is elaborate bronze vessels (see Figure 12.19). The richly decorated bronze vessels of the Shang Dynasty have been described as "the politically all-important ritual symbols" (Chang 1994, 68). The importance of these vessels went beyond the considerable effort involved in acquiring tin and copper and the skill needed to cast such elaborate forms. The bronze vessels were used in rituals that were the exclusive domain of royalty and nobility as essential tools of political authority, tying together ritual, warfare, and political power.

The excavations at Anyang have uncovered the remains of a massive burial ground with over 1,000 simple burials and 11 deep burial pits reached by ramps. Large numbers of sacrificial victims, some with their heads buried separately from their bodies, are found in the pits. The tomb of Fu Hao, the wife or consort of one of the kings, was discovered intact in the palace-temple area across the river from the burial ground. The tomb of Fu Hao included an enormous quantity of burial goods, including 440 bronzes and almost 600 jades.

Anyang was a large city. The palace was surrounded by neighbourhoods, cemeteries, and areas with workshops, particularly for the manufacture of elite items. The palace-temple area consists of large structures built on platforms of stamped earth, arranged in clusters that probably reflected their functions as residences, temples, and ceremonial areas. The buildings themselves were made of very simple materials. In contrast to the elite, who lived in houses built on platforms, most of the people outside this zone lived in small houses dug into the ground.

International teams working on the origin of the Chinese state have focused heavily on archaeological survey. Part of the reason for the emphasis on survey is the extraordinary influence of the late K.C. Chang. Chang had a remarkable ability to

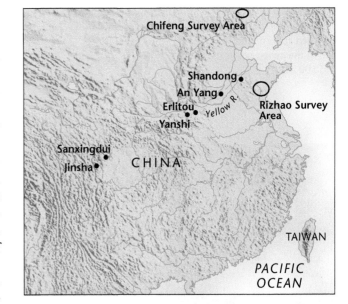

FIGURE 12.17 Map of China showing location of sites and survey areas related to early state societies.

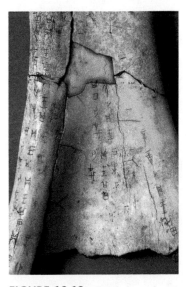

FIGURE 12.18 Oracle bone from Anyang, China. The inscription records the prediction made as well as the actual course of events.

▲▲ **Anyang** A site in northern China and the capital of the Late Shang Dynasty.

oracle bones Bones that were used in divination rituals. Inscriptions on oracle bones are a major source of written evidence about the Shang Dynasty.

Shang Dynasty The second of three powerful dynasties that emerged in northern China during the period between 2000 B.C. and 500 B.C.

FIGURE 12.19 Shang bronze vessel from Anyang, China.

FIGURE 12.20 Gilded bronze head from Sanxingdui.

synthesize data from Chinese archaeological and historical sources and was also a pioneer in developing a regional approach to archaeological research. Archaeological survey in China is not without challenges. Zhichun Jing working with colleagues in the Shangqiu region along the Yellow River to the southeast of Anyang found that during the past 1,000 years, close to 10 metres of alluvial, or river-borne, sediments were deposited across the area (Jing et al. 1997). As a result, any occupation from the Shang Dynasty is deeply buried and not visible on the surface. An extensive program of subsurface survey was carried out by drilling cores to reach the early deposits. Obviously this is a much greater effort than simply walking across a field looking for pottery and lithics. Nonetheless, subsurface survey succeeded in detecting the great 10-metre-high walls of a huge city site measuring over 9 square kilometres. This city dates to the Eastern Zhou Dynasty, which postdates the Shang.

In 1986, at the site of **Sanxingdui**, two pits filled with spectacular artifacts were found dating to the same time period as Anyang (Ge and Linduff 1990). Some of the bronzes were similar to pieces from Anyang (such as the gilded bronze head shown in Figure 12.20), but others were of a unique style that stunned experts in Chinese art. The wealth of the finds from these pits made it clear that Sanxingdui was a major centre, and subsequent research has shown that it was the location of a large urban settlement. Critical questions revolve around the relationship of Sanxingdui and Anyang.

■ Before Anyang

The **Yi-Luo Valley** in the central plains of Northern China has been identified as the political centre of the Xia and Early Shang Dynasties before the founding of Anyang (Lee 2004). **Erlitou**, a very large site in the Yi-Luo Valley, might have been the capital of the Xia Dynasty. This site, which covers 400 hectares, was inhabited between 1800 B.C. and 1600 B.C. Two large palace enclosures built on a rammed-earth terrace have been identified at Erlitou. The artifacts recovered there include a wide range of elite goods such as bronze—including the earliest bronze ritual vessels—and jade. Although the area excavated is an impressive 20,000 square metres, this is still only 0.5 percent of the total site area.

Yanshi is a similarly impressive site located 10 kilometres northeast of Erlitou. The construction of massive palace enclosures at Yanshi appears to correlate with the downfall of Erlitou. Thus the fate of these neighbouring settlements appears to be tightly linked and may be connected to the Shang conquest of the Xia that is recorded in historical documents.

The Yi-Luo River Valley Archaeological Project was launched in 1998 to explore the broader regional context for the emergence of the urban centres at Erlitou and Yanshi (see Figure 12.21). The survey area is immediately to the east of Yanshi and incorporates three tributaries of the Yi-Luo River (Liu et al. 2004). The survey found that the Early Longshan period (3000 B.C. to 2000 B.C.), which precedes the emergence of Erlitou, included two large village sites of 13 to 20 hectares. The rise of the Erlitou site is correlated with the emergence of a 60-hectare regional centre at Shaochia, an 18-hectare secondary centre, and more than forty village sites of less than 5 hectares. Combining these results with information from excavations at Erlitou, the survey team identified a four-tier settlement hierarchy with a major urban centre, two levels of secondary centres, and widely dispersed villages. These results suggest that Erlitou stood at the apex of a complex regional settlement organization. Survey results in the Yi-Luo Valley give a clear sense that developments in the urban centres of Erlitou and Yanshi had significant impact across the region as a whole.

Survey in the **Rizhao** area of Shandong Province, on the coast of the Yellow Sea, far from the Shang and Xiu capitals, found a significant increase in population

352 PART FOUR **THE DEVELOPMENT OF SOCIAL COMPLEXITY**

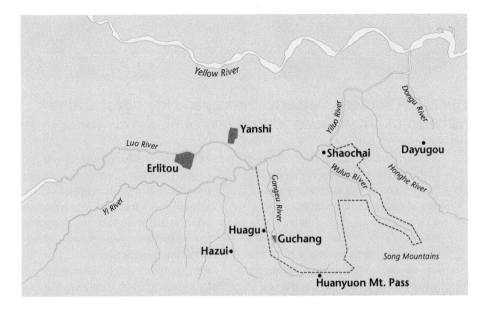

FIGURE 12.21 Map showing location of Yi-Luo Valley survey area, delineated by dashed lines, relative to the sites of Erlitou and Yanshi.

and a four-tier settlement system several centuries before the founding of Erlitou (Underhill et al. 2008). In the Rizhao area survey, two very large sites, covering between 250 and 375 hectares, were identified as Liangchengzhen in the north and Yaowangcheng in the south. Although these sites are slightly smaller than Erlitou, the survey results show that they were also urban centres at the apex of a complex settlement hierarchy. The Rizhao area survey found a significant decrease in settlement size and number of sites in the Late Longshan and Shang periods.

Located in Inner Mongolia, the **Chifeng region** is at the interface between the agricultural area of the Yellow River basin and the areas to the north and east that were occupied by societies of pastoral nomads. A survey project in the Chifeng region did not find the kind of massive settlement found in the Yi-Luo Valley or in Shandong, but even here there was a clear shift to larger settlement size and increased population around 2000 B.C. The largest single site is 23 hectares. An interesting point is that several sites also have defensive walls.

Taken together, the results of the recent survey projects make it clear that state formation in China preceded the founding of Anyang. Erlitou and Yanshi were massive urban settlements at the apex of a complex settlement hierarchy. A similar settlement system also developed to the east in Shandong in the Rizhao survey area at an earlier date. The impact of state formation extended across much of China, as is clear from the spectacular discoveries at Sanxingdui but also from the surveys in the Chifeng region of Inner Mongolia.

■ The Basis of Authority in Early China

Although military strength was critical to the power of the Shang rulers, their legitimacy rested on the unique role they fulfilled by performing rituals (Chang 1994). The power of divination was reserved for the ruler, who possessed the vessels necessary for performing rituals. The power of the rulers flowed not from their identification with a god, but with their essential role in connecting the human world with the divine. Archaeologists are able to trace the outlines of elaborate rituals of feasting and sacrifice used by Shang rulers to harness the power of their ancestors and of divine forces.

Sanxingdui A site in Sichuan Province where excavations uncovered a spectacular trove of artifacts unique in style and that are contemporary with Anyang.

Yi-Luo Valley A region where surveys have documented the complex settlement hierarchy associated with the cities of Erlitou and Yanshi, which are earlier than Anyang.

Erlitou A city in the Yi-Luo Valley that predates Anyang.

Yanshi A large settlement in the Yi-Luo Valley that appears to be slightly later than Erlitou.

Rizhao A region in Shadong Province where survey has found evidence of a complex settlement hierarchy that is earlier than the Yi-Luo River cities.

Chifeng region An area in Inner Mongolia where survey has found an increase in population around 2000 B.C.

Doing Regional Archaeological Settlement Patterns Survey in Northeast China

CHRISTIAN E. PETERSON, PHD DEPARTMENT OF ANTHROPOLOGY, UNIVERSITY OF HAWAI'I AT MĀNOA

For the better part of the last decade, my colleagues and I have been doing regional archaeological settlement patterns survey in the Western Liao River Valley of northeast China, one of four areas outside the Central Plain where complex societies arose comparably early. The first of these complex societies emerged during the Hongshan period (4500–3000 B.C.), and are best known today for their jade-yielding burials and ceremonial architecture. Although these aspects of Hongshan society have been studied for many years, until recently we knew little about the regional distribution of residential occupation in areas with ritual remains. Our work has focused on (among other things) documenting the human communities that built and used Hongshan monuments in two separate regions of the Western Liao River Valley—in Chifeng, eastern Inner Mongolia, and in Kazuo, western Liaoning Province—for comparison with those of other areas.

In both regions, we followed standard procedures for systematic pedestrian survey, covering a total of about 1,200 square kilometres in Chifeng and 200 square kilometres in Kazuo. Teams of 3–5 people walked back and forth across the landscape at intervals of 100 metres in Chifeng and 50 metres in Kazuo. Navigation was by compass, GPS, and printouts of high resolution satellite imagery of the regions, with teams covering about 1 square kilometre or more per day. As surface remains of ancient occupation were

encountered on survey, teams stopped to record the areas over which these remains were spread and to collect samples of ceramic sherds. Areas of occupation larger than the target size for each region (1 hectare in Chifeng and 0.25 hectare in Kazuo) were carved up into smaller units and collected separately to more accurately assess the size and occupational densities of multi-component settlements during different archaeological periods. All ceramics were carried back to our field lab for identification as to the archaeological period(s) represented. Sherd densities were later calculated for each collection unit by period to be used as proxies for prehistoric population. The locations and extents of collection units were drawn directly on the printed satellite imagery and later digitized into electronic maps. The resulting GIS were then linked to databases of the analyzed ceramics recovered from each collection unit and period-by-period maps of human occupation across each survey area were produced.

Upon completion of fieldwork, these maps were used to create GIS surfaces (one for each archaeological period) to help us delineate prehistoric community structure in the two survey regions. In these surfaces, concentrations of ancient occupation appear as peaks rising from flat unoccupied planes, whose bases demarcate clusters of settlements; the higher the peak, the larger the settlement cluster's estimated population. We have labelled these clusters *small*

local communities (groups of villages, hamlets, and/or dispersed farmsteads) because their residents appear to have been in more frequent interaction with one another than with their more distant neighbours. Manipulating these surfaces mathematically reveals even larger sociospatial structure (where this exists) by grouping small local communities into larger more populous ones—entities we are accustomed to calling *supra-local communities, districts,* or *polities*. Although complex societies can differ in terms of demography, composition, or internal dynamics, they are always supra-local in scale.

During the Hongshan period, the Chifeng region was home to some 4,000 to 8,000 people, while the population of the much smaller Kazuo survey area is estimated at between 750 and 1,500. In both regions, most of these people lived in settlements organized into small supra-local communities or districts; we identified about twenty of these in Chifeng, and four in Kazuo. This is the equivalent of one district every 50–60 square kilometres. These districts are visible in the distribution of settlement across the landscape in the form of concentrations of occupation separated by open or more sparsely settled areas. Each was composed of as many as ten small local communities, often with a larger one in the centre. Chifeng districts ranged from 3–5 kilometres across and had estimated populations of between 100 and 500. In Kazuo, supra-local communities

On Shang sites, elite burials exhibit a significant focus on feasting (Nelson 2003). This is a break from earlier periods, when evidence for feasting was found in burials of people from all levels of society. The emphasis on feasting at elite burials appears to indicate that during the Shang Dynasty the world of the ancestors was socially stratified. As Sarah Nelson writes, "By this point, social stratification

incorporated 100–700 people, and measured 4–8 kilometres across. In neither region is there indication of any larger or more central district that dominated others, so each supra-local community is taken to be a small independent polity or "chiefdom," although similarities in material culture indicate a high degree of interaction between them. Differentiation in Hongshan burial treatment suggests social hierarchy was the central organizing principle of these communities, while concentrations of ritual architecture in the central settlements of districts highlight the important integrative role that ceremonial activities must have played in community coalescence.

Compared to other chiefdoms, the Hongshan districts of Kazuo and Chifeng were spatially and demographically very small. Early complex societies in China's Yellow River Valley, for example, were 10 kilometres or more across and organized populations 2–5 times greater than those of their Hongshan contemporaries. Outside Asia, several well-known chiefdoms (Cahokia, Moundville, Middle Formative Basin of Mexico, Regional Classic Alto Magdalena, Early Intermediate Santa Valley, and pre-contact Hawai'i among them) had district populations ranging from 4,000 or 5,000 up into the tens of thousands, spread over areas many tens or hundreds of kilometres across. Regional populations and occupational densities in these areas were corre-

sponding higher than in the Hongshan period in northeast China. Unlike Chifeng and Kazuo, several were also the only chiefly polity present in their regions, while others were one of a small handful of polities. If the Chifeng and Kazuo survey regions are representative of the larger area of which they are a part, the entire Western Liao River Valley may have been home to thousands of supra-local communities during the fifth and fourth millennia B.C.

Our research has contributed to a better understanding of the origins of social complexity outside China's

Central Plain by documenting variation in chiefdom organization at the regional scale. The next stage of our research includes studying the organization of statuses and economic activities within Hongshan communities through remote sensing of previously identified occupation areas, the analysis of surface-collected household artifact assemblages, and stratigraphic excavation. In so doing, we hope to arrive at a more comprehensive understanding of the internal dynamics of these chiefly communities for comparison with others around the world. ▲

FIGURE 12.22   Dr. Christian Peterson on survey in the Chifeng region in 2007.

is so marked that only royalty are feasted and only the royal dead can apparently become spirits" (Nelson 2003, 87). The evidence for feasting consists mostly of the vessels recovered from excavation. Most of these are designed for drinking wine, but others are shaped for preparing and eating meat and grains. These vessels were cleaned after use and carefully stacked in the tombs.

Archaeology and Development

The Three Gorges Dam in China is only the latest and largest dam construction to cause substantial destruction of archaeological sites. Building of the massive dam across the Yangtze River was completed in 2006 and is creating a narrow reservoir that will extend over 600 kilometres. The goal of this huge project is to generate power and control flooding in the area downriver from the dam. The impact of the dam includes the displacement of over one million people. Environmentalists have raised concerns about the potential effects of this project. Moreover, the dam has also led to the flooding of hundreds of archaeological sites.

Although the scale of the Three Gorges Dam is unprecedented, the flooding of archaeological sites by artificial reservoirs is a recurrent threat. The building of the Aswan Dam in Egypt (completed in 1971) led to an international mobilization organized by UNESCO to rescue archaeological sites located along the portion of the Nile Valley that would be flooded (Hassan 2007). The transport of the Abu Simbel monumental sculp-

tures to dry ground received particular notice and demonstrated that at least some mitigation of the effects of dam construction is possible. The experience gained from the Aswan project set some guidelines for archaeological responses to dam construction. Because the scale of the threat to archaeological resources from these projects is so vast, the response requires coordinated international efforts. Initial archaeological research must also include systematic survey and detailed planning so that there is a sound basis for prioritizing which sites should be excavated.

Today, dam construction threatens archaeological sites around the world. Projects in Turkey and the Sudan have caused international concern, but there are many other works that receive only local attention. Rarely are archaeologists able to stop dam construction or even alter the design of a dam. A notable exception is the Côa Valley in Portugal, where intense lobbying by archaeologists saved the Upper Paleolithic open-air art sites in the valley just before they were to be flooded.

Archaeologists have often gained important knowledge from the opportunities afforded by dam construction. For example, the sites of Abu Hureyra and Habuba Kebira in Syria are among the sites excavated in advance of Syrian damming of the Euphrates River. Yet archeologists are painfully aware that there is no mitigation that will truly redress the damage caused by dams. Even where sites are transported or fully excavated, which happens in only a small percentage of cases, what is lost is the original context of the site and the potential for future research. These sites are a nonrenewable resource and every loss is irreversible. Archaeologists are left to act as advocates for the preservation of the archaeological record, but they are also forced to make pragmatic choices to respond to destruction that they cannot prevent. The experience with the Aswan Dam highlights the importance of strong international organizations that can mobilize an effective archaeological response to large-scale development. ●

FIGURE 12.23 Satellite photo of the Three Gorges Dam showing the reservoir flooding the valley behind the dam for a distance of more than 600 km.

FIGURE 12.24 The relocation of Abu Simbel, Egypt.

Most large sites have produced extensive evidence for sacrifice. Sacrifice appears distinct from feasting, since in many cases complete animals are interred (Jing and Flad 2005). Animals found in sacrificial pits include dogs, pigs, cattle, horses, and elephants. The numbers can be quite large. For example, at Anyang there are over 200 horses buried in 66 pits and over 220 dogs in 34 pits. Humans were also sacrificed in large numbers. There are also pits with a combination of different animals as well as pits with both human and animal sacrifices. The discoveries at Sanxingdui suggest that objects were also linked to sacrifice (see Figure 12.25). In the two large pits discovered in 1986, the objects had all been burnt and broken. The scale of the offerings in these pits is remarkable. One of them included 735 bronzes, 61 gold objects, 486 worked pieces of jade, 67 elephant tusks, and 4,600 seashells. These had been arranged in layers according to types of artifacts and had clearly not been thrown into the pit haphazardly.

FIGURE 12.25 One of the sacrificial pits from Sanxingdui with bronze vessels and ivory tusks.

■ Summing Up the Evidence

It is a fair bet that the coming decade will see significant developments in our understanding of state formation in China. The pace of fieldwork is impressive and there is an increasingly lively discussion of issues related to archaeological method and theory. A distinctive element of early Chinese states is the importance of ritual for establishing the power of the rulers. Archaeological research on feasting and sacrifice is providing important insight into how these rituals actually played out. Excavation and survey across China is beginning to undermine an approach to state formation in China that focuses exclusively on Anyang. It is now clear that state formation was a complex process that took place across a wide geographical region, stretching at the very least from Sichuan in the south to Inner Mongolia in the north. State formation also stretches back to the pre-Shan Dynasty urban sites found in the Yi-Luo Valley and Shandong.

SUMMARY

- Centralized power structures began to emerge in Minoan Crete around 1900 B.C.
- Mycenaean complex societies developed in the Peloponnese Peninsula in southern Greece and to the north in central Greece beginning around 1500 B.C.
- Palaces were at the core of both Minoan and Mycenaean society.
- Colin Renfrew proposed peer polity interaction among early state modules as the dynamic underlying the development of social complexity in the Aegean.
- Some archaeologists are beginning to question whether Minoan and Mycenaean societies fit with the idea of hierarchical states, suggesting that these societies are better understood in terms of heterarchy.

- Experimental archaeology has demonstrated that warfare using Aegean swords required considerable skill and would not have always been lethal.
- The eruption of Thera, an island in the Cyclades, resulted in the destruction of the town of Akrotiri. The nature of the impact of the Thera eruption on Minoan Crete remains the subject of debate.
- The Harappan civilization developed along the Indus River Valley. The material culture of the Harappan civilization is essentially uniform across the entire region.
- The two largest Harappan cities are Harappa and Mohenjo-Daro. These cities are characterized by a regular grid of roadways and an impressive sewage system.

- There is little evidence of monumental architecture on Harappan sites. One exception is the Great Bath at Mohenjo-Daro.
- The Harappan script is found on a range of artifacts, including seals. The script has not yet been deciphered.
- There is little evidence for the concentration of wealth in the hands of the elites of Harappan cities.
- Anyang was the capital of the Late Shang Dynasty between 1200 B.C. and 500 B.C. Excavations at Anyang have recovered large quantities of oracle bones, a massive burial ground, and the remains of a large city.
- Excavations at Sanxingdui in Sichuan Province have uncovered great hoards of remarkable artifacts contemporary with Anyang.

- Survey in the Yi-Luo Valley has revealed that the cities of Erlitou and Yanshi, which predate Anyang, were at the top of a complex settlement hierarchy.
- Survey in the Rizhao area of Shandong Province has uncovered evidence of a complex settlement hierarchy that is earlier than the Yi-Luo Valley sites.
- Survey in the Chifeng Region of Inner Mongolia has demonstrated an increase in settlement size around 2000 B.C.
- The legitimacy of Shang rulers rested on the role they played in performing rituals.
- Feasting associated with elite burials and sacrificial deposits are important features of Shang Dynasty sites.

KEY TERMS

Akrotiri, 344
Anyang, 351
Chifeng region, 353
early state modules, 338
Erlitou, 352
Great Bath, 348
Harappa, 348
Harappan period, 347
Harappan script, 348
heterarchy, 339
Indus Valley, 346
Knossos, 337
Linear B, 341
Lion Gate, 337

megaron, 341
Minoan, 337
Mohenjo-Daro, 348
Mycenaean, 337
oracle bones, 351
peer polity interaction, 338
Rizhao, 352
Sanxingdui, 352
Shang Dynasty, 351
Thera, 344
wanax, 342
Yanshi, 352
Yi-Luo Valley, 352

REVIEW QUESTIONS

1. Is the association of the Shang ruler with the performance of rituals unique or are there parallels to the role of rulers in Mesopotamia, Egypt, the Aegean, or the Indus?
2. Why do archaeologists find the absence of monumental architecture and elaborate burials in the Harappan cities surprising?
3. What is peer polity interaction and how is it applied to early Aegean states? Could this concept also apply in early contexts in China?
4. How has survey been used to understand the development of social complexity in China and the Aegean?

CANADIAN ARCHAEOLOGISTS

- Elizabeth Greene is a professor in the Department of Classics at Brock University. She is an underwater archaeologist whose research involves exploring shipwrecks in the Eastern Mediterranean, particularly off the coast of Turkey.
http://www.brocku.ca/humanities/humanities-research/humanities-research-institute/hri-associates/elizabeth-s-greene

- Zhichun Jing is a professor in the Department of Anthropology at the University of British Columbia. He has been engaged in the archaeology of the Shang Dynasty at Anyang and in the surrounding region, a project that has included the discovery of the Shang city at Huanbei.
http://www.anth.ubc.ca/people/anthropology-faculty/zhichun-jing.html

- Carl Knappett is a professor in the Department of Art at the University of Toronto. He carries out fieldwork at the Minoan site of Palaikastro. His research also includes work on material culture theory and archaeology, ceramic analysis, and network analysis. He is the author of *Thinking Through Material Culture: An Interdisciplinary Perspective* (University of Pennsylvania Press, 2005).
  www.art.utoronto.ca/people/art-history/graduate-faculty/carl-knappett

- Heather Miller, professor in the Department of Anthropology at the University of Toronto at Mississauga, has carried out studies on the technology of the Harappan societies of the Indus Valley. She currently directs a project on Islamic Caravanserai Networks in the area around the city of Peshawar, Pakistan. Her recent publications include *Archaeological Approaches to Technology* (Academic Press/Elsevier, 2007).
  www.utm.utoronto.ca/~w3hmlmil/

- Christian Peterson, professor in the Department of Anthropology at the University of Hawai'i at Manoa, began his studies in archaeology at the University of Toronto before going on to carry out graduate research at the University of Pittsburgh. He is involved in a number of research projects investigating the emergence of social complexity in Inner Mongolia.
  www.anthropology.hawaii.edu/People/Faculty/Peterson/

- Alice Yao is a professor in the Department of Anthropology at the University of Toronto at Mississauga. Her research focuses on the impact of Han Empire's conquest of frontier regions and seeks to explain the variable ways different communities and social classes responded to momentous changes in local history. She is currently directing a survey project in southwestern China.
  http://anthropology.utoronto.ca/people/faculty-1/faculty-profiles/alice-yao/

PEARSON

Visit **www.myanthrokit.com**, where you will find a variety of tools and resources to enhance your learning, including:
- Practise quizzes with Study Plans
- Videos
- Listening Activities
- And much more!

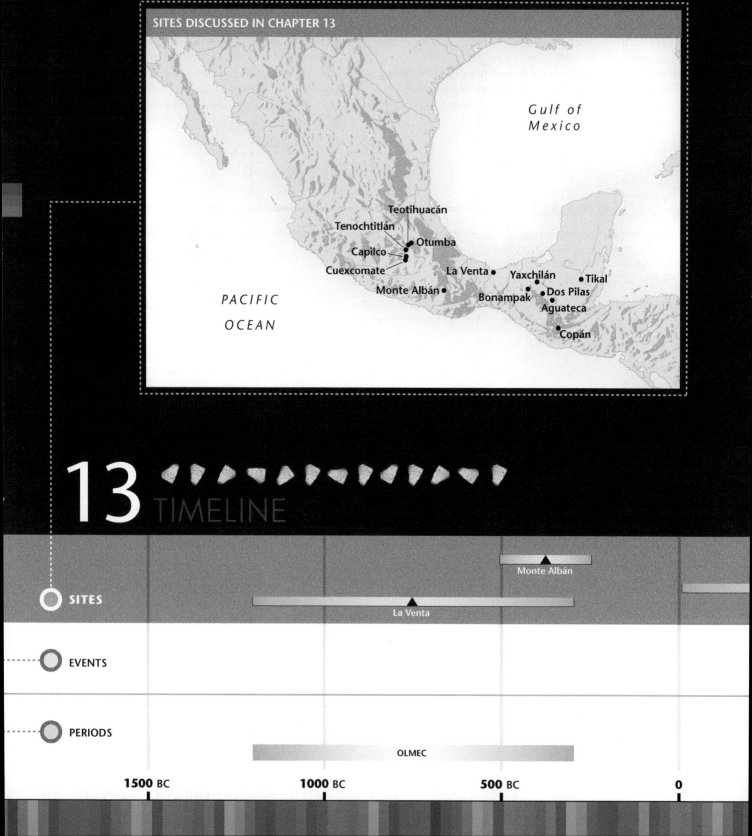

Gulf of
Mexico

Teotihuacán

Tenochtitlán

• Otumba

Capilco •

Cuexcomate

La Venta •

Yaxchilán
• Tikal

PACIFIC

Monte Albán •

Bonampak •
• Dos Pilas

Aguateca

OCEAN

• Copán

13
TIMELINE

Monte Albán

SITES

La Venta

EVENTS

PERIODS

OLMEC

1500 BC   **1000** BC   **500** BC   0

FROM CITY TO EMPIRE:
SOCIAL COMPLEXITY IN MESOAMERICA

The complex societies of Mesoamerica expand our understanding
of urbanism and the institutions that underlie both cities and empires.
After reading this chapter, you should understand:

- The archaeological evidence for the
  nature of social organization in the city
  of Teotihuacán.

- The structure of Maya cities and the
  historical record recovered from
  Maya hieroglyphic texts.

- The history and organization
  of the Aztec Empire.

Recording Maya glyphs.

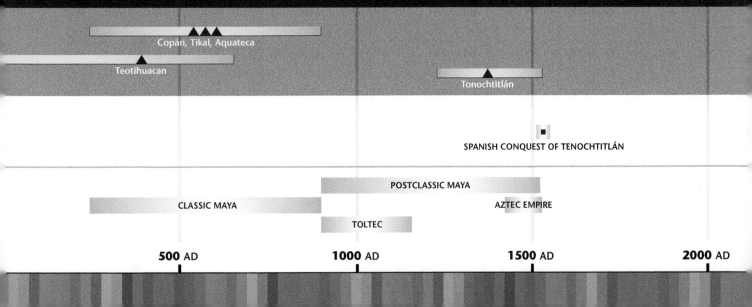

Copán, Tikal, Aquateca

Teotihuacan

Tonochtitlán

SPANISH CONQUEST OF TENOCHTITLÁN

POSTCLASSIC MAYA

CLASSIC MAYA

AZTEC EMPIRE

TOLTEC

500 AD   **1000** AD   **1500** AD   **2000** AD

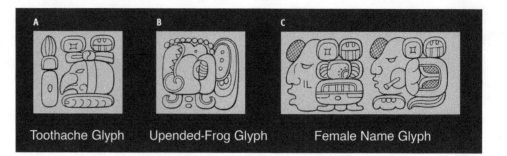

FIGURE 13.1 **A:** The toothache glyph, indicating that the date that follows is the date when a ruler took to the throne. **B:** The upended-frog glyph, indicating that the date that follows is a birth date. **C:** The name glyph of the woman on Stela 3. The profile with a cross-hatched oval over the forehead indicates that the person named was a woman.

Toothache Glyph   Upended-Frog Glyph   Female Name Glyph

In 1961, Tatiana Proskouriakoff noticed that a series of inscriptions from the Maya site of Piedras Negras featured one sign, known as the "toothache sign," along with another sign, the "upended-frog," with each placed next to the sign for a date (see Figure 13.1). The Maya calendar had already been deciphered, so Proskouriakoff was able to determine that the date associated with the upended-frog sign was twenty to thirty years earlier than the date associated with the toothache sign. On the basis of this observation, she came to the conclusion that the toothache sign indicated the date a ruler ascended to the throne, and that the upended-frog sign indicated the ruler's birth date. This modest hypothesis had major implications for the study of the ancient Maya. If Proskouriakoff was correct, then the Maya had recorded the history of their rulers and this history could be deciphered.

Proskouriakoff then turned to three stelae numbered 1 through 3 (see Figure 13.2). On the front of these large stones, the inscription is badly eroded, but on the back the well-preserved carving of a woman wearing a robe is clearly seen. Proskouriakoff found that Stelae 1 and 2 showed the upended-frog glyph (indicating the date of birth), followed by a name. The name was prefixed by a profile with a cross-hatched oval or lock of hair on the forehead, a prefix indicating that the person was a woman. The date and the name on both stelae were the same.

On the third stela, a girl kneels next to the woman. The upended-frog glyph date for the girl is thirty-three years later than the birth date of the main figure. Proskouriakoff concluded, "How can one reasonably doubt that [the] robed figures are portraits of the same person, that the person is a woman, and that her little daughter, not yet born when Stela 1 was erected, is shown on Stela 3?" (Proskouriakoff 1961, 16). Proskouriakoff had succeeded in reading a small piece of Maya history. Subsequent advances in deciphering Maya hieroglyphs came at a steady pace and today much of the history recorded by the Maya that survives can be read (a complete reading of Stela 3 from Piedras Negras can be found at http://www.pbs.org/wgbh/nova/mayacode/translate.html).

Mesoamerica is not a geographically defined region, but rather a region whose indigenous inhabitants share a number of cultural traits, including a complex calendar, an emphasis on bloodletting, and a ball game played on a special court (Coe 1993). In this chapter, we begin by briefly exploring the evidence for the emergence of social complexity and urbanism in Mesoamerica. We then take a more in-depth look at both the urban centre of Teotihuacán and the Maya cities. The last part of this chapter examines the emergence of the Aztec Empire. A number of authors have argued that there are aspects of the development of state societies in Mesoamerica that do not fit well with general models for state formation. Richard Blanton and colleagues have posited that while some Mesoamerican states were hierarchical, in others a different power strategy was dominant (Blanton et al. 1996). In a hierarchical state, there are clear patterns of dominance, with a single ruler at the apex of society holding a monopoly on power. Blanton refers to the political strategy underlying hierarchical states as

FIGURE 13.2 The back of Stela 3 from Piedras Negras, showing a woman sitting on a throne with a child beside her.

Figure 11.8 from Expedition 4 (1), Figure 5, p. 17 (1961). Reprinted by permission of University of Pennsylvania Museum.

exclusionary. Other societies developed a *corporate* political strategy in which power is shared across different sectors. In a corporate setting, social forces actually inhibit the centralization of power in a single individual. Old Kingdom Egypt presents perhaps the ultimate example of a hierarchical state with the construction of monumental funerary complexes built around the body of the king. Yet even in Old Kingdom Egypt, there were countervailing forces, most likely from the social structure organized around lineages and households. In Mesopotamia, the ruler was clearly politically dominant, but the power of the palace was balanced by that of the temple. Perhaps the best examples of an urban society with a corporate power strategy are the cities of the Indus Valley. The layout of Mohenjo-Daro and Harappa show evidence of planning and a central authority, yet there is an almost complete absence of indications of the concentration of power in the hands of a single ruler. In Mesoamerica, the city of Teotihuacán, although very different from the cities of the Indus Valley, might also be best understood in the context of corporate strategy, or even as the emergence of a corporate strategy in response to the excesses of hierarchical rulers. The rulers of Maya cities were clearly powerful individuals. But even with the Maya there are indications of tension between the ruling lineages and a political body that was more broadly representative of the elite of the city.

FIGURE 13.3 La Venta colossal Olmec head.

13.1 The Origins of Urbanism and Social Complexity

The earliest evidence of emerging political complexity in Mesoamerica is found on **Olmec** sites along the Gulf Coast of Mexico (Benson et al. 1996). Between 1200 B.C. and 300 B.C., the Olmec constructed a series of major ceremonial centres in towns with populations numbering in the thousands. The Olmec developed a highly sophisticated artistic tradition that included monumental sculptures of human heads carved out of volcanic rock, such as the sculpture from the site of La Venta, shown in Figure 13.3. These sculptures give a vivid sense of the prestige of Olmec society's leaders. Particularly significant is the headgear depicted on the sculptures, which is possibly related to competition in a ball game. Hollow clay sculptures of infants with what appear to be adult heads are often found on Olmec sites. These delicate figures stand in sharp contrast to the raw power expressed in the monumental stone sculptures raising the question of whether the figures depict leaders or divinities. The Olmec also produced spectacular sculptures from jade and other hard stones. At the site of La Venta, a cache of sixteen male figures carved from jade and serpentine was found, standing in front of a series of polished stone axes (Lauck 1996). It is possible that this scene represents a town council, a balance to the power of the rulers depicted through the monumental sculptures.

The first city in Mesoamerica was located at the site of **Monte Albán**, in the Oaxaca Valley in the Mexican highlands. Between 500 and 350 B.C., the population of Monte Albán grew first to 5,000 and then to 17,000 in neighbourhoods built around a central plaza (Blanton et al. 1993). In the period between 350 and 250 B.C., Monte Albán was surrounded by a defensive wall. The central plaza became the focus of monumental construction that included temples, a possible palace, and a ball court.

Olmec The earliest complex society in Mesoamerica. Olmec sites are located along the Gulf Coast of Mexico.

▲▲ **Monte Albán** Site of the oldest city in Mesoamerica, located in the Oaxaca Valley.

The Gender of Tomb 7 at Monte Albán

The site of Monte Albán in the Oaxaca Valley of Mexico is known as the earliest city in Mesoamerica. Tomb 7 at Monte Albán is something of an anomaly for this site. The main use of Tomb 7 dates to the Late Postclassic, a period between A.D. 900 and A.D. 1521 that is not well represented at Monte Albán. However, the spectacular discoveries made in Tomb 7 have assured it a key role in the archaeology of Mesoamerica.

Tomb 7 consists of two chambers connected by a central corridor. In the east chamber there are the remains of four people along with burial goods. In the southwest corner of this chamber a human skull covered in turquoise and shell mosaic with a knife stuck into the nasal cavity was recovered. There were also five human mandibles—lower jaws—painted red. The west chamber included four skeletons that like those recovered from the east chamber were in primary context, meaning that they had been placed in the tomb as complete corpses. At the western end of the west chamber, remains of a very different kind were recovered. These were the bones of a single individual, known as Skeleton A,

found in a seated position. Skeleton A had been buried as a mummy bundle and was the focus of the entire tomb. Skeleton A showed evidence of Paget's disease, a thickening of the skull bone that would have caused intense headaches. Skeleton A was identified as the remains of a 55-year-old male.

Sharisse and Geoffrey McCafferty have re-examined Tomb 7 and question whether Skeleton A is actually male. They raise the question of whether this identification is based on biases brought by the excavators and suggest that the data leads to a very different conclusion. It turns out that the pelvis and other parts of Skeleton A that would have made it possible to determine the sex of the skeleton were missing. The McCaffertys suggest that the identification of the skeleton as male was largely based on the thickness of the cranial bones. But the thickness of the cranial bone was altered by Paget's disease, so this trait should not be used to determine gender.

The McCafferty team then turned to the artifacts found with Skeleton A and found that these were almost all objects

associated with weaving, an activity that in Mesoamerica was carried out by women. Among these objects were pieces with the shape of a batten, a slender piece of wood used to separate the warp strings. Of the thirty-four carved eagle and jaguar bones found with Skeleton A, many look like battens, with a smoothed edge and pointed ends. Small combs and picks as well as spindle whorls were also found with Skeleton A. There was even a "false fingernail" that might have actually been a thimble. The McCaffertys suggested that these were not everyday tools but rather special forms used in the context of burial ritual. They concluded that Skeleton A was both a biological female and the bearer of symbolic attributes associated with the female gender, perhaps as the representative of a female deity. The reinterpretation of Tomb A demonstrates the value of questioning interpretations that might be based as much on our own biases as on the archaeological remains. ◆

REFERENCE: McCafferty, S.D. and G.G. McCafferty. (1994). Engendering Tomb 7 at Monte Alban: Respinning an old yarn. *Current Anthropology* 35(2): 143-166.

13.2 Teotihuacán

Beginning 2,000 years ago (A.D. 1 to A.D. 200), **Teotihuacán** grew into an enormous city covering an area of 20 square kilometres, with a population of more than 80,000 (Sugiyama 2004). Teotihuacán, shown in Figure 13.4, is located in the highland Valley of Mexico at 7,000 metres above sea level, a rich agricultural area dotted by lakes. The Teotihuacán Mapping Project surveyed the entire area of the city and carried out systematic collections of artifacts (Millon 1973; Millon et al. 1973). This project, which produced the site map shown in Figure 13.5, is perhaps the largest-scale urban survey ever undertaken.

Teotihuacán was laid out along a road known as the **Avenue of the Dead**, that stretches for 5 kilometres and runs south to north. Surveys indicate that the growth of Teotihuacán was fuelled by the depopulation of the surrounding countryside. During the period of the initial growth of Teotihuacán, between A.D. 1 and A.D. 200, the great monuments that line the Avenue of the Dead—The Pyramid of

▲▲ **Teotihuacán** An enormous city with a population of over 80,000 located in the Valley of Mexico and established around 2,000 years ago.

Avenue of the Dead A road that stretches for 5 kilometres through the centre of Teotihuacán.

the Sun, the Ciudadela, the Temple of the Feathered Serpent, and the Pyramid of the Moon—were built. While this program of monumental construction was under way, little effort was put into elaborating the residential areas of the city. The **Pyramid of the Sun** is the largest monument at Teotihuacán, rising to 64 metres and encompassing over 1 million cubic metres. A cave runs below the pyramid for about 100 metres. This natural feature was clearly of great importance, but excavations found that most of the contents of the cave had been looted in antiquity.

The **Ciudadela** is a very large compound that some archaeologists think might have housed a palace. At the back of the main courtyard in the compound is the **Temple of the Feathered Serpent** (also known as the Feathered Serpent Pyramid), so named for the carved heads of the deity that adorn the monument's surface (see Figure 13.6). Excavations in the 1980s revealed burials of sacrificial victims distributed symmetrically along the four sides of the temple. The grave goods found with these male victims suggest they held high-status positions related to the military. A series of skeletons was found with necklaces consisting of shell replicas of human upper jaws (maxillae). In one case, the necklace is made of actual human jaws (see Figure 13.7). The burials in the temple make it clear that there was a relationship between military power and prestige in Teotihuacán. They also vividly demonstrate the role of human sacrifice in Teotihuacán ritual.

Around A.D. 400, a remarkable event took place. The facade of the Temple of the Feathered Serpent was smashed and burned and then re-covered with a new layer of construction. This destruction of the facade of the temple had been preceded by a shift away from monumental construction. Beginning around A.D. 200, the residential areas of the city were reconfigured into apartment complexes, multifamily dwellings enclosed within massive walls. There is a great deal of variation between the apartment compounds, but all of the apartments were built along the same orientation as the Avenue of the Dead. It is estimated that 50 to 100 people lived in a complex. Some of the compounds have been identified as residences of groups coming from outside the Valley of Mexico. The construction of the apartments, along with the destruction of the facade of the Temple of the Feathered Serpent, might have been the result of a gradual increase in the power of kin groups at the expense of the centralized ruler. The presence of burials near sacrificial altars in the main apartment complexes might indicate the

Pyramid of the Sun The largest monument at Teotihuacán, rising to 64 metres.

Ciudadela A very large compound in Teotihuacán that includes a large courtyard where the Temple of the Feathered Serpent is located.

Temple of the Feathered Serpent Structure at the back of the Ciudadela adorned with the sculpted heads of the feathered serpent deity.

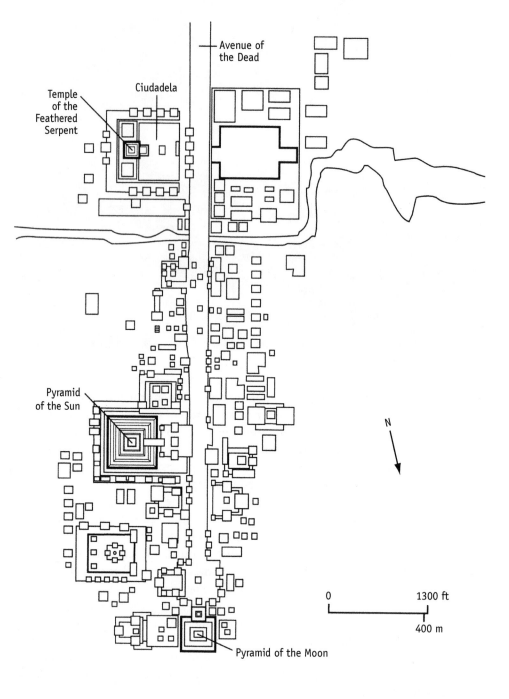

FIGURE 13.5 Map of the central area of Teotihuacán from the Teotihuacán Mapping Project.

development of ritual built around the ancestors of kin groups. These ancestral lineages would have rivaled the military cult found in the Temple of the Feathered Serpent.

Research by Christine White, Michael Spence, and colleagues has produced evidence for interactions between Téotihuacan and other parts of Mesoamerica. Tlailotlacán—a cluster of houses near the western edge of Teotihuacán—was home to a group of immigrants from the Valley of Oaxaca, 400 kilometres to the southeast. The material culture remains and burial practices found in excavations at Tlailotlacán show that the people living there maintained their Oaxacan cultural identity through 400 years of occupation. White and Spence examined a series of fifty-six burials from one of the residences excavated at Tlailotlacán. To determine whether there was a continuous flow of people between Tlailotlacán and Oaxaca, they analyzed the oxygen isotope signature of the teeth. An oxygen isotope signature reflects the characteristics of water consumed while a tooth is forming. Because the timing of the mineralization of teeth takes place by age 13, and the age of mineralization of each tooth is known, the oxygen isotope signature of a series of teeth can reveal where a person lived during childhood. In addition, isotope data provides information on the time of weaning, and analysis of the bones indicates where people lived as adults.

The picture that emerges shows that throughout the occupation of Tlailotlacán, there was a constant flow of people between the city and their Oaxacan homeland. Most children showed evidence of at least one period of time spent in Oaxaca. These trips to Oaxaca often took place before the age of weaning, which was in the range of three to four years. This means that mothers would have been travelling back and forth between Teotihuacán and Oaxaca with young children.

The tension between lineages and the military as sources of power may have been central to the dynamics of the political life of Teotihuacán (Headrick 2007). But who would have stood at the apex of political authority? To address this question we must turn to the art from Teotihuacán. There are a number of monumental sculptures from the centre of the city, but it is unclear whether these represent individuals or gods. The paintings found on the walls of buildings provide a rich body of data. Powerful military leaders, clearly identifiable by their costume, which includes an elaborate headdress, goggles, earspools, and a mirror worn behind the neck, are often depicted in these paintings (see Figure 13.8). Most of the warriors grasp a spear-thrower, or atlatl, in one hand and a bunch of darts in the other. Some of the paintings seem to depict a name glyph with an individual. In other paintings, a person holds a knife piercing a bleeding, impaled heart. The ruler, or the member of the elite, is rarely shown in isolation, but is often part of a pattern in which the same image is repeated many times. The impression is that the art is an effort to at once recognize the power of the ruling elite while also stripping them of their individual identity, suggesting that (at least at the level of artistic representation) the political office was more important than the person filling it.

Recent excavations at the **Pyramid of the Moon**, at the northern end of the Avenue of the Dead, have provided new insight into the relationship between military power and the rulers of Teotihuacán. A series of pits found within the Pyramid of the Moon complex have yielded debris from obsidian workshops (see Figure 13.9). This volcanic glass was a critical component of the Teotihuacán military prowess; the atlatl darts fired by Teotihuacán warriors were made of obsidian. The excavators at the Pyramid of the Moon found that the workshops within the compound were producing thousands of atlatl dart points (Carballo 2007). This discovery makes it clear that the function of the pyramid

FIGURE 13.6 Facade of the Temple of the Feathered Serpent, Teotihuacán.

Pyramid of the Moon A pyramid complex used for both symbolic functions and the production of military supplies and located at the north end of the Avenue of the Dead in Teotihuacán.

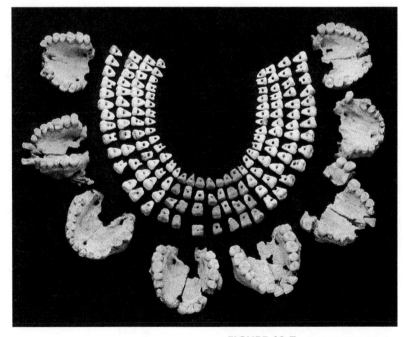

FIGURE 13.7 Necklace made of human maxillae from the Temple of the Feathered Serpent, Teotihuacán.

FIGURE 13.8 Royal image from Teotihuacán mural.

Mural with tassel headed priest, 400-600. Volcanic ash, lime coating, pigment, mud backing, 32 x 46 x 2 in. (81.3 x 116.8 x 5.1 cm) Fine Arts Museums of San Francisco, Bequest of Harald J. Wagner, 1985.104.5.

complex went beyond the symbolic to include the production of military supplies. But the distinction between military and ritual might have been artificial for the inhabitants of Teotihuacán. In other pits, the debris from the production of sacrificial knives in the shape of animals and bound prisoners was found. Obsidian was not only an essential weapons component; it was also a material with powerful symbolic resonance.

Excavations within the pyramid itself raise further questions about the military and its role in the political and ritual structure of the city. Along the main north–south axis of the pyramid, a series of burial deposits of sacrificial victims was found. Evidently, these were put in place each time the pyramid structure was expanded. These burial deposits included a careful arrangement of human and animal sacrificial victims and a range of burial goods. These are very complex deposits that resist generalization. Brief consideration of Burial 2 gives a sense of the nature of the discoveries. One adult male aged 40 to 50 was buried in a seated position near the eastern edge of the chamber. His hands were crossed behind his back and probably bound. He was wearing beads, earspools, and a pendant, all of which indicate elite status. Isotopic analysis of the skeletal remains indicates that he was not from the Valley of Mexico. Spread around the tomb were objects, including obsidian blades in the shape of people, shell pendants, the remains of a golden eagle, greenstone figurines, and jars in the shape of the storm god, Tlaloc. Finally, there were bones of a range of animals, including an eagle, a falcon, and a horned owl. Two pumas and a wolf appear to have been buried alive in cages. There are compelling reasons to interpret the animals found in the burial as representative of military units or as warriors who transform into animals in the heat of battle. The sole human skeleton appears to be a foreign warrior captured in battle and sacrificed for the consecration of the pyramid.

■ Summing Up the Evidence

The scale of Teotihuacán, along with its extensive urban planning and monumental construction, indicates a strongly centralized state. It is likely that the great monuments, including the Temple of the Feathered Serpent, Pyramid of the Sun, and

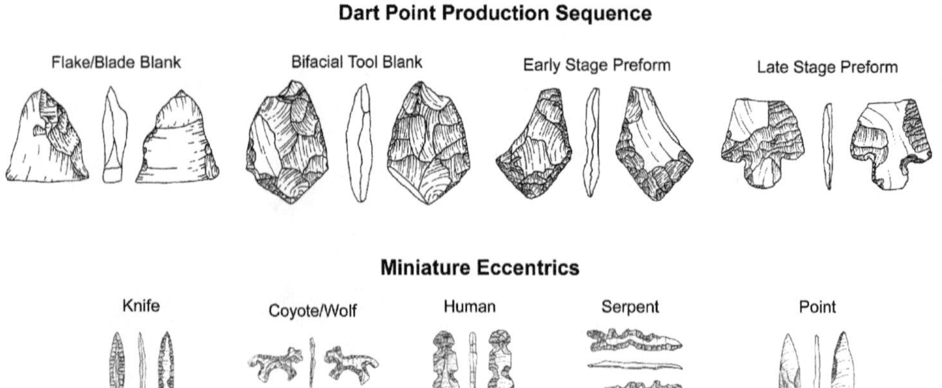

FIGURE 13.9 Drawings of obsidian artifacts recovered from pits outside the Pyramid of the Moon. The top row includes pieces discarded in the process of manufacturing dart points while the lower row are miniatures chipped into the form of tools or figures.

Dart Point Production Sequence

Flake/Blade Blank   Bifacial Tool Blank   Early Stage Preform   Late Stage Preform

Miniature Eccentrics

Knife   Coyote/Wolf   Human   Serpent   Point

Human Osteoarchaeology

Forensic scientists have become unlikely pop culture heroes. Their uncanny abilities to make deductions from the most minute (and gruesome) details appeals to our taste for the macabre and our desire for definitive answers. Human osteoarchaeologists are responsible for developing many of the methods used by forensic scientists, but their goal is not to solve a crime but rather to contribute to an archaeological understanding of the past. In the late nineteenth and early twentieth centuries, the field of human osteoarchaeology—the analysis of human skeletons recovered on archaeological sites—was an extension of physical anthropology, and the major goal of analysis was often to describe the physical attributes of populations. Today, human osteoarchaeologists use tools from the biological and medical sciences and integrate their research into broad archaeological frameworks. Among the key areas of research are quality of life (including diet and nutrition, disease, and growth and development), behaviour and lifestyle, and population history (Larsen 2006). Human osteoarchaeologists often work in close collaboration with archaeologists who study artifacts to combine evidence from the physical and cultural remains found in burials. The analyses of the complex mortuary deposits uncovered in the Pyramid of the Moon at Teotihuacán offer an excellent example of this kind of collaborative research (Spence and Pereira 2007, Sugiyama and López Luján 2007).

As in all areas of archaeological analysis, it is critical that human osteoarchaeologists be aware of the challenges posed by the nature of the type of material they study. One particular problem facing human osteoarchaeologists is *selective mortality*. As stated by James Wood and colleagues, "There is one, and perhaps only one, irrefutable fact about the cases making up a skeletal series: they are dead. We never have a sample of all the individuals who were at risk of disease or death at a given age, but only of those who did in fact die at that age" (Wood et al. 1992, 344). Essentially, we are missing that part of the population that did not succumb to disease.

In recent years, restrictions on the excavation of human skeletal remains, often the result of claims made by aboriginal communities, have had a major impact on human osteoarchaeology. In Canada, a number of projects have been able to go forward in partnership with First Nations communities. An ossuary found at the Moatfield site in the process of renovating a soccer field in North York, Ontario, led to the emergence of a particularly productive partnership (Williamson and Pfeiffer 2003, van de Merwe et al. 2003). Ossuaries are pits filled with the secondary burials of a large number of individuals. Moatfield contained the remains of eighty-seven people dated to around A.D. 1300. The Six Nations Council of Oshweken, Ontario, which is the recognized First Nations authority of the site, allowed for not only careful excavation and documentation of the ossuary but also analysis of one tooth per individual before the human remains were reburied. The resulting analyses have produced important insight into variations Iroquoian diet in relationship to sex and age. ●

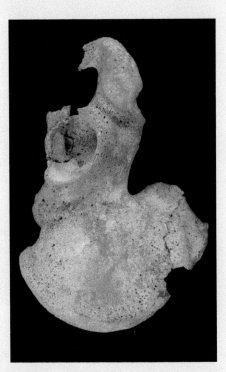

FIGURE 13.10 Analysis of teeth from the Moatfield site has provided important insight into Iroquoian diet in relationship to sex and age.

Pyramid of the Moon, were built by rulers seeking to advance their power. If this is the case, the destruction of the Temple of the Feathered Serpent and the shift to building apartment complexes speaks clearly of a strong reaction against centralizing power in favour of a corporate political structure. Is it possible that a hierarchical leader pursuing an exclusionary political strategy was not the lynchpin of this society? According to George Cowgill, "pride and a sense of citizenship, and not just submission to overawing deities and overpowering rulers, may explain much about [Teotihuacán's] stability and why there was no abundance of self-glorifying rulers" (Cowgill 1997, 153). Certainly, the forces that came together to create an urban society on an unprecedented scale for the Americas will continue to challenge archaeologists well into the future.

13.3 The Maya

The modern Maya live in an area stretching from southern Mexico through Guatemala and Belize, as well as in parts of Honduras and El Salvador. Beginning around 2,000 years ago, the Maya developed a state society with a complex writing system and large urban centres. Much of their rich history was lost under Spanish rule, which brought with it devastating disease and the systematic imposition of European culture, including the burning of most Maya books (Coe 1999). However, archaeology has made major strides in reconstructing the Maya past. The decipherment of Maya hieroglyphics has afforded spectacular insight into the detailed history of the early cities. The study of modern Maya oral traditions and cultural practices also plays a significant role in understanding the remains of the Maya past.

■ The Setting and Chronology

The Maya cities developed in the lowland zones that run from the foothills of the Sierra Madre in the south to the Caribbean Sea in the north. The Maya lowlands are divided into the tropical rain forests of the southern zone and the flat scrublands of the Yucatán in the northern zone. Most of the early cities developed along rivers and swamps in the southern zone. The northern zone became the dominant focus of Maya settlement in later periods. Maya sites in the northern zone are located near *cenotes*—sinkholes that were a critical source of water.

The main agricultural method used in the Maya region is slash-and-burn cultivation, in which the forest is cleared by burning. After a number of growing seasons, the field is abandoned and the forest is allowed to regenerate. Slash-and-burn cultivation is a shifting system of agriculture in which field systems move over time as areas are cleared, exploited, and then left fallow. The Maya also developed methods for growing crops on extensive raised fields in swamps. The use of raised fields was a critical component of the intensified agriculture needed to support large population centres. There is little evidence that Maya agriculture rested on large-scale irrigation projects. However, there is some evidence for large-scale projects; for example, canal systems that are poorly understood have been found around some cities (Demarest 2004).

The Maya cities developed during the Classic period, which dates to between A.D. 250 and A.D. 900. Around A.D. 900, many of the large cities were abandoned in what is known as the Maya Collapse. During the subsequent Postclassic period, which lasted from A.D. 900 to the arrival of the Spanish in 1519, most large Maya settlements were located in the northern Yucatán peninsula.

■ The City

The ruins of Classic-period Maya cities are covered by dense forest undergrowth. On many excavations, machetes are as important as trowels. Steep pyramids, their apexes often visible above the forest canopy, are the defining feature of the cities. These pyramids sit in the central area of the city together with royal residences, ball courts, and open plazas. Extensive survey work and excavation on Maya sites has demonstrated

FIGURE 13.11 The central area of the Maya city of Copán in a reconstruction by Tatiana Proskouriakoff. This drawing places the monuments within an empty jungle setting. Today we know that the city of Copán covered a wide area beyond the pyramids and palaces.

FIGURE 13.12 The hieroglyphic stairway at Copán.

that these cities stretched far beyond the central area to include large residential areas with populations of up to 20,000 living on small house mounds.

The central area of **Copán**, Honduras, has been the focus of intensive research. The centre of Copán includes two large pyramids and an elaborate ball court (see Figure 13.11). An inscription recounting the dynastic history of Copán runs down the entire face of the northern pyramid in what is known as the hieroglyphic stairway, (shown in Figure 13.12). This feature led from an altar at the base of the pyramid to a temple structure at the top. The inscription of the history of Copán in such a powerful setting has been interpreted as an effort to connect the troubled rulers of the late periods with the glorious achievements of the great ancestral kings (Fash 1991).

The Maya pyramids were built up over centuries as new rulers tore down and built over the temples of their predecessors (Figure 13.13). The top of the pyramids served as temple platforms, while the rulers and their families were buried within the expanding structures. Research on the Maya pyramids involves not only mapping their surface, but also tunnelling into them to find the earlier structures that were encased as the pyramid was expanded and rebuilt. At the southern pyramid of Copán, the archaeological tunnelling has resulted in the discovery of a completely intact temple from the early stages of the city's history. Unlike other structures that were destroyed before being built over, this one, known as Rosalila, appears to have been so revered that it was

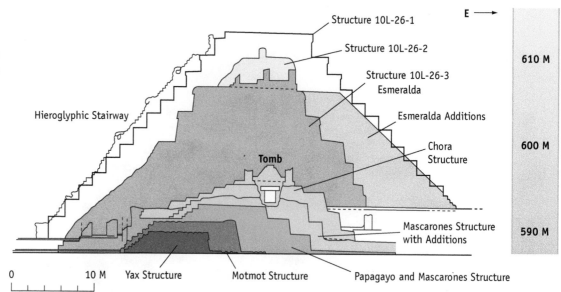

FIGURE 13.13 Cross-section of Pyramid 10L-26 at Copán. In the final stage of construction, the hieroglyphic stairway was built on the western face of the pyramid, but the cross-section shows that there were several earlier phases that included burials, each encased within a later construction.

Structure 10L-26-1
Structure 10L-26-2
Structure 10L-26-3 Esmeralda
Esmeralda Additions
Chora Structure
Hieroglyphic Stairway
Tomb
Mascarones Structure with Additions

E →
610 M
600 M
590 M

0   10 M
Yax Structure   Motmot Structure   Papagayo and Mascarones Structure

FIGURE 13.14 Eccentric flint from Rosalila, Copán.

▲▲ **Copán** A large Maya city with two large pyramids and an elaborate ball court at its centre.

▲▲ **Tikal** One of the major Maya urban centres.

encased in pristine condition. Rosalila was a rectangular edifice elaborately decorated with painted stucco figures. These sculptures present fantastic depictions of gods, birds, and snakes. In the floor of one of the rooms in Rosalila, a cache of spectacular flint artifacts in the shape of a deity were found (see Figure 13.14). These objects, known as eccentric flints, are among the finest objects of chipped stone ever made.

■ Government

Maya cities were ruled by dynasties of powerful kings. The exact timing of the emergence of kingship among the Maya is the subject of debate. The earliest king documented at the site of **Tikal** is Yax Ehb' Xook, who appears to have lived around A.D. 100 (Martin 2003). However, it is not clear that Yax Ehb' Xook was the ruler of a city. It appears that the year 378 marked a major change in the history of Tikal. The glyphs speak of the arrival of a new ruler coming from outside and ending the dynastic line. This new ruler came either from the highland Mexican city of Teotihuacán or was in some way heavily influenced by it.

The foundation of the royal dynasty at the city of Copán dates to A.D. 426. The first king of Copán, named Yax K'uk' Mo', came from outside of the city, and possibly had links to Teotihuacán. One of the burials at Copán appears to be the remains of Yax K'uk' Mo'. Skeletal analysis has shown that this individual suffered several traumas during his life, perhaps as the result of warfare or participating in ball games (Buikstra et al. 2004).

On the basis of the evidence from Tikal and Copán, it appears that the founding of the Maya cities was linked in some cases with the arrival of a ruler connected to Teotihuacán. Once established, the ruling dynasties maintained their power for generations, often hundreds of years. Monuments were frequently used to connect the ruler with the prestige of the dynasty. The hieroglyphic staircase at Copán is the most spectacular example of such monuments. The rulers of the Maya cities rarely claimed to be gods themselves; however, they were viewed as uniquely sacred individuals (Houston 2000). There is no sense of a strong distinction between the palace

TOOLBOX

Geophysical Methods

Geophysical methods are used to gain an idea of what lies below a surface without excavation. In effect, geophysical methods allow archaeologists to detect invisible features. The two main geophysical methods used by archaeologists are magnetometry and ground-penetrating radar.

Magnetometry works by detecting magnetic anomalies in the soil. These anomalies are often evidence of buried features such as tombs, pit houses, channels, and roadways (Pasquinucci and Trément 2000). In practice, a magnetometry survey involves walking along a landscape with an instrument that records magnetic readings. The data obtained are collated by computer to present a picture of subsurface anomalies that are interpreted by the archaeologist and used to guide further research.

Ground-penetrating radar (GPR) involves transmitting an electromagnetic pulse into the ground (Conyers 1997). Depending on what the pulse encounters as it travels, it is either reflected back to the surface or continues to travel until it is completely dissipated. The analyst uses GPR instruments to build up a reflection profile that provides a picture of any variation in the sediments below the ground. The reflection profile can provide information about the depth and extent of anomalies that might indicate buried archaeological features.

At the Maya site of Kaminaljuyu, Guatemala, GPR was used as a response to the pressures of excavating under salvage conditions (Valdes and Kaplan 2000). The site today is in a modern urban setting that has been heavily affected by development. Plans to build a shopping complex and a hotel in the area led to urgent salvage excavations. The GPR survey allowed archaeologists to rapidly survey areas that they would not have had time to test by excavation. The survey succeeded in locating a series of buried objects, ranging from a car muffler to significant archaeological features, including the floor of a house and two ritual caches. ●

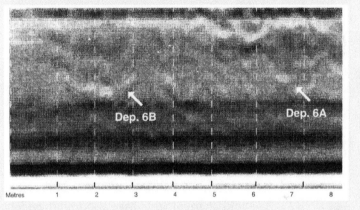

FIGURE 13.15 GPR thermal printout from Kaminaljuyu, showing the location of buried features.

---

and the temple. The dynasty was closely identified with the temple complexes at the core of the Maya city.

Although the rulers of Maya cities were able to draw on the prestige of their dynastic lineage and the sacred aspect of their office, their power was not absolute or unchallenged. There is evidence that, particularly during the later part of the Classic period, a broader aristocracy came to challenge the power of the ruler. A particularly intriguing discovery made at Copán was a building known as Popol Na, literally a *mat house*, which appears to have been the locale for meetings of a council of aristocrats. The tension between the power of the aristocracy and the royal lineage seems to have been a critical dynamic in the history of Maya cities.

■ Inequality

The burials of Maya royalty do not contain large quantities of elaborate goods. The tomb of Yax K'uk Mo', the founder of the Copán dynasty, included jade and shell ornaments, the remains of a headdress made of shells, a number of pottery vessels, and

FIGURE 13.16 Photograph of the excavation of the scribe's house at Aguateca. Can you identify the rooms shown on the plan of the house in the next figure?

a cache of eccentric flints. These are clearly high-status objects, but they are not an overwhelming display of wealth. It is possible that much greater wealth, including textiles and feathers that have not survived, were originally buried with Yax K'uk Mo'.

The development of household archaeology has begun to make an important contribution to understanding the structure of Maya society. By moving away from the monuments of the centre, household archaeologists cast light on the lives of ordinary people and study diversity among households (Robin 2003). Excavations of Maya houses have found that not all people had equal access to high-status objects. Particularly as one moves out to small agricultural hamlets, the range of artifacts becomes limited mostly to locally produced objects used in daily life. However, household archaeologists have also found evidence that high-status trade items were not restricted to elite residences.

At the site of **Aguateca**, Guatemala, archaeologists have discovered a unique window into the lives of the Maya at the very end of the Classic period (Inomata and Stiver 1998). The town of Aguateca was burned and abandoned, most probably the result of a military attack. The people were forced to flee their homes, leaving behind much of what they owned. After the houses burned, their walls collapsed, sealing the floors under rubble. In one of the houses, the tools of a scribe were discovered, providing a vivid picture of the position of scribes in Maya society (see Figure 13.16 and Figure 13.17). The scribe's rooms, in the north and centre of the building, included a large number of high-status artifacts, indicating that scribes were members of the Maya elite. It is interesting that the scribe's room contrasts with the southern part of the building, where cooking vessels and tools used in weaving were found. The excavators suggest that this was the home of a nuclear family in which the male was a scribe and the female, probably his wife, carried out tasks related to food preparation and weaving in the southern part of the building. The excavation of the house at Aguateca points to the many levels of differentiation found in state societies. On a broad scale, there are significant differences between groups within society; however, on a smaller scale, there is also differentiation within households.

▲▲ **Aguateca** A site that was abandoned and burned, probably in a military attack, leaving archaeologists with a unique record of the daily life of the Maya.

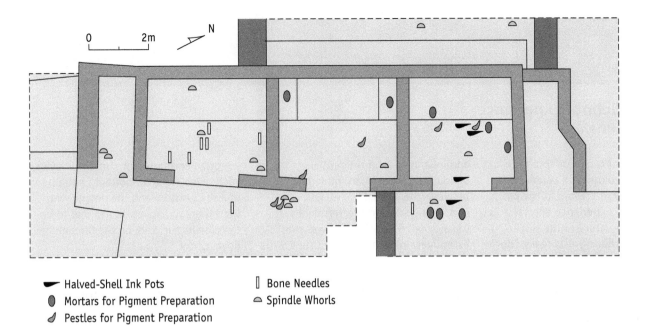

Halved-Shell Ink Pots
Mortars for Pigment Preparation
Pestles for Pigment Preparation
Bone Needles
Spindle Whorls

FIGURE 13.17 Plan of the scribe's house at Aguateca. The symbols show where different types of artifacts were found.

One aspect of wealth that is largely invisible archaeologically is richly woven cloth and other elaborate items of clothing. The contemporary Maya are renowned for their colourful clothing, which features many design elements that can be found on Classic Maya sculptures and paintings. Depictions of the Maya rulers show that in addition to wearing beautifully woven garments, they donned highly elaborate headdresses made of flowers and feathers (see the Yaxchilán lintel, Figure 13.20 on page 379).

■ Maya Hieroglyphics

Like the cuneiform writing system of Mesopotamia, the **Maya hieroglyphic** writing system developed from pictographic signs representing concepts to a system that uses these same signs to represent syllables. However, Maya scribes never discarded the pictographic meaning of signs, resulting in a highly complex writing system in which the same sign could represent either a concept or a syllable. The development of Maya script was not purely the outgrowth of economic functions. The major reason for the development of written script was to record the timing of ritual events in the lives of rulers. Whereas cuneiform writing developed out of the economic needs of the ruling elite of the cities of Mesopotamia, the Maya hieroglyphic writing developed out of the connection between rulers and ritual.

Maya script first appeared during the Early Classic period through the coalescence of three distinct traditions dating back to the end of the Olmec period (Houston 2000). The first tradition was the use of a segment of an image to represent the whole. An example found in Olmec art is the use of the eye of a jaguar to represent the animal. The progressive abstraction of these forms lies behind many of the Maya hieroglyphs.

The second tradition was the recording of a complex calendar (Fash 1991). The earliest-recorded calendar date comes from Stela C from the Olmec site of Tres Zapotes, dated to 300 B.C. The Maya calendar was an extraordinarily complex system of multiple overlapping systems. The Long Count records time from

Maya hieroglyphs A complex combination of pictographic and syllabic script that initially developed to record major events in the lives of rulers.

The Field School Experience

BY JOËLLE CHARTRAND

Whether we choose to pursue archaeology as a career or are simply interested in the past, the field school experience allows us to understand the nature of the discipline. What archaeologists really "do" is search for clues, meanings, and answers to questions about past life-ways. In 1999, I attended Trent University's Social Archaeology Research Project at the site of Minanha, Belize. At the time, I knew very little about Belize or the ancient Maya. However, intrigued and wanting to gain field experience, I enrolled in the project and made my way to rural Belize for a month of archaeology. It proved to be a very meaningful experience in my life. Captivated by the culture-history, the project's goals, and the country of Belize as a whole, I returned to contribute to research initiatives for six years. Ultimately, I completed my Master's research at Minanha and served as the project's field director.

Located in the little-explored North Vaca Plateau of west-central Belize, Minanha has been the focus of investigations for Trent University's Social Archaeology Research Program since 1999. Excavations have revealed a dense epicentre—a series of ceremonial,

administrative, and residential buildings. The site was inhabited between the Terminal Preclassic (A.D. 100–250) and the Terminal Classic (A.D. 810–900) and was most extensively inhabited in the Late Classic Period (A.D. 675–810) (Iannone 2005). Led by Dr Gyles Iannone, research at Minanha has focused on research questions aimed at understanding the state dynamics, the site's history, and how its rise and fall is tied to broader regional politics (Iannone 2005).

In my six years of work at this site, I had the opportunity to explore these ideas by participating in excavations and research initiatives. My field school experience was spent with a six-person team, excavating a pyramidal structure within the site's core. Here I developed meticulous excavation and mapping skills and started to understand how archaeologists interpret and find meaning in material culture. In subsequent research seasons, I excavated in numerous structures throughout the site. My Master's research examined the trade of ceramics and its associated interaction, based on pottery sherds found at Minanha.

Mayanists often compare their archeological experiences to the peeling of an onion, for ancient Maya structures

are often composed of numerous layers, each revealing an important component of a site's history and the people who lived there. I certainly found that to be the case in our work on the Minanha Royal Court.

Peeling the first layer in the site's Royal Court revealed a grouping of modestly constructed buildings that would have possessed pole and thatch superstructures. Peeling to the second layer proved quite laborious, involving excavating through approximately 8 metres of boulder-sized floor fill. We found countless ceramic sherds, obsidian blades, and other objects in the process. Excavation of the underlying architectural phase revealed multiple vaulted buildings, a throne room, and a rounded pyramidal structure. There was a striking difference between the two phases we excavated, which reflects shifts over time in Maya society and economy. Importantly, it was not the differences in materials or architecture that captured my attention; rather, it was the meaning of these objects and buildings—primary evidence for broader archaeological research questions. Our excavations in Minanha's Royal Court raised

a zero date (August 13, 3114 B.C., according to our calendar). In place of the seven-day week and the 365-day solar year, the Maya used a series of four units for measuring time:

1 kin = 1 day

20 kins = 1 uinal = 20 days

18 uinals = 1 tun = 360 days

20 tuns = 1 katun = 7,200 days

20 katuns = 1 baktun = 144,000 days

countless questions about the rise and fall of the court, the city-centre's history as a whole, and the way the material evidence, within and between layers, manifested itself as the result of the people who lived here in relation to the politics of the time.

Keeping broad research questions in mind, I cannot speak of my experiences at Minanha without describing the lush and scenic setting of our day-to-day efforts. Every morning, I emerged from a thatch-roofed treehouse, joining my colleagues for our daily commute to work, which consisted of a 40-minute tractor ride along an old logging road and a 30-minute hike up a mountain. Minanha is quite literally located in the middle of the Central American jungle. There really is something to be said about a workspace where the view consists of 360 degrees of tropical forest and the occasional howler monkey.

The people I worked with also helped make my time in Belize memorable. Living with a Belizean family and working alongside Belizean, Canadian, and American field workers, I had the chance to work closely with wonderful families and people whom I would not have otherwise known. Our coming together led to rich learning experiences and the development of real, long-lasting friendships. I will forever treasure my time in Belize and the friends I made while I was there.

I look forward to visiting them in the coming years. ▲

REFERENCE: G. Iannone. (2005). The rise and fall of an ancient Maya petty court. *Latin American Antiquity* 16(1): 26–44.

FIGURE 13.18 The author at the buried royal residential courtyard at Minanha.

The Maya also used a 260-day ritual calendar with 23 numbers and 20 named days, a 365-day solar calendar, and at least two other systems. The complexity of the Maya calendar reflects the centrality and significance the people attached to measuring time, matched by an intense interest in recording astronomical events.

There is very slight evidence that Maya script might also have developed out of a tradition of using written records in economic transactions. If such records existed, they must have been written on perishable materials that have not survived. One of the main sources of evidence for the use of writing to record transactions comes from drawings of a deity writing numbers on leaves.

The Maya documents that survive deal largely with the recording of events in the lives of the rulers of cities, particularly the dates when the rulers performed significant rituals. Most of the surviving texts are monuments carved in stone or inscriptions on clay vessels (see Figure 13.19). More complex religious and historical documents were probably written in books known as codices, only a small number of which have survived. Depictions of daily life are rare, although the recently discovered murals from the site of Calakmul (Vargas et al. 2009) are a striking exception. A unique expression of the wealth of Maya mythology is found in the **Popol Vuh**, which was transcribed following the Spanish conquest (Coe 1993). The Popol Vuh tells the epic tale of the hero twins Hunahpu and Xbalnque and their battle with the lords of the underworld, known as Xibalbá. The tale hinges on the skill and trickery of the twins, which allow them to vanquish the lords of the underworld before rising up through the surface of the earth and into the sky, where they become the sun and the moon. A ball game played to the death is central to the story.

■ Ritual, Violence, and Warfare

Bloodletting and sacrifice were important elements of Maya ritual (Schele and Miller 1986). Some of the most vivid scenes of bloodletting are found on a series of carvings from the site of Yaxchilán. In these scenes, the ruler and his wife are seen drawing blood from their tongues and collecting the drops on special paper (see Figure 13.20). The bloodletting brings on spectacular visions of enormous snakes with the heads of gods.

The ball game also played a major role in Maya society. The epic battle between the hero twins of the Popol Vuh and the lords of the underworld appears to be at the heart of much of Maya ritual practice. Echoing the centrality of the ball game to Maya ritual is the position of the ball court at the core of the city. The ball courts consist of a bare patch of ground, flanked on either side by a banked structure. Paul Healy's excavation of the ball court at the site of Pacbitun, Belize demonstrates that this court was in use for a period of close to 1,000 years (Healy 1992). Throughout this period, there were many phases of repair and reconfiguration, including changes to the slope of the side walls that would have had a significant effect on the way the game was played. The game was played with a heavy rubber ball that apparently had to be shot through a ring without the use of the hands. Some archaeologists have argued that, as it was in the myth of the Popol Vuh, in real life the ball game was played to the death.

FIGURE 13.19 Painted Maya pot. (A) Photograph of the vessel. (B) Rolled-out view showing the presentation of tribute to a seated lord.

(top): ©The Trustees of the British Museum/Art Resource. (bottom): ©The Trustees of the British Museum/Art Resource, NY.

A

B

However, violence in the Maya world went beyond ritual and sport. From sites such as Aguateca, there is clear evidence that cities were conquered and burned. Inscriptions record the capture of cities and the death of their rulers, and a vivid series of murals from the site of Bonampak shows scenes of prisoners being tortured and killed. It is not clear how the Maya carried out their warfare. There is no evidence of standing armies, and Maya weaponry appears to have been limited to flint spears and armour made from skins.

Recent research by Kathryn Reese-Taylor at the site of Naachtun, identified as the Maya city of Masuul, sheds light on the role of warfare in Maya politics (Reese-Taylor 2005). Information drawn from inscriptions suggests that Masuul was caught up in the conflicts between its powerful neighbours at the sites of Tikal and Calakmul. Archaeological investigations at Naachtun have uncovered a limestone defensive wall, apparently built as a response to the precarious situation of the city.

FIGURE 13.20 Limestone carved lintel from Yaxchilán, Mexico. Lady Wak Tuun is shown during a bloodletting ritual. She holds a stingray spine, a rope used in bloodletting, and bloodied paper. In front of her, a vision serpent emerges from a bowl containing strips of paper.
© The Trustees of the British Museum.

■ The Maya Collapse

Sometime around A.D. 870, the cities of the southern Maya lowlands collapsed. New construction ended, and the cities were gradually deserted. This collapse was the result of factors internal to Maya society as well as factors related to the external environment. One factor that played a role in weakening the power of the Maya rulers was the ratcheting up of cycles of violence and warfare. By the end of the Classic period, warfare was widespread and its consequences often catastrophic, as demonstrated by the burned town at Aguateca. Excavations at the large urban centre of Dos Pilas have uncovered a radical transformation of the site beginning in A.D. 761, when a defensive palisade was built around the central area with stones ripped from the temples and pyramids. The residents built a tightly packed siege village in the open plazas and began living in the area once reserved for ritual and ceremony (Demarest 2004). A number of archaeologists argue that the increasing power of the nobility led to a further weakening of the power of the rulers or even resulted in a "nobles revolt" (Fash 1991).

Ecological factors might have also contributed to the Maya collapse. The need to feed the large populations of the cities led to damage to agricultural lands, and the resulting decrease in agricultural productivity put stress on the cities. Also, a series of severe droughts occurred during the period of the Maya collapse (Haug et al. 2003). It is likely that these intense short-term climatic events played a role in the abandonment of the Classic Maya cities. However, recently published data on pollen cores from a pond near the site of Copán has raised significant questions about the linkage between environmental degradation and the Maya collapse (McNeil et al. 2010). While these cores do show deforestation during the period of the founding of Copán, there is clear evidence for the subsequent recovery of the forests. In this pollen core, there is no evidence for deforestation in the period leading up to the Maya collapse.

■ Summing Up the Evidence

Maya kings ruled over large urban centres. The emergence of both cities and state society among the Maya is closely linked with external influences, particularly from the highland city of Teotihuacán. The power of the Maya kings was based on the

Archaeology and Tourism

Copán is a critical site for the archaeology of the Maya. It is also a major tourist destination. The rapid growth of cultural tourism has obvious implications for archaeological site development and protection. But there are also more subtle issues raised by the intersection of archaeology and tourism. For example, in Honduras, the prominence of Copán and the Maya history has led to the eclipse of other aspects of the heritage of Honduras, with a resulting impact on national identity and politics (Mortensen 2007). The demands of the tourist industry can also lead to the "packaging" of archaeological sites. At the fourteenth-century site of Bagan in Burma (now known as Myanmar), reconstruction of the archaeological remains has led to widespread criticism, including a comment by one UN official that "a Disney-style fantasy version of one of the world's great religious and historical sites is being created by (the military) government" (quoted in Hudson 2008). In the case of Bagan, the reconstruction is fuelled by a combination of politics, development, and religious reverence.

The threats posed by tourist development are balanced by positive economic and cultural potential. Visiting archaeological sites gives tourists direct access to the remains of our shared cultural heritage. For local communities, particularly in areas of the world with few employment opportunities, the economic potential of archaeological tourism can be very important. The International Council on Monuments and Sites (ICOMOS) has recognized that it is critical to develop tools to enhance understanding and cooperation between the archaeological community and the tourism industry. In its 1999 International Cultural Tourism Charter the organization lays out the following principles for cultural tourism:

- Conservation should provide responsible and well-managed opportunities for members of the host community and visitors to experience and understand that community's heritage and culture at first hand.
- The relationship between heritage places and tourism is dynamic and may involve conflicting values that require careful management.
- Conservation and tourism planning for Heritage Places should ensure that the visitor experience will be worthwhile, satisfying, and enjoyable.
- Host communities and indigenous peoples should be involved in planning for conservation and tourism.
- Tourism and conservation activities should benefit the host community.
- Tourism promotion should protect and enhance cultural heritage.

This is a strong set of principles but noticeably absent is any mention of the interests of researchers, which includes archaeologists. However, in most cases research is an essential element of sustained tourist development of archaeological sites. Visitors come with questions and they expect that if a site is worth visiting it must also be worth exploring scientifically.

The strength of the ICOMOS principles is their emphasis on finding management solutions to bridge different worldviews. There is a clear sense of need for a new kind of expertise, one that combines the skills of planning and management with an understanding of the issues involved in research, conservation, heritage, and tourism. In her study of Copán, Lena Mortensen states that recent developments "straddle borders that explode the once hermeneutic circles that have traditionally controlled the production of scholarly knowledge" (Mortensen 2007, 133). The task facing archaeologists responding to the economic and political interests inherent in the rapidly growing cultural tourism industry offers a fundamental challenge to archaeological theory (for discussion of hermeneutics see p. 47). ●

FIGURE 13.21 Tourists climbing the pyramid at the Maya site of Coba, Mexico.

prestige of the royal lineage and reinforced by the king's critical ceremonial role. The prestige of the royal lineage was literally built into the city in the form of monumental inscriptions and pyramids that encased the burials of the kings. The hieroglyphic writing system was developed as a tool for recording the timing of ritual events in the lives of rulers. The eventual collapse of the Maya cities appears to have been the result of a number of factors, including warfare, ecological degradation, and external climatic events. Of these factors, the intensified warfare between cities seems to have played a decisive role.

13.4 The Aztec Empire

In 1519, Spanish soldiers arrived at the city of **Tenochtitlán**, the capital of the **Aztec Empire**. Tenochtitlán was at that time one of the largest cities in the world and the largest city ever built in Mesoamerica. The Spanish were amazed by what they saw and wrote that "some of our soldiers asked whether it was not all a dream" (Bernal Diaz del Castillo, quoted in Smith 2003). Tenochtitlán was built on an island in Lake Texcoco in the Valley of Mexico and was connected to the mainland by a series of causeways (Figure 13.22). At the centre of the city rose the great twin pyramids of the Templo Mayor, the spiritual centre of the Aztec universe.

Two years of bloody and treacherous warfare led to the final conquest of Tenochtitlán (Townsend 2000). The end of the Aztec Empire came on August 13, 1521, when, at the close of a 93-day siege, the last Aztec king, Cuauhtemoc, was captured as he tried to escape the city by canoe. In a powerful symbolic act, the Spanish built their cathedral near the ruins of the Templo Mayor in the heart of what has become Mexico City.

Some of the priests who arrived on missions to convert natives to Christianity carefully documented Aztec history, religion, and society. Among the most important historical source is a series of books known as the **Florentine Codex**, compiled by the Spanish friar **Bernardo de Sahagún** (Brumfiel 2001). The Florentine Codex consists of the interviews Sahagún carried out with Aztec informants, both in the

▲▲ Tenochtitlán The capital of the Aztec Empire and the largest indigenous city ever built in the Americas; located in the Valley of Mexico.

Aztec Empire A large Mesoamerican empire based in Tenochtitlán.

Florentine Codex A document that is a major source of information on Aztec history and culture; compiled soon after the Spanish conquest of the Aztecs.

Bernardo de Sahagún The Spanish friar who compiled the Florentine Codex.

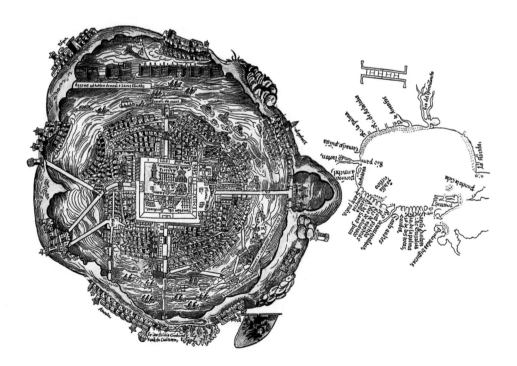

FIGURE 13.22 Spanish map of the city of Tenochtitlán, built on an island and reached by causeways. The sacred precinct of the Templo Mayor is located in the centre of the city.

Toltec Empire An empire that preceded the Aztecs in the Valley of Mexico. It is not clear whether the Toltec controlled areas beyond their capital city.

Tula The capital city of the Toltec Empire.

Aztlán The homeland, possibly mythical, of the Aztecs.

native language, Nahuatl, and in Spanish translation. This text is accompanied by extensive illustrations drawn by native artists. Illustrated books were also kept by the Aztecs themselves; however, few have survived. Archaeological research has confirmed many of the descriptions in the Florentine Codex with spectacular discoveries at the site of the Templo Mayor in Mexico City. Archaeology has also extended our understanding of the Aztec Empire by uncovering evidence of the lives of the people living in areas beyond Tenochtitlán.

■ The History of the Aztecs

The Aztecs were aware of both the Olmec and Teotihuacán and drew explicit connections to those societies. Among the precious objects found in ritual caches in the Templo Mayor was an Olmec stone mask (Matos Moctezuma 1988). A number of objects from Teotihuacán were also found in excavations at the Templo Mayor, and Aztec architecture makes frequent reference to styles that originated in Teotihuacán. The name Teotihuacán is not the original name of the city, but rather the name used by the Aztecs, which, in the Aztec language Nahuatl, means "the place where gods (or rulers) are made."

Aztec kings traced their genealogy back to the rulers of the **Toltec Empire**, which developed between A.D. 950 and A.D. 1150 after the fall of Teotihuacán (Smith 2003). The Aztec kings depict the Toltec Empire as great and powerful; however, archaeology paints a rather more modest picture. The Toltec capital, **Tula**, was the largest city of its time, but its population of 50,000 was far smaller than those of either Teotihuacán and the Aztec capital of Tenochtitlán. It is also far from clear that Tula did actually control a large empire; there is little archaeological evidence for Toltec control of regions beyond Tula.

The Aztecs traced their origins to people who migrated from afar. The location of the Aztec homeland of **Aztlán** remains unknown and is perhaps mythical (Smith 2003). There was a series of migrations from Aztlán into the Valley of Mexico during the period between A.D. 1200 and A.D. 1250. All of these migrants are known as Aztecs, after the homeland of Aztlán. The first group of Aztec migrants settled in the Valley of Mexico, while the second wave settled in the surrounding valleys. The final group to arrive was the Mexica, who had to settle for a desolate area known as "grasshopper hill." Even in this setting, the Mexica faced attack by a coalition of Tepanecs (an earlier group of settlers from Aztlán) and their allies from the town of Culhuacán (Townsend 2000). The Mexica were roundly defeated and forced to resettle in an even more desolate setting under the protection of Culhuacán. An alliance then developed between the two groups.

The Mexica approached one of the leaders of Culhuacán and asked for his daughter as a bride for the main Mexica deity, Huitzilopochtli. The Culhuacán leader complied, thus paving the way for a further strengthening of the alliance between the two groups. But when the Culhuacán chieftain was invited to festivities with the Mexica, he recognized in horror the flayed skin of his daughter on the body of the Mexica priest. The outraged people of Culhuacán chased the Mexica to uninhabited islands in Lake Texcoco. As the Mexica fled, one of their priests had a vision that they should settle at a sacred spot marked by an eagle perched on a cactus. When the Mexica found an eagle on a cactus the next day, they immediately built a crude temple, which developed over time into the Templo Mayor at the core of the great city of Tenochtitlán. Today, the Mexican flag pictures an eagle perched on a cactus, in recognition of this significant turning point in the history of Mesoamerica.

How did the Mexica go from being despised outcasts to the rulers of a great empire? One must recognize that the origins of empires are often highly mythologized; this is clearly the case for the Mexica origin stories. Nonetheless, the Mexica's rapid rise to power is remarkable. This increase in power rested on a series of conflicts and alliances with neighbouring groups, as well as on the consistent growth of Tenochtitlán as an urban centre. In 1428, an alliance between the cities of Tenochtitlán, **Texcoco**, and **Tlapocán** was established (Figure 13.23). This **Triple Alliance** allowed the rapid expansion of the area dominated by the Aztec to regions far beyond the limits of the Basin of Mexico. Within the Triple Alliance, the Mexica rulers of Tenochtitlán were dominant, and their power grew along with the empire. Among the Aztec groups that migrated to the Valley of Mexico from Aztlán, it was the outcast Mexica, the last to arrive, who came to rule over the entire Valley of Mexico and far beyond.

■ Aztec Economy

The rise of Tenochtitlán and the expansion of the Aztec Empire resulted in a dramatic increase in population in the Basin of Mexico. Archaeological surveys have shown that 40 percent of the sites in the Basin of Mexico date to the period of the expansion of the Aztec Empire (Nichols 2004). Population estimates for the Basin of Mexico during this period range between 800,000 and 1.25 million, a fourfold increase over preceding periods. The large populations of the Basin of Mexico relied on an intensification of agriculture and a system for exacting tribute from conquered territories.

Tenochtitlán relied heavily on the expansion of raised agricultural fields, known as **chinampas**, within the swamps of the lakes of the Basin of Mexico (Smith 2003). The chinampa plots are artificial islands built up between long, straight drainage canals. By periodically scraping the muck out of the canals to use as fertilizer, the productivity of the plots was maintained. Archaeological surveys on the outskirts of Mexico City have uncovered the gridlike system of Aztec chinampa drainage canals and fields. In addition to farming chinampa plots, the Aztecs constructed extensive terrace walls to farm hillsides and dug large irrigation canals to open valleys to farming.

Tributes from the conquered territories flowed into Tenochtitlán, supporting the growing population of the city and enriching the Aztec elite. An early colonial document known as the Codex Mendoza reproduces an Aztec list of tribute by

Texcoco City that was a member of the Aztec Triple Alliance.

Tlapocán City that was a member of the Aztec Triple Alliance.

Triple Alliance The pact between the cities of Tenochtitlán, Telapocán, and Texcoco that formed the basis of the Aztec Empire.

chinampas Raised agricultural beds built in swamps; critical for Aztec agriculture.

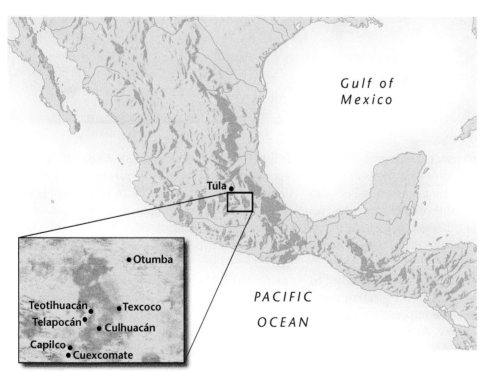

FIGURE 13.23
Map of the Aztec Empire.

FIGURE 13.24 Aztec tribute list from the Codex Mendoza. How would you describe the objects shown in this illustration?

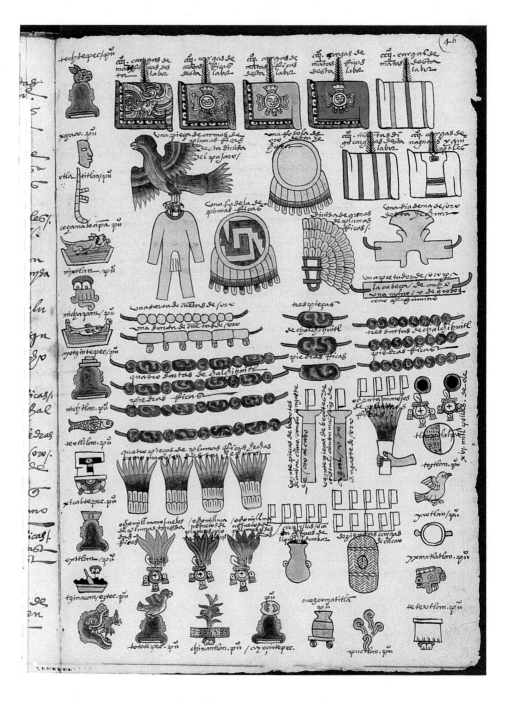

province (see Figure 13.24) (Smith 2003). Historical documents emphasize the significance of markets in the Aztec economy, as well as the role played by professional merchants known as Pochteca (Hirth 1998, Nichols et al. 2002). All provinces provided textiles of cotton and maguey, as well as warrior costumes and shields. A variety of other goods, including tropical feathers, rubber balls, wooden beams, and incense, were also major tribute items. Notably, the only foods that were major tribute items were salt, honey, chili, and cacao beans. The Aztecs lacked draft animals for transporting tribute, so all items had to be carried to Tenochtitlán by porters.

Archaeological excavations on sites outside the Basin of Mexico provide insight into the impact that the Aztec expansion had on what became the periphery of the empire. At the site of **Otumba** in the Teotihuacán Valley, an intensive survey, along with limited excavation, has provided evidence about the organization of craft production (Charlton, Nichols, and Charlton 1991). On the basis of the

Otumba A site in the Teotihuacán Valley where excavations have produced evidence about the nature of the Aztec organization of craft production.

artifacts recovered, craft workshops for production of obsidian blades, ceramic figurines, basalt grinding stone, and maguey fibre textile were identified at Otumba. One of the most spectacular discoveries provided evidence of specialized craft workshops for the production of ground stone artifacts from obsidian, including delicate earspools and lip plugs known as labrets. Because obsidian is volcanic glass, the production of ground objects requires considerable skill. It is not surprising that a large number of the ground obsidian objects that were found had been broken and discarded in the process of manufacture. There is also evidence at Otumba that cotton textiles and censers (a special type of pottery vessel used in religious practices) were made in households rather than in specialized workshops. The research at Otumba shows that the Aztec demand for tribute placed a high pressure on the peripheral territories to increase their production of specialized crafts.

Excavations at the rural sites of **Cuexcomate** and **Capilco** in Morelos, to the south of the Basin of Mexico, have uncovered evidence of how people living in rural provincial settlements experienced the Aztec expansion (Smith 2001, 2003). Capilco is the smaller of the two sites, with a total of 21 houses; Cuexcomate has over 150 houses, as well as temples and storehouses. Both these sites grew significantly during the period of Aztec expansion. Capilco expanded from an estimated population of 72 to 116, and Cuexcomate from an estimated population of 237 to 803. All of the houses excavated at these rural sites yielded artifacts used in preparing food: blades, grinding stones, and large quantities of pottery. Spindle whorls and spinning bowls used in making cotton textiles were also found in every house, along with ritual artifacts, including figurines and incense burners. Surprisingly, all of the houses contained a large number of items that were traded over a distance, such as elaborately painted pottery vessels. There was no difference in the amount of trade goods per house between Capilco and the larger town of Cuexcomate. It is interesting to note that, during the period of Aztec expansion, the amount of trade goods found in the houses at both sites actually decreased, while the number of artifacts used in making cloth found in each house increased.

The archaeological evidence from Otumba, Capilco, and Cuexcomate demonstrates the impact of the Aztec expansion on the people living beyond the Valley of Mexico. In many ways, the expansion acted as a stimulus, spurring the intensity of craft production at Otumba and leading to an increase in population at Capilco and Cuexcomate. However, the rise of power of Tenochtitlán fundamentally rerouted the exchange of trade goods within the areas under Aztec rule. The need to provide tribute required increased specialization; evidence of this was found not only at Otumba, but also in the peasant houses at Capilco and Cuexcomate, in the form of increased textile manufacture. At the same time that craft production increased, the access to trade goods of those living at sites like Capilco and Cuexcomate actually decreased. The expansion of the Aztec Empire saw increased centralization of both wealth and power in the core of the empire in the city of Tenochtitlán.

■ Ritual and Human Sacrifice

In 1978, workers were digging a trench for electrical cables near the cathedral in Mexico City when they hit a monumental stone sculpture. This fortuitous discovery led archaeologists to the core of the Aztec spiritual world: the **Templo Mayor** that once rose above the centre of Tenochtitlán. The sculpture (shown in Figure 13.25) uncovered by the electric company workers is a spectacular rendition of the dismembered body of **Coyolxauhqui**, a goddess killed by the Aztec patron deity **Huitzilopochtli** in a central event in Aztec mythology (Matos Moctezuma 1992). In this myth, a woman named Coatlicue living on the mountain of Coatepec was impregnated

Cuexcomate The larger of two rural sites in Morelos, to the south of the Basin of Mexico, that have produced insight into rural life under the Aztecs.

Capilco The smaller of two rural sites in Morelos, to the south of the Basin of Mexico, that have produced insight into rural life under the Aztecs.

Templo Mayor Double pyramid at the centre of Tenochtitlán that was the core of the Aztec world.

Coyolxauhqui A goddess killed by the Aztec patron god Huitzilopochtli in a central event in Aztec mythology.

Huitzilopochtli The Aztec patron god.

FIGURE 13.25 Excavation of the Coyolxauhqui stone.

by a ball of feathers. When Coatlicue's 400 children learned of her pregnancy, they were enraged. One of these children, Coyolxauhqui, urged her siblings to kill their mother. At the very moment the siblings approached the Coatepec mountain to carry out the murder, Huitzilopochtli was born, fully grown, and immediately dressed for war. With a magical snake, Huitzilopochtli wounded Coyolxauhqui and cut off her head. As her body fell down the mountain, it broke into pieces, as is depicted on the sculpture discovered in Mexico City. Huitzilopochtli then chased down and killed the 400 siblings.

Excavations following the discovery of the Coyolxauhqui sculpture expanded rapidly until much of the sacred precinct was uncovered. The sculpture lay at the base of a double pyramid; on the top of these were the two temples of the gods Tlaloc and Huitzilopochtli. The pyramid represents the hill of Coatepec in the architectural retelling of the defeat of Coyolxauhqui and the victory of the Aztec patron Huitzilopochtli.

The excavation of the pyramid at Templo Mayor showed that, like other Mesoamerican pyramids, it had been built in stages, with each new pyramid encapsulating its predecessor. Within the body of the pyramid, more than one hundred ceremonial caches (such as the one shown in Figure 13.26) of artifacts were found (Matos Moctezuma 1988). These caches often bring together artifacts from across the domains controlled by the Aztec Empire. The symbolic meaning of the caches is often difficult to understand; however, many appear to express the placement of the Templo Mayor at the centre of the Aztec spiritual world. Two of the caches (Caches 7 and 61) are particularly intriguing in that they are nearly identical. Both were placed in small stone-walled chambers and consist of three levels. The lowest level features strombus shells oriented from north to south. Above this is a layer of crocodile remains, and above these remains are the figures of a seated god. On the right side of these seated gods, some coral was placed, and on the left, a clay vessel was found depicting the god Tlaloc. The meaning of this arrangement is enigmatic, but it might represent levels of creation, from the sea (the shells), to the land (the crocodiles), to the heavens (the seated god).

Other caches in the Templo Mayor provide evidence of the important role human sacrifice played in Aztec ritual. Worked human skulls, known as "skull masks,"

FIGURE 13.26 Ceremonial cache found in the Templo Mayor excavations. Notice the flint knife inserted in the nasal cavity of the skull.

have been found in a number of the caches. The masks are made up of the front part of the skull. The eye sockets are filled with white shell discs, and round pieces at the centre of the shell discs represent the irises. In some cases, carefully flaked flint knives have been found inserted horizontally between the teeth of the skull or vertically into its nasal cavity.

Human sacrifice played a critical role in Aztec ritual, and the sacrifice of war captives or slaves was an important part of the ritual cycle. Historic descriptions of the Templo Mayor mention racks with large numbers of human skulls. No such large concentration of skulls has ever been found at the site; however, the excavations did uncover a large platform decorated with sculptures depicting 240 skulls.

A detailed description of a variety of human sacrificial rituals is found in the Florentine Codex. For example, sacrifices staged at the Templo Mayor commonly involved four men stretching out the victim on the sacrificial stone. His breast was then cut open by the priest, and his heart was seized and dedicated to the sun. The victim's corpse was then sent toppling down the side of the pyramid. Finally, a priest removed the head and placed it on the skull rack (Smith 2003). For the Aztecs, the act of sacrifice transformed the victim into a deity. However, as the Aztec Empire expanded, ritual sacrifice also came to play a role in projecting the empire's power and terrifying its opponents. In one case, during the reign of Ahuizotl (1486–1502), a massive slaughter took place on the occasion of the rededication of the Templo Mayor. It appears that Ahuizotl was using ritual slaughter as a particularly brutal form of propaganda.

Archaeological research on sites outside the Basin of Mexico shows that the violent ritual found in the core of the empire did not have wide currency in the peripheral regions (Brumfiel 2001). Ceramic figurines are found on most Aztec-period sites, and it is likely that they were used in household rituals (Figure 13.27). During the period of Aztec dominance, the female figurines outnumber the male figurines three to one. Few of the male figurines represent warriors. The women shown in Aztec formal art are usually depicted in a subservient, kneeling position. However, when shown in figurines, the women are usually standing and are often holding two children. The low number of figurines depicting warriors suggests that

FIGURE 13.27 An Aztec household figurine.

the ritual practices of rural people differed significantly from those of the people of Tenochtitlán. The question then is, Who was the audience for the rituals enacted at the Templo Mayor? It is likely that the goal of these rituals was at least as much to inspire a spirit of warfare in the men of fighting age within the city of Tenochtitlán as to terrify the Aztecs' subjects. Clearly, people's experience of these rituals would vary depending on their place in society. The elite and the warriors were active participants in the rituals. For the city masses, the events taking place at the Templo Mayor must have been difficult to avoid. For people in the provinces, by contrast, the rituals practised at the temple would have been a terrifying rumour few would have experienced in person.

■ Summing Up the Evidence

Since empires are characterized by social heterogeneity, different members of society have vastly differing experiences and world views. For this reason, it is important to take great care before making blanket generalizations about an empire such as that of the Aztecs. Archaeological excavations on rural sites have shown that although the impact of the Aztec Empire varied, it was significant. Surveys demonstrate that the advent of the Aztecs saw a significant rise in population in the Valley of Mexico. The Aztecs ruled through a Triple Alliance, but the city of Tenochtitlán was clearly the dominant party. Excavations in the Templo Mayor in the middle of modern Mexico City have brought archaeologists to the heart of the Aztec Empire. The evidence from these excavations vividly illustrates the ideology of warfare and human sacrifice that were essential to the empire. But there was more to Aztec ideology than violence: The discoveries at the Templo Mayor also uncover the paths the Aztecs took to connect themselves to an illustrious past. The symbolism of the sculptures connects the Aztecs to the mythological time of Huitzilopochtli. On a semimythological plane, the Templo Mayor was built on the actual spot where the Mexica refugees from Aztlán decided to make their last stand. But at the same time that the descendants of the Mexica rooted themselves in a uniquely Aztec mythical past, they also found connections with their Mesoamerican predecessors. The inclusion of Olmec and Teotihuacán objects speaks to a reverence for antiquity that is strongly reminiscent of the interest of the Aztecs' European contemporaries in the antiquities of Greece and Rome.

SUMMARY

- In a hierarchical state an exclusionary political strategy leads to a single individual holding a monopoly on power. In societies with a corporate political strategy power is shared across different sectors.

- The Olmec sites of 1200 B.C. to 300 B.C. on the Gulf Coast of Mexico are the earliest evidence of political complexity in Mesoamerica.

- By 500 B.C., the site of Monte Albán in the Oaxaca Valley had grown into a large city with a population of 5,000.

- Beginning around 2,000 years ago, Teotihuacán, in the Valley of Mexico, had grown into a city with a population of more than 80,000 people.

- The major monuments of Teotihuacán including the Pyramid of the Sun, Ciudadela and Temple of the Feathered Serpent, and the Pyramid of the Moon, were built along the Avenue of the Dead.

- Excavations of the Temple of the Feathered Serpent and the Pyramid of the Moon uncovered elaborate burials of sacrificial victims.

- Beginning around A.D. 200 the residential areas of Teotihuacán were reconfigured into apartment complexes. In the fourth century the Temple of the Feathered Serpent was destroyed before being covered over.

- The absence of individualized depictions of rulers in the art of Teotihuacán is one line of evidence suggesting that this might have been a society with a corporate political strategy.
- The Maya hieroglyphic writing system developed out of the connection between rulers and rituals.
- The core of the Maya city included royal residences, open plazas, pyramids, and ball courts.
- Maya cities were ruled by powerful dynasties. The power of the king derived from the prestige of the dynasty and the sacred aspect of kingship.
- Violence and warfare in Maya society were closely linked to rituals of bloodletting. There is clear evidence of warfare between Maya cities.
- Around A.D. 870, cities in the southern Maya lowlands collapsed.
- The Aztec capital of Tenochtitlán was built on an island in Lake Texcoco in the Valley of Mexico and had a very large population.
- Tenochtitlán fell to the Spanish in 1521. Texts such as the Florentine Codex provide extensive documentation of Aztec history, religion, and society.

- The Aztec traced their genealogy back to the Toltec Empire, which developed after the fall of Teotihuacán.
- The Aztec migrated to the Valley of Mexico from a region to the north known as Aztlán.
- The formation of a Triple Alliance between Tenochtitlán, Texcoco, and Tlapocán was a critical event in the formation of the Aztec Empire. Within this alliance, Tenochtitlán was the dominant force.
- The economy of Tenochtitlán relied on intensified agriculture, including the farming of raised fields known as chinampas.
- Excavations at the provincial sites of Otumba, Capilco, and Cuexcomate shed light on the effect of the Aztec expansion at the periphery of the empire.
- A chance discovery led archaeologists to the Templo Mayor, the massive pyramid temple that stood at the centre of Tenochtitlán. Templo Mayor was the site of rituals involving human sacrifice.

KEY TERMS

Aguateca, 374
Avenue of the Dead, 364
Aztec Empire, 381
Aztlán, 382
Bernardo de Sahagún, 381
Capilco, 385
chinampas, 383
Ciudadela, 365
Cuexcomate, 385
Copán, 372
Coyolxauhqui, 385
Florentine Codex, 381
Huitzilopochtli, 385
Maya hieroglyphs, 375
Monte Albán, 363

Olmec, 363
Otumba, 384
Popol Vuh, 378
Pyramid of the Moon, 367
Pyramid of the Sun, 365
Temple of the Feathered Serpent, 365
Templo Mayor, 385
Tenochtitlán, 381
Teotihuacán, 364
Texcoco, 383
Tikal, 372
Tlapocán, 383
Toltec Empire, 382
Triple Alliance, 383
Tula, 382

REVIEW QUESTIONS

1. What are the similarities and differences between the cities of the Indus Valley and those of Teotihuacán? Does it make sense to say these two societies shared a common political strategy?
2. How did the elite of the Maya cities use architecture to establish their position of power? How does this compare with the use of monumental architecture found in Egypt and Mesopotamia?

3. What insight does archaeology yield about the impact of Aztec expansion on people living at the periphery of the empire?

- Paul Healy is a professor in the department of Anthropology at Trent University. He has excavated sites in Mexico, Belize, Nicaragua, and Honduras including the Maya site of Pacbitun, Belize.
  www.trentu.ca/anthropology/healy.php

- Gyles Iannone, professor in the Department of Anthropology at Trent University, is a specialist in the archaeology of the ancient Maya. He has carried out a long-term field project at the site of Minanha, Belize, focused on the investigation of ancient Maya sociopolitical integration.
  http://www.trentu.ca/anthropology/iannone.php

- Geoffrey McCafferty, professor in the Department of Archaeology at the University of Calgary, has carried out a number of field projects in Mexico and Nicauragua. Granada, Nicaragua, is the current focus of his field research. He also has a long-standing interest in gender and archaeology.
  http://arky.ucalgary.ca/mccafferty/

- Kathryn Reese-Taylor, professor in the Department of Archaeology at the University of Calgary, is the director of the Naachtun Archaeological Project in the Yucatan peninsula,

Guatemala. Naachtun is one of the most remote sites in the Yucatan and one of the least known of all major Classic Maya centres. Although the site has been trenched by looters, this project is the first scientific excavation at Naachtun.
www.ucalgary.ca/~naachtun/

- Michael Spence is a Professor Emeritus at the University of Western Ontario. He has carried out research both at Téotihuacan, where he focuses on the Oaxacan enclave of Tlailotlacan, and in Ontario, where he has worked both on burials from Praying Mantis, a small Iroquoian village site, and on the use of silver by the Hopewell.
  http://anthropology.uwo.ca/spence/

- Christine White, professor in the Department of Anthropology at the University of Western Ontario, is a bioarchaeologist (human osteoarchaeologist) who uses chemical and forensic analyses of human remains to construct life histories of disease, diet, physical activity, environment, and geographical relocations on both individual and populations scales. She has conducted research in Mesoamerica, the Nile Valley, and Peru.
  http://publish.uwo.ca/~white2/About.html

PEARSON
myanthrokit™

Visit **www.myanthrokit.com**, where you will find a variety of tools and resources to enhance your learning, including:
- Practise quizzes with Study Plans
- Videos
- Listening Activities
- And much more!

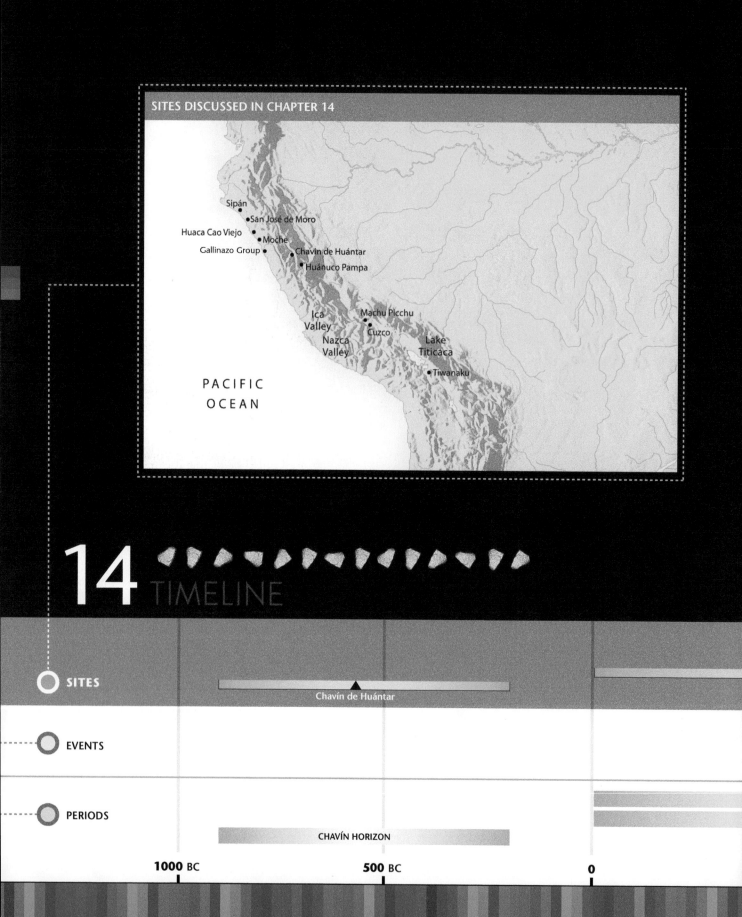

SITES DISCUSSED IN CHAPTER 14

Sipán
San José de Moro
Huaca Cao Viejo
Moche
Gallinazo Group
Chavín de Huántar
Huánuco Pampa

Ica Valley
Machu Picchu
Nazca Valley
Cuzco
Lake Titicaca
Tiwanaku

PACIFIC OCEAN

14 TIMELINE

SITES

Chavín de Huántar

EVENTS

PERIODS

CHAVÍN HORIZON

1000 BC   500 BC   0

BRINGING THE FOUR PARTS TOGETHER:
STATES AND EMPIRE IN THE ANDES

The Inca Empire developed out of a long history of social complexity in the Andes. After reading this chapter you should understand:

- The major characteristics and the archaeological interpretation of the site of Chavín de Huántar.

- The emerging understanding of social complexity in Moche and Nasca societies, including the roles of violence and feasting.

- The basic characteristics of the political and economic organization of the Inca Empire.

Machu Picchu, Peru. This spectacular site appears to meld into the mountain landscape.

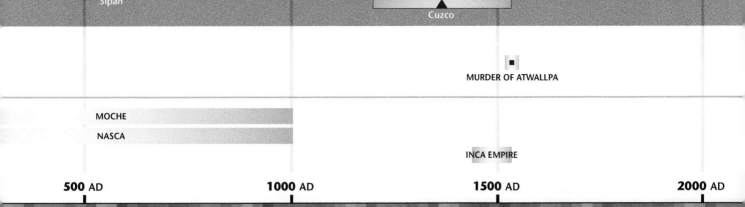

Tiwanaku

Machu Picchu

Sipan

Cuzco

MURDER OF ATWALLPA

MOCHE

NASCA

INCA EMPIRE

500 AD   **1000** AD   **1500** AD   **2000** AD

FIGURE 14.1 Outgoing staff-holders walk through the village of Tupicocha on New Year's Eve.

J ust before midnight on New Year's Eve, men from around the village of Tupicocha in the highlands of Peru slowly congregate in the centre of town (see Figure 14.1). These are the *varayuq* or staff-holders. By the end of the night, the ten varayuq will have ended their one-year term in office and turned their responsibilities over to a new set of staff-holders. The staffs are sticks of wood that have been carefully incised by the current staff-holder or his assistant. At the end of each year, the staff, which serves much like a police officer's badge, is retired and replaced with a new one. Checking to make sure that the new staffs have been properly marked is a serious business, undertaken in near silence while a crowd watches the procedure. The exchange of staffs and the annual reassignment of public offices in Tupicocha are examples of the small-scale interactions that underlie the structures of today's societies and those of the past. The use of staffs as markers of office continues an Andean tradition that goes back at least 3,000 years. Depictions of the deities from some of the earliest complex societies in the Andes include a figure holding a staff.

The environment of the Andes varies considerably (see Figure 9.9 on p. 250). The Pacific coast is a dry desert with rich marine resources and narrow zones of arable land along river valleys. Moving east from the coast, one ascends the high peaks of the Andes and the intermountain valley. Continuing east, one descends into the tropical lowlands of the Amazon Basin. The hallmark of Andean prehistory is the knitting together of these different environmental and cultural landscapes, culminating in the **Tawantinsuyu**, "the four parts together," of the Inca Empire. In this chapter, we begin at the highland site of **Chavín de Huántar**, which provides evidence for interregional connections based on the spread of a religious cult rather than on the bureaucratic organization of a state. We then move on to consider the **Nasca** and **Moche** societies, which emerged along the river valleys of the southern and northern coast of Peru. The Nasca and Moche raise further questions regarding the relationship between ritual and social structure. Finally, we will consider the history and structure of the Inca Empire.

14.1 Chavín de Huántar

The origins of social complexity in the Andean region can be traced back to the Cotton Preceramic (see Chapter 9). Cotton Preceramic sites such as Caral, Aspero, and El Paraiso reached a size of over 50 hectares close to 6,000 years ago. But many archaeologists stress the significance of the site of Chavín de Huántar as a major turning point in the development of Andean social complexity. The initial construction of the temple at Chavín is dated to 900 B.C. The temple structure was expanded around 500 B.C. before being abandoned at some point between 390 B.C. and 200 B.C. Recent reanalysis of the temple structure has produced an earlier chronology for the site according to which construction ceased around 500 B.C. (Kembel 2008). Further excavation and radiocarbon dating is needed to resolve these chronological questions.

■ The Setting and the Temple

Chavín de Huántar is located in a narrow valley in the highlands of Peru, at the confluence of the Huachesca and Mosna rivers (see Figure 14.2). The site is at an elevation of 3,150 metres above sea level, and the mountains rise steeply from the

Tawantinsuyu The Inca name for their empire; the name means "the four parts together."

▲▲ **Chavín de Huántar** A major ceremonial centre in the Andean highlands constructed around 800 B.C.

Nasca A culture that developed along the southern Pacific coast of Peru at the same time as the Moche society.

Moche A culture that developed along the Pacific coast of Peru and that flourished beginning 2,000 years ago.

FIGURE 14.2 Aerial view of Chavín de Huántar.
Chavín de Huántar and nearby village from above, image courtesy of CyArk (www.cyark.org).

valley floor. Although the soils of the valley support a range of agriculture, and the slopes above the valley floor are used for grazing llamas and alpacas, the valley itself is too narrow to have ever supported a large population.

The rivers that flow past Chavín cannot be navigated, so visitors would have arrived by foot, descending from the mountains on paths along one of the rivers. Arriving at the valley floor, travellers were met by a wall of dressed stones rising 11 metres above ground level. A row of busts of humans and animals, many of which have fangs and wear a contorted expression, projected out from this massive wall (see Figure 14.3). These heads appear to represent the transformation of a shaman into an animal form during a drug-induced trance. Working their way around this edifice, visitors reached an open area on the eastern side of the monumental complex (see Figure 14.4). At the centre of this open area was a circular courtyard sunken into the ground. Those descending into the courtyard would find themselves enclosed within the wings of the

FIGURE 14.3 One of the colossal stone heads that adorned the west wall of the temple at Chavín de Huántar.

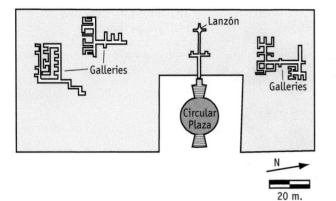

FIGURE 14.4 Plan of Chavín Old Temple. Note that the entrance to the temple structure went through the Circular Plaza that is enclosed within the two wings of the building.

Lanzón An engraved monolith at the core of the temple at Chavín de Huántar.

FIGURE 14.5 View of the Lanzón through the corridors of Chavín.

temple structure. Staring straight ahead, their eyes would be drawn to the western staircase that rose to an opening in the temple. On either side of the staircase were carved images of jaguars and mythical figures that appeared to be moving toward the temple. We do not know whether visitors would have been allowed past this point or if the interior of the temple was reserved for priests. The temple interior consists of a warren of narrow passageways, known as galleries, embedded in earth and rubble fill. The galleries create a complex maze lit only by natural light filtering in through ventilation shafts. The overall impression is that the layout of the galleries was intentionally designed to create a sense of confusion. Walking directly from the staircase leading up from the circular courtyard, the visitor reaches the intersection of two galleries (see Figure 14.5). In the centre of the intersection stands a four-metre-high granite shaft known as the **Lanzón**, carved in the form of a fanged human deity (see Figure 14.6). The play of light on the sculpted surface of the irregularly shaped rock of the Lanzón would have had a powerful effect on visitors.

The actual function of the temple at Chavín remains unclear. One intriguing proposal is that Chavín was an oracular site where people would come for prophesies or cures at the hands of the priests. There was a chamber situated directly above the Lanzón that might have served for ceremonies drawing on the power of this object. Or perhaps libations would have been poured over the Lanzón from this chamber. Surprisingly, there is only limited evidence of feasting at Chavín. This is in clear contrast to other ritual centres we have considered, such as Pueblo Bonito or Cahokia. Excavations in one of the galleries did produce a large collection of pottery vessels that are likely associated with drinking maize beer. However, even the size of the circular courtyard is inconsistent with the use of the temple as a setting for massive public gatherings.

Rather than creating a setting for bringing together large numbers of people, the design of Chavín is structured to affect the perceptions of individuals. Chavín was not a theatre where one sat back to watch; it was a construct where the visitor was immersed in sensory experience. Moving down into the circular courtyard would create a feeling of enclosure that would be accentuated by penetrating into the temple's narrow galleries. The galleries' layout creates dislocation, while the sheer size of the Lanzón gives a sense of awe. Some archaeologists have proposed that it was also possible to create powerful sound effects by controlling the flow of water through drainage channels running through the temple. In one case, it was observed that pouring water down the drainage canal below the staircase leading to the temple creates a very loud noise, more like applause (or the roar of a jaguar) than running water. The iconography of the figures at the site also makes it clear that those entering the temple were often in a drug-induced trance state. A range of psychoactive plants was available in the area around Chavín, and these plants are clearly represented in the art at the site.

■ The Chavín Horizon

The occupation site of Chavín in itself is unremarkable. The site was neither an urban centre nor the core of a state. The population of the valley during the initial stage of temple construction is estimated at 500, a number that would rise to a maximum of 1,000 at the time of the expansion of the temple, around 500 B.C. However, it is the widespread influence of Chavín that has made this site central to the study of the emergence of social complexity in the Andes. Chavín connections span the entire range of Andean environments from the Amazon Basin to the east to the coastal regions to the west. However, Chavín was not an empire, and it was not strictly political power that led to the widespread network of connections radiating out from this site. The term *Chavín Horizon* recognizes the extent of linkages to Chavín, but it leaves open the question of what underlies these connections.

Assessing the extent of connections between Chavín and the tropical lowlands to the east of the Andes is difficult because the archaeology of the Amazon Basin is poorly developed (Heckenberger and Góes Neves 2009). A number of the animals represented in Chavín art, including snakes, jaguars, crested eagles, and caymans, are native to the Amazon tropical lowlands and not found in the highlands. The crops depicted in the Chavín sculptures, including manioc, bottle gourd, and hot peppers, are also native to the lowlands and cannot be grown in the highlands around Chavín. The people of Chavín drew heavily on the mythology of Amazonia in creating their religious centre, but it does not appear that the settlement was constructed by migrants from the east. It is possible that the movement of individual charismatic or shamanistic leaders played a role in the transfer of religious beliefs from Amazonia to Chavín.

Artifacts in the Chavín style are found across the highlands and along the coastal lowlands to the west. Some of the most vivid examples of Chavín iconography come from painted textiles found on coastal sites, where dry conditions allow for

FIGURE 14.6 Detail view of the Lanzón.

the preservation of these fragile materials (see Figure 14.7). Unfortunately, many of the textiles come from looted tombs, so little can be said about their context. One group of looted textiles comes from a tomb at the coastal site of Karwa. These textiles were decorated with scenes that follow the conventions of Chavín art. However, there are significant differences between the deities depicted on the Karwa textiles and those that appear on the sculptures at Chavín. Notably, the staff god at Karwa is depicted as a female, whereas the same figure at Chavín is of indeterminate gender. The textiles found at Karwa suggest that aspects of the Chavín cult were practised on the coast at a distance of over 500 kilometres from Chavín. However, the question of how and why this belief system spread so widely is less clear. It is important to emphasize the skill involved in the painting of intricate Chavín-inspired designs on the Karwa textiles. When considering the spread of the Chavín cult, one must keep in mind that the religious system encompassed more than just a collection of mythological beliefs; the system also employed highly developed skills in making artifacts and, one presumes, in enacting rituals.

■ Summing Up the Evidence

The temple at Chavín was designed to create a powerful sensory impression on individuals or small groups visiting the site. The sacred core of the temple was the Lanzón, which stood in a strategically located gallery. Rituals at the temple involved the use of psychoactive drugs that would have further heightened the experience of this built environment. The cult of Chavín drew on mythology from the tropical lowlands to the east, and its influence extended across the highlands and down to sites along the coast. Chavín was not a city, and there is no evidence for a Chavín state. The influence of Chavín appears to have flowed from the ritual

prestige or oracular powers of the temple and the associated cult. Chavín forces us to look beyond aspects of social hierarchy and technology and seriously examine the significance of religious systems in creating the conditions for the emergence of social complexity.

14.2 Nasca and Moche

The Nasca societies of the southern coast of Peru and the Moche of the northern coast have challenged archaeologists and intrigued the general public. The Nasca and the Moche both developed around 2,000 years ago and persisted for close to 1,000 years. While some archaeologists see indications of Nasca and Moche urbanism and state bureaucracy, others are more cautious. Helaine Silverman has emphasized the importance of kinship in Andean social organization, particularly the significance of **ayllus**—or kin-based farming communities (Silverman and Proulx 2002). Lineages within the ayllus are ranked, providing for a degree of social complexity within a kinship system. Thus there is reason to be cautious about ascribing all evidence of social complexity (such as large monumental architecture) to a state society in which kinship has been eclipsed by bureaucracy.

■ Nasca

The Nasca culture developed in the narrow Nasca and Ica valleys of the southern coast of Peru. This culture is best known for **Nasca Lines**, or the large patterns they created on the desert floor. These "drawings" include depictions of humans and animals, as well as a large number of straight lines that stretch for miles along the desert (Aveni 2000). In most cases, the figures created by the lines are visible only in aerial photographs. To create the lines, the Nasca cleared black desert rocks and stacked them along the edge of a trail, leaving the lighter coloured desert surface exposed (see Figures 14.8 and 14.9). The purpose of this undertaking is a mystery that has intrigued archaeologists as well as UFO enthusiasts. Survey and aerial photography has shown that the lines are not randomly distributed across the desert floor; instead, they radiate out from a series of central points. Although some archaeologists argue that the lines served as astronomical observatories, it seems more likely that they were paths walked along in ritual processions, perhaps related to rain ceremonies. Although the ancient Nasca were unable to view their creations, they were able to experience the figures and lines sketched onto the desert floor with their bodies as they walked.

The site of **Cahuachi**, a ceremonial centre that stretches along an area 2 kilometres long, is the largest known Nasca site. Cahuachi consists of forty mounds interspersed

ayllus Kin-based farming communites that are important elements of Andean social organization.

Nasca Lines Large-scale patterns created on the desert floor near the Nasca River on the Andean coast. The Nasca lines include depictions of humans and animals as well as a large number of straight lines that stretch for miles.

▲ Cahuachi A large Nasca site that appears to have served as a centre for pilgrimage and ritual feasting.

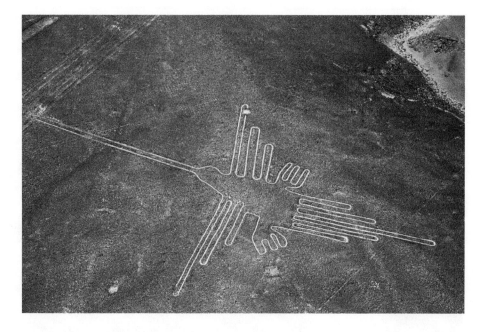

FIGURE 14.8 Aerial photograph of Nasca Lines depicting a hummingbird.

with large enclosures. Excavations have uncovered mostly ceremonial objects including caches of panpipes, engraved gourds, elaborately decorated textiles, and llama burials. There is little evidence to date of extensive habitation. Kevin Vaughn has proposed that Cahuachi was a pilgrimage site that, along with secondary ceremonial sites, served to integrate villages dispersed across the foothills of the Andes (Vaughn and Linares Grados 2006). To support this argument, Vaughn points to the prevalence of elaborately decorated polychrome pottery vessels in Nasca villages (see Figure 14.10). In excavations at the village site of Marcaya, Vaughn found polychrome pottery in all houses, although some vessel shapes were found only in elite houses. Neutron activation analysis (see Toolbox pp. 322–323) of polychrome vessels from Marcaya and other Nasca village sites identify the source for the clay used in making these vessels to a place near Cahuachi (Vaughn et al. 2006). This evidence indicates that polychrome pottery was produced at Cahuachi and then widely distributed to villages in the surrounding area, perhaps by pilgrims returning from ceremonial feasts.

FIGURE 14.9 View along one of the paths creating the hummingbird.

FIGURE 14.10 An elaborately decorated Nasca polychrome vessel from the village site of Marcaya.

FIGURE 14.11 Burial from Sipán richly adorned with gold, silver, and copper objects including beads, nosepieces, and earspools.

■ Moche

The Moche societies of the northern coast of Peru built impressive mounds, including a massive structure known as the **Huaca del Sol**, made of more than 140 million mud bricks, located at the site of Moche. Unfortunately, the looting of Moche sites has also been large scale. In the most extreme case, during the Colonial period, the Spanish diverted the Moche River to remove the mud brick and get to the gold buried inside the Huaca del Sol. The first completely intact burials were discovered in the 1980s at the site of **Sipán** in the Lambyeque Valley (see Figure 14.11). Similar discoveries were subsequently made at the site of **San José de Moro** in the Jequetepeque Valley. The wealth of burial goods found with the elite of Sipán and San José de Moro is simply amazing. Most of the objects, including worked gold, adorn the body of the main burial. Many of the specific items found in the Sipán burials can be identified in the paintings of warriors found on pottery vessels (see Figure 14.12). Before the discoveries at Sipán, these paintings were often interpreted as depictions of deities. Now they are recognized as representations of warrior elites. It is now clear that military power was essential to the social hierarchy of the Moche, and that a major goal of military conflict was the provision of victims for ritual sacrifice. The paintings on the pottery vessels show manacled prisoners being led up to a figure seated on a platform and then being killed and dismembered. The discovery of a series of murals at the site of **Huaca Cao Viejo** in the Chicama Valley showing a line of prisoners and sacrificial scenes

Huaca del Sol A massive mound made of over 140 million mud bricks, located at the site of Moche.

▲▲ **Sipán** An elite burial site on the coast of Peru that has given archaeologists a sense of the wealth and violence of Moche society.

▲▲ **San José de Moro** A Moche site where elite burials with an impressive wealth of burial goods have been discovered.

▲▲ **Huaca Cao Viejo** A Moche site where a mural showing a line of prisoners was found.

provides further support for viewing conflict and sacrifice as a key activity of the Moche elite (see Figure 14.13). Near the **Huaca de la Luna** at the site of Moche, the actual remains of sacrificial victims in various states of dismemberment were uncovered, providing visceral evidence that these rituals actually did take place.

There remains little question that violence and human sacrifice were an integral aspect of Moche ritual and society. But the scope of military action and the social context of violence remain unclear. The wealth of the Moche burials and the scale of monumental construction might point to a state society. Claude Chapdelaine has pointed out that a number of Moche sites have produced evidence of large, dense occupation, with populations estimated at a minimum of 5,000 people, suggesting that these sites were the urban centres of states (Chapdelaine, Pimentel, and Bernier 2000). Recent research by Jean-François Millaire at the Gallinazo Group site in the Viru Valley has identified evidence of a large urban occupation, with preliminary population estimates between 14,000 and 21,000 people (Millaire 2010). Radiocarbon dating suggests that the initial development of the Gallinazo Group dates back as early as 200 B.C. However, it is also possible that Moche society was essentially kinship based, with an ayllu system that allowed for hierarchy to emerge within kin groups, generating the wealth of displays found in elite burials without the bureaucracy characteristic of state societies. One essential question is whether Moche violence was political or ritual. Were these wars of conquest leading to political domination, or ritual combat limited to capturing victims for sacrifice? Jeffrey Quilter has argued that politics and ritual may not be mutually exclusive domains. He recognizes the effect of the emergence of a violent ritual cult and questions "the emotional power of participating in or watching fellow human beings transformed into chunks of rotting flesh, flayed skins, and

FIGURE 14.12 Moche fine-line pottery vessel showing warriors.

Huaca de la Luna A massive mud-brick mound at the site of Moche where actual remains of sacrificial victims were uncovered and found in various states of dismemberment.

FIGURE 14.13 Cleaning one of the murals from Huaca Cao Viejo that shows scenes of battle.

Discovering a Ceremonial Site of the Ancient Moche People

KATRINA JOOSTEN, UNIVERSITY OF TORONTO

As part of my undergraduate experience in archaeological fieldwork and methods, in the summers of 2009 and 2010, I collaborated in the excavations of an important Late Moche ceremonial site, located on the northern coast of Peru. Under the co-direction of Dr. Edward Swenson from the University of Toronto and Dr. John Warner from the University of Kentucky, our team excavated the remains of five burials with fully-articulated skeletons, which revealed a complex series of major occupation events and architectural renovations. The site we excavated is locally well-known as Huaca Colorada, which means "coloured-hill" in the indigenous Peruvian dialect Quechua. This is because the site is easily recognizable across the desert valley due to masses of pottery sherds that cover its sandy surface—one might whimsically say it appears like a glowing natural citadel in the distance.

At first I felt uneasy about excavating a site that the locals, at nearby San Lorenzo de Jatanca, refer to as the place where "spirits will eat you alive." It wasn't until the 2010 season, when some of our on-site workers requested that we have a local Peruvian Shaman perform a cleansing ritual at the site, that I experienced my first genuine awareness of the importance of heritage and local folkloric legend at archaeological sites.

Located in the very arid clime of Peru's northcoast desert region, the site has survived numerous ancient El Niño events. Some of these El Niño events were so drastic that they forced many Moche populations out of the main valley due to drought. Today the valley is known as one of the driest in the world, often considered an extension of the Atacama Desert in Chile. Following its period of last occupation, Huaca Colorada has been buried deep beneath the rolling dunes of fine grain sand, making it a very good environment for preservation—especially for human bones.

The working environment at Huaca Colorada—to sum up in a few words—is harsh, brutal, and, in an ironic way, mentally cleansing. Our daily routine began sharply at 5:30 a.m. We woke up, ate breakfast, and prepared our field kits for the day. Our personal field kits would normally included a field notebook, trowel, line levels, measuring tools, aluminum foil (for carbon date samples), string and nails, a pocket knife, bags for artifacts, sharpies and labels, and, most importantly, our sunglasses, hats, sunscreen, and water. These were heavy bags! At around 6:30 a.m., after disposing of our beat-up field vehicle at the nearest village (San Lorenzo de Jatanca), we walked 45 minutes across the desert pompa

with all of our equipment for the day, which also included buckets, screens, shovels and hatchets. It was such an exhilarating time for us, to watch the sun rise over the shadows of the Andean foothills as we stepped foot on top of the huaca, where most of our main units were set up. There we stayed, working until sometimes you felt as if you were going blind by the sand, until around 4 p.m. We loved it.

The 2010 season was especially successful because of the momentous amount of cultural material we discovered. I conducted excavations with a smaller team of three other student archaeologists, in two very large 6 × 6 metre units (Units 1 and 5). Located on top of the huaca in the approximate location where we had found three female sacrificial burials the prior year, Units 1 and 5 were on the southeast side, surrounded by Units 2 and 3 to the west. In total, we excavated over 11 6 × 6 metre units in 2010. In Units 1 and 3, we found a series of adobe brick paica holders (also called paica stands) and use-floor reconstruction events, which indicated the continuous occupation of space used for production-based activity from the site's earliest to latest phases. Paica holders are common at other contemporaneous Moche sites and have been demonstrated to function for the storage of materials used in

dismembered carcasses" (Quilter 2002, 172). Quilter implies that the violence inherent in Moche ritual would inevitably have had an effect on Moche politics.

Ultimately, resolving the question of whether the Moche were state societies requires moving beyond the centres to look at the settlements where people lived. Surveys and excavations have indicated a range of site sizes within each of the valleys, consistent with the hierarchical settlement system characteristic of a state society. However, more research is needed to understand the function of these various types of sites.

the production of an important ritual feasting drink made from fermented corn, called chicha. At Huaca Colorada, the paica holders were unusually large, with some as deep as 2 metres and as wide as 150 centimetres. As many as thirteen paica holders were found in Units 1–10 alone. Each paica holder varied slightly in construction. However what was perhaps most amazing was that they carried the signature of their builders. On the exterior plaster finish of each structure survived the actual fingerprints of their ancient Moche creators—even whole hand- and footprints survived!

Excavations revealed very interesting clues to the role of Huaca Colorada and its inhabitants in the production of ceremonial and feasting goods. The people of Huaca Colorada likely specialized in a particular combination of economic productivity, playing distinct religious roles within the overall Moche world. Among the information we discovered, of particular interest was Huaca Colorada's role in the production of copper and chicha. Taken together, our discoveries indicate that Huaca Colorada was an important locale for the political and religious power of Moche elites. ▲

FIGURE 14.14 Katrina Joosten working in the field.

■ Summing Up the Evidence

Nasca Lines and Moche human sacrifice are both evidence of societies with highly developed religious systems. The challenge for archaeologists is to understand the relationship between ritual practice and political structure in these societies. Currently, there is debate whether the Nasca and the Moche should be considered state societies. A social structure based on ayllus or hierarchically organized kinship groups provides an alternative basis for the kinds of elaborate practices found among these peoples.

Metallurgy

In rare instances, metals are found in such a pure state that they can be hammered into tools or ornaments without any processing. Artifacts made of pure, or native, copper are found on prehistoric sites in eastern North America. But most metals must first be smelted by heating ores to a high temperature. Once smelted, metals can be shaped by hammering or casting.

Copper can be smelted at relatively low temperatures, but early metalworkers rapidly realized that the material could be strengthened by mixing it with other metals to create alloys. Bronze is a copper alloy produced by mixing copper and tin or arsenic. Both copper and tin are found in limited deposits, so bronze metal production often involved extensive trade. The Ulu Burun shipwreck found off the coast of Turkey provides vivid evidence of this trade. Both tin and bronze were recovered from the hull of the ship as stacks of "oxhide" ingots (Bass 1986).

Although iron offers the advantage of being more widely available than copper or tin, the metal also needs to be heated to very high temperatures in order to be smelted. Iron metallurgy did not develop indigenously in the Americas. In Africa, archaeologists have uncovered a fascinating record of the indigenous development of iron smelting (Schmidt 1997).

Copper, bronze, and iron provided new and effective raw materials for the manufacture of both tools and weapons. However, archaeological metallurgists also stress the symbolic aspects of metal production. Dorothy Hosler (1995) has studied metal production in western Mexico under the Tarascan Empire. She found that western Mexican artisans placed an emphasis on producing objects worn by elites and used in rituals, rather than on utilitarian tools. These artisans were most interested in two physical properties of the copper alloys they worked: sound and colour. One of the most important types of artifacts produced was bells that were shaped by means of an elaborate technique known as the lost-wax method. High-status or ritual objects were made using copper alloys that had high levels of arsenic or tin. Laboratory experiments have shown that the amount of tin or arsenic found in artifacts is far higher than needed to enhance the mechanical properties of the resulting alloy. Moreover, utilitarian items did not have these high levels of arsenic or tin. Although the high levels of these metals do not alter the mechanical quality of the alloys, they do alter the colour, creating increasingly golden or silvery hues.

Historical texts about the Tarascans indicate that they saw sound and colour

FIGURE 14.15 Cleaned and reconstructed banner from Sipán.

14.3 The Inca Empire

Inca Empire An empire that thrived for over a century and at its peak ruled over 12 million people from northern Chile to Ecuador.

The **Inca Empire** that was known as Tawantinsuyu, "the four parts together," thrived for over a century, tying together a vast realm under the royal Inca in the capital city, Cuzco (D'Altroy 2002). At the peak of the empire, the Inca ruled over 12 million people in a region that stretched across 3,000 kilometres from Ecuador to northern Chile. The Inca Empire was not only massive; it also covered a highly heterogeneous

as connected. For example, they believed metallic sounds can create metallic colour. As Hosler reconstructs the process: "Smelting, that is, winning metal from its ore through heat, gives birth to sound (and song), and it also gives birth to the golden metallic colours" (Hosler 1995, 113). Looking at Tarascan metallurgy demonstrates that it is important not to reduce the study of technology to simply an examination of the utilitarian functions of tools: Often, even the most elaborate technologies are shot through with symbolic elements.

Metallurgical analysis of Moche artifacts has demonstrated that a number of techniques were used to enhance the surface qualities of objects to give them a metallic or golden sheen. The Moche occasionally used casting to form their metal artifacts, but their main technique was hammering out thin sheets of metal and using a range of methods, including soldering and welding, to join the sheets together to form complex objects. The key trick employed by Moche artisans to produce a surface that was rich in gold or silver was to use alloys in which these metals were mixed with copper. The Moche mastered two sophisticated methods to enrich the surface of their artifacts. The first method was to actually coat an artifact with a thin layer of gold using a method known today as electrochemical replacement plating (Lechtman, Erliz, and Barry 1982). In an experimental study, Heather Lechtman was able to demonstrate that the Moche dissolved gold in a solution of corrosive materials such as salt and potassium nitrate. Copper sheets could then be dipped in the boiling solution for 5 minutes, resulting in an even, thin coating of gold. Further heating was required to bond the gold layer to the underlying matrix. Analysis of an ornamental plate from the Sipán tombs has shown clear evidence for the use of this method (Hörz and Kallfass 2000). The second method used to enrich an artifact was to deplete the amount of copper at the surface of the object. This was achieved by repeatedly heating and cooling a metal sheet. In the process, copper oxides formed at the surface. These copper oxides could then be removed by soaking the sheet in a solution of acid plant juice or stale urine (ammonia), resulting in a surface that was depleted in copper relative to the underlying matrix. ●

FIGURE 14.16 Cross-section through one of the platelets making up the Sipán banner. A thin gold film is visible as a thin white line at the original surface of the piece. The outer shell of red-brown material is the product of corrosion of the copper body of the platelet that diffused through the gold film forming a crust on the surface.

region, ranging from the river valleys of the Pacific coast to the high-altitude valleys of the Andean altiplano.

In 1533, the immense and powerful kingdom of Tawantinsuyu fell to a group of 168 Spanish soldiers under the command of Francisco Pizarro. Facing an army of 80,000 Inca soldiers, Pizarro was nevertheless able to capture the Inca ruler Atawallpa and hold him for a ransom that today would amount to $50 million in jewels and melted gold. Even though the Inca paid the ransom, Pizarro executed

Ancient Agriculture and Modern Development

In the Bolivian highlands, archaeologists working at the ancient city of Tiwanaku are faced with a puzzle. One thousand years ago, Tiwanaku had a large population. A massive pyramid and sunken courtyard at the centre of the city provide a vivid indication of the Tiwanaku's power. Today, the area surrounding this ancient city is relatively underpopulated and faces many economic challenges. A team of archeologists and agricultural scientists led by Alan Kolata have been working to understand the agricultural system that sustained the urban centre of Tiwanaku. Through a combination of survey and test excavation, the team has learned that an extensive area around Tiwanaku was farmed using a system of raised fields. Ditches were excavated and the dirt piled onto the patches of ground between the ditches. Water was diverted from rivers into the complex network of artificial ditches. The result was an effective combination of irrigation and drainage. The raised fields would also provide some insulation from cold, and the stagnant water in the ditches would fill with plants that could be heaped up onto the fields as fertilizer.

Kolata and his colleagues began to wonder whether the poverty of the villagers who live in the area today is in part due to the abandonment of raised-field agriculture imposed during the colonial period. To explore this possibility, the team worked with a number of villages, developing plots of raised fields to grow potatoes and other crops. The results were promising, although several archaeologists have raised critiques of Kolata's ideas about Tiwanaku agriculture (Kolata 1996). The raised fields were productive and in many cases yielded more produce with less commercial fertilizer than the methods the villagers had been using. But the yield was dependent on the motivation of the particular group of farmers. Moreover, there is nothing in the study that suggests that raised fields are an instant cure for the economic problems of the region. However, Kolata's study has brought historical depth and ecological insight to the agricultural issues facing contemporary Bolivia. Kolata's team's research has shown that archaeologists can provide insight into the historical component of ecological issues facing rural populations. ●

FIGURE 14.17 Rehabilitated raised fields near Lakaya.

Atawallpa on July 26, 1533. The ruler's murder set off the rapid disintegration of the Inca Empire.

The early history of the Inca is shrouded in myth. The Inca believed that the god Wiraqocha created their ancestors, who then journeyed until they reached Cuzco, where they founded their capital. The initial expansion of the Inca realm appears to have taken place during the reign of the eighth ruler, Wiraqoch Inka. The history of the remaining rulers in the Inca dynasty is a succession of wars of conquest punctuated by conflicts over succession to the throne. The most violent war of succession took place immediately before the arrival of Pizarro. Waskhar and his half-brother,

Atawallpa, engaged in a long battle across much of the empire before Waskhar was captured and his family slaughtered.

■ Inca Society

One of the most intriguing aspects of Inca society was the power exerted by deceased rulers. After death, the emperor was mummified as part of an elaborate collective ritual. The mummified ruler continued to play an active role in the ceremonial and political life of Cuzco. Food was burnt in front of mummies, and, through mediums, they were able to communicate their wishes. The role of the deceased emperor was not limited to ceremonial functions. The property amassed by the emperor during his life passed to his kin-group descendants, known as **panaqa**. But the new ruler did not belong to the panaqa of the deceased king. He therefore had to go out and build his own fortune. This dynamic played an important role in the expansion of the Inca Empire, since each ruler was forced to carve out his own wealth.

The panaqa controlled considerable resources, including the royal estates of the former rulers. These estates, which included agricultural fields, pastures, forests, and mines, provided physical support for the emperor and his descendants (Niles 2004). In some cases, the estates served important ritual functions. The most famous of the royal estates is **Machu Picchu**. Located on a high mountain peak at the western end of the **Urubamba Valley**, Machu Picchu was built by Pachacuti Inca Yupanqui between 1450 and 1470 (Burger and Salazar 2004). Machu Picchu is a small walled settlement that includes royal and aristocratic complexes built in the classic Inca masonry style in which stone blocks are carefully fit together. There are also subsidiary buildings that appear to have housed the people who served the members of Pachacuti's panaqa. There is a large number of shrines, some of which are built around striking natural rock outcroppings.

Analysis of burials recovered at Machu Picchu indicates that the people who served Pachacuti's panaqa were drawn from across the empire (Burger and Salazar 2004). One of the most unusual lines of evidence comes from deformed skulls that were found at the site. In the highlands, the normal practice was to bind an infant's head with cloth strips, while on the coast it was more common to flatten the skull by tying the child's head to a cradleboard. Skeletons from Machu Picchu show both types of cranial deformation, indicating that the people buried at the site came from the coast and the highlands. The range of pottery vessels found with the burials at Machu Picchu offers further evidence of the ethnic diversity of the people buried there.

Feasting and the exchanging gifts played a central role in Inca society. At state centres, the elite spent much time hosting feasts of corn beer, coca leaves, meat, and music for their subjects (Burger and Salazar 2004). Large feasting halls often adjoined open plazas. The large feasting hall at Machu Picchu is located outside the walls and was probably used to fête local farmers. At the large Inca centre of **Hua'nuco Pampa**, over 600 kilometres north of Cuzco, two enormous halls and a series of subsidiary buildings were constructed alongside the main plaza (Morris and Thompson 1985). The substantial quantities of pottery recovered from the buildings around the plaza consist mainly of large jars, like the vessel shown in Figure 14.17, and plates, evidence that the plaza and the adjoining buildings were the site of large-scale feasting. Providing large-scale feasts is one of the most distinctive aspects of Inca political economy. This apparent demonstration of generosity challenges us to carefully consider the sources of legitimacy for the Inca Empire.

■ Building Empire

The Inca engaged in constant military campaigns to maintain and expand their empire. Integrating and controlling heterogenous conquered territories required

panaqa The collective descendants of the Inca emperor.

▲▲ **Machu Picchu** An Inca royal estate on a high mountain peak at the western end of the Urubamba Valley.

▲▲ **Urubamba Valley** The location of Machu Picchu, the most famous of the Inca royal estates.

▲▲ **Hua'nuco Pampa** An Inca centre 600 kilometres north of Cuzco.

CANADIAN research

Excavating in the Peruvian Desert

An essential element of the expansion of the Inca Empire was a policy that allowed local groups to continue traditional practices, a strategy that limited the resistance to Inca rule. However, based on research on the southern coast of Peru, Justin Jennings, an archeologist at the Royal Ontario Museum, has found that in rare cases the Inca suppressed elements of local religious practice (Jennings 2003). For thousands of years, until the arrival of the Inca, people living on the southern coast used painted tablets as offerings to the gods. The tablets were sherds of broken pots or flat pieces of stone. These simple materials were painted with geometric designs or abstract representations of

humans, animals, or celestial beings. Why would the powerful Inca Empire pay attention to such mundane objects? What possible threat could broken pots with painted designs pose?

Jennings suggests that the Inca put an end to the use of painted tablets because this practice contradicted Inca beliefs about the proper way to serve the gods, beliefs that were fundamental to the legitimacy of the Inca Empire. For the Inca, proper offerings to the gods were either consumable items like camelids, beer, and cloth or valuable objects such as gold and silver—or in some cases even people offered for sacrifice. Inca offerings also involved vocalized prayers and gestures. Because the painted tablets used markings

to give meaning to the offering and were in and of themselves of no intrinsic value this practice was an affront to the Inca religious system. Jennings suggests: "If the legitimacy of the Inca conquest was in part predicated on the spread of divinely-inspired ideas, then the *natural* right of the Empire to exit could be jeopardized if local practices that contradicted these imperial ideas were allowed to continue" (Jennings 2003, 116). Thus, the seemingly benign painted tablets of the southern coast posed a fundamental threat to the powerful Inca Empire. ◆

REFERENCE: Jennings, J. (2003). The fragility of imperialist ideology and the end of local traditions, an Inca example. *Cambridge Archaeological Journal* 13(1): 107–120.

FIGURE 14.18 Inca storage vessel.

khipu A system of knotted strings used by the Inca to record information.

effective mechanisms of administration. The Inca developed an impressive and extensive system of roads. These were critical for the movement of goods, people, and information. The Inca did not have a formal writing system; however, they did employ an elaborate method for recording information using knotted ropes known as **khipu**. In bringing together the four corners of Tawantinsuyu, the Inca showed a great deal of flexibility. In some areas, they ruled through local elites with a minimum of interference; in others, they installed distinctive administrative centres to allow for direct rule.

WARFARE. The Inca were able to field very large military forces consisting of tens of thousands of troops (D'Altroy 2003). These armies were drawn from the diverse ethnic groups belonging to Tawantinsuyu. The emperor often rode with the army, carried aloft on a litter. Weapons included arrows, sling stones, and javelins. The tactics of warfare were essentially massed frontal assaults followed by hand-to-hand combat using maces, clubs, and spears. Feigned retreats and similar tricks were often used to draw out an enemy, who could then be routed in a surprise counter-attack. Forts and garrisons were built in strategic locations. In Cuzco, the massive structure known as Saqsawaman (see Figure 14.18) appears to have served both as a temple to the sun and a fortress. An early Spanish traveller described Saqsawaman as being built of "such big stones . . . as big as pieces of mountains or crags" (Hyslop 1990, 53). The outer walls of the fortress were constructed on three terraces in a zigzag pattern designed to deter a frontal assault.

ROADS. Tawantinsuyu stretched over a vast and varied landscape. Control of the Inca Empire demanded the rapid movement of information, military force, and tribute. The Inca built a network linking together approximately 40,000 kilometres of roads (Hyslop 1984). Many of these were pre-existing roads that the Inca brought into their system. The scale of the roadways and their method of construction varied with the local topography and the importance of the road. The width of the roads varied from 1 to 4 metres, and the construction ranged from a simple line of stones leading through the desert to elaborate stone-built roads with drains to control the flow of water. Bridges were erected in many places to allow the roads to cross bodies of water. In some cases, the bridges were simple floating barges built of reeds; however, where the road needed to cross deep chasms, impressive suspension bridges were built out of reed cables woven together. The bridge built over the Apurimac River spanned 45 metres (see Figure 14.19). The floor of the bridge was 1.5 metres wide and could support a line of people and animals. The Spanish would even ride their horses over the bridge at a gallop. In some cases where a suspension bridge was not built, a cable was connected to the two sides of a chasm and a large basket was suspended from the cable. People or animals were then pulled from one bank to another by people hauling ropes attached to the basket.

FIGURE 14.19
Ruins of Saqsawaman.

One of the primary functions of the road system was as a conduit for rapid communication across Tawantinsuyu. Relay messengers were stationed every 6 to 9 kilometres. It is estimated that, as a group, these messengers could cover 240 kilometres a day. Approximately 1,000 roadside lodging and storage areas, known as *tampu*, were also built along the roads. These installations served as Inca administrative centres.

KHIPU. It would have taken many transfers of information to get a message from the northern end of Tawantinsuyu to the capital in Cuzco. Because the messengers were drawn from the diverse cultures of the Inca Empire, they might well have not spoken the same language. Furthermore, since the Inca lacked written documents, one would think that their road system would be more likely to resemble a game of broken telephone than an effective means for administering an empire. There are many situations in which a system for recording information would have been crucial for the Inca. However, they did not develop a classic writing system. In place of signs impressed in clay or written on paper, they used a system of knotted strings known as khipu.

A khipu consists of a series of coloured pendant strings tied onto a main cord. Groups of knots are tied along the pendant strings. Sometimes top cords were also tied to the main cords and subsidiary cords were attached to the pendant strings (see Figure 14.20). There are three basic types of khipu knots: a long knot with four turns, a single knot, and a figure-eight knot (see Figure 14.21).

Khipus are a highly complex system in which the number and the placement of cords and knots can be manipulated into an endless set of configurations. When one considers that the colour of the cords and even the way they were spun could also be controlled, the potential of khipus to code information seems almost limitless. Unfortunately, historic sources provide no glossary for translating or reading khipus. The system could code information, but the nature of the code remains the subject

FIGURE 14.20 Grass rope bridge spanning the Apurimac River, Peru.

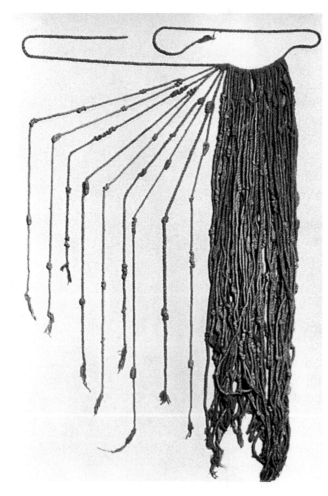

FIGURE 14.21 Inca khipu with knotted strings hanging from a main cord.

of debate. At one extreme is the theory that khipus were personal memory devices used to help jog the memory of individuals, known as *khipu kamayuq*, charged with keeping communal memory (see Figure 14.22). One khipu kamayuq could not read another's khipu. A second theory holds that khipus were a form of writing or at least a coding system for language (Urton 2003). According to this position, khipus were records—administrative texts and even histories—that could be read by Inca administrators. A third theory argues that khipus were indeed recording devices, but that they were used mostly for accounting and economic purposes (Ascher and Ascher 1981). There is support for this position as khipus are well designed to record numerical values by means of knots neatly arranged to represent numbers in decimal position. It is curious that the Inca responded to the need to manage information through the development of a code of knots rather than a script. One intriguing possibility is that the use of strings and knots to record information reflects the centrality of textiles in Andean society.

■ Summing Up the Evidence

The Inca tied together an impressively large and heterogeneous geographic region through the use of military power, an extensive road system, and an administrative apparatus that made use of khipus to keep records. It is important to emphasize that the Inca realms were not only geographically varied, but also culturally and linguistically diverse. The expansionist dynamic of the Inca was driven in large part by a system of inheritance that passed the emperor's wealth on to his descendants, known as his panaqa, rather than to his successor. As a result, each

a.

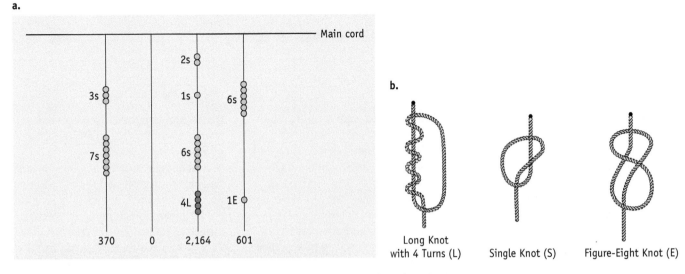

FIGURE 14.22 (a) Diagram showing how khipu knots can be used to record numbers. Letters refer to the type of knot. (b) Types of knots used in khipus.

new ruler had to accumulate his own wealth, often accomplished through military conquest. The Inca system of inheritance also resulted in frequent internal battles. The final battle of succession between Atawallpa and his half-brother, Waskhar, fatally weakened the Inca Empire on the eve of the arrival of Pizarro.

The fall of the Inca Empire is part of a global transformation that is still underway. The spread of Europeans, along with their culture and institutions, that began in the fifteenth century has had a dramatic impact on societies around the world, creating what anthropologists often refer to as a world system. The European expansion is richly documented in a wide range of written sources. Yet even here, archaeology can play a critical role through the branch of the discipline known as historical archaeology (Deetz 1996; Orser 2004). The written record was composed largely by Europeans, leaving many indigenous societies to be mistakenly perceived as "people without history" (Wolf 1982). Archaeologists can contribute to giving a voice to these people and recovering a history that is otherwise lost. Examples of such research efforts include the archaeology of indigenous people who lived during the process of European contact, as well as the archaeology of slave communities. Historical archaeologists also work in urban industrial centres, examining the changing technologies and social relations that powered European expansion. Here again, archaeologists can contribute to our understanding of aspects of society that are poorly represented in historical documents.

FIGURE 14.23 Khipu kamayuq with a khipu. Illustration from a sixteenth-century Spanish manuscript.

TOOLBOX

Tracking Ancient Diseases

Because many diseases leave no evidence on the skeleton, detecting the traces of illness in ancient populations is often extremely challenging. Even in cases where a disease does leave a clear trace on the skeleton, the interpretation of these pathologies can be ambiguous. Tuberculosis in the prehistoric Americas is a good example. In severe cases, the disease can lead to spinal deformities that can be identified on archaeological skeletons. But these same spinal deformities can be caused by infections other than tuberculosis. As a result, many researchers have been reluctant to accept skeletal evidence of tuberculosis in the Americas before European contact. It has long been thought that tuberculosis was a European disease brought to the Americas by European settlers.

Another way to trace diseases in archaeological remains is to extract tissue and identify infectious agents directly. Unfortunately, this is rarely possible. However, in a pioneering study, DNA was extracted from mummified human remains that showed lesions consistent with a diagnosis of tuberculosis (Salo et al. 1994). This study has demonstrated that tuberculosis was present in the Americas before European contact.

The Chiribaya were an agricultural group that lived on the southern Peruvian coast between A.D. 1000 and A.D. 1300. The aforementioned DNA analysis was carried out on the spontaneously mummified body of a Chiribaya woman dated to A.D. 1040. DNA was extracted from a lesion on the right lung and was then amplified with the use of PCR (polymerase chain reaction). The results showed a clear match between the DNA recovered from the mummy's lung and the DNA of modern tuberculosis.

The genetic analysis of the lineage of Tutankhamun discussed in the Toolbox on page 330 also succeeded in isolating the DNA of malaria from four mummies, including Tutankhamun's (Hawass et al. 2010). This evidence is leading to a reappraisal of the history of malaria in human populations. ●

FIGURE 14.24 Piece of mummified lung tissue showing lesions characteristic of tuberculosis.

SUMMARY

- Construction of the temple complex at Chavín de Huántar began around 900 B.C. The temple structure consists of a series of narrow passageways known as galleries.
- The Lanzón is a carved stone that stands in a strategic location in one of the central galleries at Chavín de Huántar.
- The temple complex at Chavín de Huántar was designed to create a complex sensory experience for a limited number of people.

- The Chavín Horizon spans extensive areas of the Andean highlands and coast. This phenomenon appears to reflect the spread of religious practices rather than the expansion of a political power.
- Hierarchically organized kinship groups, known as ayllus, play an important role in the social complexity of Andean societies.

- Beginning 2,000 years ago, the Nasca societies of the southern coast of Peru created the Nasca Lines, enormous patterns on the desert floor.
- The Moche were societies on the northern coast of Peru contemporary with the Nasca. The Moche built very large burial mounds, including the Huaca del Sol.
- The discovery of intact Moche burials at Sipán and San José de Moro uncovered a wealth of burial goods.
- There is considerable evidence indicating the centrality of violence and warfare to Moche society, including paintings on ceramics showing captives and sacrificial victims, murals showing captives at the site of Huaca Cao Viejo, and the remains of dismembered sacrificial victims at the Huaca de la Luna.
- The Inca Empire Tawantinsuyu covered an area that stretched over 3,000 kilometres and had a population of 12 million.
- In 1533, the Inca Empire fell to a small group of Spanish soldiers under the command of Pizarro.
- The property of the Inca emperor was passed on to his descendants, collectively known as his panaqa. The site of Machu Picchu was an estate belonging to the panaqa of Pachacuti.
- Feasting and the exchange of gifts played an important role in Inca society. At the Inca centre of Hua'nuco Pampa, two enormous halls used for feasting have been excavated.
- The Inca built an extensive network of roads to facilitate communication across the empire. The Inca used a system of knotted strings known as khipu to record information.

KEY TERMS

REVIEW QUESTIONS

1. What are ayllus and how do they affect our view of the Moche and the Nasca?
2. What is the evidence for warfare and violence in Moche society?
3. How were the Inca able to maintain their dominion over the large territories that made up Tawantinsuyu?

CANADIAN ARCHAEOLOGISTS

- Claude Chapdelaine, professor in the Department of Anthropology at the University of Montreal, has written extensively on Moche social complexity. He also carries out research on the prehistory of Quebec.
www.mapageweb.umontreal.ca/chapdelc/

- Nicole Couture, professor in the Department of Anthropology at McGill University, carries out research on the urban landscape of Tiwanaku. She is particularly interested in understanding the diversity of Tiwanaku society.
www.mcgill.ca/anthropology/faculty/fulltime/nicole_couture/

- Justin Jennings is a curator at the Royal Ontario Museum specializing in the archaeology of the Wari and Inca Empire. He is currently excavating the Wari-influenced site of Collota.
http://www.rom.on.ca/collections/curators/jennings.php

- Jean-Francois Millaire, professor in the Department of Anthropology at the University of Western Ontario, specializes in the archaeology of complex societies in the Andes. He has carried out fieldwork at Huacas de Moche, Huancaco, Huaca del Pueblo, and Huaca Santa Clara. His publications include

Moche Burrial Pattern: An Investigation into Prehispanic Social Structure (BAR International Series, 2002).

http://anthropology.uwo.ca/faculty/millaire/

- Lisa Rankin is a professor in the Department of Archaeology at Memorial University with research interests in Labrador and the lower Great Lakes. She has also carried out research on the Inca policy of Mitmaq, the movement of people around the empire by the state authrorities.

www.ucs.mun.ca/~lrankin/intro.html

- Edward Swenson, professor in the Department of Anthropology at the University of Toronto, conducts research in the Cañoncillo urban system of the Jequetepeque Valley, Peru, with the goal of understanding how transformations in public architecture related to changes in local ritual activity and the organization of domestic space.

http://anthropology.utoronto.ca/people/faculty-1/faculty-profiles/edward-r.-swenson

PEARSON
myanthrokit™

Visit **www.myanthrokit.com**, where you will find a variety of tools and resources to enhance your learning, including:
- Practise quizzes with Study Plans
- Videos
- Listening Activities
- And much more!

An archaeologist holds some of the household materials recovered from the excavation of a historical site.

EPILOGUE

BRINGING IT BACK HOME

As we arrive at the end of this book, a journey in a sense, we are filled with images from far away, both in place and in time. However, in closing, it is important to recall that archaeology is not only about exploring the unknown, but also about recognizing the traces of the past in our familiar world. Increased awareness of the past that surrounds us in our daily lives can also profoundly alter our sense of the world in which we live.

Reburial ceremony at the African burial ground in Lower Manhattan.
Nancy Siesel/The New York Times

The French historian Pierre Nora used the evocative term "Places of Memory" for locations or objects that become saturated with historical meaning (Nora 1996–1998). Places of Memory are critical touchstones for our connection with society, creating a visceral and authentic tie between present and past. The discovery of an African slave cemetery in Lower Manhattan in 1991 offers a vivid illustration of the emotional effect of the actual physical remains of the past (photo on page 417; Mack and Blakey 2004). Although historians have known that slavery was widespread in early Manhattan, the discovery of the cemetery grounded this historical knowledge in a concrete physical presence.

More recently, New York City was the site of a catastrophe of tragic scope. The events of September 11, 2001, transformed Ground Zero into one of the most profound Places of Memory of our time, a place whose physical presence raises deep emotions. Most of the traces of the past that enrich our world are neither as awful or as awe-inspiring as Ground Zero. The archaeologist James Deetz coined the phrase "In Small Things Forgotten," which he drew from a seventeenth-century appraisal of the contents of a house in Plymouth, Massachusetts. At the end of the listing of the contents, the appraiser had made a last entry: "In small things forgotten, eight shillings six-pence" (Deetz 1996, 4). One can imagine the various objects left behind that together came to a value of eight shillings six-pence. Small things forgotten are found all around us, below our feet as we walk on roads, sidewalks, and even manhole covers. Recognizing and valuing these subtle traces of the past enriches the world we live in.

Archaeologists combine attention to detail with an appreciation of the significance of context. In 2008, Matthew Cochran, a graduate student excavating in Annapolis, Maryland, recognized the significance of a football-sized lump of mud that most people would sweep aside without a second thought (Figure E.1). As Cochran worked 1.2 metres below the modern surface in levels dating to the early eighteenth century, he saw what appeared to be a flat stone surrounded by small pieces of lead shot. Recognizing that this was something unusual, he freed the rock, which turned out to be a clay bundle. A crack in the clay showed a pile of pins and nails, raising the possibility that this object might be from hoodoo rituals, African customs brought to Maryland by slaves. The bundle was then x-rayed, revealing 300 pieces of metal and a

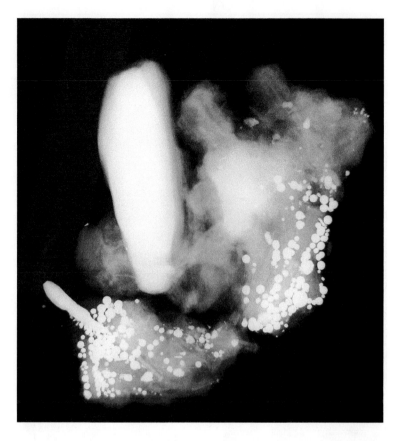

FIGURE E.2 X-ray photograph of the bundle revealing the metal objects and stone axe packed inside.

stone axe poking out through the clay (Figure E.2). This unassuming assemblage of artifacts is, on close examination, precious evidence of the ephemeral realm of African beliefs, the spiritual world of eighteenth-century slaves. Bundles of metal objects are a well-known element of West African ritual, and stone blades are associated with the god of thunder and lightning. Mark Leone of the University of Maryland, the director of the excavation at Annapolis, states that "the bundle is African in design . . . . The people who made this used local materials. But their knowledge of the charms and the spirit world probably came with them directly from Africa" (Wilford 2008).

The archaeologist's attention to detail rescued this precious object from obscurity, but without careful control of stratigraphic context the age of the object would not be known. The identification of pottery dating to the 1720s in the same level as the clay bundle is the only means of determining when the ritual act took place. However, the context tells us more than simply the age of the object. The bundle was found in a gutter at the edge of a street, not in a hidden location, but rather in an open and visible place. This suggests to Leone that in the early eighteenth century there was a degree of toleration for African ritual in the city of Annapolis. This is a beautiful example of how archaeological sensitivity to "small things forgotten" can open new windows on the past.

Archaeology trains us to look at the world in a new way. The science of archaeology has produced new understanding of the history of humanity, but it also provides us with a way of being aware of the world around us. Along with attention to detail and context, archaeology brings a questioning attitude to bear on the material world that surrounds us, a world that we often take for granted. Archaeology encourages us to see the historical layers that underlie our everyday experience. Behind our MP3 players there are the shades of the "sound system" built into the temple at Chavín de Huántar, the flutes from the Neolithic site of Jiahu, and the still earlier flutes recently recovered from the Aurignacian site of Hohle Fels, Germany.

Underlying the tools we use to recreate music rest millennia of human experimentation with sound. But we can also turn our archaeological perspective on our modern technology to ask how our MP3 player articulates with the social and technological world we inhabit. The same exercise can be extended to all aspects of our material world—from disposable coffee cups to massive skyscrapers.

What do we see when we look at the cumulative material record of human existence? In this book we approach the archaeological record as the basis for an ongoing process of archaeological research, a process that over the past 150 years has extended and enriched our understanding of humanity and history. However, what if we look at the archaeological record not as the basis for research but as something that exists with us, something that is very much part of the fabric of our lives? The social theorist Walter Benjamin developed a beautiful and harrowing image of the "angel of history" that might apply to the archaeological record. Benjamin writes of a painting by Paul Klee that shows an angel contemplating something he is about to move away from (Figure E.3). For Benjamin, this is an image of the angel of history:

"His face is turned toward the past. Where we perceive a chain of events, he sees one single catastrophe which keeps piling wreckage upon wreckage and hurls it in front of his feet" (Benjamin 1968, 257). Benjamin's angel would like to stay and heal the wreck before his eyes, but a "storm irresistibly propels him into the future to which his back is turned, while the pile of debris before him grows skyward. This storm is called progress" (Benjamin 1968, 258). Certainly the events of recent years, from New Orleans to Port au Prince, have left scenes of overwhelming devastation seared on our minds. The lethal collapse of buildings, our shelter from the elements and the constructs that shape our lives, seems to mock our faith in human achievement. Benjamin's vision is a horrifying idea of progress that cautions us not to assume that it implies improvement.

Yet, as an archaeologist, I find something lacking from Benjamin's vision. As we look back on the "wreckage of progress" that archaeologists have uncovered and continue to uncover, what do we see? There are many answers to this question, and it is largely a matter of personal perspective. What I find lacking from Benjamin's vision is a sense of the humanity of the past. The archaeological record is profoundly human. A handaxe is not only a shaped stone, but also a stone that bears the traces of every blow used to sculpt a tool, as well as the microtraces left after the tool was used. A pot bears the imprints of the hands of the person who made it and the paint strokes or incisions applied as decoration. Walls are not simply architectural spaces, but the remnants of structures in which people spent their lives.

Benjamin's vision can be balanced by the words of the late Israeli poet Yehunda Amichai. In his poem, Amichai writes of sitting by David's Tower in Jerusalem after going shopping. He becomes the point of reference for a tour guide who says, "You see that man with the baskets? Just to the right of his head there's an arch from the Roman period." In the poem, Amichai looks to the day when the guide says, "You see that arch from the Roman period? It's not important: but next to it, left and down a bit, there sits a man who's bought fruit and vegetables for his family" (Amichai 1996, 137–138). So that is where we leave our journey, not with the gold of kings or the bones of early hominins, but with a person alive in a world saturated with the past. Wherever we live, some part of us is that person.

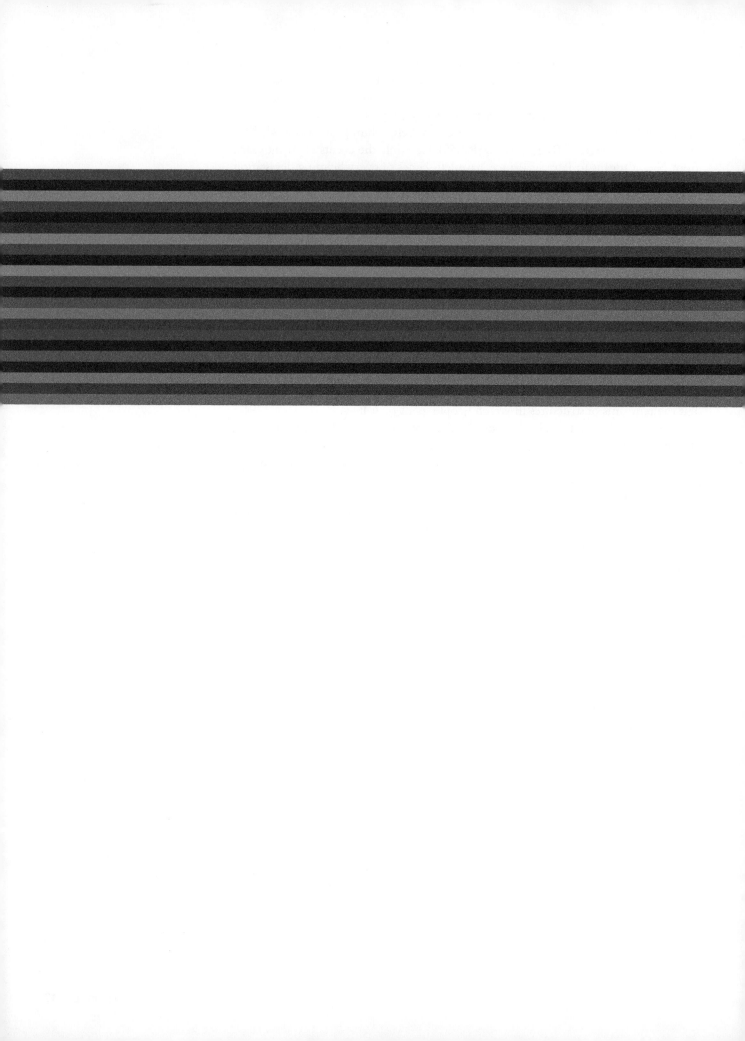

APPENDICES

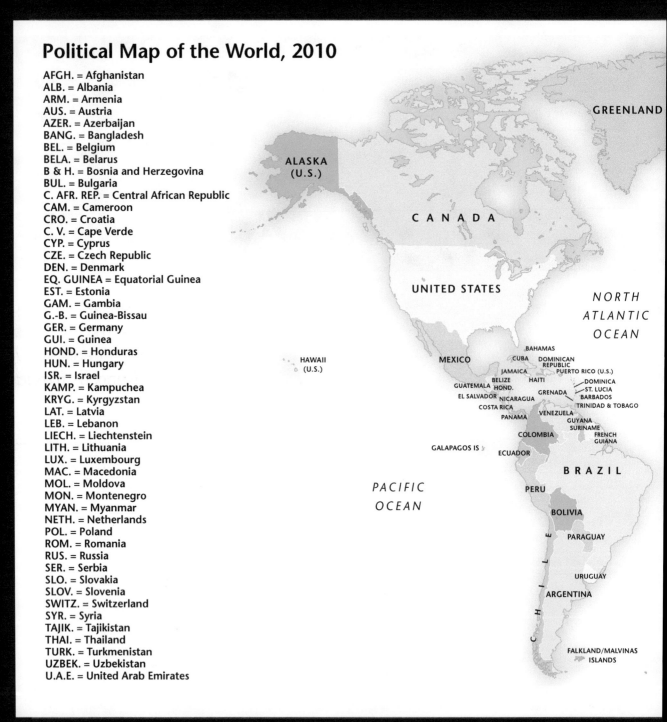

Political Map of the World, 2010

AFGH. = Afghanistan
ALB. = Albania
ARM. = Armenia
AUS. = Austria
AZER. = Azerbaijan
BANG. = Bangladesh
BEL. = Belgium
BELA. = Belarus
B & H. = Bosnia and Herzegovina
BUL. = Bulgaria
C. AFR. REP. = Central African Republic
CAM. = Cameroon
CRO. = Croatia
C. V. = Cape Verde
CYP. = Cyprus
CZE. = Czech Republic
DEN. = Denmark
EQ. GUINEA = Equatorial Guinea
EST. = Estonia
GAM. = Gambia
G.-B. = Guinea-Bissau
GER. = Germany
GUI. = Guinea
HOND. = Honduras
HUN. = Hungary
ISR. = Israel
KAMP. = Kampuchea
KRYG. = Kyrgyzstan
LAT. = Latvia
LEB. = Lebanon
LIECH. = Liechtenstein
LITH. = Lithuania
LUX. = Luxembourg
MAC. = Macedonia
MOL. = Moldova
MON. = Montenegro
MYAN. = Myanmar
NETH. = Netherlands
POL. = Poland
ROM. = Romania
RUS. = Russia
SER. = Serbia
SLO. = Slovakia
SLOV. = Slovenia
SWITZ. = Switzerland
SYR. = Syria
TAJIK. = Tajikistan
THAI. = Thailand
TURK. = Turkmenistan
UZBEK. = Uzbekistan
U.A.E. = United Arab Emirates

APPENDIX B
COMMONLY USED METRIC SYSTEM UNITS AND SYMBOLS

QUANTITY MEASURED	UNIT	SYMBOL	RELATIONSHIP		
Length, width,	millimetre	mm	10 mm	=	1 cm
distance, thickness,	centimetre	cm	100 cm	=	1 m
girth, etc.	metre	m			
	kilometre	km	1 km	=	1000 m
Mass (weight)	milligram	mg	1000 mg	=	1 g
	gram	g			
	kilogram	kg	1 kg	=	1000 g
	metric tonne	t	1 t	=	1000 kg
Time	second	s			
Temperature	degree Celsius	°C			
Area	square metre	m^2			
	hectare	ha	1 ha	=	10,000 m^2
	square kilometre	km^2	1 km^2	=	100 ha
Volume	millilitre	mL	1000 mL	=	1 L
	cubic centimetre	cm^3 or cc	1 cm^3	=	1 mL
	litre	L	1000 L	=	1 m^3

Conversion Table

TO CONVERT FROM	TO	MULTIPLY BY *
acres	hectares (ha)	0.4
feet (ft)	metres (m)	0.3
inches (in)	centimetres (cm)	2.54
miles (mi)	kilometres (km)	1.6
ounces (oz)	grams (g)	28
pounds (lb)	kilograms (kg)	0.45 or divide by 2.2
yards (yd)	metres (m)	0.9

*approximate, except for the inches-to-centimetre multiplier, which is exact.

APPENDIX C
THE HOMININ WHO'S WHO

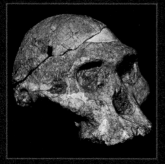

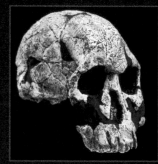

National Museums of Kenya, Nairobi.
©1985 David L. Brill.

Australopithecus

- 3.5–2.5 million years ago
- Brain size: 450–475 cc
- Found in East Africa, South Africa, and Chad
- Species include *Australopithecus bahrelghazali*, *Australopithecus afarensis*, and *Australopithecus africanus*
- Bipedal with small canines

Kenyanthropus

- 3.5 million years ago
- Brain size: 450–475 cc
- Only one species known, *Kenyanthropus platyops*
- Similar to *Australopithecus*

Paranthropus

- 2.5–1.4 million years ago
- Brain size: 450–475 cc
- Found in East Africa and South Africa
- Also known as robust *Australopithecus*. Species include *Paranthropus robustus* and *Paranthropus boisei*
- Massive molars and muscles for chewing

Homo habilis

- 2.5–1.6 million years ago
- Brain size: 500–800 cc
- Found in East Africa and South Africa
- First member of genus *Homo*
- Increased brain size

Hominoids are members of the biological superfamily that includes humans, great apes, and gibbons.

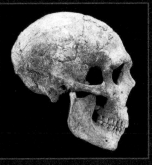

Homo erectus

- 1.9 million–45,000? years ago

- Brain size: 750–1,250 cc

- Found in Africa, Asia, and Europe (first hominin found outside of Africa)

- Early *Homo erectus* is often referred to as *Homo ergaster*

- Increased brain size

Homo neanderthalensis

- 175,000–30,000 years ago

- Brain size: 1,200–1,700 cc

- Found in Europe and the Middle East

- Some anthropologists prefer to label this group of fossils *Homo sapiens neanderthalensis*

- Large brain size, muscular, and adapted to the cold

Homo sapiens sapiens

- 160,000 years ago until today

- Brain size: 1,200–1,700 cc

- Found throughout the globe

- All living humans belong to this species, which is often referred to as "modern humans"

- Globular braincase, vertical forehead, decreased body mass

Homo floresiensis

- 38,000–18,000 years ago

- Brain size: 380 cc

- Found only on the island of Flores

- Some anthropologists question whether this is in fact a distinct species

- Small brain and body size

Hominins are members of the human lineage after it split with the chimpanzee lineage.

APPENDIX D
DATING METHODS

Radiocarbon Dating

TOOLBOX ON P. 27

- Time range: Beginning 40,000 years ago.

- Material dated: Organic remains including charcoal, bone, wood, and shell.

- The death of an organism removes it from the carbon-exchange reservoir and radioactive carbon-14 begins to decay at a steady rate. The concentration of carbon-14 relative to other isotopes of carbon is the basis for calculating the time since the death of the organism.

- Because of fluctuations in the concentration of carbon-14 in the global reservoir, carbon-14 dates have to be calibrated to arrive at a calendar date (see p. 164).

- Accelerator mass spectrometry (AMS) allows for the dating of very small samples (see p. 221).

Argon Dating

TOOLBOX ON P. 81

- Effective for dating all periods of hominin evolution.

- Materials dated: Volcanic rock and ash, as well as meteoric glass (tektites).

- Measures the accumulation of argon-40 from the decay of potassium-40. The decay of potassium-40 takes place at a constant rate. The accumulation clock is zeroed at the time of a volcanic eruption because argon diffuses out of a material at high temperatures. Consequently, after an eruption there is no argon in lava and ash. Argon then begins to accumulate as a result of the decay of potassium.

- Can be used only in areas with volcanic deposits.

Paleomagnetic Dating

TOOLBOX ON P. 80

- Effective for dating all periods of hominin evolution.

- Material dated: Sediments.

- Determines whether sediments were deposited in periods of normal or reversed polarity. Can be used to situate a stratigraphic context in the paleomagnetic time scale.

Luminescence Dating

TOOLBOX ON P. 130

- Most effective for the more recent periods of hominin evolution (since 200,000 years ago).

- Materials dated: Sediments (optically stimulated resonance, or OSL), burnt flint and pottery (thermoluminescence or TL), teeth (electron spin resonance, or ESR).

- Measures the accumulation of electrons in crystal lattices. The clock is zeroed when the material is heated (TL), when it is exposed to sunlight (OSL), or upon the initial growth of the crystal (ESR).

- The background radiation at the find must be measured with a dosimeter.

Dendrochronology

TOOLBOX ON P. 293

- Most useful for the last 10,000 years.

- Material dated: Wood.

- The ring pattern found in a piece of wood is matched to the fluctuations in a long-term chronology.

GLOSSARY

Abrigo Lagar Velho A site in Portugal where the skeleton of a modern human child dating to 24,500 years ago was discovered. The discovery is thought by some to support the hybridization model.

absolute chronology A chronology stated in terms of calendar years.

Abu Hureyra A site on the Euphrates River in Syria that was occupied during the Natufian and the Neolithic periods.

Abydos The site of the royal cemetery of Egypt during the First and Second Dynasties.

accelerator mass spectrometry (AMS) radiocarbon dating A refined method of radiocarbon dating that makes it possible to date very small samples, including plant remains.

Acheulian Lower Paleolithic stone tool industry dated in Africa between 1.7 million and 200,000 years ago, characterized by bifacial tools including handaxes and cleavers.

Adena A period of intensive mound building in the Ohio River Valley; it corresponds to the Middle Woodland culture.

Aegyptopithecus A fossil primate that lived 56-23 million years ago.

agency theory A theory that emphasizes the interaction between the agency of individuals and social structure.

Aguateca A site that was abandoned and burned, probably in a military attack, leaving archaeologists with a unique record of the daily life of the Maya.

Akhenaten A religious reformer who built the city of Amarna.

Akrotiri A Bronze Age town on the island of Thera that was buried by a catastrophic volcanic eruption.

alpacas Camelid animals domesticated in the Andean highlands; *vicuñas* are the ancestral species of alpacas.

Allumettes Island site A site on the Ontario-Quebec border where a large number of copper tools have been recovered, dating to the Archaic period.

Amarna A city built by the heretic king Akhenaten and abandoned after his reign. Excavation of this city has provided a unique horizontal exposure of an Egyptian urban centre.

Amesbury Archer A burial with a range of elite burial goods found near Stonehenge.

Amud Cave The location where a Neanderthal child was found buried with the upper jaw of a red deer.

anthropogenic deposits Deposits that result from human activity. Human activities range from building fires on ephemeral hunter–gatherer campsites to erecting the palaces and fortifications of great cities.

Anyang A site in northern China and the capital of the Late Shang Dynasty.

archaeological theory Ideas that archaeologists have developed about the past and about the ways we come to know the past.

Arcy-sur-Cure A site in northern France where excavators discovered a rich collection of ornaments, bone tools, and Châtelperronian stone tools.

Ardipithecus ramidus An early species in the hominin lineage. This species, which lived approximately 4.5 million years ago, is known from fossils originally discovered in 1992 at the site of Aramis in Ethiopia.

artifacts Objects that show traces of human manufacture.

Aterian A North African stone tool industry distinguished by the presence of points with a pronounced tang—a small projection located at the base of the point and used to secure the point to a spear handle.

attribute A particular characteristic of an artifact.

Aurignacian The earliest Upper Paleolithic period. Aurignacian industries have been found on sites across Europe and the Middle East.

australopithecine A hominin genus that lived in Africa between 4 million and 2.5 million years ago.

Avenue of the Dead A road that stretches for 5 kilometres through the centre of Teotihuacán.

ayllus Kin-based farming communites that are important elements of Andean social organization.

Aztec Empire A large Mesoamerican empire based in Tenochtitlán.

Aztlán The homeland, possibly mythical, of the Aztecs.

Banpo A large farming village located in the Yellow River Valley (China) dating to the Yangshou culture.

Beeches Pit A site in England dating to 400,000 years ago that has produced compelling evidence for the use of fire in the Lower Paleolithic.

Beringia A land bridge that connected Asia and North America during periods of low sea level.

Bernardo de Sahagún The Spanish friar who compiled the Florentine Codex.

bevel-rim bowls Small undecorated vessels made of coarse clay that are ubiquitous on Uruk-period sites.

Biache-Saint-Vaast The site in France where the oldest-known fossil of a Neanderthal, dated to 175,000 years ago, was found.

bifaces Characteristic tools of the Acheulian. Bifaces include handaxes and cleavers.

Blackwater Draw A site near Clovis, New Mexico, where spearpoints were found in levels below Folsom points.

Blombos Cave A site in South Africa where pieces of ochre with incised decoration were found in a Middle Stone Age level dated to 77,000 years ago.

bluestones A ring of standing stones at the centre of Stonehenge. The source of the stones is over 240 kilometres from Stonehenge.

Border Cave One of the South African sites where fossils of modern humans dated to between 120,000 and 70,000 years ago were discovered.

Bose A site in southern China that produced a stone tool industry that includes handaxes dated to 800,000 years ago.

Boxgrove One of the oldest known Acheulian sites in Europe; located in England and dated to 500,000 years ago.

broad spectrum adaptation Exploitation of a wide range of plant animal resources characteristic of many hunter–gatherer societies that preceded the shift to agriculture.

Cahokia A large settlement dating to the Mississippian Period located just outside of St. Louis, Missouri.

Cahuachi A large Nasca site that appears to have served as a centre for pilgrimage and ritual feasting.

Capilco The smaller of two rural sites in Morelos, to the south of the Basin of Mexico, that have produced insight into rural life under the Aztecs.

Çatalhöyük A Late Neolithic site in Turkey that includes rooms decorated with elaborate frescoes.

Cepheren A Fourth Dynasty Egyptian king who constructed a pyramid at Giza that was slightly smaller than the one constructed by Cheops. The great Sphinx is located alongside the Cepheren Valley Temple.

Cerro Juanaqueña An early agricultural site in northern Mexico with extensive evidence of terracing and other stone built features.

Chaco Canyon A canyon in New Mexico that became the centre of a regional settlement network and the site of the construction of large multistoried structures, known as Great Houses, beginning around A.D. 800.

Chacoan Network A road system that links Chaco Canyon with sites covering a large part of what is today the Four Corners region of the American Southwest.

Châtelperronian An archaeological industry found in France and northern Spain identified as transitional between the Middle Paleolithic and Upper Paleolithic.

Chauvet Cave The earliest known painted cave, dated to between 38,000 and 33,000 years ago. It is located in France.

Chavín de Huántar A major ceremonial centre in the Andean highlands constructed around 800 B.C.

Cheops A Fourth Dynasty Egyptian king who constructed the first and largest pyramid ever built, at Giza.

Chesowanja Site located in Kenya and dated to 1.4 million years ago that has produced tentative evidence for the use of fire by early hominins.

Chifeng region An area in Inner Mongolia where survey has found an increase in population around 2000 B.C.

chinampas Raised agricultural beds built in swamps; critical for Aztec agriculture.

Cishan A site in northern China that has yielded dates of 10,000 years ago for domesticated millet.

Ciudadela A very large compound in Teotihuacán that includes a large courtyard where the Temple of the Feathered Serpent is located.

Clactonian A simple flake tool industry contemporary with the Acheulian in England.

Clovis culture The period many North American archaeologists view as the initial human occupation of the Americas, dated to between 13,500 and 12,500 years ago.

Clovis first model Clovis culture, dated to 13,500 to 12,500 years ago, is the first human occupation in the Americas.

coastal migration The route some archaeologists say was used by the earliest people in the Americas to move out of Beringia instead of moving through an ice-free corridor.

community The term applied to the changes in society and settlement patterns in the transition to an agricultural way of life. This includes not only physical changes to the landscape through the construction of villages and monuments, but also a change in the way people viewed the landscape and the way the ownership of the land was conceived.

Copán A large Maya city with two large pyramids and an elaborate ball court at its centre.

Cotton Preceramic The period beginning 5,700 years ago when sites with monumental architecture flourished on the coast of Peru.

Coyolxauhqui A goddess killed by the Aztec patron god Huitzilopochtli in a central event in Aztec mythology.

Cuexcomate The larger of two rural sites in Morelos, to the south of the Basin of Mexico, that have produced insight into rural life under the Aztecs.

cultural resource management (CRM) Public archaeology carried out with the goal of mitigating the effects of development on archaeological resources.

cuneiform A writing system in which signs were impressed in wet clay. Cuneiform was used to write a range of languages, including Sumerian and Akkadian.

cylinder seals One of the methods developed by Mesopotamian scribes to mark ownership.

datum point The linchpin for the control of excavation. It serves as a reference point for all depth measurements on the site.

David Rindos An archaeologist who saw agriculture as the result of a coevolutionary process involving a symbiotic relationship between plant and animal species.

deduction Drawing particular inferences from general laws and models.

depositional unit The material deposited at a site at a particular point in time.

dhaka A mixture of clay and gravel that was used for building huts at Great Zimbabwe.

diachoronic studies Studies that make comparisons between different periods and look at processes of change through time.

dispersal An event where a single species dramatically expands its range.

DK The site at Olduvai Gorge where a stone circle was found, suggesting evidence of a temporary structure built on a home-base site.

Dmanisi The oldest known archaeological site outside of Africa, located in the Republic of Georgia and dated between 1.7 and 1.8 million years ago.

domestication The relationship between humans, on the one hand, and plants and animals, on the other, in which the humans play an integral role in the protection and reproduction of plants and animals.

Dorset A Paleo-Eskimo culture characterized by small winter village sites consisting of large rectangular structures.

Durrington Walls A site on the Avon River near Stonehenge with three monumental timber circles and evidence of occupation.

early arrival model Human occupation of the Americas began as early as 30,000 to 40,000 years ago.

Early Dynastic period The period that follows the Uruk period, during which southern Mesopotamia was home to a series of city states.

early state modules Colin Renfrew's term to describe autonomous political units.

East African Rift Valley A geological feature stretching from East Africa to the Middle East that is the richest context for the recovery of early hominin archaeological sites.

ecofacts Objects recovered from an archaeological context that are either the remains of biological organisms or the results of geological processes.

egalitarian society A society in which the only differences in status are based on skill, age, and gender.

El Niño A severe reversal of the Humboldt Current that causes a massive decline in marine resources along the Andean coast.

emic An approach to archaeological or anthropological analysis that attempts to understand the meanings people attach to their actions and culture.

empires Political entities that bring together a diverse and heterogeneous group of societies under a single ruler.

Erlitou A city in the Yi-Luo River Valley that predates Anyang.

Ester Boserup An economist whose research suggests that increased population size might have been the cause of the shift to agriculture.

etic An approach to archaeological or anthropological analysis that does not attempt to adopt the perspective of the members of the culture that are being studied.

Eurasian Acheulian A stone tool industry found on sites throughout the Middle East and Europe beginning 500,000 years ago. The handaxe is the characteristic tool of this industry.

evolutionary archaeology A range of approaches that stress the importance of evolutionary theory as a unifying theory for archaeology.

feminist archaeology An approach that focuses on the way archaeologists study and represent gender and brings attention to gender inequities in the practice of archaeology.

Fertile Crescent A ribbon of Mediterranean climate that arcs across the Middle East. It is characterized by dry summers and winter rains with enough precipitation to support vegetation ranging from woodlands to open-park woodlands.

fire-stick farming A term used by Rhys Jones to describe the aboriginal use of fire in Australia.

First Dynasty The dynasty based in Hierakonpolis and Abydos in Upper Egypt.

FLK North (FLKN) The site in Olduvai Gorge, where the remains of an elephant were found together with stone tools.

Florentine Codex A document that is a major source of information on Aztec history and culture; compiled soon after the Spanish conquest of the Aztecs.

flotation The process used to recover botanical material (wood and seeds) which involves mixing sediments vigorously in water. In the process, charred remains of seeds and wood float to the surface while the mineral sediments settle to the bottom. The charred botanical material can then be skimmed off and dried for analysis.

Frison effect Due to resharpening, the process through which the shape of stone tools changes during their use-life.

geographical information systems (GIS) Software applications that allow spatial data to be brought together and consolidated.

Gesher Benot Ya'akov An Acheulian site in Israel dating to 780,000 years ago that has produced limited evidence for the use of fire and for cracking of nuts.

Giza The site of the pyramids of Cheops, Cepheren, and Mycerinus—monuments representing the apex of pyramid construction in Old Kingdom Egypt.

Gobero A site in the Sahara alongside an ancient lake where a hunter–gatherer occupation dating between 9,700 and 8,200 years ago has been discovered.

Gran Dolina, Atapuerca A cave in Spain where stone tools and hominin remains dated to 800,000 years ago were found. These artifacts are the oldest reliable evidence of human occupation of western Europe.

Grand Plaza An artificially cleared and levelled area at the core of Cahokia located just to the south of Monk's Mound.

Gravettian The second major Upper Paleolithic archaeological period in Europe.

Great Bath An impressive structure built around a rectangular basin at the site of Mohenjo-Daro. It is one of the few monumental structures found on a Harappan site.

Great Houses Large multistoried structures located at Chaco Canyon, New Mexico, that became the centre of a regional settlement network beginning around A.D. 800.

Great Zimbabwe A large settlement in modern Zimbabwe that includes the remains of impressive stone enclosures and was built between A.D. 1300 and A.D. 1400.

Guilá Naquitz A site in Oaxaca, Mexico, that has produced the earliest evidence of domesticated plants in Mesoamerica.

Guitarrero Cave Site in the Andean highlands of Peru where excavations uncovered the earliest evidence of domesticated beans dating to 4,300 years ago.

Gunbilngmurrung A site in Australia where a beeswax figure of a turtle was found, radiocarbon dated to 4,000 years ago.

Habuba Kebira An Uruk colony located on the upper reaches of the Euphrates River in northern Syria.

Hadar Location in the East African Rift Valley where many important fossils, including the near-complete fossil of an australopithecine, and the earliest known stone tools have been discovered.

Hamoukar A site in northern Syria that has produced evidence of violent conflict that might relate to the Uruk expansion.

Harappa One of the two major urban centres of the Harappan period.

Harappan period The period between 2600 B.C. and 1900 B.C. during which urban centres developed in the Indus Valley.

Harappan script A script that has not yet been deciphered and is known mostly from small carved stone sealings used to mark vessels and bundles.

Hemudu A well-preserved rice-farming village in southern China.

hermeneutics A theory of interpretation that stresses the interaction between the presuppositions we bring to a problem and the independent empirical reality of our observations and experiences.

Herto A site in Ethiopia where the oldest known fossil of a modern human was discovered, dating to between 160,000 and 154,000 years ago.

heterarchy The relationship of elements to one another when they are not ranked.

Hierakonpolis Along with Abydos, one of the two centres of Egypt during the late Predynastic period and the First Dynasty.

Hohle Fels   A site in Germany where bone flutes and a female figurine have been discovered in levels dating to the Aurignacian.

Hohlenstein   A site in Germany where a lion-headed figure was found in levels with an Aurignacian industry.

home-base/food-sharing model   Model developed by Glynn Isaac that sees the sharing of meat at base camps as a fundamental part of the lives of early hominins.

hominins   The members of the human lineage after it split with the chimpanzee lineage.

hominoids   The biological superfamily that includes humans, great apes, and gibbons.

Homo erectus   The first hominin found on sites outside of Africa. The earliest known *Homo erectus* fossils date to the period between 1.9 and 1.5 million years ago.

Homo habilis   This hominin is the earliest species to be assigned to the genus *Homo*.

Homo sapiens   The species name for modern humans.

Hopewell   A period of intensive mound building in the Ohio River Valley; it corresponds to the Middle Woodland culture.

horizontal excavation   An excavation for which the goal is to excavate a broad area in order to expose the remains of a single point in time.

Howiesons Poort   A Middle Stone Age industry found in southern Africa that is characterized by small crescent-shaped stone tools.

Hua'nuco Pampa   An Inca centre 600 kilometres north of Cuzco.

Huaca Cao Viejo   A Moche site where a mural showing a line of prisoners was found.

Huaca de la Luna   A massive mud-brick mound at the site of Moche where actual remains of sacrificial victims were uncovered and found in various states of dismemberment.

Huaca del Sol   A massive mound made of over 140 million mud bricks, located at the site of Moche.

Huitzilopochtli   The Aztec patron god.

Humboldt Current   A current that brings cool waters from the south up along the Andean coast, accounting for the remarkable wealth of marine resources in the area.

ice-free corridor   A potential migration route for populations expanding out of Beringia, running between the Cordilleran and Laurentide ice sheets.

in situ   Archaeological material is considered to be *in situ* when it is found in the place where it was originally deposited.

Inca Empire   An empire that thrived for over a century and at its peak ruled over 12 million people from northern Chile to Ecuador.

induction   Drawing general inferences on the basis of available empirical data.

Indus Valley   An area extending along the course of the Indus River that covers much of modern Pakistan and the Kutch and Gujarat provinces of India.

intersite   Comparisons between two or more sites—for example, an analysis comparing the number of houses between sites in a region.

intrasite   Having to do with contexts within a single site—for example, an analysis comparing the sizes and contents of different houses to try to determine the social structure of a society.

isotope analysis   The study of diet through the chemical signature of bones; particularly effective in tracing the spread of maize agriculture.

Jenne-Jeno   The site of an urban centre in Mali, West Africa, that predates extensive external contact.

Jerf el Ahmar   A Pre-Pottery Neolithic A site on the Euphrates River in Syria with the remains of communal structures.

Jericho tower   A 9-metre-high structure made of undressed stone and mud brick dating to the Pre-Pottery Neolithic A.

Jomon   Japanese preagricultural societies that lived in large villages and produced elaborate pottery.

Katanda   A Middle Stone Age site in the Democratic Republic of Congo where bone harpoons have been found.

Kebara Cave   A site in Israel where excavations have produced important evidence about the nature of Neanderthal occupation of caves, as well as one of the most complete skeletons of a Neanderthal.

Kennewick man   Skeletal remains found at Kennewick, Washington, and dated to 9,200 years ago. Control and ownership of the remains have been the subject of controversy.

khipu   A system of knotted strings used by the Inca to record information.

King Djoser   The Third Dynasty Egyptian king who constructed the first pyramid, located at Saqqara.

kivas   Subterranean circular chambers found on sites in the American Southwest.

Klasies River Mouth   A Middle Age site in South Africa that has produced remains of modern humans and that offers evidence of hunting and the intensive use of fire.

Knossos   A site excavated by Arthur Evans that is the largest Minoan settlement.

Kuk Swamp   A site in highland New Guinea that has produced early evidence of agriculture.

Labrets   Large plugs placed below the lip or on the side of the mouth that were worn by people on the Northwest Coast as markers of status.

La Cotte de St. Brelade   The location on the Jersey Islands where evidence of Neanderthals hunting mammoths by stampeding them off a cliff was found.

Laetoli   Location in Tanzania where tracks of australopithecine footprints were found showing that australopithecines walked upright.

Lake Mungo   One in a series of dried-out lakes located in southern Australia where evidence of human occupation dates to between 50,000 and 46,000 years ago.

language dispersal hypothesis   The theory that the spread of agriculture across Europe was the result of a migration of farmers who spoke Indo-European languages.

Lanzón   An engraved monolith at the core of the temple at Chávin de Huántar.

Lapita   A culture that spread across a vast area of Melanesia beginning 3,500 years ago and reached as far as the islands of Samoa and Tonga.

Las Capas   A site near Tucson, Arizona, where an Archaic village and canal system have been discovered.

law of superposition   In any undisturbed depositional sequence, each layer of sediments is younger than the layer beneath it.

legitimacy   A quality or status achieved when the right of a centralized authority to have power is accepted. Legitimacy can be based on consensus or on coercion.

Lepenski Vir   An impressive Mesolithic site along the Danube River in Serbia where structures, burials, and sculptures were found.

Levallois method   A particular prepared-core technology used during the Middle Paleolithic that can often be recognized on the basis of tortoise-shaped cores.

Lewis Henry Morgan   A nineteenth-century American anthropologist who viewed the transition to agriculture as marking the boundary between the period of "savagery" and the period of "barbarism."

Linear B   A script used to write the Mycenaean language; texts in Linear B are a major source of information about the organization of Aegean society.

Linear Band Keramik   The term referring to the earliest farming communities that emerged around 7,200 years ago in central and western Europe culture; also referred to as LBK culture.

Lion Gate   An important example of Mycenaean defensive architecture.

llamas   Camelid animals domesticated in the Andean highlands; *guanacos* are the ancestral species of llamas.

Lokalalei   An archaeological site in Kenya dating to 2.3 million years ago. Analysis of refit cores from the site indicates that stone tool manufacture at this early date was more complex than anticipated.

Lower Egypt   The northern part of the Nile River Valley, including the Nile Delta.

Lower Paleolithic   The period when hominins began producing stone tools.

lunate   Tiny crescent-shaped stone tools characteristic of the Natufian.

ma'at   A concept that combines the virtues of balance and justice; it was of central importance to Egyptian society.

Machu Picchu   An Inca royal estate on a high mountain peak at the western end of the Urubamba Valley.

Mallaha   A Natufian site in northern Israel with the remains of oval stone structures.

Mapungubwe   A predecessor to Great Zimbabwe; located in South Africa, it features an elite residence situated within a walled compound.

Marpole Phase   The period when inherited status appears to have developed on the Northwest Coast, 2,400–2,100 years ago.

Marshall Sahlins   An anthropologist who described hunter–gatherers as the "original affluent society."

Maya hieroglyphs   A complex combination of pictographic and syllabic script that initially developed to record major events in the lives of rulers.

Meadowcroft Rockshelter   A site in Pennsylvania where evidence was found supporting pre-Clovis occupation of the New World.

megafauna   Species of large animals that became extinct in many areas of the world, including the Americas and Australia, toward the end of the Pleistocene.

megaron   A large hall located at the centre of the Mycenaean palace.

Mesopotamia   A region along the course of the Tigris and Euphrates Rivers centred in modern Iraq.

Mezmaiskaya Cave   The location that has produced the most recent Neanderthal fossil, dated to 30,000 years ago.

Middle Paleolithic   The archaeological period during which Neanderthals occupied Europe.

Middle Stone Age   The archaeological period of the earliest modern humans in Africa. The Middle Stone Age began between 300,000 and 200,000 years ago and ended around 40,000 years ago.

Middle to Upper Paleolithic transition   The archaeological period that saw the appearance of modern humans in Europe. It includes the development of new types of stone and bone tools and the dramatic appearance of a wide range of symbolic artifacts.

middle-range research   Research investigating processes that can be observed in the present and that can serve as a point of reference to test hypotheses about the past.

Milagro   An early agricultural village located outside Tucson, Arizona.

millet   A cereal crop domesticated in northern China in the region around the Yellow River Valley.

Minoan   A Bronze Age society located on the island of Crete.

Miocene era   The period 23 million to 5 million years ago when there was an explosion in the number of hominoid species.

mitochondrial DNA   DNA located outside of the cell nucleus; inherited exclusively from the mother.

Moche   A culture that developed along the Pacific coast of Peru and that flourished beginning 2,000 years ago.

Models for Human Occupation of the Americas   Clovis First: Clovis culture, dated to 13,500 to 12,500 years ago, is the first human occupation in the Americas; Pre-Clovis: Human occupation of the Americas predates 13,500 years ago; Early Arrival: Human occupation of the Americas began as early as 30,000 to 40,000 years ago.

modern humans   Members of the species *Homo sapiens*, which includes all living humans.

Mohenjo-Daro   One of the two major urban centres of the Harappan period.

molecular clock   Mechanism that allows the timing of the split between lineages to be calculated on the basis of the degree of genetic similarity.

Monk's Mound   A massive earthen pyramid occupying the core of the ancient settlement of Cahokia.

Monte Albán   Site of the oldest city in Mesoamerica, located in the Oaxaca Valley.

Monte Verde   A site in Chile where evidence of human occupation 15,000 years ago supports the argument that Clovis culture does not represent the first occupation of the Americas.

Mound 72   A mound at Cahokia where excavation uncovered an individual buried on a bird-shaped platform made of shells, as well as mass burials of apparently sacrificial victims.

Mycenaean   A Bronze Age society that developed on the Peloponnese Peninsula and in central Greece.

Mycerinus   The last Fourth Dynasty Egyptian king to build a pyramid at Giza; it was smaller than the other pyramids and at least partially sheathed in polished granite.

Nabta Playa   An area in the Egyptian Western desert that was the location of a series of early agricultural and preagricultural sites located along the edge of a lake.

Narmer Palette   Artifact discovered at the site of the Hierakonpolis; its two sides show the unification of Upper and Lower Egypt under King Narmer.

Nasca   A culture that developed along the southern Pacific coast of Peru at the same time as the Moche society.

Nasca lines   Large-scale patterns created on the desert floor near the Nasca River on the Andean coast. The Nasca lines include depictions of humans and animals as well as a large number of straight lines that stretch for miles.

Natufians   Societies in the Middle East that practised a broad-spectrum subsistence strategy that relied on a wide range of resources.

Nauwalabila I   The site that offers the earliest secure evidence of human occupation of Australia, dating between 60,000 and 53,000 years ago.

Nenana   The earliest culture in Beringia, dating to between 14,000 and 12,800 years ago.

Neolithic Revolution   The term V. Gordon Childe used to describe the transition to agriculture as an event that affected every aspect of human society.

Neolithic   The period in which there are polished stone tools. Also called the New Stone Age.

Netiv Hagdud   A Pre-Pottery Neolithic A site in the Jordan Valley that was a village of between 20 and 30 houses.

New Archaeology (or processual archaeology)   An approach to archaeology based firmly on scientific method and supported by a concerted effort aimed at the development of theory.

Newnans Lake   A lake in Florida where a large number of archaic canoes have been recovered.

Ngandong   Site on the island of Java where the most recent known fossil of *Homo erectus* was found, dating to between 46,000 and 27,000 years ago.

Nihewan Basin   Location in northern China where there is solid evidence of human occupation around 1.6 million years ago.

Nile Valley   A swath of lush vegetation descending from the highlands of Ethiopia and standing in sharp contrast to the surrounding desert.

nuclear DNA   DNA located in the cell nucleus; combines DNA from each parent.

Ohalo   A Kebaran site in northern Israel with excellent preservation of organic remains.

Oldowan   Lower Paleolithic stone tool industry, dated between 1.9 and 1.15 million years ago, characterized by choppers and flakes.

Olduvai Gorge   The most impressive and important location in the East African Rift Valley for the study of human evolution.

Olmec   The earliest complex society in Mesoamerica. Olmec sites are located along the Gulf Coast of Mexico.

ontogeny   The growth and development of an individual organism.

optimal foraging theory   A theory based on the assumption that the choices people make reflect rational self-interest in maximizing efficiency when collecting and processing resources.

oracle bones   Bones that were used in divination rituals. Incriptions on oracle bones are a major source of written evidence about the Shang Dynasty.

Otumba   A site in the Teotihuacán Valley where excavations have produced evidence about the nature of the Aztec organization of craft production.

oxygen isotope curve   The record of fluctuations in global climate during the Pleistocene.

Ozette Site   A site in Washington State where rapid burial led to the superb preservation of artifacts made from organic materials, including baskets, bows, and arrows.

paleoanthropologists   Scientists who study the evolutionary history of the hominoids.

Paleolithic   The period in which humans lived with now-extinct animals. Also called the Old Stone Age.

palimpsest   An archaeological site produced by a series of distinct brief occupations.

Paloma   A preagricultural village site on the coast of Peru.

panaqa   The collective descendants of the Inca emperor.

pastoral societies   Mobile societies with an economy based on herds of domesticated animals.

Pedra Furada   A site in Brazil where highly controversial evidence of human occupation, dating to 48,000 and 35,000 years ago, was found.

Pedra Pintada   A site in the Brazilian Amazon that demonstrates that there were groups contemporary with the Clovis that were living in South America in a rain-forest environment.

peer polity interaction   Colin Renfrew's term to describe the full range of exchanges taking place between autonomous socio-political units.

Pengtoushan   A site in southern China that has produced some of the earliest evidence of domesticated rice dating to approximately 9,000 years ago.

Peştera cu Oase Cave   The site in Romania where the oldest modern human remains in Europe, dating to 36,000 years ago, were found.

phylogeny   The evolutionary history of a species.

Pinnacle Point   A site on the southern coast of South Africa that has produced evidence that mollusks were part of the diet of modern humans as early as 160,000 years ago.

plastered skulls   Human skulls on which a plaster face has been modelled; found buried beneath floors on sites dating to the Pre-Pottery Neolithic B period.

Pleistocene   The geological era that began 1.8 million years ago, characterized by the frequent buildup and retreat of continental ice sheets.

Popol Vuh   A Maya myth that tells the epic tale of hero twins and their battle with the lords of the underworld.

Potlatch   A competitive feast described in ethnographic accounts of Northwest Coast society.

postdepositional processes   Events that take place after a site has been occupied.

postprocessual archaeology   A movement, led by British archaeologist Ian Hodder, which argues that archaeologists should emulate historians in interpreting the past.

Poverty Point   A Late Archaic site in Louisiana with a series of six concentric embankments.

pre-Clovis model   Human occupation of the Americas predates 13,500 years ago.

prepared-core technology   The dominant approach to tool manufacture during the Middle Paleolithic; a technique in which the person making the tools carefully shaped the core to control the form of the flakes produced.

provenience The precise context in wich an object is recovered in an excavation.

Pueblo Bonito A massive 650-room complex, the largest Great House in Chaco Canyon.

Pyramid of the Moon A pyramid complex used for both symbolic functions and the production of military supplies and located at the north end of the Avenue of the Dead in Teotihuacán.

Pyramid of the Sun The largest monument at Teotihuacán, rising to 64 metres.

Qafzeh Cave One of the sites in Israel where modern human skeletons were found in a Middle Paleolithic context.

quantification Methods used by archaeologists to represent the large quantities of material recovered in excavations and surveys.

rachis The tough part of a cereal plant that holds the seed to the stalk and keeps the seed on the plant until it is harvested.

radiation A period in which there is a rapid increase in the diversity of a single lineage. During the period between 4 million and 2 million years ago, there was a radiation in the hominin lineage.

ranked society A society in which there is a hierarchy of prestige not linked to age, gender, or ability.

relative chronology A chronology that places assemblages in a temporal sequence not directly linked to calendar dates.

rice A major cereal crop domesticated in southern China in the Yangtze and Huai River Valleys.

Rizhao A region in Shadong Province where survey has found evidence of a complex settlement hierarchy that is earlier than the Yi-Luo River cities.

Royal Tombs at Ur Tombs dating to the Early Dynastic period in which the dead were buried with a spectacular array of precious artifacts and sacrificial victims.

Sahara Desert The most dominant feature of the North African landscape today. Between 14,000 and 4,500 years ago, there was increased rainfall in the area, allowing for human occupation.

Sahelanthropus tchadensis A possible early member of the hominin lineage. Fossils of the species were discovered in Chad in levels dating to 7 million years ago.

Sahul The landmass that encompassed Australia, Tasmania, and New Guinea during periods of low sea level.

San José de Moro A Moche site where elite burials with an impressive wealth of burial goods have been discovered.

Sangiran and Perning Sites on the island of Java where fossils of *Homo erectus* dating to 1.8 million years ago were found.

Sangoan/Lupemban A Middle Stone Age industry found in Central and East Africa. Characterized by very crude heavy-duty tools, the Sangoan/Lupemban might be indicative of an adaptation to a heavily wooded environment.

Sanxingdui A site in Sichuan Province where excavations uncovered a spectacular trove of artifacts unique in style and that are contemporary with Anyang.

Saqqara The location of the stepped pyramid, the earliest constructed in Egypt. In later periods, Saqqara continued to be used as a sacred burial area.

Sarsen Circle A circle of massive upright sandstone blocks capped with lintels set up around the perimeter of Stonehenge.

Schöningen The location in Germany where 400,000-year-old wooden spears were discovered.

seriation The method of comparing the relative frequency of artifact types between contexts.

Shang Dynasty The second of three powerful dynasties that emerged in northern China during the period between 2000 B.C. and 500 B.C.

shell middens Sites built up with large accumulations of discarded shells.

Sipán An elite burial site on the coast of Peru that has given archaeologists a sense of the wealth and violence of Moche society.

Skhul Cave One of the Middle Paleolithic sites in Israel where modern human skeletons have been found.

Solutrean hypothesis The proposal that the origin of the Clovis culture was in the migration of groups from the Solutrean culture of southern France.

species A group of intimately related and physically similar organisms that can produce fertile offspring.

St. Césaire A site in France where a Neanderthal was found dating to 36,000 years ago.

states Societies in which power is organized on a supra-kin basis or by a bureaucracy that uses force.

Stonehenge A ring of massive standing stones on the Salisbury Plain, England, that was constructed beginning in the Early Neolithic and ending in the Early Bronze Age.

strata Discrete layers in a stratigraphic sequence.

stratified society A society in which access to key resources is linked to prestige.

Sunda The landmass that connected much of South East Asia during periods of low sea level.

survey An archaeological survey maps the physical remains of human activity.

synchronic studies Studies that make comparisons within a single period.

systems theory An archaeological theory that views society as an interconnected network of interacting elements.

Szeletian An archaeological industry found in Eastern Europe during the transition between the Middle Paleolithic and Upper Paleolithic. Bifacially retouched tools are characteristic of the Szeletian.

Taï Forest Location where chimpanzees use stone hammers and anvils to break open hard nuts. The tools are not manufactured, but rather used as found.

Talheim An LBK site in Germany where a pit containing a mass grave was discovered.

taphonomy The study of the processes that affect organic remains after death.

Tawantinsuyu The Inca name for their empire; the name means "the four parts together."

technology The tools used for daily tasks, including farming, food processing, and food storage.

Tehuacán Valley A valley in the Mexican highlands where excavations by Richard MacNeish recovered some of the earliest evidence of domesticated plants in Mesoamerica.

Temple of the Feathered Serpent Structure at the back of the Ciudadela adorned with the sculpted heads of the feathered serpent deity.

Templo Mayor   Double pyramid at the centre of Tenochtitlán that was the core of the Aztec world.

Tenochtitlán   The capital of the Aztec Empire and the largest indigenous city ever built in the Americas; located in the Valley of Mexico.

teosinte   A wild grass found in the highlands of Mexico; the wild ancestor of maize.

Teotihuacán   An enormous city with a population of over 80,000 located in the Valley of Mexico and established around 2,000 years ago.

Texcoco   City that was a member of the Aztec Triple Alliance.

Thera   A Cycladic island that was devastated by a major volcanic eruption during the Bronze Age.

Three-Age system   A system developed by Danish antiquarian Christian Jürgensen Thomsen that catalogues artifacts into relics of three periods—the Stone Age, the Bronze Age, and the Iron Age—based on the material of manufacture.

Thule   The archaeological culture ancestral to contemporary Inuit.

thunderstones   Objects such as ground stone axes that people in Medieval Europe believed were formed in spots where lightning struck the earth.

Tigris and Euphrates rivers   Two large rivers that were the focus for the development of Mesopotamian civilization.

Tikal   One of the major Maya urban centres.

Tim Ingold   An anthropologist who views the shift from hunting to agriculture as a shift from trust to domination.

Tlapocán   City that was a member of the Aztec Triple Alliance.

Toltec Empire   An empire that preceded the Aztecs in the Valley of Mexico. It is not clear whether the Toltec controlled areas beyond their capital city.

trilithons   Three pairs of upright sandstone blocks capped with lintels at Stonehenge located within the Sarsen Circle.

Triple Alliance   The pact between the cities of Tenochtitlán, Telapocán, and Texcoco that formed the basis of the Aztec Empire.

Tula   The capital city of the Toltec Empire.

typology   A list used to draw up an inventory of types of artifacts found by archaeologists in a particular archaeological context.

Uan Afuda   A preagricultural site in the Sahara that yielded evidence that wild sheep were kept in pens in the back of a cave.

Ubeidiya   One of the earliest archaeological sites outside of Africa, located in Israel south of the Sea of Galilee and dated between 1.4 and 1.0 million years ago.

Ulluzian   An archaeological industry found in Italy during the transition between the Middle Paleolithic and Upper Paleolithic. Arched-back knives are characteristic of the Ulluzian.

Upper Egypt   The southern Nile River Valley ending in a series of cataracts, or rapids, in the area around the modern border between Egypt and Sudan.

Upper Paleolithic   The archaeological period that saw the earliest occupation of Europe by modern humans.

urban society   A society in which people live in large cities. V. Gordon Childe developed ten criteria defining an urban society.

Urubamba Valley   The location of Machu Picchu, the most famous of the Inca royal estates.

Uruk   The oldest known city in the world, located in southern Iraq.

Uruk period   The period between 4000 and 3200 B.C. during which the first cities in Mesopotamia were developed.

vacant centre pattern   The model that sees the Hopewell earthworks as the empty core of a dispersed settlement system.

Venus figurines   Portable art objects that are found with the Gravettian industry and that depict the female body.

vertical excavation   An excavation for which the goal is to excavate a significant depth of deposits in order to expose the record of a sequence of occupation.

Vindija Cave   A site in Croatia where the discovery of Neanderthal remains have been dated to 29,000 years ago.

Wallace Line   The line that runs through Wallacea and separates the unique animals and plants of Australia from the animal and plant communities of Southeast Asia.

wanax   The title of the ruler in Linear B texts.

Watson Brake   A series of mounds in Louisiana built between 5,400 and 5,000 years ago that provide the earliest evidence of monumental construction in Eastern North America.

wet screening   The process of spraying water onto a sieve to break up sediments and move them through the mesh to make sure that all artifacts are recovered during an excavation.

Wilson-Leonard site   A site in Texas with a stratigraphic sequence that includes both Paleoindian and Archaic occupations.

Yangshao culture   A Neolithic culture in northern China that is particularly well represented in the village site of Banpo.

Yangtze and Huai River Valleys   The area of southern China where rice was domesticated.

Yanshi   A large settlement in the Yi-Luo Valley that appears to be slightly later than Erlitou.

Yellow River Valley   The area in northern China where millet was domesticated.

Yi-Luo Valley   A region where surveys have documented the complex settlement hierarchy associated with the cities of Erlitou and Yanshi, which are earlier than Anyang.

Younger Dryas   A period of global climatic stress that had a significant impact on Natufian society.

Zafarraya Cave   A site in Spain where the discovery of Neanderthal remains dated between 33,000 and 27,000 years ago suggests that, at least in this area, Neanderthals survived long after the arrival of modern humans in Europe.

Zhoukoudian   A series of caves in Longgu-shan, or Dragon Bone Hill, outside of Beijing (Peking), China, where the remains of more than 40 *Homo erectus* individuals and over 100,000 stone choppers and flakes were recovered.

ziggurat   Stepped pyramid found in many Mesopotamian temple precincts.

REFERENCES

Abu El-Haj, Nadia. *Facts on the Ground: Archaeological Practice and Territorial Self-Fashioning in Israeli Society.* Chicago: University of Chicago Press, 2001.

Adams, Robert McCormick, and Hans Nissen. *The Uruk Countryside: The Natural Setting of Urban Societies.* Chicago: University of Chicago Press, 1972.

Adcock, G.J., et al. "Mitochondrial DNA Sequences in Ancient Australians: Implications for Modern Human Origins." *Proceedings of the National Academy of Sciences* 98.2 (2001): 537–42.

Adovasio, J.M., et al. "Meadowcroft Rockshelter 1977: An Overview." *American Antiquity* 43 (1978): 632–51.

Agrawal, D.P. *The Archaeology of India.* Scandinavian Institute of Asian Studies Monograph Series. Malmö, Sweden: Curzon Press, 1985.

Ahler, Stanley A., and Phil R. Geib. "Why Flute? Folsom Point Design and Adaptation." *Journal of Archaeological Science* 27 (2000): 799–820.

Aiello, Leslie C., and Peter Wheeler. "The Expensive-Tissue Hypothesis." *Current Anthropology* 36.2 (1995): 199–221.

Aitken, M.J., Chris Stringer, and Paul Mellars. *The Origin of Modern Humans and the Impact of Chronometric Dating.* Princeton, N.J.: Princeton University Press, 1993.

Aitken, Martin J. *Science-Based Dating in Archaeology.* London: Longman, 1990.

Akins, N.J. "The Burials of Pueblo Bonito." *Pueblo Bonito Centre of the Chacoan World.* Ed. Jill E. Neitzel. Washington: Smithsonian Press, 2003. 94–106.

Alcock, Susan, et al., eds. *Empires.* Cambridge, U.K.: Cambridge University Press, 2001.

Alemseged, Z. "A juvenile early hominin skeleton from Dikika, Ethiopia." *Nature* 443 (2006): 296–301.

Algaze, Guillermo. *The Uruk World System: The Dynamics of Expansion of Early Mesopotamian Civilization.* Chicago: University of Chicago Press, 1993.

Allchin, F. Raymond, and Bridget Allchin. *The Rise of Civilization in India and Pakistan.* Cambridge World Archaeology. Cambridge, U.K.: Cambridge University Press, 1982.

Ames, Kenneth, and Herbert Maschner. *Peoples of the Northwest Coast: Their Archaeology and Prehistory.* London: Thames and Hudson, 1999.

Amichai, Yehuda. *Selected Poetry of Yehuda Amichai.* Trans. Chana Bloch and Stephen Mitchell. Berkeley, CA: University of California Press, 1996.

Andah, Bassey W. "Identifying Early Farming Traditions of West Africa." *The Archaeology of Africa: Food, Metals, and Towns.* Ed. Thurstan Shaw. London: Routledge, 1993. 240–53.

Anping, Pei. "Notes on New Advancements and Revelations in the Agricultural Archaeology of Early Rice Domestication in the Dongting Lake Region." *Antiquity* 72 (1998): 878–85.

Arensburg, B. "A Middle Paleolithic Human Hyoid Bone." *Nature* 338 (1989): 758–60.

Arnold, Bettina. "The Past as Propaganda: Totalitarian Archaeology in Nazi Germany." *Antiquity* 64 (1990): 464–78.

Arsuaga, Juan Luis de, Andy Klatt, and Juan Carlos Sastre. *The Neanderthal's Necklace: In Search of the First Thinkers.* New York: Four Walls Eight Windows, 2002.

Ascher, Marcia, and Robert Ascher. *Code of the Quipu: A Study in Media, Mathematics, and Culture.* Ann Arbor, MI.: University of Michigan Press, 1981.

Asfaw, Berhane, et al. "Australopithecus Garhi: A New Species of Early Hominid from Ethiopia." *Science* 284 (1999): 629–35.

Aveni, Anthony F. *Nasca: Eighth Wonder of the World?* London: British Museum Press, 2000.

Bafna, S. Space syntax: a brief introduction to its logic and analytical techniques. *Environment and Behavior* 35 (2003): 17–28.

Bahn, Paul G. "The 'Unacceptable Face' of the West European Upper Paleolithic." *Antiquity* 52 (1978): 183–92.

Bahn, Paul G. *Written in Bones: How Human Remains Unlock the Secrets of the Dead.* Newton Abbot, Devon: David & Charles, 2002.

Baillie, M.G.L. *A Slice Through Time: Dendrochronology and Precision Dating.* London: Batsford, 1995.

Ballard, Chris. "Writing (Pre)History: Narrative and Archaeological Explanation in the New Guinea Highlands." *Archaeology of Oceania* 38 (2003): 135–48.

Ballard, R.D., ed. *Archaeological Oceanography.* Princeton: Princeton University Press, 2008.

Ballard, R.D., et al. Iron-age shipwrecks in deep water off Ashkelon, Israel. *American Journal of Archaeology* 106 (2002): 151–68.

Balter, Vincent, et al. "Ecological and Physiological Variability of Sr/Ca and Ba/Ca in Mammals of West Europe Mid-Wurmian Food Webs." *Palaeogeography, Palaeoclimatology, Palaeoecology* 186 (2002): 127–43.

Balter, Vincent, et al. "Les Néandertaliens Étaient-Ils Essentiellement Carnivores? Résultats Préliminaires sur les Teneurs en Sr et en Ba de la Paléobiocénose Mammalienne de Saint-Césaire." *Comptes Rendus de l'Académie des Sciences: Earth and Planetary Sciences* 332 (2001): 59–65.

Banning, E. B. *Archaeological Survey. Manuals in Archaeological Method, Theory, and Technique.* New York: Kluwer Academic/Plenum Publishers, 2002.

Banning, E. B. *The Archaeologist's Laboratory: The Analysis of Archaeological Data. Interdisciplinary Contributions to Archaeology.* New York: Kluwer Academic/Plenum Publishers, 2000.

Barlow, K. Renee. "Predicting Maize Agriculture among the Fremont: An Economic Comparison of Farming and Foraging in the American Southwest." *American Antiquity* 67.1 (2002): 65–88.

Barrett, John C. *Fragments from Antiquity: An Archaeology of Social Life in Britain, 2900–1200 B.C. Social Archaeology.* Oxford, U.K.: Blackwell, 1993.

Bartstra, Gert-Jan. "*Homo erectus*: The Search for His Artifacts." *Current Anthropology* 23.3 (1982): 318–20.

Bar-Yosef, O. "The Walls of Jericho: An Alternative Interpretation." *Current Anthropology* 27.2 (1986): 157–62.

Bar-Yosef, O., et al. "The Excavations at Kebara Cave, Mt Carmel." *Current Anthropology* 33.5 (1992): 497–550.

Bar-Yosef, Ofer, et al. "Netiv Hagdud: An Early Neolithic Village Site in the Jordan Valley." *Journal of Field Archaeology* 18 (1991): 405–23.

Bar-Yosef, Ofer. *A Cave in the Desert: Nahal Hemar.* Jerusalem, Israel: Israel Museum, 1985.

Bass, George. "A Bronze Age Shipwreck at Ulu Burun: 1984 Campaign." *American Journal of Archaeology* 90 (1986): 269–96.

Bawden, Garth. *The Moche.* Malden, MA: Blackwell, 1999.

Beattie, Owen, and John Geiger. *Frozen in Time: The Fate of the Franklin Expedition.* Vancouver: Greystone Books, 1998.

Bednarik, Robert G. "Direct Dating Results from Australian Cave Petroglyphs." *Geoarchaeology: An International Journal* 13.4 (1998): 411–18.

Bednarik, Robert G. "The Dating of Rock Art: A Critique." *Journal of Archaeological Science* 29 (2002): 1213–33.

Begun, D. "Miocene Hominids and the Origins of the African Apes and Humans." *Annual Reviews in Anthropology* 39 (2010): 67–84.

Bell, Ellen E., et al. *Understanding Early Classic Copan.* Philadelphia: University of Pennsylvania Museum of Archaeology and Anthropology, 2004.

Bellwood, Peter S. *First Farmers: The Origins of Agricultural Societies.* Malden, MA: Blackwell Pub., 2005.

Bellwood, Peter, and Colin Renfrew, eds. *Examining the Farming/Language Dispersal Hypothesis.* Cambridge, U.K.: McDonald Institute, 2002.

Bender, Barbara. "Theorizing Landscapes, and the Prehistoric Landscapes of Stonehenge." *Man* 27.4 (1992): 735–55.

Bender, Barbara. *Farming in Prehistory: From Hunter–Gatherer to Food-Producer.* London: J. Baker, 1975.

Benjamin, Walter. *Illuminations: Essays and Reflections.* Trans. Harry Zohn. New York: Schocken, 1968.

Benson, Elizabeth P., et al. *Olmec Art of Ancient Mexico.* Washington, DC: National Gallery of Art, 1996.

Benson, Larry, et al. "Ancient Maize from Chacoan Great Houses: Where Was It Grown?" *Proceedings of the National Academy of Sciences* 100.22 (2003): 13111–15.

Berger, Thomas D., and Erik Trinkaus. "Patterns of Trauma among the Neanderthals." *Journal of Archaeological Science* 22.6 (1995): 841–52.

Berrin, K., and E. Pasztory, eds. *Teotihuacán: Art from the City of the Gods.* New York: Thames and Hudson, 1993.

Binford, Lewis. "Archaeological Perspectives." *New Perspectives in Archaeology.* Eds. Sally Binford and Lewis Binford. Chicago: Aldine, 1968. 5–32.

Binford, Lewis. *In Pursuit of the Past: Decoding the Archaeological Record.* New York: Thames and Hudson, 1983.

Binford, Sally and Lewis Binford, eds. *New Perspectives in Archaeology.* Chicago: Aldine, 1968.

Binnie, N.E. et al. "Shipwrecks, archaeology and zebra mussels: Is mussel attachment a threat to our submerged cultural resources?" *Proceedings of the International Aquatic Nuisance and Zebra Mussel Conference* (2000): 1–11.

Bird, M.I., et al. "Radiocarbon Analysis of the Early Archaeological Site of Nauwalabila I, Arnhem Land, Australia: Implications for Sample Suitability and Stratigraphic Integrity." *Quaternary Science Reviews* 21 (2002): 1061–75.

Blanton, R., et al. A dual-processual theory for the evolution of Mesoamerican civilization. *Current Anthropology* 31 (1996): 1–14.

Blanton, Richard E. *Ancient Mesoamerica: A Comparison of Change in Three Regions.* New York: Cambridge University Press, 1987.

Blanton, Richard, et al. *Ancient Mesoamerica: A Comparison of Change in Three Regions.* Cambridge: Cambridge University Press, 1993.

Blench, Roger. "Ethnographic and Linguistic Evidence for the Prehistory of African Ruminant Livestock, Horses, and Ponies." *The Archaeology of Africa: Food, Metals, and Towns.* ed. Thurstan Shaw. London: Routledge, 1993.

Blumenschine, Robert J., et al. "Late Pliocene Homo and Hominid Land Use from Western Olduvai Gorge, Tanzania." *Science* 299 (2003): 1217–21.

Boas, F. *The Social Organization and Secret Societies of the Kwakiutl Indians.* Washington: Reports of the United States National Museum, 1895.

Boëda, Eric, et al. "A Levallois Point Embedded in the Vertebra of a Wild Ass (Equus Africanusafricanus): Hafting, Projectiles and Mousterian Hunting Weapons." *Antiquity* 73.280 (1999): 394–402.

Boëda, Eric. "Levallois: A Volumetric Construction, Methods, and Technique." *Definition and Interpretation of Levallois Technology.* Eds. Harold Dibble and Ofer Bar-Yosef. Madison, WI: Prehistory Press, 1995. 41–68.

Bocherens, Hervé, et al. "New Isotopic Evidence for Dietary Habits of Neanderthals from Belgium." *Journal of Human Evolution* 40 (2001): 497–505.

Boesch, Christophe, and Hedwige Boesch-Achermann. *The Chimpanzees of the Taï Forest: Behavioural Ecology and Evolution.* Oxford, U.K.: Oxford University Press, 2000.

Boesch, Christophe. "Animal Behaviour: The Question of Culture." *Nature* 379 (1996): 207–08.

Boivin, N. "Rock art and rock music: petroglyphs of the South Indian Neolithic." *Antiquity* 78 (2004): 38–53.

Boone, Elizabeth Hill. "Glorious Imperium: Understanding Land and Community in Moctezuma's Mexico." *Moctezuma's Mexico: Visions of the Aztec World.* Eds. Eduardo Matos Moctezuma and David Carrasco. Boulder, CO: University of Colorado, 1992. 159–74.

Bordes, François. *A Tale of Two Caves.* New York: Harper & Row, 1972.

Boric, Dusan. "Body Metamorphosis and Animality: Volatile Bodies and Boulder Artworks from Lepenski Vir." *Cambridge Archaeological Journal* 15.1 (2005): 35–69.

Boserup, Ester. *The Conditions of Agricultural Growth.* London: George Allen and Unwin, 1965.

Bourget, Steve, and Kimberly L. Jones. *The Art and Archaeology of the Moche: An Ancient Andean Society of the Peruvian North Coast.* Austin: University of Texas Press, 2008.

Bousman, C.B., et al. The Paleoindian-Archaic transition in North America: new evidence from Texas. *Antiquity* 76 (2002): 980–90.

Bowens, Amanda. *Underwater Archaeology: The NAS Guide to Principles and Practice.* Malden, MA: Blackwell, 2009.

Bowler, James M., et al. "New Ages for Human Occupation and Climatic Change at Lake Mungo, Australia." *Nature* 421 (2003): 837–40.

Bowler, Peter J. *Theories of Human Evolution: A Century of Debate, 1844–1944.* Baltimore: Johns Hopkins University Press, 1986.

Boyd, M. and C. Surette. "Northernmost precontact maize in North America." *American Antiquity* 75.1 (2010): 117–33.

Brackenridge, Henry Marie. *Views of Louisiana Together with a Journal of a Voyage up the Missouri River, in 1811.* Chicago: Quadrangle Books, 1814 [1962].

Branch, Nick. *Environmental Archaeology: Theoretical and Practical Approaches. Key Issues in Environmental Change.* London and New York: Hodder Arnold; Distributed in the United States by Oxford University Press, 2005.

Braswell, Geoffrey E. *The Maya and Teotihuacán: Reinterpreting Early Classic Interaction.* Austin: University of Texas Press, 2003.

Brooks, A.S., et al. "Dating and Context of Three Middle Stone Age Sites with Bone Points in the Upper Semliki Valley, Zaire." *Science* 268 (1995): 548–53.

Brose, David S., and N'omi Greber, eds. *Hopewell Archaeology: The Chillicothe Conference.* Kent, OH: Kent State University Press, 1979.

Brose, David S., James A. Brown, and David W. Penney, eds. *Ancient Art of the American Woodland Indians.* New York: Abrams, 1985.

Brown, A.D. "Wetlands and Drylands in Prehistory: Mesolithic to Bronze Age Human Activity and Impact in the Severn Estuary, Southwest Britain." Ph.D. thesis. University of Reading, 2005.

Brown, James A. "Charnel Houses and Mortuary Crypts: Disposal of the Dead in the Middle Woodland Period." *Hopewell Archaeology: The Chillicothe Conference.* Eds. David S. Brose and N'omi Greber. Kent, OH: Kent State University Press, 1979.

Brown, P., et al. "A New Small-Bodied Hominin from the Late Peistocene of Flores, Indonesia." *Nature* 431 (2004): 1055–61.

Bruins, H.J., et al. "Geoarchaeological tsunami deposits at Palaikastro (Crete) and the Late Minoan IA eruption of Santorini." *Journal of Archaeological Science* 35 (2008): 191–212.

Brumfiel, Elizabeth. "Aztec Hearts and Minds: Religion and the State in the Aztec Empire." Eds. Susan Alcock, et al. Cambridge, U.K.: Cambridge University Press, 2001. 283–310.

Brumm, A., et al. "Early Stone Technology on Flores and Its Implications for Homo Floresiensisfloresiensis." *Nature* 441 (2006): 624–28.

Brunet, M., et al. "New Material of the Earliest Hominid from the Upper Miocene of Chad." *Nature* 434 (2005): 752–55.

Brunet, Michel, et al. "The First Australopithecine 2,500 Kilometers West of the Rift Valley (Chad)." *Nature* 378 (1995): 273–75.

Bryan, Frank. "A Review of the Geology of the Clovis Finds Reported by Howard and Cotter." *American Antiquity* 2 (1938, 1939): 113–30, 43–51.

Buchanan, B., M. Collard, and K. Edinborough. "Paleoindian demography and the extraterrestrial impact hypothesis." *Proceedings of the National Academy of Sciences* 105 (2008): 11651–11654.

Buikstra, J., and L. Beck, eds. *Bioarchaeology: The Contextual Analysis of Human Remains.* Amsterdam: Academic Press, 2006.

Buikstra, Jane, et al. "Tombs from the Copan Acropolis: A Life History Approach." *Understanding Early Classic Copan.* Eds. Ellen E. Bell, Marcello A. Canuto, and Robert J. Sharer. Philadelphia: University Museum, 2004. 191–214.

Bulmer, Susan. *The Prehistory of the New Guinea Highlands.* microform/.[s.n.], Auckland, 1976.

Bunn, Henry T. "A Taphonomic Perspective on the Archaeology of Human Origins." *Annual Review of Anthropology* 20 (1991): 433–67.

Burger, Richard L. "An Overview of Peruvian Archaeology." *Annual Review of Anthropology* 18 (1989): 37–69.

Burger, Richard L. *Chavin and the Origins of Andean Civilization.* London: Thames and Hudson, 1992.

Burger, Richard L., and Lucy C. Salazar. *Machu Picchu: Unveiling the Mystery of the Incas.* New Haven, CT: Yale University Press, 2004.

Cadogan, Gerald, Eleni Hatzaki, and Adonis Vasilakis. *Knossos: palace, city, state. Proceedings of the Conference in Herakleion organised by the British School at Athens and the 23rd Ephoreia of Prehistoric and Classical Antiquities of Herakleion, in November 2000, for the Centenary of Sir Arthur Evan's excavations at Knossos.* London: British School at Athens, 2004.

Cain, C.R. "Notched, Flaked and Ground Bone Artefacts from Middle Stone Age and Iron Age Layers of Sibudu Cave, KwaZulu-Natal, South Africa." *South African Journal of Science* 100 (2004): 195–97.

Cameron, Catherine. "Sacred Earthen Architecture in the Northern Southwest: The Bluff Great House Berm." *American Antiquity* 67.4 (2002): 677–96.

Cann, Rebecca L. "Tangled Genetic Routes." *Nature* 416 (2002): 32–51.

Cannon, A. and D. Yang. "Early storage and sedentism on the Pacific Northwest Coast: ancient DNA analysis of salmon remains from Namu, British Columbia." *American Antiquity* 71.1 (2006): 123–41.

Carballo, D. "Implements of state power: Weaponry and martially themed obisidian production near the Moon Pyramid, Teotihuacán." *Ancient Mesoamerica* 18 (2007): 173–190.

Carbonell, Eudald, et al. "Les Premiers Comportements Funéraires Auraient-Ils Pris Place à Atapuerca, il y a 350,000 Ans?" *L'Anthropologie* 107.1 (2003): 1–14.

Carbonell, Eudald, et al. "The Pleistocene Site of Gran Dolina, Sierra de Atapuerca, Spain: A History of the Archaeological Investigations." *Journal of Human Evolution* 37.3–4 (1999): 313–24.

Carbonell, Eudald. "Out of Africa: The Dispersal of the Earliest Technical Systems Reconsidered." *Journal of Anthropological Archaeology* 18.2 (1999): 119–36.

Carneiro, R.L. "A Theory of the Origin of the State." *Science* 169 (1970): 733–38.

Carr, Christopher, and D. Troy Case, eds. *Gathering Hopewell: Society, Ritual, and Ritual Interaction.* New York: Springer, 2006.

Carrasco, David. "Toward the Splendid City: Knowing the Worlds of Moctezuma." *Moctezuma's Mexico: Visions of the Aztec World.* Eds. Eduardo Matos Moctezuma and David Carrasco. Boulder, CO: University of Colorado, 1992. 99–148.

Castelletti, Lanfredo, Michela Cottini, and Mauro Rottoli. "Early Holocene Plant Remains from Uan Afuda Cave, Tadrart Acacus (Libyan Sahara)." *Before Food Production in North Africa.* Eds. Savino di Lernia and Giorgio Manzi. Forli, Italy: A.B.A.C.O. Edizioni, 1998. 91–102.

Castleden, Rodney. *The Making of Stonehenge.* London: Routledge, 1993.

Cauvin, Jacques, and Trevor Watkins. *The Birth of the Gods and the Origins of Agriculture. New Studies in Archaeology.* Cambridge, U.K.: Cambridge University Press, 2000.

Cessford, Craig. "A New Dating Sequence for Çatalhöyük." *Antiquity* 75 (2001): 717–25.

Chaloupka, George. *Journey in Time: The World's Longest Continuing Art Tradition: The 50,000 Year Story of the Australian Aboriginal Rock Art of Arnhem Land.* Chatswood, N.S.W.: Reed, 1993.

Chang, Kwang-chih. "Ritual and Power." *China: Ancient Culture, Modern Land.* Ed. Robert E. Murowchick. Norman, OK: University of Oklahoma Press, 1994. 60–69.

Chang, Kwang-chih. *Art, Myth, and Ritual: The Path to Political Authority in Ancient China.* Cambridge, MA: Harvard University Press, 1983.

Chang, Kwang-chih. *Shang Civilization.* New Haven, CT: Yale University Press, 1980.

Chang, Kwang-chih. *The Archaeology of Ancient China.* 4th ed. New Haven, CT: Yale University Press, 1986.

Chapdelaine, C., V. Pimentel, and H. Bernier. "A glimpse at Moche Phase III occupation at the Huacas of Moche site, northern Peru." *Antiquity* 75 (2000): 361–72.

Charlton, Thomas H., Deborah L. Nichols, and Cynthia O. Charlton. "Aztec Craft Production and Specialization: Archaeological Evidence from the City–State of Otumba, Mexico." *World Archaeology* 23.1 (1991): 98–114.

Chase, P.G. "Relationships between Mousterian Lithic and Faunal Assemblages at Combe Grenal." *Current Anthropology* 27 (1986): 69–71.

Chauvet, Jean-Marie, Eliette Brunel Deschamps, and Christian Hillaire. *Dawn of Art: the Chauvet Cave: The Oldest Known Paintings in the World.* New York: H.N. Abrams, 1996.

Chen, Tie-Mei, et al. "ESR Dating of Tooth Enamel from Yunxian Homo erectus Site, China." *Quaternary Science Reviews* 16 (1997): 455–58.

Cherry, John. "Polities and palaces: some problems in Minoan state formation." *Peer Polity Interaction and Socio-political Change.* Eds. Colin Renfrew and John Cherry. Cambridge: Cambridge University Press, 1986. 19–46.

Childe, V. Gordon. *What Happened in History?* Harmondsworth, U.K.: Penguin, 1942.

Chilton, Elizabeth, Tonya Baroody Largy, and Kathryn Curran. "Evidence for Prehistoric Maize Horticulture at the Pine Hill Site, Deerfield, Massachusetts." *Northeast Anthropology* 59 (2000): 23–46.

Chilton, Elizabeth. "'Towns They Have None': Diverse Subsistence and Settlement Strategies in Native New England." *New York State Museum Bulletin* 496 (2002): 265–88.

Chilton, Elizabeth. "Mobile Farmers of Pre-Contact Southern New England: The Archaeological and Ethnohistorical Evidence." *New York State Museum Bulletin* 494 (1999): 157–76.

Chippindale, Christopher, et al. *Who Owns Stonehenge?* London: Batsford, 1990.

Chirikure, S., and G. Pwiti. "Community involvement in archaeology and cultural heritage management: an assessment from case studies in southern Africa and elsewhere." *Current Anthropology* 49 (2008): 467–85.

Clark, David. *Analytical Archaeology.* New York: Columbia University Press, 1978.

Clark, J. Desmond, and Steven A. Brandt, eds. *From Hunters to Farmers: The Causes and Consequences of Food Production in Africa.* Berkeley, CA: University of California Press, 1984.

Clark, John E., and Mary E. Pye. *Olmec Art and Archaeology in Mesoamerica.* Washington, DC and New Haven, CT: National Gallery of Art, 2000.

Clark, R.M., et al. "Pattern of Diversity in the Genomic Region near the Maize Domestication Gene Tb1." *Proceedings of the National Academy of Sciences* 101.3 (2004): 700–07.

Clarke, R.J. "First Ever Discovery of a Well-Preserved Skull and Associated Skeleton of an Australopithecus." *South African Journal of Science* 94.10 (1998): 1–6.

Cleal, Rosamund, K.E. Walker, and R. Montague. *Stonehenge in Its Landscape. Archaeological Report.* Vol. 10. London: English Heritage, 1995.

Clermont, N., C. Chapdelaine, and J. Cinq-Mars, eds. *Île aux Allumettes: l'Archaïque supérieur dans l'Outouais.* Paléo-Québec 30. Montreal: Musée Canadien des Civilisations et Recherches Amérindiennes au Québec, 2003.

Clottes, Jean, Paul G. Bahn, and Maurice Arnold. *Chauvet Cave: The Art of Earliest Times.* Salt Lake City, UT: University of Utah Press, 2003.

Clutton-Brock, Juliet. "The Spread of Domestic Animals in Africa." *The Archaeology of Africa: Food, Metals, and Towns.* Ed. Thurstan Shaw. London: Routledge, 1993. 61–70.

Codere, H. *Fighting with property: a study of Kwakiutl potlatching and warfare, 1792–1930.* New York: J.J. Augustin, 1950.

Coe, Michael D. *Breaking the Maya Code.* New York: Thames and Hudson, 1999.

Coe, Michael D. *The Maya. Ancient Peoples and Places.* 5th ed. New York: Thames and Hudson, 1993.

Coe, Michael D., et al. *The Olmec World: Ritual and Rulership.* Princeton, N.J.: Princeton University. Art Museum, 1995.

Cohen, Claudine, and Jean-Jacques Hublin. *Boucher de Perthes, 1788–1868: Les Origines Romantiques de la Préhistoire. Un Savant, une Époque.* Paris: Belin, 1989.

Cohen, Mark Nathan. *The Food Crisis in Prehistory: Overpopulation and the Origins of Agriculture.* New Haven, CT: Yale University Press, 1977.

Coles, J.M. *Experimental Archaeology.* New York: Academic Press, 1979.

Conard, N. "A female figurine from the basal Aurignacian of Hohle Fels Cave in southwestern Germany." *Nature* 459 (2009): 248–52.

Conard, N., M. Malina, and S. Munzel. "New flutes document the earliest musical tradition in southwestern Germany." *Nature* 460 (2009): 737–40.

Conard, Nicholas. "Laminar Lithic Assemblages from the Last Interglacial Complex in Northwestern Europe." *Journal of Anthropological Research* 46.3 (1990): 243–62.

Conard, Nicholas. "Palaeolithic Ivory Sculptures from Southwestern Germany and the Origins of Figurative Art." *Nature* 426 (2003): 830–32.

Conkey, Margaret. "The Identification of Prehistoric Hunter–Gatherer Aggregation Sites: The Case of Altamira." *Current Anthropology* 21.5 (1980): 609–30.

Conklin, William J., and Jeffrey Quilter. *Chavin: Art, Architecture, and Culture.* Los Angeles: Cotsen Institute of Archaeology, University of California, 2008.

Connah, Graham. *African Civilization: Precolonial Cities and States in Tropical Africa: An Archaeological Perspective.* Cambridge, U.K.: Cambridge University Press, 1987.

Conolly J., S. Colledge, and S. Shennan. "Founder effect, drift, and adaptive change in domestic crop use in early neolithic Europe." *Journal of Archaeological Science* 35 (2008): 2797–2804.

Conyers, Lawrence B., and Dean Goodman. *Ground-Penetrating Radar: An Introduction for Archaeologists.* Walnut Creek, CA: AltaMira Press, 1997.

Copley, M.S., et al. "Direct chemical evidence for widespread dairying in prehistoric Britain." *Proceedings of the National Academy of Sciences* 100 (2003):1524–29.

Cordell, Linda. *Archaeology of the Southwest.* 2nd ed. New York: Academic Press, 1997.

Coughlin, Sean, and Mark F. Seeman. "Hopewellian Settlements at the Liberty Earthworks, Ross County, Ohio." *Ohio Hopewell Community Organization.* Eds. William S. Dancey and Paul J. Pacheco. Kent, OH: Ohio University Press, 1997. 231–50.

Coupland, Gary, Roger H. Colten, and Rebecca Case. "Preliminary Analysis of Socioeconomic Organization at the McNichol Creek site, British Columbia." *Emerging from the Mist: Studies in Northwest Coast Culture History.* Ed. R. G. Matson, Gary Coupland, and Quentin Mackie. Vancouver: UBC Press, 2003. 152–169.

Cowan, C. Wesley, and Patty Jo Watson, eds. *The Origins of Agriculture: An International Perspective.* Washington, DC: Smithsonian Institution Press, 1992.

Cowgill, G. State and society at Teotihuacán, Mexico. *Annual Review of Anthropology* 26 (1997): 129–63.

Crawford, G.W. "Agricultural origins in North China pushed back to the Pleistocene-Holocene boundary." *Proceedings of the National Academy of Sciences* 106.18 (2009): 7271–72.

Crawford, Gary W., and Chen Shen. "The Origins of Rice Agriculture: Recent Progress in East Asia." *Antiquity* 72 (1998): 858–66.

Crawford, Gary W., and David G. Smith. "Paleoethnobotany in the Northeast." *People and Plants in Ancient Eastern North America.* Ed. Paul E. Minnis. Washington, DC: Smithsonian Books, 2003. 172–257.

Crawford, Gary W., and David G. Smith. "Migration in prehistory: Princess Point and the northern Iroquoian case." *American Antiquity* 61 (1996): 782–90.

Crawford, G. and G-A. Lee. "Agricultural origins in the Korean Peninsula." *Antiquity* 77.295 (2003): 87–95.

Crawford, Gary W., David G. Smith, and Vandy E. Bowyer. "Dating the Entry of Corn (Zea Mays) into the Lower Great Lakes Region." *American Antiquity* 62.1 (1997): 112–19.

Crawford, Harriet E.W. *Sumer and the Sumerians.* Cambridge, U.K.: Cambridge University Press, 1991.

Croes, Dale. R. "Northwest Coast Wet-site Artifacts: A Key to Understanding Resource Procurement, Storage, Management, and Exchange." *Emerging from the Mist: Studies in Northwest Coast Culture History.* Ed. R. G. Matson, Gary Coupland, and Quentin Mackie. Vancouver: UBC Press, 2003. 51–75.

Crown, Patricia L., W. James Judge, and School of American Research (Santa Fe NM). *Chaco & Hohokam: Prehistoric Regional Systems in the American Southwest. School of American Research Advanced Seminar Series*. Santa Fe, NM: School of American Research Press, 1991.

Crumley, C. "Heterarchy and the analysis of complex societies." *Archaeological Papers of the American Anthropological Association* 18 (1995): 1–5.

Cullen, Bob. "Testimony from the Iceman." *Smithsonian* 33.11 (2003): 42–45.

Cutting, M. "The use of spatial analysis to study prehistoric settlement architecture." *Oxford Journal of Archaeology* 22 (2003): 1–21.

Cybulski, J. S. *A Greenville Burial Ground: Human Remains in British Columbia Coast Prehistory*. Ottawa: Archaeological Survey of Canada/ Canadian Museum of Civilization, 1993.

D'Altroy, Terence N. *The Incas. Peoples of America*. Oxford, U.K.: Blackwell Publishers, 2002.

D'Andrea, A.C., et al. "Late Jomon Cultigens in Northeastern Japan." *Antiquity* 69 (1995): 146–52.

D'Andrea, D.E., et al. "Ethnoarchaeological approaches to the study of prehistoric agriculture in the Ethiopian highlands." *The Exploitation of Plant Resources in Ancient Africa*. Ed. M. Van der Veen. New York: Plenum, 1999. 101–22.

d'Errico, F. "New Model and Its Implications for the Origin of Writing: The La Marche Antler Revisited." *Cambridge Archaeological Journal* 5.2 (1995): 163–206.

d'Errico, F., et al. "Neanderthal Acculturation in Western Europe?" *Current Anthropology* 39 (1998): S1–S43.

d'Errico, F., et al. "Archaeological evidence for the emergence of language, symbolism, and music: an alternative multidisciplinary perspective." *Journal of World Prehistory* 17 (2003): 1–70.

d'Errico, Francesco, and April Nowell. "A New Look at the Berekhat Ram Figurine: Implications for the Origins of Symbolism." *Cambridge Archaeological Journal* 10.1 (2000): 123–67.

d'Errico, Francesco, et al. "A Middle Palaeolithic Origin of Music? Using Cave-Bear Bone Accumulation to Assess the Divje Babe I Bone Flute." *Antiquity* 72 (1998): 65–80.

Dalan, Rinita A. *Envisioning Cahokia: A Landscape Perspective*. DeKalb, IL: Northern Illinois University Press, 2003.

Dancey, William S., and Paul J. "A Community Model of Ohio Hopewell Settlement." *Ohio Hopewell Community Organization*. Eds. William S. Dancey and Paul J. Pacheco. Kent, OH: Ohio University Press, 1997. 3–40.

Dancey, William S., and Paul J. Pacheco, eds. *Ohio Hopewell Community Organization*. Kent, OH: Kent State University Press, 1997.

Dart, R.A. "The Predatory Transition from Ape to Man." *International Anthropological Linguistics Review* 1.4 (1953): 201–18.

Darwin, Charles. *The Origin of Species*. London: John Murray, 1859.

David, Bruno, et al. "New Optical and Radiocarbon Dates from Ngarrabullgan Cave, a Pleistocene Archaeological Site in Australia: Implications for the Comparability of Time Clocks and for the Human Colonization of Australia." *Antiquity* 71.271 (1997): 183–88.

David, Nicholas, and Carol Kramer. *Ethnoarchaeology in Action. Cambridge World Archaeology*. Cambridge, U.K.: Cambridge University Press, 2001.

Davis, Simon J. M. *The Archaeology of Animals*. New Haven, CT: Yale University Press, 1987.

Davis, Simon J.M. *The Archaeology of Animals*. New Haven, CT: Yale University Press, 1987.

Dawson, P.C. "Space syntax analysis of Central Inuit snow houses." *Journal of Anthropological Archaeology* 21.4 (2002): 464–80.

Day, Michael H. *Guide to Fossil Man*. 4th ed. Chicago: University of Chicago Press, 1986.

Dayan, Tamar. "Early Domesticated Dogs of the Near East." *Journal of Archaeological Science* 21 (1994): 633–40.

De Heinzelin, Jean, et al. "Environment and Behavior of 2.5-Million-Year-Old Bouri Hominids." *Science* 284 (1999): 625–29.

De Lumley, Henry, et al. "Les Industries Lithiques Préoldowayennes du Debut du Pleistocene Inferieur du Site de Dmanissi en Georgie." *L'Anthropologie* 109.1 (2005): 1–182.

Deacon, H.J., and Janette Deacon. *Human Beginnings in South Africa: Uncovering the Secrets of the Stone Age*. Walnut Creek, CA: Altamira Press, 1999.

Deacon, Terrence William. *The Symbolic Species: The Co-Evolution of Language and the Brain*. New York: W.W. Norton, 1997.

Debaine-Francfort, Corinne. *The Search for Ancient China*. London: Thames & Hudson, 1999.

Deetz, James J.F. *In Small Things Forgotten: The Archaeology of Early American Life*. Garden City, N.Y.: Anchor Press/ Doubleday, 1996.

Defleur, Alban, et al. "Neanderthal Cannabalism at Moula-Guercy, Ardèche, France." *Science* 286 (1999): 128–131.

Demarest, Arthur Andrew. *Ancient Maya: The Rise and Fall of a Rainforest Civilisation. Case Studies in Early Societies, 3*. Cambridge, U.K.: Cambridge University Press, 2004.

deMenocal, P. "Cultural responses to climate change during the late Holocene." *Science* 292 (2001): 667–73.

Denham, T.P., et al. "Origins of Agriculture at Kuk Swamp in the Highlands of New Guinea." *Science* 301 (2003): 189–93.

Denham, Tim, and Chris Ballard. "Jack Golsen and the Investigation of Prehistoric Agriculture in Highland New Guinea: Recent Work and Future Prospects." *Archaeology of Oceania* 38 (2003): 129–34.

Denham, Tim. "Archaeological Evidence for Mid-Holocene Agriculture in the Interior of Papua New Guinea: A Critical Review." *Archaeology of Oceania* 38 (2003): 159–76.

Desmond, Adrian J., and James R. Moore. *Darwin's Sacred Cause: How a Hatred of Slavery Shaped Darwin's Views on Human Evolution*. Boston: Houghton Mifflin Harcourt, 2009.

Desmond, Adrian J., and James R. Moore. *Darwin*. New York: Warner Books, 1992.

Devries, T.J., et al. "Determining the Early History of El Niño." *Science* 276 (1997): 965–67.

Dhillon, N.P.S., and K. Ishiki. "Genomic Variation and Genetic Relationships in *Ipomoea* spp." *Plant Breeding* 118 (1999): 161–65.

Di Lernia, Savino, and Giorgio Manzi, eds. *Before Food Production in North Africa*. Forli, Italy: A.B.A.C.O. Edizioni, 1998.

Di Lernia, Savino. "Cultural Control over Wild Animals During the Early Holocene: The Case of Barbary Sheep in Central Sahara." *Before Food Production in North Africa*. Eds. Savino di Lernia and Giorgio Manzi. Forli, Italy: A.B.A.C.O. Edizioni, 1998. 113–26.

Diamond, Jared. *Collapse: How Societies Choose to Fail or Succeed*. New York: Viking, 2005.

Dibble, Harold. "The Interpretation of Middle Paleolithic Scraper Morphology." *American Antiquity* 52 (1987): 109–17.

Dillehay, Tom D. *Monte Verde: A Late Pleistocene Settlement in Chile*. Washington, DC: Smithsonian Institution Press, 1989.

Dillehay, Tom D. *The Settlement of the Americas: A New Prehistory*. New York: Basic Books, 2000.

Dincauze, Dena F. *Environmental Archaeology: Principles and Practices*. Cambridge: Cambridge University Press, 2000.

Dixon, E. James. *Bones, Boats, and Bison: Archaeology and the First Colonization of Western North America*. Albuquerque, NM: University of New Mexico Press, 1999.

Dixon, E. James. "Human Colonization of the Americas: Timing, Technology and Process." *Quaternary Science Reviews* 20 (2001): 277–99.

Dobres, Marcia-Anne. *Technology and Social Agency: Outlining a Practice Framework for Archaeology.* Oxford: Blackwell, 2000.

Dobres, Marcia-Anne, and John E. Robb. *Agency in Archaeology.* London and New York: Routledge, 2000.

Dolukhanov, P., et al. "The chronology of Neolithic dispersal in Central and Eastern Europe." *Journal of Archaeological Science* 32 (2005): 1441–58.

Dominguez-Rodrigo, Manuel, et al. "Woodworking Activities by Early Humans: A Plant Residue Analysis on Acheulian Stone Tools from Peninj (Tanzania)." *Journal of Human Evolution* 40 (2001): 289–99.

Dominguez-Rodrigo, Manuel. "Hunting and Scavenging by Early Humans: The State of the Debate." *Journal of World Prehistory* 16.1 (2002): 1–54.

Donald, Lelana. *Aboriginal Slavery on the Northwest Coast of North America.* Berkeley: University of California Press, 1997.

Driessen, J., and C.F. Macdonald. *The Troubled Island: Minoan Crete before and after the Santorini Eruption.* Liege: Universite de Liege, 1997.

Duarte, Cidalia, et al. "The Early Upper Paleolithic Human Skeleton from the Abrigo Do Lagar Velho (Portugal) and Modern Human Emergence in Iberia." *Proceedings of the National Academy of Sciences* 96 (1999): 7604–09.

Duller, G.A.T. "Dating Methods: The Role of Geochronology in Studies of Human Evolution and Migration in Southeast Asia and Australasia." *Progress in Physical Geography* 25.2 (2001): 267–76.

Dumond, Don. *The Eskimos and Aleuts.* London: Thames and Hudson, 1987.

Edwards, P. "Wadi Hammeh 27: An Early Natufian Site at Pella, Jordan." *The Natufian Culture in the Levant.* Eds. O. Bar-Yosef and François Valla. Ann Arbor, MI: International Monographs in Prehistory, 1991. 123–48.

Ehrhardt, K.L. "Copper working technologies, contexts of use, and social complexity in the Eastern Woodlands of native North America." *Journal of World Prehistory* 22 (2009): 213–35.

Ellis, C., P.A. Timmins, and H. Martelle. "At the crossrods and periphery: The Archaic archaeological record of southern Ontario." *Archaic Societies: Diversity and Complexity Across the Midcontinent.* Eds. T.E. Emerson, D.L. McElrath, and A.C. Fortier. Albany: SUNY Press, 2009.

Elton, Sarah, Laura C. Bishop, and Bernard Wood. "Comparative Context of Plio-Pleistocene Hominin Brain Evolution." *Journal of Human Evolution* 41 (2000): 1–27.

Enloe, J.G. "Food Sharing in the Paleolithic: Carcass Refitting at Pincevent." *Piecing Together the Past: Applications of Refitting Studies in Archaeology.* Eds. J.L. Hofman and J.G. Enloe. Vol. 578. Oxford: BAR International Series, 1992. 296–315.

Enloe, James G. "Food Sharing Past and Present: Archaeological Evidence for Economic and Social Interactions." University of Iowa, 2003. http://www.uiowa.edu/~zooarch/bffoodshare2003.pdf.

Eubanks, Mary. "An Interdisciplinary Perspective on the Origin of Maize." *Latin American Antiquity* 12.1 (2001): 91–98.

Evans, John G., and T.P. O'Connor. *Environmental Archaeology: Principles and Methods.* 2nd ed. Stroud, U.K.: Sutton, 2005.

Eyre-Walker, A., et al. "Investigation of the Bottleneck Leading to the Domestication of Maize." *Proceedings of the National Academy of Sciences* 95 (1998): 4441–46.

Fagan, Brian M. *Eyewitness to Discovery: First-Person Accounts of More Than Fifty of the World's Greatest Archaeological Discoveries.* Oxford, U.K.: Oxford University Press, 1996.

Fajardo, D.S., D.R. La Bonte, and R.L. Jarret. "Identifying and Selecting for Genetic Diversity in Papua New Guinea Sweet Potato *Ipomoea batatas* (L.) Lam. Germplasm Collected as Botanical Seed." *Genetic Resources and Crop Evolution* 49 (2002): 463–70.

Fash, William Leonard. *Scribes, Warriors, and Kings: The City of Copán and the Ancient Maya. New Aspects of Antiquity.* London: Thames and Hudson, 1991.

Faupl, Peter, Wolfram Richter, and Christoph Urbanek. "Dating of the Herto Hominin Fossils." *Nature* 426 (2003): 621–22.

Fforde, C., J. Hubert, and P. Turnbull, eds. *The Dead and Their Possessions: Repatriation in Principle, Policy, and Practice.* Vol. 43. London: Routledge, 2002.

Fiedel, Stuart, and Gary Haynes. "A Premature Burial: Comments on Grayson and Meltzer's 'Requiem for Overkill.'" *Journal of Archaeological Science.* 31 (2004): 121–31.

Fiedel, Stuart. "Artifact Provenience at Monte Verde: Confusion and Contradictions." *Scientific American Discovery Archaeology* 1.6 (1999): 1–14.

Field, Judith, et al. "Archaeology and Australian Megafauna." *Science* 294 (2001): 696–702.

Field, Judith, Richard Fullagar, and Garry Lord. "A Large Area Archaeological Excavation at Cuddie Springs." *Antiquity* 75.290 (2001): 696–702.

Finney, Ben. "Myth, experiment, and the reinvention of Polynesian voyaging." *American Anthropologist* 93 (1991): 383–404.

Firestone, R.B., et al. "Evidence for an extraterrestrial impact 12,900 years ago that contributed to the megafaunal extinctions and the Younger Dryas cooling." *Proceedings of the National Academy of Sciences* 104 (2007): 16016–21.

Fitton, J. Lesley. *Minoans.* London: British Museum Press, 2002.

Fladmark, K.R. "Routes: Alternate Migration Corridors for Early Man in North America." *American Antiquity* 44.1 (1979): 55–69.

Flannery, Kent, ed. *Guila Naquitz: Archaic Foraging and Early Agriculture in Oaxaca, Mexico.* New York: Academic Press, 1986.

Flannery, Kent. "Culture History V. Culture Process: A Debate in American Archaeology." *Scientific American* 217 (1967): 119–22.

Flannery, Kent. "The Origins of Agriculture." *Annual Review of Anthropology* 1973 (1973): 271–310.

Flenley, John, and Paul G. Bahn. *The Enigmas of Easter Island: Island on the Edge.* 2nd ed. Oxford, U.K.: Oxford University Press, 2003.

Ford, Richard I. "Corn Is Our Mother." *Corn and Culture in the Prehistoric New World.* Eds. Sissel Johannessen and Christine A. Hastorf. Boulder, CO: Westview Press, 1994. 513–526.

Formicola, V., and A. Buzhilova. "Double Child Burial from Sunghir (Russia): Pathology and Inferences for Upper Paleolithic Funerary Practices." *American Journal of Physical Anthropology* 124.3 (2004): 189–98.

French, E.B. *Mycenae: Agamemnon's Capital; the Site in Its Setting.* Stroud: Tempus, 2002.

Fried, Morton H. *The Evolution of Political Society: An Essay in Political Anthropology.* New York: Random House, 1967.

Frison, G.C. "A Late Paleoindian animal trapping net from Northern Wyoming." *American Antiquity* 51 (1986): 352–61.

Frison, G.C. *Survival by Hunting: Prehistoric Human Predators and Animal Prey.* Berkeley: University of California Press, 2004.

Frison, George C. "Paleoindian Large Mammal Hunters on the Plains of North America." *Proceedings of the National Academy of Sciences* 95 (1998): 14576–83.

Fritz, Gayle J. "Gender and the Early Cultivation of Gourds in Eastern North America." *American Antiquity* 64.3 (1999): 417–29.

Galaty, Michael L., and William A. Parkinson. *Rethinking Mycenaean Palaces II.* Los Angeles: Cotsen Institute of Archaeology at UCLA, 2007.

Gamble, Clive. *Timewalkers: The Prehistory of Global Colonization.* Stroud, U.K.: A. Sutton, 1993.

Gargett, Robert. "Grave Shortcomings: The Evidence for Neanderthal Burial." *Current Anthropology* 30.2 (1989): 157–90.

Garlake, Peter S. *Great Zimbabwe.* London: Thames and Hudson, 1973.

Gaudzinski, Sabine. "On Bovid Assemblages and Their Consequences for the Knowledge of Subsistence Patterns in the Middle Palaeolithic." *Proceedings of the Prehistoric Society* 62 (1996): 19–39.

Ge, Yan, and Katheryn Linduff. Sanxingdui: a new Bronze Age site in southwest China. *Antiquity* 64 (1990): 505–13.

Gebel, Hans Georg, et al. "Ba'ja Hidden in the Petra Mountains. Preliminary Results of the 1997 Investigations." *The Prehistory of Jordan II: Perspectives from 1997.* Eds. Hans Georg Gebel, Zeidan Kafafi, and Gary O. Rollefson. Berlin: Ex Oriente, 1997. 221–62.

Geneste, Jean-Michel, and Hugues Plisson. "Hunting Technologies and Human Behavior: Lithic Analysis of Solutrean Shouldered Points." *Before Lascaux: The Complex Record of the Early Upper Paleolithic.* Eds. Heidi Knecht, Anne Pike-Tay, and Randall White. Boca Raton, FL: CRC Press, 1993. 117–35.

Gero, Joan M., and Margaret Wright Conkey. *Engendering Archaeology: Women and Prehistory. Social Archaeology.* Oxford, U.K.: B. Blackwell, 1991.

Gibbons, Ann. "Ancient Island Tools Suggest *Homo erectus* Was a Seafarer." *Science* 279 (1998): 1635–37.

Gibson, Jon L. *The Ancient Mounds of Poverty Point: Place of Rings.* Gainesville, FL: University of Florida Press, 2000.

Gichuki, Simon Templar, et al. "Genetic Diversity in Sweet Potato (*Ipomoea batatas*)." *Genetic Resources and Crop Evolution* 50 (2003): 429–37.

Gifford-Gonzalez, Diane. "Early Pastoralists in East Africa: Ecological and Social Dimensions." *Journal of Anthropological Archaeology* 17 (1998): 166–200.

Glazko, Galina V., and Masatoshi Nei. "Estimation of Divergence Times for Major Lineages of Primate Species." *Molecular Biological Evolution* 20.3 (2003): 424–34.

Goebel, Ted, Michael R. Waters, and Margarita Dikova. "The Archaeology of Ushki Lake, Kamchatka, and the Pleistocene Peopling of the Americas." *Science* 301 (2003): 501–05.

Goebs, K. "Kingship." *The Egyptian World.* Ed. T. Wilkinson. New York: Routledge, 2009. 275–95.

Goldberg, P., et al. "Site Formation Processes at Zhoukoudian, China." *Journal of Human Evolution* 41.5 (2001): 483–530.

Goldberg, Paul, and Richard Macphail. *Practical and theoretical geoarchaeology.* Malden, MA: Blackwell, 2006.

Golson, J., and D.S. Gardner. "Agriculture and Sociopolitical Organization in New Guinea Highlands Prehistory." *Annual Review of Anthropology* 19 (1990): 395–417.

Gordon, Arnold L., Claudia F. Giulivi, and A. Gani Ilahude. "Deep Topographic Barriers within the Indonesian Seas." *Deep-Sea Research Part II* 50 (2003): 2205–28.

Goren, Y., A.N. Goring-Morris, and I. Segal. "The Technology of Skull Modelling in the Pre-Pottery Neolithic B (PPNB): Regional Variability, the Relation of Technology and Iconography and Their Archaeological Implications." *Journal of Archaeological Science* 28 (2001): 671–90.

Goren, Yuval, et al. *Inscribed in Clay: Provenance Study of the Amarna Tablets and Other Ancient Near Eastern Texts.* Tel Aviv: Emery and Claire Yass Publications in Archaeology, 2004.

Goren-Inbar, Naama, et al. "Pleistocene Milestones on the Out-of-Africa Corridor at Gesher Benot Ya'aqov, Israel." *Science* 289 (2000): 944–47.

Goring-Morris, A.N., and A. Belfer-Cohen. "The Articulation of Cultural Processes and Late Quaternary Environmental Changes in Cisjordan." *Paleorient* 23.2 (1998): 71–93.

Gould, S.J. "On Replacing the Idea of Progress with an Operational Notion of Directionality." *Evolutionary Progress?* Ed. Matthew H. Nitecki. Chicago: University of Chicago Press, 1988. 319–38.

Gould, S.J., and R.C. Lewontin. "The Spandrels of San Marco and the Panglossian Paradigm: A Critique of the Adaptationist Programme." *Proceedings of the Royal Society of London,* series B 205 (1979): 581–98.

Gowlett, J., et al. "Early Archaeological Sites, Hominid Remains and Traces of Fire from Chesowanja, Kenya." *Nature* 294 (1981): 125–29.

Granger, D.E., and P.F. Muzikar. "Dating sediment burial with in-situ-produced cosmogenic nuclides: theory, techniques, and limitations." *Earth and Planetary Science Letters* 188 (2001): 269–81.

Grayson, Donald K. *The Establishment of Human Antiquity.* New York: Academic Press, 1983.

Grayson, Donald K., and David J. Meltzer. "Clovis Hunting and Large Mammal Extinction: A Critical Review of the Evidence." *Journal of World Prehistory* 16.4 (2002): 313–59.

Grayson, Donald K., and David J. Meltzer. "North American Overkill Continued?" *Journal of Archaeological Science* 31 (2004): 133–36.

Green, Ernestene L. *Ethics and Values in Archaeology.* New York: Free Press, 1984.

Green, R., et al. Analysis of one million base pairs of Neanderthal DNA. *Nature* 440 (2006): 330–36.

Green, R., et al. "A complete Neanderthal mitochondrial genome sequence determined by high-throughput sequencing." *Cell* 134 (2008): 416–26.

Greenfield, H.J. "The Secondary Products Revolution: the past, the present and the future." *World Archaeology* 42.1 (2010): 29–54.

Gregg, M.W., et al. "Subsistence practices and pottery use in Neolithic Jordan: molecular and isotopic evidence." *Journal of Archaeological Science* 36 (2009): 937–46.

Gremillion, Kristen J. "Early Agricultural Diet in Eastern North America: Evidence from Two Kentucky Rockshelters." *American Antiquity* 61.3 (1996): 520–36.

Gremillion, Kristen J. "Eastern Woodlands Overview." *People and Plants in Ancient Eastern North America.* Ed. Paul E. Minnis. Washington, DC: Smithsonian Books, 2003. 17–50.

Griffin, James B. "Eastern North American Archaeology: A Summary." *Science* 156 (1967): 175–91.

Grønnow, Bjarne. "The Saqqaq Tool Kit—Technological and Chronological Evidence from Qeqertasussuk, Disko Bugt." *The Paleo-Eskimo Cultures of Greenland: New Perspectives in Greenlandic Archaeology.* Ed. Bjarne Grønnow. Strandgade: Danish Polar Center, 1996. 17–34.

Groube, Les, et al. "A 40,000 Year-Old Human Occupation Site at Huon Peninsula, Papua New Guinea." *Nature* 324 (1986): 453–55.

Guidon, N., et al. "Nature and Age of the Deposits in Pedra Furada, Brazil: Reply to Meltzer, Adovasio & Dillehay." *Antiquity* 70 (1996): 408–21.

Guilaine, Jean. *Premiers Paysans du Monde: Naissances des Agricultures. Collection des Hespérides.* Paris: Errance, 2000.

Guthrie, R. Dale. "Rapid Body Size Decline in Alaskan Pleistocene Horses before Extinction." *Nature* 426 (2003): 169–71.

Gutierrez, Manuel, et al. "Exploitation d'un Grand Cétacé au Paléolithique Ancien: Le Site de Dungo V a Baia Farta (Benguela, Angola)." *Comptes Rendus de l'Academie des Sciences: Earth and Planetary Sciences* 332 (2001): 357–62.

Haaland, Randi. "Sedentism, Cultivation, and Plant Domestication in the Holocene Middle Nile Region." *Journal of Field Archaeology* 22 (1995): 157–74.

Haberle, Simon G. "The Emergence of an Agricultural Landscape in the Highlands of New Guinea." *Archaeology of Oceania* 38 (2003): 149–58.

Hallo, William W., and William Kelly Simpson. *The Ancient Near East: A History.* New York: Harcourt Brace Jovanovich, 1971.

Hard, Robert, and John R. Roney. "The Transition to Farming on the R'o Casas Grandes and in the Southern Jornada Mogollon Region." *The Late Archaic: Across the Borderlands.* Ed. Bradley J. Vierra. Austin, TX: University of Texas, 2005. 141–86.

Hard, Robert, and John Roney. "A massive terraced village complex in Chihuahua, Mexico, 3,000 years before present." *Science* 279 (1998): 1661–64.

Hardy, D.A. *Thera and the Aegean World III : Proceedings of the Third International Congress, Santorini, Greece.* London: Thera Foundation, 1990.

Harlan, Jack R. "The Tropical African Cereals." *The Archaeology of Africa: Food, Metals, and Towns.* Ed. Thurstan Shaw. London: Routledge, 1993. 53–59.

Harlan, Jack R. *The Living Fields: Our Agricultural Heritage.* Cambridge, U.K.: Cambridge University Press, 1995.

Harris, David R., et al. *The Archaeology of V. Gordon Childe: Contemporary Perspectives.* London: UCL Press, 1994.

Harris, Edward C. *Principles of Archaeological Stratigraphy.* New York: Academic Press, 1989.

Harrison, Peter D. *The Lords of Tikal: Rulers of an Ancient Maya City. New Aspects of Antiquity.* London: Thames and Hudson, 1999.

Hassan, Fekri. "The Aswan High Dam and the International Rescue Nubia Campaign." *African Archaeological Review* 24 (2007): 73–94.

Hastorf, Christine A. "Recent Research in Paleoethnobotany." *Journal of Archaeological Research* 7.1 (1999): 55–103.

Hastorf, Christine A. "The Cultural Life of Early Domestic Plant Use." *Antiquity* 72 (1998): 773–888.

Hastorf, Christine A., and Virginia Popper, eds. *Current Paleoethnobotany: Analytical Methods and Cultural Interpretations of Archaeological Plant Remains.* Chicago: University of Chicago, 1988.

Haug, Gerald H., et al. "Climate and the Collapse of Maya Civilization." *Science* 299 (2003): 1731.

Hayashida, F. "Archaeology, ecological history, and conservation." *Annual Review of Anthropology* 34 (2005): 43–65.

Hayden, Brian. "Nimrods, Piscators, Pluckers, and Planters: The Emergence of Food Production." *Journal of Anthropological Archaeology* 9 (1990): 31–69.

Hayden, Brian, Edward Bakewell, and Rob Gargett. "The world's longest-lived corporate group: Lithic analysis reveals prehistoric social organization near Lillooet, British Columbia." *American Antiquity* 61 (1996): 341–56.

Haynes, C. Vance. "Younger Dryas "black mats" and the Rancholabrean termination in North America." *Proceedings of the National Academy of Sciences* 105 (2008): 6520–25.

Haynes, C. Vance, et al. "A Clovis Well at the Type Site 11,500 B.C.: The Oldest Prehistoric Well in America." *Geoarchaeology: An International Journal* 14.5 (1999): 455–70.

Haynes, C. Vance, Richard E. Reanier, and William P. Barse. "Dating a Paleoindian Site in the Amazon in Comparison with Clovis Culture." *Science* 275 (1997): 1948–52.

Haynes, Gary. *The Early Settlement of North America: The Clovis Era.* Cambridge, U.K.: Cambridge University Press, 2002.

Headrick, Annabeth. *The Teotihuacán Trinity: The Sociopolitical Structure of an Ancient Mesoamerican City.* Austin: University of Texas Press, 2007.

Healy, P.F. "The ancient Maya ballcourt at Pacbitun, Belize." *Ancient Mesoamerica* 3 (1992): 229–39.

Heckenberger, M., and E. Goes Neves. "Amazonian archaeology." *Annual Review of Anthropology* 38 (2009): 251–66.

Hedges, S. Blair. "A Start for Population Genomics." *Nature* 408 (2000): 652–53.

Hegmon, M., and S. Kulow. "Painting as agency, style as structure: Innovations in Mimbres pottery designs from Southwest New Mexico." *Journal of Archaeological Method and Theory* 12 (2005): 313–34.

Heizer, Robert F. *Man's Discovery of His Past; Literary Landmarks in Archaeology.* Englewood Cliffs, N.J.: Prentice-Hall, 1962.

Hendon, Julia A., and Rosemary A. Joyce. *Mesoamerican Archaeology: Theory and Practice. Blackwell Studies in Global Archaeology* 1. Malden, MA: Blackwell, 2004.

Henshilwood, C.S., and J. Sealy. "Bone Artifacts from the Middle Stone Age at Blombos Cave, Southern Cape, South Africa." *Current Anthropology* 38 (1997): 890–95.

Henshilwood, C.S., et al. "Emergence of Modern Human Behavior: Middle Stone Age Engravings from South Africa." *Science* 295 (2002): 1278–80.

Hide, Robin. *Pig Husbandry in New Guinea: A Literature Review and Bibliography.* Canberra, Australia: Australian Centre for International Agriculture Research, 2003.

Higgs, E.S., ed. *Papers in Economic Prehistory.* Cambridge, U.K.: Cambridge University Press, 1972.

Higham, Charles, and Tracey L.-D. Lu. "The Origins and Dispersal of Rice Cultivation." *Antiquity* 72.278 (1998): 867–77.

Higham, Tom, Christopher Bronk Ramsey, and Clare Owen, eds. *Radiocarbon and Archaeology.* Oxford, U.K.: Oxford University School of Archaeology, 2004.

Hill, James. "Broken K Pueblo: Patterns of Form and Function." *New Perspectives in Archaeology.* Ed. Sally Binford and Lewis Binford. Chicago: Aldine, 1968. 103–42.

Hirth, K. "The distributional approach: A new way to identify marketplace exchange in the archaeological record." *Current Anthropology* 39 (1998): 451–76.

Hodder, Ian. *Reading the Past.* Cambridge, U.K.: Cambridge University Press, 1986.

Hodder, Ian. *The Archaeological Process: An Introduction.* Oxford, U.K.: Blackwell, 1999.

Hodder, Ian. *The Domestication of Europe: Structure and Contingency in Neolithic Societies. Social Archaeology.* Oxford, U.K.: Blackwell, 1990.

Hodder, Ian and Robert Preucel, eds. *Contemporary Archaeology in Theory.* Oxford: Blackwell, 1996.

Holl, Augustin F. C. "Livestock Husbandry, Pastoralisms, and Territoriality: The West African Record." *Journal of Anthropological Archaeology* 17 (1998): 143–65.

Holl, Augustin F. C. "The Dawn of African Pastoralisms: An Introductory Note." *Journal of Anthropological Archaeology* 17.2 (1998): 81–165.

Hooton, Earnest Albert. *Apes, Men, and Morons.* G.P. Putnam, New York, 1937.

Horz, G, and M. Kallfass. "The treasure of gold and silver artifacts from the Royal Tombs of Sipan, Peru: a study on the Moche metalworking techniques." *Materials Characterization* 45 (2000): 391–420.

Hosler, Dorothy. "Sound, Color, and Meaning in the Metallurgy of Ancient West Mexico." *World Archaeology* 27.1 (1995): 100–15.

Houston, Stephen D. "Into the Minds of Ancients: Advances in Maya Glyph Studies." *Journal of World Prehistory* 14.2 (2000): 121–201.

Hovers, Erella, William H. Kimbel, and Yoel Rak. "The Amud 7 Skeleton—Still a Burial. Response to Gargett." *Journal of Human Evolution* 39 (2000): 253–60.

Howard, Edgar B. "An Outline of the Problem of Man's Antiquity in North America." *American Anthropologist* 38 (1936): 394–413.

Hublin, J.J., et al. "The Mousterian Site of Zafarrya (Andalucía, Spain): Dating and Implications on the Paleolithic Peopling Processes of Western Europe." *Comptes Rendus de l'Académie des Sciences,* Serie IIa 321.10 (1995): 931–37.

Huckell, Bruce B., and J. David Kilby, eds. *Readings in Late Pleistocene North America and Early Paleoindians: Selections from American Antiquity.* Washington, DC: Society for American Archaeology, 2004.

Hudson, B. "Restoration and reconstruction of monuments at Bagan (Pagan), Myanmar (Burma), 1995–2008." *World Archaeology* 40 (2008): 553–71.

Huffman, O. Frank. "Geologic Context and Age of the Perning/Mojokerto *Homo erectus,* East Java." *Journal of Human Evolution* 40 (2001): 353–62.

Huffman, Thomas. "Mapungubwe and Great Zimbabwe: The origin and spread of social complexity in southern Africa." *Journal of Anthropological Archaeology* 28 (2009): 37–54.

Humle, Tatyana, and Tetsuro Matsuzawa. "Ant-Dipping among the Chimpanzees of Bossou, Guinea, and Some Comparisons with Other Sites." *American Journal of Primatology* 58 (2002): 133–48.

Hunt, Gavin R. "Manufacture and Use of Hook-Tools by New Caledonian Crows." *Nature* 379.6562 (1996): 249–51.

Hunt, Gavin R., and Russell D. Gray. "Diversification and Cumulative Evolution in New Caledonian Crow Tool Manufacture." *The Royal Society* 270 (2003): 867–74.

Hunter, John, and Ian Ralston. *The Archaeology of Britain: An Introduction from the Upper Palaeolithic to the Industrial Revolution.* London: Routledge, 1999.

Hyodo, Masayuki, et al. "Paleomagnetic Dates of Hominid Remains from Yuanmou, China, and Other Asian Sites." *Journal of Human Evolution* 43 (2002): 27–41.

Hyslop, John, and American Council of Learned Societies. *Inka Settlement Planning.* Austin, TX: University of Texas Press, 1990.

Hyslop, John. *The Inka Road System. Studies in Archaeology.* Orlando, FL: Academic Press, 1984.

Imamura, Keiji. *Prehistoric Japan: New Perspectives on Insular East Asia.* Honolulu: University of Hawaii Press, 1996.

Ingman, M., et al. "Mitochondrial Genome Variation and the Origin of Modern Humans." *Nature* 408 (2000): 708–13.

Ingold, Tim. *Hunters, Pastoralists, and Ranchers: Reindeer Economics and their Transformations.* Cambridge, U.K.: Cambridge University Press, 1980.

Ingold, Tim. *The Perception of the Environment: Essays on Livelihood, Dwelling and Skill.* London: Routledge, 2000.

Inomata, Takeshi, and Laura R. Stiver. "Floor Assemblages from Burned Structures at Aguateca, Guatemala: A Study of Classic Maya Households." *Journal of Field Archaeology* 25.4 (1998): 431–52.

Isaac, Barbara. "Implementation of NAGPRA: The Peabody Museum of Archaeology and Ethnology, Harvard." *The Dead and Their Possessions: Repatriation in Principle, Policy and Practice.* Eds. C. Fforde, J. Hubert, and P. Turnbull. London: Routledge, 2002. 160–70.

Jablonski, David. "Extinction: Past and Present." *Nature* 427 (2004): 589.

Jacknis, Ira. "Repatriation as Social Drama: The Kwakiutl Indians of British Columbia, 1992–1980." *American Indian Quarterly* 20.2 (1996): 274–86.

Janes, Robert R. *Archaeological Ethnography among Mackenzie Basin Dene, Canada.* Calgary, AB: Arctic Institute of North America, the University of Calgary, 1983.

Jansen, M. "Water Supply and Sewage Disposal at Mohenjo-Daro." *World Archaeology* 21.2 (1989): 177–92.

Jantz, R.L., and Douglas W. Owsley. "Variation among Early North American Crania." *American Journal of Physical Anthropology* 114 (2001): 146–55.

Jarrige, J.F. *Les Cités Oubliées de L'indus.* Paris: Musée National des Arts Asiatiques Guimet, 1989.

Jennings, J. "The fragility of imperialist ideology and the end of local traditions, an Inca example." *Cambridge Archaeological Journal* 13.1 (2003): 107–20.

Jing, Y., and R. Flad. "New zooarchaeological evidence for changes in Shang Dynasty animal sacrifice." *Journal of Anthropological Archaeology* 24 (2005): 252–70.

Jing, Z., George Rapp, and T. Gao. "Geoarchaeological aids in the investigation of Early Shang Civilization on the floodplain of the Lower Yellow River, China." *World Archaeology* 29 (1997): 36–50.

Jones, Rhys, and J. Allen. *Archaeological Research in Kakadu National Park.* Canberra, Australia: Australian National Parks and Wildlife Service, 1985.

Joyce, R., and J. Lopiparo. "PostScript: Doing agency in archaeology." *Journal of Archaeological Method and Theory* 12 (2005): 365–74.

Joyce, Rosemary A. "Academic Freedom, Stewardship and Cultural Heritage: Weighing the Interests of Stakeholders in Crafting Repatriation Approaches." *The Dead and Their Possessions: Repatriation in Principle, Policy, and Practice.* Eds. C. Fforde, J. Hubert and P. Turnbull. London: Routledge, 2002. 99–107.

Juzhong, Zhang, and Wang Xiangkun. "Notes on the Recent Discovery of Ancient Cultivated Rice at Jiahu, Henan Province: A New Theory Concerning the Origin of Oryza Japonica in China." *Antiquity* 72 (1998): 897–901.

Kaessmann, H., and S. Paabo. "The Genetical History of Humans and the Great Apes." *Journal of Internal Medicine* 251 (2002): 1–18.

Kaplan, Lawrence, and Thomas F. Lynch. "Phaseolus (Fabaceae) in Archaeology: AMS Radiocarbon Dates and Their Significance for Pre-Columbian Agriculture." *Economic Botany* 53.3 (1999): 261–72.

Kappelman, John. "The Evolution of Body Mass and Relative Brain Size in Fossil Hominids." *Journal of Human Evolution* 30 (1996): 243–76.

Katzenberg, Anne M., et al. "Stable Isotope Evidence for Maize Horticulture and Paleodiet in Southern Ontario." *American Antiquity* 60 (1995): 335–50.

Keatinge, Richard W., ed. *Peruvian Prehistory.* Cambridge, U.K.: Cambridge University Press, 1988.

Keefer, David K., et al. "Early Maritime Economy and El Niño Events at Quebrada Tacahuay, Peru." *Science* 281 (1998): 1833–35.

Keeley, Lawrence. "Technique and Methodology in Microwear Studies: A Critical Review." *World Archaeology* 5 (2001): 323–36.

Kehoe, A. "The invention of prehistory." *Current Anthropology* 43 (1991): 467–76.

Keightley, David N. "Sacred Characters." *China: Ancient Culture, Modern Land.* Ed. Robert E. Murowchick. Norman, OK: Oklahoma University Press, 1994. 70–79.

Keightley, David N. *The Ancestral Landscape: Time, Space, and Community in Late Shang China,* ca. 1200–1045 B.C. Berkeley, CA: University of California Center for Chinese Studies, 2000.

Kelley, Jane H., and Ronald Williamson. "The positioning of archaeology within anthropology: A Canadian historical perspective." *American Antiquity* 61.1 (1996): 5–20.

Kelly, R. "The three sides of a biface." *American Antiquity* 53 (1988): 717–34.

Kemp, Barry J. *Ancient Egypt: Anatomy of a Civilization.* London: Routledge, 1991.

Kenoyer, Jonathan M. *Ancient Cities of the Indus Valley Civilization*. 1st Ed. Karachi and Islamabad, Pakistan: Oxford University Press and American Institute of Pakistan Studies, 1998.

Kenyon, K. *Excavations at Jericho, Vol. 3: The Architecture and Stratigraphy of the Tell*. London: British School of Archaeology in Jerusalem, 1981.

Kidd, Kenneth E. *The Excavation of Ste Marie I*. Toronto: University of Toronto Press, 1949.

Kidder, Alfred Vincent, and Samuel James Guernsey. *Archeological Explorations in Northeastern Arizona*. Washington, DC: Govt. Print. Off., 1919.

Killian, Gerald. *David Boyle: From Artisan to Archaeologist*. Toronto: University of Toronto Press, 1983.

Killen, J.T. "Critique: a view from the tablets." *Rethinking Mycenaean Palaces II*, Ed. Michael Galaty and William Parkinson. Cotsen Institute, Los Angeles, 2007.

Kimbel, W.H., et al. "Late Pliocene *Homo* and Oldowan Tools from Hadar Formation (Kada Hadar Member), Ethiopia." *Journal of Human Evolution* 289 (1996): 550–61.

Kinahan, John. "The Rise and Fall of Nomadic Pastoralism in the Central Namib Desert." *The Archaeology of Africa: Food, Metals, and Towns*. ed. Thurstan Shaw. London: Routledge, 1993. 373–85.

King, Maureen L., and Sergei B. Slobodin. "A Fluted Point from the Uptar Site, Northeastern Siberia." *Science* 273 (1996): 634–36.

Kirch, Patrick. *The Lapita Peoples: Ancestors of the Oceanic World*. Oxford: Blackwell, 1997.

Kirch, Patrick. *On the Road of the Winds: An Archaeological History of the Pacific Islands before European Contact*. Berkeley: University of California Press, 2000.

Kislev, Mordechai, Anat Hartmann, and O. Bar-Yosef. "Early Domesticated Fig in the Jordan Valley." *Science* 312 (2006): 1372–74.

Kittler, R., M. Kayser, and M. Stoneking. "Molecular evolution of *Pediculus humanus* and the origin of clothing." *Current Biology* 13 (2003): 1414–17.

Klein, Richard G. "Whither the Neanderthals?" *Science* 299 (2003): 1525–26.

Klein, Richard G., and Blake Edgar. *The Dawn of Human Culture*. New York: Wiley, 2002.

Knappett, C. "The Neglected Networks of Material Agency: Artefacts, Pictures and Texts." *Material Agency*. Eds. C. Knappett and L. Malafouris. New York: Springer, 2008. 139–156.

Knappett, C., T. Evans, and R. Rivers. "Modelling maritime interactions in the Aegean Bronze Age." *Antiquity* 89 (2008): 1009–24.

Knecht, Heidi, Anne Pike-Tay, and Randall Keith White. *Before Lascaux: The Complex Record of the Early Upper Paleolithic*. Boca Raton, FL: CRC Press, 1993.

Knuth, Gigil. *Archaeology of the Musk-Ox Way*. Paris: Sorbonne, 1967.

Kolata, Alan L. *Tiwanaku and Its Hinterland: Archaeology and Paleoecology of an Andean Civilization. Smithsonian Series in Archaeological Inquiry*. Washington, DC: Smithsonian Institution Press, 1996.

Kolata, Alan L. *The Tiwanaku: Portrait of an Andean Civilization*. Cambridge, MA: Blackwell, 1993.

Kolata, Alan L. *Tiwanaku and Its Hinterland: Archaeology and Paleoecology of an Andean Civilization*. Washington, D.C.: Smithsonian Institute Press, 1996.

Kooyman, B. *Understanding Stone Tools and Archaeological Sites*. Calgary: University of Alberta Press, 2000.

Kramer, Carol. *Village Ethnoarchaeology: Rural Iran in Archaeological Perspective*. New York: Academic Press, 1982.

Krings, Matthias, et al. "DNA Sequence of the Mitochrondrial Hypervariable Region II from the Neanderthal Type Specimen." *Proceedings of the National Academy of Sciences* 96 (1999): 5581–85.

Lambers, K., et al. "Combining photogrammetry and laser scanning for the recording and modelling of the Late Intermediate Period site of Pinchango Alto, Palpa, Peru." *Journal of Archaeological Science* 34 (2007): 1702–12.

Langbroek, Marco, and Wil Roebroeks. "Extraterrestrial Evidence on the Age of the Hominids from Java." *Journal of Human Evolution* 38 (2000): 595–600.

Lanpo, Jia, and Huang Weiwen. *The Story of Peking Man: From Archaeology to Mystery*. Oxford: Oxford University Press, 1990.

Larsen, C.S. "The changing face of bioarchaeology: an interdisciplinary science." *Bioarchaeology: The Contextual Analysis of Human Remains*, Ed. J. Buikstra and L. Beck. Amsterdam: Academic Press, 2006. 359–74.

Larson, Edward J. *Summer for the Gods: The Scopes Trial and America's Continuing Debate Over Science and Religion*. New York: Basic Books, 1997.

Lauck, Rebecca Gonzalez. "La Venta: An Olmec Capital." *Olmec Art of Ancient Mexico*. Eds. Elizabeth P. Benson and Beatriz de la Fuente. Washington, DC: National Gallery of Art, 1996. 73–82.

Lavallée, Danièle. *The First South Americans: The Peopling of a Continent from the Earliest Evidence to High Culture*. Salt Lake City, UT: University of Utah Press, 2000.

Laville, Henri, Jean Philippe Rigaud, and James Sackett. *Rock Shelters of the Perigord: Geological Stratigraphy and Archaeological Succession. Studies in Archaeology*. New York: Academic Press, 1980.

Leakey, Mary D. *Olduvai Gorge: Excavations in Beds I and II, 1960–1963*. Olduvai Gorge; 3. Cambridge: Cambridge University Press, 1971.

Leakey, Mary D., and John Michael Harris, eds. *Laetoli, a Pliocene Site in Northern Tanzania*. Oxford, U.K.: Clarendon Press and Oxford University Press, 1987.

Leakey, Mary D., et al. "New Four Million Year Old Hominid Species from Kanpoi and Allia Bay, Kenya." *Nature* 393 (1995): 62–66.

Leakey, Meave G., et al. "New Hominid Genus from Eastern Africa Shows Diverse Middle Pliocene Lineages." *Nature* 410 (2001): 433–40.

Leakey, Richard E., and Alan Walker. *The Nariokotome Homo erectus Skeleton*. Cambridge, MA: Harvard University Press, 1993.

Lebot, V. "Biomolecular Evidence for Plant Domestication in Sahul." *Genetic Resources and Crop Evolution* 46 (1999): 619–28.

Lechtman, H., A. Erliz, and E. Barry. "New perspectives on Moche metallurgy: Techniques of gilding copper at Loma Negra, Northern Peru." *American Antiquity* 47 (1982): 3–30.

Lee, Richard B. *The Dobe Ju/'Hoansi. Case Studies in Cultural Anthropology*. 3rd ed. South Melbourne, Australia: Wadsworth Thomson Learning, 2003.

Lee, Yun Kuen. "Control strategies and polity competition in the lower Yi-Luo Valley, North China." *Journal of Anthropological Archaeology* 23 (2004): 175–92.

Lehner, Mark. *The Complete Pyramids*. New York: Thames and Hudson, 1997.

Leone, Mark, Parker Potter, and Paul Shackel. "Toward a Critical Archaeology." *Current Anthropology* 28.3 (1987): 283–302.

Lepofsky, D. and N. Lyons. "Modeling ancient plant use on the Northwest Coast: towards an understanding of mobility and sedentism." *Journal of Archaeological Science* 30 (2003): 1357–71.

Lepper, Bradley T., and Richard W. Yerkes. "Hopewellian Occupations at the Northern Periphery of the Newark Earthworks: The Newark Expressway Sites Revisited." *Ohio Hopewell Community Organization*. Eds. William S. Dancey and Paul J. Pacheco. Kent, OH: Ohio University Press, 1997. 175–206.

Leroi-Gourhan, André. *Pincevent: Campement Magdalénien de Chasseurs de Rennes. Guides Archéologiques de la France*, 3. Paris: Ministère de la Culture, Direction du Patrimoine, 1984.

Leroi-Gourhan, Arlette. "The Flowers Found with Shanidar IV, a Neanderthal Burial in Iraq." *Science* 190.4214 (1975): 562–64.

Lewontin, Richard C. *Human Diversity.* Scientific American Library: [Distributed by] W.H. Freeman, New York, 1982.

Li, Xueqin, et al. "The Earliest Writing? Sign Use in the Seventh Millennium B.C. at Jiahu, Henan Province, China." *Antiquity* 77.295 (2002): 31–44.

Lieberman, Daniel E. "Another Face in Our Family Tree." *Nature* 410 (2001): 419–20.

Lieberman, L., and F.L.C. Jackson. "Race and three models of human origin." *American Anthropologist* 97 (1995): 231–42.

Lillios, Katina. "Objects of memory. The ethnography and archaeology of heirlooms." *Journal of Archaeological Method and Theory* 6.2 (1999): 235–62.

Linares, O. "African Rice (*Oryza glaberrima*): History and Future Potential." *Proceedings of the National Academy of Science* 99.25 (2002): 16360–65.

Linduff, K., R. Drennan, and G. Shelach. "Early complex societies in NE China: The Chifeng International Collaborative Archaeological Research Project." *Journal of Field Archaeology* 29 (2004): 45–73.

Liu, Li, and Xingcan Chen. *State Formation in Early China.* London: Duckworth, 2003.

Liu, Li, et al. "Settlement patterns and development of social complexity in the Yiluo Region, North China." *Journal of Field Archaeology* 29 (2004): 75–100.

Lloyd, Seton. *The Archaeology of Mesopotamia: From the Old Stone Age to the Persian Conquest.* London: Thames and Hudson, 1978.

Londo, J., et al. "Phylogeography of Asian Wild Rice, *Oryza rufipogen*, Reveals Multiple Independent Domestications of Cultivated Rice, *Oryza sativa*." *Proceedings of the National Academy of Science* 103.25 (2006): 9578–83.

Lordkipanidze, David, et al. "The Earliest Toothless Hominin Skull." *Nature* 434 (2005): 717–18.

Loring Brace, C., et al. "Old World Sources of the First New World Human Inhabitants: A Comparative Craniofacial View." *Proceedings of the National Academy of Sciences* 98.17 (2001): 10017–22.

Losier, L.M., J. Pouliot, and M. Fortin. "3D geometrical modeling of excavation units at the archaeological site of Tell 'Acharneh (Syria)." *Journal of Archaeological Science* 34 (2007): 272–88.

Lourandos, Harry. *Continent of Hunter–Gatherers: New Perspectives in Australian Prehistory.* Cambridge, U.K.: Cambridge University Press, 1997.

Lu, H. et al. "Earliest domestication of common millet (*Panicum miliaceum*) in East Asia extended to 10,000 years ago." *Proceedings of the National Academy of Sciences* 106.18 (2009): 7367–72.

Lu, Tracey L.D. "Some Botanical Characteristics of Green Foxtail (*Setaria viridis*) and Harvesting Experiments on the Grass." *Antiquity* 72.278 (1998): 902–07.

Lu, Tracey L.D. *The Transition from Foraging to Farming and the Origin of Agriculture in China.* Bar International Series. Vol. 774. Oxford, U.K.: BAR, 1999.

Lynch, Thomas F., ed. *Guitarrero Cave: Early Man in the Andes.* New York: Academic Press, 1980.

Lyons, Diane, and A. Catherine D'Andrea. "Griddles, ovens and agricultural origins: An ethnoarchaeological study of bread baking in Highland Ethiopia." *American Anthropologist* 105.3 (2003): 515–30.

Maag, C. "Ohio Indian mounds: hallowed ground and a nice par 3." *New York Times,* (November 25, 2005).

Mabry, Jonathan B. "Changing Knowledge About the First Farmers in Southeastern Arizona." *The Late Archaic: Across the Borderlands.* ed. Bradley J. Vierra. Austin, TX: University of Texas Press, 2005. 41–83.

MacGillivray, J.A. *Minotaur: Sir Arthur Evans and the Archaeology of the Minoan Myth.* New York: Hill and Wang, 2000.

Mack, M.E., and M.L. Blakey. "The New York African Burial Ground Project: Past Biases, Current Dilemmas, and Future Research Opportunities." *Historical Archaeology* 38.1 (2004): 10–17.

Magid, Anwar A., and Isabella Caneva. "Economic Strategy Based on Food-Plants in the Early Holocene Central Sudan: A Reconsideration." *Before Food Production in North Africa.* Eds. Savino di Lernia and Giorgio Manzi. Forli, Italy: A.B.A.C.O. Edizioni, 1998. 79–90.

Mallory-Greenough, L., J.D. Greenough, and J.V. Owen. "The Origin and Use of Basalt in Old Kingdom Funerary Temples." *Geoarchaeology* 15.4 (2000): 315–30.

Mandryk, Carole A.S., et al. "Late Quaternary Paleoenvironments of Northwestern North America: Implications for Inland Versus Coastal Migration Routes." *Quaternary Science Reviews* No. 20 (2001): 301–14.

Manning, S.W., et al. "Chronology for the Aegean Late Bronze Age 1700–1400 B.C." *Science* 312.5773 (2006): 565–69.

Marean, C., et al. "Early human use of marine resources and pigment in South Africa during the Middle Pleistocene." *Nature* 449 (2007): 905–08.

Marshack, Alexander. "Upper Paleolithic Notation and Symbol." *Science* 178 (1972): 817–28.

Marshall, Fiona, and Elisabeth Hildebrand. "Cattle before Crops: The Beginnings of Food Production in Africa." *Journal of World Prehistory* 16.2 (2002): 99–143.

Marshall, John. "A New Chapter in Archaeology: The Prehistoric Civilisation of the Indus." *Illustrated London News* (January 7, 1928).

Martin, R.D., et al. "Comment on 'the Brain of Lb1, *Homo floresiensis*.'" *Science* 312 (2006): 999.

Martin, Simon. "In Line of the Founder: A View of Dynastic Politics at Tikal." *Tikal: Dynasties, Foreigners, and Affairs of State.* Ed. Jeremy Sabloff. Santa Fe, NM: SAR Press, 2003.

Martindale, Andrew. "A Hunter–Gatherer Paramount Chiefdom: Tsimshian Developments through the Contact System." *Emerging from the Mist: Studies in Northwest Coast Culture History.* Ed. R. G. Matson, Gary Coupland, and Quentin Mackie. Vancouver: UBC Press, 2003. 12–50.

Martindale, A. and I. Jurakic. "Northern Tsimshian elderberry use in the late pre-contact to post-contact era." *Canadian Journal of Archaeology* 28 (2004): 254–80.

Mason, R.B. and L. Cooper. "Petrographic Analysis of Bronze Age Pottery from Tell Hadidi, Syria." *Levant* 31 (1999): 135–47.

Mathieu, James. *Experimental Archaeology: Replicating Past Objects, Behaviors, and Processes.* Oxford: Archaeopress, 2002.

Matos Moctezuma, Eduardo, and Michel Zabé. *Treasures of the Great Temple.* Eng. language ed. La Jolla, CA: ALTI Pub., 1990.

Matos Moctezuma, Eduardo. "Aztec History and Cosmovision." *Moctezuma's Mexico: Visions of the Aztec World.* Eds. David Carrasco and Eduardo Matos Moctezuma. Boulder, CO: University of Colorado, 1992. 3–99.

Matos Moctezuma, Eduardo. *The Great Temple of the Aztecs: Treasures of Tenochtitlán.* New Aspects of Antiquity. London: Thames and Hudson, 1988.

Matson, R.G. "The Spread of Maize Agriculture in the U.S. Southwest." *Examining the Farming/Language Dispersal Hypothesis.* Eds. Peter Bellwood and Colin Renfrew. Cambridge, U.K.: McDonald Institute for Archaeology, 2003. 341–56.

Matson, R.G. and Gary Coupland. *The Prehistory of the Northwest Coast.* New York: Academic Press, 1995.

Matsuoka, Y., et al. "A Single Domestication for Maize Shown by Multilocus Microsatellite Genotyping." *Proceedings of the National Academy of Sciences* 99.9 (2002): 6080–84.

Matthews, Roger. *The Archaeology of Mesopotamia: Theories and Approaches. Approaching the Ancient World.* London and New York: Routledge, 2003.

McBrearty, Sally, and Alison Brooks. "The Revolution That Wasn't: A New Interpretation of the Origin of Modern Human Behavior." *Journal of Human Evolution* 39.5 (2000): 453–563.

McCafferty, S.D. and G.G. McCafferty. "Engendering Tomb 7 at Monte Alban: Respinning an old yarn." *Current Anthropology* 35.2 (1994): 143–66.

McCauley, J.F. et al.. "Subsurface Valleys and Geoarchaeology of the Eastern Sahara." *Science* 218 (1982): 1004–20.

McDonald, Mary M.A. "Early African Pastoralism: View from Dakhleh Oasis (South Central Egypt)." *Journal of Anthropological Archaeology* 17 (1998): 124–42.

McElhinny, M.W. "Paleomagnetism: Continents and Oceans." *International Geophysics Series* 73 (2000): 333–76.

McGhee, Robert. *Ancient People of the Arctic.* Vancouver: UBC Press, 1996.

McGovern, Patrick, et al. "The Archaeological Origin and Significance of the Dolphin Vase as Determined by Neutron Activation Analysis." *Bulletin of the American Schools of Oriental Research* 296 (1994): 31–43.

McGuire, Bill. *The Archaeology of Geological Catastrophes.* London: Geological Society, 2000.

McGuire, Randall H. *Archaeology as Political Action.* Berkeley: University of California Press, 2008.

McIntosh, Roderick J. *The Peoples of the Middle Niger: The Island of Gold. Peoples of Africa.* Malden, MA: Blackwell Publishers, 1998.

McIntosh, Susan, and Roderick J. McIntosh. "Cities without Citadels: Understanding Urban Origins Along the Middle Niger." *The Archaeology of Africa: Food, Metals, and Towns.* Ed. Thurstan Shaw. London: Routledge, 1993. 622–41.

McKeown, Francis P. "Implementing a 'True Compromise': The Native American Graves Protection and Repatriation Act after Ten Years." *The Dead and Their Possessions: Repatriation in Principle, Policy, and Practice.* Eds. C. Fforde, J. Hubert, and P. Turnbull. London: Routledge, 2002. 108–32.

McNeil, C.L., D.A. Burney, and L.P. Burney. "Evidence disputing deforestation as the cause for the collapse of the ancient Maya polity of Copan, Honduras." *Proceedings of the National Academy of Sciences* 107.3 (2010): 1017–22.

Mellaart, James. *Çatal Hüyük: A Neolithic Town in Anatolia.* London: Thames and Hudson, 1967.

Mellars, Paul, and Chris Stringer. *The Human Revolution: Behavioural and Biological Perspectives on the Origins of Modern Humans.* Princeton, NJ: Princeton University Press, 1989.

Mellars, Paul. *The Neanderthal Legacy: An Archaeological Perspective from Western Europe.* Princeton, NJ: Princeton University Press, 1996.

Meltzer, David J., et al. "On the Pleistocene Antiquity of Monte Verde, Southern Chile." *American Antiquity* 62.4 (1997): 659–63.

Meltzer, David J., James M. Adovasio, and Tom D. Dillehay. "On a Pleistocene Human Occupation at Pedra Furada, Brazil." *Antiquity* 68 (1994): 695–714.

Mercader, Julio, et al. "4,300-year-old chimpanzee sites and the origins of percussive stone technology." *Proceedings of the American Academy of Sciences* 104.9 (2007): 3043–48.

Mercader, J. "Mozambican grass seed consumption during the Middle Stone Age." *Science* 326 (2009): 1680–83.

Mercader, Julio, Melissa Panger, and Christophe Boesch. "Excavation of a Chimpanzee Stone Tool Site in the African Rainforest." *Science* 296 (2002): 1452–55.

Meskell, Lynn, and Peter Pels. *Embedding Ethics.* Oxford, U.K. and New York: Berg, 2005.

Metcalf, Mary. "Construction and Labor at Pueblo Bonito: Center of the Chacoan World." *Pueblo Bonito: Center of the Chacoan World.* Ed. Jill E. Neitzel. Washington, DC: Smithsonian Institution Press, 2003.

Michab, M., et al. "Luminescence Dates for the Paleoindian Site of Pedra Pintada, Brazil." *Quaternary Geochronology* 17 (1998): 1041–46.

Millaire, J.F. "Primary state formation in the Virú Valley, North Coast of Peru." *Proceedings of the National Academy of Science* 107.14 (2010): 6186–91.

Miller, Gifford H., et al. "Pleistocene Extinction of *Genyornis newtoni*: Human Impact on Australian Megafauna." *Science* 283 (1999): 205–08.

Miller, Heather. *Archaeological Approaches to Technology.* New York: Academic/Elsevier, 2007.

Millon, R., R. Drewitt, and G. Cowgill. *Urbanization at Teotihuacán, Mexico.* Austin: University of Texas Press, 1973.

Millon, Rene. "Teotihuacán: Completion of Map of Giant Ancient City in the Valley of Mexico." *Science* 170 (1970): 1077–82.

Milner, George R. *The Cahokia Chiefdom: The Archaeology of a Mississippian Society. Smithsonian Series in Archaeological Inquiry.* Washington, DC: Smithsonian Institution Press, 1998.

Milo, R.G. "Evidence for Hominid Predation at Klasies River Mouth, South Africa, and Its Implications for the Behaviour of Early Modern Humans." *Journal of Archaeological Science* 25 (1998): 99–133.

Minnegal, Monica, and Peter D. Dwyer. "Intensification and Social Complexity in the Interior Lowlands of Papua New Guinea: A Comparison of Bedamuni and Kubo." *Journal of Anthropological Archaeology* 17 (1998): 375–400.

Minnis, Paul E., ed. *People and Plants in Ancient Eastern North America.* Washington, DC: Smithsonian Books, 2003.

Miracle, Preston. "Through the Clovis Barrier." *Antiquity* 73 (1999): 944–47.

Mitchell, P. "Practicing archaeology at a time of climatic catastrophe." *Antiquity* 82 (2008): 1093–103.

Mithen, Steven. "Technology and Society During the Middle Pleistocene: Hominid Group Size, Social Learning, and Industrial Variability." *Cambridge Archaeological Journal* 4.1 (1994): 3–32.

Molloy, B. *The Cutting Edge: Studies in Ancient and Medieval Combat.* Stroud: Tempus, 2007.

Molloy, B. "Martial arts and materiality: a combat archaeology perspective on Aegean swords of the fifteenth and fourteenth centuries B.C." *World Archaeology* 40 (2008): 116–34.

Monks, Greg. "The Cultural Taphonomy of Nuu-chah-nulth Whale Bone Assemblages." *Emerging from the Mist: Studies in Northwest Coast Culture History.* Ed. R. G. Matson, Gary Coupland, and Quentin Mackie. Vancouver: UBC Press, 2003. 188–212.

Montgomery, John. *Tikal: An Illustrated History: The Ancient Maya Capital.* New York: Hippocrene Books, 2001.

Moore, A. M. T., Gordon C. Hillman, and A. J. Legge. *Village on the Euphrates: From Foraging to Farming at Abu Hureyra.* Oxford, U.K.: Oxford University Press, 2000.

Moore, M.W., et al. "Continuities in stone flaking technology at Liang Bua, Flores, Indonesia." *Journal of Human Evolution* 57 (2009): 503–26.

Morgan, Lewis Henry. *Ancient Society: Or, Researches in the Lines of Human Progress from Savagery, through Barbarism to Civilization.* Chicago: C.H. Kerr, 1877.

Morin, E. "Evidence for declines in human population densities during the early Upper Paleolithic in western Europe." *Proceedings of the National Academy of Science* 105.1 (2008): 48–53.

Morlan, Richard E. "Current Perspectives on the Pleistocene Archaeology of Eastern Beringia." *Quaternary Research* 60 (2003): 123–32.

Moro Abadía, O. "Art, crafts, and Paleolithic art." *Journal of Social Archaeology* 6.1 (2010): 119–41.

Morris, Craig, and Adriana Von Hagen. *The Inka Empire and Its Andean Origins.* New York: Abbeville, 1993.

Morris, Craig, and Donald E. Thompson. *Huánuco Pampa: An Inca City and Its Hinterland.* London: Thames and Hudson, 1985.

Mortensen, L. "Working borders: the contexts of Copan archaeology." *Archaeologies: Journal of the World Archaeological Congress* 3 (2007): 132–52.

Morwood, M., et al. "Archaeology and Age of a New Hominin from Flores in Eastern Indonesia." *Nature* 431 (2004): 1087–91.

Moser, S., et al. "Transforming archaeology through practice: strategies for collaborative archaeology and the community archaeology project at Quseir." *World Archaeology* 34 (2002): 220–48.

Muke, John, and Herman Mandui. "In the Shadows of Kuk: Evidence for Prehistoric Agriculture at Kana, Wahgi Valley, Papua New Guinea." *Archaeology of Oceania* 38 (2003): 177–85.

Murowchick, Robert E. *China: Ancient Culture, Modern Land. Cradles of Civilization.* North Sydney, Australia: Weldon Russell, 1994.

Murray, Tim. *Archaeology of Aboriginal Australia: A Reader.* St. Leonards, AUS: Allen & Unwin, 1998.

Muzzolini, A. "The Emergence of a Food-Producing Economy in the Sahara." *The Archaeology of Africa: Food, Metals, and Towns.* Ed. Thurstan Shaw. London: Routledge, 1993. 227–39.

Nadel, D., ed. *Ohalo Ii-II: A 23,000 Year-Old Fisher–Hunter–Gatherers' Camp on the Shore of the Sea of Galilee.* Haifa, Israel: Hecht Museum, 2002.

Naveh, Danny. "PPNA Jericho: A Socio-Political Perspective." *Cambridge Archaeological Journal* 13.1 (2003): 83–96.

Neitzel, Jill E. *Pueblo Bonito: Center of the Chacoan World.* Washington, DC: Smithsonian Institution Press, 2003.

Nelson, D.E., et al. "New Dates on Northern Yukon Artifacts: Holocene Not Upper Pleistocene." *Science* 232 (1986): 749–50.

Nelson, S.M. "Feasting the ancestors in early China." *The Archaeology and Politics of Food and Feasting in Early States and Empires.* Ed. T.L. Bray. New York: Kluwer, 2003. 65–89.

Nettle, Daniel. "Linguistic Diversity of the Americas Can Be Reconciled with a Recent Colonization." *Proceedings of the National Academy of Sciences* 96 (1999): 3325–29.

Neumann, Katharina. "New Guinea: A Cradle of Agriculture." *Science* 301 (2003): 180–81.

Nichols, D., et al. "Neutrons, markets, cities, and empires: A 1,000-year perspective on ceramic production and distribution in the Post-classic Basin of Mexico." *Journal of Anthropological Archaeology* 21 (2002): 25–82.

Nichols, Deborah L. "Rural and Urban Landscapes of the Aztec State." *Mesoamerican Archaeology: Theory and Practice.* Eds. Rosemary A. Joyce and Julia A. Hendon. Oxford, U.K.: Blackwell, 2004. 265–95.

Nichols, Deborah L., and Thomas H. Charlton. *The Archaeology of City–States: Cross-Cultural Approaches. Smithsonian Series in Archaeological Inquiry.* Washington, DC: Smithsonian Institution Press, 1997.

Niles, Susan A. "The Nature of Inca Royal Estates." *Machu Picchu: Unveiling the Mystery of the Incas.* Eds. Richard L. Burger and Lucy C. Salazar. New Haven, CT: Yale University Press, 2004.

Nissen, Hans. "Uruk: Key Site of the Period and Key Site of the Problem." *Artefacts of Complexity: Tracking the Uruk in the Near East.* Ed. J.N. Postgate. London: British School of Archaeology in Iraq, 2002. 1–17.

Nitecki, Matthew H. *Evolutionary Progress.* Chicago: University of Chicago Press, 1988.

Noonan, J.P., et al. "Sequencing and analysis of Neanderthal genomic DNA." *Science* 314 (2006): 1113–18.

Nora, Pierre. *Realms of Memory: Rethinking the French Past.* New York: Columbia University Press, 1996–1998.

O'Brien, M., and R.L. Lyman. "Evolutionary archeology: current status and future prospects." *Evolutionary Anthropology* 11 (2002): 26–36.

O'Connell, James, and Jim Allen. "When Did Humans First Arrive in Greater Australia and Why Is It Important to Know?" *Evolutionary Anthropology* 6.4 (1998): 132–46.

O'Connor, D. *Abydos: Egypt's First Pharaohs and the Cult of Osiris.* New York: Thames and Hudson, 2009.

O'Sullivan, Paul B., et al. "Archaeological Implications of the Geology and Chronology of the Soa Basin, Flores, Indonesia." *Geology* 29.7 (2001): 607–10.

Odell, George. "Stone Tool Research at the End of the Millennium: Classification, Function, and Behavior." *Journal of Archaeological Research* 9.1 (2001): 45–100.

Oppenheim, A. Leo, and Erica Reiner. *Ancient Mesopotamia: Portrait of a Dead Civilization.* Rev. ed. Chicago: University of Chicago Press, 1977.

Orser, Charles. *Historical Archaeology.* Upper Saddle River, NJ: Prentice Hall, 2004.

Ovchinnikov, Igor V., et al. "Molecular Analysis of Neanderthal DNA from the Northern Caucasus." *Nature* 404 (2000): 490–93.

Owsley, Douglas W., and Richard L. Jantz. "Archaeological Politics and Public Interest in Paleoamerican Studies: Lessons from Gordon Creek Woman and Kennewick Man." *American Antiquity* 66.4 (2001): 565–75.

Panagiotakis, M. "Contacts between Knossos and the Pediada Region in Central Crete." *Knossos: Palace, City, State.* Eds. E. Cadogan, E. Hatzaki, and A. Vasilakis. London: British School at Athens, 2004. 177–86.

Panger, Melissa A., et al. "Older Than the Oldowan? Rethinking the Emergence of Hominin Tool Use." *Evolutionary Anthropology* 11 (2002): 235–45.

Parker Pearson, M. "The age of Stonehenge." *Antiquity* 81 (2007): 617–39.

Parker Pearson, M., and Ramilisonina. "Stonehenge for the ancestors: the stones pass on the message." *Antiquity* 72 (1998): 308–26.

Parker Pearson, M., et al. "Who was buried at Stonehenge?" *Antiquity* 83 (2009): 23–29.

Parker Pearson, et al. *The Stonehenge Riverside Project Summary Interim Report 2005.* Published online at http://www.shef.ac.uk/content/1/c6/02/21/27/PDF-Interim-Report-2005-summary.pdf (2005).

Parkington, J., D. Morris, and N. Rusch. *Karoo Rock Engravings.* Cape Town: Creda, 2008.

Partridge, T.C., et al. "Lower Pliocene Hominid Remains from Sterkfontein." *Science* 300 (2003): 607–12.

Pasquinucci, Marinella, Frédéric Trément, and POPULUS Project. *Non-Destructive Techniques Applied to Landscape Archaeology. Archaeology of Mediterranean Landscapes* 4. Oxford, U.K. and Oakville, CT: Oxbow Books; David Brown Book Co. [distributor], 2000.

Patty Jo Watson, Steven LeBlanc, and Charles Redman. *Archaeological Explanation: The Scientific Method in Archaeology.* New York: Columbia University Press, 1984.

Pauketat, Timothy R. "Resettled Farmers and the Making of a Mississippian Polity." *American Antiquity* 68.1 (2003): 39–66.

Pauketat, Timothy R. *Ancient Cahokia and the Mississippians. Case Studies in Early Societies* 6. Cambridge, U.K.: Cambridge University Press, 2004.

Pauketat, Timothy R., et al. "The Residues of Feasting and Public Ritual at Early Cahokia." *American Antiquity* 67.2 (2002): 257–79.

Pavlov, Pavel, John Inge Svendsen, and Svein Indrelid. "Human Presence in the European Arctic Nearly 40,000 Years Ago." *Nature* 413 (2001): 64–67.

Pearson, Richard, and Anne Underhill. "The Chinese Neolithic: Recent Trends in Research." *American Anthropologist* 89 (1987): 807–22.

Pearson, Richard. "Social Complexity in Chinese: Coastal Neolithic Sites." *Science* 213 (1981): 1078–86.

Peretto, Carlo. "The First Peopling of Southern Europe: The Italian Case." *Comptes Rendus Palevol,* 5. 1–2 (2006): 283–90.

Perlés, Catherine. *The Early Neolithic in Greece: The First Farming Communities in Europe. Cambridge World Archaeology.* Cambridge, U.K.: Cambridge University Press, 2001.

Perry, Linda. "Starch Granule Size and the Domestication of Manioc (*Manihot esculenta*) and Sweet Potato (*Ipomoea batatas*)." *Economic Botany* 56.4 (2001): 335–49.

Phillipson, David W. "The Antiquity of Cultivation and Herding in Ethiopia." *The Archaeology of Africa: Food, Metals, and Towns.* Ed. Thurstan Shaw. London: Routledge, 1993. 344–57.

Pigeot, Nicole. *Magdaléniens d'Étiolles: Économie de Débitage et Organisation Sociale (l'Unité d'Habitation U5).* Paris: Editions du Centre National de la Recherche Scientifique, 1987.

Pikirayi, Innocent. *The Zimbabwe Culture: Origins and Decline in Southern Zambezian States.* Walnut Creek, CA: AltaMira Press, 2001.

Pineda, Rosa Fung. "The Late Preceramic and Initial Period." *Peruvian Prehistory.* Ed. Richard W. Keatinge. Cambridge, U.K.: Cambridge University Press, 1988. 67–98.

Pinter, N., and S. Ishman. "Impacts, mega-tsunami, and other extraordinary claims." *GSA Today* 18 (2008): 37–38.

Piperno, D. R., and K. V. Flannery. "The Earliest Archaeological Maize (*Zea mays* L.) from Highland Mexico: New Accelerator Mass Spectrometry Dates and Their Implications." *Proceedings of the National Academy of Sciences of the United States of America* 98.4 (2001): 2101–03.

Pitulko, V. V., et al. "The Yana RHS Site: Humans in the Arctic before the Last Glacial Maximum." *Science* 303 (2004): 52–56.

Plog, Stephen. *Ancient Peoples of the American Southwest.* London: Thames and Hudson, 1997.

Plug, I. "Resource Exploitation: Animal Use During the Middle Stone Age at Sibudu Cave, KwaZulu-Natal, South Africa." *South African Journal of Science* 100. 151–158 (2004).

Pollock, Susan. *Ancient Mesopotamia: The Eden That Never Was. Case Studies in Early Societies.* Cambridge, U.K.: Cambridge University Press, 1999.

Pope, Geoffrey. "Bamboo and Human Evolution." *Natural History* 98.10 (1989): 48–57.

Portal, Jane. *The Terracotta Warriors.* London: British Museum, 2007.

Postgate, J. N. *Artefacts of Complexity: Tracking the Uruk in the Near East.* Iraq Archaeological Reports; 5 [S.l]: British School of Archaeology in Iraq, 2002.

Postgate, J. N. *Early Mesopotamia: Society and Economy at the Dawn of History.* Rev. ed. London and New York: Routledge, 1994.

Potts, Richard. *Early Hominid Activities at Olduvai. Foundations of Human Behavior.* New York: A. de Gruyter, 1988.

Preece, R. C., et al. "Humans in the Hoxnian: habitat, context and fire use at Beeches Pit, West Stow, Suffolk, UK." *Journal of Quaternary Science* 21 (2006): 485–96.

Prentice, Guy. "Origins of Plant Domestication in the Eastern United States: Promoting the Individual in Archaeological Theory." *Southeastern Archaeology* 5 (1986): 103–19.

Preston, Douglas. "Fossils & the Folsom Cowboy." *Natural History* 106.1 (1997): 16–21.

Proctor, Robert. "From Anthropologie to Rassenkunde: Concepts of race in German physical anthropology." *Bones, Bodies, Behavior: Essays on Biological Anthropology.* Ed. G. Stocking. Madison: University of Wisconsing, 1988. 138–79.

Proskouriakoff, Tatiana. "The Lords of the Maya Realm." *Expedition* 4.1 (1961): 14–21.

Proskouriakoff, Tatiana. *An Album of Maya Architecture.* New ed. Norman, OK: University of Oklahoma Press, 1963.

Quilter, Jeffrey. "Moche politics, religion, and warfare." *Journal of World Prehistory* 16 (2002): 145–95.

Quilter, Jeffrey, et al. "Subsistence Economy of El Paraíso, an Early Peruvian Site." *Science* 251 (1991): 277–83.

Quilter, Jeffrey. "Architecture and Chronology at El Paraíso, Peru." *Journal of Field Archaeology* 12 (1985): 279–97.

Quilter, Jeffrey. *Life and Death at Paloma: Society and Mortuary Practices in a Preceramic Peruvian Village.* Iowa City, IA: University of Iowa Press, 1989.

Radovanovic, Ivana. "Houses and Burials at Lepenski Vir." *European Journal of Archaeology* 3.3 (2000): 330–49.

Rasmussen, M. et al. "Ancient human genome sequence of an extinct Palaeo-Eskimo." *Nature* (2010): 757–62.

Rawson, Jessica. "The first emperor's tomb: the afterlife universe." *The First Emperor: China's Terracotta Army.* Ed. Jane Portal. London: British Museum, 2007. 114–52.

Raymond, J. Scott. "A View from the Tropical Forest." *Peruvian Prehistory.* ed. Richard W. Keatinge. Vol. 279–302. Cambridge, U.K.: Cambridge University Press, 1988.

Reese-Taylor, K. "Naachtun: A lost city of the Maya." Posted on BBC: *Archaeology in Depth* http://www.bbc.co.uk/history/archaeology/excavations_techniques/maya_naachtun_01.shtml, 2005.

Reitz, Elizabeth J. "Faunal Remains from Paloma, an Archaic Site in Peru." *American Anthropology* 90 (1988): 310–22.

Reitz, Elizabeth Jean, and Elizabeth S. Wing. *Zooarchaeology.* Cambridge: Cambridge University Press, 2008.

Renfrew, Colin. "Introduction: peer polity interaction and socio-political change." *Peer Polity Interaction and Socio-political Change.* Ed. Colin Renfrew and John Cherry. Cambridge: Cambridge University Press, 1986. 1–18.

Renfrew, Colin, and John F. Cherry. *Peer Polity Interaction and Socio-political Change.* Cambridge: Cambridge University Press, 1986.

Renfrew, Colin, Peter Forster, and Mathew Hurles. "The Past within Us." *Nature Genetics* 26 (2000): 253–54.

Renfrew, Colin. *Archaeology and Language: The Puzzle of Indo-European Origins.* New York: Cambridge University Press, 1990.

Renfrew, Colin. *Social Archaeology.* Edinburgh, U.K.: Edinburgh University Press, 1984.

Richards, M. P., et al. "Stable Isotope Evidence of Diet at Neolithic Çatalhöyük, Turkey." *Journal of Archaeological Science* 30 (2003): 67–76.

Richards, Michael P., et al. "Neanderthal Diet at Vindija and Neanderthal Predation: The Evidence from Stable Isotopes." *Proceedings of the National Academy of Sciences* 97.13 (2000): 7663–66.

Rindos, David. *The Origins of Agriculture: An Evolutionary Perspective.* San Diego, CA: Academic Press, 1984.

Roberts, Mark, and Simon Parfitt. *Boxgrove: A Middle Pleistocene Hominid Site at Eartham Quarry, Boxgrove, West Sussex.* London: English Heritage, 1999.

Roberts, Richard G., et al. "New Ages for the Last Australian Megafauna: Continent-Wide Extinction about 46,000 Years Ago." *Science* 292 (2001): 1888–90.

Roberts, Richard G., et al. "The Human Colonisation of Australia: Optical Dates of 53,000 and 60,000 Years Bracket Human Arrival at Deaf Adder Gorge, Northern Territory." *Quaternary Science Reviews* 13 (1994): 575–83.

Roberts, Richard, et al. "Luminescence Dating of Rock Art and Past Environments Using Mud-Wasp Nests in Northern Australia." *Nature* 387 (1997): 696–99.

Robertshaw, Peter. "The Beginnings of Food Production in Southwestern Kenya." *The Archaeology of Africa: Food, Metals, and Towns.* Ed. Thurstan Shaw. London: Routledge, 1998. 358–71.

Robin, Cynthia. "New Directions in Classic Maya Household Archaeology." *Journal of Archaeological Research* 11.4 (2003): 307–56.

Robinson, K. and D.W. Griffiths. *Investigations of a Potential Shipwreck site, Temlar Channel, Clayquot Sound, B.C.* Tofino, British Columbia: Tonquin Foundation, 2005.

Roche, H., et al. "Early Hominid Stone Tool Production and Technical Skill 2.34 Myr Ago in West Turkana, Kenya." *Nature* 399 (1999): 57–60.

Rohling, E.J., et al. "Magnitudes of Sea-Level Lowstands of the Past 500,000 Years." *Nature* 394 (1998): 162–65.

Roksandic, M., et al. "Interpersonal Violence at Lepenski Vir Mesolithic/ Neolithic Complex of the Iron Gates Gorge (Serbia-Romania)." *American Journal of Physical Anthropology* 129.3 (2006): 339–48.

Rollefson, Gary O. "Ritual and Social Structure In Neolithic 'Ain Ghazal." *Life in Neolithic Farming Communities.* Ed. I Kuijt. New York: Plenum, 2000. 165–90.

Roosevelt, A.C., et al. "Paleoindian Cave Dwellers in the Amazon: The Peopling of the Americas." *Science* 272 (1996): 373–84.

Rosen, Steven. "Paradigms and politics in the terminal Pleistocene archaeology of the Levant." *Perspectives on the Past: Theoretical Biases in Mediterraean Hunter–Gatherer Research.* Ed. Geoffrey Clark. Philadelphia: University of Pennsylvania Press, 1991.

Roth, A.M. *Egyptian Phyles in the Old Kingdom: The Evolution of a System of Social Organization. Studies in Ancient Oriental Civilization.* Vol. 48. Chicago: Oriental Institute of the University of Chicago, 1991.

Rothman, Mitchell S. "Studying the Development of Complex Society: Mesopotamia in the Late Fifth and Fourth Millennia B.C." *Journal of Archaeological Research* 12.1 (2004): 75–119.

Rothman, Mitchell S. *Uruk Mesopotamia and Its Neighbors: Cross-Cultural Interactions in the Era of State Formation. School of American Research Advanced Seminar Series.* Santa Fe, NM: School of American Research Press, 2001.

Russon, Anne E. "Return of the Native: Cognition and site-specific expertise in orangutan rehabilitation." *International Journal of Primatology* 23.3 (2001): 461–78.

Ruvolo, M. "Genetic Diversity in Hominid Primates." *Annual Review of Anthropology* 26 (1997): 515–40.

Ruvolo, Maryellen. "Molecular Phylogeny of the Hominoids: Inferences from Multiple Independent DNA Sequence Data Sets." *Molecular Biological Evolution* 14.3 (1997): 248–65.

Sabloff, Jeremy, and Gordon Willery. *A History of American Archaeology.* San Francisco: Freeman, 1980.

Sahlins, Marshall David. *Stone Age Economics.* Chicago: Aldine-Atherton, 1972.

Salomon, F. "How an Andean "writing without words" works." *Current Anthropology* 42 (2001): 2–27.

Sandweiss, Daniel H., et al. "Geoarchaeological Evidence from Peru for a 5000 Years B.P. Onset of El Ni–o." *Science* 273 (1996): 1531–32.

Sandweiss, Daniel H., et al. "Quebrada Jaguay: Early South American Maritime Adaptations." *Science* 281 (1998): 1830–32.

Sandweiss, Daniel H., et al. "Variation in Holocene El Ni–o Frequencies: Climate Records and Cultural Consequences in Ancient Peru." *Geology* 29.7 (2001): 603–06.

Santos, G.M., et al. "A Revised Chronology of the Lowest Occupation Layer of Pedra Furada Rock Shelter, Brazil: The Pleistocene Peopling of the Americas." *Quaternary Science Reviews* 22 (2003): 2303–10.

Saraydar, Stephen C. *Replicating the Past: The Art and Science of the Archaelogical Experiment.* Long Grove: Waveland Press, 2008.

Sassaman, Kenneth. "Structure and practice in the Archaic Southeast." *North American Archaeology.* Ed. Timothy Pauketat and DIana DiPaolo Loren. Malden: Blackwell, 2005. 79–107.

Saunders, J.W., et al. "A mound complex in Louisiana at 5,400–5,000 years before present." *Science* 277 (1997): 1796–99.

Scarre, Christopher. *The Seventy Wonders of the Ancient World: The Great Monuments and How They Were Built.* New York: Thames & Hudson, 1999.

Scarre, Christopher, and Geoffrey Scarre. *The Ethics of Archaeology: Philosophical Perspectives on Archaeological Practice.* Cambridge, U.K.: Cambridge University Press, 2006.

Scarre, Christopher, and Graeme Lawson, eds. *Archaeoacoustics.* Cambridge: McDonald Institute for Archaeological Research, 2006.

Schaepe, David. "Rock Fortification: Archaeological Insights into Pre-Contact Warfare and Sociopolitical Organization Among the Sto:lo of the Lower Fraser River Canyon, B.C." *American Antiquity* 71.4 (2006): 671–706.

Scham, S., and A. Yahya. "Heritage and reconciliation." *Journal of Social Archaeology* 3 (2003): 399–416.

Schele, Linda, and L. Miller. *The Blood of Kings: Dynasty and Ritual in Maya Art.* New York and Fort Worth, TX: G. Braziller and Kimbell Art Museum, 1986.

Schick, Kathy D., et al. "Continuing Investigations into the Stone Tool-Making and Tool-Using Capabilities of a Bonobo *(Pan Paniscus)*." *Journal of Archaeological Science* 26 (1999): 821–32.

Schick, Kathy, and Nicholas Toth. *Making Silent Stones Speak: Human Evolution and the Dawn of Technology.* New York: Simon & Schuster, 1993.

Schiffer, Michael B. *Formation Processes of the Archaeological Record.* 1st ed. Albuquerque, NM: University of New Mexico Press, 1987.

Schirmer, Wulf. "Some Aspects of Building at the 'Aceramic–Neolithic' Settlement of Cayonu Tepesi." *World Archaeology* 21.3 (1990): 365–87.

Schmidt, K. "Gobekli Tepe and the Early Neolithic Sites of the Urfa Region: A Synopsis of New Results and Current Views." *Neo-lithics* 10.1 (2001): 9–11.

Schmidt, Peter R. *Iron Technology in East Africa: Symbolism, Science, and Archaeology.* Bloomington, IN: Indiana University Press, 1997.

Schmidt, Peter R., and Roderick J. McIntosh. *Plundering Africa's Past.* Bloomington, IN: Indiana University Press, 1996.

Schmitz, Ralf W., et al. "The Neanderthal Type Site Revisited: Interdisciplinary Investigations of Skeletal Remains from the Neander Valley, Germany." *Proceedings of the National Academy of Sciences* 99.20 (2002): 13342–47.

Schnapp, Alain. *The Discovery of the Past.* New York: Harry N. Abrams, 1997.

Schreiber, Katharina. "The Wari Empire of Middle Horizon Peru: The Epistemological Challenge of Documenting an Empire without Documentary Evidence." *Empires.* Eds. Susan Alcock, et al. Cambridge, U.K.: Cambridge University Press, 2001.

Schwartz, Jeffrey H., and Ian Tattersall. "Whose Teeth?" *Nature* 381 (1996): 201–02.

Scott, K. "The Large Mammal Fauna." *La Cotte de St. Brelade 1961–1978.* Eds. P. Callow and J.M. Cornford. Norwich, U.K.: Geo Books, 1986. 109–38.

Sebastian, Lynne. *The Chaco Anasazi: Sociopolitical Evolution in the Prehistoric Southwest. New Studies in Archaeology.* Cambridge, U.K.: Cambridge University Press, 1992.

Semah, François, et al. "Did Early Man Reach Java During the Late Pliocene?" *Journal of Archaeological Science* 27 (2000): 763–69.

Semaw, S. "The World's Oldest Stone Artefacts from Gona, Ethiopia: Their Implications for Understanding Stone Technology and Patterns of Human Evolution between 2.6–1.5 Million Years Ago." *Journal of Archaeological Science* 27 (2000): 1197–214.

Semaw, S., et al. "2.5-Million-Year-Old Stone Tools from Gona, Ethiopia." *Nature* 385 (1997): 333–34.

Sereno, P., et al. "Lakeside cemeteries in the Sahara: 5,000 years of Holocene population and environmental change." *PLOS One* 3 (2008): 1–22.

Service, Elman Rogers. *Primitive Social Organization: An Evolutionary Perspective.* 2nd ed. New York: Random House, 1971.

Service, Elman. *Origins of the State and Civilization.* New York: Norton, 1975.

Shanks, Michael, and Christopher Y. Tilley. *Social Theory and Archaeology.* Cambridge, U.K.: Polity Press, 1987.

Shanks, Michael, and Christopher Y. Tilley. *Re-Constructing Archaeology: Theory and Practice. New Studies in Archaeology.* Cambridge, U.K. and New York: Cambridge University Press, 1987.

Shea, John, Zachary Davis, and Kyle Brown. "Experimental Tests of Middle Paleolithic Spear Points Using a Calibrated Crossbow." *Journal of Archaeological Science* 28.8 (2001): 807–16.

Shen, G., et al. "Age of Zhoukoudian *Homo erectus* determined with 26Al/10Be burial dating." *Nature* 458 (2009): 198–200.

Silverberg, Robert. *Mound Builders of Ancient America: The Archaeology of a Myth.* Athens, OH: Ohio University Press, 1986.

Silverman, Helaine, and Donald A. Proulx. *The Nasca.* Malden, MA: Blackwell, 2002.

Sklenar, K. *Archaeology in Central Europe: The First 500 Years.* Leicester, U.K.: Leicester University Press, 1983.

Smalley, J. and M. Blake. "Sweet beginnings: Stalk sugar and the domestication of maize." *Current Anthropology* 44.5 (2003) 675–705.

Smith, Andrew B. "Keeping People on the Periphery: The Ideology of Social Hierarchies between Hunters and Herders." *Journal of Anthropological Archaeology* 17 (1998): 201–15.

Smith, Bruce D. "Low-Level Food Production." *Journal of Archaeological Research* 9.1 (2001): 1–43.

Smith, Bruce D. "The Initial Domestication of *Cucurbita pepo* in the Americas 10,000 Years Ago." *Science* 276 (1997): 932–34.

Smith, Bruce D. *The Emergence of Agriculture.* New York: Scientific American Library, 1995.

Smith, Bruce D., and C. Wesley Cowan. "Domesticated Crop Plants and the Evolution of Food Production Economies in Eastern North America." *People and Plants in Ancient Eastern North America.* Ed. Paul E. Minnis. Washington, DC: Smithsonian Books, 2003. 105–25.

Smith, C.E. "Plant Remains from Guitarrero Cave." *Guitarrero Cave: Early Man in the Andes.* Ed. Thomas F. Lynch. New York: Academic Press, 1980. 87–119.

Smith, Claire, and H. Martin Wobst, eds. *Indigenous Archaeologies: Decolonizing Theory and Practice.* London: Routledge, 2005.

Smith, Colin, et al. "Not Just Old but Old and Cold?" *Nature* 410 (2001): 771–72.

Smith, Fred H., et al. "Direct Radiocarbon Dates for Vindija G1 and Velika Pecina Late Pleistocene Hominid Remains." *Proceedings of the National Academy of Science* 96.22 (1999): 12281–86.

Smith, Michael Ernest. *The Aztecs. Peoples of America.* 2nd ed. Malden, MA: Blackwell Pub., 2003.

Snow, Dean. "Migration in prehistory: The northern Iroquoian Case." *American Antiquity* 60 (1995): 59–79.

Society for American Archaeology, SAA. *Principles of Archaeological Ethics.* http://www.saa.org/public/resources/ethics.html (2005).

Soffer, O., J.M. Adovasio, and D.C. Hyland. "The 'Venus' Figurines: Textiles, Basketry, Gender, and Status in the Upper paleolithic." *Current Anthropology* 41.4 (2000): 511–37.

Solis, Ruth Shady, Jonathan Haas, and Winifred Creamer. "Dating Caral, a Preceramic Site in the Supe Valley on the Central Coast of Peru." *Science* 292 (2001): 723–26.

Sonett, Charles P. "The Present Status of Understanding of the Long-Period Spectrum of Radiocarbon." *Radiocarbon after Four Decades.* Eds. R.E. Taylor, A. Long, and R.S. Kra. New York: Springer Verlag, 1992. 50–61.

Souden, David. *Stonehenge Revealed.* London: Collins & Brown; in association with English Heritage, 1997.

Spector, Janet. "What This Awl Means: Toward a Feminist Archaeology." *Engendering Archaeology: Women and Prehistory.* Eds. Joan Gero and Margaret Conkey. Oxford, U.K.: Blackwell, 1991. 388–406.

Speller, C. et al. "Ancient mitochondrial DNA analysis reveals complexity of indigenous North American turkey domestication." *Proceedings of the National Academy of Sciences* 107.7 (2010): 2807–12.

Spence, M.W., and G. Pereira. "The human skeletal remains of the Moon Pyramid, Teotihuacán." *Ancient Mesoamerica* 18 (2007): 147–57.

Spencer, Frank. *Piltdown: A Scientific Forgery.* London: Oxford University Press, 1990.

Spindler, Konrad. *Der Mann Im Eis: Neue Funde Und Ergebnisse. Man in the Ice,* V. 2. Wien and New York: Springer-Verlag, 1995.

Spindler, Konrad. *The Man in the Ice: The Discovery of a 5,000-Year-Old Body Reveals the Secrets of the Stone Age.* Toronto: Doubleday Canada, 1994.

Spooner, N.A. "Human Occupation at Jinmium, Northern Australia: 116,000 Years Ago or Much Less?" *Antiquity* 72.275 (1998): 173–78.

Squier, Ephraim G., and Edwin Davis. *Ancient Monuments of the Mississippi Valley. Smithsonian Classics of Anthropology.* Washington, DC: Smithsonian Institution, 1848.

Srejovic, D. *Europe's First Monumental Sculpture: New Discoveries at Lepinski Vir.* New York: Stein and Day, 1972.

Stafford, C. Russel, and Steven D. Creasman. "The Hidden Record: Late Holocene Landscapes and Settlement Archaeology in the Lower Ohio River Valley." *Geoarchaeology: An International Journal* 17.2 (2002): 117–40.

Stafford, Michael D., et al. "Digging for the Color of Life: Paleoindian Red Ochre Mining at the Powars II Site, Platte County, Wyoming, USA." *Geoarchaeology: An International Journal* 18.1 (2003): 71–90.

Stanford, Craig. *The Hunting Ape: Meat Eating and the Origins of Human Behavior.* Princeton, NJ: Princeton University Press, 1999.

Stanford, Dennis, and Bruce Bradley. "The Solutrean Solution: Did Some Ancient Americans Come from Europe?" *Discovering Archaeology* 2.1 (2000): 54–55.

Steadman, S. "Recent research in the archaeology of architecture: beyond the foundations." *Journal of Archaeological Research* 4 (1996): 51–93.

Steele, James. "Stone Legacy of Skilled Hands." *Nature* 399 (1999): 24–25.

Stein, Gil. *Rethinking World-Systems: Diasporas, Colonies, and Interaction in Uruk Mesopotamia.* Tucson, AZ: University of Arizona Press, 1999.

Stiner, Mary C., et al. "Paleolithic Population Growth Pulses Evidenced by Small Animal Exploitation." *Science* 283 (1999): 190–93.

Stock, J.T., et al. "F-81 Skeleton for Wadi Mataha, Jordan and Its Bearing on Human Variability in the Epipaleolithic of the Levant." *American Journal of Physical Anthropology* 128.2 (2005): 453–65.

Storck, P., and A. Spiess. "The Significance of New Faunal Identifications Attributed to an Early Paleoindian (Gainey Complex) Occupation at the Udora Site, Ontario, Canada." *American Antiquity* 59 (1994): 121–42.

Storck, Peter L. *Journey to the Ice Age: Discovering an Ancient World.* Vancouver, BC: UBC Press in association with the Royal Ontario Museum, 2004.

Stordeur, D., et al. "Les Bâtiments Communautaires de Jerf el Ahmar et Mureybet Horizon PPNA (Syrie)." *Paléorient* 26.1 (2000): 29–44.

Storm, Paul. "The Evolution of Humans in Australasia from an Environmental Perspective." *Palaeogeography, Palaeoclimatology, Palaeoecology* 171 (2001): 363–83.

Straus, L.G. "Solutrean Settlement of North America? A Review of Reality." *American Antiquity* 65.2 (2000): 219–26.

Stringer, C.B., and P. Andrews. "Genetic and Fossil Evidence for the Origin of Modern Humans." *Science* 239 (1988): 1263–68.

Stringer, C.B., et al. "Neanderthal exploitation of marine mammals in Gibraltar." *Proceedings of the National Academy of Sciences* 105 (2008): 14319–24.

Stringer, Chris, and Robin McKie. *African Exodus: The Origins of Modern Humanity.* 1st Owl Books ed. New York: Henry Holt, 1998.

Sugiyama, S., and L. Lopez Lujan. "Dedictory burial/offering complexes at the Moon Pyramid, Teotihuacán." *Ancient Mesoamerica* 18 (2007).

Sugiyama, S., and R. Cabrera Castro. "The Moon Pyramid project and the Teotihuacán state polity." *Ancient Mesoamerica* 18 (2007).

Sugiyama, Saburo. "Governance and Polity at Classic Teotihuacán." *Mesoamerican Archaeology: Theory and Practice.* Eds. Julia A. Hendon and Rosemary A. Joyce. Oxford, U.K.: Blackwell, 2004. 97–123.

Sutton, Mark Q., Brooke S. Arkush, and Joan S. Schneider. *Archaeological Laboratory Methods: An Introduction.* 2nd ed. Dubuque, IA: Kendall/Hunt Pub. 1998.

Suwa, Gen, et al. "The First Skull of *Australopithecus boisei.*" *Nature* 389 (1997): 489–92.

Swedlund, Alan, and Duane Anderson. "Gordon Creek Woman Meets Kennewick Man: New Interpretations and Protocols Regarding the Peopling of the Americas." *American Antiquity* 64.4 (1999): 569–76.

Swedlund, Alan, and Duane Anderson. "Gordon Creek Woman Meets Spirit Cave Man: A Response to Comment by Owsley and Jantz." *American Antiquity* 68.1 (2003): 161–67.

Swisher, C.C., et al. "Age of the Earliest Known Hominids in Java, Indonesia." *Science* 263.5150 (1994): 1118–21.

Swisher, C.C., et al. "Latest *Homo Erectus* of Java: Potential Contemporaneity with *Homo Sapiens sapiens* in Southeast Asia." *Science* 274 (1996): 1870–1874.

Tankersley, Kenneth B. "Sheriden: A Clovis Cave Site in Eastern North America." *Geoarchaeology: An International Journal,* 12.6 (1997): 713–24.

Tattersall, Ian, and Jeffrey H. Schwartz. "Hominids and Hybrids: The Place of Neanderthals in Human Evolution." *Proceedings of the National Academy of Science* 96 (1999): 7117–19.

Tattersall, Ian, and Jeffrey H. Schwartz. *Extinct Humans.* 1st ed. Boulder, CO: Westview Press, 2000.

Taylor, R.E., A. Long, and R.S. Kra, eds. *Radiocarbon after Four Decades: An Interdisciplinary Perspective.* New York: Springer Verlag, 1992.

Taylor, R.E., and Martin J. Aitken, eds. *Chronometric Dating in Archaeology.* New York: Plenum, 1997.

Taylor, R.E., et al. "Radiocarbon Analyses of Modern Organics at Monte Verde, Chile: No Evidence for a Local Reservoir Effect." *American Antiquity* 64.3 (1999): 455–60.

Taylor, Walter W. *A Study of Archaeology.* Carbondale, IL: Southern Illinois University Press, 1948.

Tchernov, Eitan, and François Valla. "Two New Dogs, and Other Natufian Dogs, from the Southern Levant." *Journal of Archaeological Science* 24 (1997): 65–95.

Tehrani, J. and M. Collard. "Investigating cultural evolution through biological phylogenetic analyses of Turkmen textiles." *Journal of Anthropological Archaeology* 21 (2002): 443–63.

Templeton, Alan R. "Out of Africa Again and Again." *Nature* 416 (2002): 45–47.

Thieme, Hartmut. "Lower Paleolithic Hunting Spears from Germany." *Nature* 385 (1997): 807–10.

Thomas, David Hurst. *Skull Wars: Kennewick Man, Archaeology, and the Battle for Native American Identity.* New York: Basic Books, 2000.

Thomas, J., et al. "The date of the Greater Stonehenge cursus." *Antiquity* 83 (2009): 40–53.

Thomas, Julian. *Archaeology and Modernity.* London: Routledge, 2004.

Thomas, Julian. *Rethinking the Neolithic.* Cambridge, U.K.: Cambridge University Press, 1991.

Thomas, Julian. *Time, Culture, and Identity: An Interpretive Archaeology.* London: Routledge, 1996.

Thomas, Julian. *Understanding the Neolithic.* Rev. 2nd ed. London: Routledge, 1999.

Thornton, Russel. "Repatriation as Healing the Wounds of the Trauma of History: Cases of Native Americans in the United States of America." *The Dead and Their Possessions: Repatriation in Principle, Policy, and Practice.* Eds. C. Fforde, J. Hubert, and P. Turnbull. London: Routledge, 2002. 17–24.

Tieme, Chen, et al. "The Problems in ESR Dating of Tooth Enamel of Early Pleistocene and the Age of Longgupo Hominid, Wushan, China." *Quaternary Science Reviews* 20 (2001): 1041–45.

Tilley, Christopher and Michael Shanks. *Social Theory and Archaeology.* Albuquerque, NM: University of New Mexico Press, 1987.

Tobias, Phillip V. "Encore Olduvai." *Science* 299 (2003): 1193–94.

Tomasello, Michael. *The Cultural Origins of Human Cognition.* Cambridge, MA: Harvard University Press, 1999.

Toth, Nicholas, et al. "Pan the Tool-Maker: Investigations into the Stone Tool-Making and Tool-Using Capabilities of a Bonobo (*Pan paniscus*)." *Journal of Archaeological Science* 20 (1993): 81–91.

Townsend, Richard F. *The Aztecs.* London: Thames and Hudson, 2000.

Tozzer, Alfred M., et al. *Landa's Relaci—n de las Cosas de Yucatán: A Translation. Papers of the Peabody Museum of American Archaeology and Ethnology,* Harvard University; V. 18. Cambridge, MA: The Peabody Museum, 1941.

Trigger, Bruce G. *A History of Archaeological Thought.* Cambridge, U.K.: Cambridge University Press, 1989.

Trigger, B. "Monumental Architecture: A Thermodynamic Explanation of Symbolic Behaviour." *World Archaeology* 22.2 (1990): 119–32.

Trigger, Bruce G. *Understanding Early Civilizations: A Comparative Study.* Cambridge, U.K.: Cambridge University Press, 2003.

Trinkaus, Erik, and Pat Shipman. *The Neanderthals: Changing the Image of Mankind.* New York: Knopf, 1993.

Trinkaus, Erik, et al. "An Early Modern Human from the Pestera Cu Oase, Romania." *Proceedings of the National Academy of Science* 100 (2003): 11231–36.

Turnbull, C.J. "The Augustine Site: A mound from the Maritimes." *The Archaeology of Eastern North America* 4 (1976): 50–62.

Underhill, Anne, et al. "Changes in regional settlement patterns and the development of complex societies in southeastern Shandong, China." *Journal of Anthropological Archaeology* 27 (2008): 1–29.

Underhill, Peter A., et al. "Y Chromosome Sequence Variation and the History of Human Populations." *Nature Genetics* 26 (2000): 358–61.

Urton, Gary. *Signs of the Inka Khipu: Binary Coding in the Andean Knotted-String Records. The Linda Schele Series in Maya and Pre-Columbian Studies.* Austin: University of Texas Press, 2003.

Valdes, Juan Antonio, and Jonathan Kaplan. "Ground-Penetrating Radar at the Maya Site of Kaminaljuyu, Guatemala." *Journal of Field Archaeology* 27.3 (2000): 329–42.

Valdez, Lidio M., and J. Ernesto Valdez. "Reconsidering the Archaeological Rarity of Guinea Pig Bones in the Central Andes." *Current Anthropology* 38.5 (1997): 896–97.

Valladas, H., et al. "Thermoluminescence Dating of Mousterian Proto-Cro-Magnon Remains from Israel and the Origin of Modern Man." *Science* 331 (1988): 614–16.

Van den Bergh, G.D. "The Liang Bua faunal remains: a 95 k.yr. sequence from Flores, East Indonesia." *Journal of Human Evolution* 57 (2009): 527–37.

Van den Bergh, Gert D., John de Vos, and Paul Y. Sondaar. "The Late Quaternary Paleogeography of Mammal Evolution in the Indonesian Archipelago." *Palaeogeography, Palaeoclimatology, Palaeoecology* 171 (2001): 385–408.

van der Merwe, et al. "The Moatfield ossuary: isotopic dietary analysis of an Iroquoian community, using dental tissue." *Journal of Anthropological Archaeology* 22 (2003): 245–61.

Van Oosterzee, Penny. *Dragon Bones: The Story of Peking Man.* Cambridge, MA: Perseus Publishing, 2000.

Van Schaik, Carel P., et al. "Orangutan Cultures and the Evolution of Material Culture." *Science* 299 (2003): 102–05.

Van Tilburg, JoAnne. *Easter Island: Archaeology, Ecology, and Culture.* Washington, DC: Smithsonian Institution Press, 1994.

Vandermeersch, Bernard. *Les Hommes Fossiles de Qafzeh, Israël. Cahiers de Paléontologie.* Paris: Editions du Centre National de la Recherche Scientifique, 1981.

Vastokas, Joan M., and Romas K. Vastokas. *Sacred Art of the Algonkians: A Study of the Peterborough Petroglyphs.* Peterborough: Mansard Press, 1973.

Vaughn, K.J. "Households, crafts, and feasting in the ancient Andes: the village context of early Nasca craft consumption." *Latin American Antiquity* 15 (2004): 61–88.

Vaughn, K.J., and M. Linares Grados. "Three thousand years of occupation in Upper Valley Nasca: Excavations at Upanca." *Latin American Antiquity* 17 (2006): 595–612.

Vaughn, K.J., C. Conlee, H. Neff, and K. Schreiber. "Ceramic production in ancient Nasca: provenance analysis of pottery from the Early Nasca and Tiza cultures through INAA." *Journal of Archaeological Science* 33 (2006): 681–89.

Verhoeven, Marc. "Ritual and Ideology in the Pre-Pottery Neolithic B of the Levant and Southeast Anatolia." *Cambridge Archaeological Journal* 12.2 (2002): 233–58.

Vitelli, Karen D., and Chip Colwell-Chanthaphonh. *Archaeological Ethics.* 2nd ed. Lanham, MD: AltaMira Press, 2006.

Vos, John de. "Dating Hominid Sites in Indonesia." *Science* 266 (1994): 1726.

Wadley, L. "Vegetation Changes between 61,500 and 26,000 Years Ago: The Evidence from Seeds in Sibudu Cave, KwaZulu-Natal." *South African Journal of Science* 100 (2004): 167–73.

Walker, C. B. F. *Cuneiform. Reading the Past;* V. 3. Berkeley, CA and London: University of California Press and British Museum, 1987.

Waller, S. "Intentionality of rock-art placement deduced from acoustical measurements and echo myths." *Archaeoacoustics.* Ed. C. Scarre and G. Lawson. Cambridge: McDonald Institute, 2006. 31–40.

Walter, R.C., et al. "Early Human Occupation of the Red Sea Coast of Eritrea During the Last Interglacial." *Nature* 405 (2000): 65–69.

Wang, J., et al. "Research on digitizing processing of the terracotta warriors and horses of the Qin dynasty." *Proceedings of the 2003 Internation Conference on Geometric Modeling and Graphics* (2003).

Wanpo, Huang, et al. "Early *Homo* and Associated Artefacts from Asia." *Nature* 378 (1995): 275–78.

Wanpo, Huang, et al. "Whose Teeth?" *Nature* 381 (1996): 201–02.

Wasylikowa, K., et al. "Examination of Botanical Remains from Early Neolithic Houses at Nabta Playa, Western Desert, Egypt, with Special Reference to Sorghum Grains." *The Archaeology of Africa: Food, Metals, and Towns.* Ed. Thurstan Shaw. London: Routledge, 1993. 154–63.

Watchman, A.L., and R. Jones. "An Independent Confirmation of the 4 Ka Antiquity of a Beeswax Figure in Western Arnhem Land, Northern Australia." *Archaeometry* 44.1 (2002): 145–53.

Watchman, A.L., et al. "Micro-Archaeology of Engraved and Painted Rock Surface Crusts at Yiwarlarlay (the Lightning Brothers Site), Northern Territory, Australia." *Journal of Archaeological Science* 27 (2000): 315–25.

Waters, Michael R., Steven L. Forman, and James M. Pierson. "Diring Yuriakh: A Lower Paleolithic Site in Central Siberia." *Science* 275 (1997): 1281–84.

Watkins, Joe. "The Politics of American Archaeology: Cultural Resources, Cultural Affiliation, and Kennewick." *Indigenous Archaeologies: Decolonizing Theory and Practice.* Eds. Claire Smith and H. Martin Wobst. London: Routledge, 2005. 189–206.

Watkins, Trevor. "The Origins of House and Home?" *World Archaeology* 21.3 Architectural Innovation (1990): 336–47.

Watson, Patty Jo, and Mary Kennedy. "The Development of Horticulture in the Eastern Woodlands of North America: Women's Role." *Engendering Archaeology: Women and Prehistory.* Eds. Joan Gero and Margaret Conkey. Oxford, U.K.: Blackwell, 1991. 255–75.

Watson, Patty Jo, Steven A. LeBlanc, and Charles L. Redman. *Archaeological Explanation: The Scientific Method in Archaeology.* New York: Columbia University Press, 1984.

Watts, C. "On meditatin and material agency in Peircean Semeiotic." *Material Agency.* Eds. C. Knappett and L. Malafouris. New York: Springer, 2008. 187–207.

Wells, H.G. *The Time Machine and the The Invisible Man.* New York: New American Library, 1984.

Wendorf, Fred, and Romuald Schild. "Nabta Playa and Its Role in Northeastern African Prehistory." *Journal of Anthropological Archaeology* 17 (1998): 97–123.

Wendorf, Fred, et al. "The Use of Plants During during the Early Holocene in the Egyptian Sahara: Early Neolithic Food Economies." *Before Food Production in North Africa.* Eds. Savino di Lernia and Giorgio Manzi. Forli, Italy: A.B.A.C.O. Edizioni, 1998. 71–78.

Wetterstrom, Wilma. "Foraging and Farming in Egypt: The Transition from Hunting and Gathering to Horticulture in the Nile Valley." *The Archaeology of Africa: Food, Metals, and Towns.* Ed. Thurstan Shaw. London: Routledge, 1993. 165–225.

Wheatley, David, and Mark Gillings. *Spatial Technology and Archaeology: The Archaeological Applications of GIS.* London and New York: Taylor & Francis, 2002.

Wheeler, Mortimer. *Archaeology from the Earth.* Harmondsworth, U.K.: Penguin Books, 1954.

Wheeler, R.J., et al. "Archaic period canoes from Newnans Lake, Florida." *American Antiquity* 68 (2003): 533–51.

White, C., et al. "Demography and ethnic continuity in the Tlailotlacán enclave of Teotihuacán: The evidence from stable oxygen isotopes." *Journal of Archaeological Science* 23 (2004): 385–403.

White, Randall. "Beyond Art: Toward an Understanding of the Origins of Material Representation in Europe." *Annual Review of Anthropology* 21 (1992): 537–64.

White, Randall. "Husbandry and Herd Control in the Upper Paleolithic." *Current Anthropology* 30.5 (1989): 609–32.

White, T., et al. "*Ardipithecus ramidus* and the Paleobiology of early Hominids." *Science* 326.64 (2009): 75–86.

White, Tim D., et al. "Pleistocene *Homo sapiens* from Middle Awash, Ethiopia." *Nature* 423 (2003): 742–52.

White, Tim, Gen Suwa, and Berhane Asfaw. "*Australopithecus ramidus*, a New Species of Early Hominid from Aramis, Ethiopia." *Nature* 371 (1994): 306–12.

White, Tim, Gen Suwa, and Berhane Asfaw. "Corrigenda: *Australopithecus ramidus*, a New Species of Early Hominid from Aramis, Ethiopia." *Nature* 375 (1995): 88.

Whiten, A., et al. "Cultures in Chimpanzees." *Nature* 399 (1999): 682–85.

Whittle, Alasdair. *Europe in the Neolithic: The Creation of New Worlds.* Cambridge, U.K.: Cambridge University Press, 1996.

Wilford, John Noble. "Under Maryland street, ties to African past." *New York Times* (October 20, 2008).

Willcox, George. "Measuring Grain Size and Identifying Near Eastern Cereal Domestication: Evidence from the Euphrates Valley." *Journal of Archaeological Science* 31 (2004): 145–50.

Willey, Gordon R., and Philip Phillips. *Method and Theory in American Archaeology.* Chicago: University of Chicago Press, 1958.

Williamson, B.S. "Middle Stone Age Tool Function from Residue Analysis at Sibudu Cave." *South African Journal of Science* 100 (2004): 174–78.

Williamson, R.F. and S. Pfeiffer. *Bones of the Ancestors: The Archaeology and Oesteobiography of the Moatfield Ossuary.* Archaeological Survey of Canada. Mercury Series Paper 163. Quebec: Canadian Museum of Civilization, 2003.

Wills, W.H., and Thomas C. Windes. "Evidence for Aggregation and Dispersal During the Basketmaker III Period in Chaco Canyon, New Mexico." *American Antiquity* 54 (1989): 347–69.

Windes, Thomas C. "This Old House: Construction and Abandonment at Pueblo Bonito." *Pueblo Bonito: Center of the Chacoan World.* Ed. Jill E. Neitzel. Washington, DC: Smithsonian Press, 2003. 14–32.

Wittfogel, Karl. *Oriental Despotism: A Comparative Study of Total Power.* New Haven, CT: Yale University Press, 1957.

Wobst, H.M. "The Archaeo-Ethnology of Hunter–Gatherers or the Tyranny of the Ethnographic Record in Archaeology." *American Antiquity* 43.2 (1978): 303–09.

Wolf, Eric R. *Europe and the People without History.* Berkeley, CA: University of California Press, 1982.

Wolpoff, Milford H., and Rachel Caspari. *Race and Human Evolution.* New York: Simon & Schuster, 1997.

Wolpoff, Milford H., and Rachel Caspari. *Race and Human Evolution.* New York: Simon & Schuster, 1997.

Wood, B., and M.C. Collard. "The Human Genus." *Science* 284 (1999): 65–71.

Wood, Bernard, and Alan Turner. "Out of Africa and into Asia." *Nature* 378.6554 (1995): 239–40.

Wood, Bernard, and Brian G. Richmond. "Human Evolution: Taxonomy and Paleobiology." *Journal of Anatomy* 196 (2000): 19–60.

Wood, Bernard. "The Oldest Whodunnit in the World." *Nature* 385 (1997): 292–93.

Wood, James, et al. "The osteological paradox: problems of inferring prehistoric health from skeletal samples." *Current Anthropology* 33 (1992): 343–70.

Wrangham, Richard, et al. "The Raw and the Stolen: Cooking and the Ecology of Human Origins." *Current Anthropology* 40.5 (1999): 567–94.

Wright, Henry T., and Gregory A. Johnson. "Population, Exchange, and Early State Formation in Southwestern Iran." *American Anthropologist* 77 (1975): 267–89.

Wright, J.V "The prehistoric transportation of goods in the St. Lawrence River basin." *Prehistoric Exchange Systems in North America.* Eds. T.G. Baugh and J.E. Ericson. NY: Plenum, 1994. 47–71.

Yamei, Hou, et al. "Mid-Pleistocene Acheulean-Like Stone Technology of the Bose Basin, South China." *Science* 287.5458 (2000): 1622–26.

Yellen, J.E., et al. "A Middle Stone Age Worked Bone Industry from Katanda, Upper Semliki Valley, Zaire." *Science* 268 (1995): 553–56.

Yesner, David R. "Human Dispersal into Interior Alaska: Antecedent Conditions, Mode of Colonization, and Adaptations." *Quaternary Science Reviews* 20 (2001): 315–27.

Yi, Soojin, Darrell L. Ellsworth, and Wen-Hsiung Li. "Slow Molecular Clocks in Old World Monkeys, Apes, and Humans." *Molecular Biological Evolution* 19.12 (2002): 2191–98.

Yoffee, Norman. *Myths of the Archaic State: Evolution of the Earliest Cities, States, and Civilizations.* Cambridge, U.K.: Cambridge University Press, 2005.

Young, Biloine W., and Melvin L. Fowler. *Cahokia, the Great Native American Metropolis.* Urbana, IL: University of Illinois Press, 2000.

Zazula, Grant D., et al. "Ice-Age Steppe Vegetation in East Beringia." *Nature* 423 (2003): 603.

Zazula, G.D. et al. "A late Pleistocene steppe bison (*Bison priscus*) partial carcass from Tsiigehtchi, Northwest Territories, Canada." *Quaternary Science Reviews* 28 (2009): 2734–42.

Zerubavel, Y. *Recovered Roots: Collective Memory and the Making of Israeli National Tradition.* Chicago: University of Chicago Press, 1995.

Zettler, Richard L., Lee Horne, and Donald P. Hansen. *Treasures from the Royal Tombs of Ur.* Philadelphia: University of Pennsylvania Museum of Archaeology and Anthropology, 1998.

Zhang, Juzhong, et al. "Oldest Playable Musical Instruments Found at Jiahu Early Neolithic Site in China." *Nature* 401 (1999): 366–68.

Zhijun, Zhao. "The Middle Yangtze Region in China Is One Place Where Rice Was Domesticated: Phytolith Evidence from the Diaotonghuan Cave, Northern Jiangxi." *Antiquity* 72.278 (1998): 885–97.

Zhu, R.X., et al. "New Evidence on the Earliest Human Presence at High Northern Latitudes in Northeast Asia." *Nature* 431 (2004): 559–62.

Zhu, Rixiang, et al. "Magnetostratigraphic Dating of Early Humans in China." *Earth-Science Reviews* 61 (2002): 341–59.

Zilhao, J. "The Rock Art of the Coa Valley, Portugal: Significance, Conservation, and Management." *Conservation and Management of Archaeological Sites* 2.4 (1998): 193–206.

Zollikofer, C. P. E., et al. "Virtual Cranial Reconstruction of *Sahelanthropus tchadensis*." *Nature* 434.7034 (2005): 755–59.

Zvelebil, Mark. "Demography and Dispersal of Early Farming Populations at the Mesolithic–Neolithic Transition: Linguistic and Genetic Implications." *Examining the Farming/Language Dispersal Hypothesis.* Eds. Peter Bellwood and Colin Renfrew. McDonald Institute Monographs. Cambridge, U.K.: McDonald Institute, 2002.

FIGURE AND PHOTO CREDITS

Archaeological Journal (2000) 10: 123-167, Figure 1, E. d'Errico and A. Nowell. Reprinted with permission of Cambridge University Press.; Page 100 Ken Mowbray/Photo Courtesy of Ken Mowbray/ American Museum of Natural History; Page 102 Arensburg, Schepartz, Tillier, Vandermeersch, and Rak "A reappraisal of the anatomical basis for speech in middle paleolithic hominids." From: American Journal of Physical Anthropology 83:137-146. ©1990 American Association of Physical Anthropologists. Reprinted by permission of Wiley-Liss, Inc., a subsidiary of John Wiley ©Sons, Inc.; Page 103 Most recent Science used to illustrate an article on Neanderthal Genetics PALEOGENETICS: The Dawn of Stone Age Genomics Elizabeth Pennisi (17 November 2006) Science 314 (5802), 1068. [DOI: 10.1126/science.314.5802.1068] Johannes Krause Dept. Genetics. Reprinted with permission of Johannes Krause, Max-Planck Institute for Evolutionary Enthropology; Page 104 Dmitri Kessel/ Time Life Pictures/Dmitri Kessel/Time Life Pictures/Getty Images, Inc.; Page 105 Harold L. Dibble/Courtesy Harold L. Dibble; Page 106 Science Vol. 134, No. 3482, (Sept. 22, 1961), Fig. 6, p. 808 in an article entitled "Mousterian Cultures in France" by Francois Bordes. American Association for the Advancement of Science (AAAS); Page 107 American Antiquity 52(1): 109-117, Fig. 2. Reprinted by permission of the Society of the American Archaeology from American Antiquity 52(1); Page 108 Courtesy of Michael Chazan and Alexandra Sumner; Page 110 Philippe Plailly/©Philippe Plailly/Eurelios/LookatScience; Page 111 Antiquity Publications Ltd./"A Levallois point embedded in the vertebra of a wild ass" by Eric Boeda et al., Antiquity 73: 394-402, Figure 5 (1999). Reprinted by kind permission of Antiquity Publications Ltd.; Page 113 Paul Goldberg; Page 115 Courtesy of Ariane Burke, Professor, Université de Montréal; Page 116 Journal of Human Evolution 26, Y. Rak et al., Figure 2, 313-324 (1994), with permission from Elsevier.; Page 117 Reproduced with permission from Defleuer et. al Science 286:128-131, Figure 2b (1999) American Association for the Advancement of Science. Courtesy of Lynne Schepartz.

Chapter 5
Page 121 Kenneth Garrett/National Geographic Image Collection; Page 122 Sisse Brimberg/National Geographic Image Collection; Page 123 David Brill/©2001 David L. Brill/Atlanta; Page 124 Institue for Human Evolution University of Witwatersrand/Experimental hafting of Howiesons Poort microliths. Image first published in Lombard, M. & Pargeter, J. 2008. Journal of Archaeological Science 35: 2523-2531; Page 125 Yellen et al., Science, 268:553-556, Figure 1 (1995). Reprinted with permission from AAAS. Photography courtesy of Chip Clark; Page 127 From the Field by Michael S. Bisson, McGill University/print with permission; Page 128 Image courtesy of Chris Henshilwood & Francesco d'Errico; Page 125 American Museum of Natural History; Page 135 Courtesy of Randall White/New York University; Page 137 From Denise de Sonneville-Bordes, Upper Paleolithic Cultures in Western Europe, Science 18 October 1963: Vol. 142. no. 3590, pp. 347–355. Copyright ©1963, The American Association for the Advancement of Science. Reprinted with permission from AAAS; Page 138 Gianni Dagli Orti/©Gianni Dagli OrtI/ CORBIS All Rights Reserved; Page 139 Philippe Plailly/Eurelios Photographic Press Agency; Page 140 (left) Ulmer Museum; Page 140 (right) H. Jensen/Front and side views of the recently discovered female figurine from the Aurignacian levels of Hohle Fels. Photographer: H. Jensen. ©University of Tübingen; Page 141 (right) H. Jensen/A well-preserved flute found in the Aurignacian levels of Hohle Fels/ Photographer: H. Jensen. ©University of Tübingen; Page 141 (left) Ira Block/Ira Block/NGS Image Collection; Page 142 La Marche

Antler. "A New model and its implications for the origin of writing: the La Marche Antler revisited," Cambridge Archaeological Journal (1994) 5(2): 163-206, Fig. 19. Reprinted with the permission of Cambridge University Press; Page 143 Ministere de la Culture et des Communication; Page 145 Reprinted from Current Anthropology 30(5): 609-632 (b. redrawn by Bahn from Bahn 1978:190) with permission from the University of Chicago Press; Page 146 Courtesy of Michael Chazan; Page 147 © Robert Estall photo agency/Alamy.

Chapter 6
Page 151 Tony Heald/Nature Picture Library; Page 152 Denver Museum of Nature & Science; Page 155 (top) Courtesy of Dr. Mark Moore/University of New England, Australia.; Page 155 (bottom) Courtesy Gert van den Bergh/University of Wollongong; Page 157 Cary Wolinsky/Aurora Photos, Inc.; Page 158 Steven David Miller/ Nature Picture Library; Page 159 This image belongs to the Anthropology Photographic Archive, the Department of Anthropology, The University of Auckland; Page 160 Monte Costa/Photo Resource Hawaii; Page 161 Jerry Jacka/Courtesy Arizona State Museum ©Jerry Jacka Photography; Page 162 Cast by (Peter Bostrom of Lithic Casting Laboratory, Troy, Illinois) of Gault site engraved stone. Courtesy of the Gault Project, TARL, UT. Austin.; Page 166 (top) Courtesy Thomas D. Dillehay; Page 166 (bottom) Stratigraphy of Pedra Pintada. Science 272 (April 19, 1996), p. 373-384, Fig. 5. American Association for the Advancement of Science (AAAS); Page 167 (top) Reproduced with permission from A. C. Roosevelt et al, Science 272, Page 373-384, fig. 6A (19 April 1996) American Association for the Advancement of Science; Page 167 (bottom) Stone tools from Pedra Pintada. Science 272 (April 19, 1996), p. 373-384, Fig. 6a. American Association for the Advancement of Science (AAAS); Page 169 Harry DiOrio/Syracuse Newspapers/The Image Works; Page 171 Susan Blaire/Courtesy of Susan Blair/The University of New Brunswick; Page 173 Chase Studio/ Photo Researchers, Inc.; Page 176 (left) Joe Ben Wheat/University of Colorado Museum, Joe Ben Wheat Photo.; Page 176 (right) From Journal of Archaeological Science 27:799–820, "Why Flute? Folsom Point Design and Adaptation," Figs. 4c&d and 5d&e, (2001). Reprinted with permission of Elsevier. Page 177 (right) Figure 3 reprinted from Bousman et al. 2002 Antiquity 76:980-990.; Page 177 (left) Adapted from Antiquity (2002) Vol. 76 (2940) Bousman et al. Fig. 2 (p. 982) http://antiquity.ac.uk/ant/076/Ant0760980.htm; Page 178 Max Friesen, University of Toronto; Page 179 Mask © Canadian Museum of Civilization, Artifact KbFk-7:308, S90-3114.

Part Three
Page 184 Douglas Mazonowicz/Berna Villiers; Page 185 Jason Laure/The Image Works; Page 188 (top) Maria Stenzel/National Geographic Image Collection; Page 188 (bottom) Jameson/Courtesy Department Library Services, American Museum of Natural History; Page 189 Vroman/Peabody Museum, Harvard University; Page 190 Stephen Sharnoff/National Geographic Image Collection.

Chapter 7
Page 193 Photo Courtesy of Gary Rollefson/Whitman; Page 194 Pictures of Record, Inc.; Page 195 Reproduced with the permission of the PUSH project; Page 196 Michael Chazan; Page 197 Michael Chazan/Michael Chazan; Page 198 Courtesy of Michael Chazan; Page 199 (top) Courtesy of Brigham Young University and Joel C. Janetski/BYU Museum of Art; Page 199 (bottom) Photo courtesy of J. Perrot, Centre de recherche français de Jérusalem; Page 200 "Evidence of domestication of the Dog 12,000 Years Ago in the Natufian of Israel" by Simon Davis, et al. Nature 276:608-610 (1978) Reprinted

by permission from Macmillan Publisher Ltd.; Page 201 Courtesy of Godi Laron/Kfar Hahoresh Archives and Nigel Goring-Morris/SMU Southern Methodist Univetiry; Page 202 B. ARNAUD/Eurelios Photographic Press Agency; Page 203 Frontispiece from Village on the Euphrates by AMT Moore, GC Hillman, and AJ Legge, p. 226, Figure 8.43 Copyright ©2002. Reprinted by permission of Oxford University Press, Inc.; Page 205 (top left) Courtesy Nigel Goring-Morris; Page 205 (top right) Courtesy Nigel Goring-Morris; Page 205 (bottom) Erich Lessing/Art Resource, NY; Page 193 Y. Langsam/Reproduced with permission from Kislev et al., Science 312:1372-1374, Figure 1 (2006). Image by Y. Langsam/American Association for the Advancement of Science. Page 208 (top) Philippe PLAILLY/Eurelios Photographic Press Agency; Page 208 (bottom) Courtsy De. Joy McCorriston; Page 209 Courtesy Avi Gopher; Page 210 Gianni Dagli Orti/©Gianni Dagli Orti/CORBIS All Rights Reserved; Page 212 Erich Lessing/Art Resource, N.Y.; Page 213 "Neolithic transition in Europe: The radiocarbon record revisited" Antiquity 77 (295): 45-62.

Chapter 8

Page 217 Service Historique de la Marine, Vincennes, France/Lauros/Giraudon/Bridgeman Art Library; Page 218 Tony Linck/Ohio Dept. of Natural Resources; Page 219 Courtesy fo Hugh Iltis/Doebly Lab/University of Wisconsin, Madison; Page 220 Reproduced with permission from Smith, Science 276:932-934 Fig. 2 (9 May 1997) American Association for the Advancement of Science; Page 221 From Science-based Dating in Archaeology by M.J. Aitken. Copyright ©1990. Reprinted by permission of Pearson Education; Page 223 Courtesy of Desert Archaeology Inc.; Page 224 Courtesy of Desert Archaeology Inc.; Page 226 Hillel Burger/Copyright President and Fellows of Harvard College 1995. All rights reserved. © 2006 Harvard University Peabody Museum—Harvard University, 26-7-10 95879 T85. Photograph by Hillel Burger.; Page 227 (A) Maria Montoya and Julian Martinez (San Ildefonso Pueblo, Native American, ca. 1887-1980; 1879-1943). "Jar". c. 1939. Blackware. 11 ? × 13 in. (dia.). The National Museum of Women in the Arts, Washington, DC. Gift of Wallace and Wilhelmina Holladay.; Page 227 (B, C, D, E, F) New Mexico Department of Tourism; Page 228 (left) Jon L. Gibson, The Ancient Mounds of Poverty Point: Place of Rings, 2001, Page 82, figure 5.2. Copyright ©2001. Reprinted courtesy of the University Press of Florida; Page 228 (right) Neg. No. 329206. Photo by J. Bird. Courtesy Dept. of Library Services, American Museum of Natural History; Page 229 Courtesy of the Louisiana Division of Archaeology.; Page 231 Werner Forman Archive Ltd; Page 232 The Ohio Historical Society; Page 233 (left) Dario Pignatelli/©Dario Pignatelli/Reuters; Page 233 (right) James Q. Jacobs/jqjacobs.net; Page 234 Reprinted by permission of the Society of the American Archaeology from Antiquity 60 (1995); Page 237 Courtesy Elizathe S. Clinton, Univesity of Massachusetts Amherst.

Chapter 9

Page 241 Neil Palmer/Alamy Images; Page 244 (top) Image courtesy of Dr. Paul Sereno; Page 244 (middle) Image courtesy of Dr. Paul Sereno; Page 245 Catherine D'Andrea, Ph.D.; Nabta Playa E-75-6. Journal of Anthropological Archaeology 17:97–123, Fig. 2. Elsevier; Page 246 Jean-Loôc LE QUELLEC/Eurelios Photographic Press Agency; Page 247 Adrian Arbib/CORBIS- NY; Page 248 map of Kuk Swamp excavation. SCIENCE 301:189-193 (2003). Denham et al. Fig. 2 B, C, & D. 19 June 2003. Plan of Kuk swamp excavation. SCIENCE 301:189-193 (2003). Denham et al. Fig 2 B, C, & D. 19 June 2003. American Association for the Advancement of Science (AAAS); Page 249 (top) CAMR/A. B. Dowsett/Photo Researchers,

Inc.; Page 249 (bottom) Andrew Syred/Science Photo Library/Photo Researchers, Inc.; Page 250 Fig. 9.9, Cross section of the Andes. Richard Burger (1992) Chavin and the Origins of Andean Civilization, fig. 11, p. 21. London: Thames and Hudson. Richard Burger; 22 Jiahu flutes. Nature 401 (23 September 1999) 366-368, fig. 1. Blackwell; Page 251 The Granger Collection, New York; Page 252 A. Ramey/Woodfin Camp & Associates, Inc.; Page 253 Jeffrey Quilter/Life and Death of Paloma by Jeffrey Quilter, p. 59, ©1989, Iowa City: University of Iowa Press. Photograph by Jeffrey Quiter; Page 254 Oscar Biffi/©Oscar Biffi/LATINPHOTO.org; Page 255 Jar, with string decor. Japan, Neolithic. Mid Jomon period (2500-1600 BCE). ca. 2000BCE. Terracotta, 37.5 × 31.2 cm. Inv.: MA3355. Photo: P. Pleynet. Musee des Arts Asiatiques-Guimet, Paris, France. ©Réunion des Musées Nationaux/Art Resource, NY; Page 256 "Oldest Playable Musical Instruments Found in Jiahu Early Neolithic Site in China" by Juzhong Zhang et al. (1999). Nature 401: 366-368, Figure 1. Reprinted by permission from Macmillan Publihsers Ltd.; Page 257 Proceedings of the National Academy of Sciences 101 (Dec. 21, 2004), pp. 17593-17598, Fig. 1 PNAS; Page 258 Lowell Georgia/©Georgia/CORBIS All Rights Reserved; Page 259 Ellen Rooney/Robert Harding World Imagery.

Part Four

Page 265 Sarah Leen/National Geographic Image Collection; Page 267 (top) Thomas Lunt/Maori Woman from New Zealand Image #32775. Photo Thomas Lunt. Courtesy Dept. of Library Services, American Museum of Natural History; Page 267 (bottom) Getty Images, Inc. - PhotoDisc; Page 268 Neg./Transparency no. 328739. Courtesy Dept. of Library Services, American Museum of Natural History.; Page 269 ANCIENT ART & ARCHITECTURE//DanitaDelimont.com; Page 270 AP Wide World Photos.

Chapter 10

Page 273 Adam Woolfitt/CORBIS - NY; Page 274 Steve Allen Travel Photography/Alamy Images; Page 275 (top) Figure, Kwak-waka'wakw, before 1973. Courtesy UBC Museum of Anthropology, Vancouver, Canada. Photo: Derek Tan # A17154; Page 275 (bottom) Courtesy of the Makah Cultural and Research Center and Janet Friedman; Page 277 Farid Rahemtulla, University of Northern British Columbia; Page 278 Lily Jackson, Gitksan woman, next to split salmon hanging from a drying rack, © Canadian Museum of Civilization, photo Marius Barbeau, 1920, 49443; Page 279 Labret © Canadian Museum of Civilization, D2002-007359, Artifact VII-A-192 c; Page 280 (top) British Museum AN30866 © The Trustees of the British Museum. All rights reserved.; Page 280 (bottom) These figures are reprinted with permission of the Publisher from Emerging from the Mist: Studies in Northwest Coast Culture History by Matson, R.G., Gary Coupland, and Quentin Mackie, eds. © University of British Columbia Press 2003. All rights reserved by the Publisher.; Page 282 (in text) William Wordsworth poem on Stonehenge; Page 282 Constable, John (1776-1837) Victoria & Albert Museum, London, UK/The Bridgeman Art Library; Page 283 (all) Courtesy of English Heritage Photo Library; Page 284 Lawrence Mogdale/Photo Researchers, Inc.; Page 285 National Geographic Image Collection; Page 286 Kenneth Geiger/©Kenneth Geiger/National Geographic Stock/with permission from Salisbury & South Wiltshire Museum, UK; Page 287 Adam Stanford/Aerial-Cam - Detailed Aerial Photography; Page 288 NASA; Page 289 (top) Richard A. Cooke/©Richard A. Cooke/CORBIS All Rights Reserved; Page 289 (bottom) Smithsonian National Museum of Natural History; Page 290 Rota/2A6738 Photo by Rota. Printed with permission of

American Museum of Natural History Library; Page 291 (left) Courtesy of Nasa/Marshall Space Flight Center; Page 291 (right) Georg Gerster/Georg Gerster/Photo Researchers, Inc.; Page 293 "Courtesy of the Laboratory of Tree-Ring Research, University of Arizona"; Page 294 Otis Imboden Jr./Otis Imboden Jr./NGS Image Collection; Page 295 Biloine Whiting Young and Melvin Fowler (2000) Cahokia: The Great Native American Metropolis. Urbana: University of Illinois Press Fig. 27, p. 265. Courtesy of the Illinois State Archaeological Survey at the University of Illinois; Page 296 Cahokia: The Great Native American Metropolis by Biloine Whiting Young and Melvin Fowler, Figure 15, p.138 Urbana: University of Illinois Press (2000) Reprinted courtesy of the Illinois State Museum photographic archives.; Page 297 Peter Bostrom/Peter Bostrom, Courtesy of Cahokia Mounds Historic Site, Collinsville, Illinois.; Page 298 (top) Neil Beer/Getty Images Inc. - Stone All-stock; Page 298 (margin) Great Zimbabwe Site Museum, Zimbabwe; Page 299 National Archives of South Africa; Page 300 Roderick J. McIntosh, Rice University; Page 301 africanpictures/AKG-Images.

Chapter 11

Page 305 Kenneth Garrett/National Geographic Image Collection; Page 306 ©Copyright The British Museum; Page 307 ANCIENT ART & ARCHITECTURE /DanitaDelimont.com; Page 308 ©Reuters/Corbis; Page 309 Richard Ashworth/Robert Harding World Imagery; Page 310 (margin) Erich Lessing/AKG-Images; Page 310 (bottom) 11.10 Susan Pollock, Melody Pope, Cheryl Coursey (1996). Househeled production at the Uruk Mound, Abu Salabikh, Iraq. American Journal of Archaeology 100(4): 638-698. Figure 4, Top, Page 689. Published by the American Institute of Archaeology; Page 311 (top) ©Bettmann/CORBIS All Rights Reserved; Page 311 (bottom) ©The Trustees of the British Museum/ Art Resource, NY; Page 312 Queen Puabi's headdress from the Royal Tombs at Ur, Iraq, Image #150028, reprinted by permission of University of Pennsylvania Museum; Page 313 (top) Ashmolean Museum. Oxford, UK/Bridgeman Art Library; Page 313 (bottom) Dagli Orti; Page 314 Early Mesopotamia, Nicholas Postage, Copyright 1992 Routledge. (P. Amiet, Glyptique susienne Paris 1972, no 539) Reproduced by permission of Taylor & Francis Books UK.; Page 315 Fig. 11.14, Habuba Kebira Gullermo Algaze (1993) The Uruk World System. Chicago: University of Chicago Press. Page 317 Michael Chazan/Photo courtesy of Michael Chazan; Page 318 Art Resource, N.Y.; Page 320 Dagli Orti/[The Art Archive/Dagli Orti]; Page 322 Dagli Orti/[The Art Archive/Musée du Louvre Paris/Dagli Orti]; Page 323 Courtesy of Stanley Klassen.; Page 324 (top) Figure 12.1, from Ancient Egypt: Anatomy of a Civilization by Barry Kemp, Figure 11. Copyright (c) 1989 Routledge. Reproduced by permission of Taylor & Francis Books UK; Page 324 (bottom) Sylvia Cordaiy Photo Library Ltd/Alamy Images; Page 325 Space Imaging Europe/ Photo Researchers, Inc.; Page 326 (top) Michael Chazan/Photo courtesy of Michael Chazan; Page 326 (bottom) Michael Chazan/ Photo courtesy of Michael Chazan; Page 329 Michael Chazan/ Photo courtesy of Michael Chazan; Page 330 Kenneth Garrett/ KENNETH GARRETT/National Geographic Stock; Page 331 Werner Forman/Art Resource, NY.

Chapter 12

Page 335 O. Louis Mazzatenta/National Geographic Image Collection; Page 336 Eddie Gerald/Eddie Gerald; Page 338 (left) Courtesy of the Institute of Nautical Archaeology, Texas A&M University/Photo by Don A. Frey; Page 338 (right) Woods Hole Oceanographic Institution/Courtesy of H. Singh, J. Howland ©WHOI, IFE, Ashkelon

Excavations; Page 340 Deutches Arch. Inst./Lion's Gate—Athens. Deutsches Archaeologisches Institut, Athens, D-DAI-ATH-Mykene 63; Page 341 (top) Jean Soutif/LookatSciences; Page 341 (bottom) Piet de Jong, The Throne Room of the Megaron. Courtesy The Department of Classics, University of Cincinnati.; Page 342 Getty Images/De Agostini Editore Picture Library; Page 343 From THE USE OF SPATIAL ANALYSIS TO STUDY PREHISTORIC SETTLEMENT ARCHITECTURE by Marion Cutting, Oxford Journal of Archaeology 22(1). Copyright ©2003 Blackwell Publishing Ltd. Reprinted by permission of John Wiley and Sons; Page 344 (top) Gustavo Tomsich/©Gustavo Tomsich/CORBIS All Rights Reserved; Page 344 (bottom) National Archeological Museum, Athens/Art Resource, NY; Page 345 Dagli Orti/Picture Desk, Inc./Kobal Collection; Page 347 Chris Sloan. Courtesy J. M. Kenoyer; Page 348 Borromeo/Borromeo/Art Resource, NY; Page 349 (all) Georg Helmes; Page 350 Georg Helmes; Page 351 Lowell Georgia/CORBIS-NY; Page 352 (top) Richard Lambert/©Réunion des Musées Nationaux/Art Resource, NY; Page 352 (bottom) O. Louis Mazzatenta/ National Geographic Image Collection; Page 355 Photo used courtesy of The Chifeng International Collaborative Archaeological Research Project; Page 356 (left) NASA; Page 356 (right) Nenadovic/ UN/DPI/Nenadovic; Page 357 China Photos/Getty Images, Inc.

Chapter 13

Page 361 Kenneth Garrett/National Geographic Image Collection; Page 362 (top) Expedition 4(1), figs. 2-4a, p. 17 (1961). Reprinted by permission of University of Pennsylvania Museum; Expedition 4(1) 1961, Figure 5, p. 17, "The Lords of the Maya Realm:" by Tatiana Proskouriakoff; University Museum, University of Pennsylvania; Page 362 (bottom) Figure 11.8 from Expedition 4 (1), Figure 5, p. 17 (1961). Reprinted by permission of University of Pennsylvania Museum; Page 363 Papers of Robert F. Heizer (heizer_287), National Anthropological Archives, Smithsonian Institution; Page 365 Elizabeth Barrows Rogers/Mexican Government Tourism Office; Page 366 ©1996 Harry N. Abrams, Inc.; Page 367 (top) Project of the Feathered Serpent Pyramid, Arizona State University and the National Institute of Anthropology and History in Mexico; Page 367 (bottom) Project of the Feathered Serpent Pyramid, Arizona State University and the National Institute of Anthropology and History in Mexico; Page 368 (top) Mural with tassel headed priest, 400-600 Volcanic ash, lime coating, pigment, mud backing, 32 × 46 × 2 in. (81.3 × 116.8 × 5.1 cm) Fine Arts Museums of San Francisco, Bequest of Harald J. Wagner, 1985.104.5; Page 368 (bottom) Illustrations by David Carballo/University of Alabama; Page 369 D. Merrett/ S. Pfeiffer; Page 371 (top) Peabody Museum, Harvard University; Page 371 (bottom) Kenneth Garrett/National Geographic Image Collection; William Fash (1991) Scribe, Warriors, and Kings. London: Thames and Hudson, pl. VII, p. 110 William Fash; Page 372 (top) William Fash (1991) Scribe, Warriors, and Kings. London: Thames and Hudson, fig. 48, p. 95; Page 372 (bottom) Kenneth Garrett/ National Geographic Image Collection; Page 373 Kaminaluyu deposit 6 GPR thermal printout from Journal of Field Archaeology 27(3): 329–342, Fig. 10 (Autumn 2000). Reproduced with permission of the Trustees of Boston University. All rights reserved. Journal of Field Archaeology Boston University 675 Commonwealth Avenue Boston, MA 02215; Page 374 Journal of Field Archaeology 25 (1998): 431-452 Figure 3. Courtesy of Vanderbilt University Press; Page 375 Journal of Field Archaeology 25 (1998): 431-452. Figure 6; Page 377 Courtesy of Joëlle Chartrand; Page 378 (A and B) ©The Trustees of the British Museum/Art Resource; Page 379 ©The Trustees of the British Museum; Page 380 Sarah Cummins/Rough Guides Dorling

Kindersley; Page 381 The Granger Collection; Page 384 Bodleian Library, University of Oxford, #MS. Arch.Selden.A. 1, fol.46r; Page 386 David Hiser/Getty Images Inc. - Stone Allstock; Page 387 (top) David Hiser/Getty Images Inc. - Stone Allstock; Page 387 (bottom) Elizabeth M. Brumfiel/Photo Courtesy of Elizabeth Brumfiel.

Chapter 14
Page 393 Pete Oxford/Nature Picture Library; Page 394 Frank Salomon/Courtesy of Frank L Salomon; Page 395 (top) Chavin de Huantar and nearby village from above, image courtesy of CyArk (www.cyark.org); Page 395 (bottom) Charles Lenars/Image by ©Charles & Josette Lenars/CORBIS; Page 396 (top) ccrma.stanford.edu/groups/chavin. Kembel, Silvia Rodriguez, 2001. Architectural Sequence and Chronology at Chavin de Huantar, Peru. Ph.D. Dissertation, Department of Anthropological Sciences, Stanford University. Figure 2.11, Page 256. Located at http://kembel.com/silvia/chavin. Reproduced by permission of the author; Adapted from Richard Burger 1992 Chavin and the Origins of Andean Civilization. Thames and Hudson, p. 131, figure 120, ccrma.stanford.edu/group/chavin/Richard Burger; Page 396 (bottom) Charles & Josette Lenars/©Charles & Josette Lenars/ CORBIS All Rights Reserved; Page 397 Charles Lenars/©Charles & Josette Lenars/CORBIS All Rights Reserved; Page 398 Textile Fragment. Peru; Chavin. Precolumbian, 4th-3rd BCE. Cotton, refined iron earth pigments, H. 5 3 4 × W. 12 1 4in. (14.6 × 31.1cm). Bequest of Jane Costello Goldberg, from the Collection of Arnold I. Goldberg, 1986 (1987.394.704). The Metropolitan Museum of Art, New York, NY/©The Metropolitan Museum of Art/Art Resource, NY; Page 399 (top) David Nunuk/Photo Researchers, Inc.; Page 399 (bottom) David Nunuk/Photo Researchers, Inc.; Page 400 (left) Photo courtesy of Kevin Vaughn; Page 400 (right) Nathan Benn/ ©Nathan Benn/Alamy; Page 401 (top) Ira Block/National Geographic Image Collection; Page 401 (bottom) Ira Block/©Ira

Block/National Geographic Stock; Page 403 Photo by: Mubeen Muhtar; Page 404 Dr. Gerhard Hoerz/Used with permission of Dr. G. Hoerz and M. Kallfass; Page 405 Dr. Gerhard Hoerz/Used with permission of Dr. G. Hoerz and M. Kallfass; Page 406 Kenneth Garrett/Kenneth Garrett/National Geographic Stock; Page 408 Peruvian School/British Museum, London, UK/The Bridgeman Art Library; Page 409 Jeremy Horner/©Jeremy Horner/CORBIS All Rights Reserved; Page 410 (top) Robert Frerck/©2004 Robert Frerck, Odyssey Productions, Chicago; Page 410 (bottom) The Granger Collection, New York; Page 411 (top) Marcia Ascher and Robert Ascher (1981) Code of the Quipu. Fig. 2.13 and 2.11, p. 29 and 30. Ann Arbor: Univ. of Michigan Press; Page 411 (bottom) The Granger Collection; Page 412 National Academy of Sciences, U.S.A./WL. Salo, AC Aufderheide. J Buikstra, and TA Holcomb./ National Academy of Sciences, U.S.A.

Epilogue
Page 416 Kevin Fleming/Kevin Fleming; Page 417 Nancy Siesel/The New York Times; Page 418 University of Maryland; Page 419 University of Maryland; Page 420 Israel Museum Jerusalem/Photo Courtesy of the Israel Museum by David Harris.

Appendix
Page 428 (left) Gallo Images/Corbis; Page 428 (middle right) National Museums of Kenya, Nairobi. ©1985 David L. Brill.; Page 428 (middle left) Meave Leaky, Fred Spoor/Kenya National Museum; Page 428 (right) Original housed in National Museum of Kenya, Nairobi. ©1994 David L. Brill; Page 429 (left) Brill Atlanta; Page 429 (middle right) Israel Antiquities Authority, Rockefeller Museum. ©1995 David L. Brill. David L. Brill/Brill Atlanta.; Page 429 (middle left) Israel Antiquities Authority, Rockefeller Museum. ©1995 David L. Brill. David L. Brill/Brill Atlanta.; Page 429 (right) National Geographic Image Collection.

Note: An *n* following a page reference indicates a note; an *f* following a page reference indicates a figure.

SUBJECT INDEX

Note: An *n* following a page reference indicates a note; an *f* following a page reference indicates a figure.

teosinte, 219, 219f
Teotihuacán, 364–370, 366f
terminal moraine, 92
test pit survey, 50
Texcoco, 383
Thera, 344, 345–346
Thermal Infrared Multispectral Scanner (TIMS), 291, 291f, 292
thermoluminescence (TL), 130
Three-Age system, 37, 40
Three Gorges Dam (China), 356, 356f
3D modelling, 316
Thule, 179
thunderstones, 35–36
Thutmose IV, King of Egypt, 35, 35f
Tigris River, 306
Tikal, 372
time, organization of, 37
time scale, 26
Tiwanaku (Bolivia), 406
Tla'amin-Simon Fraser University Archaeology and Stewardship Program, 28
Tlailotlacán, 366–367
Tlapocán, 383
Tlingit, 274
Toltec Empire, 382
Tomb 7 at Monte Albán, 364
Tomb of Ty at Saqqara, 320, 320f
Tonquin, 339
tools
    see also specific tools
    animals, and tool use, 74–75
    archaeological evidence, 75–77
    bone tools, 124–125, 125f, 137, 138f
    copper tools, 177
    Lower Paleolithic, 99
    Middle Stone Age, 124–125
    military supplies, 367–368
    origin of tool use, 74–77
    primate tool use, 76
    stone tools. See stone tools
    wooden spears, 99, 111
toothache glyph, 362, 362f
toothless man from Dmanisi, 64, 64f
tortoise-shaped cores, 109
tourism, 380
trade routes, 322–323
trances, 143–144
transitional industries, 134–135
treasure hunters, 39
tree rings, 25–26, 164, 293
Trent University, 376
tribe societies, 266
trilithons, 284
Trinil (Java), 86
Triple Alliance, 383
Troy (of the Iliad), 39, 39f
Tsiigehtchic (Northwest Territories), 162
Tsimshian, 274, 275

tuberculosis, 412
tuffs, 67
Tula, 382
Tupicocha (Peru), 394, 394f
turkeys, 225
Tutankhamun, 32f, 330, 412
typology, 22–24
"tyranny of the ethnographic record," 23

U

Uan Afuda (Libya), 243, 246
Uan Muhuggiag (Africa), 244
Ubeidiya (Israel), 85–86
Ulluzian, 134
Ulu Burun (Turkey), 338f, 339, 404
Umm el Tlel (Syria), 111, 111f
Umm Sayhun (Jordan), 197
"unchanging savage," 39
underwater archaeology, 338–339
UNESCO, 300
United States, 22, 24–25
    see also North America; specific United States sites
upended-frog glyph, 362, 362f
Upper Egypt, 318
Upper Paleolithic
    artwork, 139–144
    body ornamentation, 144
    cave art, 142–144
    chronology, 136–137
    defined, 130
    explaining the Upper Paleolithic, 146
    fishing, 145
    human burials, 138
    hunting, 145
    Middle to Upper Paleolithic transition, 131–135
    mobiliary art, 139–142
    site structure, 144–145
    stone tool industries, 136–137, 136t
    subsistence, 145
    tools, 137, 137f
Upper Sangiran Formation, 87
urban society, 267
Urubamba Valley, 407
Uruk (Iraq), 309–310
Uruk period, 309, 310
use-wear analysis, 111, 139
Ushki (Siberia), 165

V

vacant centre pattern, 231
Valtorta (Spain), 184f
Vanguard Cave (Gibraltar), 111
Venus figurines, 140–141, 141f, 143, 144
Vértesszölös (Hungary), 96
vertical excavation, 11, 11f, 12
Vindija Cave (Croatia), 102–103, 136

violence, 342–344, 378–379, 402
Virú Valley (Peru), 42
Vogelherd (Germany), 140
volcanos, 25

W

Wadi Hammeh (Jordan), 198, 199
Wadi Mataha (Jordan), 196–197, 199f
Wadi Ziqlab (Jordan), 201
Wallace Line, 153, 155
Walpi Pueblo (Arizona), 189
wanax, 342
warfare, 281, 314–315, 342–344, 378–379, 408–409
water buffalo, 255
Watson Brake (Louisiana), 177–178
"Wave of Advance," 211
Western Liao River Valley (China), 354–355
wet screening, 16
White Dog Cave (Arizona), 224
wiggles, 164
Wilson-Leonard site (Texas), 176, 177f
Wisconsin effigy mounds, 218
Wisconsin glaciation, 168
Wonderwerk Cave (South Africa), 18
wooden spears, 99, 111
woodhenge, 297
writing, 313–314, 319–321, 348–349, 375–378

X

Xian (China), 335f, 336, 336f
Xiaochangliang (China), 70

Y

Y chromosome, 134
Yana River (Siberia), 170
Yangshao culture, 258
Yangtze River Valley (China), 255, 256
Yanshi (China), 352, 353
Yax Ehb' Xook, 373
Yax K'uk Mo', 373, 374
Yaxchilán, 378, 379f
Yellow River Valley (China), 255
"Yellow Steatite Figurine," 127f
Yi-Luo River Valley Archaeological Project, 352
Yi-Luo Valley (China), 352, 353, 353f
Ying Zheng, 336
Younger Dryas, 198, 199
Yuku (New Guinea), 248

Z

Zafarraya Cave (Spain), 136
Zhoukoudian (China), 70, 97–98
ziggurat, 309, 309f
zoo-archaeologists. See faunal analysis